Appraisal and Criticism in Economics

Appraisal and Criticism in Economics

A BOOK OF READINGS

Edited by
Bruce J. Caldwell
University of North Carolina at Greensboro

Boston
ALLEN & UNWIN
London   Sydney

Allen & Unwin, Inc.,
Fifty Cross Street, Winchester, Mass. 01890, USA

George Allen & Unwin (Publishers) Ltd,
40 Museum Street, London WC1A 1LU, UK

George Allen & Unwin (Publishers) Ltd,
Park Lane, Hemel Hempstead, Herts HP2 4TE, UK

George Allen & Unwin Australia Pty Ltd,
8 Napier Street, North Sydney, NSW 2060, Australia

First published in 1984

Library of Congress Cataloging in Publication Data

Main entry under title:
   Appraisal and criticism in economics.
Bibliography: p.
1. Economics—Methodology—Addresses, essays, lectures.
I. Caldwell, Bruce J.
HB131.A66 1984   330   84−12394
ISBN 0−04−330343−9
ISBN 0−04−330344−7 (pbk.)

British Library Cataloguing in Publication Data

   Appraisal and criticism in economics.
1. Economics—Methodology
I. Caldwell, Bruce J.
330′01′8   HB131
ISBN 0−04−330343−9
ISBN 0−04−330344−7 Pbk

Printed in Great Britain by Mackays of Chatham

Contents

PREFACE

What is economic methodology? Is it what economists do? Or perhaps what they say they do? Or maybe what they say they ought to do? And is there any relationship among the three?

Why should we bother to study methodology? Don't we learn how to become economists by 'doing' economics, rather than by talking about it? Has any economist ever changed the way he approached his subject after reading methodology? Does methodology matter?

What right do methodologists have to tell 'real' scientists what proper scientific procedure is? Aren't they a bit like priests giving marital advice? But if there is no normative role for methodology, what can methodologists do besides describe scientific behavior?

If methodology is essentially a descriptive discipline, what framework is best for describing what economists do? Is the philosophy of science helpful? How about the sociology of science? Or does argumentation in economics come down to a matter of rhetoric? Can we get beyond Stigler's jaundiced dictum that economics is what economists do? Do we want to?

Questions. If you decide to take the risk, and read the writings of economists on methodology, then you had better be prepared to be barraged by questions. Even worse, though some of the questions have answers, it seems that others, and these are often the most important ones, do not. Indeed it is a special characteristic of methodological work that you can spend years simply trying to pose a question correctly. If you are not the type of person who can feel comfortable carrying around a lot of unanswered questions in your head, you probably will not enjoy methodology very much.

If this were not bad enough, the pursuit of this prickly subject will earn you few rewards. Some colleagues will be openly hostile, but most will be simply indifferent. This is because your work, which is to analyze and explicate scientific procedure, *is* very different from their work, which is to do economics. Explaining the purpose of methodology to an economist is a lot like an economist trying to explain a theoretical model of the hog cycle to a hog farmer. No matter how long or how fast the economist talks, the hog farmer just can't help believe that raising pigs involves working for a living, while talking about pigs is, well, just talk.

So I will not try to convince you that studying methodology is necessarily good for you. It *can* be good for you, if it is undertaken as a complement to the study of economics. Let me digress briefly on this point.

One can be a very good economist (though often a rather narrow and complacent one) even if one has never read any methodology. Conversely, some of the worst drivel in the methodological literature has been penned by those who made the mistake of never having seriously studied economics first. And it is even possible for some very good economists to write some awful things about methodology, though hopefully this is less likely today than it was in the positivist era. (It was more common then for methodological work to bear little resemblance to the actual practice of economics.) The study of methodology is most likely to bear fruit for those who, having already committed themselves to a careful study of economics, are willing to entertain questions about the foundations of their discipline. It is in this last case that the expected returns from studying methodology are the highest.

Whatever one thinks about methodology, an explosion of interest in the field has occurred recently, as a brief glance at the Bibliography establishes. I will not speculate about why this explosion has taken place, though I suspect that internal rather than external forces are more important in explaining it. I have tried to make the Bibliography as comprehensive as possible, though I am sure that there are omissions, and for this I apologize. If there is one portion of this book that is most likely to become dated, it is the Bibliography. If present trends predict the future, the Bibliography will double in ten years!

Given the sheer size of the literature, I feel compelled to explain how I came up with the selections that comprise this book. First, I limited myself to articles and books written in the last fifty years. That literature was divided into two parts, which I labeled positivist and post-positivist. Then the selection process began in earnest. It was a painful task. The first criterion I used was an obvious one: quality. But the number of articles and excerpts that survived the first cut was still very large.

For the positivist section, I then applied some admittedly arbitrary selection rules. First, I decided to choose from the writings of economists who focused on 'mainstream' methodological topics, rather than from those whose work challenged the orthodoxy. Thus, the contributions of people like Mises, Hayek, Sweezy, Marcuse, Myrdal, Robinson, Galbraith, Heilbroner, Lowe, Shackle, Simon and a host of others are excluded. Next, I chose readings in which methodological questions were directly addressed, rather than those in which differences in opinion about an issue in economics turned into a methodological debate. Nearly all great debates in economics end up being fought on the methodological plane. In a volume such as this, it would not be difficult to begin including such classic debates as the Lester−Machlup exchange, or Friedman's many debates with his critics on testing Keynesian and monetarist models. The hard part would be knowing where to stop.

Turning to the post-positivist section, making choices became even more torturous. Even so, some of the selections were straightforward: Boland's piece on Friedman's instrumentalism and McCloskey's article on the rhetoric of economists are already minor classics. As for the rest, all that I can say is that I have chosen articles that I thought were very good, and that I tried in each of the sections to juxtapose a variety of sometimes antagonistic views. The emphasis throughout is on methodological debate, and for that I make no apology.

I would like to thank my research assistant, Randall Austin, for his many contributions to this project. Vicky Sparrow and Becky Askew's speedy typing helped me get this book to my editor on time. And finally, I offer my thanks to the Acquisitions Editor at Allen & Unwin, Nick Brealey, for having enough confidence in me to risk a book of readings in so arcane a subject as economic methodology, and for being a good friend. Bourbon and hot sausage forever!

Greensboro, North Carolina   *BRUCE J. CALDWELL*

March 1984

Acknowledgements

I thank all of the authors, and the estate of Fritz Machlup, for granting their permissions to reprint the articles published in this volume. I also gratefully acknowledge the editors of the following presses for granting their permission to reprint.

Augustus M. Kelley, Publishers, for permission to reprint Chapters I, II and IV of T. W. Hutchison, *The Significance and Basic Postulates of Economic Theory*, 1960

The *Southern Economic Journal*, for permission to reprint the following articles:

Fritz Machlup, 'The Problem of Verification in Economics' *SEJ*, July 1955, pp. 1−21.

Terence Hutchison, 'Professor Machlup on Verification in Economics', *SEJ*, April 1956, pp. 476−83.

Fritz Machlup, 'Rejoinder to a Reluctant Ultra-Empiricist', *SEJ*, April 1956, pp. 483−93.

Bruce Caldwell, 'A Critique of Friedman's Methodological Instrumentalism', *SEJ*, October 1980, pp. 366−74.

The American Economic Association for its permission to reprint the following articles:

Ernest Nagel, 'Assumptions in Economic Theory', *American Economic Review Papers and Proceedings*, May 1963, pp. 211−19.

Paul Samuelson, 'Discussion', *American Economic Review Papers and Proceedings* ,May 1963, pp. 231−6.

Fritz Machlup, 'Professor Samuelson on Theory and Realism', *American Economic Review*, September 1964, pp. 733−6.

Paul Samuelson, 'Theory and Realism: A Reply', *American Economic Review*, September 1964, pp. 736−9.

Lawrence Boland, 'A Critique of Friedman's Critics', *Journal of Economic Literature*, June 1979, pp. 503−22.

Edward E. Leamer, 'Let's Take the Con Out of Econometrics', *American Economic Review*, March 1983, pp. 31−43.

Donald McCloskey, 'The Rhetoric of Economics', *Journal of Economic Literature*, June 1983, pp. 481−517.

Melvin Reder, 'Chicago Economics: Permanence and Change', *Journal of Economic Literature*, March 1982, pp. 1−38.

Harvey Leibenstein, 'A Branch of Economics Is Missing: Micro-Micro Theory', *Journal of Economic Literature*, June 1979, pp. 477−502.

Lawrence Boland, 'On the Futility of Criticizing the Neoclassical Maximization Hypothesis', *American Economic Review*, December 1981, pp. 1031−6.

Bruce Caldwell, 'The Neoclassical Maximization Hypothesis: Comment', *American Economic Review*, September 1983, pp. 824−7.

ACKNOWLEDGEMENTS

Lawrence Boland, 'The Neoclassical Maximization Hypothesis: Reply', *American Economic Review*, September 1983, pp. 828–30.

Kyklos, for permission to reprint Alan Musgrave, '"Unreal Assumptions" in Economic Theory: The F-Twist Untwisted', 1981, pp. 377–87. The following material:

Mark Blaug, *The Methodology of Economics: Or How Economists Explain*, 1980, Chapter 15, pp. 253–64.

Brian Loasby, 'Hypothesis and Paradigm in the Theory of the Firm', *Economic Journal*, December 1971, pp. 863–85.

Rod Cross, 'The Duhem–Quine Thesis, Lakatos and the Appraisal of Theories in Macroeconomics', *Economic Journal*, June 1982, pp. 320–40.

was printed by permission of Cambridge University Press.

M. E. Sharpe, Inc., for permission to publish the following exchange from the *Journal of Post-Keynesian Economics:*

E. Roy Weintraub, 'Substantive Mountains and Methodological Molehills', *JPKE*, Winter 1982–83, pp. 295–303.

Sheila Dow, 'Substantive Mountains and Methodological Molehills: A Rejoinder', *JPKE*, Winter 1982–83, pp. 304–8.

The *Review of Social Economy*, for permission to reprint Elba Brown, 'The Neoclassical and Post-Keynesian Research Programs: The Methodological Issues', *RSE*, October 1981, pp. 111–32.

The University of Chicago Press, for permission to reprint Milton Friedman, 'The Methodology of Positive Economics', *Essays in Positive Economics*, 1953.

PART I

THE POSITIVIST EPOCH – CLASSICAL CITATIONS

Editor's introduction

The term 'positivism' has three denotations, two of which depend on the addition of a modifer. *Classical* positivism denotes a nineteenth-century doctrine, often associated with the writings of Auguste Comte and Ernst Mach. *Logical* positivism was developed by a group of philosophers and scientists in Vienna in the middle of the 1920s. Members of the Vienna Circle included, among others, Moritz Schlick, Herbert Feigl, Kurt Godel, Otto Neurath and Rudolf Carnap.

Logical positivism was a radically empirical philosophy of science. By the middle of the 1930s, most of the advocates of this extreme variant of positivism realized that it was an untenable position, and began working out the details of a modified version. After the hiatus of World War II, the more reasonable empirical philosophy of science, logical empiricism, emerged. Though there is no such animal as a 'pure logical empiricist', men whose names have been associated with this tradition include the later Carnap, A. J. Ayer, Carl Hempel, Richard Braithwaite and Ernest Nagel. To the extent that logical empiricism is associated with an analytical approach to questions in the philosophy of science, it still has many followers. Since the late 1950s, however, advocates of an alternative approach to the philosophy of science have become increasingly influential. Indeed, the writings of Karl Popper, Thomas Kuhn, Imre Lakatos, Paul Feyerabend, Stephen Toulmin, Joseph Agassi, Larry Lauden and other advocates of the 'growth of knowledge' approach may arguably be viewed as representing a new orthodoxy in the philosophy of science. (For more detailed accounts of the rise and fall of logical positivism and logical empiricism, see Blaug, 1980b, Caldwell, 1982, Suppe, 1977, and citations listed therein.)

The denotation of positivism in its unmodified form is more difficult. I shall use the term loosely. Though classical positivism is excluded from my definition, both logical positivism and logical empiricism are included, as well as other expressly empirical positions in twentieth-century philosophy of science, such as operationalism and behaviorism.

For those who like arbitrary precision, I shall date the beginning of the positivist epoch in economics as 1938. In that year, the empiricist gauntlet was unmistakably thrown down with the publication of Terence Hutchison's *The Significance and Basic Postulates of Economic Theory*. It is less easy to date the end of the epoch, if indeed it has ended. If you ask a working economist what science is, and why what he is doing qualifies as scientific, his answer will be peppered with positivist buzz-words. The rhetoric of economics, to use Donald McCloskey's felicitous phrase, is still dominated by the phraseology of logical positivism and logical empiricism. It is only among economic methodologists (and, more recently, a growing band of fellow travellers) that the death of positivism is old news.

If 'positivist' is a term to be used derisively today, three decades ago it was a term of approbation, at least among orthodox economic methodologists. (Of course, there is always an exception. Fritz Machlup was educated in Vienna, and as a result he had a far deeper understanding of the origins and variety of methodological positions than did his peers.) This is not to say that economists writing about methodology in the positivist epoch all agreed about what it meant to be a positivist science. To the contrary, disagreement was the norm, as is evidenced in the selections to follow. We begin with excerpts from Hutchison's book. Next comes his exchange with Machlup on the necessity of testing assumptions. Finally, there is Friedman's famous essay, and a handful of the critical responses to it.

Some of the most quoted (and quotable!) phrases in the methodological literature are contained in these selections. There is Hutchison's claim that the proposition of economic science must be at least 'conceivably testable'. There is Machlup's accusation that such views make Hutchison an 'ultra-empiricist', and Hutchison's vigorous denial of the charge. There is Friedman's bizarre claim that 'the more significant the theory, the more unrealistic the assumptions'. There is Samuelson's famous discussion of Friedman's methodology, published a full decade later, in which he labels his perennial opponent's position the 'F-twist', a label that has stuck. And, finally, there is Samuelson's own peculiar position that scientists never explain behavior, 'by theory or any other hook'.

I conclude with a personal note. It was in the second week of graduate school that I first read Friedman and Samuelson on methodology. After numerous rereadings, I still felt baffled. The same questions kept recurring: Were they serious? Did they really mean what they said? Or did the words they used have different meanings from normal usage? At the dissertation stage, I resolved to find the answers to these questions. In subsequent readings, I found some answers, as well as many more questions. More important, I discovered that economic methodology is truly a strange and wonderful field, and that it was well worth the effort to try to figure it out. I sincerely hope that some of the readers of these pages may have a similarly rich experience.

1

Positivism Enters Economic Methodology

Terence Hutchison, *The Significance and Basic Postulates of Economic Theory*, 2nd edn, New York: Kelley, 1960 (first published 1938), Chapters I, II and IV.

Editor's comments

In the opening chapter of his famous book, Terence Hutchison states the goal of his analysis: to lay down explicit scientific criteria by which to judge the claims of economics. He hopes his exercise will rid economics of 'quackery, prejudice, and propaganda', and transform the discipline from a 'pseudo-science' into a science. The criterion he adopts is that the 'finished propositions' of economic science be, at a minimum, conceivably testable. Hutchison cites the work of many economists in making his case, but other names are also present: Schlick, Mach, Poincaré, Popper, Hempel. The linking of methodological questions in economics to answers formulated by philosophers of science had begun. This practice has continued into the present.

Hutchison begins with the claim that the 'propositions of pure theory' are absolutely necessary and certain. Their unconditional necessity has a price, however: such propositions are completely lacking in empirical content. Unlike others who had claimed that the deduced statements of economic theory are obvious and self-evident generalizations about reality, for Hutchison such statements are merely symbols to be manipulated in a theoretical structure. Only when the premises of economic theory are established empirically as true will economics become an empirical science.

Hutchison gives extended attention to the 'fundamental assumption' of economic theory, that of maximizing behavior. If the assumption is to have any meaning, an additional assumption about the agent's state of knowledge is necessary. 'Perfect foresight' is usually assumed, since it alone guarantees that maximizing behavior will indeed result in the agent attaining a maximum. Hutchison rejects the use of such an obviously empirically false assumption, and recommends that economists begin detailed empirical investigations of individual and market behavior to see how choice actually takes place.

Hutchison's work is interesting on a number of levels. Note first the importance he attaches to the question of expectations. This is not untypical; a number of economists grappled with the problem of knowledge and its acquisition in the 1930s. Though interest in this topic dwindled as the Keynesian Revolution gained momentum, the idea that the formation of expectations is a crucial issue in economics was to re-emerge with a vengeance some thirty years later.

Next, what relation exists between Hutchison's recommendations and subsequent changes in the practice of economics? His book was not well received (Frank Knight's 1941 review in the *Journal of Political Economy* is a study in academic invective), yet it seems he anticipated perfectly the movement toward empirical studies that took off in the post-war decades. I say 'anticipated' because it is doubtful that economics took this turn as a result of Hutchison's book. The question nevertheless remains: what forces were responsible for this development, which, together with the 'mathematization' of economics, constitute the defining characteristics of the practice of economics in this century? What would a 'rational reconstruction' of this revolution in economics look like? Is it really a revolution? In his 1978 book *On Revolutions and Progress in Economic Knowledge*, Hutchison answers this last question (with characteristic modesty, given his role) in the negative.

Finally, the questions raised by Hutchison provided an agenda for subsequent debates among economic methodologists in the positivist epoch. What is the logical status of the rationality assumption? Is it a self-evident postulate about phenomenal reality? Or is it a testable, empirical statement? If the latter, must it be actually tested, and, if so, how? Other alternative formulations are possible: perhaps assumptions are chosen for their tractability in a theoretical structure. What is the precise relationship between theoretical and empirical work in economics? Is economics in its essential form a series of deductions from postulates, or is it a body of empirical generalizations, or perhaps something else altogether? Even if we disagree with the answers he gave, we can thank Terence Hutchison for raising these questions in a clear and forceful way.

I

INTRODUCTION

1. THE PRESENT POSITION OF ECONOMIC "METHODOLOGY"

THE purpose of this essay is to help in elucidating the significance of that body of "pure theory" the possession of which distinguishes Economics from the other social sciences. It is concerned, therefore, to arrive at a clear definition of "pure theory" enabling one to mark off clearly propositions which belong to "pure theory" from those that do not, to investigate the source of the validity of these propositions, to clarify their relation to the assumptions or postulates on which they rest, including, in particular, the "ceteris paribus" assumption, and finally to clarify these assumptions themselves by analysing the main concepts (for example, "equilibrium", "expectation", "sensible" or "rational conduct", "utility"), which they contain.

Despite the quantity of literature on such fundamental problems as these, few economists—least of all probably those like Kaufmann, Mackenroth, Morgenstern, Myrdal, and Robbins who in recent years have particularly contributed to their discussion—would claim that they are satisfactorily and definitively settled, even with that relative definitiveness which is the most that any scientist claims for his results.

3

INTRODUCTION

The central conclusion of this essay has been advanced over and over again throughout the history of Economics. For the difficulty is not that of finding some new theory or standpoint—*on ne saurait rien imaginer de si étrange et si peu croyable, qu'il n'ait été dit par quelque philosophe*—but that of bringing conclusive and definitive arguments in favour of one as against the others—" conclusive ", that is, not necessarily *absolutely* (whatever that would mean), but according to some agreed scientific criterion. Nor further is it the case that the foundations of economic science have been found necessarily to be precarious, but rather that it is not at all clear precisely what they are. To this lack of fundamental clarity can be attributed to a certain extent the ferocious and interminable character of the many controversies that rage among economists themselves on the one hand, and on the other hand much of the uncertainty as to the significance of their results with which economists face the outside world.

Unfortunately, however, methodological writings and the discussion of *Grundprobleme* from every conceivable philosophical standpoint—Idealist, Materialist, Phenomenological, Transcendentalist, Neo-Kantian, etc., etc.—have, not unjustifiably, won a bad reputation among economic scientists. As Professor Schumpeter with particular reference to German conditions complains : [1] " Long enough have we searched after new paths, explored philosophical backgrounds, quarrelled over methods, represented and championed fundamental ' standpoints ' and ' positions ', and in general pursued economic theory as though it was philosophy, containing fundamentally different systems about which each has his own dogma ". In the less

4

THE PRESENT POSITION OF ECONOMIC " METHODOLOGY "

philosophically-minded Anglo-Saxon countries it is
hardly surprising that many have turned their backs
in impatience on " this noisy conflict of half-truths
angrily denying one another ", and have abandoned
the interminable wranglings and controversies of the
" methodologists " and " philosophers " for seemingly
more constructive work. But this evasion can only be
temporary. For it can fairly be insisted that no advance
in the elegance and comprehensiveness of the theoretical superstructure can make up for the vague and
uncritical formulation of the basic concepts and
postulates, and sooner or later—and at the moment it
seems to be *sooner*—attention will have to return to
the foundations.

What are the roots, then, and what is the way out
of this dilemma of, on the one hand, the obvious
pressing necessity for the critical clarification of the
basic concepts and postulates, and on the other hand
the interminable inconclusiveness of the controversies
over the " methodological " and " philosophical "
foundations ? A road must be found which leads
definitively and conclusively forward and not simply
round in a circle.

Of the literature on these problems it may be com-
mented, first, that even to-day much of it appears to
be concerned rather to attack or defend some particular
" school ", or to lay down a " method " in the abstract,
rather than with the detailed analysis and criticism
of fundamental propositions in accordance with a
definite criterion to which scientific propositions must
attain. Here, as elsewhere, it is usually found easier
when there is a lack of clarity about the particular to
discourse on the general.[2] Secondly, as Professor
Morgenstern recently pointed out,[3] the results of the

5

revolutionary developments in recent decades of the science of Logic and logical analysis have scarcely been made use of at all. Since Mill, Jevons, J. N. Keynes, and W. E. Johnson, when Economics and Logic were closely associated, there has been a division of scientific labour, and against the gains of increased specialisation there may be losses to be set off.

But there is a far more important and fundamental reason than either of these for the inconclusiveness of the discussions of the " philosophical foundations of Economics ", and that is the obscurity as to whether the object in view is the " philosophical " discussion of " philosophical " questions, or rather the solution of " scientific " problems according to a definite " scientific " criterion. These vague and highly ambiguous adjectives " philosophical " and " scientific " are being used here in a sharply and clearly separable sense and the distinction is of fundamental importance for our discussion.

2. " SCIENTIFIC " AND " PHILOSOPHICAL " PROBLEMS

The scientist's activity may be described as the taking over of the apparatus, results, and solutions of his predecessors, the testing and, if necessary, the rejecting of them according to agreed criteria, when possible their improvement and development, and the taking up of new problems—which he, in his turn, passes on to his successors. It is reasonable to speak of the " advance " of science owing to the possibility of taking some results as, at any rate temporarily, agreed upon and settled, and of then proceeding to new problems and solutions. But one can scarcely more appropriately speak of the *advance* of philosophy

6

from Plato to Hegel than one can of the advance of poetry from Homer to Shakespeare, certainly not as one can speak of the advance of Biology from Aristotle to Mendel or even of Economics from Petty to Marshall. The reason why scientists, unlike philosophers, can build on and advance their predecessors' work rather than each being simply " influenced " by it and starting afresh right from the beginning at the same problems with some completely new system, is that " scientists " have definite, agreed, and relatively conclusive criteria for the testing of propositions, solutions, and theories which " philosophers " do not accept. It is this acceptance of the testing of propositions according to definite criteria which is the source of that steady secular piecemeal agreement and advance of " science ", and its cumulative, international, impersonal, and " coral-reef-like " growth.

This distinction between the " scientific " and " philosophical " procedure may be developed by means of a simple example.[4]

Two economists might have an argument as to whether the cheque system did or did not exist in Paraguay. They might be prepared to settle the dispute by referring to some book they accepted as authoritative. But if there was no such book they could themselves go to Paraguay and investigate, and there is no reason to suppose that they would not soon come to complete agreement as to whether, on their definition of the terms, the " cheque system " existed in " Paraguay " or not. Nor is there any difference in principle if their argument did not relate to present-day Paraguay but to Paraguay in the fifteenth century before or after Christ, and if owing to the inconclusiveness and ambiguity of the evidence one economist

7

INTRODUCTION

conjectured that " cheques " then did exist and the other that they did not. They could at any rate agree as to precisely what the evidence was, record that it gave rise to different interpretations, and that, failing the discovery of some new evidence, there was nothing else at all to be said. But supposing that the two economists had found that in present-day Paraguay the cheque system *did* exist, and actually had a cheque before them. Then, having settled the scientific dispute, they might begin a philosophical dispute. One of them might argue that they had not got the real cheque-an-sich before them, which was a transcendental cheque and for ever inaccessible, but only the idea or appearance of a cheque ; while the other might argue that, on the contrary, this printed slip of paper was the real essential cheque, and that ideas did not really exist, or that he did not know what a real cheque was, as the only ultimate reality for him was his own private subjective experience of seeing and touching a cheque and he had no idea whether someone else had the same real experiences or any experience at all. And so on. . . .

So long as the two economic scientists remained in their own scientific field their problem was one which could be brought to a definite test and ultimately settled one way or the other, and disagreement could thus in the end be removed. When, however, the two investigators went outside the scientific field, there was no such test. There was no agreed method of finding out whether their respective propositions were " true " or " false ", or of indicating what would have to be the case if one or the other was " true " or " false ", and there is therefore no reason to suppose that the disputants would necessarily ever come to agreement—as in fact in two thousand years philo-

8

sophers never have. Further, if they *did* happen to agree it would be quite a different kind of " agreement " from that of two scientists who have accepted the result of an agreed test.[5] If such intersubjective tests could not satisfactorily be made, there could be no science. A world is quite conceivable in which they could not, just as no statistics or even agreed estimates can yet at any rate be obtained as to many social phenomena. It is simply an empirical fact that over large areas satisfactory agreement can be and is arrived at by such tests.

The scientist proceeds by means of the two inextricably interconnected activities of empirical investigation and logical analysis, the one, briefly, being concerned with the behaviour of facts, and the other with the language in which this is to be discussed. It is this latter activity as carried out in the science of Economics which it is largely the purpose of this book to analyse and itself to carry on. But if the finished propositions of a science, as against the accessory purely logical or mathematical propositions used in many sciences, including Economics, are to have any empirical content, as the finished propositions of all sciences except of Logic and Mathematics obviously must have,[6] then these propositions must *conceivably* be capable of empirical testing *or be reducible to such propositions* by logical or mathematical deduction. They need not, that is, actually be tested or even be *practically* capable of testing under present or future technical conditions or conditions of statistical investigation, nor is there any sense in talking of some kind of " absolute " test which will " finally " decide whether a proposition is " absolutely " true or false. But it must be possible to indicate intersubjectively

9

what is the case if they are true or false : their truth or falsity, that is, must make some conceivable empirically noticeable difference, or some such difference must be directly deducible therefrom.

3. SCIENCE AND PSEUDO-SCIENCE

We suggest that the economic scientist is transgressing the frontiers of his subject whenever he resorts to, or advances as possessing some empirical content, propositions which, whatever emotional associations they may arouse, can never conceivably be brought to an intersubjective empirical test, and of which one can never conceivably say that they are confirmed or falsified, or which cannot be deduced from propositions of which that can conceivably be said. It makes no difference to such a transgression whether the proposition is an expression of ethical uplift or persuasion, political propaganda, poetic emotion, psychological " association ", or metaphysical " intuition " or speculation. If there is any object in pursuing an activity one calls " scientific ", and if the word " science " is not simply to be a comprehensive cloak for quackery, prejudice, and propaganda, then there must be a definite objective criterion for distinguishing propositions which may be material for science from those that are not, and there must be some effective barrier for excluding expressions of ethical or political passion, poetic emotion or metaphysical speculation from being mixed in with so-called " science ".

The most sinister phenomenon of recent decades for the true scientist, and indeed for Western civilisation as a whole, may be said to be the growth of

10

SCIENCE AND PSEUDO-SCIENCE

Pseudo-Sciences no longer confined to hole-and-corner cranks or passive popular superstitions, but organised in comprehensive militant and persecuting mass-creeds, attempting simply to justify crude prejudice and the lust for power. There is, however, one criterion by which the scientist can keep his results pure from the contamination of pseudo-science and there is one test with which he can always challenge the pseudo-scientist—a test which at once ensures precision and exposes the vague concepts and unsupported general-isations on which the pseudo-scientist always relies. As three scientists have insisted, who work in a field which is possibly in greater danger and in even greater need of a definite barrier against the rising tide of pseudo-science than is Economics : " The essence of science is the appeal to fact ".[7] This is an appeal which the scientist must always be ready and eager to see made, and where this appeal cannot conceivably be made there is no place for the scientist as such.

We have tried here very briefly to indicate the only principle or distinction practically adoptable which will keep science separate from pseudo-science, a prin-ciple in fact which, though only consciously and precisely formulated in recent years, has always more or less unconsciously been practised by scientists, and the employment of which in rejecting all propositions and concepts which do not fulfil it (e.g. the concept of " Absolute Space ") has been synchronous with the advance of science. To say that, in general, the natural sciences are less controversy-ridden, less split up into warring " schools " or " orthodox " and " unorthodox " parties, into " bourgeois ", " Nordic ", " Jewish ", and " workers' " sciences, and enjoy a greater area of common agreement, is simply to say that in general

11

INTRODUCTION

this principle has, for various reasons, received earlier and fuller recognition here than in the social sciences —partly because, in the former, statistics and observations are at present on the whole technically easier to obtain, and partly because objective tests are more readily accepted since human passions and desires are not so closely involved in the former as in the latter.

We are not attempting here to exalt " scientific " propositions or problems above " non-scientific " ones. We do not argue that the meteorologist's " knowledge " of a sunset is either somehow superior or inferior to the poet's or artist's " knowledge ". Nor do we insist that this is *necessarily* exactly the most suitable defining line between these two planes of science and of non-science—though we prefer it to any other terminological suggestion we have seen.[8] We are simply concerned with a vitally necessary distinction, label it how one will. It is not the place here to argue for the adoption of this principle any further, or to render our brief formulation of it more precise. We leave this to specialist works on the Logic of Science and scientific method and on the tactics for the scientist to adopt against his intellectual enemies. Our object in this introduction is simply to indicate as shortly as possible the general attitude in which the particular problems of the succeeding chapters will be approached, and we believe that this will emerge sufficiently clearly. It is these particular scientific problems which are our concern rather than general methodological issues. We are not concerned so much to advocate a particular disciplinary principle or criterion for the scientist as to show what are the consequences for economic science when this principle that we suggest is followed out. In that sense the

12

SCIENCE AND PSEUDO-SCIENCE

validity of our conclusions is independent of the question as to whether this principle is accepted. In Chapter V we shall be particularly concerned to apply it to the concepts of utility and social utility.

In the main this essay is addressed to economists who already broadly accept the criterion we propose, though not necessarily the precise wording of this sketchy formulation of it, and who are prepared to see it applied rigidly and unwaveringly to the particular concepts and postulates of theoretical Economics, not simply out of an aesthetic pleasure in rigour for its own sake, but for the highly practical and important reason that only through this principle have we at once a method of reaching agreement and a barrier against the pseudo-scientist. We therefore decline debate with those who do not hold with this criterion just as we should refuse to play chess with someone with whom we could not agree as to the rules, and we say with Pareto, who among economists seems to have been one of the first and most emphatic to insist on our principle : " Throughout the course of these pages, we are in the logico-experimental field. I intend to remain absolutely in that field and refuse to depart from it under any inducement whatsoever. If, therefore, the reader desires a judge other than objective experience, he should stop reading this book, just as he would refrain from proceeding with a case before a court to which he objected. If people who are disposed to argue the propositions mentioned desire a judge other than objective experience, they will do well to declare exactly what their judge is to be, and if possible (it seldom is) to make themselves very clear on the point." [9]

There are certainly writers on Economics who are

13

INTRODUCTION

not prepared to accept this criterion and the discipline it implies. Professor Sombart, for example, makes a distinction between what he calls the method of Natural science and the method of Moral science (*Geisteswissenschaft*). Although this distinction derives originally from Mill's distinction between Natural and Moral sciences, by English writers it never appears to have been regarded as much more than a useful classification, significant particularly, perhaps, with regard to the different possibilities of prognosis in the two types of sciences. In most of the English standard works on Logic and Scientific Method, although a number of them have been written by authorities who had a particular interest in and understanding of the problems of the social sciences—for example, Jevons' *Principles of Science* and Johnson's *Logic*—the idea of some fundamental difference in method and criteria is not mentioned ; or else the contrary is obviously implied, that there is but one scientific procedure— that applied with most success up till now in the natural sciences, as, for example, the quotation from Mill at the head of this chapter says. Bentham also, perhaps the greatest English pioneer in social science, is exceedingly explicit on this point. But in Germany the doctrine that the social or moral sciences have quite other criteria and methods than the natural sciences, employing philosophical and artistic elements, is dominant to the point of orthodoxy, and the criterion we have proposed here for economic scientists would almost certainly be called " naturalistic " and inadequate for a social science. The " naturalistic " conception is at any rate very explicitly rejected by Professor Sombart. We do not want to argue over such a rejection, as this controversy over the *naturwissen-*

14

16

schaftliche and geisteswissenschaftliche methods is just one of those interminable and inconclusive contro-versies which never trouble the practical scientist faced with a particular concrete problem and which we want to keep clear of in this book. We may, how-ever, indicate one or two of Professor Sombart's con-clusions, as the contrast may make our own more clear.[10]

He is perfectly clear that in rejecting the criteria and method of " natural science " in order to include philosophical and poetical elements and the know-ledge of " essences " (*Wesenserkenntnis*) he is giving up the prospect of the progress of the " moral " sciences and of their being of much practical use or applicability. They are to be " a luxury ", ," tragically torn between science, philosophy, and art ". Unlike, however, the natural sciences, they are to press on to an " understanding " of the " essence " of things. (It is significant that there is no English technical term for the German *verstehen* here.)[11] Against those who deliberately choose this path with a clear knowledge of the consequences we have no objection to make—*atque idem jungat vulpes et mulgeat hircos.* It is permissible to enquire, however, of those who thus reject the criterion we advocate as to what definite procedure they have for ever reaching agreement on any con-clusion and whether they possess any intersubjective criterion for raising their so-called scientific (*geistes-wissenschaftliche*) propositions above any sort of quackery and propaganda. It may further be remarked that it may not, possibly, be entirely a coincidence that precisely those academic circles in Europe which have most traditionally and conclusively rejected our " naturalistic " scientific criterion as unsuited for the moral or social sciences which are to aim higher at "understanding" the "essence" of the phenomena they deal with, have found themselves most powerless against the ravings of Pseudo-science and have even in a few cases positively facilitated or assisted its growth. Here at least there seem to be traces of an unholy alliance of undisciplined metaphysical yearnings with propagandist Pseudo-science, of the longing for the infinite with the will to power, a combination so typical of a certain philosophical direction.

4. THE SCOPE AND PROGRAMME OF THIS ESSAY

Sciences never begin with problems which come logically first—if they did they would probably make very slow progress—but they start at a "common-sense" level and have to build *upwards* their structure of laws and relations, and *downwards* their foundations —the latter task being by criticism and analysis to test and make precise the common-sense notions they start with, and to assure a logically firm and secure basis for the superstructure.[2] If one cares to call this latter activity—of which Einstein's criticism and revision of the fundamental concepts of Physics is an obvious example—"philosophical" or "methodo-logical", as against the "scientific" work on the superstructure of science, one may. We do not regard this terminology as useful, however, for the "philo-sopher" and "methodologist" of a science, if his work is to be of use to the scientist as such, must accept and discipline himself to exactly the same criteria of empirical testability and logical consistency as the "scientific" worker on the superstructure.

Nor further can any clear line be drawn between

16

THE SCOPE AND PROGRAMME OF THIS ESSAY

the problems of the infra-common-sense foundations and the supra-common-sense superstructure—the two are inextricably interconnected—and only the most complete confusion can ensue when those who do not accept the criteria of the scientist try and solve the basic problems of his science for him. It is sometimes argued that there are metaphysical assumptions underlying all sciences which the self-conscious and profound scientist must work back to and formulate, or that no science is safer than the metaphysical assumptions on which it rests. Actually we happen to believe that this notion of " metaphysical assumptions " has been shown to be completely misconceived. But even if this were not so—*posito non concesso*—we should urge that the metaphysical discussion should be kept strictly separate from the scientific, which should be pushed back as far as it could according to its own methods and criteria.

To be of use to the scientist the " methodological " problems must be worked out in closest co-operation with the scientific worker at the more advanced stage of the scientific structure of production and, within the limits implied in the scientific criteria, solely with an eye to his problems. The discussion of " methodological " questions—for the scientist at any rate—only has sense in connection with the practical problems of science.[1] Of course any economic scientist or " methodologist " will almost certainly save himself much thinking, many mistakes, and possibly his going completely off the rails, by making the fullest use of the modern works of specialists in Logic and the Logic of Science, who accept the same criteria as himself ; but the critical analysis of the basic concepts of economic science must be carried through to the end

17

INTRODUCTION

within the science itself and according to the scientific criteria, not according to the criteria of outside philosophers.

To the objection of a rather Anglo-Saxon type that it is better to settle the problems of the basic concepts by " sound instinct and common sense " without entering into " philosophical refinements " (to which attitude that of business men and popular newspapers to economic theory may be compared), it would be answered that it is precisely the task of science to supersede crude common-sense notions by critical analysis, and further that it is the unsatisfactory state of the foundations beneath the common-sense surface which is the most serious and crippling deficiency of contemporary economic science, since other deficiencies lie rather in the nature of the subject matter as compared with that of natural sciences and may never be thoroughly overcome in the same way.[14]

In concluding this introductory chapter we wish to emphasise once again that this book is concerned to seek solutions of certain basic problems of economic science in accordance with the criteria we have here outlined. It is not concerned to urge or to appear to urge any ultimate " necessity " or " absoluteness " about these criteria, although, not attempting to hide our personal intellectual tastes, we have tried to indicate here some consequences of their adoption on the one hand and their rejection on the other.

NOTES

1. Cf. J. Schumpeter, Introduction to E. Barone's *Grundzüge der theoretischen Nationalökonomie*, p. 7.

2. Cf. J. Schumpeter, *Wesen und Hauptinhalt der theoretischen Nationalökonomie*, p. xiii : " In allgemeinen methodologischen

18

NOTES

Werken ist von konkreten Problemen meist gar nicht die Rede ; vielmehr bewegt sich die Diskussion in allgemeinen Behauptungen ".

3. Cf. O. Morgenstern, *Zeitschrift für Nationalökonomie*, 1936, p. 1.

4. Cf. R. Carnap's essay, *Scheinprobleme in der Philosophie.*

5. Cf. J. Schumpeter, *op. cit.* p. 24 : " Aber müssen wir wirklich warten bis sich die Menschheit über diese Fragen klar geworden ist ? In diesem Falle müsste man die Ökonomie überhaupt aufgeben, da manche derselben sicherlich erst mit dem letzten Atemzuge des letzten Menschen verstummen werden."

6. This seems to us obvious. But the contrary view that Economics is, or ought to be, not an empirical science at all but a formal science just like Mathematics and Logic is held by a number of authorities led by Professor L. von Mises. Cf. *Grundprobleme der Nationalökonomie* and his lecture in *Actes du Congr s International de Philosophie*, Paris, 1937. In future references we may, for reasons of brevity, omit this obvious qualification to the Principle of Testability : that a scientific proposition may not itself be empirically testable *directly*, but may be reducible by direct deduction to an empirically testable proposition or propositions (cf. propositions of Physics about electrons, a and β particles, etc.).

7. Cf. J. Huxley, A. C. Haddon, and A. M. Carr-Saunders, *We Europeans : A Survey of " Racial " Problems*, p. 287.

8. We prefer this terminology—" science " and " non-science "—for the distinction, to that of " sense " and " nonsense " which used to be employed by writers of the former Vienna circle. To speak, however, of " scientific " propositions may well be misleading if it is not clear that all that is meant is that they might *conceivably* be recognised as scientifically " true ", not that they necessarily are so. The most fantastic proposition—*e.g.* the National Income of England is £1 per annum—might *conceivably* be material for science since it is empirically testable by statistical investigation.

9. Cf. V. Pareto, *The Mind and Society*, p. 14, and *Manuel d'Économie Politique*, p. 28.

10. Cf. W. Sombart, *Die Drei Nationalökonomien*, pp. 337-42 : " Deshalb kann man auch mit gutem Fug in den Naturwissenschaften von einem ' Fortschritt ' reden. Dass das Wissen kein Wesenswissen sondern nur ein Regelwissen ist, macht diesen ' Fortschritt ' möglich. Die Geisteswissenschaften können dieses Ideal schon deshalb nicht haben . . . da zu dem blossen Sachwissen

19

INTRODUCTION

noch andere Bestandteile hinzutreten : just philosophische und künstleriche, so dass jedes vollkommene Erzeugnis geisteswissenschaftlichen Schaffens sich uns immer auch als ein philosophisches und Kunstwerk darstellt. . . . In dieser unausgesetzten Spannung zwischen den Anforderungen der Wissenschaft und der Verlorenheit an Philosophie und Kunst tritt das innerste Wesen der Geisteswissenschaften zutage, liegt aber auch ihre Tragik begründet. . . . Sie sind ein Luxus im wahrsten Sinne des Wortes."

11. Among writers on Economics, Gottl and Spann, in addition to Sombart, have particularly devoted themselves to the theory of *verstehen* without, for the non-philosophical reader, coming to any very clear or agreed results. What is common to all these writers appears to be a certain contempt for the natural sciences, and a wish to detract from the authority they enjoy and to obtain more respect for their own activities by explaining that the natural scientist never " understands " the " essence " of what he studies. We agree with Professor Sombart that Spann is right in calling his work Economic Philosophy and not Economic Science.

12. Cf. B. Russell, *Introduction to Mathematical Philosophy*, p. 2.

13. Cf. J. Schumpeter, *op. cit.* p. 7.

14. Cf. M. Weber, *Gesammelte Aufsätze zur Wissenschaftslehre*, p. 206.

20

II

THE PROPOSITIONS OF PURE THEORY

1. PROPOSITIONS OF PURE THEORY

THE term " pure theory " is one commonly and rather loosely used by economists, but for the purposes of more precise analysis it is better replaced by the concept of the *type of proposition* of which " pure theory " consists.

By a " proposition of pure theory ", then, we understand one of the form " Under perfect competition firms are of optimum size ", or " With an increase in M, and with V and T remaining the same, P rises ", or " If p then q ", or " p ⊃ q ".

Propositions of pure theory, on our definition, are to be sharply marked off from two other types of proposition. They are to be distinguished, *first*, from propositions of the form " Conditions of perfect competition hold in this or that market, therefore firms are of optimum size ", or " M has risen and V and T have remained the same, therefore P has risen ", or " *Since* p *therefore* q ". These might suitably be called " propositions of *applied* theory ".

In this latter type of proposition the premise " p " is asserted as true empirically, while in " propositions of pure theory " no empirical assertion as to the truth of p or q individually is made. The statement made is that of a certain relation between the premise

23

p and the conclusion q. " *Since* p *therefore* q " is equivalent to two propositions, (1) the proposition of pure theory " If p then q ", and (2) the empirical synthetic proposition " p is true " (and, if one likes, thirdly, the further assertion as true of the empirical synthetic proposition q). An adequate symbolism makes the distinction between the proposition of pure theory, p ⊃ q and ⊢p. p⊃q, perfectly clear,[1] and shows that the latter consists of two quite separate propositions either of which may be " true " individually while the other is " false ".

We have been assuming that the premise " p " is an empirical synthetic proposition. For the particular distinction we are here drawing it makes no difference if " p " is an analytical proposition or a definition, for example, " All economic conduct is *ex definitione* rational ". The obviously fundamental distinction in the significance of " If p then q " when " p " is a definition, and " If p then q " when " p " is an empirical synthetic proposition, will be examined later.

The " truth " or " consistency ", then, of " propositions of pure theory " is quite independent of the question of fact as to whether the premise (of course when it is an empirical synthetic proposition) is empirically true or not, though it is on this question of fact that its applicability depends.[2] In this sense, propositions of pure theory are independent of all facts, which can be of any conceivable kind without their *consistency* being affected. We may compare a proposition of pure theory with the empirical assertion of the truth of a premise to the following distinction between a proposition of pure geometry and a proposition of applied geometry : " Thus a geometrical principle, when applied to a concrete presented object,

24

PROPOSITIONS OF PURE THEORY

is *a priori* and certain in the form ' If this plot of ground is triangular and our space is Euclidean, then the sum of these angles is 180 degrees '. But when the hypothesis is dropped and we assert ' The sum of these angles is 180 degrees ', the judgment is probable only, because there is no *a priori* and complete assurance that the concept ' Euclidean triangle ' is genuinely applicable to this plot ".[3] As Jevons put it : " If a triangle be right-angled the square on the hypotenuse will undoubtedly equal the sum of the squares on the other two sides ; but I can never be sure that a triangle is right-angled ".[4]

These quotations bring us to the second type of proposition from which propositions of pure theory must be sharply distinguished, that is, from propositions like " If the clouds are grey it is going to rain ", or " If you offer a man unconditionally *either* one shilling *or* one pound he will take the pound ", or " If one has only seven loaves and a few little fishes, one cannot feed and satisfy four thousand hungry people ". For this type of proposition we may invent the symbol p s q.

It is a defect of ordinary language that there is not necessarily any distinction, as regards the outward form, between p ⊃ q, a deductive inference, and p s q an inductive inference.[5] The latter does not signify any logically " necessary " relation between p and q but a *conceivably* falsifiable, even if *in fact* not falsified inductive generalisation, the falsification of which, however miraculous and absolutely unprecedented, is nevertheless conceivable, and the negation of which produces no contradiction in terms. In loose every-day language a proposition may be ambiguous as between the two types. For example, before the dis-

25

THE PROPOSITIONS OF PURE THEORY

covery of black swans in Australia the proposition
" All swans are white " might have been defined as
an inductive generalisation conceivably falsifiable, or
as a definition that creatures that were not white
were not to be called " swans ". But these are obviously quite as much two different propositions as
the propositions " This is a dear 'house " when it is
equivalent to " This is a charming house ", and " This
is a dear house " when it is equivalent to " This is an
expensive house ", and equally in both cases any one
who understands what he is talking about must be
able to indicate which he means. But whereas, with
the former type of ambiguity, a house may be both
charming and expensive without a contradiction in
terms, a proposition cannot *both* be conceivably falsifiable by empirical observation, and *not* be thus conceivably falsifiable.

This, it is perhaps necessary to emphasise, is a
matter of deliberate definition. We propose this as a
" division by dichotomy ", as it is called, or exhaustive
twofold classification of all propositions which have
" scientific " sense. According to our definitions of the
terms—and we suggest that they are quite normal and
straightforward—either a proposition which has sense
is conceivably falsifiable by empirical observation or
it is not. If it is not thus falsifiable it does not, if true,
forbid any conceivable occurrence, but only a contradiction in terms. Propositions obtain their empirical
content simply in so far as, if true, they *exclude*,
restrict, or *forbid* something (*e.g.* " This table is
wooden ", if true, *forbids* or *excludes* " This table is
of iron ", etc.). Therefore a proposition with empirical
content or an empirical proposition must, by definition, be conceivably falsifiable, that is, if true, *exclude*

26

THE " NECESSITY " OF PROPOSITIONS OF PURE THEORY

some conceivable possibility. Conversely, a proposition with sense, the validity of which does not depend on any empirical observation, cannot, by definition, exclude any conceivable possibility, and is therefore devoid of empirical content. The price of the unconditional necessity and certainty of propositions of pure logic and mathematics (and of propositions of pure theory) is, therefore, complete lack of empirical content.[6] According to our proposed definition all propositions with scientific sense, then, are either conceivably falsifiable by empirical observation or not, and none can be both.

It has been necessary to analyse this classification in such detail because it has been argued that those who adopt it " deny the existence " of some conceivable type or types of proposition. We make no such empirical proposition, but simply propose a classification which cannot be " true " or " false " but simply convenient or inconvenient. We suggest that, at any rate for the purposes of the economic scientist, it is the most obviously convenient classification,[7] and we propose to make use of it for this essay.

2. THE " NECESSITY " OF PROPOSITIONS OF PURE THEORY

Before pursuing our logical analysis any further we may turn aside for a moment to an inductive confirmation that it is leading us in the right direction. It seems to have escaped emphasis that throughout the history of economic theory there is a persistent record of accusations and counter-accusations of " circularity " and " assuming what one requires to prove ". Hardly any of the well-known theories of economists

27

THE PROPOSITIONS OF PURE THEORY

from the Physiocrats onwards have escaped such a characterisation at one time or another.[8] In recent years the term " tautology " came to be applied, apparently with a derogatory innuendo (usually " a sheer ", " a mere ", or " no more than a " tautology), to various propositions of deductive theory, for example the Quantity Theory of Money and different variations of it in terms of saving and investment, the marginal productivity theory of interest, and other propositions.

It was not quite clear what was meant by this terminology or what other form of proposition apart from " mere tautologies " it was intended to arrive at by the procedure of pure theory. Possibly the purely " subjective " psychological characteristic of " obviousness " or " self-evidence " was being confused with logical type. Because the proposition $2 \times 2 = 4$ is to most people probably obvious or " self-evident ", while the proposition $17 \times 37 = 629$ is probably not, this does not imply that they are of different logical type. Similarly, though the proposition " If there is an increase in M, and V and T remain the same, there will be a proportionate increase in P " is " obviously a tautology " recording a terminological agreement, the proposition " Under perfect competition firms are of optimum size ", though possibly at first not obviously so, possesses the same logical character. Though certainly it would be fantastic to deduce a fact about the nature of the costs of a firm from a purely geometrical argument, this is not what has been done in this latter proposition. No empirical proposition recording a fact about costs has been stated; attention has been called, simply, to the relations between definitions—a " fact " of linguistic usage if one likes.[9]

28

THE "NECESSITY" OF PROPOSITIONS OF PURE THEORY

If necessary, we can follow out the deduction of this proposition in detail. We start from the assumption, first, that the firms act "sensibly". This is defined as balancing marginal cost against marginal revenue—or to include that—an, in a certain degree, arbitrary procedure, because there are many alternative definitions of "sensible" that might be given under which we could *not* say that sensible firms balanced marginal cost against marginal revenue. But obviously, rather than go through this process of definition we might have started with this as our initial assumption—that the firms balance marginal cost against marginal revenue. Similarly with the second assumption, which is "equilibrium". This term is defined, as applied to the firm, as having average cost equal to price. We might, then, here also have started with this as an initial assumption. The third assumption is "perfect competition". In ordinary life these words might mean all sorts of things. But in Economics, though originally it was arbitrary, the accepted definition of the term is "conditions such that the demand, or average revenue curve, for the individual firm is perfectly elastic". As we are accepting this conventional definition we might have made it one of our initial assumptions. But this, by definition (and in no other way), implies that marginal revenue equals price. It appears, then, that in a sense, instead of going through this arbitrary process of assigning definitions, we might have started straight off by saying, "Let us assume marginal cost is equal to marginal revenue, is equal to price, is equal to average cost". Here we may fit in the now accepted, but originally arbitrary, definitions of the terms marginal and average cost. These are such that they

29

THE PROPOSITIONS OF PURE THEORY

can only be equal when average cost is at a minimum. Again, we might have started with this as our one assumption. But there is now a recognised definition for " working at minimum average cost "—that is, " being of optimum size ". Our conclusion was thus assumed when we made our assumptions, and was reached by assigning definitions.

If we assume these assumptions and definitions our conclusion is already assumed—the proof is the process of recognising what we have assumed in our definitions. " Propositions which form part of logic, or *which can be proved by logic*, are all tautologies. . . . Such propositions, therefore, are really concerned with symbols, because they are only concerned with symbolic manipulations." [10]

In formulating a system of definitions one is in one and the same process formulating a series of analytical-tautological propositions of pure theory. Unless one is prepared to contradict oneself—that is, use language inconsistently by defining a concept in one way and then using it in another—once one has formulated a system of definitions one must agree to the resulting propositions of pure theory. Purely theoretical analysis consists in the manipulation of concepts in accordance with the rules laid down in their definitions. The assigning of definitions, therefore, obviously plays a key rôle in the construction of pure theory.

The selection of good definitions which make possible the development of useful deductive chains is indisputably a creative scientific achievement, but the selection of a definition does not involve an issue of truth or falsity in the same sense that an empirical synthetic proposition is either true or false.[11] A definition may be misleading, inappropriate, or incon-

30

THE " NECESSITY " OF PROPOSITIONS OF PURE THEORY

venient, and if a scientist prefers using one definition or system of definitions to another there is no way of ultimately confuting him so long, of course, as he uses them consistently. In this sense, though the use of this adjective seems sometimes to encounter resistance, definitions are " arbitrary ".[11] The convenience or inconvenience of a definition will turn mainly on the actual facts to which it is to be applied, in Economics on what statistics may or may not be available.

Whether in introducing a new term altering, sharpening, or confirming the sense of an old one, a definition lays down a convention made by the scientist, who imposes it as a government does a traffic regulation. It is this law-giving element in the assignment of definitions which is the source of the " necessity " or " inevitability " so often claimed for propositions of pure theory, which at bottom are necessary and inevitable because we make them so— the reverse of what is the case with empirical generalisations, which, in a sense, are imposed on us by the behaviour of the facts.

Although theoretical economists have sometimes emphasised that they are aware that propositions of pure theory are concerned with definitions, not with facts, nevertheless in Economics, as apparently in Philosophy, Mathematics, and other sciences, countless controversies and confusions have resulted from the use of the " material " rather than the " formal " mode of expression.[13] Take, for example, propositions such as " Value *is* this ", " Costs *really are* this ", " No, they are that ",[14] " What *is* saving or capital or the stationary state ? " The form of these propositions leads one to the misleading notion that one is treating of something other than a question of language—put

31

THE PROPOSITIONS OF PURE THEORY

crudely, that one is talking about things and not about words. It appears that these propositions must be definitely right or wrong, and that there must be one correct answer to the questions. But when they are expressed in the accurate "*formal*" mode, for example, " In the Marxian language-system value is defined as follows . . .", or " I propose that in the language-system (economic theory) which economists are constructing the word 'saving' be defined as follows . . .", it is clear at once that the issue is fundamentally one of convenience, of how the definition fits in with others in the language, and is not one of absolute rightness or wrongness. When the relativity of a proposition such as " Perfect competition is, etc. . . ." to a particular language-system is admitted, and placed in the foreground from the start, there is more chance of profitable discussion and less of beating the air.

It would be completely fallacious to conclude that because we have insisted that various disputes — in fact *all purely theoretical* disputes which do not turn on questions of fact—are purely *verbal*, that therefore we are necessarily saying that they are *trivial*. On the contrary, it is arguable that, particularly with regard to the theory of the trade cycle, for example, attention to the question of arriving at an accepted and unified system of definitions would be amply rewarded, instead of continuing with each writer having his own private terminology and imagining that he has found out something new about the trade cycle—some " Fundamental Relation " or other—when he has simply added to the already vastly excessive number of terminologies. But constructive verbal discussion can only begin when it is perfectly clear that it is verbal and purely verbal.

Similarly when we, or quotations we have cited,

32

have spoken of propositions of pure theory as " simply " or " only " concerned with symbolic or terminological manipulations, we are, of course, not trying to level a deliberate insult at propositions of pure theory or those who work at them, and to scorn them as being concerned simply with trivialities. But it is the feeling that important scientific work is being somehow belittled and analysed out of existence which seems often to be behind the resistance to such analysis as this, when no alternative logico-scientific analysis of analytical propositions devoid of unscientific mysticism is put forward.

3. THE USE AND SIGNIFICANCE OF PROPOSITIONS OF PURE THEORY

Let us turn from examining what we have called propositions of pure theory from the point of view of *the source of their necessity* to an examination of *their use and significance*. The rôle of analytical propositions in science has been clearly summarised by Schlick as follows :

" The construction of any strictly deductive science is, as it were, a game with symbols. In an abstract science like the theory of numbers, for example, it is simply the enjoyment of this game for its own sake which is the motive for the building of a deductive structure. But in geometry, on the other hand, and to an even greater extent in other sciences the interest above all lies in certain other perceptual (*anschauliche*) objects to which there is a possibility of linking the net of concepts. In general, then, we concern ourselves with the abstract only in order to apply the results to the concrete. But in the moment of transferring a rela-

33

THE PROPOSITIONS OF PURE THEORY

tion of concepts to perceptual examples the exact rigour is no longer preserved. For if any object is given us, how can we ever know with absolute certainty that they stand to one another in precisely those relations which are laid down in the postulates through which we define our concepts ? " [15]

Being unconditionally true and neither confirmable nor contradictable by an empirical synthetic proposition, propositions of pure theory cannot tell us anything new in the sense of telling us new facts about the world. But they call attention to implications of our definitions which might otherwise have escaped our attention, and reveal unexpected relations between our definitions which are thus explained and clarified.[16] " Pure theory " affords us a sharp clear-cut language or system of definitions with which to approach the problems which the facts of the world raise. Just as theoretical physicists and astronomers have the task of explaining everything we say by implication if we assert the law of gravitation,[17] so theoretical economists have the task of explaining what we say by implication if we assert the various assumptions of economic analysis.

Propositions of pure theory enable us, further, to pass at once from one empirical synthetic proposition to another. Just as the proposition of pure mathematics "$7 \times 17 = 119$" enables me to pass at once from the empirical proposition " My bookcase contains 7 rows with 17 books in each row " to the further empirical proposition " My bookcase contains 119 books ", so the proposition of pure theory " Under perfect competition firms are of optimum size " enables one to pass at once from the proposition " Competition is perfect in this market " to the pro-

34

position " The firms competing in this market are of optimum size ". Their use thus depends on one's being able to establish an empirical proposition as true. In some kind of perfectly fluid world even mathematics would be inapplicable.

Theoretical analysis thus compensates us, in a certain way, for the fact that our brains are not all-powerful.[18] With all-powerful brains we would need no pure theory to work out the relations and implications of our definitions or empirical premisses. We would just have a dictionary in which all our concepts —" perfect competition ", " monopoly ", " saving ", etc.—were clearly defined and, after reading it through, would perceive at one glance all the most subtle inter-relations. As it is, pure theory, by consistent uncontradictory use of the economic vocabulary and by building up the vocabulary further, brings home to us what the implications of our definitions are.

A sharply and clearly defined system of concepts enables sharp and clear answers to be obtained from empirical investigation. The " man in the street " asks whether " wages " have risen since 1920, and getting four or five different answers, concludes that " one can prove anything by statistics ". This is quite a correct conclusion if one is proceeding without sharply defined concepts. An economist distinguishing between " money " wages and " real " wages, wages per hour and wages per month, can squeeze the maximum of definiteness and clarity out of the available statistics. The constant object of the scientist, it has been said, is to compel the facts of experience to answer his questions definitely " Yes " or " No ",[19] and he can only do this with a clear-cut language-system. As the classic advocate of induction admitted : *prudens*

35

THE PROPOSITIONS OF PURE THEORY

interrogatio dimidium scientiae—a half, but only a half, for, to quote Poincaré, " all that the scientist creates in a fact is the language in which he enunciates it ".

Every single step in a deductive chain is trivial. Long deductive chains lose their trivial, but not their analytical-tautological character. To criticise a proposition of pure theory *as such* as tautological, or circular, or as assuming what it requires to prove, is beside the point. The *applicability* of the assumptions of a piece of pure theory may be criticised; but this is purely a question of fact, having nothing to do with the *form* of a proposition of pure theory, which *must* necessarily be " tautological ", " circular ", and " assume what it proves "—for what it proves must be contained in the assumptions, and cannot be obtained from any other source. As Professor Lewis puts it : " The test of circularity is a valuable test of any deductive development of logic. That the principles proved are precisely the principles used in the demonstration of them is here a matter for congratulation. That the method of our proof coincides with the results of it, is a test of both method and result. It is not a test of truth, however, it is a test of formal or methodo logical consistency." [20]

4. THE HYPOTHETICAL METHOD

To a far greater extent than any other science, except perhaps Geometry, Economics makes use of what has been called the " hypothetical " or " isolating " method. That is, much of the economist's work is devoted to investigating not directly the problems of the world as it is, but simplified cases and examples

36

THE HYPOTHETICAL METHOD

which, it is claimed, " throw light on the real problems ". Communities of perfect competition, with " neutral " money, communities in some sense " static " or " dynamic ", the behaviour of a Robinson Crusoe and other " conjectural history ", as Sir James Steuart called it, of every description is investigated.[21]

The same or a similar method was that called " the hypothetical experiment " by Cairnes.[22] As a modern writer puts it, " Economic theory is a laboratory for the economist " ; [23] or, to take a fuller description by Böhm-Bawerk : " Just as the experimenter artificially simplifies the conditions under which he tests the workings of certain forces or materials, and excludes the disturbing ' frictions ' of the world as it is, so the deductive, but by no means *a priori*, theorist isolates in this thought the workings of certain typical social or economic forces to examine them first free of disturbances in their purity, and out of the partial knowledge obtained in this way gradually pieces together his knowledge of the full and varied empirical reality. His simplified and simplifying premisses are in the same sense real as the contents of the experimenter's test-tube." [24]

It is clearly very necessary here, when it is claimed, apparently, that the simplified hypothetical " experiment " of the deductive theorist is a full substitute for the laboratory experiments of the natural scientist, to emphasise the distinction drawn at the beginning of the chapter between a proposition of pure theory— a *deductive* inference or logical implication—and an *inductive* inference won by experiential observation, for, in our imperfect everyday language, they may both be worded in the same way (" If p then q ").[25]

The result of an empirical experiment, however

37

THE PROPOSITIONS OF PURE THEORY

isolated and artificial the conditions under which it is carried out, is recorded in a synthetic empirical proposition. It is always conceivable that if the experiment were repeated the result might be different, and either a generalisation based on previous similar experiments would be falsified, or some disturbing element or a " mistake " might be recorded.

It may perhaps be psychologically useful in some cases for an investigator to imagine and describe to himself the workings of some particular model community representing an extreme case. But this cannot be anything more than a preliminary thought-clearing exercise, and it would be fantastic to suggest that one could thus achieve the concrete results obtainable from laboratory experiment for which this procedure constitutes a substitute.

But the procedure of the so-called " hypothetical experiment " is completely different. Here certain simplifying assumptions are made, and then what we have called " propositions of pure theory " *without any empirical content*, are arrived at by pure deduction. When it is stated, for example, that static equilibrium analysis " examines in isolation part of the forces operating in the real world ", which tend to regain equilibrium like water in a tank when disturbed,[26] clearly there is a danger of propositions of the type $p \supset q$ being confused with propositions of the type $p \, s \, q$. Cairnes used, incidentally, for demonstrating a hypothetical experiment, that " mere tautology ", as it has been called, the Quantity Theory of Money, examining the " effects " on P of a rise in M when V and T remained the same.[27] This is one variety of many different kinds of attempts to read some empirical content into propositions of pure theory, to give them,

38

THE HYPOTHETICAL METHOD

as Professor Myrdal puts it, " einen scheinbaren Inhalt von Wirklichkeitserkenntnis ".[28] We discuss in the next chapter attempts to assign to them prognostic value, the statement of a causal connection, and, above all, their being called " laws ". Such attempts are no doubt partly due to this type of analysis usually being mainly carried on in the *material* rather than the strictly accurate *formal* mode of expression. The argument usually begins " We assume conditions of perfect competition . . ." or " Imagine a community . . .", instead of " The term ' perfect competition ' being defined as follows, it logically implies . . ."

The very terms " assume " and " assumption " may give a misleadingly " material " appearance to " purely theoretical " discussions, as though one was really considering an empirical possibility, by way of a model (as when in everyday language one says " Assuming it rains to-morrow "), and not simply analysing definitions.[29]

That " pure theory " is so often carried on in everyday language instead of the formal abstract language of mathematics may also give it a misleadingly " material " appearance, as the constant mention of markets, consumers, prices, goods, and so on inevitably calls up images in our minds which divert attention from the purely formal nature of the argument. It is necessary constantly to remember that " theories which make a proposition of logic appear substantial are always false ".[30]

In so far, then, as the propositions of hypothetical analysis are propositions of pure theory—that is, in so far as the assumptions on which they are based are not asserted as facts—to that extent hypothetical propositions say nothing about facts but about the

39

THE PROPOSITIONS OF PURE THEORY

way in which we discuss the facts. Hypothetical analysis or pure theory creates, as Ramsey put it, a " language for the discussing of the facts ".[31] All these relations between symbols say nothing about real experience ; they are but part of the instrument for mastering it. All these analyses of hypothetical simplified communities—in so far as the resulting propositions are of the form we have discussed (however misleadingly they may appear to be dealing with " things " and not " words " by beginning " Let us *assume* such-and-such *conditions* " or " Let us imagine a community where . . ., etc.")—are concerned with language. They are concerned in no way with some mystical " real " connection between facts which we discover by deductive thinking. Rather they have no direct connection with facts but flow from the way in which we talk about the facts.[32]

5. THE " CETERIS PARIBUS " ASSUMPTION

As an example of the use of the ceteris paribus assumption we may take the proposition " If the price at which a good is sold rises, ceteris paribus the amount of the good demanded declines ". Is this an empirical generalisation which can conceivably be false without any contradiction, or is it an analytical-tautological proposition ?

This, usually, is not made clear, and perhaps such propositions are sometimes meant in one way, sometimes in another. One can only ask in each particular case whether the validity of the ceteris paribus proposition in question depends on facts, or whether, on the other hand, the denial of it simply shows that one does not understand by the terms " rise in price "

40

THE " CETERIS PARIBUS " ASSUMPTION

and " amount demanded " what the language of economists understands.[33]

If the proposition " If the price at which a good is sold rises, ceteris paribus the amount of the good demanded declines " is an empirical generalisation, so it can only have a clear scientific meaning if it is indicated under what conditions it would be true, or under what false. Further, it is desirable that the difference be shown between *this* empirical generalisation (*with* ceteris paribus) and the *other* empirical generalisation, " If the price at which a good is sold rises the amount of the good demanded declines " (*without* ceteris paribus).

Ceteris paribus propositions *can* be interpreted in this way. But if they are to be so interpreted—as empirical generalisations—then they are usually very vaguely and unclearly formulated. For no attempt is made, usually, to indicate under what conditions they are true and under what false, and the meaning of the vital qualification " ceteris paribus " is left hopelessly imprecise. The ceteris paribus assumption, just as much as any other, must be precisely formulated if the propositions it qualifies are to have any clear meaning. The *intention* of the assumption obviously is to lessen the falsifiability of the too often falsified generalisation " If the price of a good rises, the amount sold declines ". But exactly *how far* is its falsifiability thus lessened, and if it remains an empirical proposition, what conceivable possibilities of falsification remain?

On the other hand, it seems more probable that ceteris paribus propositions are frequently treated as analytical-tautological propositions, the example taken in this case explaining a relation between the definitions of " rise in price " and " amount demanded "

41

THE PROPOSITIONS OF PURE THEORY

at different points on a demand curve of a particular shape—a purely logical or geometrical relation. Then it is inconceivable that its truth or falsity (as against its applicability) can be established by any facts, since it is without factual content. In this case one simply determines whether, in fact, the ceteris paribus assumption is true or false, by observing whether or not the price has risen appropriately or not—a circular procedure. This appears to be the interpretation favoured by Menger,[34] though it involves a very elastic conception of " *cetera* ". For example, if the well-known case of poor people buying *more* bread when the price of it rises in no way falsifies our proposition, this involves a considerable stretching of the assumption " ceteris paribus ".

Thus interpreted the ceteris paribus clause is an accessory assumption of pure theory, and ceteris paribus propositions may be analysed in the same way as the propositions of pure theory have been. The ceteris paribus assumption makes out of an empirical proposition that is concerned with facts, and therefore conceivably can be false, a necessary analytical-tautological proposition. For a mathematical solution (by tautological transformations) the number of equations must be equal to the number of unknowns. The ceteris paribus assumption sweeps all the unknowns together under one portmanteau assumption for a logical " solution ".

In Physics and Chemistry, where there are far more discovered empirical regularities, the ceteris paribus assumption is not used in the same way. For if the assumption is broadly true, or if, as is rather the case, the " *cetera* " in the natural sciences themselves act in accordance with known laws, then the ceteris

42

THE " CETERIS PARIBUS " ASSUMPTION

paribus assumption is more or less given one, and a true premise can always be dropped. For in a certain sense it is only necessary to make an assumption when one does not know it is true, or knows that it is untrue. This is the peculiar dilemma —apparently unique throughout science—of the " isolating ", " assumption-making " procedure of economic theory where there are few empirical generalisations known to be true.

In the natural sciences certain fundamental propositions can be taken either to be analytical-tautological or to be empirical generalisations, exactly as the ceteris paribus propositions may be so taken. For example, originally the proposition " All gases expand on warming " was probably arrived at by empirical experiments. But if to-day an experiment was made with something which as regards the other ways in which it was tested behaved like a " gas " but did not expand on warming, one would at first be inclined to suggest that some mistake had been made in the experiment. But if after repeated experiments this " gas " did not expand, scientists would be faced with a choice. Either they must say " Our law that all gases expand on warming is destroyed, and we must find a new law ", or they could say " This stuff which does not expand on warming is no ' gas ', for *by definition* a ' gas ' *must* expand on warming ; we must find some other name for this ". The choice of this second course on all conceivable occasions would mean that the proposition " All gases expand on warming " was not an empirical law at all, but an analytical-tautological definition which was always true because it was not allowed to be false. From the mere wording and form of the proposition

43

THE PROPOSITIONS OF PURE THEORY

one cannot say whether it is the one or the other. One can only find out by a test case when scientists are forced to choose one alternative or the other.[35]

According to Edgeworth, " The treating as constant of what is variable is the source of most of the fallacies in Political Economy ",[36] and it is the danger of the ceteris paribus assumption that it particularly facilitates such fallacies. It is quite probably true that in more cases than not a rise in price is in fact followed by a decrease in demand, but this of course might not be so ; and whether it is so or not can only be decided by statistical investigation. Our proposition with ceteris paribus does not tell us this. In fact the ceteris paribus clause seems sometimes so to be used that one might equally significantly and correctly advance the proposition that ceteris paribus a rise in price is followed by an *increase* in demand, as the proposition that ceteris paribus it is followed by a *decrease*. " Ceteris paribus this follows that " seems to come to mean simply " *In many cases* this follows that ", and however often it may not, the reply is that the proposition only said " in many cases " (or ceteris paribus), and this was simply one of the other cases (or " ceteris paribus " did not hold).

In the recent developments of the " dynamic " pure theory of employment the ceteris paribus assumption appears sometimes to have been applied to propositions which standing alone (without " ceteris paribus ") are quite probably more often empirically false than true, but when it is added are meant to get away with some kind of exact and significant empirical content.

Mr. Keynes gives an example of the use of the ceteris paribus clause on these lines.[37] He contrasts the two

44

THE " CETERIS PARIBUS " ASSUMPTION

propositions: (1) "A decreased readiness to spend . . . will ceteris paribus increase investment ", and (2) " A decreased readiness to spend . . . will ceteris paribus diminish employment ". Are these empirical or analytical propositions—that is, what is the precise content of " ceteris paribus " ? If they are empirical, then it is difficult to see what the qualification " ceteris paribus " can mean other than " usually ". Then we have two propositions : " A decreased readiness to spend will usually " either (1) " increase investment " or (2) " diminish employment "—two rather vague impressionist generalisations ; and though one *may* be more often true than the other, neither is of much scientific value compared with statistical investigations as to what, *in fact*, *does* follow a decreased readiness to spend in different cases, pending the results of which it seems difficult to justify an exclusive insistence on one as against the other.

If, on the other hand, these propositions are analytical, there is of course no question of one being " true " and the other " false ", and no particular reason for contrasting them, since neither says anything about *what in fact follows* a decreased readiness to spend. " Ceteris paribus " is simply used differently for the two equations. In the first *total outlay* is included among the " ceteris " that remain the same, so that a decrease in one division of it (consumption spending) mathematically implies an increase in the other division (investment). In the second equation *employment on capital goods* is assumed to remain the same, so that a decrease in employment on consumption goods mathematically implies a decrease in total employment.

Either of these interpretations is possible and there

45

THE PROPOSITIONS OF PURE THEORY

may be others. In the first place such a use of the
" ceteris paribus " clause leaves it quite ambiguous
as to what kind of proposition is being put forward.
In the second place it appears to give to what is
either simply an empirically empty analytical proposition, or a very vague and statistically unsupported
empirical generalisation, an air of some kind of precise and widely valid empirical content.

We suggest that the ceteris paribus assumption
can only be safely and significantly used in conjunction with an empirical generalisation verified as true
in a large percentage of cases but occasionally liable
to exceptions of a clearly describable type.

NOTES

1. Cf. L. S. Stebbing, *A Modern Introduction to Logic*, 2nd
edition, p. 212.
2. F. Kaufmann, *Methodenlehre der Sozialwissenschaften*,
pp. 38-57.
3. Cf. C. I. Lewis, *Mind and the World Order*, p. 313.
4. Cf. W. S. Jevons, *Principles of Science*, vol. i. p. 270. Also
A. Einstein, *Geometrie und Erfahrung*, p. 3 ; J. Nicod, *La Géo-
métrie et le monde sensible*, p. 14.
5. M. Schlick, *Allgemeine Erkenntnislehre*, 2, A, p. 43.
6. Cf. H. Feigl, *Theorie und Erfahrung in der Physik*, p. 11,
and A. D. Ritchie, *Scientific Method*.
7. We emphasise very strongly that we are simply proposing a
classification and not claiming that any conceivable type of proposition " does or does not exist ". Neo-Kantian philosopher-
economists may object that this classification is inconvenient
as it passes over the Kantian synthetic propositions *a priori*,
which cannot be fitted into it without distortion. We do not
wish to go into the general philosophical or logical problems of
Kantian criticism and exegesis on this point, though we happen
to believe that all genuine problems here have been conclusively
settled (cf. for example M. Schlick's *Allgemeine Erkenntnislehre*).
We are concerned simply with a convenient classification *for
economic scientists* and find that all the propositions of Economics

46

NOTES

that we are concerned with in this book, including the Economic Principle (*vide* Chapter IV)—provided of course they are precisely and unambiguously formulated—at once fit into our classification. As regards the Economic or "maximum" principle it may be noted that Kant himself, it appears, would not have considered it a vastly significant proposition, and almost certainly not a synthetic one *a priori*, to judge by his comments on the concept of "Glückseligkeit", *Kritik der Urteilskraft*, § 83 : "Der Mensch . . . ändert diesen (Begriff der Glückseligkeit) so oft, dass die Natur, wenn sie auch seiner Willkür gänzlich unterworfen wäre, doch schlechterdings kein bestimmtes allgemeines und festes Gesetz annehmen könnte, um mit diesem schwankenden Begriff, und so mit dem Zweck, den jeder sich willkürlicherweise vorsetzt, übereinzustimmen ". Cf. also the "neo-Kantian" T. H. Green's criticism of the Utilitarian principle : Introduction to Hume's *Treatise of Human Nature*, vol. ii. pp. 3-27.

If advocates of synthetic propositions *a priori* would agree and formulate—as they have not done yet, being content largely with generalisations—a number of these synthetic propositions *a priori* very precisely indeed, then we could begin to consider how they fit into our classification, which corresponds with that of most standard works on scientific method. An explanation would further be desirable as to how the "truth" of these propositions can be tested, if this cannot be done either by empirical verification or logical consistency, and whether or no they have empirical content and are conceivably falsifiable empirically. For the scientist just dogmatic assertion or question-begging phrases like "self-evidence" are hardly satisfactory. One neo-Kantian economist (cf. H. Bernadelli, *Economica*, 1936, p. 446 ; see also F. Kaufmann's apt reply, 1937, p. 337) admits that one is here led up against a brick wall, and concludes logically, but rather depressingly for the scientist, that as regards synthetic propositions *a priori* ' so long as their source remains undiscovered all sciences which are built on philosophical or mathematical principles—and there is none which is not—hang so to speak in the air ". When one finds oneself in this position it may be better than insisting that the wall is not, or some day will not be, or ought not to be, there, to consider whether, possibly, one has not been on the wrong road from the start. A hopeless confusion over the term *a priori* in Economics also arises over its being somehow mixed up with " introspection " (*vide* below, V. 1-2).

8. See below, III. 1.
9. Cf. J. Robinson, *Economics of Imperfect Competition*, p. 95.

47

THE PROPOSITIONS OF PURE THEORY

10. Cf. B. Russell, *Analysis of Matter*, p. 171, and P. M. Eaton, *Symbolism and Truth*, p. 227.

11. Cf. P. Frank, *Das Kausalgesetz und seine Grenzen*, p. 1.

12. Cf. L. Rougier, *La Structure des théories déductives*, p. 86 ; W. Dubislav, *Die Definition*, p. 112 ; and on the other hand, L. S. Stebbing, *op. cit.* p. 427 : " It is because definitions are not arbitrary that they are useful ". The disagreement is obviously an unimportant terminological one.

13. Cf. R. Carnap, *Logische Syntax der Sprache*, pp. 210 and 225, and *Philosophy and Logical Syntax*, pp. 46-81.

14. The " cost " controversy presents one of the most perfect examples of decades of argument over a purely verbal issue— though of course not necessarily the less important for that. Compare the following statement of the issues : " As is well known, Marshall and (up to a recent date) most of his followers insisted that costs, in the last analysis, were something real and absolute—a conception independent of utility. Wicksteed and the Austrians, on the other hand, denied that they were anything but foregone alternatives " (L. C. Robbins, Introduction to P. Wicksteed's *Commonsense of Political Economy*, p. xviii). Professor L. M. Fraser's *Economic Thought and Language* brings many such purely verbal controversies to light.

15. Cf. M. Schlick, *Allgemeine Erkenntnislehre*, p. 35.

16. Cf. A. J. Ayer, *Language, Truth, and Logic*, p. 104.

17. Cf. H. Hahn, *Logik, Mathematik, Naturerkennen*, p. 19.

18. Cf. R. M. Eaton, *General Logic*, p. 474.

19. Cf. K. Popper, *Logik der Forschung*, pp. 207-8.

20. Cf. C. I. Lewis, *Mind and the World Order*, p. 240.

21. W. Eucken, *Kapitaltheoretische Untersuchungen*, p. 7, clearly describes the hypothetical method and its importance : " Wenn ein isolierter Staat vorhanden, wenn das Land überall gleich fruchtbar ist, und wenn die übrigen von Thünen gesetzten Annahmen gegeben sind, dann muss der Standort der einzelnen Betriebssysteme sich da und dort befinden. Wenn ein Mann als Eremit lebt, wenn er bestimmte Bedürfnisse und ein bestimmtes technisches Wissen besitzt, wenn er über eine bestimmte Arbeitskraft verfügt und wenn noch mehrere andere Bedingungen gegeben sind, dann muss er auf bestimmte Weise bestimmte Produkte in bestimmter Menge herstellen. Der einzelne theoretische Satz enthält also ein hypothetisches allgemeingültiges Urteil über einen notwendigen Bedingungszusammenhang, *die moderne nationalökonomische Theorie als Ganzes stellt das in sich geschlossene einheitliche Gesamtsystem solcher Urteile dar.*" (Our italics.)

48

NOTES

22. Cf. J. E. Cairnes, *Character and Logical Method of Political Economy*, 2nd edition, p. 90.

23. Cf. E. Phelps Brown, *The Framework of the Pricing System*, p. 32.

24. Cf. E. von Böhm-Bawerk, *Gesammelte Schriften*, p. 193, and also F. von Wieser, *Gesammelte Abhandlungen*, p. 19.

25. See above, Section 1.

26. See below, IV. 6.

27. Cf. J. E. Cairnes, *op. cit.* pp. 90-91.

28. Cf. G. Myrdal, *Beiträge zur Geldtheorie*, ed. F. A von Hayek, pp. 485-6.

29. In addition to the laboratory experiment and the so-called " hypothetical experiment " there is the *Gedankenexperiment*. This is simply letting one's fancy conceive what *might* happen if one tried some " real " laboratory experiment. *By itself* it yields no results at all ; it is simply the preliminary thinking-out of a possibly significant laboratory experiment and must always be followed up by that if it is to be proved valuable. Cf. E. Mach, *Erkenntnis und Irrtum*, ch. xi., and W. Dubislav, *Naturphilosophie*, pp. 60-62.

30. Cf. L. Wittgenstein, *Tractatus Logico-Philosophicus*, p. 155 ; J. Jörgensen, *Principles of Logic*, vol. iii. pp. 116-17, and L. Rougier, *op. cit.*, *passim*.

31. Cf. F. P. Ramsey, *The Foundations of Mathematics*, p. 212.

32. Cf. H. Hahn, *op. cit.* p. 15.

33. Cf. K. Adjukiewicz, *Erkenntnis*, 1934, p. 263.

34. Cf. C. Menger, *Untersuchungen über die Methode*, pp. 57-9 : " Das Gesetz, dass der erhöhte Bedarf an einer Ware eine Steigerung der Preise, und zwar dass ein bestimmtes Mass der Steigerung des Bedarfes, auch eine ihrem Masse nach bestimmte Steigerung der Preise zur Folge habe, ist demnach, an der Wirklichkeit in ihrer vollen Komplikation geprüft, unwahr—unempirisch. Was beweist dies aber anders, als dass Ergebnisse der exakten Forschung an der Erfahrung im obigen Sinne eben nicht ihren Prüfstein finden ? *Das obige Gesetz ist trotz alledem wahr, durchaus wahr*, und von der höchsten Bedeutung für das theoretische Verständnis der Preiserscheinungen." (Our italics.)

35. Cf. K. Popper, *op. cit.* p. 230, and P. Frank, *op. cit.* pp. 241-50.

36. Quoted by O. Morgenstern, *Limits of Economics*, heading to ch. iii.

37. Cf. J. M. Keynes, *General Theory of Employment, Interest and Money*, p. 185.

49

IV

THE BASIC POSTULATES OF PURE THEORY
EXPECTATIONS, RATIONAL CONDUCT,
AND EQUILIBRIUM

1. THE " FUNDAMENTAL ASSUMPTION "

THROUGHOUT its history, the idea of some " Fundamental Assumption ", some basic " Economic Principle " about human conduct from which much or
most of Economics can ultimately be deduced, has
been deeply rooted in the procedure of economic
theory. Some such notion is still, in many quarters,
dominant at the present time. For example, it has
recently been stated that the task of Economics is
" to display the structure and working of the economic cosmos as an outgrowth of the maximum
principle ".[1] This " fundamental maximum principle ", which should obviously receive very careful
formulation and empirical verification, has been
framed in different ways in the history of economic
theory, from the profit-seeking Ricardian business
man down to the " rational " consumer balancing
marginal utilities. Sometimes more emphasis has
been laid on the purely hypothetical nature of the
principle as a starting-point for a deductive argument,
while sometimes it is urged rather that the principle
is in fact, roughly at any rate, an empirically true
generalisation.[2]

83

THE BASIC POSTULATES OF PURE THEORY

But at the present day, far from there appearing to be any definite agreement as to the precise formulation of this " Fundamental Assumption ", there appears not even to be complete agreement as to whether it is necessary or in fact used at all.[3] The clarification of these problems, and the resolving of the at any rate superficial contradiction in the procedure of text-books which begin their exposition of the theory of value with the assumption that everyone acts " rationally " or " sensibly ", and then in a later chapter base their explanation of economic fluctuations on " mistakes ", fluctuations of optimism and pessimism, or the casino-like nature of the capital market, is a necessary preliminary to the task of co-ordinating the theory of output and employment with the theory of price or value. For this co-ordination, if it can usefully be carried through at all, can only take place by bringing the two theories under a common set of assumptions, which involves finding out and formulating more precisely what the assumptions of the two theories are.[4]

2. " PERFECT EXPECTATION " AND THE FUNDAMENTAL ASSUMPTION

In spite of other variations there is one remarkable characteristic common to nearly all formulations of the " Fundamental Principle " from its origins in Utilitarian doctrines down to the present time. One of Bentham's formulations was : " Nature has placed mankind under the governance of two sovereign masters, pain and pleasure. It is for them alone to point out what we ought to do, as well as to determine what we shall do ".[5] Ricardo expressed the

84

" PERFECT EXPECTATION " AND FUNDAMENTAL ASSUMPTION

principle in a particular connection thus : " Whilst every man is free to employ his capital where he pleases, he will naturally seek for it that employment which is most advantageous ; he will naturally be dissatisfied with a profit of 10 per cent, if by removing his capital he can obtain a profit of 15 per cent ".[6] J. S. Mill speaks of the fundamental assumption " that man is a being who is determined, by the necessity of his nature, to prefer a greater portion of wealth to a smaller in all cases. . . ." [7] Finally, a modern formulation : " The fundamental assumption of economic analysis is that every individual acts in a sensible manner, and it is sensible for the individual to balance marginal cost against marginal gain . . . sensible conduct leads to the maximisation of money gains ".[8]

The common characteristic of all these different formulations—chosen quite at random—of the Fundamental Assumption, is that as they stand they appear further to postulate, and only are applicable if the further postulate is made, that all expectations are perfectly correct. They therefore pass over all the problems of economy in the world as it is, which may be said to arise from precisely this factor of uncertainty and imperfect foresight. They all make no mention of the question *how* one is to maximise one's returns. They simply say that it is " rational ", " sensible ", or " natural " to do this, assuming, presumably, that one *knows* how this can be done. To decisions which are not of this certain automatic kind they have no applicability. The absence of uncertainty in the conditions analysed emerges clearly from the formulae themselves. According to Bentham, pleasure and pain completely determine one's

85

THE BASIC POSTULATES OF PURE THEORY

actions. There is no question as to *which* line of conduct leads to pleasure and which to pain—this is apparently known for certain. Similarly with Ricardo, there is no uncertainty as to the relative advantages of different lines of investment. The assumption is tacitly made that it is perfectly foreseen that one will yield 10 per cent and the other 15 per cent, and people " naturally " select 15 per cent. With Mill again the problem as to *which* line of conduct will yield " the greater portion of wealth " is not mentioned as existing, and his principle that men " naturally " prefer this to a smaller portion only begins to have sense when it is assumed that people can foresee perfectly which line of conduct leads to the greater portion—an assumption which Mill apparently tacitly slips in. Again, in the last quotation there is, as it stands, no question as to *how* one is to maximise one's money gains. This is known, and one simply acts " sensibly " on one's certain knowledge.

Where uncertainty is present, as is in principle the case with any piece of conduct in this world, economic or otherwise, one cannot, strictly speaking, seek the most advantageous employment for one's capital or act so as to maximise one's returns. One can only act in accordance with one's *expectations* as to the " maximum " conduct, and the expectations of the most clever and " rational " may, in the world as it is, turn out to be incorrect. The terms " sensible " and " rational " cannot, then, be applied to conduct under conditions of perfect foresight in the same sense in which they are usually loosely applied to conduct in the world as it is. It is taken for granted as " natural " that people prefer a greater

86

PERFECT EXPECTATION " AND FUNDAMENTAL ASSUMPTION

satisfaction, in the widest sense, to a lesser one when they *know for certain* which line of conduct leads to the greater and which to the lesser. But in the world as it is, where this is not known, the terms " rational " and " sensible " are usually applied to the *expectations or the process of arriving at the expectations* that one line of conduct will yield more satisfaction than an alternative. When an investment is called " stupid " or " irrational " it is not usually meant that the investor in question was deliberately aiming at less than the maximum return open to him, but that it was " stupid " of him *to expect* that he would maximise his returns in that way. This use of such terms is, of course, excluded from application under conditions where *all* expectations are alike perfect.

So long as one is concerned with a world where the choice is always an automatic one between a return which is *certainly* maximum and others which are *certainly* smaller, the assumption that people *expect* to maximise their returns and the assumption that they *actually do* maximise them come to the same thing. But where the consequences of all decisions can be perfectly foreseen, the maximum principle clearly works itself out in a very special way which must be fundamentally distinguished from the only way in which it can work itself out when there is any uncertainty present, that is, under conditions where people cannot conceivably *know* or *calculate* but can only more or less vaguely *guess*, which out of many possible lines of conduct will lead to the fulfilment of the principle. This vital distinction is only glossed over by assuming that people " tend " or " seek " to fulfil the maximum principle, and has been entirely passed over even when this principle has been formu-

87

THE BASIC POSTULATES OF PURE THEORY

lated with the term " expect ".[9] An analysis of a world with any uncertainty in it, and particularly an analysis which takes into account the factor of money (which can be construed as a sign that uncertainty is present, or even as a measure of its amount),[10] cannot start from the same assumption of " sensible " or " rational " conduct as that applicable in a world without uncertainty, with which, consciously and explicitly or not, the bulk of pure economic theory from Ricardo onwards appears to have been concerned.

With uncertainty absent, economic life is " problemless " and automatic, and people would become more or less automata. As Professor Knight has pointed out : " With uncertainty absent, man's energies are devoted altogether to doing things ; it is doubtful whether intelligence itself would exist in such a situation ; in a world so built, it seems likely that all organic readjustment would become mechanical, all organisms automata ".[11] The Economic Man had perfect expectation. He was a pleasure machine because his life was purely mechanical.[12] To say that this sort of conceptual marionette manipulated by the theoretical economist as a preliminary thought-clearing exercise is " rational " or " has perfect foresight " is apt to be misleading. One might as well speak of the parts of a mechanical model " acting sensibly " or " having perfect expectation " when the mechanism works smoothly as designed.[13]

The problemless mechanical nature of the conditions analysed by the usual Theory of Value is brought out very clearly in the following description of its procedure : " When the fundamental assumption " (that everyone acts sensibly and maximises

88

"PERFECT EXPECTATION" AND FUNDAMENTAL ASSUMPTION

his returns) " is made, every economic tendency can be analysed by a series of questions. What would a sensible man do in such a case ? ... A technique which would study the economic effects of neuroses and confused thinking would be considerably more complicated than the technique here set out." [14] The Theory of Value, that is, is confined to economic tendencies where there is one definite, unambiguous, and correct answer to the question " How am I to maximise my returns ? "—conditions in which it might fairly be called neurotic or confused not to maximise them. It is inapplicable where there is any uncertainty about the answer to this question —which is, in principle, always the case in the world as it is.[15] Anyone in the world as it is, even the most brilliant economist, would be grateful for any information which would lead to his maximising his returns, and all he can do is to act in the way which he *expects* will maximise them, and can hardly be called neurotic or confused if his expectations are wrong. As Wicksteed put it : " We are bound to act upon estimates of the future, and since wise as well as foolish estimates may be falsified, the mere failure of correspondence between the forecast and the event does not in itself show that the forecast was an unwise one ".[16]

Passing over the difficulties in the interpretation of the term " wealth ", it may perhaps be a broadly true generalisation " that everyone desires to obtain additional wealth with as little sacrifice as possible ",[17] or " that every person will choose the greater apparent good ",[18] or that " man directs his actions so as to maximise the sum of his satisfaction ".[19] But this tells one nothing as to how, in fact, they set about fulfilling their desires, or, dropping the assumption

89

of perfect expectation, how even it is " sensible " or " rational " for them to do so.[20]

3. THE DEMAND FOR CAPITAL GOODS AND FOR CONSUMPTION GOODS UNDER THE FUNDAMENTAL ASSUMPTION

There has recently been much discussion of expectation and uncertainty as affecting the demand for capital instruments. Here the attempt to make use of a definition of " rational " conduct which only has sense when perfect foresight is also assumed, has been found to lead to a more or less useless circular theory of interest. If it is *known for certain*—as Ricardo apparently tacitly assumed his entrepreneur knew for certain—that an extra £100 worth of machinery will add £3 annually to net output, and if the investors are acting " sensibly ", and applying the machinery everywhere just up to the point where it pays and only just pays, then the rate of interest is 3 per cent per annum.[21] The weak link in this circular chain (perfectly descriptive of a world with no uncertainty, but defined to include interest) is that obviously investors actually *never do nor can know* how much an additional £100 worth of machinery will yield, and can only act on their *expectations*: " The most important confusion concerning the meaning and significance of the marginal efficiency of capital has ensued on the failure to see that it depends on the *prospective* yield of capital and not merely on its current yield." [22] This is clearly traceable to the inappropriate use of a definition of " rational " conduct which tacitly assumes perfect foresight. But as is frequently pointed out in discussions of the definitions

90

DEMAND FOR " CAPITAL " AND " CONSUMPTION " GOODS

of " capital " and " consumption " goods, the defining line between the two must be very arbitrarily drawn —at any rate if one is drawing one's distinction in accordance with the length of the period of time which the good takes to consume. There is a " capital " element in *all* goods, in that all goods take *some* time to consume. The act of purchase and the act of consumption of a good cannot be coterminous in time. This can conveniently be made part of the definition of the term " consumption of a good or service ". Therefore expectations concerning the future must be considered as affecting the demand for " consumption " goods as well as that for " capital " goods. Risk, uncertainty, and more or less correct expectations about the future are not the peculiar characteristics of enterprise or capital investment, but pervade all action, economic or otherwise, in the world as we know it. The common text-book distinction between present goods and future goods (instead of more immediately and more distantly future goods) inaccurately neglects the complete continuity between the two. This not very obscure but fundamental point has been clearly put by Schönfeld : " Just as all economy is a provision for the future, so the determination of what is the economically most appropriate disposition of resources is something directed to the future. There is no difference in principle whether this future is immediate or remote. In this sense the disposition of resources for the so-called satisfaction of present needs is a provision for the immediate future." [23]

It is precisely because they take no account of the uncertainty factor that the analyses of " rational " consumers' behaviour, and " consumers' equilibrium ",

91

THE BASIC POSTULATES OF PURE THEORY

where people balance the utility of one more lump of sugar against one more biscuit, seem so very fanciful and *wirklichkeitsfremd*. It is not necessarily because the quantities discussed are too small. If one is confronted with a chocolate, a cigarette, an aspirin tablet, and a biscuit (or even smaller quantities), of known quality, *to consume here and now*, one can arrange them fairly definitely in an order. But unless one can perfectly foresee one's tastes this time to-morrow or next week, in what order one will prefer such small quantities when the time comes to consume them can only be forecasted in the very roughest way.[24] The " perfect expectation " analysis of " rational " consumers' conduct is only very roughly applicable when, as is mostly the case, goods, first, take some time to consume, and secondly when the consumption is not begun as soon as the purchase is made—since in the intervening period anything may happen to upset one's calculations.[25]

So far we have been using an over-simplified notion of " the period of consumption " of a good. We have been considering only what may be called the period of " direct consumption " ; that is, the period of time at the end of which the good or service is physically worn out or used up. But " the period over which an object yields consumption is not necessarily that of its own existence as a good ".[26] It has been pointed out that the " period of production " of a glass of beer may be construed as in one sense going *back* to the Creation. So the " period of consumption " may be construed as extending *forward* to the Day of Judgment. Among the " net advantages " or disadvantages of a glass of beer may be that, by making one's driving unsteady, it may involve

92

DEMAND FOR " CAPITAL " AND " CONSUMPTION " GOODS

one in a fatal motor smash which will profoundly affect the lives of one's children, one's children's children, and so *ad infinitum*. There is no need to resort to far-fetched examples to demonstrate that any of one's most trivial everyday actions, economic or otherwise, may have indefinitely far-reaching consequential ramifications. So far as people take them into consideration at all, their economic decisions will be affected by more or less vague expectations as to the possibility of such ramifications.

The expectations, then, on which any economic decision is based *may* concern literally any conceivable event in the future history of the world. But corresponding to the distinction between " direct " and " indirect " periods of consumption, it may have some clarificatory value to distinguish between " direct " and " indirect " factors in expectation. By " *direct* " factors in expectation we mean expectation as to the bare physical and technical qualities of a good or service—of a box of cigars, a machine, or the work of a labourer. Such qualities are always *conceivably* capable of physical measurement at the end of the direct period of consumption when the good or service has been physically applied or used up. On the other hand " *indirect* " factors in expectation *may* relate to any conceivable occurrence either *during* the period of " direct " consumption, or at any time after it. Obvious " indirect " factors in expectation in relation to consumption goods are expectations as to the future of one's own tastes, and as to the future prices or obtainability of the goods if they are preservable (cf. food-hoarding against expected shortage). As regards capital instruments and labour, obvious " indirect " factors are the expected future prices of the goods

93

they produce, and of the labour or capital instruments with which they are technically required to co-operate in production ; further, if there is any element of oligopoly, the further price policy of competitors may be considered. Finally it is clear that an individual's whole expenditure policy, and division of his income between " saving " and " consumption ", may well depend on what he expects his income to be in the future, which depends on his expectations as to the future of general economic conditions in his country, which depends on his expectations as to the future economic and political history of the world. (Compare the Victorian attitude to the future of the world and " saving " with that of to-day.)

4. " PERFECT EXPECTATION " AND EQUILIBRIUM

Though in most expositions of the Theory of Value any discussion of expectations has been completely lacking, several writers have argued that some such postulate as " perfect expectation " is necessary for equilibrium theory.[27] On the other hand, Professor Morgenstern [28] has shown that such a postulate may give a nonsensical indeterminate situation the very reverse of equilibrium. (Compare, for example, a game of chess in which both players foresaw each other's moves and tried to adjust their own accordingly, or else foresaw *their own moves as well* but by some fatal Cassandra-like compulsion were not able to alter them even if leading to defeat.) Professor Morgenstern goes on to argue that the theory of equilibrium must somehow get on without this postulate if it is not to collapse in a contradiction, and comments : " wie unüberlegt in der theoretischen

94

" PERFECT EXPECTATION " AND EQUILIBRIUM

Ökonomie oft von grundlegenden Annahmen dort gesprochen wird, wo es lediglich um Unsinn handelt ". So far no attempt appears to have been made either to contest these conclusions or to show how equilibrium theory can dispense with the " perfect expectation " postulate.

It is important to notice that the " perfect expectation " postulate is not a postulate as to how people under conditions of equilibrium actually behave, but is introduced simply as an *explanation* of their behaviour. It is the general answer one would receive if one was able to question members of a community in static equilibrium as to how they came to behave in the way they did. What is necessary for equilibrium is only that people behave in a certain way, and it is not strictly necessary to go into the question as to how or why they should behave in this way any more than with any other hypothetical simplified example. The case has been considered of a community producing and consuming only one commodity [29]—bananas—and it is not necessary to enter into the question as to how and why a community should live on such a diet. There may be no satisfactory answer as to how or why they should behave in this way ; it is enough for the purposes of the simplified example that they do. If we find that people could not possibly behave as in the simplified example—that is, live solely on bananas—and be constituted like ourselves, the contradiction does not lie in the example as such, but in our procedure. We create certain conceptual automata " motivated " necessarily in a way different from ourselves, and then, with unconscious anthropomorphism, try to ask them why it is they behave like that, while the only answer

95

THE BASIC POSTULATES OF PURE THEORY

to such a question ultimately is that they do so
because we make them when we define the position
of equilibrium. It is as though one was to sketch
out the plans for, or actually construct (as one could
actually construct a mechanical model of a community
in static equilibrium) some piece of mechanism, say
a cuckoo clock, and then ask the cuckoo whether it
was because it had perfect expectation of the time
that it appeared exactly at each hour.[30]

In some cases the economist will consider it enough
simply to ascertain what people's conduct in certain
situations is, or to establish a correlation between it
and other social phenomena. But in other cases,
for a satisfactory scientific explanation the economist
will want to ascertain how this conduct came about,
that is, with what other conduct—" expectations "
or " beliefs "—it was correlated, and how in turn
these latter came to be held.[31] As, therefore, the equilibrium concept is designed to help in the explanation
of people's behaviour as it is, and as *Gedankenexperi-
mente* with extreme cases are sometimes useful for the
analysis of the facts as they are, the anthropomorphis-
ing of the mechanical model by enquiry as to what
" expectations " or " motives " the behaviour of an
equilibrium community could reasonably be correlated with, may possess some clarificatory value
provided we keep in mind its ultimate contradictori-
ness and the fact that people *might* behave in any
particular way for any reasons, or without any particular reasons at all. For, at any rate at present, little
is known of significance about the " reasons " behind
different types of economic conduct. In any case, if
one does not attribute expectations to a person one
can hardly call his conduct " sensible " or " rational ".

96

" PERFECT EXPECTATION " AND EQUILIBRIUM

Expectations are correlated with behaviour in the market in accordance with the maximum principle. A person forms particular expectations as to the future course of events (his tastes, prices, consumers' demand, etc.), and from these arrives at the expectation that a particular line of conduct will lead to the maximum returns. A person with perfect expectation is able at once to dispose of his resources in accordance with the principle that people act in the way which they expect will lead to the maximum returns, for his expectations will tell him certainly and unambiguously which line of conduct will lead to this result. This would not be possible where two or more people have perfect expectations about one another's conduct and then try to adjust their own conduct in accordance with the maximum principle. A game of chess or bridge with all players having perfect expectations of one another's play and then adjusting their own, could not be played.

The example might be put forward of two duopolists both of whom foresaw that the other possessed full knowledge of the theory of duopoly and was going to fix his price at the monopoly price, fixed their own prices at the monopoly price, and thus, in a certain sense, maximised their profits.[32] But this is not really a case of perfect expectation and consequent adjustment of conduct in accordance with the maximum principle. If one of the two duopolists perfectly foresees that his rival is going to fix his price at the monopoly price over a definite period of time—if this is *given* to him—he is not acting in accordance with the maximum principle in fixing his own price at the same level. If it is replied that he does not do this because he knows perfectly well that if he does not fix his own

97

THE BASIC POSTULATES OF PURE THEORY

price at the monopoly price his rival will of course alter his correspondingly, then he had not originally perfect foresight as to his rival's price policy, for with perfect foresight he must have certainly known *unconditionally* his rival's price policy over the period of time in question.

The impossibiLty of "monopolistic" conduct based on perfect expectations is not simply a high improbability but a *logical* impossibility, a self-contradictory paradox, like the Cretan saying that all Cretans are liars. A person's conduct cannot both be given to someone else who may adjust his own accordingly, and still be adjustable by the person himself. Just the same is the case if it is not a question of two individuals facing each other, but of each individual member of a mass facing the average opinion of the mass, as in Mr. Keynes'[33] description of the professional speculator working out what average opinion expects average opinion expects, average opinion expects . . . (etc. *ad infinitum*) future prices will be. The game of Old Maid —as Mr. Keynes describes speculation—obviously could not be played when each player had perfect expectation. For if they were seeking to maximise their profits and had control over their conduct, each player in turn whose perfect expectations told him he would have the Old Maid would not play.

Perfect expectation therefore is incompatible, in an interdependent economic system, with people acting in the way they expect will maximise their profits and at the same time more than one person adjusting his conduct in accordance with his (perfect) expectations of the other's conduct—that is, it is incompatible with more than one person acting "monopolistically" with perfect expectation.[34] Perfect ex-

98

" PERFECT EXPECTATION " AND EQUILIBRIUM

pectation is only compatible with " competitive " conditions—that is, conditions where no one person's conduct can affect the conduct, and the result of the calculations on which it is based, of another.[35]

If, then, the assumption of perfect expectations, which appears to be implicit in many formulations of the " Fundamental Principle ", must be dropped for oligopolistic analysis, some other definite assumption about some sort of imperfect expectations and the correlated conduct must take its place, if any attempt at " explaining " oligopolists' conduct is to be made. If one's interests are purely geometrical or algebraical one need not worry about how one's demand and supply curves can be drawn up. But then it is hardly justifiable to call the conduct recorded by them " sensible " or to suppose that it *necessarily* ever occurs in practice ; it is simply one out of an infinite number of types of conceivable behaviour. A " biologist " might pursue his science, not by enquiring what the laws of heredity or genetics are, but by working out an infinite number of conceivable formulae.

One might assume that though people are acting under oligopolistic conditions, where each individual's conduct has some appreciable effect on price and market conditions, they none of them take the effects of their own conduct on their rivals' conduct in any way into account.[36] That is, they behave like bridge-players who play the card which seems to them best without any consideration of the effects that their play has on the subsequent play of the other people at the table. Though such conduct may conceivably be " sensible " in the special sense of being based on the expectation that it will lead to the fulfilment of the maximum principle, such an expectation can hardly be called

99

THE BASIC POSTULATES OF PURE THEORY

sensible in any less special sense of the term, nor does the assumption of it appear very realistic.

The difficulty is simply that under oligopolistic conditions there is no one clear and unambiguous answer to the question " How would a sensible man act in such a situation ? " [37] Such a question is not very helpful. His action all depends on his necessarily imperfect expectations about the conduct of other people. Though one can argue in a vague impressionist way *a priori* that some assumptions are more reasonable than others, if one wants to find out how or on what expectations oligopolists in fact behave, the only way is to " look and see ".[38] It cannot be directly deduced from some " Fundamental Principle ", any more than, except in a very few cases, one can deduce how a hand of bridge will be played, or even how it would be " rational " to play it, with given cards simply from the principle that all the players are " sensible " and are out to maximise their points. Outside competitive conditions, any " equilibrium " position or position of rest which may occur is a conventional one, arrived at along its own particular path—which might well have been different— and which will last just as long as the conventions which support it happen to last.

So far we have not attempted, in discussing perfect expectation, to decide whether or not it is the only condition of expectation which is reasonably correlatable with the behaviour of an individual or community in the condition of " equilibrium ". On the one hand there are various possible conditions which an individual or a community might be in, which might be called " equilibrium ". On the other hand it is necessary to distinguish clearly between *perfect*

100

" PERFECT EXPECTATION " AND EQUILIBRIUM

expectation and simply *correct and undisappointed* expectations.

" Perfect ", " correct ", and " undisappointed " expectations appear often to have been used more or less interchangeably as a necessary or even defining characteristic of equilibrium.[39] But in quite ordinary senses of the words, " undisappointed " expectations may well not have been " correct ", and " correct " expectations may well not have been " perfect ". By perfect expectation we mean, practically, omniscience about the future. A man with perfect expectation must at least have certain knowledge about everything that is relevant to his decisions—and this *may* possibly be anything in the whole future history of the world—and he must at any rate know about everything else that it is irrelevant. On the other hand a man's expectations as to the results of a line of conduct may be quite *correct*, and he may also expect that he will maximise his returns by adopting it, but he may not have heard of other possibilities which would be more profitable to him, and therefore, though his expectations about the line of conduct he adopts are quite correct, he is not acting in the most lucrative possible way. This kind of blissful ignorance is probably a common condition. The distinction between " correct " and " undisappointed " expectations is of small importance. A man's expectations about the line of conduct he adopts may be quite correct and he may get exactly what he counted on, but because *in the meantime* possibilities have been suggested to him of which he was ignorant before, he may be *disappointed* that he did not act in another way.

But whether expectations are perfect or imperfect,

101

THE BASIC POSTULATES OF PURE THEORY

correct or incorrect, undisappointed or disappointed, has nothing whatever to do, logically, with whether they are *constant* or *changing*, and on this depends whether or not there is any change in an individual's conduct or any endogenous [40] change in an economic system. Expectations are constant when people believe that the expectations and the correlated conduct of the previous period will lead to the maximum returns in the next period. Whether expectations have just been incorrect or disappointed or the reverse does not imply either that they will be changed or held to, or, necessarily, that it would be "rational" to change or hold to them. Because of the tacit or explicit assumption of perfect expectation, endogenous changes, in the usual exposition of equilibrium analysis, appear generally to be regarded as more or less automatic. When the assumption of perfect expectation is dropped it is seen that whether or not there is an endogenous change depends on the much less automatic factor of whether people's expectations are constant or not. It is the assumption of perfect expectation, further, which brings it about that in the absence of other changes elsewhere there will be no further change in the disposition of resources when the position of equilibrium has been attained. When this assumption is removed this peculiar characteristic of the " equilibrium " position is also removed, for an (incorrect) change may be made in the disposition of resources which *would have been* in their " maximum " " equilibrium " position if it had not been made.

If expectations are perfect they must necessarily also be correct, undisappointed, in " static " conditions constant, and in " dynamic " conditions

102

" PERFECT EXPECTATION " AND EQUILIBRIUM

changing. Further, people with perfect expectation must be in their " maximum " position, that is, they could not obtain greater returns anywhere else. But if expectations are *not* perfect, any combination of one of the alternatives from each of the pairs, correct or incorrect, undisappointed or disappointed, constant or changing, is possible. If we drop the division of " correct " expectations into disappointed and undisappointed as being of little interest, this leaves eight possible conditions of expectations and correlated conduct—four when people are actually in their " maximum " positions, and four when they are not : correct and constant, correct and changing, incorrect and constant, incorrect and changing. For if expectations are not perfect it is quite possible for someone to be in his " maximum " position, not to realise it, be disappointed, and change. While in the world as it is nobody could be found with quite perfect expectations in our sense, a good number, probably, could be found in each of the eight " imperfect " conditions we have classified.

Any favourable or maximum position may be arrived at by " luck " or by " judgment " or by any mixture of the two. Though it might well happen that an *individual* was in his " maximum " position more or less by accident, that is, not having been led to it by perfect expectation, it is obviously fantastically improbable that all the members of a *community* could for any length of time be all in their respective maximum conditions by accident, *without* perfect expectation or a combination of luck and nearly perfect expectation. We agree therefore that, on the whole, perfect expectation is the most reasonable state of knowledge and expectation to be attributed

103

THE BASIC POSTULATES OF PURE THEORY

to, or correlated with, that harmonious optimum condition which has always been the ideal of Economic Liberalism. We agree, further, that the term " equilibrium " is best reserved for this condition, but we do not agree with making " perfect expectation " a *defining characteristic* of it.[41] For this involves defining " equilibrium ", not by the actions and conditions of an individual or community, but by the knowledge which led them to these actions and conditions. It seems that " equilibrium " is best reserved for the optimum maximum condition whether or not the individual or community has been led to it by perfect expectation.

There is one further slight ambiguity about the term " equilibrium ". In a sense, no single economic action takes place except when or where there is " disequilibrium ". " Equilibrium ", that is, only holds where there is, and so long as there is, complete inactivity. But the term seems often to be used of a condition lasting while economic action is taking place. That is, a community or individual is not necessarily in " disequilibrium " in the moment before any economic activity, if this activity is leading to the maximum returns.

5. THE ASSUMPTION OF A " TENDENCY " TOWARDS EQUILIBRIUM

The position of equilibrium has always been the very central concept of economic analysis. *A priori* one cannot say more than that this is just one out of an infinite number of conceivable positions. The only justification for the special concern with this position and the treatment of disequilibrium, change

104

ASSUMPTION OF A " TENDENCY " TOWARDS EQUILIBRIUM

and development, as simply temporary aberrations from the normal, can be that in fact the economic conditions under which we live in some sense " tend " towards it. This is the very crux of equilibrium theory. Professor von Hayek goes as far as to say : " There seems to be no possible doubt that the only justification for this " (special concern with equilibrium analysis) " is the existence of a tendency towards equilibrium. It is only with this assertion that economics ceases to be an exercise in pure logic and becomes an empirical science." [42] Is this as a justification satisfactory ?

We have seen that the only way to make sense of most formulations of the Fundamental Assumption is to add the assumption of " perfect expectation ". With this assumption added we are assuming also, at the same time, permanent equilibrium under competitive conditions, and the disappearance of money. The early writers regarded the equilibrium condition —that is, complete expectations—as constantly at hand, as a position on which society was constantly verging. [43] Until fairly recently it was considered that if a comparison was made between economic life and the water in a tank which is constantly being disturbed, but which could soon sink to a position of " rest " when the disturbance was removed, enough had been said to justify almost exclusive preoccupation with equilibrium analysis. [44] It was overlooked that it is an experimentally testable empirical truth that water sinks to an equilibrium level if left undisturbed, while there is no corresponding empirical truth or even suggested experiment with regard to an economic system. To justify special preoccupation with the position of equilibrium it is necessary to assert as an

105

THE BASIC POSTULATES OF PURE THEORY

empirically testable truth that there is a tendency towards this position in our economic system, or that readjustment in general comes quicker than new disturbances occur.

But there is an ambiguity in speaking of a " tendency towards " a certain condition which is not always kept clear in this connection. It may mean that the position *actually is* regularly arrived at, or it may simply mean that although there is a " tendency " towards this position, this " tendency " is always counterbalanced by other " tendencies " which result in the position never in fact being reached at all, or even necessarily approximated to. This is the sense in which to-day most economists appear to speak of the tendency towards equilibrium. For example : " We make no assumption that final equilibrium is necessary. We assume that there are operative in different parts of the system certain tendencies which make for the restoration of an equilibrium in respect to certain limited points of reference. But we do not assume that the composite effect of these tendencies will necessarily be equilibrating." [45]

This interpretation of the assumption of a " tendency towards equilibrium " at once gives away the case for any special preoccupation with this condition rather than with any other conceivable condition of the economic system. There is no assumption, here, that we necessarily ever come anywhere near an equilibrium condition. One might assume that there was a " tendency ", in this sense, for the population of England to dwindle to nothing (through diseases, wars, etc.), or to become indefinitely large (through births and a falling death-rate, etc.), or to attain to any other conceivable figures—though the

106

ASSUMPTION OF A " TENDENCY " TOWARDS EQUILIBRIUM

" tendencies " to these positions were always offset by opposing tendencies. If, therefore, the special study of the equilibrium position rather than any other conceivable position is to be justified by the empirical truth of the assumption of a "tendency" towards equilibrium, this must mean a tendency in the former, *significant* sense ; that is, it must be the case that we are always in equilibrium or fairly often approximating to it to make a special study of it of particular interest.[46] At least one is entitled to expect those who justify their special study of the equilibrium condition on the grounds— in their usual rather metaphysical language—that they are " examining in isolation a part of the forces acting in the real world ", to give some empirical indication as to the " strength " of these forces under existing conditions as compared with the strength of the opposing " forces ", or at least to make it clear that whether their analysis is of any conceivable application depends on this issue. It is hardly a sufficient justification of equilibrium analysis, and completely begs the question of its applicability, to claim—as someone engaged in the exclusive study of conditions in England with a population of 0, 1000, or 1000,000,000 might claim—that, though it is of course counteracted by opposing " tendencies " so that the condition never sets in or is necessarily approximated to, there is always a " tendency " towards it.

The assumption of a tendency towards equilibrium implies, on the usual definition, the assumption of a tendency towards perfect expectations, competitive conditions, and the disappearance of money. To get anything like a precise answer to the question as to what extent this assumption is true or untrue would

107

THE BASIC POSTULATES OF PURE THEORY

require vastly complicated empirical investigations. Possibly it was nearer the truth in the nineteenth century than it is to-day. In some markets, obviously expectations are more nearly perfect than in others. Probably the more " oligopolistic " markets become, the less perfect expectations become, for then there is an important addition to the number of factors about which, up till now at any rate, only fairly uncertain expectations can be formed—that is, the behaviour of rival oligopolists. The lengthening of the processes of production would also probably increase uncertainty and disequilibrium. On the other hand there is, on the whole, probably a tendency for communities to *learn*, which does more than simply keep pace with the changes in conditions. But whether ultimately, if more correct prognoses come to be made, these will not defeat their own end by themselves bringing about further changes and thus rendering themselves false, whether or how far, that is, there is a definite relation between the prognoses of social science and the social facts, remains an open sociological question which can hardly be of more than speculative interest until there are more data in the form of recognised and disseminated economic and sociological prognoses.

At present, at any rate, the " perfect expectation " assumption of equilibrium analysis begs all our questions, and we conclude with a recent investigator : " To attempt to retain the partial equilibrium approach by introducing such assumptions as ' the future is completely foreseen ' or that money remains neutral, amounts in effect to an exclusion of the whole problem. The question is on the contrary just to what degree, under realistic assumptions concern-

108

ASSUMPTION OF A "TENDENCY" TOWARDS EQUILIBRIUM

ing the anticipations of the entrepreneurs, the future is shown to be foreseen, and furthermore, to what extent total 'monetary' categories disrupt the adjustment towards a partial equilibrium." [47]

6. "SUBJECTIVE" AND "OBJECTIVE" RATIONALITY

The "Fundamental Assumption" as usually formulated, if it is to have any sense, must be supplemented by the assumption of perfect expectation. The element in the "Fundamental Assumption" thus formulated, in the Economic Man, in the "maximum principle", and the like, applicable to a world with any uncertainty and imperfect foresight, that is, to a world in which any *economic* as against perhaps simply *technical* problems may be said to exist, is the principle that people act in the way they *expect* will maximise their returns, profits, or net advantages. This is the "general" principle of which the assumption of perfect expectation is a very peculiar special case. Everybody's conduct is in this sense "subjectively" rational (though we use this term only at once to suggest that it is misleading and unsuitable), however "irrational" and nonsensical the *expectations* on which it is based. How far people act in an "objectively" rational way must remain quite indefinite, because in the first place, in a world full of uncertainty and with economic science still able to afford very little guidance, most decisions in economic life *have* to be taken without recourse to anything which can suitably be called "objective rationality" —though it is in accordance with some such objective criterion or other that the term is applied to expectations or the process of arriving at them in everyday life.

109

THE BASIC POSTULATES OF PURE THEORY

The term " rational " simply means, normally, being guided in a certain way by past experience ; the question is in precisely *what* way. A complete " objective rationality " in economic conduct requires a complete economic science which can tell one with " certainty " exactly what the effects of one decision or the other will be, and even then a sceptic can argue that it is not necessarily " rational " to act even in accordance with the most confirmed and certain of scientific prognoses. Nor can the calculus of probability, rather vaguely appealed to by Bentham and subsequent writers, be of the slightest assistance in most economic decisions, for there is simply no basis for any sort of calculation.[48] Judgments as to the " objective rationality " or " irrationality " of economic conduct or expectation can on the whole only be fragmentary and negative.

There is, however, one class of expectations, possibly not uncommon, which could quite definitely and objectively be called irrational—that is, *contradictory* expectations. Under uncertain conditions economic calculation—if it can be called that under such conditions, since the very term seems to imply some automatic " certain " basis—takes the form of considering the various relevant factors, direct and indirect, which occur to one in deciding one's choice, and then selecting that line of conduct which, given these expectations, will lead to the maximising of returns. If the expectations as to the various relevant factors—even simply those that happen to occur to one—are not sufficiently pondered, it is quite possible that all the *strictly logical implications* contained in them are not realised and are not seen to be in contradiction to the maximising

110

" SUBJECTIVE " AND " OBJECTIVE " RATIONALITY

of returns by the line of conduct chosen. One of the expectations *must* be falsified then, and it will be pure luck if it is not that as to the maximising of returns.

The Law of Motivation,[49] as the principle of "subjective rationality " may more suitably be called, is undoubtedly the core of empirical truth in the Economic Man and similar generalisations about human conduct. Though we agree that there is no principle of any considerable significance that will serve as a basis for a realistic deductive economic theory, we do not, therefore, precisely agree with Professor Mackenroth that there is no such principle at all. It appears an empirically true and testable generalisation that people act in the way which they expect will maximise their returns, even if this was only the *ex post* rationalisation of their habits. This generalisation could, if it was worth while, be more precisely formulated and a more precise method of testing it be given. Roughly, one can test it simply by asking anyone whether they expect that if they were to employ their money or resources in any other way than that in which they are at the moment doing or about to do, they expect that they would increase their returns. If they reply that they *do* expect that they would increase their returns—understood, if one likes, in the widest sense to include the " satisfaction " of the masochist and altruist—by employing their resources in another way, then they are offending against the principle of subjective rationality or the Law of Motivation. But it would appear a waste of time for an economist, at any rate, to attempt to define this principle more precisely, as the significant content of this generalisation as a fundamental

111

THE BASIC POSTULATES OF PURE THEORY

assumption for a deductive economic theory is in any case negligible.

One can, of course, draw the usual conclusions that people will balance expected marginal cost against expected marginal gain, and will have no tendency to change their conduct when the expected marginal return from resources in each direction is equal, and so on. But out of an almost circular postulate only almost circular conclusions can be drawn. But what is always wanted is *what* expectations people have, that is, in what way they expect they will maximise their returns, and therefore in what way they will behave. This Law of Motivation tells one nothing whatever about this.

The orthodox " perfect expectation " Theory of Value was all more or less empty when it was based on the assumption that everyone maximised *his utility*, because of the difficulty in defining this term in any but a more or less circular and empty way. On the other hand, the principle seemed to have some content and to permit of deductions of some content about the behaviour of entrepreneurs, and their price, production, wage, and employment policies. For without too great inaccuracy entrepreneurs might be said to aim at maximising their money profits, which seemed a definite enough criterion to decide their policies (though even here, in the interests of accuracy, some economists are in favour of making this proposition more or less circular, insisting that the entrepreneurs' aim is not maximum money profits, but maximum satisfaction from the " net advantages "). Looked at retrospectively *ex post*, profits are a fairly definitely calculable sum. As, however, it is clearly not the " objective " re-

112

" SUBJECTIVE " AND " OBJECTIVE " RATIONALITY

sulting *ex post* profits but the " subjective " *ex ante* expectations which determine entrepreneurs' policy,[50] and which are in a common metaphor the " mainspring " of economic activity, unless one makes a definite assumption about expectations, " maximising profits " is quite an empty conception telling one nothing about how entrepreneurs will in fact behave. With the assumption of complete expectations no relevant distinction between *ex post* and *ex ante* profits existed, next year's profits being as definitely and objectively known as last year's. But dropping the assumption of complete expectations, the problem remains as to what expectations people hold and how they come to hold them. To make assumptions as to expectations and therefore as to conduct, unless these assumptions are empirically confirmed, is, in dealing with economic problems fundamentally, to beg the question and assume what one wants to find out, which is always just what people's expectations and correlated behaviour in different situations are.

It has long been recognised that, when economists assume that people behave " rationally ", no assumption is made as to the nature of the goods—bread, opium, bibles, or instruments of self-torture—which it is " rational " to choose, no such distinction being feasible. Similarly (as we have argued) no generalisation is possible either as to what is, in some sense, the *objectively rational* way of arriving at one's expectations, or as to *how people do, in fact,* arrive at their expectations that one line of expenditure will yield them better returns than another. Whether and to what extent entrepreneurs behave " competitively " or " monopolistically ",[51] whether and to what extent people's decisions are dominated

113

THE BASIC POSTULATES OF PURE THEORY

by present prices as against the whole expected future course of prices ; to what extent people's economic actions are taken on the spur of the moment, or according to a detailed plan ; how far people come to any particular expectation at all or act unreflectingly according to habit ; to what extent people learn from past economic mistakes and disappointments ; how and to what extent people behave in any way one chooses to call objectively rational—are questions which cannot be answered by any general " Fundamental Assumption " or " Principle ". Although in some cases rough *a priori* reasoning may yield results which turn out fairly accurately when tested, *ultimately* all such questions as these can only be decided satisfactorily by extensive empirical investigation of each question individually.

The Law of Motivation says nothing about how people behave in any market, nor anything about the expectations or the process of arriving at the expectations correlated with behaviour in the market. It only says something as to how people will react if questioned in a particular way as to their behaviour in the market. It is, however, an empirical generalisation capable of being tested empirically and of being falsified, possessing therefore *some* empirical content, however insignificant this may be. It is not simply an empirically empty definition, which is what is sometimes offered as a " Fundamental Principle " of economic conduct.

7. THE FUNDAMENTAL ASSUMPTION AS A DEFINITION

Since the revolution in the Theory of Value of 1871 economists have been trying to formulate a

114

fundamental " maximum principle " of economic conduct applicable to consumers, to take the place of the Ricardian business man guided only by the desire for money profits. To render this principle not obviously false they have had steadily to widen it, and thus to diminish its empirical content. First it had to be agreed that it was not necessarily " rational " for the consumer to seek to maximise merely his *material* wealth—" spiritual " wealth must also be included. Then in order to elude the charge of hedonism the conduct of altruists and masochists had to be admitted as "rational". The economic principle thus became less and less falsifiable. Fewer and fewer, if any, types of economic conduct remained which were not subsumed under it, and almost none were excluded or could falsify it. Its empirical content, therefore, simultaneously grew smaller and smaller.[52] To say that a piece of economic conduct was " rational " came to mean little, if anything, more than that it was a piece of economic conduct. The cruder classical generalisations about the ubiquity of the money-making motive, though in a probably high percentage of cases false, did have some empirical significance. Ricardo's instinct was right when he wrote : [53] " It is self-interest which regulates all the speculations of trade ; and, where that can be clearly and satisfactorily ascertained, we should not know where to stop if we admitted any other rule of action ". He was wrong in believing apparently that self-interest could often with much accuracy be " clearly and satisfactorily ascertained ".

Finally it came to be openly stated that the " Fundamental Principle " was not conceivably falsifiable and devoid of *all* empirical content, a circularity, a

115

THE BASIC POSTULATES OF PURE THEORY

matter of definition, a linguistic proposal. It was assumed or stated that everybody behaves " rationally " or " sensibly ", and " rationally " or " sensibly " was defined as how people do in fact behave. All economic conduct is *ex definitione* rational or sensible. It would be contradictory to speak of " irrational " economic conduct, or if one does " one means only that one's fellow men do not act as one considers right ".[54]

It is sometimes argued, even when it is thus stated as a circularity or definition, that the Fundamental Assumption cannot be empty because of all that economists have succeeded in deducing out of it.[55] Certainly its being a circularity does not preclude any number of deductions being made from it. But all the propositions thus deduced will be equally circular and empirically empty. If the Fundamental Assumption that everybody acts rationally is circular, so is the proposition that people balance marginal cost against marginal gain circular, and all the further deductions will simply be different ways of saying that people behave " rationally ", that is, as they do behave. If one thinks it worth while, one can say " people behave as they do behave " in as many different ways as one likes, but one will not learn anything further about their behaviour; for the empirical content of the assumption and all the conclusions will be the same—that is, nothing. " From a tautology only tautologies follow." [56]

With a definition there is no question of verifiability or falsifiability. One can, if one likes, say " Economic conduct = ' Rational ' or ' sensible ' economic conduct. Def.", if one is consistent in this linguistic usage. As a terminological suggestion,

116

THE FUNDAMENTAL ASSUMPTION AS A DEFINITION

however, it simply seems superfluous, inappropriate, and misleading. It is superfluous, because if one takes economic behaviour as given, one's task is to examine it as it is, and there is no point in adding the adjective " rational " or " sensible ", which is *by definition* purely redundant. It is inappropriate because we all know—and this is often particularly emphasised precisely by those who insist that all economic conduct is or " must be " rational—that, in the everyday " objective " sense of the terms, much economic conduct is the very reverse of " rational " or " sensible " : that is, is based on quite incorrect and " stupid " expectations. Lastly it is misleading because it may appear that some generalisation of empirical content is being made about economic conduct from which conclusions of empirical content may be deduced, while all that is being done is to set out a definition.

In defence of this terminology it has been suggested that it is necessary to make it clear in this way that the Fundamental Principle of Economics is in no sense a value-utterance exalting any one type of economic conduct above another.[57] But it is not clear, to say the least, why, in order to exclude value-utterances concerning one piece of economic behaviour as compared with another, it is necessary to deliver what, in appearance at any rate, is a sweeping and vague value-utterance about *all* economic behaviour. It is like suggesting that a book-reviewer not wishing to deliver himself of value-utterances, cannot content himself with simply giving an account of books and the facts about them, but must insist that *all* books are, and " must be ", by definition good, or " rational " and " sensible " books.

117

8. A METHODOLOGICAL CONCLUSION

A broader methodological conclusion would appear to follow from the above. In so far as one is dissatisfied with purely " static ", a-monetary analysis omitting the uncertainty factor—which alone may be said to create any problems of conduct economic or otherwise—the method of deduction from some " Fundamental Assumption " or " principle " of economic conduct is more or less useless, because no relevant " Fundamental Assumption " can, on our present knowledge, be made.

The whole conception of Economics, as held for example by Senior, as a science resting on a very few general propositions (or " four Fundamental propositions ", the first being " that every person is desirous to obtain with as little sacrifice as possible, as much as possible of the articles of wealth "),[58] is shown to be entirely inadequate. Because the uncertainty factor was passed over it was possible to believe with Robert Lowe [59] that " If you place a man's ear within the ring of pounds, shillings and pence his conduct can be counted on to the greatest nicety ". Only so long as more or less tacit assumptions as to expectations were being made did the use of such a method as the deduction of chains of conclusions from one or a compact number of fundamental assumptions seem applicable. When assumptions as to expectations are more or less explicitly introduced, there come, quite rightly, accusations of " circularity ", " begging the question ", and " assuming what one requires to prove ", which have been a rather conspicuous feature of recent controversies over the theory of money and employment and the de-

118

A METHODOLOGICAL CONCLUSION

velopment of some kind of " dynamic " pure theory.[60]

According to Professor von Hayek,[61] the immediately pressing questions in this field are how entrepreneurs react to the expectations of particular price-changes, how the expectations of entrepreneurs are formed, and how given price-changes affect entrepreneurs' expectations. Clearly the answers to such questions cannot be deduced from some " Fundamental Assumption " or conjectured at all accurately *a priori*. They are questions of economic psychology to which an answer will be sought in vain in a few empty utilitarian phrases. If one wants to find out the answer to such questions, one must admit with Richard Jones : [62] " I really know of but one way to attain our object, and that is to look and see ". As a prominent investigator has recently concluded : " Thus, logically speaking, the door is open for all kinds of reactions ; and it is only a question of fact which one is the most frequent and typical ",[63] or as another puts it : " When the *a priori* yields nothing, it may be well to revert to observed facts. . . . When we examine the fundamental facts of human nature, when we regard the economic motive in its simplest terms, in order to discover whether prices are likely to rise or fall as activity is increased, nothing whatever is vouchsafed us. . . . Those theorists who seek to make economics more scientific by eschewing the uncertainties which are necessarily attached to empirical methods are in fact taking the path which leads away from science to pure scholastic." [64]

Before there can be any more " realistic " analysis some idea must be formed of what the more realistic assumptions are on which it is to be based,[65] unless

119

THE BASIC POSTULATES OF PURE THEORY

deductive theorists are simply going to continue building up their analysis on any assumptions—say as to the wage-policy of trade unions when there is a rise in prices—which appeal to them impressionistically *a priori*, or which are " tractable " ; that is, make possible a fascinating display of mathematical or geometrical ingenuity, or which merely fit in with their political views.[66]

The objection has been made to statistical investigations, questionnaires to consumers and entrepreneurs, the examination of family budgets and the like, that the results of such arduous researches are subject to a high degree of inaccuracy, can easily be " cooked ", and in any case would not tell us much that we did not know already. The answer to such an objection is quite simple. If, as one is perfectly free to do, one considers that the results obtainable by the only possible scientific method open to one are not of sufficient interest to reward the effort of the investigation, then one must give up the scientific handling of these problems altogether and leave them to others of different intellectual tastes.

NOTES

1. Cf. A. C. Pigou, *Economics of Stationary States*, p. 4.
2. Cf. A. Fey, *Der Homo Oeconomicus in der klassischen Nationalökonomie*, p. 122.
3. Cf. J. Robinson, *Economics is a Serious Subject*, p. 10.
4. Cf. P. N. Rosenstein-Rodan, *Economica*, 1936, p. 279.
5. Cf. J. Bentham, *Works*, edited Bowring, vol. i. p. 1. Cf. also J. Bonar, *Philosophy and Political Economy*, p. 225 : " But the older Utilitarians were bound by their principles to assume that the individual was infallible in following his interest " ; and the similar criticism of W. R. Sorley, *History of English Philosophy*, p. 223.

120

NOTES

6. Cf. D. Ricardo, *Principles of Political Economy and Taxation*, ch. iv. In a passage most illuminating for his methods and postulates and scientific criteria, Ricardo does appear explicitly to make the " perfect expectation " assumption : " The first point to be considered is, what is the interest of countries in the case supposed ? The second, what is their practice ? Now it is obvious that I need not be greatly solicitous about this latter point ; it is sufficient for my purpose if I can clearly demonstrate that the interest of the public is as I have stated it. It would be no answer to me to say that men were ignorant of the best and cheapest mode of conducting their business and paying their debts, because that is a question of fact not of science, and might be urged against almost every proposition in Political Economy " (*Letters of Ricardo to Malthus*, ed. Bonar, p. 18). The only possible interpretation of this passage which might be paralleled in the writings of the Physiocrats, seems to be that economists are not to concern themselves with what actually happens in the economic world, as this is simply a question of fact, and not of science. The *scientist* assumes that people are omniscient as to their interests and are out to maximise their money returns, and deduces conclusions dependent on these and other such postulates. Where we agree with Ricardo is that " almost every proposition in Political Economy " conforms to his notions of a scientific proposition.

7. Cf. J. S. Mill, *Essays on Some Unsettled Questions*, p. 138.

8. Cf. J. Robinson, *Economics of Imperfect Competition*, pp. 241-2.

9. Mr. G. F. Shove explicitly introduced expectations into some formulae for the theory of value without discussing the conception at any length (*vide Economic Journal*, 1930, pp. 97-8).

10. Cf. J. R. Hicks, *Zeitschrift für Nationalökonomie*, 1933, p. 445, and Rosenstein-Rodan, *op. cit.* p. 271.

11. Cf. F. H. Knight, *Risk, Uncertainty and Profit*, p. 268.

12. Cf. R. von Keller, *Die Kausalzusammenhänge in der Konjunkturbewegung*, pp. 15-16.

13. Cf. *vide infra*, Section 5.

14. Cf. J. Robinson, *op. cit.* p. 15.

15. Cliff Leslie (*Essays in Political and Moral Philosophy*, p. 229), and later some of the Institutionalist critics, came very near to exposing this limitation in the " orthodox " Theory of Value. Cf. Z. C. Dickenson, *Economic Motives*, pp. 240-46 : " When we come to the market-place we find dealers absorbed in calculations which are reasoning, discovery, invention, rather than choosing

121

THE BASIC POSTULATES OF PURE THEORY

among utilities. Their desire to make the largest profit possible, within the rules of the game, is fairly constant ; the problem is *how* to make it. . . . As we have reiterated in many connections there is no *a priori* rule as to the accuracy for any individual's calculations. None can be completely accurate, for nobody knows *all* the consequences which will follow from any of his acts. Each of us is liable to be deceived as to the durability or stylishness of the clothes we buy. If any theorems of the accepted economic principles are dependent on the assumption of human infallibility in inferring the ultimate consumption utilities from concrete goods . . . of course those theorems are doomed." Cf. also T. Veblen, *The Place of Science in Modern Civilisation*, p. 227.

16. Cf. P. Wicksteed, *The Common Sense of Political Economy*, p. 121.

17. Cf. N. Senior, *Political Economy*, 6th edition, pp. 26-8.

18. Cf. W. S. Jevons, *Theory of Political Economy*, p. 18.

19. Cf. H. H. Gossen, *Entwicklung des Gesetzes des menschlichen Verkehrs*, p. 3.

20. The doctrine of Opportunity Cost is often expressed in a way which seems tacitly to postulate perfect foresight. The cost, it is said, to Robinson Crusoe of a hammer was the amount of fish he could have caught with the same expenditure of effort ; or the cost of the satisfaction from sixpence worth of cigarettes is the satisfaction one might have got from sixpence worth of chocolate, etc. " Cost here, as anywhere, means nothing but advantages to be derived from the use of given resources in other directions " (F. A. von Hayek, *Collectivist Economic Planning*, p. 6). But since the resources are never used in the other directions, how, failing perfect foresight, can one *know precisely and for certain* what they would have yielded ? How can Robinson Crusoe ever do more than make a forever unverifiable guess at what the " cost " of his hammer was ? that is, how much satisfaction his fish, whatever number he would have caught, would have afforded him. Failing some sort of perfect knowledge, what *would* have happened if someone had acted differently can only be the subject of speculation. For this reason the conception, *ex post*, of maximising returns is practically of little significance. It obviously has little or no sense to say that any particular individual, Lord Nuffield, the local greengrocer, or the winner of the Irish Sweepstake " maximised their returns ".

21. Cf. J. M. Keynes, *General Theory of Employment, Interest, and Money*, pp. 139-40. In a footnote Mr. Keynes asks the question, " But was he [Marshall] not wrong in supposing that the

122

marginal productivity theory of wages is equally circular ? " Since any purely theorctical deduction *as such* must necessarily be circular, the charge of "circularity" appears usually to mean that the assumption is untrue and unrealistic and the theory therefore inapplicable. In this sense the marginal productivity theory of wages would appear to be less "circular" than the marginal productivity theory of interest, since the assumption that the marginal productivity of the worker is equated to the wage would appear to be more probably generally true than that the marginal productivity of capital is equated to the rate of interest, *because the former can more easily be done.* Workers on short contracts can quickly be taken on or thrown off to adjust a divergence between the wage and marginal productivity, but such adjustments cannot be made with capital sunk in machines of long life. On the other hand, to judge from the following quotation, the assumption of the marginal productivity theory of wages (*i.e.* correct expectations as to the productivity of labour) is as unlikely and difficult as that of the marginal productivity theory of capital, which is therefore no more " circular " than the marginal productivity theory of wages : " The judgment or estimation as to the value of a man is a probability judgment of a complex nature, indeed. More or less based on experience and observation of the outcome of his predictions, it is doubtless principally after all simply an intuitive judgment or 'unconscious induction', as one prefers " (F. H. Knight, *op. cit.* p. 229).

22. Cf. J. M. Keynes, *op. cit.* p. 141 ; also G: Myrdal, *Beiträge zur Geldtheorie,* ed. F. A. von Hayek, p. 394.

23. Cf. L. Schönfeld, *Grenznutzen und Wirtschaftsrechnung,* p. 6. Cf. also G. Mackenroth, *Theoretische Grundlagen der Preisbildungsforschung und Preispolitik,* 1932, p. 134 ; O. Morgenstern, *Wirtschaftsprognose,* p. 36 ; and P. N. Rosenstein-Rodan, article " Grenznutzen " in *Handwörterbuch der Staatswissenschaften.*

24. The very term "utility" is ambiguously used for *both* ex-ante desire measured by demand price, *and* ex-post satisfaction, as though the two necessarily correspond. Professor Pigou (*Economics of Welfare,* 3rd edition, p. 24), mentioning that lack of correspondence between the two might have great practical importance, concludes that in fact it has not, and may be disregarded (except for the well-known case of the underestimation of future satisfactions, to compensate which he proposes State action). He would thus appear to be making what amounts to an assumption of roughly perfect expectation.

25. Cf. L. Schönfeld, *op. cit.* p. 28.

123

THE BASIC POSTULATES OF PURE THEORY

26. Cf. F. H. Knight, *Essays in Honour of Cassel*, p. 330, and L. M. Fraser, *Economic Thought and Language*, p. 177.

27. Cf. F. H. Knight, *Risk, Uncertainty and Profit*, p. 197 ; J. R. Hicks, *op. cit.* p. 445 ; A. C. Pigou, *op. cit.* p. 76.

28. Cf. O. Morgenstern, *Zeitschrift für Nationalökonomie*, 1935, p. 337 ff.

29. Cf. J. M. Keynes, *Treatise on Money*, vol. i. p. 176.

30. The contradiction in this procedure emerges clearly from Professor Knight's discussion of static equilibrium. On pp. 76-7 (*op. cit.*) his marionettes start as " normal human beings . . . familiar in a modern Western nation . . . acting with ordinary human motives . . . knowing what they want and seeking it intelligently ". But by p. 268 they have become, as quoted above, " mechanical automata ".

31. We may say at once that, though it may be difficult to find a precise and satisfactory definition, we do not regard the proposition " A expects or believes x " as being not conceivably testable, and therefore on our standards extra-scientific. See below, V. 3.

32. Cf. O. Morgenstern, *op. cit.* p. 354.

33. Cf. J. M. Keynes, *op. cit.* p. 156.

34. Cf. A. C. Pigou, *op. cit.* pp. 87-8. The emphasis in recent years on the unity of the Theory of Value under competitive and monopolistic conditions and the uniformity of the basic assumptions is apt to conceal the fundamental distinction between competitive and monopolistic conduct, or conduct " heeding " or " heedless " of rivals.

35. This conclusion would appear to be in correspondence with the conclusion that under monopolistic conditions there is no determinate equilibrium. Cf. A. C. Pigou, *op. cit.* p. 227, and H. von Stackelberg, *Marktform und Gleichgewicht*, pp. 94-8, *et passim*. The conception of equilibrium as essentially a *competitive* equilibrium in the classical writers, and J. B. Clark, for example, was *logically* sound, though the idea of some force breaking down all monopolies in the long run was *empirically* far-fetched.

36. Cf. J. Robinson, *op. cit.* pp. 21-3 ; and on the other hand E. R. Chamberlin, *Theory of Monopolistic Competition*, pp. 31 and 46, and H. von Stackelberg, *op. cit.* pp. 86 ff.

37. *Vide supra*, Section 2.

38. This is apparently what Edgeworth had in mind when he said that normally under monopoly there is not a sufficient number of conditions to render economic equilibrium determinate, and that in a world of monopolies there would be no occupation

124

for abstract economists, who would have to make way for empiricists (cf. *Collected Papers*, vol. i. pp. 136-8). J. S. Mill in an interesting passage may have been making the same point : " . . . only through the principles of competition has political economy any pretension to the character of a science. So far as rents, profits, wages, prices are determined by competition, laws may be assigned for them. Assume competition to be their exclusive regulator, and principles of broad generality and scientific precision may be laid down according to which they will be regulated. The political economist justly deems this his proper business : and, as an abstract of hypothetical science, political economy cannot be required to do, and indeed cannot do, anything more " (*Principles*, People's Edition, p. 147).

39. Cf. J. R. Hicks, *op. cit.* p. 445 : " Die Vorbedingung für Gleichgewicht in diesem weitesten Sinne ist *vollständige Voraussicht.* Ungleichgewicht ist somit die Enttäuschung der Erwartungen." But if complete expectations cannot be disappointed, " undisappointed " expectations may very well be incomplete. See also the quotation in the next note but one.

40. By an endogenous change we mean a change in people's market behaviour ; by an exogenous change, which of course will often be correlated with an endogenous one, any other type of change. It is not clear whether changes in individuals' holdings of cash, or in their " monetary " conduct, is " endogenous " or " exogenous ", but this lack of clarity does not affect greatly our use of the term here. See the discussion in G. Haberler, *Prosperity and Depression*, pp. 8-10.

41. Cf. F. A. von Hayek, *Economica*, p. 41 : " Correct foresight . . . is a defining characteristic of equilibrium ".

42. Cf. F. A. von Hayek, *op. cit.* p. 43. Cf. also E. Lundberg, *The Theory of Economic Expansion*, p. 2.

43. Cf. F. H. Knight, *op. cit.* p. 152.

44. Cf. J. B. Clark, *The Distribution of Wealth*, pp. 279 and 408-9, by whom this rather question-begging comparison was often used.

45. Cf. L. Robbins, *Nature and Significance of Economic Science*, 2nd edition, p. 102.

46. Professor von Hayek (*op. cit.* p. 49) appears to hold, on the other hand, that the assumption of a tendency towards equilibrium is true in the former significant sense, *i.e.* that we are usually in, or interestingly near, equilibrium.

47. Cf. E. Lundberg, *op. cit.* p. 24.

48. Cf. J. M. Keynes, *op. cit.* pp. 162-3.

125

THE BASIC POSTULATES OF PURE THEORY

49. Cf. M. Schlick, *Fragen der Ethik*, p. 27 ff., on the *Motivationsgesetz*.

50. Cf. G. Myrdal, *op. cit.* p. 437.

51. Cf. A. C. Pigou, *op. cit.* pp. 87-8.

52. For the relation between falsifiability and empirical content cf. K. Popper, *Logik der Forschung*, pp. 13 and 43. Popper brings out very clearly that it is the function of a scientific law to " forbid " some conceivable types of occurrence : " Nicht umsonst heissen die Naturgesetze ' Gesetze ' : Sie sagen umso mehr, je mehr sie verbieten ". A circularity or tautology " forbids " nothing. It is " true " whatever occurs, and therefore empirically empty. Cf. also C. G. Hempel and P. Oppenheimer, *Der Typusbegriff im Lichte der neuen Logik*, Leiden, pp. 105-6 : " Typologische Systeme, in denen keine denkbare Mischform der zugrundegelegten Typenmerkmale als empirisch ausgeschlossen bezeichnet wird, enthalten überhaupt keine empirischen Gesetze und haben daher nicht den Charakter wissenschaftlicher Theorien ".

53. Cf. D. Ricardo, *Letters to Malthus* (ed. Bonar), p. 18 n.

54. Cf. L. von Mises, *Grundprobleme der Nationalökonomie*, pp. 32-3 and 139, and J. Robinson, *op. cit.* pp. 211-12.

55. Cf. L. von Mises, *op. cit.* p. 50.

56. Cf. L. Wittgenstein, *Tractatus Logico-Philosophicus*, p. 167.

57. Cf. L. Robbins, *op. cit.* p. 93.

58. Cf. M. Bowley, *Nassau Senior*, pp. 43-8. Dr. Bowley emphasises the similarity between the doctrines of Senior—" the most important writer on scope and method among the classical economists "—and the contemporary doctrines of Professor von Mises and his followers.

59. Quoted by Cliff Leslie, *op. cit.* p. 202.

60. F. Lutz (*Das Konjunkturproblem in der Nationalökonomie*) brings out very clearly the point that there can be no deductive theory based on assumptions of mistaken conduct, but he comes to exactly the opposite conclusion to us that a theory of the trade cycle and fluctuations must be constructed on an assumption of rational unmistaken conduct—implying presumably perfect expectation. We cannot help fearing that such an attempt is bound to lead to the dilemma of the classical economists who set out to examine the problem of " overproduction " on the tacit assumption that no such thing could occur.

61. *Nationalökonomisk Tidskrift*, 1935, p. 191.

62. *Literary Remains*, p. 568, quoted by H. Wagenführ, *Der Systemgedanke in der Nationalökonomie*, p. 160.

63. Cf. G. Haberler, *Prosperity and Depression*, p. 242.

126

NOTES

64. Cf. R. F. Harrod, *The Trade Cycle*, pp. 38-9.

65. O. Morgenstern, *Zeitschrift für Nationalökonomie*, 1935, p. 356, and C. F. Roos, *Dynamic Economics*, p. 68.

66. *Vide* Appendix for examples of " political " assumptions.

Without entering into the particular criticisms of different accounts of the rate of interest with which it is concerned, the following general criticism of impressionist assumptions in dynamic theories makes some very relevant points : " It is impossible to over-emphasise the truism that existence and non-existence of an effective discount of the future remain nothing more than tentative postulates, until appropriate statistical analysis establishes the one or the other postulate as a fact. For generations followers of the classical doctrine have *assumed* that time-preference is a strong determinant of saving and dis-saving ; now Mr. Keynes *assumes* that time-preference is not important as a determinant of dis-saving and new savings. These conflicting opinions are both based only upon intuition and personal experience, which are at best untrustworthy criteria, and the more so when in conflict. Both Mr. Keynes and the classicists seem to have fallen prey to what has, in another connection, been called the ' Ricardian vice '."—G. R. Holden, *Quarterly Journal of Economics*, 1938, p. 294.

127

2

The Testability and Testing of Assumptions — Machlup vs. Hutchison

Fritz Machlup, 'The Problem of Verification in Economics', *Southern Economic Journal*, vol. 22, no. 1, July 1955, pp. 1–21.

Terence Hutchison, 'Professor Machlup on Verification in Economics', *Southern Economic Journal*, vol. 22, no. 4, April 1956, pp. 476–83.

Fritz Machlup, 'Rejoinder to a Reluctant Ultra-Empiricist', *Southern Economic Journal*, vol. 22, no. 4, April 1956, pp. 483–93.

Editor's comments

In 'The Problem of Verification in Economics', Fritz Machlup views himself as the great reconciler, who treads the middle path between a priorists like Mises, Knight and Robbins and ultra-empiricists like Hutchison. (Significantly, no one else is mentioned in this latter group.) The verification problem is simply stated: must all propositions in a scientific system be verified, or at least verifiable? A priorists claim that, because economics consists of a series of deductions from necessary and self-evident truths, empirical testing is unnecessary. Ultra-empiricists insist that all propositions in a theoretical structure must be tested, including the assumptions. Machlup's intermediate position is that only the deduced, lower-level hypotheses of a theory should be tested. Predictions, not assumptions, are the loci of testing in science.

Hutchison is clearly upset with Machlup's charge that he is an ultra-empiricist. He points out that 'conceivable testability' is all that he called for in his book, and he demands that Machlup show him exactly what the 'indirect testing' of assumptions would entail. In his reply, Machlup obliges him rather well.

Though the crucial issue of 'conceivable testability' is neatly sidestepped by both of the combatants, much may be learned from this exchange. It seems to me that Machlup carried the day, for two reasons. First, his command of the philosophical literature permitted him to take a position that was quite compatible with prevailing views in the philosophy of science of his day. By the 1950s, the logical positivist prescription that all scientific statements require independent testing had been replaced by the logical empiricist view that theories may contain untestable statements that gain indirect support when the theory as a whole is tested. This 'indirect testability' thesis is wholly consistent with Machlup's emphasis on testing lower-level hypotheses. Second, Machlup buttressed his philosophical claims with concrete examples drawn from economics. His skillful blending of ideas drawn from philosophy and economics provides a good example of one way to make a significant contribution to the field of methodology.

We may close with a question that will aid our transition to the next group of readings. Many economists have lumped the views of Machlup and Friedman together, and given them the label of positivist. Is either Machlup or Friedman a positivist? How are their positions similar, and how are they different?

Volume XXII   Number I

The SOUTHERN ECONOMIC JOURNAL
July 1955

THE PROBLEM OF VERIFICATION IN ECONOMICS*

FRITZ MACHLUP

The Johns Hopkins University

I

It will be well for us first to clear the ground lest we get lost in the rubble of past discussions. To clear the ground is, above all, to come to a decision as to what we mean by verification and what it can and cannot do for our research and analysis.

The Meaning of Verification

A good book of synonyms will have the verb "verify" associated with the more pretentious verbs "prove," "demonstrate," "establish," "ascertain," "confirm," and with the more modest verbs "check" and "test." The verbs in the former group would usually be followed by a "that"—"we shall prove that . . ."—the verbs in the latter group by a "whether"—"we shall check whether. . . ." Besides this difference between "verify that" and "verify whether," there is the difference between verification as a process and verification as an affirmative result of that process. By using *"test"* for the former and *"confirmation"* for the latter we may avoid confusion. Where the distinction is not necessary, "verification" is an appropriate weasel-word, meaning both test and confirmation.

Verification in research and analysis may refer to many things including the correctness of mathematical and logical arguments, the applicability of formulas and equations, the trustworthiness of reports, the authenticity of documents, the genuineness of artifacts or relics, the adequacy of reproductions, translations and paraphrases, the accuracy of historical and statistical accounts, the corroboration of reported events, the completeness in the enumeration of circumstances in a concrete situation, the reliability and exactness of observations, the reproducibility of experiments, the explanatory or predictive value of generalizations. For each of these pursuits, the term verification is used in various disciplines. But we intend to confine ourselves to the last one mentioned: the verification of the explanatory or predictive value of hypothetical generalizations.

Although definitions are sometimes a nuisance rather than an aid, I shall try my hand at one, and say that verification in the sense most relevant to us—the

* A paper presented at the Annual Conference of the Southern Economic Association in Biloxi, Mississippi, on November 19, 1954. The author is indebted to several of his colleagues, but chiefly to Dr. Edith Penrose, for criticism and suggestions leading to improvements of style and exposition.

1

2   FRITZ MACHLUP

testing of generalizations—is *a procedure designed to find out whether a set of data of observation about a class of phenomena is obtainable and can be reconciled with a particular set of hypothetical generalizations about this class of phenomena.*

Truth and Reality

I have carefully avoided the words "truth" and "reality," although the Latin *veritas* forms the root of the term defined. I eschewed references to truth and reality in order to stay out of strictly epistemological and ontological controversies. Not that such discussions would be uninteresting or unimportant; he who never studies metaphysical questions, and even prides himself on his unconcern with metaphysics, often does not know how much in fact he talks about it. To stay away from metaphysics one has to know a good bit about it.

The function of words chosen—testing, checking, confirming—is precisely to enable us to leave the concepts of truth and reality in the background. If I should slip occasionally and say that a proposition is "true" or a phenomenon is "real," this should be taken merely as an unguarded way of speaking; for I mean to say only that there seems to be considerable "support" or "evidence" for the proposition in view of a marked *correspondence* or consistency between that proposition and statements about particular observations.

Special and General Hypotheses

My definition of verification related only to hypothetical generalizations. But the status of *special hypotheses about single events or unique situations* (and their causes, effects, and interrelations) also calls for examination, for it is with these that economic history and most of applied economics are concerned. Such special hypotheses—to establish the "facts"—are of course also subject to verification, but the rules and techniques are somewhat different from those of the verification of general hypotheses.

In a murder case we ask "who done it?" and the answer requires the weighing of several alternative special hypotheses. Such special hypotheses may be mental constructions of unobserved occurrences which could have taken place in conjunction with occurrences observed or conclusively inferred. It is an accepted rule that a special hypothesis will be rejected if it is contradicted by a single inconsistency between a firmly established observation and any of the things that follow logically from the combination of the special hypothesis and the factual assumptions of the argument.

But this weighing and testing of special hypotheses in the light of the known circumstances of the case always involves numerous *general* hypotheses. For example, the generalization that "if a man is at one place he cannot at the same time be at another place" may be of utmost importance in verifying a suspicion that Mr. X was the murderer. And whenever observations have to be interpreted and special hypotheses applied to reach a conclusion about what are the "concrete facts," the argument will presuppose the acceptance of numerous general theories or hypotheses linking two or more (observed or inferred) "facts" as possible (or probable) causes and effects. This is the reason why it has to be said

over and over again that most of the facts of history are based on previously
formed general hypotheses or theories. Although this has been an important
theme in the discussion of the relation between theory and history, and one of
the central issues in the *Methodenstreit* in economics, it is not an issue in our discussion today. At the moment we are concerned with the verification of general
hypotheses and theories, not of propositions concerning individual events or
conditions at a particular time and place. But this much ought to be said here:
to establish or verify "historical facts," we must rely on the acceptance of numerous general hypotheses (theories); and to verify general hypotheses we must rely
on the acceptance of numerous data representing "facts" observed or inferred
at various times and places. We always must take something for granted, no
matter how averse we are to "preconceptions."

Theories, Hypotheses, Hunches, Assumptions, Postulates

No fixed lines can be drawn between theories, hypotheses, and mere hunches,
the differences being at best those of degree. There are degrees of vagueness in
formulation, degrees of confidence or strength of belief in what is posed or stated,
degrees of acceptance among experts, and degrees of comprehensiveness or range
of applicability.[1]

A hunch is usually vague, sometimes novel, original, often incompletely formulated; perhaps more tentative than a hypothesis, although the difference may lie
just in the modesty of the analyst. A hypothesis may likewise be very tentative;
indeed, some hypotheses are introduced only for didactic purposes, as provisional
steps in an argument, in full knowledge of their inapplicability to any concrete
situation and perhaps in preparation for a preferred hypothesis. Distinctions
between hypotheses and theories have been suggested in terms of the strength of
belief in their applicability or of the comprehensiveness (range) of their applicability.[2] But so often are the words theory and hypothesis used interchangeably that there is not much point in laboring any distinguishing criteria.

Perhaps it should be stressed that every hypothesis may have the status of an
"assumption" in a logical argument. An assumption of a rather general nature
which is posited as a "principle" for an argument or for a whole system

---

[1] The belief that a "hunch" is something fundamentally different from a "theory" may
be responsible for certain antitheoretical positions of some historians and statisticians.
Those who claimed the priority and supremacy of fact-finding over "theoretical speculation" might have accepted the contention that you cannot find facts without having some
hunch. But this is practically all that the theorists meant when they claimed that theory
must precede fact-finding, whether historical or statistical, and that history without theory,
and measurement without theory are *impossible*. There are kinds of fact-finding which presuppose full-fledged theories; some simpler kinds may start with vague hunches.

[2] "A hypothesis is an assumption . . . tentatively suggested as an explanation of a phenomenon." Morris R. Cohen and Ernest Nagel, *An Introduction to Logic and Scientific
Method* (New York: Harcourt, Brace, 1938), p. 205.—"A hypothesis . . . is . . . a theory
which has, at present at least, a limited range of application. It is promoted to the status
of a theory if and when its range is deemed sufficiently large to justify this more commenda-
tory appelation." Henry Margenau, "Methodology of Modern Physics," *Philosophy of
Science*, Vol. II (January 1935), p. 67.

4   FRITZ MACHLUP

of thought, but is neither self-evident nor proved, is often called a "postulate." Just as there may be a connotation of tentativeness in the word "hypothesis," there may be a connotation of arbitrariness in the word "postulate."[3] But since no fundamental assumption in an empirical discipline is definitive, and since all are more or less arbitrary, it is useless to insist on subtle distinctions which are (for good reasons) disregarded by most participants in the discussion.[4]

Confirmation versus Non-Disconfirmation

How is a hypothesis verified? The hypothesis is *tested* by a two-step procedure: first deducing from it and the factual assumptions with which it is combined all the conclusions that can be inferred, and second, confronting these conclusions with data obtained from observation of the phenomena concerned. The hypothesis is *confirmed* if reasonable correspondence is found between the deduced and the observed, or more correctly, if no irreconcilable contradiction is found between the deduced and the observed. Absence of contradictory evidence, a finding of non-contradiction, is really a negation of a negation: indeed, one calls a hypothesis "confirmed" when it is merely *not dis*confirmed.

Thus, the procedure of verification may yield findings compelling the rejection of the tested hypothesis, but never findings that can "prove" its correctness, adequacy or applicability.[5] As in a continuing sports championship conducted by elimination rules, where the winner stays in the game as long as he is not defeated but can always be challenged for another contest, no empirical hypothesis is safe forever; it can always be challenged for another test and may be knocked out at any time. The test results, at best, in a "confirmation till next time."

Several logicians use the word "falsification" for a finding of irreconcilable contradiction; and since a hypothesis can be definitely refuted or "falsified," but not definitely confirmed or "verified," some logicians have urged that we speak only of "falsifiable," not of verifiable propositions. Because the word "falsification" has a double meaning, I prefer to speak of refutation or disconfirmation. But the dictum is surely right: testing an empirical hypothesis results either in its disconfirmation or its non-disconfirmation, never in its definitive confirmation.

[3] Cf. Wayne A. Leeman, "The Status of Facts in Economic Thought," *The Journal of Philosophy*, Vol. XLVII (June 1951), p. 408.—Leeman suggests that economists prefer the term "assumption" because it "escapes . . . the undesirable connotations" of the terms "hypothesis" and "postulate."

[4] "So far as our present argument is concerned, the things (propositions) that we take for granted may be called indiscriminately either hypotheses or axioms or postulates or assumptions or even principles, and the things (propositions) that we think we have established by admissible procedure are called theorems." Joseph A. Schumpeter, *History of Economic Analysis* (New York: Oxford University Press, 1954), p. 15.

[5] There are no rules of verification "that can be relied on in the last resort. Take the most important rules of experimental verification: reproducibility of results; agreement between determinations made by different and independent methods; fulfillment of predictions. These are powerful criteria, but I could give you examples in which they were all fulfilled and yet the statement which they seemed to confirm later turned out to be false. The most striking agreement with experiment may occasionally be revealed later to be based on mere coincidence. . . ." Michael Polanyi, *Science, Faith and Society* (London: Cumberlege, 1946), p. 13.

Even if a definitive confirmation is never possible, the number of tests which a hypothesis has survived in good shape will have a bearing on the confidence people have in its "correctness." A hypothesis confirmed and re-confirmed any number of times will have a more loyal following than one only rarely exposed to the test of experience. But the strength of belief in a hypothesis depends, even more than on any direct empirical tests that it may have survived, on the place it holds within a hierarchical system of inter-related hypotheses. But this is another matter, to be discussed a little later.

Nothing that I have said thus far would, I believe, be objected to by any modern logician, philosopher of science, or scientist. While all points mentioned were once controversial, the combat has moved on to other issues, and only a few stragglers and latecomers on the battlefield of methodology mistake the rubble left from long ago for the marks of present fighting. So we shall move on to issues on which controversy continues.

II

Which kinds of propositions can be verified, and which cannot? May unverified and unverifiable propositions be legitimately retained in a scientific system? Or should all scientific propositions be verified or at least verifiable? These are among the controversial issues—though my own views are so decided that I cannot see how intelligent people can still quarrel about them, and I have come to believe that all good men think as I do, and only a few misguided creatures think otherwise. But I shall restrain my convictions for a while.

Critizing extreme positions is a safe pastime because one may be sure of the support of a majority. But it is not for this reason but for the sake of a clear exposition that I begin with the presentation of the positions which *extreme apriorism*, on the one side, and *ultra-empiricism*, on the other side, take concerning the problem of verification in economics.

Pure, Exact, and Aprioristic Economics

Writers on the one side of this issue contend that economic science is a system of *a priori* truths, a product of pure reason,[6] an exact science reaching laws as universal as those of mathematics,[7] a purely axiomatic discipline,[8] a system of pure deductions from a series of postulates,[9] not open to any verification or refutation on the ground of experience.[10]

[6] "The ultimate yardstick of an economic theorem's correctness or incorrectness is solely reason unaided by experience." Ludwig von Mises, *Human Action: A Treatise on Economics* (New Haven: Yale University Press, 1949), p. 858.

[7] "There is a science of economics, a true and even exact science, which reaches laws as universal as those of mathematics and mechanics." Frank H. Knight, "The Limitations of Scientific Method in Economics," in R. G. Tugwell, ed., *The Trend of Economics* (New York: Crofts, 1930), p. 256.

[8] "Economic theory is an axiomatic discipline. . . ." Max Weber, *On the Methodology of the Social Sciences* (Glencoe, Ill.: Free Press, 1949), p. 43.

[9] "Economic analysis . . . consists of deductions from a series of postulates. . . ." Lionel Robbins, *An Essay on the Nature and Significance of Economic Science* (London: Macmillan, 2nd ed., 1935), p. 99.

[10] "What assigns economics its peculiar and unique position in the orbit of pure knowl-

FRITZ MACHLUP

We must not attribute to all writers whose statements were here quoted or paraphrased the same epistemological views. While for Mises, for example, even the fundamental postulates are *a priori* truths, necessities of thinking,[11] for Robbins they are "assumptions involving in some way simple and indisputable facts of experience."[12] But most of the experience in point is not capable of being recorded from external (objective) observation; instead, it is immediate, inner experience. Hence, if verification is recognized only where the test involves objective sense-experience, the chief assumptions of economics, even if "empirical," are not independently verifiable propositions.

This methodological position, either asserting an *a priori* character of all propositions of economic theory or at least denying the independent objective verifiability of the fundamental assumptions, had been vigorously stated in the last century by Senior[13] and Cairnes,[14] but in essential respects it goes back to John Stuart Mill.

Mill, the great master and expositor of inductive logic, had this to say on the method of investigation in political economy:

> Since . . . it is vain to hope that truth can be arrived at, either in Political Economy or in any other department of the social science, while we look at the facts in the concrete, clothed in all the complexity with which nature has surrounded them, and endeavor to elicit a general law by a process of induction from a comparison of details; there remains no other method than the *a priori* one, or that of 'abstract speculation.'[15]

> By the method *a priori* we mean . . . reasoning from an assumed hypothesis; which is not a practice confined to mathematics, but is of the essence of all science which admits of general reasoning at all. To verify the hypothesis itself *a posteriori*, that is, to examine whether the facts of any actual case are in accordance with it, is no part of the business of science at all but of the *application* of science.[16]

This does not mean that Mill rejects attempts to verify the results of economic analysis; on the contrary,

> We cannot . . . too carefully endeavor to verify our theory, by comparing, in the particular cases to which we have access, the results which it would have led us to predict, with the most trustworthy accounts we can obtain of those which have been actually realized.[17]

---

edge and of the practical utilization of knowledge is the fact that its particular theorems are not open to any verification or falsification on the ground of experience." Ludwig von Mises, *op. cit.*, p. 858.

[11] Ludwig von Mises, *op. cit.*, p. 33.

[12] Lionel Robbins, *op. cit.*, p. 78, also pp. 99–100.

[13] Nassau William Senior, *Political Economy* (London: Griffin, 3rd ed., 1854), pp. 5, 26–29.

[14] John E. Cairnes, *The Character and Logical Method of Political Economy* (London: Macmillan, 1875), especially pp. 74–85, 99–100.

[15] John Stuart Mill, "On the Definition of Political Economy; and on the Method of Investigation Proper to It" in *Essays on Some Unsettled Questions of Political Economy* (London, 1844, reprinted London School of Economics, 1948), pp. 148–49.

[16] *Ibid.*, p. 143.

[17] *Ibid.*, p. 154.

The point to emphasize is that Mill does not propose to put the *assumptions* of economic theory to empirical tests, but only the *predicted results that are deduced from them.* And this, I submit, is what all the proponents of pure, exact, or aprioristic economic theory had in mind, however provocative their contentions sounded.[18] Their objection was to verifying the basic assumptions in isolation.

Ultra-Empirical Economics

Opposed to these tenets are the ultra-empiricists. "Empiricist" is a word of praise to some, a word of abuse to others. This is due to the fact that there are many degrees of empiricism. Some economists regard themselves as "empiricists" merely because they oppose radical apriorism and stress the dependence of theory on experience (in the widest sense of the word); others, because they demand that the results deduced with the aid of theory be compared with observational data whenever possible; others, because they are themselves chiefly concerned with the interpretation of data, with the testing of hypotheses and with the estimates of factual relationships; others, because they are themselves engaged in the collection of data or perhaps even in "field" work designed to produce "raw" data; others, because they refuse to recognize the legitimacy of employing at any level of analysis propositions not independently verifiable. It is the last group which I call the ultra-empiricists.[19] Then there are the ultra-ultra-empiricists who go even further and insist on independent verification of all assumptions by objective data obtained through sense observation.

The ultra-empiricist position is most sharply reflected in the many attacks on the "assumptions" of economic theory. These assumptions are decried as unverified, unverifiable, imaginary, unrealistic. And the hypothetico-deductive system built upon the unrealistic or unverifiable assumptions is condemned either as deceptive or as devoid of empirical content,[20] without predictive or

[18] "Aprioristic reasoning is purely conceptual and deductive. It cannot produce anything else but tautologies and analytic judgments." While this sounds like an "empiricist's" criticism of the aprioristic position, it is in fact a statement by Mises. (*Op. cit.*, p. 38.) Mises emphasizes that "the end of science is to know reality," and that "in introducing assumptions into its reasoning, it satisfies itself that the treatment of the assumptions concerned can render useful services for the comprehension of reality." (*Ibid.*, pp. 65–66.) And he stresses that the choice of assumptions is directed by experience.

[19] It is in this last meaning that empiricism has usually been discussed and criticized in philosophy. In the words of William James, radical empiricism "must neither admit into its constructions any element that is not directly experienced, nor exclude from them any element that is directly experienced. For such a philosophy, *the relations that connect experiences must themselves be experienced relations, and any kind of relation experienced must be accounted as 'real' as anything else in the system.*" William James, *Essays in Radical Empiricism* (New York: Longmans, Green, 1912), pp. 42–43.

[20] "That 'propositions of pure theory' is a name for ... propositions not conceivably falsifiable empirically and which do not exclude ... any conceivable occurrence, and which are therefore devoid of empirical content. . . ." T. W. Hutchison, *The Significance and Basic Postulates of Economic Theory* (London: Macmillan, 1938), p. 162.

FRITZ MACHLUP

explanatory significance,[21] without application to problems or data of the real world.[22] Why deceptive? Because from wrong assumptions only wrong conclusions follow. Why without empirical significance? Because, in the words of the logician Wittgenstein, "from a tautology only tautologies follow."[23]

If the ultra-empiricists reject the basic assumptions of economic theory because they are not independently verified, and reject any theoretical system that is built on unverified or unverifiable assumptions, what is the alternative they offer? A program that begins with facts rather than assumptions.[24] What facts? Those obtained "by statistical investigations, questionnaires to consumers and entrepreneurs, the examination of family budgets and the like."[25] It is in research of this sort that the ultra-empiricists see "the only possible scientific method open" to the economist.[26]

This, again, is the essence of the ultra-empiricist position on verification: the ultra-empiricist is so distrustful of deductive systems of thought that he is not satisfied with the indirect verification of hypotheses, that is, with tests showing that the results deduced (from these hypotheses and certain factual assumptions) are in approximate correspondence with reliable observational data; instead, he insists on the independent verification of all the assumptions, hypothetical as well as factual, perhaps even of each intermediate step in the analysis. To him "testable" means "directly testable by objective data obtained by sense-observation," and propositions which are in this sense "non-testable" are detestable to him.

The Testability of Fundamental Assumptions

The error in the antitheoretical empiricist position lies in the failure to see the difference between *fundamental* (heuristic) hypotheses, which are not inde-

[21] ". . . that propositions of pure theory, by themselves, have no prognostic value or 'causal significance.' " T. W. Hutchison, *op. cit.*, p. 162.—The clause "by themselves" makes Hutchison's statement unassailable, because nothing at all has causal significance by itself; only in conjunction with other things can anything have causal significance. But if Hutchison's statement means anything, it means an attack against the use of empirically unverifiable propositions in economic theory, regardless of their conjunction with other propositions. Indeed, he states that "a proposition which can never *conceivably* be shown to be true or false . . . can *never* be of any use to a scientist" (*ibid.*, pp. 152-53).

[22] With regard to the "fundamental assumption" of economic theory concerning "subjectively rational" and "maximizing" behavior, Hutchison states that "the empirical content of the assumption and all the conclusions will be the same—that is, nothing." *Ibid.*, p. 116.

[23] Ludwig Wittgenstein, *Tractatus Logico-Philosophicus* (London: Routledge & Kegan Paul, 1951), p. 167.

[24] ". . . if one wants to get beyond a certain high level of abstraction one has to begin more or less from the beginning with extensive empirical investigation." T. W. Hutchison, *op. cit.*, p. 166.

[25] *Ibid.*, p. 120. This does not answer the question: "what facts?" Precisely what data should be obtained and statistically investigated? What questions asked of consumers and entrepreneurs?

[26] *Ibid.*, p. 120. I could have quoted from dozens of critics of economic theory, from adherents of the historical, institutional, quantitative schools, and these quotations might be even more aggressive. I have selected Hutchison because he is the critic best informed about logic and scientific method.

pendently testable, and *specific* (factual) assumptions, which are supposed to correspond to observed facts or conditions; or the differences between hypotheses on different levels of generality and, hence, of different degrees of testability.

The fundamental hypotheses are also called by several other names, some of which convey a better idea of their methodological status: "heuristic principles" (because they serve as useful guides in the analysis), "basic postulates" (because they are not to be challenged for the time being), "useful fictions" (because they need not conform to "facts" but only be useful in "as if" reasoning), "procedural rules" (because they are resolutions about the analytical procedure to be followed), "definitional assumptions" (because they are treated like purely analytical conventions).

A fundamental hypothesis serves to bring together under a common principle of explanation vast numbers of very diverse observations, masses of data of apparently very different sort, phenomena that would otherwise seem to have nothing in common. Problems like the explanation of the movements in wages in 13th and 14th century Europe, of the prices of spices in 16th century Venice, of the effects of the capital flows to Argentina in the 19th century, of the consequences of German reparation payments and of the devaluation of the dollar in the 1930's; problems like the prediction of effects of the new American quota on Swiss watches, of the new tax laws, of the increase in minimum wage rates, and so forth,—problems of such dissimilarity can all be tackled by the use of the same fundamental hypotheses. If these hypotheses are successful in this task and give more satisfactory results than other modes of treatment could, then we accept them and stick by them as long as there is nothing better—which may be forever.

That there is no way of subjecting fundamental assumptions to independent verification should be no cause of disturbance. It does not disturb the workers in the discipline which most social scientists so greatly respect and envy for its opportunities of verification: physical science. The whole system of physical mechanics rests on such fundamental assumptions: Newton's three laws of motion are postulates or procedural rules for which no experimental verification is possible or required; and, as Einstein put it, "No one of the assumptions can be isolated for separate testing." For, he went on to say, "physical concepts are free creations of the human mind, and are not, however it may seem, uniquely determined by the external world."[27]

Much has been written about the meaning of "explanation." Some have said that the mere *description* of regularities in the co-existence and co-variation of observed phenomena is all we can do and will be accepted as an *explanation* when we are sufficiently used to the regularities described.[28] There is something to this view; but mere resignation to the fact that "it always has been so" will not for long pass as explanation for searching minds. The feeling of relief and satisfied curiosity—often expressed in the joyous exclamation "ah haahh!"—comes to most analysts only when the observed regularities can be deduced from

[27] Albert Einstein and Leopold Infeld, *The Evolution of Physics* (New York: Simon and Schuster, 1938), p. 33.

[28] Cf. P. W. Bridgman, *The Logic of Modern Physics* (New York: Macmillan, 1927), p. 43.

FRITZ MACHLUP

general principles which are also the starting point—foundation or apex, as you like—of many other chains of causal derivation. This is why Margenau, another physicist, said that an explanation involves a "progression into the constructional domain. We explain by going 'beyond phenomena.' "[29] But this clearly implies that the explanatory general assumptions cannot be empirically verifiable in isolation.

Logicians and philosophers of science have long tried to make this perfectly clear. Although appeals to authority are ordinarily resorted to only where an expositor has failed to convince his audience, I cannot resist the temptation to quote two authorities on my subject. Here is how the American philosopher Josiah Royce put it:

> One often meets with the remark that a scientific hypothesis must be such as to be more or less completely capable of verification or of refutation by experience. The remark is sound. But equally sound it is to say that a hypothesis which, just as it is made, is, without further deductive reasoning, capable of receiving direct refutation or verification, *is not nearly as valuable to any science as is a hypothesis whose verifications, so far as they occur at all, are only possible indirectly, and through the mediation of a considerable deductive theory,* whereby the consequences of the hypothesis are first worked out, and then submitted to test.[30]

And here is the same idea in the words of the British philosopher of science, Richard B. Braithwaite:

> For science, as it advances, does not rest content with establishing simple generalizations from observable facts. It tries to explain these lowest-level generalization by deducing them from more general hypotheses at a higher level. . . . As the hierarchy of hypotheses of increasing generality rises, the concepts with which the hypotheses are concerned cease to be properties of things which are directly observable, and instead become 'theoretical' concepts—atoms, electrons, fields of force, genes, unconscious mental processes—which are connected to the observable facts by complicated logical relationships.[31]

And he states that "the empirical testing of the deductive system is effected by testing the lowest-level hypotheses in the system."[32]

Assumptions in Economics, Pure and Applied

Examples of *fundamental assumptions* or "high-level generalizations" in economic theory are that people act rationally, try to make the most of their opportunities, and are able to arrange their preferences in a consistent order; that entrepreneurs prefer more profit to less profit with equal risk.[33] These are

---

[29] Henry Margenau, *The Nature of Physical Reality* (New York: McGraw-Hill, 1950), p. 169.

[30] Josiah Royce, "The Principles of Logic," in *Logic, Encyclopaedia of the Philosophical Sciences*, Vol. I (London: Macmillan, 1913), pp. 88–89.

[31] Richard Bevan Braithwaite, *Scientific Explanation: A Study of the Function of Theory, Probability and Law in Science* (Cambridge: University Press, 1953), p. ix.

[32] *Ibid.*, p. 13.

[33] For most problems of an enterprise economy no exact specifications about "profit"

assumptions which, though empirically meaningful, require no independent empirical tests but may be significant steps in arguments reaching conclusions which are empirically testable.

Examples of *specific assumptions* are that the expenditures for table salt are a small portion of most households' annual budgets; that the member banks are holding very large excess reserves with the Federal Reserve Banks; that there is a quota for the importation of sugar which is fully utilized. Examples of *deduced "low-level hypotheses"* are that a reduction in the price of table salt will not result in a proportionate increase in salt consumption; that a reduction in the discount rates of the Federal Reserve Banks will at such times not result in an increase in the member banks' lending activities; that a reduction in sugar prices abroad will not result in a reduction of domestic sugar prices. All these and similar specific assumptions and low-level hypotheses are empirically testable.

Perhaps a few additional comments should be made concerning the fundamental assumptions, particularly the postulate of rational action, the "economic principle" of aiming at the attainment of a maximum of given ends. Any independent test of this assumption by reference to objective *sense*-experience is obviously impossible. Those who accept findings of introspection as sufficient evidence may contend that the fundamental assumption can be, and constantly is, verified. Those who accept findings of interrogation (that is, replies to questions put to large numbers of introspectors) as "objective" evidence may contend that the assumption of "maximizing behavior" is independently testable. But such a test would be gratuitous, if not misleading. For the fundamental assumption may be understood as an idealization with constructs so far removed from operational concepts that contradiction by testimony is ruled out; or even as a complete fiction with only one claim: that reasoning *as if* it were realized is helpful in the interpretation of observations.[34]

Economists who are still suspicious of non-verifiable assumptions, and worry about the legitimacy of using them, may be reassured by this admission: The fact that fundamental assumptions are not directly testable and cannot be refuted by empirical investigation does not mean that they are beyond the pale of the so-called "principle of permanent control," that is, beyond possible challenge, modification or rejection. These assumptions may well be rejected, but only together with the theoretical system of which they are a part, and only when a more satisfactory system is put in its place; in Conant's words, "a theory is only overthrown by a better theory, never merely by contradictory facts."[35]

(whose? for what period? how uncertain? etc.) will be needed. There are some special problems for which "specific assumptions" concerning profit are needed. Needless to say, the assumption about entrepreneurs will be irrelevant for problems of centrally directed economies.

[34] Or, again in a different formulation: the fundamental assumption is a resolution to proceed in the interpretation of all data of observation as if they were the result of the postulated type of behavior.

[35] James B. Conant, *On Understanding Science* (New Haven: Yale University Press, 1947), p. 36.

12   FRITZ MACHLUP

III

What I have said and quoted about assumptions and hypotheses on various "levels" of abstraction may itself be too abstract, too remote from our ordinary terms of discourse, to be meaningful to many of us. Perhaps it will be helpful to try a graphical presentation of a simple model of an analytical system combining assumptions of various types.

A Model of an Analytical Apparatus

The design for the model was suggested by the usual metaphors about an analytical "apparatus," "machine," or "engine of pure theory." Something goes into a machine and something comes out. In this case the input is an assumption concerning some "change" occurring and causing other things to happen, and the output is the "Deduced Change," the conclusion of the (mental) operation. The machine with all its parts furnishes the connection between the "assumed cause," the input, and the "deduced effect," the outcome. The main point of this model is that *the machine is a construction of our mind, while the assumed and deduced changes should correspond to observed phenomena, to data of observation, if the machine is to serve as an instrument of explanation or prediction.* In explanations the analytical machine helps select an adequate "cause" for an observed change; in predictions it helps find a probable "effect" of an observed change.[36]

The machine consists of many parts, all of which represent assumptions or hypotheses of different degrees of generality. The so-called *fundamental assumptions* are a fixed part of the machine; they make the machine what it is; they cannot be changed without changing the character of the entire machine. All other parts are exchangeable, like coils, relays, spools, wires, tapes, cylinders, records, or mats, something that can be selected and put in, and again taken out to be replaced by a different piece of the set. These exchangeable parts represent *assumptions about the conditions* under which the Assumed Change must operate. Some of the parts are exchanged all the time, some less frequently, some only seldom. Parts of type A, the Assumed Conditions as to "type of case," are most frequently exchanged. Parts of type B, the Assumed Conditions as to "type of setting," will stay in the machine for a longer time and there need be less variety in the set from which they are selected. Parts of type C, the Assumed Conditions as to "type of economy," are least exchangeable, and there will be only a small assortment of alternative pieces to choose from.

Now we shall leave the engineering analogies aside and discuss the status of all these assumptions regarding the operational and observational possibilities and the requirements of verification.

Verified Changes under Unverified Conditions

Both the Assumed Change and the Deduced Change should be empirically verifiable through correspondence with data of observation. At least one of the two has to be verifiable if the analysis is to be applied to concrete cases. Hence

---

[36] On the problem of prediction versus explanation see the chapter on "Economic Fact and Theory" in my book *The Political Economy of Monopoly* (Baltimore: Johns Hopkins Press, 1952), pp. 455 ff.

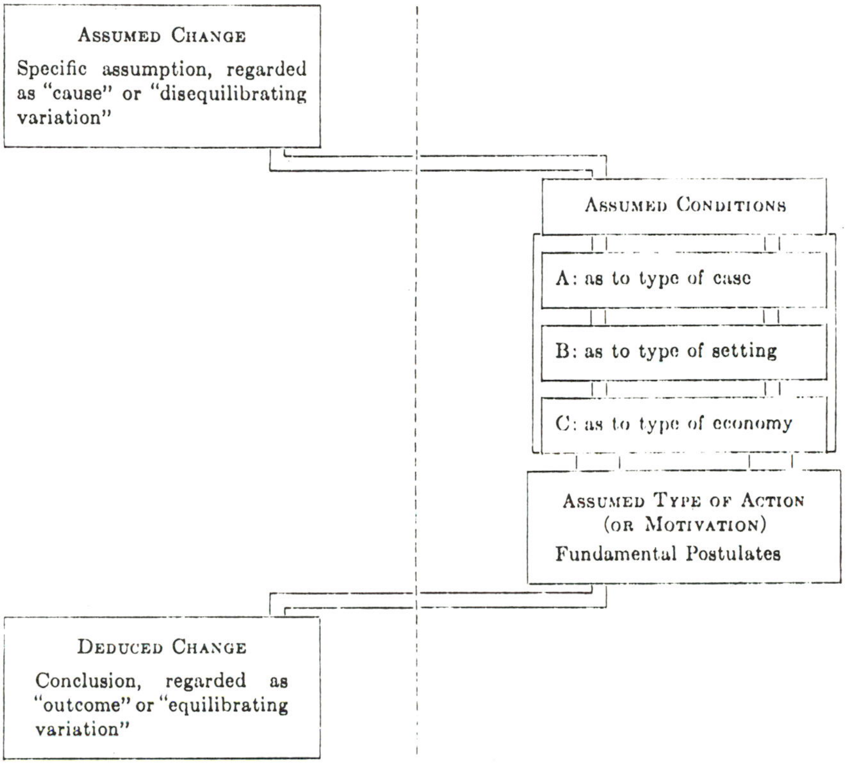

FIG. 1. A MODEL OF THE USE OF AN ANALYTICAL APPARATUS

On the right side is the "machine of pure theory," a mental *construction* for heuristic purposes; on the left side are assumptions of independent and dependent variables whose *correspondence* with data of observation may be tested.

the concepts employed to describe the changes should, if possible, be operational. This raises no difficulty in the case of most kinds of *Assumed Change* in whose effects we are interested, for example: changes in tax rates, customs duties, foreign-exchange rates, wage rates, price supports, price ceilings, discount rates, open-market policies, credit lines, government expenditures, agricultural crops— matters covered in reports and records. There are difficulties concerning some other kinds of Assumed Change, such as improvements in technology, greater optimism, changed tastes for particular goods—things for which recorded data are often unavailable. As regards the *Deduced Change* the requirement that it be operational will usually be met, because we are interested chiefly in effects upon prices, output, income, employment, etc.,—magnitudes reported in statistical series of some sort. To be sure, the figures may be unreliable and the statistical concepts may not be exact counterparts to the analytical concepts, but we cannot be too fussy and must be satisfied with what we can get.

In principle we want both Assumed Change and Deduced Change to be capable of being compared with recorded data so that the correspondence between the theory and the data can be checked. The analysis would be neither wrong nor invalid, but it would not be very useful if it were never possible to identify the concrete phenomena, events, and situations, to which it is supposed to apply. Once we have confidence in the whole theoretical system, we are willing to apply it to concrete cases even where only one of the two "changes," either the "cause" or the "effect," is identifiable in practice, rather than both. For example, we are prepared to base policy decisions on explanations or predictions where one of the phenomena cannot be isolated in observation from the complex of simultaneous variations. For purposes of verification of the entire theory, however, we shall have to identify both the phenomena represented by the Assumed Change and the Deduced Change—although such verification may be practical only on rare occasions.

We need not be particularly strict concerning the verification of the *Assumed Conditions*. Regarding them, a casual, perhaps even impressionistic empiricism will do, at least for most types of problems. The Assumed Conditions refer to personal characteristics, technological or organizational circumstances, market forms, enduring institutions—things of rather varied nature. Few of the Conditions are observable, except through communication of interpretations involving a good deal of theorizing by the parties concerned. Often the Conditions are not even specified in detail, but somehow taken for granted by analysts working in a familiar milieu. All of the Conditions are hypothetical parameters, assumed to prevail at least for the duration of the process comprising all the actions, interactions and repercussions through which the Assumed Change is supposed to cause the Deduced Change.

Assumed Conditions of Type A, that is, as to *"type of case,"* refer to conditions which may vary from case to case and influence the outcome significantly, but are sufficiently common to justify the construction of "types" for theoretical analysis. Here is a list of examples: type of goods involved (durable, non-durable, perishable; inferior, non-inferior; taking up substantial or negligible parts of buyer's budget; substitutable, complementary; etc.); cost conditions (marginal cost decreasing, constant, increasing; joint costs, etc.); elasticity of supply or demand (positive, negative, relatively large, unity, less than unity); market position (perfect, imperfect polypoly; collusive, uncoordinated oligopoly; perfect, imperfect monopoly); entry (perfect, imperfect pliopoly); expectations (elastic, inelastic; bullish, bearish; certain, uncertain); consumption propensity (greater, smaller than unity); elasticity of liquidity preference (infinite, less than infinite, zero).

Assumed Conditions of Type B, that is, as to "type of setting," refer to conditions which may change over brief periods of time—say, with a change of government or of the political situation, or during the business cycle—and are apt to influence the outcome in definite directions. A list of examples will indicate what is meant by conditions prevailing under the current "setting": general business outlook (boom spirit, depression pessimism); bank credit availability (banks loaned up, large excess reserves); central bank policy (ready to monetize government securities, determined to maintain easy money policy, willing to let interest rates rise); fiscal policy (expenditures fixed, adjusted to tax revenues, geared to unemployment figures; tax rates fixed, adjusted to maintain revenue, etc.); farm program (support prices fixed, flexible within limits, etc.); antitrust policy (vigorous prosecution of cartelization, etc.); foreign aid program; stabilization fund rules; trade union policies.

Assumed Conditions of Type C, that is, as to *"type of economy,"* refer to conditions which may vary from country to country and over larger periods of time, but may be assumed to be "settled" for a sufficiently large number of cases to justify taking these conditions as constant. Examples include legal and social institutions; private property; freedom of contract; corporation law; patent system; transportation system; enforcement of contracts; ethics of law violations; social customs and usages; monetary system (gold standard, check system, cash holding habits).

Assumed Conditions are exchangeable because the effects of an Assumed Change may have to be analysed under a variety of conditions: for example, with different degrees or forms of competition, different credit policies, different tax structures, different trade union policies, etc. But it may also be expedient, depending on the problem at hand, to regard a variation of an Assumed Condition as an Assumed Change, and *vice versa*. For example, the problem may concern the effects of a wage rate increase under various market conditions or, instead, the effects of a change in market position under conditions of automatic wage escalation; the effects of a change in monetary policy with different tax structure, or the effects of a change in the tax structure under different monetary policies.

After listing the many examples of the various types of Assumed Conditions it will probably be agreed that a rigid verification requirement would be out of place. Usually the judgment of the analyst will suffice even if he cannot support it with more than the most circumstantial evidence or mere "impressions." Suppose he deals with a simple cost-price-output problem in a large industry, how will the analyst determine what "type of case" it is with regard to "market position?" Lacking the relevant information, he may first try to work with a model of perfect polypoly[37]—although he knows well that this cannot fit the real situation—and will note whether his deduced results will be far off the mark. He may find the results reasonably close to the observed data and may leave it at that. For to work with a more "realistic" assumption may call for so many additional assumptions for which no relevant information is available that it is preferable and unobjectionable to continue with a hypothesis contrary to fact. When a simpler hypothesis, though obviously unrealistic, gives consistently

---

[37] Under perfect polypoly the individual seller assumes that his own supply will not affect any other seller or the market as a whole and, thus, that he could easily sell more at the same price and terms. This condition was also called "pure competition," "perfect competition," or "perfect market" (although it has little to do with any effort of "competing" or with any property of the "market"). See Fritz Machlup, *The Economics of Sellers' Competition* (Baltimore: Johns Hopkins Press, 1952), pp. 85–91, and pp. 116 ff.

satisfactory results, one need not bother with more complicated, more realistic hypotheses.

Ideal Type of Action, Unverified but Understood

While solid empirical verification is indicated for the Assumed Change, and casual empirical judgments are indicated for the Assumed Conditions, the *Assumed Type of Action* forms the fundamental postulates of economic analysis and thus is not subject to a requirement of independent verification.

Various names have been suggested for the fundamental postulates of economic theory: "economic principle," "maximization principle," "assumption of rationality," "law of motivation," and others. And their logical nature has been characterized in various ways: they are regarded as "self-evident propositions," "axioms," "*a priori* truths," "truisms," "tautologies," "definitions," "rigid laws," "rules of procedure," "resolutions," "working hypotheses," "useful fictions," "ideal types," "heuristic mental constructs," "indisputable facts of experience," "facts of immediate experience," "data of introspective observation," "private empirical data," "typical behavior patterns," and so forth.

Some of these characterizations are equivalent to or consistent with each other, but some are not. How can a proposition be both *a priori* and empirical, both a definition and a fact of experience? While this cannot be, the distinctions in this particular instance are so fine that conflicts of interpretation seem unavoidable. Logicians have long debated the possibility of propositions being synthetic and yet *a priori*, and physicists are still not quite agreed whether the "laws" of mechanics are analytical definitions or empirical facts. The late philosopher Felix Kaufmann introduced as a middle category the so-called "rules of procedure," which are neither synthetic in the sense that they are falsifiable by contravening observations nor *a priori* in the sense that they are independent of experience;[38] they are and remain accepted as long as they have heuristic value, but will be rejected in favor of other rules (assumptions) which seem to serve their explanatory functions more successfully.

If this debate has been going on in the natural sciences, how could it be avoided in the social sciences? If issues about "self-evident," "inescapable," or "indisputable" insights arose concerning the physical world, how much more pertinent are such issues in the explanation of human action, where man is both observer and subject of observation! This, indeed, is the essential difference between the natural and the social sciences: that in the latter the facts, the data of "observation," are themselves results of interpretations of human actions by human actors.[39] And this imposes on the social sciences a requirement which does not

[38] Felix Kaufmann, *Methodology of the Social Sciences* (New York: Oxford University Press, 1944), pp. 77 ff, especially pp. 87–88.

[39] ". . . the object, the 'facts' of the social sciences are also opinions—not opinions of the student of the social phenomena, of course, but opinions of those whose actions produce his object. . . . They [the facts] differ from the facts of the physical sciences in being . . . beliefs which are as such our data . . . and which, moreover, we cannot directly observe in the minds of the people but recognize from what they do and say merely because we have

exist in the natural sciences: that all types of action that are used in the abstract models constructed for purposes of analysis be "understandable" to most of us in the sense that we could conceive of sensible men acting (sometimes at least) in the way postulated by the ideal type in question. This is the crux of Max Weber's methodology of the social sciences, and was recently given a refined and most convincing formulation by Alfred Schuetz.[40]

Schuetz promulgates three postulates guiding model construction in the social sciences: the postulates of "logical consistency," of "subjective interpretation," and of "adequacy." The second and third of these postulates are particularly relevant here:

> In order to explain human actions the scientist has to ask what model of an individual mind can be constructed and what typical contents must be attributed to it in order to explain the observed facts as the result of the activity of such a mind in an understandable relation. The compliance with this postulate warrants the possibility of referring all kinds of human action or their result to the subjective meaning such action or result of an action had for the actor.
>
> Each term in a scientific model of human action must be constructed in such a way that a human act performed within the life world by an individual actor in the way indicated by the typical construct would be understandable for the actor himself as well as for his fellowmen in terms of common-sense interpretation of everyday life. Compliance with this postulate warrants the consistency of the constructs of the social scientist with the constructs of common-sense experience of the social reality.[41]

Thus, the fundamental assumptions of economic theory are not subject to a requirement of independent empirical verification, but instead to a requirement of understandability in the sense in which man can understand the actions of fellowmen.[42]

IV

We are ready to summarize our conclusions concerning verification of the assumptions of economic theory. Then we shall briefly comment on the verification of particular economic theories applied to predict future events, and on the verification of strictly empirical hypotheses.

Verifying the Assumptions

First to summarize: We need not worry about independent verifications of the fundamental assumptions, the Assumed Type of Action; we need not be

---

ourselves a mind similar to theirs." F. A. v. Hayek, "Scientism and the Study of Society," *Economica, New Series*, Vol. V (August 1942), p. 279. Reprinted F. A. v. Hayek, *The Counter-Revolution of Science* (Glencoe, Ill.: Free Press, 1952).

[40] Alfred Schuetz, "Common-Sense and Scientific Interpretation of Human Action," *Philosophy and Phenomenological Research*, Vol. XIV (September 1953), pp. 1-38. *Idem.*, "Concept and Theory Formation in the Social Sciences," *The Journal of Philosophy*, Vol. LI (April 1954), pp. 257-273.

[41] Schuetz, "Common-Sense, etc.," p. 34.

[42] Disregard of this requirement is, in my view, the only serious flaw in the otherwise excellent essay on "The Methodology of Positive Economics" by Milton Friedman, *Essays in Positive Economics* (Chicago: University of Chicago Press, 1953), pp. 3-43.

very particular about the independent verifications of the other intervening assumptions, the Assumed Conditions, because judgment based on casual empiricism will suffice for them; we should insist on strict independent verifications of the assumption selected as Assumed Change and of the conclusion derived as Deduced Change; not that the theory would be wrong otherwise, but it cannot be applied unless the phenomena to which it is supposed to apply are identifiable. *Simultaneous verifications of Assumed Change and Deduced Change count as verification—in the sense of non-disconfirmation—of the theory as a whole.*

Now it is clear why some writers insisted on the *a priori* nature of the theory and at the same time on its empirical value for the area of Applied Economics; for one may, if one wishes, regard the theory, or model, as a construction *a priori*, and the directions for its use, the instructions for its applications,[43] as an empirical appendage in need of verification. Returning to the analogy of the analytical machine, one may say that the machine and its parts are always "correct," regardless of what goes on around us, whereas the *choice* of the exchangeable parts and the *identification* of the events corresponding to the Assumed and Deduced changes may be wrong.

Testing the Predictive Values of Theories

We have examined the empiricists' charges against the theorists—charges of contemptuous neglect of the requirement of verification—and have concluded that these charges must be dismissed insofar as they refer to a failure to verify all assumptions directly and in isolation from the rest of the theory. We must yet examine another count of the charge of insufficient attention to verification: an alleged failure to test the correspondence between Deduced (predicted) and Observed outcomes. These kinds of tests are obligatory.

If verification of a theory takes the form of testing whether predictions based on that theory actually come true, one might think that this can be done in economics no less than in the physical sciences. It cannot, alas, because of the non-reproducibility of the "experiments" or observed situations and courses of events in the economy. For, while certain types of events, or "changes," recur in the economy often enough, they recur rarely under the same conditions. If some significant circumstances are different whenever a phenomenon of the same class recurs, each recurrence is virtually a "single occurrence." Economic theory applied to single events, or to situations significantly different from one another, cannot be tested as conclusively as can physical theory applied to reproducible occurrences and conditions.

Not long ago I was challenged to admit that my theories, even though applied to ever-changing circumstances, could be tested provided I were prepared to make unconditional predictions which could be compared with actual outcomes. Of course, I could only dare make unconditional predictions—without hedging about probability and confidence limits—where I was absolutely certain that my diagnosis of the situation (i.e., of *all* relevant circumstances) *and* my foreknowl-

---

[43] Cf. Milton Friedman, *op. cit.*, pp. 24–25.

edge of government and power group actions *and* the theory on which the prediction rests were all perfectly correct. Suppose that I was so foolhardy as to be sure of all this and that I did make a number of unconditional predictions. Still, unless reliable checks were possible to verify separately every part of my diagnosis and of my anticipations regarding government and power group actions, my theory could not be tested. There could be lucky "hits" where wrong diagnoses would compensate for mistakes due to bad theories; there could be unlucky "misses" where wrong diagnoses spoiled the results of good theorizing. Despite a large number of good hits the theories in question could not be regarded as confirmed, even in the modest sense of not being disconfirmed, because a joint and inseparable test of diagnosis, anticipations, and theory says nothing about the theory itself.

Where the economist's prediction is *conditional*, that is, based upon specified conditions, but where it is not possible to check the fulfillment of all the conditions stipulated, the underlying theory cannot be disconfirmed whatever the outcome observed. Nor is it possible to disconfirm a theory where the prediction is made with a stated *probability* value of less than 100 percent; for if an event is predicted with, say, 70 percent probability, any kind of outcome is consistent with the prediction.[44] Only if the same "case" were to occur hundreds of times could we verify the stated probability by the frequency of "hits" and "misses."

This does not mean complete frustration of all attempts to verify our economic theories. But it does mean that the tests of most of our theories will be more nearly of the character of *illustrations* than of verifications of the kind possible in relation with repeatable controlled experiments or with recurring fully-identified situations. And this implies that our tests cannot be convincing enough to compel acceptance, even when a majority of reasonable men in the field should be prepared to accept them as conclusive, and to approve the theories so tested as "not disconfirmed," that is, as "O. K."

Strictly Empirical Hypotheses

All this seems to circumscribe rather narrowly the scope of empirical verification, if not empirical research, in economics. But to draw such a conclusion would be rash. For there is a large body of economics apart from its theoretical or "hypothetico-deductive" system: namely, the empirical relationships obtained through correlation of observations, but not derivable, or at least not yet derived, from higher-level generalizations. Every science has such a body of strictly empirical hypotheses, no matter how fully developed or undeveloped its theoretical system may be.

I define a strictly empirical hypothesis as a proposition predicating a regular relationship between two or more sets of data of observation that cannot be

---

[44] This statement, it should be noted, refers to *general* theories which are part of a hypothetico-deductive system, not to strictly empirical hypotheses obtained by statistical inference. The predictions in question can never be in precise numerical terms, because no numerical magnitudes can be deduced from the assumptions of the type used in "general theory."

deduced from the general hypotheses which control the network of interrelated inferences forming the body of theory of the discipline in question. The distinction is made in almost all disciplines; it is best known as the distinction between "empirical laws" and "theoretical laws," though several other names have been used to denote the two types of scientific propositions. The philosopher Morris Cohen spoke of "concrete laws" in contrast to "abstract laws." Felix Kaufmann, though using the terms empirical and theoretical laws, characterized the former as "strict laws," the latter as "rigid laws." The physicist Henry Margenau contrasted "epistemic" or "correlational laws" with "constitutive," "exact," or "theoretical" laws. And Carl Menger, the founder of the Austrian School and protagonist in the *Methodenstreit*, distinguished "empirical laws" from "exact laws," the latter dealing with idealized connections between pure constructs, the former with "the sequences and coexistences of real phenomena."[45]

The study of the "sequences and coexistences" of the real phenomena depicted in statistical records yields correlational and other empirical findings which have to be tested and modified whenever new data on the same class of phenomena become available. While the constructs and deductions of the theoretical systems will influence the selection, collection and organization of empirical data, the particular relationships established between these data by means of correlation analysis and other statistical techniques are not deducible from high-level assumptions and can neither confirm nor disconfirm such assumptions. But these relationships, especially the numerical estimates of parameters, coefficients, or constants, are themselves subject to verification by new observations.

Verification of Empirical Hypotheses

Every one of us has lately been so much concerned with statistical demand curves, saving and consumption functions, investment functions, import elasticities and import propensities that a description of these and similar research activities is not necessary. The trouble with the verification of the empirical hypotheses derived by means of statistical and econometric analysis is that successive estimates on the basis of new data have usually been seriously divergent. Of course, such variations over time in the numerical relationships measured are not really surprising: few of us have expected these relationships to be constant or even approximately stable. Thus when new data and new computations yield revised estimates of economic parameters, there is no way of telling whether the previous hypotheses were wrong or whether things have changed.

That the numerical relationships described by these empirical hypotheses may be subject to change—to unpredictable change—alters their character in an essential respect. Hypotheses which are strictly limited as to time and space are not "general" but "special" hypotheses, or *historical propositions*. If the relationships measured or estimated in our empirical research are not universal but historical propositions, the problem of verification is altogether different—so different that according to intentions expressed in the introduction we should

[45] Carl Menger, *Untersuchungen über die Methode der Socialwissenschaften und der Politischen Oekonomie insbesondere* (Leipzig: Duncker & Humblot, 1883), pp. 28, 36.

not be concerned with it. For we set out to discuss verification of *generalizations*, not of events or circumstances confined to particular times and places. If all propositions of economics were of this sort, the dictum of the older historical school, that economics cannot have "general laws" or a "general theory," would be fully vindicated.

If a hypothesis about the numerical relationship between two or more variables was formulated on the basis of statistical data covering a particular period, and is later compared with the data of *another period*, such a comparison would be in the nature of a verification only if the hypothesis had been asserted or expected to be a universal one, that is, if the measured or estimated relationships had been expected to be constant. In the absence of such expectations the test of a continuing "fit" (between hypothesis and new data) is just a comparison between two historical situations, an attempt to find out whether particular relationships were stable or changing. A genuine verification of a previously formulated hypothesis about a given period calls for comparisons with additional data relating to the *same period*, to check whether the previous observations and their previous numerical description had been accurate. In brief, a historical proposition can only be verified by new data about the historical situation to which it refers. This holds also for geographic propositions and comparisons between different areas.

However, although the changeable "structures"[16] estimated by statistical and econometric researchers are nothing but historical propositions, there are probably limits to their variations. For example, we may safely generalize that the marginal propensity to consume cannot in the long run be greater than unity; or that the elasticity of demand for certain types of exports of certain types of countries will not in the long run be smaller than unity. Statements about definite limits to variations of special or historical propositions are again general hypotheses; they are not strictly empirical but universal in that they are deducible from higher-level generalizations in the theoretical system of economics. The various successive estimates of changeable structures may then be regarded as verifications of general hypotheses according to which certain parameters or coefficients must fall within definite limits. Since these limits are usually rather wide, verification will of course not be the rigorous kind of thing it is in the physical sciences with its numerical constants and narrow margins of error.

But neither this nor anything else that has been said in this article should be interpreted as intending to discourage empirical testing in economics. On the contrary, awareness of the limits of verification should prevent disappointments and present challenges to the empirical worker. May he rise to these challenges and proceed with intelligence and fervor by whatever techniques he may choose.

[16] In the sense used by Tjallong Koopmans and other econometricians.

COMMUNICATIONS

PROFESSOR MACHLUP ON VERIFICATION IN ECONOMICS

According to Professor Machlup it is significant to distinguish two schools of thought on the subject of verification in economics, which he describes as the "A Priori" and the "Ultra-Empiricist." Of the "Ultra-Empiricist" he writes: "This again is *the essence of the ultra-empiricist position on verification: the ultra-empiricist is so distrustful of deductive systems of thought that he is not satisfied with the indirect verification of hypotheses, that is, with tests showing that the results deduced (from these hypotheses and certain factual assumptions) are in approximate correspondence with reliable observational data*; instead, he insists on the independent verification of all the assumptions, hypothetical as well as factual, perhaps even of each intermediate step in the analysis." (Italics added.)[1] In fact Ultra-empiricists "refuse to recognise the legitimacy of employing at any level of analysis propositions not independently verifiable" (p. 7).

Professor Machlup claims that he could give "dozens" of examples of the "Ultra-Empiricist" position. The one he chooses to cite is that outlined in my book *The Significance and Basic Postulates of Economic Theory (1938)*. He makes it clear that he is not concerned so much with extracting a single statement or two which is at fault, but with the position represented throughout the book— ("I have selected Hutchison" Professor Machlup writes).

I find I wrote (*op. cit.*, p. 9): "If the finished propositions of a science, as against the accessory purely logical or mathematical propositions used in many sciences, including Economics, are to have any empirical content, as the finished propositions of all sciences except of Logic and Mathematics obviously must have, (6) then these propositions must *conceivably* be capable of empirical testing *or be reducible to such propositions* by logical or mathematical deduction. They need not, that is, actually be tested or even be *practically* capable of testing under present or future technical conditions or conditions of statistical investigation, nor is there any sense in talking of some kind of "absolute" test which will "finally" decide whether a proposition is "absolutely" true or false. But it must be possible to indicate intersubjectively what is the case if they are true or false; their truth or falsity, that is, must make some conceivable empirically noticeable difference, or some such difference must be directly deducible therefrom." (Italics as in original.) The note (6) attached to this passage ran: "This seems to us obvious. But the contrary view that Economics is, or ought to be, not an empirical science at all but a formal science just like Mathematics and Logic is (1937) held by a number of authorities led by Professor L. von Mises. Cf. *Gründprobleme der Nationalökonomie* and his lecture in *Actes du Congrès Internationale de Philosophie*, Paris, 1937. In future references we may, for reasons of brevity, omit this obvious qualification to the Principle of Testability: that a scientific proposition may not itself be empirically testable *directly*, but may be reducible by direct deduction

[1] Cf. F. Machlup, "The Problem of Verification in Economics," *Southern Economic Journal*, July 1955, p. 8.

to an empirically testable proposition or propositions (cf. propositions of Physics about electrons, α and β particles, etc.)."

This was the first and only relatively full account of the position on verification which I tried to expound in my book. This passage now seems to me rather old-fashioned, and even slightly crude and ungrammatical in the way it is formulated. But one thing it indubitably is *not*, and that is an example of what Professor Machlup calls "Ultra-empiricism." In fact it explicitly denies what he describes as "the essence of the ultra-empiricist position on verification."

Fortunately I do not have to rely on my own interpretation of my writings of eighteen years ago, if any interpreting is necessary. In his work *Economic Theory and Method* (recently published in a new English edition), Professor F. Zeuthen makes it clear that he is quoting me in diametrically the opposite sense to Professor Machlup, (and I venture to assume that Professor Zeuthen would not have chosen to quote me in that sense, or any other, if there had seemed to him to be any question of the direction my argument was taking). Professor Zeuthen writes: "If statements about reality are to have a meaning, and if they are not direct statements as to individual observations, it must be possible, by means of logical transformations to translate them at least into possible observations. There must be a possibility of verifying their reality or the reality of their consequences. In a rationalized theory, as, for instance, in micro-physics, it is still not considered necessary to be able to translate each individual statement into the language of reality, if only verification of a certain complex of statements is possible. In this connection we may also quote Paul Samuelson: 'By a meaningful theorem I mean simply a hypothesis about empirical data which could conceivably be refuted, if only under ideal conditions.'... Direct or indirect measurability (or the possibility of other factual testing) is a necessary condition for the avoidance of mystery, where everyone may have his own ideas as to the same words. Scientific statements about reality must be verifiable by others. As Hutchison says, they must 'conceivably be capable of empirical testing or be reducible to such propositions by logical or mathematical deductions. If there is no conceivable possibility of proving if an assertion is right, it is of a mystical character' " (*op. cit.*, pp. 8–9).

I am afraid it seems to me that—doubtless through my own fault—Professor Machlup completely failed to understand the position I was trying to outline, particularly since not a single one of the very brief passages of mine which he quoted seems to me, when taken in context, to make the point which Professor Machlup seems to imagine it makes.[2] Professor Zeuthen may be easier to follow,

[2] I don't wish to claim any particular wisdom or rectitude for my propositions, only that Professor Machlup has not interpreted accurately what he very briefly quotes. For example (a) Professor Machlup quotes me as writing "that propositions of pure theory, by themselves, have no prognostic value," and states that this proposition, "as it stands," is "unassailable." However, in his determination to assail the unassailable, Professor Machlup proceeds to interpret "propositions of pure theory, by themselves, have no prognostic value" as meaning "an attack against the use of empirically unverifiable propositions in economic theory regardless of their conjunction with other propositions." (b) Professor Machlup writes, "With regard to the 'fundamental assumption' of economic theory con-

and it might help to elucidate Professor Machlup's categories if he could explain whether Professor Zeuthen fell into the category of "Ultra-Empiricists," or that of "A Priorists"; or indeed how the other important contributors in the last decade, to the methodology of economics, such as Samuelson, Lange, Little and Friedman are to be placed in relation to these categories.[3]

While the trouble with Professor Machlup's "Ultra-Empiricist" category simply seems to be that the one example he gives falls quite obviously outside it, the trouble with his "A-Priorist" category seems to be that it is much too elastic and comprehensive to be significant, while at least one or two of the various authorities Professor Machlup describes as "A-Priorists" might well have much preferred to be called "empiricists," if they were to be called anything. Professor Machlup agrees that his term covers writers of very different epistemological views, ranging from J. S. Mill to Mises. After telling us (p. 5) that he is simply concerned with two "extreme positions" Professor Machlup proceeds, while indeed defining "Ultra-Empiricism" in extreme terms, to leave "A-Priorism" very elastic. In fact it is very hard to tell whether his two categories are meant to describe two extremes, with a large third middle ground in between; or whether "A-Priorism" is being so stretched as to include all the middle ground up to the frontier line of "Ultra-Empiricism," the former comprising all those who are prepared to recognize "indirect" methods of verification or confirmation, and the latter those who explicitly reject indirect verification and insist on "direct" in-

---

cerning 'subjectively rational' and maximising behaviour, Hutchison states that 'the empirical content of the assumption and all the conclusions will be the same—that is nothing." Here I would simply like to quote my complete sentence which was concerned with Professor Mises' apparently circular method of formulating the fundamental assumption (not with other methods): "If one thinks it worth while, one can say 'people behave as they do behave' in as many different ways as one likes, but one will not learn anything further about their behaviour; for the empirical content of the assumption and all the conclusions will be the same—that is nothing."

[3] Cf. the following passage from Prof. Zeuthen's chapter on Material and Method in Economics, *op. cit.*, pp. 14–15: "How the conception of economics as an empirical, i.e., a logical-empirical science is compatible with a considerable amount of deduction and theorizing will be apparent from the following statement by O. Lange: 'Theoretical economics puts the pattern of uniformity in a coherent system. This is done by presenting the laws of economics as a deductive set of propositions derived by the rules of logic (and of mathematics) from a few basic propositions. The basic propositions are called assumptions or postulates, the derived propositions are called theorems. Theoretical economics thus appears (like all other theoretical sciences) as a deductive science. This, however, does not make it a branch of pure mathematics or logic. Like the rest of economics, economic theory is an empirical science. *Its assumptions or postulates are approximative generalizations of empirical observations; e.g., the assumption that business enterprises act so as to maximise their money profit.* Some inaccuracy of approximation (e.g., some considerations, like safety, may keep enterprises from maximizing money profit) is accepted for the sake of greater simplicity. The theorems, in turn, are subjected to test by empirical observation. A deductive set of theorems to be subjected to empirical test is also called a theory, hypothesis, or a model. We can thus say that theoretical economics provides hypotheses or models *based on generalizations of observations and subject to empirical test.* Since the assumptions (postulates) underlying a model are only approximative, the theorems do not correspond directly to results of empirical observations.' " (Italics added.)

dependent verification or confirmation only (assuming Professor Machlup can give an example of this category).[4]

However, it seems doubtful whether any distinction which is made to turn on whether or not "indirect" verification or testing is accepted, could be at all serviceable—even if it were more lucidly defined, less questionably labelled, and less erroneously exemplified. Supposing (A) I have tested and confirmed (1) that a plot of ground forms a right-angled triangle, and (2) that the two shorter sides are 30 and 40 yards long; and supposing (B) that I have checked my calculation or deduction via the Pythagoras theorem that the longest side is 50 yards long. Professor Machlup apparently insists that there are "dozens" of economists who would *deny* that the performance of these measurements and tests, as to the two shorter sides and the right angle, entitled me to regard as to that extent tested and verified the proposition (C) that the third side was 50 yards long? These "dozens" of "Ultra-Empiricist" economists (whose existence I beg leave to doubt) would continue to regard proposition (C) as a completely unconfirmed piece of speculative guess-work until I had tested or confirmed it "directly" and "independently" by separately measuring the 50-yard side (which might conceivably for technical reasons be very difficult or practically impossible).

Anyhow, it would not seem to be committing some incredibly naive and dangerous methodological error if I *did* attempt to test (C) directly and independently by a separate measurement, provided this was technically or practically possible. Whether (C) was tested directly or indirectly would be a matter of practical convenience and of the degree of confirmation aimed at. It is not clear how any serious controversial point can arise here, or how in such a case any very interesting distinction can be made to turn on whether or not the "indirect" testing of (C) is acceptable or not.

So much for the critical-historical elements in Professor Machlup's paper. Perhaps, now I have started, I may go on to express one or two doubts about his more positive thesis. The point at issue,—and there is a point at issue,—lies rather in Professor Machlup's conception of "fundamental assumptions" or "high-level generalizations" *in economics*. The only example he gives of this special type of proposition is "the fundamental assumption" that "people act rationally, try to make the most of their opportunities, and are able to arrange their preferences in a consistent order; that entrepreneurs prefer more profit with equal risk" (pp. 10–11). These are all variations on the ubiquitous assump-

---

[4] One function of this elastic category "A Priorist," which is first described as "extreme" but which is then stretched to include J. S. Mill, seems to be to cast an aura of respectable moderation on the certainly highly "extreme" political and methodological dogmatizing of Professor L. Mises. There have been previous examples in the last decade or so of associates or disciple of Professor Mises volunteering such explanations as that when Mises said "impossible" he really meant "possible," or when he said "a priori" he really meant "empirical." Now, according to Professor Machlup, when Professor Mises held that in economics "the fundamental postulates are *a priori* truths, necessities of thinking" (p. 6) "*all*" he "had in mind however provocative (his) contentions seemed" as an "objection . . . to verifying the basic assumptions in isolation."

tion, the central assumption in 'micro-economic' analysis, of 'maximising' or "rational" action. It might be helpful to know whether Professor Machlup can cite any other examples of a "fundamental assumption" in economics beyond this one and its variants. If so, the point at issue might well be illuminated, while if not, it would stand out in a pretty clearly defined way as turning on the status and nature of this proposition about "maximising" and/or "rational" conduct.[5] We should like to note here that Professor Machlup describes this "fundamental assumption" as "empirically meaningful," which would appear to mean "conceivably falsifiable empirically"; or, at any rate, Professor Machlup does not interpret this fundamental assumption as a more or less disguised definition, without empirical content, that is, as simply saying that people maximise what they maximise, or that economic conduct must, by definition, be rational—(as Professor Mises appears to hold).

Now the main difficulty with this fundamental assumption, throughout its history,—since, roughly speaking, Bentham,—has been that of knowing just what content, if any, it has been meant to possess, just when, where, and how far it is applicable, and therefore just what the significance may be of the conclusions about human activities which can logically be deduced from it. At one time this fundamental assumption was formulated to the effect that the consumer "maximised his satisfaction" or "utility," the firm its "profits," or even that society, in certain conditions, maximised its aggregate "social satisfaction" or "utility" or "welfare." What was necessary, in the first instance, with such formulations of this fundamental assumption, was more *clarity* rather than more confirmation or verification, that is, not any actual testing so much as a specification of what a test would amount to, or of the more precise circumstances under which the generalisation was to be regarded as "confirmed" or "disconfirmed."

Professor Machlup goes on to describe this fundamental assumption of "maximising" or "rational" action, and its variants, as "assumptions which, though empirically meaningful, require no independent empirical tests but may be significant steps in arguments reaching conclusions which are empirically testable."

---

[5] Professor M. Friedman (*Essays in Positive Economics*, p. 16n) commenting on Professor Machlup's presentation of the marginal productivity doctrine (*American Economic Review*, Sept. 1946, pp. 519-54) notes that "in Machlup's emphasis on the logical structure, he comes perilously close to presenting the theory as a pure tautology, though it is evident at a number of points that he is aware of this danger and anxious to avoid it." I must say that Professor Machlup's "anxiety" on this point might well have seemed more pressing both in 1946 and in 1955. Anyone who was "anxious" could easily set about relieving his anxiety by giving an outline specification of the empirical content of the maximisation-of-returns hypothesis for the case in which he was concerned, that is, by indicating the conditions by which the hypothesis could be tested in a particular individual case. Professor Mises, of course, is not in the least "anxious" on this score: quite the reverse, he repudiates all anxiety by claiming that all economic action is "rational"—by definition presumably—and Professor Machlup seems at times most anxious to defend Professor Mises' position. We would note, in addition, that the point of view we are advocating is summed up very succinctly by Professor Friedman as follows (*op. cit.*, p. 41): "It is necessary to be more specific about the content of existing economic theory and to distinguish among its different branches."

It can certainly be agreed that actual independent tests may not be *"required."* But if one claims that a proposition is "empirically meaningful," or a "significant step," one *is* "required" to indicate where that significance begins and ends, what "work," if any, the proposition can and does do, and just why it is not a superfluous fifth wheel on the car—(as any such proposition as "all economic action, being rational, maximises whatever it maximises" certainly is).[6]

Of course it does not matter in principle whether the specification of the conditions of a test of this fundamental assumption is obtained "directly" and "independently," or by working back "indirectly" from the specified tests of the conclusions to the assumption from which the conclusions are deduced. According to Professor Machlup these conclusions *are* "empirically testable," that is, reasonably specific descriptions are available of what constitutes a test of them. What he does not show is how "empirically testable" conclusions about human actions can be deduced with logical inevitability from "empirically meaningful" assumptions about human actions, while these assumptions are to be regarded by themselves as either not conceivably, or not possibly, or not practically, or only "gratuitously" and "misleadingly," testable—(which of these adverbs he he really means, Professor Machlup never quite makes clear). In fact, what exactly is the contrast that Professor Machlup seems to be implying between "empirically meaningful" and "empirically testable," with regard to propositions about economic actions? At this point Professor Machlup rides off on analogies from physical theories without demonstrating that there is any relevant analogy in economic theory. In the social sciences there are, of course, considerable difficulties all along the line in testing *any* proposition. Professor Machlup does nothing to show that it is in any respect more difficult to confirm or "disconfirm" assumptions, "fundamental" or otherwise, about human actions in economic theorising, than it is to confirm or "disconfirm" the conclusions about human actions. The comparatively simple maximising theories of human action in microeconomics cannot in this respect relevantly be compared with the theories of physics. Methodological generalisations and analogies from physics are liable to be of rather limited significance in the interpretation and elucidation of specific

---

[6] Cf. the chapter 'The Analysis of Consumers' Behaviour' in *Welfare Economics*, by I. M. D. Little (p. 14 ff.). On the maximisation hypothesis as applied to the consumer, Mr. Little writes (pp. 20-21): "Where the chief difficulty lies is in the interpretation of the axiom 'the individual maximises utility'. . . . In the past economists have often been attacked on the grounds that their theories only applied to selfish people; such attacks were brushed aside as absurd. But they were not absurd. It was the economists who were wrong in suggesting that positive economics had any necessary connexion with satisfactions at all. Nor could the economist argue that he had some positive objective tests which showed him to whom the theory applied, and to whom it did not apply, and that it didn't matter whether it was really a test of satisfaction or not. He could not make this reply because no such test had been suggested. . . . One economist has tried to get over this difficulty by saying that it does not matter what a man tries to maximise, so long as he tries to maximise something, say his weight or his misery. But this amounts to a determination to say that whenever the economist *can* explain a man's behaviour then that man must be maximising *something*. It gives no indication whatever as to when the theory can be applied and when not."

economic theories and propositions.[7] In short, while admitting the principle of indirect verification, we cannot agree to the kind of loose and sweeping appeal to it which Professor Machlup seems to be making. Much more particularity and precision seems to be desirable.

Let us take the example where economists have for decades tried to draw the most sweeping and consequential practical conclusions from theories built round the fundamental assumption of maximizing or rational actions, that is, the theory of welfare economics and of consumers' behaviors. When we take a conclusion such as that of Walras (and many others) that "free competition procures within certain limits the maximum of utility for society," exactly the reverse procedure to that claimed as essential by Professor Machlup seems to be "required." It hardly seems very promising when confronted with such a "conclusion" to try to test it "directly." On the contrary, exactly reversing the process insisted upon by Professor Machlup, one must work back from the "conclusion" to the assumptions, and in particular the "fundamental" assumption about the individual consumer and producer, and enquire what would constitute a test of this fundamental assumption.

Again, Professor Machlup mentions, as a variant of the fundamental assumption, that "consumers can arrange their preferences in an order." How was this formulation arrived at and how did it come to replace for most economists (including, apparently, Professor Machlup) the earlier formulations in terms of "maximizing utility"? Simply thanks to the increasingly rigorous insistence by a long line of economists—(Fisher, Pareto, Slutsky, Hicks and Allen, Samuelson, and Little)—that the fundamental assumption of the theory of consumers' behaviour be testable.

When, on the other hand, Professor Machlup formulates the fundamental assumption to the effect that "people act rationally," it is not in the least clear what would constitute a test of this assumption and whether even it is testable. Not knowing how it can be tested, one cannot tell at all precisely what can be deduced from it. Nevertheless, brandishing this generalisation that all economic

---

[7] Cf. Little (*op. cit.*, pp. 2–4) on welfare economics: "In contrast to the undoubted validity of the formal deduction, what are called the foundations of the theory have always been shrouded in darkness. What are the foundations of a theory? The answer is, those postulates from which the theorems are deduced." In physics "it does not really matter in the least whether one believes that such words as 'electrons' and 'molecule' stand for entities of a peculiar kind, or whether one believes that they are merely words which serve a useful practical purpose. . . . But drawing analogies between physics and other studies can result in harm. . . . The analogy with physics breaks down in two important ways, which should lead one to suspect that what holds for one may not hold for the other. First, the concepts of physics about which people are not clear, do not appear in the conclusions. The conclusions are about macroscopic or microscopic objects, not about electrons. By contrast, in welfare economics, the conclusions are about welfare. Secondly, physicists' conclusions are verified or falsified; ours are not. . . . I do suggest that the reality of the theory (of welfare economics) has been badly overestimated by economists." These arguments apply to a lesser but none the less a very important extent—to the "maximising of utility" and the theory of the consumer, and even to the "maximising of profits" and the theory of the firm.

action was (or even must be) "rational" some economists—notably Professor Mises, whom Professor Machlup seems so concerned to defend—have proceeded to claim that wholesale political conclusions were logically deducible from it, and were thus to be regarded as established conclusions of economic science.[8] It is not difficult to understand why those wishing to propagate sweeping political dogmas as the established logical conclusions of scientific economic theory, should resist the claim that some procedure for testing should be described for these conclusions, and/or for the assumptions, including the fundamental assumption, from which they were deduced. I am afraid that Professor Machlup's doctrines on verification and verifiability in economics are not merely questionable in themselves as an account of the structure of micro-economic theory, but may be used in defence of a kind of politico-intellectual obscurantism that seeks to avoid not merely the empirical testing of its dogmas, but even the specification of what would constitute tests.

London School of Economics   T. W. HUTCHISON

REJOINDER TO A RELUCTANT ULTRA-EMPIRICIST

From the tone of Professor Hutchison's reply to my article I infer that he was hurt by my characterization of his position as one of ultra-empiricism. I am sorry that I hurt or angered him; I am glad that he rejects, at least on principle, the position which I called ultra-empiricism; and I am puzzled by many of his comments which still strike me as ultra-empiricist.

I agree fully with Professor Hutchison that his opening statement—on page 9 of his book and on page 476 of his note above—is a rejection of what I call ultra-empiricism. Whereas ultra-empiricists require direct empirical testing of propositions used as fundamental assumptions in a theoretical system, Professor Hutchison in this declaration seems satisfied with the *conceivable* testability of

[8] Cf. *Kritik des Interventionismus*, pp. 23–24, and *Liberalismus*, pp. 3, 78 and 170: "Liberalism is the application of the doctrines of science to the social life of men. . . . Liberalism and Political Economy were victorious together. No other politico-economic ideology can in any way be reconciled with the science of Catallactics. . . . One cannot understand Liberalism without Political Economy. For Liberalism is applied Political Economy, it is state and social policy on a scientific basis. . . . Liberalism starts from the pure sciences of Political Economy and Sociology which within their systems make no valuations and which say nothing about what ought to be or what is good or bad, but only ascertain what is an how it is. If this science shows that of all conceivable possible organisations of society only one, that resting on private property in the means of production, is capable of existing, because none of the others can be carried through, there is nothing in this which justifies the term optimism. . . . He who recommends a third type of social order of regulated private property, can only deny altogether the possibility of scientific knowledge in the field of Economics." Cf. also W. H. Hutt, *Economists and the Public*, p. 367: "Our plea is in short for that economic liberty which was dimly visualised by the Classical economists, and whose coincidence with the *summum bonum* has been an implication of the subsequent teachings of economic orthodoxy. We have attempted to show that expert, dispassionate and disinterested thought on these matters has been the preserve of those whose gropings in a world of divergent beliefs and arguments (beset on all sides by the lure of interests) have led them to the path of orthodox tradition."

the deduced *consequences* of these propositions. I might have quoted his statement on this point in support of my position that direct testing is not required—had he not in effect repudiated it by much of what followed it in his book. And he does it again in his note, as I shall attempt to show presently.

But do we really mean the same thing when we speak of "indirect testing"? Perhaps the crucial misunderstanding lies right here. Professor Hutchison mentions that a proposition not itself empirically testable directly must be "reducible by *direct* deduction to an empirically testable proposition or propositions." (Emphasis supplied.) This formulation suggests a requirement that the implications of any single proposition be tested independently of those of other propositions with which it is conjoined to constitute a "case." In fact, however, the *conjunction of logically independent propositions and derivation of their joint consequences* is the essence of indirect testing.

If assumption A can neither be subjected to any direct empirical test nor reduced "by direct deduction to an empirically testable proposition," its indirect verification can be accomplished by combining it with an assumption B which is directly testable; if a consequence C can be deduced from the conjunctive hypothesis A *plus* B—but not from either one alone—and if C is empirically tested, A is regarded as having passed the indirect test.

I suspect that Professor Hutchison does not accept the validity of indirect verification in this sense. Unfortunately, he makes no reference to my detailed exposition and schematic representation of the conception and operation of indirect testing. Silent on this, he professes to accept indirect testing and then proceeds to demand direct (independent) tests. I had pointed out that fundamental postulates, such as the maximization principle, are "not subject to a requirement of independent verification"; they are considered as verified, together with the whole theory of which they are a part, when the deduced consequences of their conjunction with an evident and substantive change and with assumed conditions relevant to the case are shown to correspond to observed events. Thus, if the fundamental postulate (e.g., that firms prefer more profit to less profit at equal risks[1]) is combined with assumptions about economic institutions and conditions (e.g., certain forms of competition) and with assumptions about certain substantive changes (e.g., the imposition of import quotas on certain products); and if we deduce from this conjunction of assumptions certain consequences (e.g., increases in the excess of domestic over foreign prices); and if these deduced consequences are found to be in relatively good correspondence with observed events (e.g., increases in the excess of domestic over foreign prices of bicycles) subsequent to actual changes of the kind in question (e.g., the imposition of import quotas on bicycles); then the theory is regarded as verified, and the fundamental postulate is regarded as verified with it.

Now, those who do not accept this "indirect verification" of the fundamental postulate but demand that the assumption of attempted profit maximization be

[1] On the problem of differences of risk and uncertainty in connection with differences in profits see my book *The Economics of Sellers' Competition* (Baltimore: Johns Hopkins Press, 1952), pp. 53-56.

empirically tested independently of the other propositions (about competition, import quotas, and bicycle prices) are the "ultra-empiricists" discussed in my article. If he understands this, I wonder whether Professor Hutchison will still deny membership in the society of ultra-empiricists or whether instead he will be eager to confirm it.

That Professor Hutchison misunderstands the essence of indirect verification is suggested by his example about the length of the unmeasured side of a triangular plot of land. If he had referred to the Pythogoras theorem as the general proposition in need of verification and to the lengths of the sides of his plot as the independently verifiable propositions, he might have come nearer to our problem, the validation of the use of universal propositions. What he really showed was (a) that he had confidence in the reliability of the Pythagoras theorem, (b) that he was sure his plot was reasonably close to a perfect right-angled triangle, and (c) that his measurements of the two short sides were reasonably accurate. The whole example has little to do with the question of the direct or indirect verification of fundamental assumptions employed in general theory.

That Professor Hutchison is not satisfied with the indirect verification of such universal propositions employed as fundamental postulates in general theory can be seen from several comments. For example, he contends (p. 478) that I have failed to state whether they are "conceivably falsifiable empirically" or rather definitions "without empirical content." (I had said they were "heuristic principles," "procedural rules," etc. See pp. 9 and 16). Then he demands (p. 478) "a specification of what a test would amount to, or of the more precise circumstances under which the generalization [of maximizing conduct] was to be regarded as 'confirmed' or 'disconfirmed.' " (I had stated repeatedly that the test consisted in checking the correspondence of observed events with the "assumed changes" and the "deduced changes" of the entire theoretical model. See especially p. 18.) It is quite obvious that Professor Hutchison, contrary to his initial declaration, wants more than indirect testing of the fundamental postulates of general theory.

Professor Hutchison asks whether my category of apriorism in economics is "so stretched to include all the middle ground up to the frontier line of 'ultra-Empiricism.' " (Since he also questions that I could name any "example of this category," he must believe that on my classification all economists are apriorists!) The answer is that I know very few "extreme apriorists" (e.g., Professor von Mises). The middle ground between the extreme positions is very large indeed; of the economists whom Professor Hutchison asked me to classify, it includes Zeuthen, Samuelson, Lange, and Friedman; none of them holds that no conceivable kind of experience could ever cause him to give up his theory, and none of them wants his fundamental assumptions empirically tested independently of the propositions with which they are combined when the theory is applied.

Professor Hutchison asks whether I can cite any other fundamental assumption in economics "beyond" that of "maximizing or rational action." It all depends on what one regards as fundamental. Perhaps the assumption that only limited outputs can be obtained from given resources should be called fundamental; it "underlies" all economic problems, but it does not always become a relevant step in the argument. Perhaps still other (or narrower) assumptions should be proposed for inclusion, though frankly I had not intended it.

If the question referred to the possible replacement of, rather than addition to, the assumption of maximizing conduct, my answer would be that substitutes have been proposed, but not successfully. Some writers on the equilibrium of the firm (theory of output and price) have advanced "security of survival" and similar postulates in lieu of profit maximization (for the enterprise economy), but the proposed substitutes were less simple and less comprehensive. Yet, I grant the possibility that better postulates may be proposed, and therefore I have described the "Fundamental Postulates" as "Assumed Type of Action (or Motivation)" instead of limiting them to that of "maximizing conduct."[2]

In his comments on the nature and significance of the maximization postulate Professor Hutchison conveys the impression that he recognizes as scientifically legitimate only two kinds of statements: propositions which by empirical tests can, at least conceivably, be proved to be false, and definitions without empirical content. If so, he rejects a third category of propositions used in most theoretical systems: the heuristic postulates and idealized assumptions in abstract models of interdependent constructs useful in the explanation and prediction of observable phenomena.

Such propositions are neither "true or false" nor empirically meaningless. They cannot be false because what they predicate is predicated about ideal constructs, not about things or events of reality. Yet they are not empirically "meaningless," because they are supposed to "apply" or correspond broadly to experienced events. They cannot be "falsified" by observed facts, or even be "proved inapplicable," because auxiliary assumptions can be brought in to establish correspondence with almost any kind of facts; but they can be superseded by other propositions which are in better agreement with these facts without recourse to so many auxiliary assumptions.

Logicians have long recognized this intermediate category of propositions, which are neither *a priori* nor *a posteriori* in the strict sense of these terms.[3] (One may, with Friedman, prefer to say that a theoretical system has two parts, an analytical one demonstrating valid inferences, and a synthetic one stating correct applications.[4]) I had mentioned this category of propositions in my article (p. 16), but Professor Hutchison chose to disregard my remarks on this issue.

It was necessary to bring this up again because Professor Hutchison said

---

[2] The assumption of maximizing conduct of the householder may, of course, be broken down into several parts—that each person has preferences, that these preferences are consistent (transitive) and can be orderly arranged, that he wishes to follow these preferences in deciding on his actions, etc.—and it is possible to call each of these a separate postulate. This, I suppose, is not questioned here.

[3] They were called "procedural rules" by Felix Kaufmann, "complex-analytic propositions" by Wm. P. Montague, "constitutive, non-epistemic" propositions by Henry Margenau.

[4] Milton Friedman, *Essays in Positive Economics* (Chicago: University of Chicago Press, 1953), pp. 24-25.

(p. 478) that if I called the fundamental assumption (of maximizing behavior) "empirically meaningful" I should mean it to be "conceivably falsifiable empirically." I do not. Resolutions to analyse certain aspects of experience with the aid of a heuristic postulate, or even of a pure fiction, are not "falsifiable" but nevertheless "empirically meaningful."[5]

At another point (pp. 478–479) Professor Hutchison realizes that I did not mean that the fundamental assumptions about human actions should or could be empirically tested, and he asks me to show "how 'empirically testable' conclusions about human actions can be deduced" from those untested or untestable fundamental assumptions. I thought I had shown it with sufficient clarity; of course, the conclusions are deduced not from the fundamental assumptions in isolation but from their conjunction with other assumptions including some whose correspondence with factual observation is established.

I can easily comply with Professor Hutchison's request by pointing to the illustration I gave above, where I showed how a relative price increase for bicycles was the empirically testable consequence deduced from the partly untested or untestable assumptions. But Professor Hutchison repeats that I had done "nothing to show that it is in any respect more difficult to confirm or 'disconfirm' assumptions, 'fundamental' or otherwise, about human actions in economic theory, than it is to confirm or 'disconfirm' the conclusions about human action." Can there be any doubt that a direct empirical test of the motivations behind businessmen's actions, such as a test whether their decisions are made in an attempt to maximize profits, would be "more difficult," to say the least, than a test that higher prices are paid for bicycles?

Perhaps it was confusing when, in addition to stating that these fundamental assumptions *need not* be independently verified empirically, I also indicated that they *cannot* be so verified. Some economists who agree that no independent verification is required would none the less hold that such verification is *possible;* and others would contend that any special tests are *unnecessary* because the assumptions are *self-evident* statements of common experience. Common experience, however, tells us merely that we (that is, I and those with whom I have talked about it) *can* follow our preferences in choosing among the alternatives open to us and that we usually do it. Common experience, moreover, tells those of us who are or were in business that we *usually* attempt to make such decisions as would promise us the highest returns, but it does not tell us that *all* businessmen do so in *all* their actions, Indeed we know, also from common experience, that there are times when many businessmen refrain from following the most profitable courses of action and instead act to meet some demands of "patriotism" or to obey the moral suasion of governmental authorities. Are there any objective tests

---

[5] Some may wonder how one may possibly interpret the "fundamental assumptions" alternatively as rules of procedure (imperative statements), definitions (resolutions), useful fictions, and "true" empirical propositions. The answer lies in the convertibility of propositions. The following formulation may suggest how it can be done: "In analysing problems of this sort *let us proceed* by assuming that things will work *as if* businessmen were always attempting to maximize their money profits (and perhaps they actually do!)".

possible by which the assumption of profit maximization could be verified independently of the uses to which the assumption is put in economic theory?

We could *conceivably* place researchers into every business office to analyse every decision that is made and check the motivations behind it. This would not be quite reliable unless our researchers were invisible, had invisible lie detectors or perhaps mind-reading apparatus. In case we are satisfied with what is *practically possible*, we could have exceptionally competent and skillful survey researchers examine in carefully devised interviews a sample of the decisions made by a sample of businessmen. The object would be to establish the relative frequency of decisions consistent with profit maximization: In what percentage of their decisions do businessmen believe that they are acting in the best (long-term) interest of their firm (that is, of its owners)? Surely, some businessmen do so some of the time; probably, most businessmen do so most of the time. But we would certainly not find that all of the businessmen do so all of the time. Hence, the assumption of consistently profit-maximizing conduct is contrary to fact. .

Of course, no proposition about empirical facts can be absolutely certain; but here we are defending an assumption of which we are certain that it does not always conform to the facts. If the deviations are insignificant we can safely neglect them. But we do not know *how* significant they might be, especially because the relative strength of non-profit objectives changes with the conditions of the time, changes probably also with the kind of decisions, and changes perhaps also with several other factors. What then should be done? Just what is being done: to accept maximizing conduct as a heuristic postulate and to bear in mind that the deduced consequences may sometimes be considerably out of line with observed data. We can, to repeat, test empirically whether the outcome of people's actions is most of the time reasonably close to what one would expect *if* people always acted as they are unrealistically assumed to act. Again, the "indirect verification" or justification of the postulate lies in the fact that it gives fairly good results in many applications of the theory.

Professor Hutchison has several questions concerning the assumption of maximizing conduct; we shall call it for short the Assumption (with capital A). He asks (a) "just what content, if any, it has been meant to possess," (b) "just when, where, and how far it is applicable," (c) "what a test [of it] would amount to," (d) under what circumstances it "was to be regarded as 'confirmed' or 'disconfirmed.' " And he finds that I am "required" to indicate (e) the range of the "significance" of the Assumption, (f) "what 'work,' if any," it can do, and (g) "just why it is not a superfluous fifth wheel on the car." I shall attempt brief answers to all seven questions.

(a) I am not sure what sort of "content" it is that is in question. Does "content" refer to specific data of experience that have gone "into" the Assumption and are now an integral part of it, as in the case of a universal proposition whose subject can be defined by complete enumeration? In this sense the Assumption has no determinate "content." Or, rather, is the question whether the Assumption is to apply to empirical data of a certain class, and whether it would matter if it did or did not apply? In this sense the "content" of the assumption of profit maximization can readily be illustrated. Suppose (1) the government announces that price reductions would be in the national interest, (2) wage rates have just been raised, (3) raw-material prices have gone up, (4) no changes in technology have occurred for many years, and (5) aggregate demand has not changed. Should we expect product prices to rise or to fall? If firms did not attempt to maximize profits, they might well act in accordance with what the government publicizes to be in the national interest, and prices would be reduced. The Assumption does make a difference.

(b) The applicability—"when, where and how far"—of the Assumption, or rather of theories based on it, can be "prescribed" in broadly formulated directives, but there will always be a wide margin for the use of good judgment. The "directions for use" may be different for explanations of past events and for predictions of future events. In general, for purposes of prediction, we should *not* apply the Assumption to particular households or to particular firms, but only to large numbers of households or firms, or rather to cases where the deduced events, such as changes in prices, outputs, consumption, exports, imports, etc., are regarded as the outcome of actions and interactions of large numbers of firms and households. We should apply it only with reservations in times when strong moral suasion is exerted to make people disregard their usual preferences or interests, such as in war time when patriotic objectives are strongly pressed.

(c) Our discussion of the "kind of test" to which the Assumption should be subjected has probably been sufficient to warrant our conclusion that the test of the pudding lies in the eating and not in its ingredients. If we find no better theory to explain or predict changes in prices, outputs, etc., etc., and if our present theory does no worse than it has been doing, we may consider our Assumption as warranted.

(d) The Assumption will of course never be considered as "confirmed" for good, but only until further notice. Under what circumstances is the Assumption to be regarded as "disconfirmed"? When a theory not using this Assumption is proposed and is shown to work equally well for a wider range of problems, or with a smaller number of variables or provisos, or more reliably or more accurately for the same range of problems and with the same number of variables or qualifications—then the Assumption will have outlived its usefulness and will be sent to the limbo of "disconfirmed propositions." (And even this need not be beyond recall.)

(e) May I take the "range of the significance" to mean the same thing as the "when, where, and how far" of the applicability of the Assumption? If so, I may refer to what I said under (b). These answers, however, are strictly confined, as was my article, to positive economics, that is, to explanations and predictions of economic changes and events. Normative or evaluative economics has been outside the scope of my discussion; hence, I am not examining the significance of the Assumption for welfare economics. To give a simple example, we have been concerned with questions like "what consequences can be expected from the removal of a tariff," not with questions like "whether these consequences would be desirable" and "whether the tariff ought to be removed."

(f) The kind of "work" the Assumption does for us was indicated under (a), where its "content" was discussed.[6] Let me add two more illustrations, (A) from the theory of the household, and (B) from the theory of the firm and industry. (A) Suppose (1) the tastes for foodstuffs are given, (2) the substitutability between vinegar and lemon in salad dressings, the complementarity between salad dressings and salads, and the income elasticities of demand for both are all given with the tastes, (3) the prices of lettuce and other salads are reduced, (4) disposable incomes rise, and (5) the price of vinegar is increased. If we trust the Assumption we can predict increased consumption or increased prices of lemons (or longer queues if lemon prices are fixed, and more bootlegging if lemons are rationed). Without the Assumption we cannot say anything, for if people do not follow their preferences, act inconsistently and haphazardly, "given" scales of preference mean nothing. (B) Assume (1) the technological conditions of production are given, (2) entry into the textile industry is open, (3) the supply of productive services required for textiles is elastic, and (4) the demand for grey goods increases. On the basis of the Assumption we can explain or predict a larger output of grey goods; without the Assumption we cannot. If businessmen like smaller profits just as well as bigger profits, or even better, why should any manufacturer increase his output when demand increases? If businessmen are not tempted by opportunities to make more profit, why should anybody take up the production of grey goods? It is hard to understand how any doubt can be entertained as to "what work" the Assumption does for us.

(g) The question whether the Assumption is not really "superfluous" is, I believe, disposed of with our description of the "work" it does for us. To be sure, the same work might possibly be done by a different assumption—and we know that many versions of the fundamental "Type of Action" have been used over the years—but I doubt whether the difference can be very great. But while the Assumption might be replaced by an alternative, it cannot be eliminated without replacement; it is not a redundant part in the theory. It is perhaps possible to put an indefinite number of "behavior functions" in the place of our Assumption, with the stipulation that all consumers will consistently stick to these functions. Such a stipulation would be neither simpler nor more realistic than the Assumption; and since the required knowledge of all behavior functions would be a heavy burden for the theory of consumer behavior, this whole approach is distinctly inferior to the traditional theory. The latter has yielded a large number of generalizations as "deduced consequences" even without knowledge of the exact preference systems of consumers, merely on the basis of some very general properties of such preference systems. As for the theory of production in an enterprise economy, the Assumption appears to be indispensable. Never could a behavioristic approach provide all the millions of "entrepreneurial behavior functions" which would be needed to do the job that is now done by the simple postulate of profit maximization.

A few minor misunderstandings remain to be cleared up. The assumption

---

[6] I prefer to speak of "the work it does" rather than of "the content it has"; both are metaphors, to be sure, but the latter, I think, is quite infelicitous.

that "consumers can arrange their preferences in an order" is not, as Professor Hutchison believes (p. 479), a "variant" of the fundamental assumption, "replacing" earlier formulations in terms of "maximizing utility." Nor has it been proposed "thanks to the insistence" of Hicks and Allen, Samuelson, and Little to make the theory testable. Instead, the phrase was used by Robbins[7] and can be traced back to Čuhel[8] and the earlier Austrians; and it was proposed in order to spell out the logical prerequisites of maximizing utility.

In a footnote (p. 481) Professor Hutchison approvingly quotes I. M. D. Little concerning certain differences between physics and economics in the use of fundamental assumptions. One of the differences singled out for emphasis is supposed to be that the "concepts . . . about which people are not clear"—pure constructs, idealizations, and postulates—"do not appear in the conclusions" in physics, but do so in "welfare economics." I have not discussed welfare economics and do not intend to do so. But that the controversial, "untested" assumptions "do not appear in the conclusions" holds, as I have demonstrated, for positive economics no less than for physics.

In another footnote (p. 480) Professor Hutchison believes that he has found an ally in Professor Friedman, who held that I had come "perilously close" to a tautological formulation of the theory. But by pressing his demand for an independent empirical test of the profit maximization postulate Professor Hutchison has placed himself right in the center of the target of Friedman's attack. It was the main theme of Friedman's methodological essay that fundamental assumptions do their work even if they are contrary to fact, and that it is a mistake to attempt empirical tests for them besides those of the findings derived from the theory of which they are a part.

There is, furthermore, the charge of "tautology," which is implied in some of Professor Hutchison's strictures against my work and is made explicit in the quotation from Friedman. The judgment that a certain theory is "purely tautological" may mean rather different things: that the theory is underdetermined and can yield no specificable conclusions; that some of the important variables are unknowable or changing in undetermined ways; that the *ceteris paribus* clause is used without specifying the *cetera* or their significance for the outcome; that the deduced conclusions can never be tested against data of experience; that the theory constitutes an internally consistent and closed system; that some of the assumptions are "empirically empty." I shall comment here only on the last two meanings of the charge.

A fully developed theoretical system will always be "an internally consistent set of assumptions and definitions, such that each proposition is capable of being logically deduced from the assumptions and definitions (in the manner of a theorem)."[9] This was, and probably still is, recognized by Professor Hutchison,

---

[7] Lionel Robbins, *An Essay on the Nature and Significance of Economic Science* (London: Macmillan, 1932), pp. 56, 86, and elsewhere.

[8] Franz Čuhel, *Zur Lehre von den Bedürfnissen* (Wien, 1908), pp. 186–216.

[9] Arnold M. Rose, *Theory and Method in the Social Sciences* (Minneapolis: University of Minnesota, 1954), p. 263.

who once wrote that pure theory must necessarily be of a form such that "what it proves must be contained in the assumptions and cannot be obtained from any other sources." Hence, "to criticize a proposition of pure theory *as such* as tautological, or circular, or as assuming what it requires to prove, is beside the point."[10]

The assumptions that consumers act to "maximize their expected satisfaction" and entrepreneurs act to "maximize their expected profits" are sometimes considered as "empirically empty" or "tautological" because (a) we cannot know whether or not the consumers and entrepreneurs really believe that their actions are the best of the alternatives considered, (b) whatever they do can thus be interpreted as being what they consider to be "the best under the circumstances," and (c) as long as we do not know their tastes, preferences, and alternative anticipations, we cannot deduce any particular way of acting from the assumptions standing by themselves.

The point, however, is that the assumptions do not stand by themselves but are combined with other assumptions, including some about certain substantive changes which are observable by us as well as by the consumers or firms concerned. Our theory does not tell or explain what the decision makers have been doing, or have preferred to do, or have avoided to do before the changes in question occurred; it deals only with the ways in which decisions will be changed by the occurrence and its repercussions. No matter how many pounds of lemons consumers have been purchasing, they will try to purchase more; the theory tells us this from the assumptions furnished. No matter how many yards of grey goods manufacturers have been producing, they will produce more; the theory can tell us this on the basis of the assumptions supplied.[11] An assumption apparently quite "empty" or without empirical implications as long as it stands alone may become of definite empirical significance when combined in a model with other assumptions.

Finally, there is that polemical red herring dragged across the trail: veiled charges of sympathizing with controversial value judgments, "indirect" accusations based on guilt by association with others accused directly. I was first inclined to overlook it, because I thought that silence on my part would be the most eloquent response. I have been persuaded, however, that my rejoinder would be sadly incomplete without a comment on this confusion, innocent or deliberate, between positive economics and political evaluation.

Not a single passage or sentence in my article could in fairness be interpreted as dealing with political implications, value judgments, policy advice, welfare economics. Yet, in the last pages of his reply Professor Hutchison throws a heavy barrage against alleged welfare implications of my argument. Furious salvos are

[10] T. W. Hutchison, *The Significance and Basic Postulates of Economic Theory* (London: Macmillan, 1938), p. 36.

[11] See my reply to R. A. Gordon, who had interpreted methodological subjectivism as leaving "theory saying that businessmen do what they do because they do it." Fritz Machlup, *The Economics of Sellers' Competition* (Baltimore: Johns Hopkins Press, 2952), p. 36.

fired against the "maximum of utility for society" in connection with Walras and free competition, and against "wholesale political conclusions" in connection with Mises and liberal economic policies.

If Professor Hutchison really believes that my "doctrines on verification and verifiability" can be used (and are designed?) to "propagate sweeping political dogmas" and to defend "politico-intellectual obscurantism" he does precisely what he apparently considers objectionable in others: he confuses normative (ethical) judgments with positive propositions of economic theory. Yet, at the same time he claims to be an advocate of Professor Friedman's dictum that "It is necessary to be more specific about the content of existing economic theory and to *distinguish among its different branches.*[12] Would that Professor Hutchison practiced what he advocates.

The Johns Hopkins University   FRITZ MACHLUP

A NOTE ON TESTING THE TRANSITIVITY AXIOM

Recently Pfouts[1] in discussing the testing of certain fundamental assumptions in the theory of ordinal utility has stated "that if we can show empirically that the transitivity rule is not obeyed by individual consumers then there is something wrong with the existing theory of consumer's preferences." Pfouts cites the results of May[2] as preliminary evidence indicating a tendency toward nontransitivity in human choice.

It is the purpose of this note to clarify the conditions under which the transitivity axiom would be refuted and to make clear the type of tests under which the axiom could never be refuted. The transitivity condition stated in Pfouts' terminology is that if $X_i R X_j$, and $X_j R X_k$, then it must follow that $X_i R X_k$, where R indicates the relation "preferred or indifferent to." But we must recognize that in ordinal utility theory $X_k R X_i$ and even $X_j R X_i$ are also allowable relationships provided that all the R's in the relations represent the condition of "indifference." In fact in ordinary utility theory one can use the definition that indifference exists between X_i and X_j if and only if $X_i R X_j$ and $X_j R X_i$.

We are now able to appreciate that any binary choice experiment, and May's in particular, in which the individual being tested *must* make a choice between X_i and X_j only demonstrates the relation R; the existence of a cyclical pattern $X_i R X_j R X_k R X_i$ in no way contradicts the axiom of transitivity. An equivalent statement of the transitivity condition to be tested which pinpoints the critical test to be made is that if $X_i R X_j$, $X_j R X_k$, then not $X_k P X_i$, where P indicates the relation "preferred to."

We may easily demonstrate by an intuitive approach that cyclical choice patterns of R are admissible. Consider an individual who is indifferent to X_i,

[12] Milton Friedman, *op. cit.*, p. 41. Emphasis supplied.

[1] R. W. Pfouts, "Prolegomena to the Testing of Utility Theory," *Southern Economic Journal*, Vol. XXII, October 1955, pp. 178–188.

[2] K. O. May, "Transitivity, Utility and Aggregation in Preference Patterns," *Econometrica*, Vol. XXII, January 1954, pp. 1–13.

3

Realism of Assumptions and Descriptivism

Milton Friedman, 'The Methodology of Positive Economics', in *Essays in Positive Economics*, Chicago: University of Chicago Press, 1953, pp. 3–43.

Ernest Nagel, 'Assumptions in Economic Theory', *American Economic Review Papers and Proceedings*, vol. 53, May 1963, pp. 211–19.

Paul Samuelson, 'Problems of Methodology – Discussion', *American Economic Review Papers and Proceedings*, vol. 53, May 1963, pp. 231–6.

Fritz Machlup, 'Professor Samuelson on Theory and Realism', *American Economic Review, vol. 54, September 1964, pp. 733–6.*

Paul Samuelson, 'Theory and Realism: A Reply', American Economic Review, vol. 54, September 1964, pp. 736–9.

Editor's comments

We come at last to Milton Friedman, whose 'The Methodology of Positive Economics' is the most famous piece of methodological writing in economics. The secondary literature on Friedman's article is enormous and variegated, so no summary of his arguments will be attempted here. A few comments on the other articles are in order.

Ernest Nagel's brief discussion is one of the first efforts by a philosopher of science (and a distinguished philosopher, at that) to analyze the methodological writings of an economist. It is packed with ideas and warrants careful study. Nagel meticulously defines the types of statements that scientific theories contain, using categories drawn from logical empiricist philosophy of science. He notes the difficulties that are often encountered in establishing the truth or falsity of statements containing theoretical terms, and that such difficulties have led some to embrace an instrumental view of theories. Nagel's most important contribution, however, is to show that Friedman uses the term 'realism' ambiguously. Because of his lack of clarity on this point, Friedman's position on the status and role of theory in economics becomes equally uncertain, as Nagel easily demonstrates. And *that* ambiguity is why subsequent commentators have been able to attribute so many divergent views to Friedman. To muddy the waters further, very few of Friedman's critics and interpreters picked up on Nagel's important insight. And *that* unforgiveable omission is why Boland was able to write some fifteen years later that no one had interpreted Friedman correctly.

But we are getting ahead of ourselves. Nagel concludes that Friedman is right for the wrong reasons, that, despite the economist's mis-steps, Friedman is right in believing that theories are tested by comparing their implications, or predictions, with the data. (Not surprisingly, this particular belief is in perfect accordance with logical empiricist philosophy of science.) Less generous is Paul Samuelson, whose discussion is a farrago of humorous (though occasionally biting) disparagement, natural science name-dropping, and symbolic logic. Though he means the last to be his substantive contribution, it is in the early pages of his note that Samuelson makes his mark by coining the memorable term 'F-twist'. As for the rest of his comment, it is an inventive piece of choplogic that elicited its own set of critical responses.

Only one exchange is reprinted here, and again we find Fritz Machlup trying to correct the methodological miscreance of his peers. In his comment, Machlup cleverly points out the inconsistencies between Samuelson's past theoretical work and his methodological pronouncements. More important is Machlup's argument that Samuelson's position implies a rejection of a role for theory in economics. In his remarkable reply, Samuelson is able to insult the Austrians, footnote Kuhn, Hanson and Polyani, and embrace a descriptivist view of theories, a view that was last popular at the end of the nineteenth century. And this in less than four pages!

Samuelson's solecisms raise some questions. How could such a renowned theorist be such an awful methodologist? Was his problem that he paid too much attention to the writings of philosophers, or not enough? Is there no interface between the scribbling of methodologists and the practice of economists? I hope that the readings in Part II will aid us in formulating some answers.

The Methodology of Positive Economics*

IN HIS admirable book on *The Scope and Method of Political Economy* John Neville Keynes distinguishes among "a *positive science* . . . [,] a body of systematized knowledge concerning what is; a *normative* or *regulative science* . . . [,] a body of systematized knowledge discussing criteria of what ought to be . . . ; an *art* . . . [,] a system of rules for the attainment of a given end"; comments that "confusion between them is common and has been the source of many mischievous errors"; and urges the importance of "recognizing a distinct positive science of political economy."[1]

This paper is concerned primarily with certain methodological problems that arise in constructing the "distinct positive science" Keynes called for—in particular, the problem how to decide whether a suggested hypothesis or theory should be tentatively accepted as part of the "body of systematized knowledge concerning what is." But the confusion Keynes laments is still so rife and so much of a hindrance to the recognition that economics can be, and in part is, a positive science that it seems well to preface the main body of the paper with a few remarks about the relation between positive and normative economics.

I. THE RELATION BETWEEN POSITIVE AND NORMATIVE ECONOMICS

Confusion between positive and normative economics is to some extent inevitable. The subject matter of economics is regarded by almost everyone as vitally important to himself and within the range of his own experience and competence; it is

---

* I have incorporated bodily in this article without special reference most of my brief "Comment" in *A Survey of Contemporary Economics,* Vol. II (B. F. Haley, ed.) (Chicago: Richard D. Irwin, Inc., 1952), pp. 455–57.

I am indebted to Dorothy S. Brady, Arthur F. Burns, and George J. Stigler for helpful comments and criticism.

1. (London: Macmillan & Co., 1891), pp. 34–35 and 46.

3

the source of continuous and extensive controversy and the occasion for frequent legislation. Self-proclaimed "experts" speak with many voices and can hardly all be regarded as disinterested; in any event, on questions that matter so much, "expert" opinion could hardly be accepted solely on faith even if the "experts" were nearly unanimous and clearly disinterested.[2] The conclusions of positive economics seem to be, and are, immediately relevant to important normative problems, to questions of what ought to be done and how any given goal can be attained. Laymen and experts alike are inevitably tempted to shape positive conclusions to fit strongly held normative preconceptions and to reject positive conclusions if their normative implications—or what are said to be their normative implications—are unpalatable.

Positive economics is in principle independent of any particular ethical position or normative judgments. As Keynes says, it deals with "what is," not with "what ought to be." Its task is to provide a system of generalizations that can be used to make correct predictions about the consequences of any change in circumstances. Its performance is to be judged by the precision, scope, and conformity with experience of the predictions it yields. In short, positive economics is, or can be, an "objective" science, in precisely the same sense as any of the physical sciences. Of course, the fact that economics deals with the interrelations of human beings, and that the investigator is himself part of the subject matter being investigated in a more intimate sense than in the physical sciences, raises special difficulties in achieving objectivity at the same time that it provides the social scientist with a class of data not available to the physical sci-

2. Social science or economics is by no means peculiar in this respect—witness the importance of personal beliefs and of "home" remedies in medicine wherever obviously convincing evidence for "expert" opinion is lacking. The current prestige and acceptance of the views of physical scientists in their fields of specialization—and, all too often, in other fields as well—derives, not from faith alone, but from the evidence of their works, the success of their predictions, and the dramatic achievements from applying their results. When economics seemed to provide such evidence of its worth, in Great Britain in the first half of the nineteenth century, the prestige and acceptance of "scientific economics" rivaled the current prestige of the physical sciences.

The Methodology of Positive Economics   5

entist. But neither the one nor the other is, in my view, a fundamental distinction between the two groups of sciences.[3]

Normative economics and the art of economics, on the other hand, cannot be independent of positive economics. Any policy conclusion necessarily rests on a prediction about the consequences of doing one thing rather than another, a prediction that must be based—implicitly or explicitly—on positive economics. There is not, of course, a one-to-one relation between policy conclusions and the conclusions of positive economics; if there were, there would be no separate normative science. Two individuals may agree on the consequences of a particular piece of legislation. One may regard them as desirable on balance and so favor the legislation; the other, as undesirable and so oppose the legislation.

I venture the judgment, however, that currently in the Western world, and especially in the United States, differences about economic policy among disinterested citizens derive predominantly from different predictions about the economic consequences of taking action—differences that in principle can be eliminated by the progress of positive economics—rather than from fundamental differences in basic values, differences about which men can ultimately only fight. An obvious and not unimportant example is minimum-wage legislation. Underneath the welter of arguments offered for and against such legislation there is an underlying consensus on the objective of achieving a "living wage" for all, to use the ambiguous phrase so common in such discussions. The difference of opinion is largely grounded on an implicit or explicit difference in predictions about the efficacy of this particular means in furthering the agreed-on end. Proponents believe (predict) that legal minimum wages diminish poverty by raising the wages of those receiving less than the minimum wage as well as of some receiving more than the

3. The interaction between the observer and the process observed that is so prominent a feature of the social sciences, besides its more obvious parallel in the physical sciences, has a more subtle counterpart in the indeterminacy principle arising out of the interaction between the process of measurement and the phenomena being measured. And both have a counterpart in pure logic in Gödel's theorem, asserting the impossibility of a comprehensive self-contained logic. It is an open question whether all three can be regarded as different formulations of an even more general principle.

minimum wage without any counterbalancing increase in the number of people entirely unemployed or employed less advantageously than they otherwise would be. Opponents believe (predict) that legal minimum wages increase poverty by increasing the number of people who are unemployed or employed less advantageously and that this more than offsets any favorable effect on the wages of those who remain employed. Agreement about the economic consequences of the legislation might not produce complete agreement about its desirability, for differences might still remain about its political or social consequences; but, given agreement on objectives, it would certainly go a long way toward producing consensus.

Closely related differences in positive analysis underlie divergent views about the appropriate role and place of trade-unions and the desirability of direct price and wage controls and of tariffs. Different predictions about the importance of so-called "economies of scale" account very largely for divergent views about the desirability or necessity of detailed government regulation of industry and even of socialism rather than private enterprise. And this list could be extended indefinitely.[4] Of course, my judgment that the major differences about economic policy in the Western world are of this kind is itself a "positive" statement to be accepted or rejected on the basis of empirical evidence.

If this judgment is valid, it means that a consensus on "correct" economic policy depends much less on the progress of normative economics proper than on the progress of a positive economics yielding conclusions that are, and deserve to be, widely accepted. It means also that a major reason for dis-

4. One rather more complex example is stabilization policy. Superficially, divergent views on this question seem to reflect differences in objectives; but I believe that this impression is misleading and that at bottom the different views reflect primarily different judgments about the source of fluctuations in economic activity and the effect of alternative countercyclical action. For one major positive consideration that accounts for much of the divergence see "The Effects of a Full-Employment Policy on Economic Stability: A Formal Analysis," *infra,* pp. 117–32. For a summary of the present state of professional views on this question see "The Problem of Economic Instability," a report of a subcommittee of the Committee on Public Issues of the American Economic Association, *American Economic Review,* XL (September, 1950), 501–38.

The Methodology of Positive Economics   7

tinguishing positive economics sharply from normative economics is precisely the contribution that can thereby be made to agreement about policy.

II. Positive Economics

The ultimate goal of a positive science is the development of a "theory" or "hypothesis" that yields valid and meaningful (i.e., not truistic) predictions about phenomena not yet observed. Such a theory is, in general, a complex intermixture of two elements. In part, it is a "language" designed to promote "systematic and organized methods of reasoning."[5] In part, it is a body of substantive hypotheses designed to abstract essential features of complex reality.

Viewed as a language, theory has no substantive content; it is a set of tautologies. Its function is to serve as a filing system for organizing empirical material and facilitating our understanding of it; and the criteria by which it is to be judged are those appropriate to a filing system. Are the categories clearly and precisely defined? Are they exhaustive? Do we know where to file each individual item, or is there considerable ambiguity? Is the system of headings and subheadings so designed that we can quickly find an item we want, or must we hunt from place to place? Are the items we shall want to consider jointly filed together? Does the filing system avoid elaborate cross-references?

The answers to these questions depend partly on logical, partly on factual, considerations. The canons of formal logic alone can show whether a particular language is complete and consistent, that is, whether propositions in the language are "right" or "wrong." Factual evidence alone can show whether the categories of the "analytical filing system" have a meaningful empirical counterpart, that is, whether they are useful in analyzing a particular class of concrete problems.[6] The simple example of "supply" and "demand" illustrates both this point and the pre-

5. Final quoted phrase from Alfred Marshall, "The Present Position of Economics" (1885), reprinted in *Memorials of Alfred Marshall,* ed. A. C. Pigou (London: Macmillan & Co., 1925), p. 164. See also "The Marshallian Demand Curve," *infra,* pp. 56–57, 90–91.

6. See "Lange on Price Flexibility and Employment: A Methodological Criticism," *infra,* pp. 282–89.

ceding list of analogical questions. Viewed as elements of the
language of economic theory, these are the two major categories
into which factors affecting the relative prices of products or
factors of production are classified. The usefulness of the dichotomy depends on the "empirical generalization that an enumeration of the forces affecting demand in any problem and of the
forces affecting supply will yield two lists that contain few items
in common."[7] Now this generalization is valid for markets like
the final market for a consumer good. In such a market there
is a clear and sharp distinction between the economic units that
can be regarded as demanding the product and those that can be
regarded as supplying it. There is seldom much doubt whether
a particular factor should be classified as affecting supply, on
the one hand, or demand, on the other; and there is seldom much
necessity for considering cross-effects (cross-references) between the two categories. In these cases the simple and even
obvious step of filing the relevant factors under the headings
of "supply" and "demand" effects a great simplification of the
problem and is an effective safeguard against fallacies that
otherwise tend to occur. But the generalization is not always
valid. For example, it is not valid for the day-to-day fluctuations
of prices in a primarily speculative market. Is a rumor of an
increased excess-profits tax, for example, to be regarded as a
factor operating primarily on today's supply of corporate equi-
ties in the stock market or on today's demand for them? In
similar fashion, almost every factor can with about as much
justification be classified under the heading "supply" as under
the heading "demand." These concepts can still be used and
may not be entirely pointless; they are still "right" but clearly
less useful than in the first example because they have no meaningful empirical counterpart.

Viewed as a body of substantive hypotheses, theory is to be
judged by its predictive power for the class of phenomena which
it is intended to "explain." Only factual evidence can show
whether it is "right" or "wrong" or, better, tentatively "accepted" as valid or "rejected." As I shall argue at greater length
below, the only relevant test of the *validity* of a hypothesis is

7. "The Marshallian Demand Curve," *infra,* p. 57.

The Methodology of Positive Economics   9

comparison of its predictions with experience. The hypothesis is rejected if its predictions are contradicted ("frequently" or more often than predictions from an alternative hypothesis); it is accepted if its predictions are not contradicted; great confidence is attached to it if it has survived many opportunities for contradiction. Factual evidence can never "prove" a hypothesis; it can only fail to disprove it, which is what we generally mean when we say, somewhat inexactly, that the hypothesis has been "confirmed" by experience.

To avoid confusion, it should perhaps be noted explicitly that the "predictions" by which the validity of a hypothesis is tested need not be about phenomena that have not yet occurred, that is, need not be forecasts of future events; they may be about phenomena that have occurred but observations on which have not yet been made or are not known to the person making the prediction. For example, a hypothesis may imply that such and such must have happened in 1906, given some other known circumstances. If a search of the records reveals that such and such did happen, the prediction is confirmed; if it reveals that such and such did not happen, the prediction is contradicted.

The validity of a hypothesis in this sense is not by itself a sufficient criterion for choosing among alternative hypotheses. Observed facts are necessarily finite in number; possible hypotheses, infinite. If there is one hypothesis that is consistant with the available evidence, there are always an infinite number that are.[8] For example, suppose a specific excise tax on a particular commodity produces a rise in price equal to the amount of the tax. This is consistent with competitive conditions, a stable demand curve, and a horizontal and stable supply curve. But it is also consistent with competitive conditions and a positively or negatively sloping supply curve with the required compensating shift in the demand curve or the supply curve; with monopolistic conditions, constant marginal costs, and stable demand curve, of the particular shape required to produce this result; and so on indefinitely. Additional evidence with which the

8. The qualification is necessary because the "evidence" may be internally contradictory, so there may be no hypothesis consistent with it. See also "Lange on Price Flexibility and Employment," *infra*, pp. 282–83.

hypothesis is to be consistent may rule out some of these possibilities; it can never reduce them to a single possibility alone capable of being consistent with the finite evidence. The choice among alternative hypotheses equally consistent with the available evidence must to some extent be arbitrary, though there is general agreement that relevant considerations are suggested by the criteria "simplicity" and "fruitfulness," themselves notions that defy completely objective specification. A theory is "simpler" the less the initial knowledge needed to make a prediction within a given field of phenomena; it is more "fruitful" the more precise the resulting prediction, the wider the area within which the theory yields predictions, and the more additional lines for further research it suggests. Logical completeness and consistency are relevant but play a subsidiary role; their function is to assure that the hypothesis says what it is intended to say and does so alike for all users—they play the same role here as checks for arithmetical accuracy do in statistical computations.

Unfortunately, we can seldom test particular predictions in the social sciences by experiments explicitly designed to eliminate what are judged to be the most important disturbing influences. Generally, we must rely on evidence cast up by the "experiments" that happen to occur. The inability to conduct so-called "controlled experiments" does not, in my view, reflect a basic difference between the social and physical sciences both because it is not peculiar to the social sciences—witness astronomy—and because the distinction between a controlled experiment and uncontrolled experience is at best one of degree. No experiment can be completely controlled, and every experience is partly controlled, in the sense that some disturbing influences are relatively constant in the course of it.

Evidence cast up by experience is abundant and frequently as conclusive as that from contrived experiments; thus the inability to conduct experiments is not a fundamental obstacle to testing hypotheses by the success of their predictions. But such evidence is far more difficult to interpret. It is frequently complex and always indirect and incomplete. Its collection is often arduous, and its interpretation generally requires subtle

The Methodology of Positive Economics 11

analysis and involved chains of reasoning, which seldom carry real conviction. The denial to economics of the dramatic and direct evidence of the "crucial" experiment does hinder the adequate testing of hypotheses; but this is much less significant than the difficulty it places in the way of achieving a reasonably prompt and wide consensus on the conclusions justified by the available evidence. It renders the weeding-out of unsuccessful hypotheses slow and difficult. They are seldom downed for good and are always cropping up again.

There is, of course, considerable variation in these respects. Occasionally, experience casts up evidence that is about as direct, dramatic, and convincing as any that could be provided by controlled experiments. Perhaps the most obviously important example is the evidence from inflations on the hypothesis that a substantial increase in the quantity of money within a relatively short period is accompanied by a substantial increase in prices. Here the evidence is dramatic, and the chain of reasoning required to interpret it is relatively short. Yet, despite numerous instances of substantial rises in prices, their essentially one-to-one correspondence with substantial rises in the stock of money, and the wide variation in other circumstances that might appear to be relevant, each new experience of inflation brings forth vigorous contentions, and not only by the lay public, that the rise in the stock of money is either an incidental effect of a rise in prices produced by other factors or a purely fortuitous and unnecessary concomitant of the price rise.

One effect of the difficulty of testing substantive economic hypotheses has been to foster a retreat into purely formal or tautological analysis.[9] As already noted, tautologies have an extremely important place in economics and other sciences as a specialized language or "analytical filing system." Beyond this, formal logic and mathematics, which are both tautologies, are essential aids in checking the correctness of reasoning, discovering the implications of hypotheses, and determining whether supposedly different hypotheses may not really be equivalent or wherein the differences lie.

But economic theory must be more than a structure of tautol-

9. See "Lange on Price Flexibility and Employment," *infra, passim*.

ogies if it is to be able to predict and not merely describe the consequences of action; if it is to be something different from disguised mathematics.[10] And the usefulness of the tautologies themselves ultimately depends, as noted above, on the acceptability of the substantive hypotheses that suggest the particular categories into which they organize the refractory empirical phenomena.

A more serious effect of the difficulty of testing economic hypotheses by their predictions is to foster misunderstanding of the role of empirical evidence in theoretical work. Empirical evidence is vital at two different, though closely related, stages: in constructing hypotheses and in testing their validity. Full and comprehensive evidence on the phenomena to be generalized or "explained" by a hypothesis, besides its obvious value in suggesting new hypotheses, is needed to assure that a hypothesis explains what it sets out to explain—that its implications for such phenomena are not contradicted in advance by experience that has already been observed.[11] Given that the hypothesis is

10. See also Milton Friedman and L. J. Savage, "The Expected-Utility Hypothesis and the Measurability of Utility," *Journal of Political Economy,* LX (December, 1952), 463–74, esp. pp. 465–67.

11. In recent years some economists, particularly a group connected with the Cowles Commission for Research in Economics at the University of Chicago, have placed great emphasis on a division of this step of selecting a hypothesis consistent with known evidence into two substeps: first, the selection of a class of admissible hypotheses from all possible hypotheses (the choice of a "model" in their terminology); second, the selection of one hypothesis from this class (the choice of a "structure"). This subdivision may be heuristically valuable in some kinds of work, particularly in promoting a systematic use of available statistical evidence and theory. From a methodological point of view, however, it is an entirely arbitrary subdivision of the process of deciding on a particular hypothesis that is on a par with many other subdivisions that may be convenient for one purpose or another or that may suit the psychological needs of particular investigators.

One consequence of this particular subdivision has been to give rise to the so-called "identification" problem. As noted above, if one hypothesis is consistent with available evidence, an infinite number are. But, while this is true for the class of hypotheses as a whole, it may not be true of the subclass obtained in the first of the above two steps—the "model." It may be that the evidence to be used to select the final hypothesis from the subclass can be consistent with at most one hypothesis in it, in which case the "model" is said to be "identified"; otherwise it is said to be "unidentified." As is clear from this way of describing the concept of "identification," it is essentially a special case of the more general

The Methodology of Positive Economics　　13

consistent with the evidence at hand, its further testing involves deducing from it new facts capable of being observed but not previously known and checking these deduced facts against additional empirical evidence. For this test to be relevant, the deduced facts must be about the class of phenomena the hypothesis is designed to explain; and they must be well enough defined so that observation can show them to be wrong.

The two stages of constructing hypotheses and testing their validity are related in two different respects. In the first place, the particular facts that enter at each stage are partly an accident of the collection of data and the knowledge of the particular investigator. The facts that serve as a test of the implications of a hypothesis might equally well have been among the raw material used to construct it, and conversely. In the second place, the process never begins from scratch; the so-called "initial stage" itself always involves comparison of the implications of an earlier set of hypotheses with observation; the contradiction of these implications is the stimulus to the construction of new

---

problem of selecting among the alternative hypotheses equally consistent with the evidence—a problem that must be decided by some such arbitrary principle as Occam's razor. The introduction of two substeps in selecting a hypothesis makes this problem arise at the two corresponding stages and gives it a special cast. While the class of all hypotheses is always unidentified, the subclass in a "model" need not be, so the problem arises of conditions that a "model" must satisfy to be identified. However useful the two substeps may be in some contexts, their introduction raises the danger that different criteria will unwittingly be used in making the same kind of choice among alternative hypotheses at two different stages.

On the general methodological approach discussed in this footnote see Tryvge Haavelmo, "The Probability Approach in Econometrics," *Econometrica,* Vol. XII (1944), Supplement; Jacob Marschak, "Economic Structure, Path, Policy, and Prediction," *American Economic Review,* XXXVII, (May, 1947), 81–84, and "Statistical Inference in Economics: An Introduction," in T. C. Koopmans (ed.), *Statistical Inference in Dynamic Economic Models* (New York: John Wiley & Sons, 1950); T. C. Koopmans, "Statistical Estimation of Simultaneous Economic Relations," *Journal of the American Statistical Association,* XL (December, 1945), 448–66; Gershon Cooper, "The Role of Economic Theory in Econometric Models," *Journal of Farm Economics,* XXX (February, 1948), 101–16. On the identification problem see Koopmans, "Identification Problems in Econometric Model Construction," *Econometrica,* XVII (April, 1949), 125–44; Leonid Hurwicz, "Generalization of the Concept of Identification," in Koopmans (ed.), *Statistical Inference in Dynamic Economic Models.*

hypotheses or revision of old ones. So the two methodologically distinct stages are always proceeding jointly.

Misunderstanding about this apparently straightforward process centers on the phrase "the class of phenomena the hypothesis is designed to explain." The difficulty in the social sciences of getting new evidence for this class of phenomena and of judging its conformity with the implications of the hypothesis makes it tempting to suppose that other, more readily available, evidence is equally relevant to the validity of the hypothesis—to suppose that hypotheses have not only "implications" but also "assumptions" and that the conformity of these "assumptions" to "reality" is a test of the validity of the hypothesis *different from* or *additional to* the test by implications. This widely held view is fundamentally wrong and productive of much mischief. Far from providing an easier means for sifting valid from invalid hypotheses, it only confuses the issue, promotes misunderstanding about the significance of empirical evidence for economic theory, produces a misdirection of much intellectual effort devoted to the development of positive economics, and impedes the attainment of consensus on tentative hypotheses in positive economics.

In so far as a theory can be said to have "assumptions" at all, and in so far as their "realism" can be judged independently of the validity of predictions, the relation between the significance of a theory and the "realism" of its "assumptions" is almost the opposite of that suggested by the view under criticism. Truly important and significant hypotheses will be found to have "assumptions" that are wildly inaccurate descriptive representations of reality, and, in general, the more significant the theory, the more unrealistic the assumptions (in this sense).[12] The reason is simple. A hypothesis is important if it "explains" much by little, that is, if it abstracts the common and crucial elements from the mass of complex and detailed circumstances surrounding the phenomena to be explained and permits valid predictions on the basis of them alone. To be important, therefore, a hypothesis must be descriptively false in its assumptions; it

12. The converse of the proposition does not of course hold: assumptions that are unrealistic (in this sense) do not guarantee a significant theory.

The Methodology of Positive Economics   15

takes account of, and accounts for, none of the many other attendant circumstances, since its very success shows them to be irrelevant for the phenomena to be explained.

To put this point less paradoxically, the relevant question to ask about the "assumptions" of a theory is not whether they are descriptively "realistic," for they never are, but whether they are sufficiently good approximations for the purpose in hand. And this question can be answered only by seeing whether the theory works, which means whether it yields sufficiently accurate predictions. The two supposedly independent tests thus reduce to one test.

The theory of monopolistic and imperfect competition is one example of the neglect in economic theory of these propositions. The development of this analysis was explicitly motivated, and its wide acceptance and approval largely explained, by the belief that the assumptions of "perfect competition" or "perfect monopoly" said to underlie neoclassical economic theory are a false image of reality. And this belief was itself based almost entirely on the directly perceived descriptive inaccuracy of the assumptions rather than on any recognized contradiction of predictions derived from neoclassical economic theory. The lengthy discussion on marginal analysis in the *American Economic Review* some years ago is an even clearer, though much less important, example. The articles on both sides of the controversy largely neglect what seems to me clearly the main issue—the conformity to experience of the implications of the marginal analysis—and concentrate on the largely irrelevant question whether businessmen do or do not in fact reach their decisions by consulting schedules, or curves, or multivariable functions showing marginal cost and marginal revenue.[13] Perhaps these

13. See R. A. Lester, "Shortcomings of Marginal Analysis for Wage-Employment Problems," *American Economic Review*, XXXVI (March, 1946), 62–82; Fritz Machlup, "Marginal Analysis and Empirical Research," *American Economic Review*, XXXVI (September, 1946), 519–54; R. A. Lester, "Marginalism, Minimum Wages, and Labor Markets," *American Economic Review*, XXXVII (March, 1947), 135–48; Fritz Machlup, "Rejoinder to an Antimarginalist," *American Economic Review*, XXXVII (March, 1947), 148–54; G. J. Stigler, "Professor Lester and the Marginalists," *American Economic Review*, XXXVII (March, 1947), 154–57; H. M. Oliver, Jr., "Marginal Theory and Business Behavior," *American Economic Review*, XXXVII (June, 1947), 375–83; R. A. Gordon,

16   *Essays in Positive Economics*

two examples, and the many others they readily suggest, will serve to justify a more extensive discussion of the methodological principles involved than might otherwise seem appropriate.

III. CAN A HYPOTHESIS BE TESTED BY THE REALISM OF ITS ASSUMPTIONS?

We may start with a simple physical example, the law of falling bodies. It is an accepted hypothesis that the acceleration of a body dropped in a vacuum is a constant—g, or approximately 32 feet per second per second on the earth—and is independent of the shape of the body, the manner of dropping it, etc. This implies that the distance traveled by a falling body in any specified time is given by the formula $s = \frac{1}{2} gt^2$, where s is the distance traveled in feet and t is time in seconds. The application of this formula to a compact ball dropped from the roof of a building is equivalent to saying that a ball so dropped behaves *as if* it were falling in a vacuum. Testing this hypothesis by its assumptions presumably means measuring the actual air pressure and deciding whether it is close enough to zero. At sea level the air pressure is about 15 pounds per square inch. Is 15 sufficiently close to zero for the difference to be judged insignificant? Apparently it is, since the actual time taken by a compact ball to fall from the roof of a building to the ground is very close to the time given by the formula. Suppose, however, that a feather is

---

"Short-Period Price Determination in Theory and Practice," *American Economic Review*, XXXVIII (June, 1948), 265–88.

It should be noted that, along with much material purportedly bearing on the validity of the "assumptions" of marginal theory, Lester does refer to evidence on the conformity of experience with the implications of the theory, citing the reactions of employment in Germany to the Papen plan and in the United States to changes in minimum-wage legislation as examples of lack of conformity. However, Stigler's brief comment is the only one of the other papers that refers to this evidence. It should also be noted that Machlup's thorough and careful exposition of the logical structure and meaning of marginal analysis is called for by the misunderstandings on this score that mar Lester's paper and almost conceal the evidence he presents that is relevant to the key issue he raises. But, in Machlup's emphasis on the logical structure, he comes perilously close to presenting the theory as a pure tautology, though it is evident at a number of points that he is aware of this danger and anxious to avoid it. The papers by Oliver and Gordon are the most extreme in the exclusive concentration on the conformity of the behavior of businessmen with the "assumptions" of the theory.

dropped instead of a compact ball. The formula then gives wildly inaccurate results. Apparently, 15 pounds per square inch is significantly different from zero for a feather but not for a ball. Or, again, suppose the formula is applied to a ball dropped from an airplane at an altitude of 30,000 feet. The air pressure at this altitude is decidedly less than 15 pounds per square inch. Yet, the actual time of fall from 30,000 feet to 20,000 feet, at which point the air pressure is still much less than at sea level, will differ noticeably from the time predicted by the formula— much more noticeably than the time taken by a compact ball to fall from the roof of a building to the ground. According to the formula, the velocity of the ball should be gt and should therefore increase steadily. In fact, a ball dropped at 30,000 feet will reach its top velocity well before it hits the ground. And similarly with other implications of the formula.

The initial question whether 15 is sufficiently close to zero for the difference to be judged insignificant is clearly a foolish question by itself. Fifteen pounds per square inch is 2,160 pounds per square foot, or 0.0075 ton per square inch. There is no possible basis for calling these numbers "small" or "large" without some external standard of comparison. And the only relevant standard of comparison is the air pressure for which the formula does or does not work under a given set of circumstances. But this raises the same problem at a second level. What is the meaning of "does or does not work"? Even if we could eliminate errors of measurement, the measured time of fall would seldom if ever be precisely equal to the computed time of fall. How large must the difference between the two be to justify saying that the theory "does not work"? Here there are two important external standards of comparison. One is the accuracy achievable by an alternative theory with which this theory is being compared and which is equally acceptable on all other grounds. The other arises when there exists a theory that is known to yield better predictions but only at a greater cost. The gains from greater accuracy, which depend on the purpose in mind, must then be balanced against the costs of achieving it.

This example illustrates both the impossibility of testing a theory by its assumptions and also the ambiguity of the concept "the assumptions of a theory." The formula $s = \frac{1}{2} gt^2$ is valid for bodies falling in a vacuum and can be derived by analyzing the behavior of such bodies. It can therefore be stated: under a wide range of circumstances, bodies that fall in the actual atmosphere behave *as if* they were falling in a vacuum. In the language so common in economics this would be rapidly translated into: the formula assumes a vacuum. Yet it clearly does no such thing. What it does say is that in many cases the existence of air pressure, the shape of the body, the name of the person dropping the body, the kind of mechanism used to drop the body, and a host of other attendant circumstances have no appreciable effect on the distance the body falls in a specified time. The hypothesis can readily be rephrased to omit all mention of a vacuum: under a wide range of circumstances, the distance a body falls in a specified time is given by the formula $s = \frac{1}{2} gt^2$. The history of this formula and its associated physical theory aside, is it meaningful to say that it assumes a vacuum? For all I know there may be other sets of assumptions that would yield the same formula. The formula is accepted because it works, not because we live in an approximate vacuum—whatever that means.

The important problem in connection with the hypothesis is to specify the circumstances under which the formula works or, more precisely, the general magnitude of the error in its predictions under various circumstances. Indeed, as is implicit in the above rephrasing of the hypothesis, such a specification is not one thing and the hypothesis another. The specification is itself an essential part of the hypothesis, and it is a part that is peculiarly likely to be revised and extended as experience accumulates.

In the particular case of falling bodies a more general, though still incomplete, theory is available, largely as a result of attempts to explain the errors of the simple theory, from which the influence of some of the possible disturbing factors can be calculated and of which the simple theory is a special case. However, it does not always pay to use the more general theory because the extra accuracy it yields may not justify the extra cost of using it, so the question under what circumstances the simpler theory works "well enough" remains important. Air pressure is one, but only one, of the variables that define these circumstances; the shape of the body, the velocity attained, and still other variables are relevant as well. One way of interpreting the variables other than air pressure is to regard them as determining whether a particular departure from the "assumption" of a vacuum is or is not significant. For example, the difference in shape of the body can be said to make 15 pounds per square inch significantly different from zero for a feather but not for a compact ball dropped a moderate distance. Such a statement must, however, be sharply distinguished from the very different statement that the theory does not work for a feather because its assumptions are false. The relevant relation runs the other way: the assumptions are false for a feather because the theory does not work. This point needs emphasis, because the entirely valid use of "assumptions" in *specifying* the circumstances for which a theory holds is frequently, and erroneously, interpreted to mean that the assumptions can be used to *determine* the circumstances for which a theory holds, and has, in this way, been an important source of the belief that a theory can be tested by its assumptions.

Let us turn now to another example, this time a constructed one designed to be an analogue of many hypotheses in the social sciences. Consider the density of leaves around a tree. I suggest the hypothesis that the leaves are positioned as if each leaf deliberately sought to maximize the amount of sunlight it receives, given the position of its neighbors, as if it knew the physical laws determining the amount of sunlight that would be received in various positions and could move rapidly or instantaneously from any one position to any other desired and unoccupied position.[14] Now some of the more obvious implications of this hypothesis are clearly consistent with experience: for example, leaves are in general denser on the south than on the north side of trees but, as the hypothesis implies, less so or not at all on the northern

14. This example, and some of the subsequent discussion, though independent in origin, is similar to and in much the same spirit as an example and the approach in an important paper by Armen A. Alchian, "Uncertainty, Evolution, and Economic Theory," *Journal of Political Economy*, LVIII (June, 1950), 211–21.

slope of a hill or when the south side of the trees is shaded in some other way. Is the hypothesis rendered unacceptable or invalid because, so far as we know, leaves do not "deliberate" or consciously "seek," have not been to school and learned the relevant laws of science or the mathematics required to calculate the "optimum" position, and cannot move from position to position? Clearly, none of these contradictions of the hypothesis is vitally relevant; the phenomena involved are not within the "class of phenomena the hypothesis is designed to explain"; the hypothesis does not assert that leaves do these things but only that their density is the same *as if* they did. Despite the apparent falsity of the "assumptions" of the hypothesis, it has great plausibility because of the conformity of its implications with observation. We are inclined to "explain" its validity on the ground that sunlight contributes to the growth of leaves and that hence leaves will grow denser or more putative leaves survive where there is more sun, so the result achieved by purely passive adaptation to external circumstances is the same as the result that would be achieved by deliberate accommodation to them. This alternative hypothesis is more attractive than the constructed hypothesis not because its "assumptions" are more "realistic" but rather because it is part of a more general theory that applies to a wider variety of phenomena, of which the position of leaves around a tree is a special case, has more implications capable of being contradicted, and has failed to be contradicted under a wider variety of circumstances. The direct evidence for the growth of leaves is in this way strengthened by the indirect evidence from the other phenomena to which the more general theory applies.

The constructed hypothesis is presumably valid, that is, yields "sufficiently" accurate predictions about the density of leaves, only for a particular class of circumstances. I do not know what these circumstances are or how to define them. It seems obvious, however, that in this example the "assumptions" of the theory will play no part in specifying them: the kind of tree, the character of the soil, etc., are the types of variables that are likely to define its range of validity, not the ability of the leaves to do complicated mathematics or to move from place to place.

The Methodology of Positive Economics   2 1

A largely parallel example involving human behavior has been used elsewhere by Savage and me.[15] Consider the problem of predicting the shots made by an expert billiard player. It seems not at all unreasonable that excellent predictions would be yielded by the hypothesis that the billiard player made his shots *as if* he knew the complicated mathematical formulas that would give the optimum directions of travel, could estimate accurately by eye the angles, etc., describing the location of the balls, could make lightning calculations from the formulas, and could then make the balls travel in the direction indicated by the formulas. Our confidence in this hypothesis is not based on the belief that billiard players, even expert ones, can or do go through the process described; it derives rather from the belief that, unless in some way or other they were capable of reaching essentially the same result, they would not in fact be *expert* billiard players.

It is only a short step from these examples to the economic hypothesis that under a wide range of circumstances individual firms behave *as if* they were seeking rationally to maximize their expected returns (generally if misleadingly called "profits")[16] and had full knowledge of the data needed to succeed in this attempt; *as if*, that is, they knew the relevant cost and demand functions,

15. Milton Friedman and L. J. Savage, "The Utility Analysis of Choices Involving Risk," *Journal of Political Economy,* LVI (August, 1948), 298. Reprinted in American Economic Association, *Readings in Price Theory* (Chicago: Richard D. Irwin, Inc., 1952), pp. 57–96.

16. It seems better to use the term "profits" to refer to the difference between actual and "expected" results, between *ex post* and *ex ante* receipts. "Profits" are then a result of uncertainty and, as Alchian (*op. cit.,* p. 212), following Tintner, points out, cannot be deliberately maximized in advance. Given uncertainty, individuals or firms choose among alternative anticipated probability distributions of receipts or incomes. The specific content of a theory of choice among such distributions depends on the criteria by which they are supposed to be ranked. One hypothesis supposes them to be ranked by the mathematical expectation of utility corresponding to them (see Friedman and Savage, "The Expected-Utility Hypothesis and the Measurability of Utility," *op. cit.*). A special case of this hypothesis or an alternative to it ranks probability distributions by the mathematical expectation of the money receipts corresponding to them. The latter is perhaps more applicable, and more frequently applied, to firms than to individuals. The term "expected returns" is intended to be sufficiently broad to apply to any of these alternatives.

The issues alluded to in this note are not basic to the methodological issues being discussed, and so are largely by-passed in the discussion that follows.

calculated marginal cost and marginal revenue from all actions open to them, and pushed each line of action to the point at which the relevant marginal cost and marginal revenue were equal. Now, of course, businessmen do not actually and literally solve the system of simultaneous equations in terms of which the mathematical economist finds it convenient to express this hypothesis, any more than leaves or billiard players explicitly go through complicated mathematical calculations or falling bodies decide to create a vacuum. The billiard player, if asked how he decides where to hit the ball, may say that he "just figures it out" but then also rubs a rabbit's foot just to make sure; and the businessman may well say that he prices at average cost, with of course some minor deviations when the market makes it necessary. The one statement is about as helpful as the other, and neither is a relevant test of the associated hypothesis.

Confidence in the maximization-of-returns hypothesis is justified by evidence of a very different character. This evidence is in part similar to that adduced on behalf of the billiard-player hypothesis—unless the behavior of businessmen in some way or other approximated behavior consistent with the maximization of returns, it seems unlikely that they would remain in business for long. Let the apparent immediate determinant of business behavior be anything at all—habitual reaction, random chance, or whatnot. Whenever this determinant happens to lead to behavior consistent with rational and informed maximization of returns, the business will prosper and acquire resources with which to expand; whenever it does not, the business will tend to lose resources and can be kept in existence only by the addition of resources from outside. The process of "natural selection" thus helps to validate the hypothesis—or, rather, given natural selection, acceptance of the hypothesis can be based largely on the judgment that it summarizes appropriately the conditions for survival.

An even more important body of evidence for the maximization-of-returns hypothesis is experience from countless applications of the hypothesis to specific problems and the repeated failure of its implications to be contradicted. This evidence is extremely hard to document; it is scattered in numerous memorandums, articles, and monographs concerned primarily with specific concrete problems rather than with submitting the hypothesis to test. Yet the continued use and acceptance of the hypothesis over a long period, and the failure of any coherent, self-consistent alternative to be developed and be widely accepted, is strong indirect testimony to its worth. The evidence *for* a hypothesis always consists of its repeated failure to be contradicted, continues to accumulate so long as the hypothesis is used, and by its very nature is difficult to document at all comprehensively. It tends to become part of the tradition and folklore of a science revealed in the tenacity with which hypotheses are held rather than in any textbook list of instances in which the hypothesis has failed to be contradicted.

IV. THE SIGNIFICANCE AND ROLE OF THE "ASSUMPTIONS" OF A THEORY

Up to this point our conclusions about the significance of the "assumptions" of a theory have been almost entirely negative: we have seen that a theory cannot be tested by the "realism" of its "assumptions" and that the very concept of the "assumptions" of a theory is surrounded with ambiguity. But, if this were all there is to it, it would be hard to explain the extensive use of the concept and the strong tendency that we all have to speak of the assumptions of a theory and to compare the assumptions of alternative theories. There is too much smoke for there to be no fire.

In methodology, as in positive science, negative statements can generally be made with greater confidence than positive statements, so I have less confidence in the following remarks on the significance and role of "assumptions" than in the preceding remarks. So far as I can see, the "assumptions of a theory" play three different, though related, positive roles: (*a*) they are often an economical mode of describing or presenting a theory; (*b*) they sometimes facilitate an indirect test of the hypothesis by its implications; and (*c*), as already noted, they are sometimes a convenient means of specifying the conditions under which the theory is expected to be valid. The first two require more extensive discussion.

A. THE USE OF "ASSUMPTIONS" IN STATING A THEORY

The example of the leaves illustrates the first role of assumptions. Instead of saying that leaves seek to maximize the sunlight they receive, we could state the equivalent hypothesis, without any apparent assumptions, in the form of a list of rules for predicting the density of leaves: if a tree stands in a level field with no other trees or other bodies obstructing the rays of the sun, then the density of leaves will tend to be such and such; if a tree is on the northern slope of a hill in the midst of a forest of similar trees, then . . . ; etc. This is clearly a far less economical presentation of the hypothesis than the statement that leaves seek to maximize the sunlight each receives. The latter statement is, in effect, a simple summary of the rules in the above list, even if the list were indefinitely extended, since it indicates both how to determine the features of the environment that are important for the particular problem and how to evaluate their effects. It is more compact and at the same time no less comprehensive.

More generally, a hypothesis or theory consists of an assertion that certain forces are, and by implication others are not, important for a particular class of phenomena and a specification of the manner of action of the forces it asserts to be important. We can regard the hypothesis as consisting of two parts: first, a conceptual world or abstract model simpler than the "real world" and containing only the forces that the hypothesis asserts to be important; second, a set of rules defining the class of phenomena for which the "model" can be taken to be an adequate representation of the "real world" and specifying the correspondence between the variables or entities in the model and observable phenomena.

These two parts are very different in character. The model is abstract and complete; it is an "algebra" or "logic." Mathematics and formal logic come into their own in checking its consistency and completeness and exploring its implications. There is no place in the model for, and no function to be served by, vagueness, maybe's, or approximations. The air pressure is zero, not "small," for a vacuum; the demand curve for the product of a competitive

The Methodology of Positive Economics   25

producer is horizontal (has a slope of zero), not "almost horizontal."

The rules for using the model, on the other hand, cannot possibly be abstract and complete. They must be concrete and in consequence incomplete—completeness is possible only in a conceptual world, not in the "real world," however that may be interpreted. The model is the logical embodiment of the half-truth, "There is nothing new under the sun"; the rules for applying it cannot neglect the equally significant half-truth, "History never repeats itself." To a considerable extent the rules can be formulated explicitly—most easily, though even then not completely, when the theory is part of an explicit more general theory as in the example of the vacuum theory for falling bodies. In seeking to make a science as "objective" as possible, our aim should be to formulate the rules explicitly in so far as possible and continually to widen the range of phenomena for which it is possible to do so. But, no matter how successful we may be in this attempt, there inevitably will remain room for judgment in applying the rules. Each occurrence has some features peculiarly its own, not covered by the explicit rules. The capacity to judge that these are or are not to be disregarded, that they should or should not affect what observable phenomena are to be identified with what entities in the model, is something that cannot be taught; it can be learned but only by experience and exposure in the "right" scientific atmosphere, not by rote. It is at this point that the "amateur" is separated from the "professional" in all sciences and that the thin line is drawn which distinguishes the "crackpot" from the scientist.

A simple example may perhaps clarify this point. Euclidean geometry is an abstract model, logically complete and consistent. Its entities are precisely defined—a line is not a geometrical figure "much" longer than it is wide or deep; it is a figure whose width and depth are zero. It is also obviously "unrealistic." There are no such things in "reality" as Euclidean points or lines or surfaces. Let us apply this abstract model to a mark made on a blackboard by a piece of chalk. Is the mark to be identified with a Euclidean line, a Euclidean surface, or a Euclidean solid?

Clearly, it can appropriately be identified with a line if it is being used to represent, say, a demand curve. But it cannot be so identified if it is being used to color, say, countries on a map, for that would imply that the map would never be colored; for this purpose, the same mark must be identified with a surface. But it cannot be so identified by a manufacturer of chalk, for that would imply that no chalk would ever be used up; for his purposes, the same mark must be identified with a volume. In this simple example these judgments will command general agreement. Yet it seems obvious that, while general considerations can be formulated to guide such judgments, they can never be comprehensive and cover every possible instance; they cannot have the self-contained coherent character of Euclidean geometry itself.

In speaking of the "crucial assumptions" of a theory, we are, I believe, trying to state the key elements of the abstract model. There are generally many different ways of describing the model completely—many different sets of "postulates" which both imply and are implied by the model as a whole. These are all logically equivalent: what are regarded as axioms or postulates of a model from one point of view can be regarded as theorems from another, and conversely. The particular "assumptions" termed "crucial" are selected on grounds of their convenience in some such respects as simplicity or economy in describing the model, intuitive plausibility, or capacity to suggest, if only by implication, some of the considerations that are relevant in judging or applying the model.

B. THE USE OF "ASSUMPTIONS" AS AN INDIRECT TEST OF A THEORY

In presenting any hypothesis, it generally seems obvious which of the series of statements used to expound it refer to assumptions and which to implications; yet this distinction is not easy to define rigorously. It is not, I believe, a characteristic of the hypothesis as such but rather of the use to which the hypothesis is to be put. If this is so, the ease of classifying statements must reflect unambiguousness in the purpose the hypothesis is designed to serve. The possibility of interchanging theorems and axioms in an abstract model implies the possibility of interchanging "implications" and "assumptions" in the substantive hypothesis corresponding to the abstract model, which is not to say that any implication can be interchanged with any assumption but only that there may be more than one set of statements that imply the rest.

For example, consider a particular proposition in the theory of oligopolistic behavior. If we assume (*a*) that entrepreneurs seek to maximize their returns by any means including acquiring or extending monopoly power, this will imply (*b*) that, when demand for a "product" is geographically unstable, transportation costs are significant, explicit price agreements illegal, and the number of producers of the product relatively small, they will tend to establish basing-point pricing systems.[17] The assertion (*a*) is regarded as an assumption and (*b*) as an implication because we accept the prediction of market behavior as the purpose of the analysis. We shall regard the assumption as acceptable if we find that the conditions specified in (*b*) are generally associated with basing-point pricing, and conversely. Let us now change our purpose to deciding what cases to prosecute under the Sherman Antitrust Law's prohibition of a "conspiracy in restraint of trade." If we now assume (*c*) that basing-point pricing is a deliberate construction to facilitate collusion under the conditions specified in (*b*), this will imply (*d*) that entrepreneurs who participate in basing-point pricing are engaged in a "conspiracy in restraint of trade." What was formerly an assumption now becomes an implication, and conversely. We shall now regard the assumption (*c*) as valid if we find that, when entrepreneurs participate in basing-point pricing, there generally tends to be other evidence, in the form of letters, memorandums, or the like, of what courts regard as a "conspiracy in restraint of trade."

Suppose the hypothesis works for the first purpose, namely, the prediction of market behavior. It clearly does not follow that it will work for the second purpose, namely, predicting whether there is enough evidence of a "conspiracy in restraint of trade"

17. See George J. Stigler, "A Theory of Delivered Price Systems," *American Economic Review,* XXXIX (December, 1949), 1143–57.

to justify court action. And, conversely, if it works for the second purpose, it does not follow that it will work for the first. Yet, in the absence of other evidence, the success of the hypothesis for one purpose—in explaining one class of phenomena—will give us greater confidence than we would otherwise have that it may succeed for another purpose—in explaining another class of phenomena. It is much harder to say how much greater confidence it justifies. For this depends on how closely related we judge the two classes of phenomena to be, which itself depends in a complex way on similar kinds of indirect evidence, that is, on our experience in other connections in explaining by single theories phenomena that are in some sense similarly diverse.

To state the point more generally, what are called the assumptions of a hypothesis can be used to get some indirect evidence on the acceptability of the hypothesis in so far as the assumptions can themselves be regarded as implications of the hypothesis, and hence their conformity with reality as a failure of some implications to be contradicted, or in so far as the assumptions may call to mind other implications of the hypothesis susceptible to casual empirical observation.[18] The reason this evidence is indirect is that the assumptions or associated implications generally refer to a class of phenomena different from the class which the hypothesis is designed to explain; indeed, as is implied above, this seems to be the chief criterion we use in deciding which statements to term "assumptions" and which to term "implications." The weight attached to this indirect evidence depends on how closely related we judge the two classes of phenomena to be.

Another way in which the "assumptions" of a hypothesis can facilitate its indirect testing is by bringing out its kinship with other hypotheses and thereby making the evidence on their validity relevant to the validity of the hypothesis in question. For example, a hypothesis is formulated for a particular class

18. See Friedman and Savage, "The Expected-Utility Hypothesis and the Measurability of Utility," *op. cit.*, pp. 466–67, for another specific example of this kind of indirect test.

of behavior. This hypothesis can, as usual, be stated without specifying any "assumptions." But suppose it can be shown that it is equivalent to a set of assumptions including the assumption that man seeks his own interest. The hypothesis then gains indirect plausibility from the success for other classes of phenomena of hypotheses that can also be said to make this assumption; at least, what is being done here is not completely unprecedented or unsuccessful in all other uses. In effect, the statement of assumptions so as to bring out a relationship between superficially different hypotheses is a step in the direction of a more general hypothesis.

This kind of indirect evidence from related hypotheses explains in large measure the difference in the confidence attached to a particular hypothesis by people with different backgrounds. Consider, for example, the hypothesis that the extent of racial or religious discrimination in employment in a particular area or industry is closely related to the degree of monopoly in the industry or area in question; that, if the industry is competitive, discrimination will be significant only if the race or religion of employees affects either the willingness of other employees to work with them or the acceptability of the product to customers and will be uncorrelated with the prejudices of employers.[19] This hypothesis is far more likely to appeal to an economist than to a sociologist. It can be said to "assume" single-minded pursuit of pecuniary self-interest by employers in competitive industries; and this "assumption" works well in a wide variety of hypotheses in economics bearing on many of the mass phenomena with which economics deals. It is therefore likely to seem reasonable to the economist that it may work in this case as well. On the other hand, the hypotheses to which the sociologist is accustomed have a very different kind of model or ideal world, in which single-minded pursuit of pecuniary self-interest plays a much less important role. The indirect evidence available to the sociologist on

19. A rigorous statement of this hypothesis would of course have to specify how "extent of racial or religious discrimination" and "degree of monopoly" are to be judged. The loose statement in the text is sufficient, however, for present purposes.

this hypothesis is much less favorable to it than the indirect evidence available to the economist; he is therefore likely to view it with greater suspicion.

Of course, neither the evidence of the economist nor that of the sociologist is conclusive. The decisive test is whether the hypothesis works for the phenomena it purports to explain. But a judgment may be required before any satisfactory test of this kind has been made, and, perhaps, when it cannot be made in the near future, in which case, the judgment will have to be based on the inadequate evidence available. In addition, even when such a test can be made, the background of the scientists is not irrelevant to the judgments they reach. There is never certainty in science, and the weight of evidence for or against a hypothesis can never be assessed completely "objectively." The economist will be more tolerant than the sociologist in judging conformity of the implications of the hypothesis with experience, and he will be persuaded to accept the hypothesis tentatively by fewer instances of "conformity."

V. Some Implications for Economic Issues

The abstract methodological issues we have been discussing have a direct bearing on the perennial criticism of "orthodox" economic theory as "unrealistic" as well as on the attempts that have been made to reformulate theory to meet this charge. Economics is a "dismal" science because it assumes man to be selfish and money-grubbing, "a lightning calculator of pleasures and pains, who oscillates like a homogeneous globule of desire of happiness under the impulse of stimuli that shift him about the area, but leave him intact";[20] it rests on outmoded psychology and must be reconstructed in line with each new development in psychology; it assumes men, or at least businessmen, to be "in a continuous state of 'alert,' ready to change prices and/or pricing rules whenever their sensitive intuitions . . . detect a change in demand and supply conditions";[21] it

20. Thorstein Veblen, "Why Is Economics Not an Evolutionary Science?" (1898), reprinted in *The Place of Science in Modern Civilization* (New York, 1919), p. 73.

21. Oliver, *op. cit.*, p. 381.

The Methodology of Positive Economics   31

assumes markets to be perfect, competition to be pure, and commodities, labor, and capital to be homogeneous.

As we have seen, criticism of this type is largely beside the point unless supplemented by evidence that a hypothesis differing in one or another of these respects from the theory being criticized yields better predictions for as wide a range of phenomena. Yet most such criticism is not so supplemented; it is based almost entirely on supposedly directly perceived discrepancies between the "assumptions" and the "real world." A particularly clear example is furnished by the recent criticisms of the maximization-of-returns hypothesis on the grounds that businessmen do not and indeed cannot behave as the theory "assumes" they do. The evidence cited to support this assertion is generally taken either from the answers given by businessmen to questions about the factors affecting their decisions—a procedure for testing economic theories that is about on a par with testing theories of longevity by asking octogenarians how they account for their long life—or from descriptive studies of the decision-making activities of individual firms.[22] Little if any evidence is ever cited on the conformity of businessmen's actual market behavior—what they do rather than what they say they do—with the implications of the hypothesis being criticized, on the one hand, and of an alternative hypothesis, on the other.

22. See H. D. Henderson, "The Significance of the Rate of Interest," *Oxford Economic Papers*, No. 1 (October, 1938), pp. 1–13; J. E. Meade and P. W. S. Andrews, "Summary of Replies to Questions on Effects of Interest Rates," *Oxford Economic Papers*, No. 1 (October, 1938), pp. 14–31; R. F. Harrod, "Price and Cost in Entrepreneurs' Policy," *Oxford Economic Papers*, No. 2 (May, 1939), pp. 1–11; and R. J. Hall and C. J. Hitch, "Price Theory and Business Behavior," *Oxford Economic Papers*, No. 2 (May, 1939), pp. 12–45; Lester, "Shortcomings of Marginal Analysis for Wage-Employment Problems," *op. cit.*; Gordon, *op. cit.* See Fritz Machlup, "Marginal Analysis and Empirical Research," *op. cit.*, esp. Sec. II, for detailed criticisms of questionnaire methods.

I do not mean to imply that questionnaire studies of businessmen's or others' motives or beliefs about the forces affecting their behavior are useless for all purposes in economics. They may be extremely valuable in suggesting leads to follow in accounting for divergencies between predicted and observed results; that is, in constructing new hypotheses or revising old ones. Whatever their suggestive value in this respect, they seem to me almost entirely useless as a means of *testing* the validity of economic hypotheses. See my comment on Albert G. Hart's paper, "Liquidity and Uncertainty," *American Economic Review*, XXXIX (May, 1949), 198–99.

Essays in Positive Economics

A theory or its "assumptions" cannot possibly be thoroughly "realistic" in the immediate descriptive sense so often assigned to this term. A completely "realistic" theory of the wheat market would have to include not only the conditions directly under-lying the supply and demand for wheat but also the kind of coins or credit instruments used to make exchanges; the personal characteristics of wheat-traders such as the color of each trader's hair and eyes, his antecedents and education, the number of members of his family, their characteristics, antecedents, and education, etc.; the kind of soil on which the wheat was grown, its physical and chemical characteristics, the weather prevaliing during the growing season; the personal characteristics of the farmers growing the wheat and of the consumers who will ulti-mately use it; and so on indefinitely. Any attempt to move very far in achieving this kind of "realism" is certain to render a theory utterly useless.

Of course, the notion of a completely realistic theory is in part a straw man. No critic of a theory would accept this logical extreme as his objective; he would say that the "assumptions" of the theory being criticized were "too" unrealistic and that his objective was a set of assumptions that were "more" realistic though still not completely and slavishly so. But so long as the test of "realism" is the directly perceived descriptive accuracy of the "assumptions"—for example, the observation that "busi-nessmen do not appear to be either as avaricious or as dynamic or as logical as marginal theory portrays them"[23] or that "it would be utterly impractical under present conditions for the manager of a multi-process plant to attempt . . . to work out and equate marginal costs and marginal revenues for each pro-ductive factor"[24]—there is no basis for making such a distinc-tion, that is, for stopping short of the straw man depicted in the preceding paragraph. What is the criterion by which to judge whether a particular departure from realism is or is not accept-able? Why is it more "unrealistic" in analyzing business be-havior to neglect the magnitude of businessmen's costs than the

23. Oliver, *op. cit.*, p. 382.

24. Lester, "Shortcomings of Marginal Analysis for Wage-Employment Prob-lems," *op. cit.*, p. 75.

color of their eyes? The obvious answer is because the first makes more difference to business behavior than the second; but there is no way of knowing that this is so simply by observing that businessmen do have costs of different magnitudes and eyes of different color. Clearly it can only be known by comparing the effect on the discrepancy between actual and predicted behavior of taking the one factor or the other into account. Even the most extreme proponents of realistic assumptions are thus necessarily driven to reject their own criterion and to accept the test by prediction when they classify alternative assumptions as more or less realistic.[25]

The basic confusion between descriptive accuracy and analytical relevance that underlies most criticisms of economic theory on the grounds that its assumptions are unrealistic as well as the plausibility of the views that lead to this confusion are both strikingly illustrated by a seemingly innocuous remark in an article on business-cycle theory that "economic phenomena are varied and complex, so any comprehensive theory of the business cycle that can apply closely to reality must be very complicated."[26] A fundamental hypothesis of science is that appearances are deceptive and that there is a way of looking at or interpreting or organizing the evidence that will reveal superficially disconnected and diverse phenomena to be manifestations of a more fundamental and relatively simple structure. And the test of this hypothesis, as of any other, is its fruits—a test that science has

25. E.g., Gordon's direct examination of the "assumptions" leads him to formulate the alternative hypothesis generally favored by the critics of the maximization-of-returns hypothesis as follows: "There is an irresistible tendency to price on the basis of average total costs for some 'normal' level of output. This is the yardstick, the short-cut, that businessmen and accountants use, and their aim is more to earn satisfactory profits and play safe than to maximize profits" (*op. cit.*, p. 275). Yet he essentially abandons this hypothesis, or converts it into a tautology, and in the process implicitly accepts the test by prediction when he later remarks: "Full cost and satisfactory profits may continue to be the objectives even when total costs are shaded to meet competition or exceeded to take advantage of a sellers' market" (*ibid.*, p. 284). Where here is the "irresistible tendency"? What kind of evidence could contradict this assertion?

26. Sidney S. Alexander, "Issues of Business Cycle Theory Raised by Mr. Hicks," *American Economic Review*, XLI (December, 1951), 872.

so far met with dramatic success. If a class of "economic phenomena" appears varied and complex, it is, we must suppose, because we have no adequate theory to explain them. Known facts
cannot be set on one side; a theory to apply "closely to reality,"
on the other. A theory is the way we perceive "facts," and we
cannot perceive "facts" without a theory. Any assertion that
economic phenomena *are* varied and complex denies the tentative
state of knowledge that alone makes scientific activity meaningful; it is in a class with John Stuart Mill's justly ridiculed statement that "happily, there is nothing in the laws of value which
remains [1848] for the present or any future writer to clear up;
the theory of the subject is complete."[27]

The confusion between descriptive accuracy and analytical
relevance has led not only to criticisms of economic theory on
largely irrelevant grounds but also to misunderstanding of
economic theory and misdirection of efforts to repair supposed defects. "Ideal types" in the abstract model developed by economic
theorists have been regarded as strictly descriptive categories
intended to correspond directly and fully to entities in the real
world independently of the purpose for which the model is being
used. The obvious discrepancies have led to necessarily unsuccessful attempts to construct theories on the basis of categories
intended to be fully descriptive.

This tendency is perhaps most clearly illustrated by the interpretation given to the concepts of "perfect competition" and
"monopoly" and the development of the theory of "monopolistic"
or "imperfect competition." Marshall, it is said, assumed "perfect competition"; perhaps there once was such a thing. But
clearly there is no longer, and we must therefore discard his
theories. The reader will search long and hard—and I predict
unsuccessfully—to find in Marshall any explicit assumption about
perfect competition or any assertion that in a descriptive sense
the world is composed of atomistic firms engaged in perfect
competition. Rather, he will find Marshall saying: "At one
extreme are world markets in which competition acts directly
from all parts of the globe; and at the other those secluded

27. *Principles of Political Economy* (Ashley ed.; Longmans, Green & Co., 1929),
p. 436.

The Methodology of Positive Economics   35

markets in which all direct competition from afar is shut out, though indirect and transmitted competition may make itself felt even in these; and about midway between these extremes lie the great majority of the markets which the economist and the business man have to study."[28] Marshall took the world as it is; he sought to construct an "engine" to analyze it, not a photographic reproduction of it.

In analyzing the world as it is, Marshall constructed the hypothesis that, for many problems, firms could be grouped into "industries" such that the similarities among the firms in each group were more important than the differences among them. These are problems in which the important element is that a group of firms is affected alike by some stimulus—a common change in the demand for their products, say, or in the supply of factors. But this will not do for all problems: the important element for these may be the differential effect on particular firms.

The abstract model corresponding to this hypothesis contains two "ideal" types of firms: atomistically competitive firms, grouped into industries, and monopolistic firms. A firm is competitive if the demand curve for its output is infinitely elastic with respect to its own price for some price and all outputs, given the prices charged by all other firms; it belongs to an "industry" defined as a group of firms producing a single "product." A "product" is defined as a collection of units that are perfect substitutes to purchasers so the elasticity of demand for the output of one firm with respect to the price of another firm in the same industry is infinite for some price and some outputs. A firm is monopolistic if the demand curve for its output is not infinitely elastic at some price for all outputs.[29] If it is a monopolist, the firm is the industry.[30]

As always, the hypothesis as a whole consists not only of this abstract model and its ideal types but also of a set of rules, mostly

28. *Principles,* p. 329; see also pp. 35, 100, 341, 347, 375, 546.

29. This ideal type can be divided into two types: the oligopolistic firm, if the demand curve for its output is infinitely elastic at some price for some but not all outputs; the monopolistic firm proper, if the demand curve is nowhere infinitely elastic (except possibly at an output of zero).

30. For the oligopolist of the preceding note an industry can be defined as a group of firms producing the same product.

implicit and suggested by example, for identifying actual firms with one or the other ideal type and for classifying firms into industries. The ideal types are not intended to be descriptive; they are designed to isolate the features that are crucial for a particular problem. Even if we could estimate directly and accurately the demand curve for a firm's product, we could not proceed immediately to classify the firm as perfectly competitive or monopolistic according as the elasticity of the demand curve is or is not infinite. No observed demand curve will ever be precisely horizontal, so the estimated elasticity will always be finite. The relevant question always is whether the elasticity is "sufficiently" large to be regarded as infinite, but this is a question that cannot be answered, once for all, simply in terms of the numerical value of the elasticity itself, any more than we can say, once for all, whether an air pressure of 15 pounds per square inch is "sufficiently" close to zero to use the formula $s = \frac{1}{2}gt.^2$ Similarly, we cannot compute cross-elasticities of demand and then classify firms into industries according as there is a "substantial gap in the cross-elasticities of demand." As Marshall says, "The question where the lines of division between different commodities [i.e., industries] should be drawn must be settled by convenience of the particular discussion."[31] Everything depends on the problem; there is no inconsistency in regarding the same firm as if it were a perfect competitor for one problem, and a monopolist for another, just as there is none in regarding the same chalk mark as a Euclidean line for one problem, a Euclidean surface for a second, and a Euclidean solid for a third. The size of the elasticity and cross-elasticity of demand, the number of firms producing physically similar products, etc., are all relevant because they are or may be among the variables used to define the correspondence between the ideal and real entities in a particular problem and to specify the circumstances under which the theory holds sufficiently well; but they do not provide, once for all, a classification of firms as competitive or monopolistic.

An example may help to clarify this point. Suppose the problem is to determine the effect on retail prices of cigarettes of an

31. *Principles*, p. 100.

increase, expected to be permanent, in the federal cigarette tax. I venture to predict that broadly correct results will be obtained by treating cigarette firms as if they were producing an identical product and were in perfect competition. Of course, in such a case, "some convention must be made as to the" number of Chesterfield cigarettes "which are taken as equivalent" to a Marlborough.[32]

On the other hand, the hypothesis that cigarette firms would behave as if they were perfectly competitive would have been a false guide to their reactions to price control in World War II, and this would doubtless have been recognized before the event. Costs of the cigarette firms must have risen during the war. Under such circumstances perfect competitors would have reduced the quantity offered for sale at the previously existing price. But, at that price, the wartime rise in the income of the public presumably increased the quantity demanded. Under conditions of perfect competition strict adherence to the legal price would therefore imply not only a "shortage" in the sense that quantity demanded exceeded quantity supplied but also an absolute decline in the number of cigarettes produced. The facts contradict this particular implication: there was reasonably good adherence to maximum cigarette prices, yet the quantities produced increased substantially. The common force of increased costs presumably operated less strongly than the disruptive force of the desire by each firm to keep its share of the market, to maintain the value and prestige of its brand name, especially when the excess-profits tax shifted a large share of the costs of this kind of advertising to the government. For this problem the cigarette firms cannot be treated *as if* they were perfect competitors.

Wheat farming is frequently taken to exemplify perfect competition. Yet, while for some problems it is appropriate to treat cigarette producers as if they comprised a perfectly competitive industry, for some it is not appropriate to treat wheat producers as if they did. For example, it may not be if the problem is the differential in prices paid by local elevator operators for wheat.

Marshall's apparatus turned out to be most useful for problems in which a group of firms is affected by common stimuli,

32. Quoted parts from *ibid.*

and in which the firms can be treated *as if* they were perfect competitors. This is the source of the misconception that Marshall "assumed" perfect competition in some descriptive sense. It would be highly desirable to have a more general theory than Marshall's, one that would cover at the same time both those cases in which differentiation of product or fewness of numbers makes an essential difference and those in which it does not. Such a theory would enable us to handle problems we now cannot and, in addition, facilitate determination of the range of circumstances under which the simpler theory can be regarded as a good enough approximation. To perform this function, the more general theory must have content and substance; it must have implications susceptible to empirical contradiction and of substantive interest and importance.

The theory of imperfect or monopolistic competition developed by Chamberlin and Robinson is an attempt to construct such a more general theory.[33] Unfortunately, it possesses none of the attributes that would make it a truly useful general theory. Its contribution has been limited largely to improving the exposition of the economics of the individual firm and thereby the derivation of implications of the Marshallian model, refining Marshall's monopoly analysis, and enriching the vocabulary available for describing industrial experience.

The deficiencies of the theory are revealed most clearly in its treatment of, or inability to treat, problems involving groups of firms—Marshallian "industries." So long as it is insisted that differentiation of product is essential—and it is the distinguishing feature of the theory that it does insist on this point—the definition of an industry in terms of firms producing an identical product cannot be used. By that definition each firm is a separate industry. Definition in terms of "close" substitutes or a "substantial" gap in cross-elasticities evades the issue, introduces fuzziness and undefinable terms into the abstract model where they have no place, and serves only to make the theory analytically meaningless—"close" and "substantial" are in the same category

33. E. H. Chamberlin, *The Theory of Monopolistic Competition* (6th ed.; Cambridge: Harvard University Press, 1950); Joan Robinson, *The Economics of Imperfect Competition* (London: Macmillan & Co., 1933).

The Methodology of Positive Economics   39

as a "small" air pressure.[34] In one connection Chamberlin implicitly defines an industry as a group of firms having identical cost and demand curves.[35] But this, too, is logically meaningless so long as differentiation of product is, as claimed, essential and not to be put aside. What does it mean to say that the cost and demand curves of a firm producing bulldozers are identical with those of a firm producing hairpins?[36] And if it is meaningless for bulldozers and hairpins, it is meaningless also for two brands of toothpaste—so long as it is insisted that the difference between the two brands is fundamentally important.

The theory of monopolistic competition offers no tools for the analysis of an industry and so no stopping place between the firm at one extreme and general equilibrium at the other.[37] It is therefore incompetent to contribute to the analysis of a host of important problems: the one extreme is too narrow to be of great interest; the other, too broad to permit meaningful generalizations.[38]

VI. Conclusion

Economics as a positive science is a body of tentatively accepted generalizations about economic phenomena that can be used to predict the consequences of changes in circumstances.

34. See R. L. Bishop, "Elasticities, Cross-elasticities, and Market Relationships," *American Economic Review*, XLII (December, 1952), 779–803, for a recent attempt to construct a rigorous classification of market relationships along these lines. Despite its ingenuity and sophistication, the result seems to me thoroughly unsatisfactory. It rests basically on certain numbers being classified as "large" or "small," yet there is no discussion at all of how to decide whether a particular number is "large" or "small," as of course there cannot be on a purely abstract level.

35. *Op. cit.*, p. 82.

36. There always exists a transformation of quantities that will make either the cost curves or the demand curves identical; this transformation need not, however, be linear, in which case it will involve different-sized units of one product at different levels of output. There does not necessarily exist a transformation that will make both pairs of curves identical.

37. See Robert Triffin, *Monopolistic Competition and General Equilibrium Theory* (Cambridge: Harvard University Press, 1940), esp. pp. 188–89.

38. For a detailed critique see George J. Stigler, "Monopolistic Competition in Retrospect," in *Five Lectures on Economic Problems* (London: Macmillan & Co., 1949), pp. 12–24.

Progress in expanding this body of generalizations, strengthening our confidence in their validity, and improving the accuracy of the predictions they yield is hindered not only by the limitations of human ability that impede all search for knowledge but also by obstacles that are especially important for the social sciences in general and economics in particular, though by no means peculiar to them. Familiarity with the subject matter of economics breeds contempt for special knowledge about it. The importance of its subject matter to everyday life and to major issues of public policy impedes objectivity and promotes confusion between scientific analysis and normative judgment. The necessity of relying on uncontrolled experience rather than on controlled experiment makes it difficult to produce dramatic and clear-cut evidence to justify the acceptance of tentative hypotheses. Reliance on uncontrolled experience does not affect the fundamental methodological principle that a hypothesis can be tested only by the conformity of its implications or predictions with observable phenomena; but it does render the task of testing hypotheses more difficult and gives greater scope for confusion about the methodological principles involved. More than other scientists, social scientists need to be self-conscious about their methodology.

One confusion that has been particularly rife and has done much damage is confusion about the role of "assumptions" in economic analysis. A meaningful scientific hypothesis or theory typically asserts that certain forces are, and other forces are not, important in understanding a particular class of phenomena. It is frequently convenient to present such a hypothesis by stating that the phenomena it is desired to predict behave in the world of observation *as if* they occurred in a hypothetical and highly simplified world containing only the forces that the hypothesis asserts to be important. In general, there is more than one way to formulate such a description—more than one set of "assumptions" in terms of which the theory can be presented. The choice among such alternative assumptions is made on the grounds of the resulting economy, clarity, and precision in presenting the hypothesis; their capacity to bring indirect evidence to bear on the validity of the hypothesis by suggesting

The Methodology of Positive Economics   41

some of its implications that can be readily checked with observation or by bringing out its connection with other hypotheses dealing with related phenomena; and similar considerations.

Such a theory cannot be tested by comparing its "assumptions" directly with "reality." Indeed, there is no meaningful way in which this can be done. Complete "realism" is clearly unattainable, and the question whether a theory is realistic "enough" can be settled only by seeing whether it yields predictions that are good enough for the purpose in hand or that are better than predictions from alternative theories. Yet the belief that a theory can be tested by the realism of its assumptions independently of the accuracy of its predictions is widespread and the source of much of the perennial criticism of economic theory as unrealistic. Such criticism is largely irrelevant, and, in consequence, most attempts to reform economic theory that it has stimulated have been unsuccessful.

The irrelevance of so much criticism of economic theory does not of course imply that existing economic theory deserves any high degree of confidence. These criticisms may miss the target, yet there may be a target for criticism. In a trivial sense, of course, there obviously is. Any theory is necessarily provisional and subject to change with the advance of knowledge. To go beyond this platitude, it is necessary to be more specific about the content of "existing economic theory" and to distinguish among its different branches; some parts of economic theory clearly deserve more confidence than others. A comprehensive evaluation of the present state of positive economics, summary of the evidence bearing on its validity, and assessment of the relative confidence that each part deserves is clearly a task for a treatise or a set of treatises, if it be possible at all, not for a brief paper on methodology.

About all that is possible here is the cursory expression of a personal view. Existing relative price theory, which is designed to explain the allocation of resources among alternative ends and the division of the product among the co-operating resources and which reached almost its present form in Marshall's *Principles of Economics*, seems to me both extremely fruitful and deserving of much confidence for the kind of economic system that characterizes Western nations. Despite the appearance of considerable controversy, this is true equally of existing static monetary theory, which is designed to explain the structural or secular level of absolute prices, aggregate output, and other variables for the economy as a whole and which has had a form of the quantity theory of money as its basic core in all of its major variants from David Hume to the Cambridge School to Irving Fisher to John Maynard Keynes. The weakest and least satisfactory part of current economic theory seems to me to be in the field of monetary dynamics, which is concerned with the process of adaptation of the economy as a whole to changes in conditions and so with short-period fluctuations in aggregate activity. In this field we do not even have a theory that can appropriately be called "the" existing theory of monetary dynamics.

Of course, even in relative price and static monetary theory there is enormous room for extending the scope and improving the accuracy of existing theory. In particular, undue emphasis on the descriptive realism of "assumptions" has contributed to neglect of the critical problem of determining the limits of validity of the various hypotheses that together constitute the existing economic theory in these areas. The abstract models corresponding to these hypotheses have been elaborated in considerable detail and greatly improved in rigor and precision. Descriptive material on the characteristics of our economic system and its operations have been amassed on an unprecedented scale. This is all to the good. But, if we are to use effectively these abstract models and this descriptive material, we must have a comparable exploration of the criteria for determining what abstract model it is best to use for particular kinds of problems, what entities in the abstract model are to be identified with what observable entities, and what features of the problem or of the circumstances have the greatest effect on the accuracy of the predictions yielded by a particular model or theory.

Progress in positive economics will require not only the testing and elaboration of existing hypotheses but also the construction of new hypotheses. On this problem there is little to say on a

The Methodology of Positive Economics   43

formal level. The construction of hypotheses is a creative act of inspiration, intuition, invention; its essence is the vision of something new in familiar material. The process must be discussed in psychological, not logical, categories; studied in autobiographies and biographies, not treatises on scientific method; and promoted by maxim and example, not syllogism or theorem.

ASSUMPTIONS IN ECONOMIC THEORY

By ERNEST NAGEL
Columbia University

Sound conclusions are sometimes supported by erroneous arguments, and the error is compounded when a sound conclusion is declared to be mistaken on the ground that the argument for it is mistaken. This general observation must serve as my *apologia* for venturing to discuss an important and much debated methodological issue in economics, though not myself an economist. In his well-known essay, "The Methodology of Positive Economics,"[1] Professor Milton Friedman defends the use of abstract (and in particular, neoclassical) theory in economic analysis, in effect by defending the principle that the adequacy of a theory must be judged, not by assessing what he calls the "realism of its assumptions," but rather by examining the concordance of the theory's logical consequences with the phenomena the theory is designed to explain—a principle which many economists continue to reject, frequently because arguments similar to his seem to them mistaken. I also think that his argument provides no firm support for this principle; and, indeed, my paper is a critique of his defense of it. However, the relevance of my paper is not, I think, limited to Professor Friedman's essay, for I hope to show that despite the inconclusiveness of his argument his conclusion is sound.

I

Since the notions of theory and assumption are central in discussions of the principle at issue, it is convenient to begin by noting some distinctions.

1. The word theory is often used in the social sciences (including economics) rather loosely, to designate almost any general statement, however narrow its intended range of application may be. Thus, the label is commonly given to empirical generalizations (often stated in the form of equations obtained with the help of techniques of curve fitting) that are simply extrapolations from observed statistical regularities, and are asserted to hold only for behaviors occurring in a given community during some particular historical period. On the other hand, many economists (including Professor Friedman) employ the word far more selectively, and approximately in the sense associated with it when it occurs in such phrases as "the Newtonian theory of motion."

---

[1] It is published in his *Essays in Positive Economics* (Chicago, 1953). All page references, unless otherwise noted, are to this book.

211

It is in this second sense that theory will be used in this paper. Accordingly, an economic theory (e.g., the neoclassical theory of consumer choice) is a set of statements, organized in a characteristic way, and designed to serve as partial premises for explaining as well as predicting an indeterminately large (and usually varied) class of economic phenomena. Moreover, most if not all the statements of a theory have the form of generalized conditionals, which place no spatiotemporal restrictions on the class of phenomena that may be explained with their help. For example, the law of diminishing returns can be expressed in this form: If the quantity of a factor of production is augmented by equal increments, but the quantities of all other factors are kept constant, then the resulting increments in the product will eventually diminish. Space is lacking for discussing adequately the anatomy of theories, but a few additional features distinctive of them must be briefly mentioned.[2]

2. In a given codification of a theory, the statements belonging to it can be divided into three subgroups. The first consists of statements which count as the fundamental ones, and are often called the theory's "assumptions" (or basic "hypotheses"); the second subgroup contains the statements that are logically deducible as theorems from statements in the first. However, the term "assumption" is sometimes also used to refer to the antecedent clause of a conditional theoretical statement in either of these subgroups. This is the way Professor Friedman seems to use the word when, in discussing Galileo's law for freely falling bodies (i.e., "if a body falls toward the earth in a vacuum, its instantaneous acceleration is constant"), he asks whether this law does in fact "assume" that bodies actually fall through a vacuum.

The third subgroup of theoretical statements can also be readily characterized, if we recall that many (and perhaps all) statements in the first two subgroups contain expressions which designate nothing actually observable and are not explicitly definable in terms of expressions that do. Familiar examples of such expressions (for easy reference I will call them "theoretical terms") are "vacuum" in Galileo's law, "gene" in biological theory, and "elasticity of demand at a point" in neoclassical economic theory. Theoretical terms signify either various entities that cannot be specified except by way of some theory which postulates their existence, or certain ideal limits of theoretically endless processes. It is therefore evident that statements containing such terms cannot possibly explain or predict the course of actual events, unless a sufficient number of theoretical terms (but not necessarily all of them) are co-ordinated with observable traits of things.

[2] A more detailed analysis is contained in my *The Structure of Science* (New York, 1961), especially Chaps. 5 and 6.

Thus, although the theoretical terms "instantaneous acceleration" and "perfectly divisible commodity" describe nothing that can be identified in experience, the expressions do in fact correspond to empirically determinable features in certain actual processes as a consequence of various rules employed (usually tacitly) by physicists and economists. In addition to the two subgroups already mentioned, a theory will in general therefore also contain a third subgroup of statements (though commonly not fully formulated) that indicate among other things such correspondences. It must be emphasized, however, that these statements do not define theoretical terms by way of terms signifying observable traits, so that theoretical terms cannot be eliminated from formulations in which they occur with the help of these statements.[3]

3. One further point deserves mention in this connection. In most disciplines, theoretical formulations (particularly those in the first two subgroups) are normally treated as statements about some subject matter, so that as in the case of other statements questions about the truth or falsity of such formulations are regarded as significant though difficult to answer. On the other hand, theoretical formulations are sometimes denied the status of "genuine" statements and are said to be simply rules which are instrumental for drawing inferences from genuine statements but which cannot be properly characterized as true or false. It is impossible in the space available to examine the merits of these opposing views on the status of theories. I have mentioned them to call attention to the fact that a defense of the methodological principle under discussion is intelligible only on the supposition that economic theory is a set of genuine statements, so that considerations of their truth or falsity are not irrelevant to the objectives of economic analysis.

II

Professor Friedman rests his argument for the methodological principle on some general reflections concerning the nature of theories *überhaupt*. He notes that a theory cannot explain a class of phenomena, unless it abstracts a small number of "common and crucial elements" (in terms of which the phenomena may be predicted) from the mass of differing circumstances in which the phenomena are embedded. Ac-

---

[3] This point is of major importance. Professor Friedman also recognizes a category of statements in a theory roughly equivalent to the third subgroup of theoretical statements distinguished above; but he appears to believe that theoretical terms can be eliminated with the help of statements in this category. The point at issue cannot be adequately discussed in short compass, but an example will perhaps make clear why such a belief is dubious. Quantum theory is stated in terms of various theoretical terms, referring to such elementary particles as electrons. However, although physicists are certainly able to apply quantum theory to observable processes with the aid of statements in the third subgroup, such statements of correspondence do not permit the elimination of terms like "electron" from quantum theory.

cordingly, the assumptions of a satisfactory theory are inescapably "descriptively false" or "unrealistic," so that it is pointless to assess the merits of a theory by asking whether or not its assumptions' are realistic. The relevant question is whether or not the theory yields predictions which are "sufficiently good approximations for the purpose at hand."[4]

However, an assumption may be unrealistic in at least three senses important for the argument, though Professor Friedman does not distinguish them.

1. A statement can be said to be unrealistic because it does not give an "exhaustive" description of some object, so that it mentions only some traits actually characterizing the object but ignores an endless number of other traits also present. However, no finitely long statement can possibly formulate the totality of traits embodied in any concretely existing thing; and it is difficult to imagine what a statement would be like that is not unrealistic in this sense, or what conceivable use such a statement could have. But in any event, it is with this rather trivial sense of the word in mind that Professor Friedman seems frequently to defend the legitimacy of unrealistic assumptions in economic theory;[5] and although it is not clear whether any economists have maintained a contrary thesis, his defense is fully conclusive.

2. A statement may be said to be unrealistic because it is believed to be either false or highly improbable on the available evidence. Such lack of realism can sometimes be established on the basis of what Professor Friedman calls a "directly perceived descriptive inaccuracy"; but in general, statements can be shown to be false only "indirectly," by first deducing from them some of their logical consequences (or implications), and then comparing the latter with "directly" observed matters of fact. Since it is usually not possible to establish the falsity of theoretical statements directly, Professor Friedman correctly stresses the relevance of this indirect procedure for ascertaining whether a theory is unrealistic. Nevertheless, as he recognizes and even illustrates,[6] the distinction between an assumption and its implications is a sharp one only in a given formulation of a theory —an implication of some assumption in one formulation may in another formulation be a premise implying that assumption. Accordingly, his repeated claim that an assumption can be rightly tested for its realism only indirectly obviously needs qualification.

But in any event, if by an assumption of a theory we understand one of the theory's fundamental statements (i.e., those belonging to

[4] Pp. 14-15.
[5] Pp. 18, 25, 32, 35.
[6] Pp. 26-27.

the first of the three subgroups previously noted), a theory with an unrealistic assumption (in the present sense of the word, according to which the assumption is false) is patently unsatisfactory; for such a theory entails consequences that are incompatible with observed fact, so that on pain of rejecting elementary logical canons the theory must also be rejected. On the other hand, a universal conditional neither asserts nor presupposes that the conditions explicitly stated in its antecedent clause are actually realized; accordingly, a theoretical statement having this logical form is not proved to be false by showing that the specifications in its antecedent are not embodied in some given spatiotemporal region (or for that matter, in any region). Professor Friedman is therefore quite right in maintaining that a theory is not necessarily erroneous merely because its assumptions are unrealistic— provided that he is taken to mean by an "assumption of a theory," as he sometimes appears to mean, an antecedent clause of some theoretical statement. However, a theory whose assumptions are in this sense unrealistic for a given domain is simply inapplicable in that domain, though it may be applicable in another. But what is to be said of a theory whose assumptions are ostensibly unrealistic for every domain? The aspect of this question that is especially relevant to Professor Friedman's essay is best treated after the third sense of unrealistic has been explained.

3. In many sciences, relations of dependence between phenomena are often stated with reference to so-called "pure cases" or "ideal types" of the phenomena being investigated. That is, such theoretical statements (or "laws") formulate relations specified to hold under highly "purified" conditions between highly "idealized" objects or processes, none of which is actually encountered in experience. For example, the law of the lever in physics is stated in terms of the behavior of absolutely rigid rods turning without friction about dimensionless points; similarly, a familiar law of pricing in economics is formulated in terms of the exchange of perfectly divisible and homogenous commodities under conditions of perfect competition. Statements of this kind contain what have previously been called "theoretical terms," which connote what are in effect the limits of various nonterminating series and which are not intended to designate anything actual. Such statements may be said to be unrealistic but in a sense different from the two previously noted. For they are not distinguished by their failure to provide exhaustive descriptions, nor are they literally false of anything; their distinguishing mark is the fact that when they are strictly construed, they are applicable to nothing actual.

However, laws of nature formulated with reference to pure cases are not therefore useless. On the contrary, a law so formulated states how phenomena are related when they are unaffected by numerous factors, whose influence may never be completely eliminable but whose effects generally vary in magnitude with differences in the attendant circumstances under which the phenomena actually recur. Accordingly, discrepancies between what is asserted for the pure case and what actually happens can be attributed to the influence of factors not mentioned in the law. Moreover, since these factors and their effects can often be ascertained, the influence of the factors can be systematically classified into general types; and in consequence, the law can be viewed as the limiting case of a set of other laws corresponding to these various types, where each further law states a modified relation of dependence between the phenomena because of the influence of factors that are absent in the pure case. In short, unrealistic theoretical statements (in the third sense of the word) serve as a powerful means for analyzing, representing, and codifying relations of dependence between actual phenomena.

III

Professor Friedman's discussion of unrealistic assumptions in examples of theoretical statements drawn from physics and biology sheds important light on his defense of such assumptions in economic theory. It will therefore be useful to examine his account of one of these examples.

1. In his discussion of Galileo's law, Professor Friedman notes that the law is stated for bodies falling in a vacuum, but also declares that the law "works" in a large number of cases (i.e., it is in sufficiently good agreement for certain purposes with the actual behavior of bodies in these cases), though not in others. He therefore suggests that the law can be restated to read: Under a wide range of circumstances, bodies that fall in the actual atmosphere behave *as if* they were falling in a vacuum. Indeed, he seems to think that the law can be rephrased without mentioning a vacuum, as follows: Under a wide range of circumstances, the distance a body falls in a specified time is given by the formula $s = \frac{1}{2}gt^2$. Accordingly, he maintains that the circumstances in which the law works (and is therefore acceptable) must be specified as "an essential part" of the law, even though this specification (and in consequence also the law) may need revision in the light of further experience.[7]

However, as has already been indicated, the term "vacuum" is a theoretical one, so that Galileo's law in its standard version is formulated for pure cases of falling bodies. Professor Friedman's proposed paraphrase which omits all mention of a vacuum thus rests on the supposition that theoretical terms can in general be replaced by non-

[7] Pp. 18-19.

theoretical ones, without altering the meaning and function of the statements containing them. But the possibility of such a replacement is dubious on formal grounds alone; and what is more important, the suggestion that unless theoretical terms can thus be eliminated the statements containing them are scientifically otiose, overlooks the rationale for stating laws in terms of pure cases. In point of fact, the proposed paraphrase mistakenly assumes that Galileo's law can be assigned the functions actually performed by statements of correspondence (belonging to the third subgroup of theoretical statements) without impairing the effectiveness of the standard formulation for achieving systematic generality in theoretical physics.

2. The example Professor Friedman uses for the most part in his defense of unrealistic assumptions in economics is the familiar "rational maximization of returns" hypothesis in the theory of the firm. However, he states it as follows: "Under a wide range of circumstances, individual firms behave *as if* they were seeking rationally to maximize their expected returns and had full knowledge of the data needed to succeed in this attempt."[8] He freely admits that as a rule businessmen lack such knowledge and do not perform the intricate calculations required for ascertaining the indicated maximum. Indeed, he declares that "the apparent immediate determinants of business behavior" could be anything at all; e.g., ingrained habit or a chance influence. He nevertheless claims that these admitted facts do not affect the validity of the hypothesis. The relevant evidence, according to him, is the large set of facts in good agreement with various implications of the hypothesis, including the fact that firms whose actions are markedly inconsistent with it do not survive for long.

It is pertinent to ask, however, whether the operative premise from which these implications really follow is perhaps the supposition, suggested by Professor Friedman's discussion, that is rendered by: "Under a wide range of circumstances, the behavior of individual firms brings them returns approximately equal to a certain magnitude (called the maximum of expected returns by economists)"; or whether the operative premise is the hypothesis as he formulates it. On the first alternative, most of the matters mentioned in his "as if" formulation are irrelevant to the substantive content of the hypothesis. In particular, the hypothesis must then not be understood as either asserting or implying that firms conduct their affairs in order to achieve some objective. To be sure, the statement of the hypothesis contains the expression "the maximum of expected returns"; nevertheless, this expression simply designates a set of rules used by economists rather than by firms for calculating a certain magnitude. In short, the hy-

[8] P. 21.

pothesis in this case is a somewhat loosely expressed empirical generalization about the returns firms actually receive as the outcome of
their overt behavior, and it specifies no determinants in explanation of
that behavior.[9] Accordingly, although the hypothesis is not an exhaustive description of anything, it is not clear in what sense other than
this trivial one the hypothesis is in this case unrealistic if, as Professor
Friedman claims, it is in good agreement with experience. On the
second alternative, however, it is difficult to avoid reading the hypothesis as saying that firms do seek to maximize their returns in a rational
manner, since otherwise it appears to be asserting nothing whatsoever.
But the hypothesis must then be understood as dealing with pure cases
of economic behavior, requiring the use of theoretical terms in its
formulation which cannot be replaced by nontheoretical expressions.
Accordingly, the various facts Professor Friedman freely admits but
thinks are irrelevant may in this case be quite pertinent in assessing
the merits of the hypothesis.

Professor Friedman's essay does not indicate explicitly which alternative renders the hypothesis as he understands it. In consequence, the
essay is marked by an ambiguity that perhaps reflects an unresolved
tension in his views on the status of economic theory. Is he defending
the legitimacy of unrealistic theoretical assumptions because he thinks
theories are at best only useful instruments, valuable for predicting
observable events but not to be viewed as genuine statements whose
truth or falsity may be significantly investigated? But if this is the
way he conceives theories (and much in his argument suggests that it
is), the distinction between realistic and unrealistic theoretical assumptions is at best irrelevant, and no defense of theories lacking in realism
is needed. Or is he undertaking that defense in order to show that
unrealistic theories cannot only be invaluable tools for making predictions but that they may also be reasonably satisfactory explanations
of various phenomena in terms of the mechanisms involved in their
occurrence? But if this is his aim (and parts of his discussion are
compatible with the supposition that it is), a theory cannot be viewed,
as he repeatedly suggests that it can, as a "simple summary" of some
vaguely delimited set of empirical generalizations with distinctly specified ranges of application.[10]

Curiously enough, something like the notion that theories can be
viewed in this manner underlies one criticism of Professor Friedman's

[9] In particular, the hypothesis does not include the assumption, integral to many formulations of neoclassical theory, that firms are purposive agents, whose decisions are based
on rationally formed estimates of the relative advantages and risks associated with alternative courses of action open to them. See, for example, Frank H. Knight, *Risk, Uncertainty
and Profit* (London, 1957), and Paul A. Samuelson, *Foundations of Economic Analysis*
(Cambridge, Mass., 1947), Chap. III.
[10] P. 24.

defense of the maximization-of-returns hypothesis. Thus Professor Koopmans argues that if (as Professor Friedman holds) the fact that firms whose behavior diverges from it are not likely to survive is a basis for accepting the hypothesis, "we should postulate that basis itself and not the profit maximization which it implies in certain circumstances."[11] This seems like a recommendation that since a basis for accepting Newtonian gravitational theory is the fact that observed regularities in the motions of the planets are in agreement with various special laws deduced from the theory, we should postulate those regularities rather than the theory—a recommendation that would replace the theory by the empirical evidence for the theory. Such a proposal not only rejects the conception that theories have an explanatory function; it also overlooks the irreplacable role theories have in scientific inquiry in suggesting how empirical generalizations may need to be corrected, as well as in directing and systematizing further empirical research. Unless I have seriously misunderstood Professor Friedman's essay, he would reject a proposal of this sort. Nevertheless, at various points in his argument he seems to construe theoretical statements in a manner that is almost indistinguishable from what is implied by such a proposal. I have therefore tried in this paper to show where his argument lacks cogency, as well as to indicate why the main thesis he is ostensibly defending is nonetheless sound.

[11] Tjalling C. Koopmans, *Three Essays on the State of Economic Science* (New York, 1957), p. 140.

Papandreou's paper. Unreality of premises is not a virtue in scientific theory; it is a necessary evil—a concession to the finite computing capacity of the scientist that is made tolerable by the principle of continuity of approximation.

Working scientists employ the principle of continuity all the time. Unfortunately, it has no place in modern statistical theory. The word "significant" has been appropriated by the statisticians to mean "unlikely to have arisen by chance." Now, in testing extreme hypotheses—ideal types—we do not primarily want to know whether there are deviations of observation from theory which are "significant" in this sense. It is far more important to know whether they are significant in the sense that the approximation of theory to reality is beyond the limits of our tolerance. Until this latter notion of significance has been properly formalized and incorporated in statistical methodology, we are not going to accord proper methodological treatment to extreme hypotheses. The discussion at this session has not provided the solution, but it has identified this problem as one of central methodological importance for economics.

PAUL A. SAMUELSON: When Maxwell's Demon rank orders scientific disciplines by their "fruitfulness" and by their propensity to engage in methodological discussion, he finds a negative correlation and a strong inverse relationship. It is as if a science could lift itself by its own bootstraps: by maintaining a superlative silence on method, a science can become superlatively fruitful and accurate. Like many "as if" statements this is nonsense. It is more correct, albeit not very informative, to say that soft sciences spend time in talking about method because Satan finds tasks for idle hands to do. Nature does abhor a vacuum and hot air fills up more space than cold. When libertines lose the power to shock us, they take up moral pontification to bore us.

But, of course, I jest. Methodological discussion, like calisthenics and spinach, is good for us, and Dr. Nagel deserves our thanks for taking the time away from other sciences to help straighten us economists out. It is the Lord's work, and we are grateful.

As I understand his paper, Nagel comes to save Milton Friedman from himself. Nagel believes that "theory" does have an important role to play in economics and any discipline, but that Friedman's attempt in his essay on positive economics to vindicate the importance of abstract theory involves mistakes which might themselves be wrongly held against theory's establishable role.

I think Nagel's paper is valuable in pointing out certain errors in the stated claims for theory. I think, within the limits imposed by his need for brevity, it performs the constructive function of sketching some valid arguments for the useful role of theories in an empirical science. But Professor Nagel is too polite. He has not, to my mind, vindicated against itself that which was special and distinctive in the Friedman methodology; instead he seems to have jettisoned what might be called the special "Friedman Twist." And rightly so, I am afraid.

Let me first state some valid interpretations of the "as if" character of using theory to help organize our descriptions of empirical reality. Then point out some illegitimate interpretations.

When a writer on positive economics says that hypotheses or theories should be judged on their "consequences"—or their ability to describe well and organize well empirical observations—he is saying something valuable. Valuable, but perhaps not new. Pragmatists have long insisted that a theory's worth is measured by the consequences of believing it rather than something else or nothing else. Scientists and philosophers who never read Peirce, James, Dewey, Mach, Bridgman, or Carnap have enunciated this same view.

Heinrich Hertz said that a belief in Maxwell's theory of light meant nothing more and nothing less than that the observable measurements agreed with the partial differential equations of Maxwell. (With the advent of quantum mechanics and wave theory the situation became one of *reductio non ad absurdum*: physicists didn't know or much care what it was that was waving in Schrodinger's equation, a probability or what not, so long as the facts of refraction and emission could be described well by this mnemonic model.) Poincaré said that the whole content of classical dynamics was summed up in the hypothesis that certain sets of second-order differential equations exhibited solutions that to a good approximation duplicated the behavior of celestial bodies and terrestrial particles. Pascal made generous use of Occam's Razor in his "explanation" of why "nature abhors a vacuum [period or up to 30 inches of mercury and 30 feet of water]" was an inferior theory to one which assumes that there is an equilibrium balance reached between the "weight" of the unseen atmosphere and the seen mercury and water columns. When Newton wrote down his system of the world, he explicitly said what would have to be translated into modern terminology as, "I don't care to speculate why *n*-bodies behave in accordance with the inverse-square law of gravity and acceleration; I am content to show what are the implications of this law in contrast to the implications of variant hypotheses, and to present my calculations demonstrating agreement with the observations of moons, apples, and planets."

So long as light rays continue to act so as to go from place to place by the paths of least time, except as a figure of speech no one insisted that they exercised conscious, self-conscious, deliberative will. At worst, some scientists who were Deists, or Sunday poets, said that God or Nature acted like a Great Economizer.

None of the above is banal or trite. As against other authorities who insisted on seeking "more ultimate explanations," these writers said what needed to be said and Professor Friedman is a welcome recruit to their camp. But what I and other readers believe is his new twist—which from now on I shall call the "F-Twist," avoiding his name because this may be, and I hope it is, a misinterpretation of his intention—is the following: A theory is vindicable if (some of) its consequences are empirically valid to a useful degree of approximation; the (empirical) unrealism of the theory "itself," or of its "assumptions," is quite irrelevant to its validity and worth.

At points, the F-Twist seems to go even farther and claim: It is a positive merit of a theory that (some of) its content and assumptions be unrealistic since only if it is not tailored closely to one small bit of reality can it give a useful fit to a wide spread of empirical situations. Unless we explain complex reality by something simpler than itself we have accomplished little (period or by theorizing).

The last part of this F-Twist is separable from its basic part. While I believe that this last part is misphrased and that its germ of truth should be stated in other terms, brevity forbids my discussing it here and forces me to concentrate on the basic F-Twist, which is fundamentally wrong in thinking that unrealism in the sense of factual inaccuracy even to a tolerable degree of approximation is anything but a demerit for a theory or hypothesis (or set of hypotheses). Some inaccuracies are worse than others, but that is only to say that some sins against empirical science are worse than others, not that a sin is a merit or that a small sin is equivalent to a zero sin.

To a philosopher or scientist, the F-Twist is of no great moment and its discussion might perhaps be bypassed. To present-day economics—and I daresay to Professor Friedman—its validity would be of considerable moment. For, as Rotwein (*Q.J.E.*, 1959) and others have hinted, the nonpositivistic Milton Friedman has a strong effective demand which a valid F-Twist brand of positivism could supply. The motivation for the F-Twist, critics say, is to help the case for (1) the perfectly competitive laissez faire model of economics, which has been under continuous attack from outside the profession for a century and from within since the monopolistic competition revolution of thirty years past; and (2), but of lesser moment, the "maximization-of-profit" hypothesis, that mixture of truism, truth, and untruth.

If Dr. Friedman tells us this was not so; if his psychoanalyst assures us that his testimony in this case is not vitiated by subconscious motivations; even if Maxwell's Demon and a Jury in Heaven concur—still it would seem a fair use of the F-Twist itself to say: "Our theory about the origin and purpose of the F-Twist may be 'unrealistic' (a euphemism for 'empirically dead wrong'), but what of that. The consequence of our theory agrees with the fact that Chicagoans use the methodology to explain away objections to their assertions."

This, however, is cheap humor. It is hard lines to hoist a man on his own petard, while at the same time arguing that there exists no such valid petard. I must be brief in explaining why the F-Twist lacks validity. Many of these arguments can actually be found in Friedman's essay, as Nagel has noted; but that may only indicate a noble inconsistency rather than invulnerability. Besides, I am discussing the F-Twist, not any person's views, and by any other name, such as the S-Twist, it would be just as bad.

1. Define a "theory" (call it B) as a set of axioms, postulates, or hypotheses that stipulate something about observable reality. (If no conceivable observation can even in principle refute, confirm, or touch or bear upon the axiom system taken as a whole, then B is not economics, astronomy, physics, biology, or anything properly called science. It might be a model of language,

logic, mathematics, mathematical probability or geometry, or game-playing—but that is something different.)

2. A reader of Friedman might be forgiven for lapsing into thinking that the thing called B has consequences (call them C) that somehow come after it or are implied by it and (*sic*) are somehow different from it.

3. That same reader might be forgiven for thinking that just as B has consequences C that come after it, it also has some things which are somehow antecedent to it called its "assumptions" (and which we can label A).

4. The F-Twist says that the empirical realism, at least up to some "tolerable degree of approximation," of C is important. If C is empirically valid (realistic) then B is important even if A—and for that matter B itself—is not empirically valid (is unrealistic in the sense of being empirically at variance with known or knowable facts, at any tolerable level of approximation).

5. If C is the complete set of consequences of B, it is identical with B. B implies itself and all the things that itself implies. There can be no factual correctness of C so defined that is not also enjoyed by B. The minimal set of assumptions that give rise to B are identical with B, and if A is given this interpretation, its realism cannot differ from that of the theory B and consequence C.

6. But now consider a proper subset of C, which contains some but not all of the implications of B and which we may call $C-$. And consider a widened set of assumptions that includes A as a proper subset, so that it implies A (and B and C and $C-$) but is not fully implied by A. Call this $A+$.

In symbolic notation we can say

$$A + \supset A \equiv B \equiv C \supset C-$$

7. Now, suppose that C has complete (or satisfactory) empirical validity. Then bully for it. And bully for the theory B and for its assumption A.

8. We cannot say bully for $A+$ in the same sense—unless its full content, which we may call $A+ \equiv B+ \equiv C+$, also have empirical validity. If that part of $C+$ which is not in C is unrealistic in the sense of being impirically false at the required level of approximation, then $A+$ is definitely the worse for it. The invalidity of part of $A+$ is not irrelevant to its worth. If only the A subset of $A+$ is valid, then so much the worse for $(A+) - (A)$ and for $A+$.

If as often happens we do not have evidence on the factual inaccuracy or accuracy for $A+$, we simply reserve judgment about it, and keep saying bully for A. If no evidence can bear on $(A+) - (A)$, then we use Occam's Razor and concentrate on $A \equiv B \equiv C$ above, forgetting $A+$.

9. It should be unnecessary for me to explain why the empirical validity of $C-$ does not, of itself, import any luster to $A \equiv B \equiv C$—unnecessary because this is the same logical case as I have just disposed of.

This completes my demonstration that the F-Twist is fallacious. I shall illustrate briefly with some examples, primarily economic.

Let B be maximizing ordinal utility (satisfying certain regularity conditions) subject to a budget constraint defined by given income and prices.

Let C be the Weak and Strong Axioms of revealed preference, which are stated in testable form involving $\Sigma P_j Q_j$, price-quantity data. My above arguments will show how misleading it is to think such tests are in any genuine sense "indirect" ones.

It happens that C implies B as well as being implied by it. It is nonsense to think that C could be realistic and B unrealistic, and nonsense to think that the unrealism of B could then arise and be irrelevant.

But suppose the Weak Axiom, $C-$, is valid and the Strong Axiom is definitely not. If the F-Twist means anything, it says, "Never mind that B is unrealistic; its consequence $C-$ is realistic and that is all that counts."

Surely this is nonsense. B has been shown to be empirically false. That $C-$, one of its implications, is valid does not in any way atone for the fact that $(C) - (C-)$ is definitely false. Only that part of B which is $C-$ has been vindicated by the validity of $C-$. That other part $(B) - (B-)$, has been refuted. The only sensible thing to do, I mean the only thing to do, is jettison $(B) - (B-)$ and replace as your theory $B-$. If you say, "But $B-$ is a truncated fragment of the organic whole B, and it is odd to call $B-$ my theory," I simply reply: "How do you define organic wholes, and anyway I'd rather have the valid tail of a theory than have an invalid dog's body attached to that tail. What is required is not Occam's Razor so much as God's Hatchet."

Similar examples could be given where it is a question of maximizing profit and not utility. Let me add as an aside that I should be astonished to find a beast who consistently satisfied the Weak Axiom and consistently violated the Strong Axiom. That beast has a nonintegrable preference field. While I can see why a man with a mind should exercise it consistently, I fail to see why a beast with no mind should satisfy the Weak Axiom or even consistency of demand choices. I am here applying Samuelson's Razor, which, unlike Occam's which is primarily aesthetic, is based on a lifetime of sad experience: All economic regularities that have no common-sense core that you can explain to your wife will soon fail. This cannot be said of all that you can explain to her; so my statement is not an empty one. It is considerations like this which make me think that the Alchian doctrine of survival adds something to the maximization hypothesis.

Almost all the remarks about the $S = \dfrac{1}{2} g t^2$ law for falling bodies that Friedman thinks support his thesis seem to me misleading. They could as well, or poorly, apply to a purely empirical theory that says: The first terms in a Taylor's expansion for motion of a body at rest released at $S = 0$ are of the form $S = 0 + 0t + \dfrac{1}{2} g t^2 +$ remainder. Galileo's simple theory, $S''(t) = + g$, has a subset of consequences that is in tolerable agreement with some facts; e.g., for t "small," $S''(t) = + g$. But it, B, is vastly inferior as every parachute jumper, golfer, and schoolboy knows, to B^* which says $S'' = - f(S') + g, f(0) = 0, f'(S') > 0$ and which correctly predicts $S'''(t) \neq 0$ and, $t \xrightarrow{\lim} \infty S'(t) =$ a constant; etc., etc.

To reject, as I was taught to do in Chicago, monopolistic competition on the ground that it is not a "nice, simple, unified" theory like that of perfect competition, is like insisting that $f(S') \equiv 0$ because that is simpler and more manageable. If perfect competition is the best simple theory in town, that is no excuse for saying we should regard it as a good theory if it is not a good theory. To use the F-Twist to minimize its imperfections or irrelevancies is, as I have argued, simply wrong.

We must not impose a regularity—or approximate regularity—in the complex facts which is not there. Good science discerns regularities and simplicities that are there in reality—I almost said "out there." Epicycles are more horrid than perfect circles, but the ancient astronomers were right to abandon perfect circles and not say, "Well, even if wrong or imperfect, they are the best wheels in town."

Post-Copernicans were also wrong to go to the stake for the belief that Keplerian ellipses, B, were a more correct theory than epicycles, $B*$. Relativism should have told both sides that this was a nonsense issue. Actually, $B*$ is merely a representation of B and deductively $B \equiv B*$. However, to imperfect human minds the $B*$ formulation "looks" simpler and has the great mnemonic virtues of "economical description" which Mach rightly recognizes as the essence of good science. Mach has few friends today: physicists who confuse the psychological process of arriving at notions with the validity of those notions find him sterile. I should record that my experience with economics led me to notions that seem much like Mach's.

There is a final point, which was perhaps not made explicitly by Nagel, Friedman, or Mach and yet which I feel I share with Einstein and practitioners of harder sciences.

Experience suggests that nature displays a mysterious simplicity if only we can discern it. This is a bonus and need not have been so. And unrealistic, abstract models often prove useful in the hunt for these regularities. (Sometimes they prove misleading to a whole generation of searchers.)

This psychological usefulness should not be confused with empirical validity. Black coffee may be useful to physicists, mathematicians, economists, and artists. But coffee is coffee. Such abstract models are like scaffolding used to build a structure; the structure must stand by itself. If the abstract models contain empirical falsities, we must jettison the models, not gloss over their inadequacies.

The empirical harm done by the F-Twist is this. In practice it leads to Humpty-Dumptiness. Lewis Carroll had Humpty-Dumpty use words any way he wanted to. I have in mind something different: Humpty-Dumpty uses the F-Twist to say, "What I choose to call an admissible amount of unrealism and empirical invalidity is the tolerable amount of unrealism."

The fact that nothing is perfectly accurate should not be an excuse to relax our standards of scrutiny of the empirical validity that the propositions of economics do or do not possess.

Professor Samuelson on Theory and Realism

In a discussion of "Problems of Methodology" at an AEA meeting [4], Paul Samuelson embarks on a critique of theories which employ unrealistic assumptions. He concludes with this strong indictment of "unrealistic, abstract models": "If the abstract models contain empirical falsities, we must jettison the models, not gloss over their inadequacies" [4, p. 236].

Let us first indicate how Samuelson reaches this judgment. He defines a theory "as a set of axioms, postulates, or hypotheses that stipulate something about observable reality [4, p. 233]. Denoting the theory as B, the "consequences" derived from it as C, and the "assumptions" antecedent to it as A, he argues that A, B, and C must actually be identical in meaning, mutually implying one another. Thus, he holds, if the assumptions are empirically false, and the theory therefore unrealistic, the deduced consequences cannot possibly be empirically valid. In other words, an unrealistic theory cannot yield realistic consequences.

Samuelson also considers the possibility that the assumptions are *wider* than the theory, and that the theory is *wider* than the consequence, so that there is a subset $C-$ of C, while A is a subset of $A+$. In this case $A+$ may imply B, without B implying $A+$; and C may imply $C-$, without $C-$ implying C. If $C-$ happens to be empirically valid, does this "validate" the wider theory B, or the even wider set of assumptions, $A+$? Samuelson explicitly rejects this. He regards as "nonsense" the claim that the validity of $C-$ justifies holding an unrealistic theory B, let alone the completely unwarranted set of assumptions $A+$.

What Samuelson does here is to reject *all theory*. A theory, by definition, is much wider than any of the consequences deduced. If the consequences were to imply the "theory" just as the theory implies the consequences, that theory would be nothing but another form of the empirical evidence (named "consequence") and could never "explain" the observed, empirical facts.

In addition, Samuelson errs in another way. We never deduce a consequence from a theory alone. We always combine the postulated relationships (which constitute the theory) with an assumption of some change or event and then we deduce the consequence of the *conjunction* of the theoretical relationships and the assumed occurrence. Thus, we do not infer C or $C-$ from B, but rather from the conjunction of B and some occurrence O. If $C-$ can be deduced from B *cum* O; and if both O and $C-$ are found to *correspond* to data of observaton which can be regarded as the empirical counterparts (referents, proxies) of the theoretical O and $C-$; then we rule that the theory B has sustained the test. This test does not prove that B is "true," but we have no reason to "jettison" B—unless we have a better theory B'.

Let us now leave aside the argument by which Samuelson reached his decision against "unrealistic, abstract models" and theories; let us, instead, confront Samuelson's judgment with Samuelson's pattern of theorizing when he discusses, not methodology, but substantive propositions of economics. Let us choose the brilliant performance with which he demonstrated an important proposition in the theory of international trade.

In his ingenious papers on international factor-price equalization [2] [3], Samuelson shows "that free commodity trade will under certain specified conditions, *inevitably* lead to *complete* factor-price equalisation" [2, p. 181]. He admits that "it would be folly to come to any startling conclusions on the basis of so simplified a model and such abstract reasoning," but he submits—very rightly, in my opinion—that "strong simple cases often point the way to an element of truth present in a complex situation" [2, p. 181].

What are his assumptions, hypotheses, conditions? Here is the list:

1. There are but two countries, America and Europe.
2. They produce but two commodities, food and clothing.
3. Each commodity is produced with two factors of production, land and labour. The production functions of each commodity show "constant returns to scale". . . .
4. The law of diminishing marginal productivity holds. . . .
5. The commodities differ in their "labour and land intensities". . . .
6. Land and labour are assumed to be qualitatively identical inputs in the two countries and the technological production functions are assumed to be the same in the two countries.
7. All commodities move perfectly freely in international trade, without tariffs or transport costs, and with competition effectively equalizing the market price-ratio of food and clothing. No factors of production can move between the countries.
8. Something is being produced in both countries of both commodities with both factors of production. . . .

From this he concludes: "Under these conditions, real factor prices must be exactly the same in both countries (and indeed the proportion of inputs used in food production in America must equal that in Europe, and similarly for clothing production)" [2, p. 182].

In his "intuitive proof" he goes so far as to state this: "I have *established unequivocally* the following facts:

Within any country: (a) a high ratio of wages to rents will cause a definite decrease in the proportion of labour to land in both industries; (b) to each determinate state of factor proportion in the two industries there will correspond one, and only one, commodity price ratio and a unique configuration of wages and rent; and finally, (c) that the change in factor proportions incident to an increase in wages/rents must be followed by a one-directional increase in clothing prices relative to food prices" [clothing being the more labor-using commodity, food the more land-using commodity] [2, p. 187].

It may be fair to state that Samuelson had characterized the problem as "a purely logical one" [2, p. 182]. But he sometimes uses language of empirical operations, for example, when he speaks of "observing the behaviour of a representative firm." It should be clear, however, that what he "observes" is merely the logical consequence of a set of assumptions; that the "behaviour" is purely fictitious; and that his representative firm is only an ideal type, a theoretical construct. Let me quote the sentence: ". . . if we *observe* the *behaviour* of a *representative firm* in one country it will be exactly the same in all essentials as a representative firm taken from some other country —regardless of the difference in total factor amounts and relative industrial concentration—provided only that factor-price ratios are really the same in the two markets" [2, pp. 187-88, emphasis supplied].

At the end of his discussion Samuelson evaluates some important qualifications which he finds help to "reconcile results of abstract analysis with the obvious facts of life concerning the extreme diversity of productivity and factor prices in different regions of the world" [2, p. 196]. These "qualifications" to the theorem furnish Samuelson with the "causes" of the factor-price diversities. In other words, he does not hesitate, quite rightly in my view, to explain the observed facts of life—factor-price differentials—by the divergences of real conditions from the ideal ones which form the basis of the factor-price equalization theorem.

Would the Samuelson of the *A-B-C* argument against unrealistic, abstract models approve of the Samuelson of the intuitive proof of the factor-price equalization theorem? Frankly, I do not know. Perhaps both Samuelsons make a distinction between a theorem and a theory, meaning by the former a proposition deduced from counterfactual assumptions and postulates, and by the latter a proposition stipulating something about observable reality. But the Samuelson of the *Foundations of Economic Analysis,* who preceded both other Samuelsons, did pledge allegiance to a program emphasizing "the derivation of *operationally meaningful* theorems" [1, p. 3].

Since, according to Samuelson, a theorem deduced from counterfactual hypotheses cannot yield empirically true consequences, and does not contain operationally defined terms, it is not immediately clear just what an "operationally meaningful theorem" is supposed to be. If it is supposed to be a "strong simple case" pointing the way to "an element of truth present in a complex situation" [2, p. 181], then we have no quarrel. For, I submit, this is what the bulk of economic theory does. It is based on counterfactual assumptions, contains only theoretical constructs and no operational concepts, and yields results which, we hope, point to elements of truth present in complex situations. To call such theorems "operationally meaningful" is to confer on them a designation which is slightly deceptive; but in any case it gives them the recognition which Samuelson, as critic of the Friedman position, or "the F-twist," wants to deny.

I conclude that Samuelson, one of the most brilliant theorists in present-day economics, produces his best work when he deduces from unrealistic assumptions general theoretical propositions which help us interpret some of the empirical observations of the complex situations with which economic life confronts us.

FRITZ MACHLUP*

* The author is professor of economics and international finance at Princeton University.

REFERENCES

1. Paul Samuelson, *Foundations of Economic Analysis*. Cambridge, Mass. 1947.
2. ———, "International Factor-Price Equalisation Once Again," *Econ. Jour.*, June 1949, *59*, 181-97.
3. ———, "International Trade and the Equalisation of Factor Prices," *Econ. Jour.*, June 1948, *58*, 163-84.
4. ———, "Problems of Methodology—Discussion," *Am. Econ. Rev., Proc.*, May 1963, *53*, 231-36.

Theory and Realism: A Reply

1. The art of jujitsu is to direct your opponent's strength against himself. As I read Fritz Machlup's attempt to use my earlier writings on international factor-price equalization and on operationally meaningful theorems to annihilate my recent contention that the contrafactual content of a theory is its shame and not its glory, I am all admiration for his pretty footwork. Indeed I feel like the friend of Abraham Lincoln, who said he could have foregone the pleasure of being run out of town on a rail if it weren't for the honor of it.

But the issue is a serious one, and I must record the impression that, after examining Machlup's argument, I see no reason to change my view or to acknowledge any inconsistency between my precept and my practice.

2. Let the issue be clear. No one expects that anything be *perfect*, much less a simplified theory. All scientists settle for some degree of approximation; and, by gad, they had better! However, the whole force of my attack on the F-twist (which I believe is not well rendered by the first sentence that got quoted from my paper) is that the doughnut of empirical correctness in a theory constitutes its worth, while its hole of untruth constitutes its weakness. I regard it as a monstrous perversion of science to claim that a theory is *all the better for its shortcomings;* and I notice that in the luckier exact sciences, no one dreams of making such a claim.

In connection with slavery, Thomas Jefferson said that, when he considered that there is a just God in Heaven, he trembled for his country. Well, in connection with the exaggerated claims that used to be made in economics for the power of deduction and a priori reasoning—by classical writers, by Carl Menger, by the 1932 Lionel Robbins (first edition of *The Nature and Significance of Economic Science*), by disciples of Frank Knight, by Ludwig von Mises—I tremble for the reputation of my subject. Fortunately, we have left that behind us. Still there is no reason to encourage tolerance of falsification of empirical reality, much less glorify such falsification.

3. My position is so innocuous as to be platitudinous. Yet from it, Machlup believes, must follow a rejection by me of all theory. (In my copy the last two words are double-underlined!) He says: "A theory, by definition, is much wider than any of the consequences deduced." By whose definition? Machlup's? God's? Webster's? Well, not by mine—as those who read my earlier note will have seen. And I have to confess to an even sharper disagreement with Dr. Machlup on this issue.

Scientists never "explain" any behavior, by theory or by any other hook. Every description that is superseded by a "deeper explanation" turns out upon careful examination to have been replaced by still another description, albeit possibly a more useful description that covers and illuminates a wider area. I can illustrate by what everyone will agree is the single most successful "theory" of all time. I refer to Newton's theory of universal gravitation.

Kepler's ellipses gave better descriptions of the planets than did the epicycles of the Greeks. Newton showed that second-order differential equations relating the accelerations of bodies to the inverse square of their distances from neighboring bodies could still better *describe* astronomical observations. After Newton had described "how," he did not waste his time on the fruitless quest of "why?" but went on to run the Mint and write about religion. Nor has anyone since Newton provided "the explanation."

The second greatest achievement of scientific theory was Maxwell's formulation of electromagnetism. Heinrich Hertz, the great discoverer of radio waves, made my methodological point in the strongest terms when he said, "All of Maxwell's theory boils down to the simple question of whether the observable measurements on light and waves do or do not satisfy Maxwell's partial differential equations."

My third and final example illustrates how a stubborn fact can kill a pretty theory. Mercury's orbit never quite agreed with Newtonian gravitation. An F-twister would have said: "So much the worse for the fact. The theory is even the better for its inadequacy." That, of course, is rot. One would not jettison Newton's theory until a better one was found to replace it, for the very good reason that Newton did describe many facts *correctly*. But any specialist on the perihelion of Mercury would prefer to use mechanical extrapolations to reliance on the false theory. Then along came Albert Einstein. His special theory of relativity described well (but did not "explain") a host of facts, including the perihelion of Mercury. For velocities small compared to the speed of light, Newton's theory came close to duplicating Einstein's. But when the factual chips were down, the simpler Newtonian equations had to be replaced by the Einstein-Lorenz equations *because the facts called for this*.

4. About my 1948 factor-price equalization analysis I can be brief. From certain empirical hypotheses taken as postulates, by cogent logic I *deduced* as theorems certain other empirical properties. After the demonstration, the implications were obvious. When one looks at the complicated real world, one finds it obvious that the hypotheses of the syllogism are far from valid; and, also, the consequences are far from valid. This is indeed a matter for regret and full disclosure of inaccuracy should be made. Nevertheless, and here I imagine Dr. Machlup and I for once will agree, a strong polar case like this one can often shed useful light on factual reality.

Thus, writing before the Marshall Plan and at a time when many were despairing of Europe's future, I was led by my factor-price model to make the diffident suggestion that moving goods by trade might be able to do nearly as much for living standards as moving Europeans to Australia and elsewhere. Any validity to such a lucky insight would have to be attributed to the degree of realism of the model, and I can only pray for my brain children that they be ever more realistic.

5. Since the emphasis of my *Foundations of Economic Analysis* on "operationally meaningful theorems" has been brought up, it gives me the opportunity to use my strength against my friendly critic. The doctrines of revealed preference provide the most literal example of a theory that has been stripped down to its bare implications for empirical realism: Occam's Razor has cut away every zipper, collar, shift, and fig leaf. In 1938 I had shown that the regular theory of utility maximization implied, for the two-good case, no more and no less than that "no two-observed points on the demand functions should ever reveal the following contradiction of the Weak Axiom":

$$P_1^a Q_1^a + P_2^a Q_2^a > P_1^a Q_1^b + P_2^a Q_2^b$$
$$P_1^b Q_1^b + P_2^b Q_2^b > P_1^b Q_1^a + P_2^b Q_2^a$$

In *Foundations*, I showed that the complete theory of regular utility for *any* number of goods could be exhausted by the empirical hypothesis that the following Slutsky-Hicks matrix of compensated-substitution terms be singular, symmetric, and nonpositive definite of rank $n-1$. *I.e.*, the demand functions $Q_i = Q_i(P_1, \cdots, P_n, I)$ satisfy

$$S = [S_{ij}] = \left[\frac{\partial Q_i}{\partial P_j} + Q_j \frac{\partial Q_i}{\partial I} \right] = [S_{ji}]$$

$$\sum_{j=1}^{n} S_{ij} P_j \equiv 0$$

$$\sum_1^n \sum_1^n S_{ij} P_i P_j x_i x_j < 0 \qquad \text{for } x_i \neq \lambda P_i, \quad \lambda \neq 0$$

In 1950, Professor H. S. Houthakker, in a brilliant maiden work, strengthened the Weak Axiom to show that the whole conventional theory, for any number of goods, boils down (aside from obvious regularity conditions of continuity and smoothness) to the testable requirement that one never observe the following contradiction of the Strong Axiom:

$$\sum P^a Q^a > \sum P^a Q^b, \quad \sum P^b Q^b > \sum P^b Q^c, \cdots, \sum P^z Q^z > \sum P^z Q^a.$$

I beg that Dr. Machlup take me literally and seriously when I assert that the conventional theory has *no* wider implications than these prosaic factual implications. Once the two formulations had been rigorously proved to imply each other mutually, that issue was settled.

6. The F-twist, in the crude form set up and massacred by me, represents an unlamented lost cause. Let me conclude by mentioning some genuinely puzzling methodological problems that Dr. Machlup and I might continue to argue about fruitfully.

a. Quine, Polanyi, Kuhn, Hanson,[1] and other students of science have

---

[1] W. V. O. Quine, *From a Logical Point of View* (New York, 1961), Ch. 2, "Two Dogmas of Empiricism"; M. Polanyi, "Tacit Knowing," *Reviews of Modern Physics*, Oct. 1962, *34*, 601-16; T. Kuhn, *The Structure of Scientific Revolutions* (Chicago 1962); N. R. Hanson, *Patterns of Discovery* (Cambridge, U.K. 1961).

been propounding variants of the view that what is a fact (and what is a truism!) is a very subjective thing. While I should guess that much of this discussion involves a confusion between the psychological problem of forming scientific notions and the valid findings of science, undoubtedly there are deep problems here that need further study.

b. Scientists constantly utilize parables, paradigms, strong polar models to help understand more complicated reality. The degree to which these do more good than harm is always an open question, more like an art than a science.

c. Finally, in some areas at least, Nature seems to show an inexplicable simplicity. This is a brute fact, more or less of a bonus, which if it had not existed could not have been expected. As a result, the working scientist learns as a matter of routine experience that he should have faith that the more beautiful and more simple of two equally (inaccurate) theories will end up being a more accurate describer of wider experience.

This bit of luck vouchsafed the theorist should not be pushed too far, for the gods punish the greedy.

PAUL A. SAMUELSON*

* The author is professor of economics at the Massachusetts Institute of Technology.

Diminishing Returns and Linear Homogeneity: Comment

In a recent issue of this journal, G. Warren Nutter [3] has provided a mathematical specification of a production function which seeks to justify the practice common in many price theory books of drawing the short-run product curve with a point of inflection *and* a maximum point, while assuming the long-run curve to involve constant returns to scale. He cites as the reason for his communication part of my footnote invitation to those who draw the curve in this way to *specify* their function [2, p. 126, n. 3] and a statement by Professors Stonier and Hague [5, p. 229] in which they flatly assert that the marginal product of the variable factor will always diminish when returns to scale are constant. (Both my footnote and its context make clear that a maximum point is also contemplated.)

Although Nutter implies that my view is identical to that of Stonier and Hague, he is wrong: My position is simply that "a thorough search of the literature has failed to reveal a single case in which a writer has *specified* a linearly homogeneous production function which produces such a total product curve." Nor has Nutter cited any examples. Indeed it can be done, but he, too, is unsuccessful in his *ex post* attempt to specify a function which will produce diagrams such as those contained in George Stigler's book [4, p. 115, Fig. 46] or in Richard Leftwich's book [1, p. 111, Fig. 34; p. 124, Fig. 36], which may presumably be taken as representative examples. Both depict the short-run curve as having a maximum point.

Nutter's entry, which he asserts is representative of a family which does exist and makes economic sense, is:

$$(1) \qquad x = 22a^{1/4}b^{3/4} - 20a^{1/3}b^{2/3},$$

PART II

METHODOLOGY IN THE POST-POSITIVIST ERA

Editor's introduction

In the middle of the twentieth century, a revolution quietly began in the philosophy of science. At the present time, it seems to have been a success. Positivism has been overthrown, and the 'growth of knowledge' approach appears to be the heir apparent, although other pretenders to the throne exist. The revolution has spread to the provinces of the special sciences. Its impact on the writings of economic methodologists has been profound. (Again, for surveys of the philosophical issues, see Blaug, 1980b, Caldwell, 1982, or Suppe, 1977.)

For one thing, the sheer number of contributions to the methodological literature has increased dramatically. The diversity of topics treated and approaches taken has also grown. Perhaps most exciting, the quality of methodological work has improved. These trends made my job as editor both easier and harder: I had a wide range of excellent material to choose from; but narrowing my selection to the handful of articles that follow was a painful task. Though I feel that the articles I have chosen are all excellent representatives of particular genres of methodological work, they are only the tip of the iceberg of a rich and varied literature.

The readings are divided into five groups, which are arranged thematically.

The first contains three articles on Friedman's methodology. The authors attempt to clarify, explicate or criticize Friedman's famous essay, using insights drawn from the philosophy of science. The reinterpretation of past methodological positions, using ideas developed in the philosophy of science, is a common theme in current methodological work.

The second set of readings contains an exchange between Lawrence Boland and me on possible criticisms of the maximization hypothesis. We agree that the hypothesis is untestable as currently stated, though we disagree about the reasons why it is untestable. We also disagree about what it means to criticize a hypothesis.

The third chapter contains two articles in which the growth of knowledge approaches of Thomas Kuhn and Imre Lakatos are applied to specific research programs in economics. This type of analysis began almost twenty years ago in economics, and in the early days often involved 'revolution counting' (how many scientific revolutions have occurred in economics?) or comparing the relative merit of the Kuhnian and Lakatosian models for describing past episodes of theory change. Economists now are less enamored with such holistic vision of scientific development. Even so, there are insights to be gained when such exercises are handled well, as these two selections amply illustrate.

Meta-methodological questions are taken up in the fourth group of readings, and two very different answers are given to the question: If positivism is dead, whither methodology? Mark Blaug argues that methodology must prescribe behavior, and that Popper's falsificationism is the appropriate prescriptive methodology for economics. Donald McCloskey disagrees completely. He maintains that economists talk nonsense when they debate such grand methodological issues; the real methodology of economics is rhetoric, and the sooner we recognize that noble heritage, the better. That these answers to a seemingly straightforward question are so different from one another shows how unsettled certain areas of methodological investigation are today.

The final chapter contains a potpourri of contributions. The 'tight prior' of neoclassical equilibrium theorizing is explicated in the first reading. In subsequent articles, alternative research programs, and alternative methodological approaches, are investigated. There is criticism and debate that reach across paradigms, and there is the description of salient features of particular alternatives to the orthodoxy. Finally, there is an entertaining piece that hints at a new area of investigation. The chapter is appropriately labelled 'A Diversity of Themes in Contemporary Methodology'.

The authors whose work is gathered together on these pages come from a wide variety of backgrounds. There are philosophers and theorists, econometricians and historians of thought. Some have worked intensively in the area of economic methodology, others might think it strange that I have included their work in this book of readings. What the authors share in common is this: each has combined a particular area of expertise with a desire to understand some fundamental aspect of economic science. The answers that come forth, indeed the types of questions asked, are as varied as the specializations of the authors. That no single answers have yet emerged may be taken by some as a sign of the hopeless confusion that permeates methodology. For me, it is a sign that the age of methodological naiveté is over. We have finally begun to recognize the complexity of the questions, and that is an unambiguous step towards maturity.

4

On Reinterpreting Friedman

Lawrence Boland, 'A Critique of Friedman's Critics', *Journal of Economic Literature*, vol. 17, June 1979, pp. 503–22.
Bruce Caldwell, 'A Critique of Friedman's Methodological Instrumentalism', *Southern Economic Journal*, vol. 47, October 1980, pp. 366–74.
Alan Musgrave, '"Unreal Assumptions" in Economic Theory: The F-Twist Untwisted', *Kyklos*, vol. 34, 1981, pp. 377–87.

Editor's comments

Even in flux there is constancy. An illustration of this truism is our profession's continuing fascination with Milton Friedman's 'The Methodology of Positive Economics'. The piece has been occasionally praised but more often assailed; it has been analyzed and assessed by dozens of economists; the famous and the obscure have offered their observations; the endless rounds of repudiation, reinterpretation and rehabilitation persist.

There is passion in this secondary literature. It is therefore appropriate to begin with one of the most provocative of the recent contributions, Lawrence Boland's 'A Critique of Friedman's Critics'. The seventh sentence of the article reads, '*Every* critic of Friedman's essay has been wrong'. As we read further, however, we see that Boland's claims are not really so controversial. He argues that Friedman is an instrumentalist, and that because none of Friedman's critics explicitly attacks his instrumentalism all of their assaults have failed.

I think that this part of Boland's argument is correct. In the second reading, I take the next logical step and offer some criticisms of Friedman's methodology. I view my article as a footnote to Boland's, one in which it is shown that instrumentalism can be and has been criticized. In later exchanges on separate but related topics, Boland has questioned my definition of criticism, and I have questioned his. (These questions are taken up in the next section.) It is a tribute to Friedman that his article can still generate debate, and on such a wide range of topics.

The final selection is by a philosopher. It is a beautiful piece: concise, lucid and thoughtful. Twenty years earlier, another philosopher, Ernest Nagel, had demonstrated that Friedman was ambiguous in his usage of the phrase 'realism of assumptions'. Nagel focused on the word 'realism' in his analysis of the problem. Musgrave's attempt to distinguish among the types of assumptions used by economists is another step forward. His comments on Friedman's 'lapse' into instrumentalism also provide a nice counterpoint to the first two articles. If Friedman's lapse was unnecessary, the door is open for yet another rehabilitation of Friedman, this one on non-instrumentalist grounds!

Journal of Economic Literature
Vol. XVII (June 1979), pp. 503–522

A Critique of
Friedman's Critics

By Lawrence A. Boland

Simon Fraser University

*I wish to thank Milton Friedman, Mark Blaug, David Laidler, Roger
Ransom, and my colleagues Terence Brown, Steve Easton, Zane Spin-
dler, and Herb Grubel for suggestions and criticisms of an earlier
draft. I am particularly grateful to Allan Sleeman of Western Washington University and Donna Wilson of Simon Fraser University
for their editorial assistance.*

Milton Friedman's essay, "Method-ology of Positive Economics" [4, 1953], is considered authoritative by al-most every textbook writer who wishes to discuss the methodology of economics. Nevertheless, virtually all the journal arti-cles that have been written about that es-say have been very critical. This is a rather unusual situation. The critics condemn Friedman's essay, but virtually all the textbooks praise it. Why should honest textbook writers ignore the critics? It will be argued here that the reason is quite clear. *Every* critic of Friedman's essay has been wrong. The fundamental reason why all of the critics are wrong is that their criticisms are not based on a clear, correct, or even fair understanding of his essay. Friedman simply does not make the mis-takes he is accused of making. His meth-odological position is both logically sound and unambiguously based on a coherent philosophy of science—Instrumentalism.

In order to defend Friedman from his critics, I shall outline some necessary back-ground knowledge—a clear understand-ing of the nature of logic and the philoso-phy of Instrumentalism—and then pre-sent a reader's guide to his essay. Based on this background knowledge and the reader's guide, I shall survey and com-ment upon the major critics of Friedman's methodology. I shall conclude with a sug-gestion as to how a fair criticism would proceed.

1. *The Usefulness of Logic*

1.1 Modus ponens: *Logic's Only Useful Property*

Aristotle was probably the first to sys-temize the principles of logic; most of them were common knowledge in his time. Logic has not changed much since then, although some presentations lead one to think that our logic is different.

503

504   *Journal of Economic Literature, Vol. XVII (June 1979)*

Modern writers too often discuss logic as if it had nothing to do with truth. But such a view of logic is an error. In Aristotle's view logic was the study of the principles of true and *successful* argument.[1]

Recognizing that arguments consist only of individual statements joined together with an "and" or an "or," Aristotle was concerned with determining what kinds of statements are admissible into logical arguments. He posited some rules that are in effect necessary conditions for the admissibility of statements into a logical argument. These rules, which later became known as the axioms or cannons of logic, cannot be used to justify an argument; they can only be used to criticize or reject an argument on the grounds of inadmissibility.[2]

The only purpose for requiring arguments to be logical is to connect the truth of the premises or assumptions to the truth of the conclusions. Merely joining together a set of admissible statements does not necessarily form a logical argument; the only criterion for whether an admissible argument is logical is whether it is a sufficient argument in favor of its conclusions in the following sense. *If* your argument is logical, then whenever *all* of your assumptions (or premises) are true *all* of your conclusions will be true as well.

To prove that an argument is logical, one must be able to demonstrate its sufficiency. Whenever one establishes the logical sufficiency of a formal (or abstract) argument, one can use that formal argument as a part of a larger empirical (or contingent) argument that is *in favor* of the truth of any particular conclusion of the formal argument.[3] That is to say, whenever you offer an empirical argument in favor of some proposition, you are purporting both that the form of the argument is logically valid *and* that your assumptions are true. In this sense, logical validity is a necessary (but not sufficient) condition for an empirical argument to be true.

Using a formal argument in favor of the truth of any of its conclusions by arguing from the truth of its assumptions is said to be using the argument in the affirmative mode—or more formally, in *modus ponens*. The ability to use any argument successfully in *modus ponens* is the primary necessary condition for the argument's logical validity or consistency (or for short, its "logicality"). However, this is not the only necessary condition for an argument's logicality. Whenever *modus ponens* is assured for a given argument, that argument can always be used in a denial or criticism of the truth of its assumptions. Specifically, *if* your argument is logical, then any time *any one* conclusion is false *not all* of your assumptions can be true (*i.e.*, at least one assumption must be false).[4] Using this mode of argument against the truth of one's assumptions by arguing from the falsity of a conclusion is called *modus tollens*. Whenever one successfully criticizes an argument by using *modus tollens*, one can conclude that either an assumption is false *or* the argument is not logical (or both).

---

[1] However, he also explained how one can win an argument by cheating—for example, by concealing the direction of the argument.

[2] Specifically, Aristotle said that in order for an argument to be logical, *the premises must not violate any of the following axioms:* First is the *axiom of identity, viz.*, different statements cannot use different definitions of the same words; second is the *axiom of the excluded-middle, viz.*, statements that cannot be true or false, or can be something else, are prohibited; and finally, the *axiom of non-contradiction, viz.*, statements cannot be allowed to be both true and false. Thus, any argument that contains such prohibited statements cannot qualify as a *logical* argument.

[3] Previously proven mathematical theorems are the major source of the formal proofs used in economics.

[4] These logical conditions are not independent of the axioms of logic. Each condition presumes that the statements of the argument are admissible. For example, each condition presumes that if a statement is not true it must be false.

1.2 *Beyond* modus ponens

In order to distinguish *modus ponens* from its corollary *modus tollens*, not only must we explicitly refer to truth and falsity, but we must also specify the *direction* of the argument. Heuristically speaking, *modus ponens* "passes" the truth *forward* from the assumptions to the conclusions.[5] *Modus tollens*, on the other hand, "passes" the falsity *backward* from the conclusions to one or more of the assumptions.[6] The important point here, which I shall argue is implicitly recognized by Friedman in his essay, is that if one changes the direction (forward or backward) of either valid mode of using a logical argument, then the logicality of one's argument ceases to be useful or methodologically significant. Specifically, any use of *modus ponens* in *reverse* is an example of what logic textbooks call "the Fallacy of Affirming the Consequent." Similarly, any use of *modus tollens* in *reverse* is an example of what is called "the Fallacy of Denying the Antecedent." It is especially important to note that truth cannot be "passed" backward nor can falsity be "passed" forward.[7]

The major point to be emphasized here is that while the truth of assumptions and conclusions is connected in the use of a logical argument in *modus ponens*, the truth of the same assumptions and conclusions is not connected if they are used in *reverse modus ponens*. Similarly, their falsity is not connected when used in *reverse modus tollens*.

I think an explicit recognition of the two *reverse* modes of argument is essential for a clear understanding of Friedman's essay. Any methodological criticism which presumes that any formal argument that can be used in *modus tollens* can also be validly used in *reverse modus ponens* is a serious methodological error. Recognition of this methodological error, an error which Friedman successfully avoids, is essential for an appreciation of his rejection of the necessity of testing (as I will show in *Section* 3).

1.3 *Objectives of an Argument: Necessity vs. Sufficiency*

Finally, there is another aspect of the logicality of an argument that is reflected in Friedman's essay. It has to do with the "necessity" and the "sufficiency" of statements or groups of statements. In some cases one is more concerned with the sufficiency of an argument; in other cases one is more concerned with the necessity of its assumptions. To illustrate, consider the following *extreme* dichotomization. There

---

[5] I say "heuristically" because otherwise it is quite incorrect to consider "truth" to be some*thing* that can be passed around. Properly speaking, "truth" is a property of statements only; that is, there is no "truth" without a statement that is true. And, the verb "to pass" suggests the passage of time as well as the involvement of direction, but the intention is to avoid the time aspects. The verb "to connect" preserves the timelessness, but it does not suggest direction.

[6] But usually when there are many assumptions, one does not know which assumption "caused" the false conclusion.

[7] To illustrate, since this may seem counterintuitive to someone unfamiliar with formal logic, let us consider a simple example of an argument, the statements of which individually do not violate the axioms of logic. Let the assumptions be

A_1: "All males have negatively sloped demand curves."
A_2: "Only males have negatively sloped demand curves."
A_3: "All my demand curves are negatively sloped."

And let the conclusion that would follow as a matter of logic alone be

---

C: "I am a male."

Now let us say we do not know whether the assumptions are true or false. But, let us say we know that the conclusion is true. Does knowing that the conclusion of a logical argument is true enable us to say that we also know that any of the assumptions are true? Unfortunately not. As the above illustrative argument demonstrates, even if the conclusion is true all the assumptions can be false! In other words, although one's argument is logical, one still cannot use its logicality to assert that the assumptions are true on the basis of a known true conclusion. Note also that this example shows that the falsity of any assumption is not necessarily "passed" on to the individual conclusions.

are basically two different affirmative types of argument: the conjunctive and the disjunctive.

Conjunctive type of argument: Because statement A_1 is true, *and* A_2 is true, *and* A_3 is true, *and* . . . , one can conclude that the statement C_1 is true.

Axiomatic consumer theory might be an example of such an argument where the A's include statements about the utility function and the existence of maximization is the conclusion. On the other hand,

Disjunctive type of argument: Because statement R_1 is true, *or* R_2 is true, *or* R_3 is true, *or* . . . , one can conclude that the statement C_2 is true.

A politician's reasons for why he is the best candidate might be an example of this type of argument. These two ways of arguing can be most clearly distinguished in terms of what is required for a *successful refutation* of each type of argument. The conjunctive type of argument is the easiest to refute or criticize. Ideally, a pure conjunctive argument consists of assumptions *each of which is offered as a necessary condition.* It is the conjunction of *all* of them that is *just* sufficient for the conclusion to follow. If any one of the assumptions were false, then the sufficiency of the argument would be lost. To refute a pure conjunctive argument, one needs only to refute *one* assumption. The disjunctive argument, on the other hand, is very difficult to refute. Because in the extreme case such an argument, in effect, offers every assumption as a *solitarily sufficient condition* for the conclusion to follow, none of the assumptions are necessary. If someone were to refute only *one* of the assumptions, the argument is not lost. In order to defeat a pure disjunctive argument, one must refute *every* assumption—clearly a monumental task.[8]

[8] This is even more important if we distinguish between the two different purposes for building arguments. A disjunctive argument might be used by a pure politician who wishes to convince us to vote

2. "Instrumentalism" and the Relationship between Logic, Truth, and Theories

2.1 The Problem of Induction

The discussion so far has not worried about how one knows the truth of the assumptions (or conclusions). Unfortunately, logic is of little help in determining the truth of a statement. Logic can only help by "passing" along known truths. This limitation of traditional logic leads to a consideration of the so-called *problem of induction:* the problem of finding a *form* of logical argument where (a) its conclusion is a *general* statement, such as one of the true "laws" of economics (or nature), or its conclusion is the choice of the true theory (or model) from among various competitors; and (b) its assumptions include *only* singular statements of *particulars* (such as observation reports). With an argument of this form one is said to be arguing inductively from the truth of particulars to the truth of generals. (On the other hand, a deductive form of argument proceeds from the truth of generals to the truth of particulars.) If one could solve the problem of induction, the true "laws" or general theories of economics could then be said to be induced logically from the particulars. But not only must one solve the problem of induction one must also acquire access to all the particulars needed for the application of the solution. Any "solution" that requires an infinity of particulars is at best impractical and

for him or his policy. A conjunctive argument might be the objective of a pure theorist who offers his argument as a test of his understanding of the world or the economy. If the theorist's understanding of the world is correct, he should be able to explain or predict certain relevant phenomena; the assumptions used will represent his understanding (for example, the so-called "laws" of economics, physics, etc.). If a prediction turns out wrong, with the use of *modus tollens* one can say there is something wrong with his understanding of the world. A pure politician, contrarily, may not care *why* someone votes for him or his policy so long as the vote is in his favor. *Success* is the politician's primary objective.

at worst an illusion. The requirement of an infinity of true particulars in order to provide the needed true assumptions for the application of *modus ponens* means in effect that such an inductive argument would not carry the force of *modus ponens*.

One might ask, just what determines whether or not a form of argument is logical? But I have already discussed this question above. Recall from *Section* 1.1 that the criterion or necessary condition for any logical argument is that it must be capable of fulfilling the promise of *modus ponens*. However, as far as anyone knows *modus ponens* is assured only by a "deductive" form of argument.

2.2 *"Inductivism"*

One can identify (at least) three different views of the relationship between logic, truth, and theories. The "inductivists" say that theories can be true and all true theories (or assumptions) are the result of applying inductive logic to observations. "Conventionalists" deny that a theory can be inductively proven, and they furthermore consider it improper to discuss the truth status of a theory. "Instrumentalists," such as Friedman, are only concerned with the usefulness of the conclusions derived from any theory. Unlike conventionalists, instrumentalists may allow that theories or assumptions can be true but argue that it does not matter with regard to the usefulness of the conclusions.

A clear understanding of inductivism, I think, is essential for the appreciation of every modern methodological point of view. Even when economists only argue deductively (that is, by using *modus ponens* and including assumptions that are necessarily in the form of general statements), it might still be asked, how do they know that the "laws" or other general statements used are true? The inductivist philosophers have always taken the position that there is a way to prove the truth of the needed general statements (as con-

clusions) using only assumptions of the form of singular statements (*e.g.,* observations). Such inductivists often think the only problem is to specify which kinds of singular statements will do the job, *i.e.,* those which are unambiguously true and capable of forming a sufficient argument for the truth of a given statement or conclusion.

What kinds of statements must economists rely on? Clearly, biased personal reports will not do even if their conjunction could be made to be sufficient. For this reason inductivist philosophers and many well known economists (following John Neville Keynes) distinguish between "positive" statements, which can be unambiguously true, and "normative" ones, which cannot. Singular positive statements would supposedly work because they can be objectively true. But, normative statements are necessarily subjective, hence they would not carry the same logical guarantee of unambiguous truth.

Contrary to the hopes of the inductivists, even though one can distinguish between positive and normative statements, there is no inductive logic that will guarantee the sufficiency of any finite set of singular statements. There is no type of argument that will validly proceed from assumptions that are singular to conclusions that are general statements. Specifically, there is no conjunction of a *finite* number of true singular statements from which unambiguously true general statements will validly follow with the assurance of *modus ponens*. Thus, distinguishing between positive and normative statements (as most economists do today) will not by itself solve the problem of induction[9]; and for this reason Friedman tries to go *beyond* this distinction.

[9] Few economists today are serious inductivists; yet most follow Friedman's lead by stressing the importance of distinguishing between normative and positive statements. It might be argued that for some economists the use of this distinction is merely an unexamined inductivist ritual.

2.3 The "Conventionalist" Alternative to Inductivism

Since no one has yet solved the problem of induction, one is always required to assume the truth of his premises or assumptions. In response to the failure to solve the problem of induction, some philosophers and economists go as far as to avoid using the world "truth" at all. They may, however, attempt to determine the "validity" of a theory or argument, since logic can (at least) help in that determination. Too often, many economists who are unaware of these methodological problems create much confusion by using the word "validity" when they mean "truth" (*e.g.,* see Friedman [4, 1953, pp. 10*ff*]). Their formal alternative to avoiding the word "truth" is to take the position that "truth" is a matter of convention; philosophers who take such a position are thus called "conventionalists." They view theories as being convenient catalogues or "filing systems" for positive reports. Of course, catalogues cannot be properly called true or false. They are to be judged or compared only by criteria of convenience such as simplicity or degrees of approximation or closensss of "fit," etc.

Conventionalism forms the foundation for most methodological discussions in economics today (*e.g.,* which criterion is best, simplicity or generality?). It is also the primary source of methodological problems because its usual application is built upon a fundamental contradiction. Conventionalists presume that it is possible to discuss logical validity without reference to truth or falsity. Yet, as noted above, the fundamental aspect of logic that defines "validity" (namely, the assurance of *modus ponens* or *modus tollens*) requires an explicit recognition of (a concept of) truth or falsity.[10] Conventional-

ism does not offer a solution to the problem of induction; it only offers a way to avoid discussing such philosophical obstacles. Although Friedman accepts and employs several conventionalist concepts, to his credit he constructs a methodological approach that goes beyond the sterile philosophy of conventionalism.

2.4 Instrumentalism and the Usefulness of Logic

For the purposes of discussing Friedman's point of view, one can consider any theory to be an argument in favor of some given propositions or towards specific predictions. As such a theory can be considered to consist only of a conjunction of assumption statements, *i.e.,* statements, each of which is *assumed* (or asserted) to be true. In order for the argument to be sufficient it must be a deductive argument, which means that at least some of the assumptions must be in the form of general statements. But, without an inductive logic, this latter requirement seems to raise in a modified form the methodological problems discussed above. When can one assume a theory is true? It is such difficulties that Friedman's essay attempts to overcome [4, 1953].

So long as a theory does its intended job, there is no apparent need to argue in its favor (or in favor of any of its constituent parts). For some policy-oriented economists, the intended job is the generation of true or successful predictions. In this case a theory's predictive success is always a sufficient argument in its favor. This view of the *role* of theories is called "instrumentalism." It says that theories are convenient and useful ways of (logically) generating what have turned out to be true (or successful) predictions or con-

---

[10] Truth substitutes, such as probabilities, will not do. Stochastic models, in which the assumptions are

in the form of probability distribution statements, usually cannot provide the logical force of either *modus ponens* or *modus tollens.* This point was stressed by early econometricians, but is usually ignored in most econometrics textbooks.

clusions. Instrumentalism is the primary methodological point of view expressed in Friedman's essay.

For those economists who see the object of science as finding the *one* true theory of the economy, their task cannot be simple. However, if the object of building or choosing theories (or models of theories) is only to have a theory or model that provides true predictions or conclusions, *a priori* truth of the assumptions is not required *if* it is already known that the conclusions are true or acceptable by some conventionalist criterion.[11] Thus, theories do not have to be considered true statements about the nature of the world, but only convenient ways of systematically generating the already known "true" conclusions.

In this manner instrumentalists offer an alternative to the conventionalist's response to the problem of induction. Instrumentalists consider the truth status of theories, hypotheses, or assumptions to be irrelevant for any practical purposes so long as the conclusions logically derived from them are successful. Although conventionalists may argue about the nature or the possibility of determining the truth status of theories, instrumentalists simply do not care. Some instrumentalists may personally care or even believe in the powers of induction, but such concern or belief is considered to be separate from their view of the role of theories in science.

For the instrumentalists, who think they have solved the problem of induction by ignoring truth, *modus ponens* will necessarily be seen to be irrelevant. This is because they do not begin their analysis with a search for the true assumptions but rather for true or useful (*i.e.*, successful) conclusions. *Modus tollens* is likewise ir-

relevant because its use can only begin with false conclusions. This also means that like the pure disjunctive argument, the instrumentalist's argument is concerned more with the sufficiency of any assumptions than with their necessity. This is because any analysis of the sufficiency of a set of assumptions begins by assuming the conclusion is true and then asks what set of assumptions will do the logical job of yielding that conclusion. Furthermore, any valid or fair criticism of an instrumentalist can only be about the suffiency of his argument. The only direct refutation allowable is one that shows that a theory is insufficient, *i.e.*, inapplicable. Failing that, the critic must alternatively provide his own sufficient argument, which does the same job.

By identifying three distinct philosophical views of theories, I am not trying to suggest that one must choose one (that would merely be reintroducing the problem of induction at a new level). Few writers have ever thought it necessary to adhere to just one view. Most writers on methodology in economics make some use of each view. For this reason it is sometimes necessary to sort out these views in order to make sense of methodological essays. I hope to show that even a superficial understanding of these philosophical views will help form a clear understanding of Friedman's essay [4, 1953].

3. A Reader's Guide to Friedman's Essay

3.1 An Overview

Friedman's essay is rather long and rambling [4, 1953]. However, he does manage to state his position regarding all of the issues I have discussed so far. Because the essay is long, it is hard to focus on its exact purpose, but I think it can best be understood as an instrumentalist's argument for instrumentalism. As such it tries to give a series of sufficient reasons for the acceptance of instrumentalism. And further-

---

[11] This was seen above as the limitation of *reverse modus ponens* in the illustrative argument about males and negatively sloped demand curves.

more, it can be fairly judged only on the basis of the adequacy or sufficiency of each reason for that purpose. We are told that the essay's motivation is to give us a way to overcome obstacles to the construction of a "distinct positive science" centering on the problem of "how to decide whether a suggested hypothesis or theory should be tentatively accepted as part of the 'body of systemized knowledge [of] . . . what is' " [4, p. 3]. The "distinct positive science," we are told, is essential for a policy science [4, pp. 5, 6–7]. This methodological decision problem is, in fact, an inductivist's problem.[12] Implicitly Friedman recognizes that we do not have an inductive logic [4, p. 9], and he offers what he considers to be an acceptable alternative. Basically Friedman's solution (to the problem of induction) is that our acceptance of a hypothesis for the purposes of policy application should be made a matter of "judgement." Judgements, he says, cannot be made *a priori* in the absence of a true inductive science.

3.2 *"Positive vs. Normative Economics": The Problem of Induction in Instrumentalist Terms*

In the introduction Friedman expresses his interest in the problem of induction and then, in Section I, he restates the problem in instrumentalist terms [4, p. 4]. He says the task of positive economics is to

> provide a system of generalizations that can be used to make correct predictions about the consequences of any change in circumstances. Its performance is to be judged by the precision, scope, and conformity with experience of the predictions it yields. [4, p. 4.]

The inductivist's distinction between positive and normative statements is the most important part of inductivism that is retained by Friedman. And he brings with

that distinction the inductivist's claim that normative economics depends on positive economics, but positive economics does not necessarily depend on the normative [4, p. 5]. In this light he notes that even methodological judgements about policy are also positive statements to be accepted on the basis of empirical evidence [4, pp. 6–7].

3.3 *"Positive Economics": Conventionalist Criteria Used with an Instrumentalist Purpose*

Friedman begins Section II with a mild version of conventionalism by saying that a theory (*i.e.*, a set of assumptions) can be viewed as a language whose

> function is to serve as a filing system for organizing empirical material . . . and the criteria by which it is to be judged are those appropriate to a filing system. [4, p. 7.]

But his viewing a theory as a language has its limitations. I would think that a distinguishing feature of all languages is that they are intended to be both consistent and complete (*e.g.*, there should be nothing that cannot be named or completely described); and this would preclude empirical applications as the theory would, in effect, yield only tautologies. To avoid this he adopts the now popular opinion that we must add "substantive hypotheses" [4, p. 8]. But here he again raises an inductivist's problem: how do we choose the substantive hypotheses? Friedman answers that positive statements ("factual evidence") can determine acceptance. He clearly indicates that he does understand the fundamentals of logic by implicitly using *modus tollens*. He says that a

> hypothesis is rejected if its predictions are contradicted. . . . [4, p. 9.]

But what about *modus ponens?* Well, that is considered inapplicable because there is no inductive logic. Friedman, using the word "validity" when he means "not in-

---

[12] Which would easily be solved if we only had an inductive logic.

consistent with facts" (which happens to be a necessary condition of true hypotheses), says

> The validity of a hypothesis in this sense is not by itself a sufficient criterion for choosing among alternative hypotheses. Observed facts are necessarily finite in number; possible hypotheses, infinite. [4, p. 9.]

In other words, one cannot directly solve the problem of induction.

All this means that the main task of a positive economics is left unfulfilled. At this point Friedman says that we need additional criteria (beyond consistency with the facts) if we are going to be able to choose [4, p. 9]. Here he poses the problem of choosing between *competing* hypotheses or theories, *all* of which have already been shown to be consistent with available positive evidence (that is, none of them have been shown to be false using *modus tollens*). The criteria with which he claims there is "general agreement" are the "simplicity" and the "fruitfulness" of the substantive hypotheses [4, p. 10].[13] However, these are not considered to be abstract philosophical (*i.e.*, conventionalist) criteria but rather they, too, are empirically based, hence can be expressed in instrumentalist terms: "Simpler" means requires less empirical "initial knowledge" (the word "initial" refers here to the process of generating predictions with something like *modus ponens*). "More fruitful" means more applicable and more precise [4, p. 10]. The possibility of a trade-off is not discussed.

Friedman explicitly rejects the necessity of requiring the "testing" of substantive hypotheses before they are used simply because it is not possible. But here it should be noted that his rejection of testing is partly a consequence of his use of the word "testing." Throughout his essay "testing" always means "testing for truth (in some sense)." It never means "testing in order to reject" as most of his critics seem to presume. That is, for Friedman a *successful* test is one which shows a statement (*e.g.*, an assumption, hypothesis, or theory) to be true; and, of course, a minimum condition for a successful test is that the statement not be inconsistent with empirical evidence (see [4, pp. 33–34]).[14]

Appreciating the success orientation of Friedman's view is essential to an understanding of his methodological judgements. For Friedman, an instrumentalist, hypotheses are chosen because they are successful in yielding true predictions. In other words, hypotheses and theories are viewed as instruments for successful predictions. It is his assumption that there has been a prior application of *modus tollens* (by evolution, see [4, p. 22]), which eliminates unsuccessful hypotheses (ones that yield false predictions), and which allows one to face only the problem of choosing between successful hypotheses. *In this*

---

[13] Note here, although Friedman uses conventionalist criteria, it is for a different purpose. For a conventionalist the criteria are used as truth status substitutes; in conventionalism one finds that theories are either better or worse. In this sense, Friedman can be seen to pose the problem of choosing among theories already classified as "better" in his sense (successful predictions).

[14] I stress, this is the view Friedman uses *in his essay*. In recent correspondence Professor Friedman has indicated to me his more general views of testing in which success might be either a confirmation or a disconfirmation. But he still would question the meaningfulness of "testing in order to reject."

Although Friedman seldom uses the word "truth," it should be noted that throughout he consistently uses the word "validity" (by which he always means at least "not inconsistent with the available facts") in the same sense that "truth" plays in *modus ponens* seemingly while also recognizing that *modus ponens* is assured only when applied to "truth" in the absolute or universal sense (*i.e.*, without exceptions). Technically speaking his use of the word "validity" may lead one to the incorrect identification of "truth" with "logical validity." In this regard, applications of Friedman's methodology are often confused with orthodox conventionalism. This confusion can be avoided by remembering that "validity" is a necessary (but not sufficient) condition of empirical "truth"—hence, validity and truth are not identical—and by recognizing that someone can believe his theory is true, even though he knows he cannot prove that it is true.

sense, his concentrating on successful predictions precludes any further application of *modus tollens*. And similarly, any possible falsity of the assumptions is thereby considered irrelevant. Such a consideration is merely an appreciation of the logical limitations of what I called *reverse modus tollens* (above, Section 1.2). And since he has thus assumed that we are dealing exclusively with successful predictions (*i.e.*, true conclusions), nothing would be gained by applying *modus ponens* either. This is a straightforward appreciation of the limitations of what I called *reverse modus ponens*. Knowing for sure that the hypotheses (or assumptions) are true is essential for a practical application of *modus ponens*, but such knowledge, he implies, is precluded by the absence of an inductive logic [4, pp. 12–14].

By focusing only on successful hypotheses, Friedman correctly reaches the conclusion that the application of the criterion of "simplicity" is relevant. He says there is virtue in a simple hypothesis *if* its application requires less empirical information. One reason a simple hypothesis can require less information, Friedman says, is that it is descriptively false [4, pp. 14–15]. (For example, a linear function requires fewer observations for a fit than does a quadratic function.) This raises the question of "unrealistic" descriptions versus "necessary" abstractions. Friedman explicitly recognizes that some economists (presumably, followers of Lionel Robbins) hold a view contrary to his. For them the "significance" of a theory is considered to be a direct result of the descriptive "realism" of the assumptions. But Friedman claims

> the relation between the significance of a theory and the "realism" of its "assumptions" is almost the opposite. . . . Truly important and significant hypotheses will be found to have "assumptions" that are wildly inaccurate descriptive representations of reality, and, in general, the more significant the theory, the more

> unrealistic the assumptions (in this sense). . . .
> [4, p. 14.]

Clearly, this latter judgement is based on the additional criteria of importance and significance that presume a purpose for theorizing. Namely, that theories are only constructed to be instruments of policy. Those economists who do not see policy application as the only purpose of theorizing can clearly argue with that judgement. But nevertheless, in terms of the economy of information, his conclusion is still correct with respect to choosing between *successful* hypotheses that are used as policy instruments.

3.4 *"Realism of Assumptions" vs. the Convenience of Instrumentalist Methodology*

In his Section III, Friedman continues to view successful "testing" to be "confirming," and for this reason he concludes that testing of assumptions is irrelevant for true conclusions (since *modus ponens* cannot be used in reverse). Having rejected the necessity of testing for the truth of assumptions, Friedman examines the question of the relevance of the falsity of assumptions for the various uses of theories. That is, what if one could show that an assumption is false? Does it matter? Friedman argues again [4, p. 18] that the falsity of the assumptions does not matter *if the conclusions are true*. He correctly says: one can say there must be an assumption that is false *whenever* some particular conclusion is false *(modus tollens)*, but one cannot say any assumptions are true *because* any conclusion is true (*reverse modus ponens*, again) [4, p. 19].

This leads Friedman to discuss the possibility that a false assumption might be applied as part of an explanation of some observed phenomenon. Here he introduces his famous version of the "as if" theory of explanation. He says that as long as the observed phenomenon can be considered to be a logical conclusion from the argument containing the false assumption in question, the use of that assumption should be acceptable. In particular, if we are trying to explain the *effect* of the assumed behavior of some individuals (*e.g.*, the demand curve derived with the assumption of maximizing behavior), *so long as the effect is in fact observed and it would be the effect if they were in fact to behave as we assume,* we can use our behavioral assumption even when the assumption is false. That is, we can continue to claim the observed effect of the individuals' (unknown but assumed) behavior is *as if* they behaved as we assume. Note carefully, the individuals' *behavior* is not claimed to be *as if* they behaved as we assume, but rather it is the *effect* of their behavior that is claimed to be *as if* they behave according to our assumption. Failure to distinguish between the effect and the behavior itself has led many critics to misread Friedman's view. His view does not violate any logical principles in this matter.

So far the choice between competing hypotheses or assumptions has been discussed with regard to currently available observations, *i.e.*, to existing evidence. But a more interesting question is the usefulness of any hypothesis in the future; past success will not guarantee future success. This presents a problem for the methodological conclusions that Friedman has, for the most part, presented correctly up to this point. He offers some weak arguments to deal with this problem. The first is an adaptation of a Social-Darwinist view that repeated success in the face of competition temporarily implies satisfaction of "the conditions for survival" [4, p. 22]. Unfortunately, he does not indicate whether these are necessary conditions, which they must be if his argument is to be complete. He adopts another Social-Darwinist view, which claims that past success of our theory is relative to other competitors,

thereby claiming a revealed superiority of our theory. This unfortunately presumes either that the other theories have not survived as well or that the comparative advantage cannot change. The former presupposition, however, would be ruled out by his prior commitment to discussing the problem of choosing between successful theories [4, p. 23]. The latter merely begs the question. Finally he unnecessarily adds the false conventionalist theory of confirmation that says the absence of refutation supports the (future) truth of a statement [4, pp. 22–23].

3.5 *"The Positive Aspects of Assumptions" Are Positive Aspects of Instrumentalist Methodology*

If assumptions do not need to be true, why would one bother worrying about them? Or, in other words, what role do assumptions play? Friedman says their role is positive [4, p. 23]. Assumptions: (a) are useful as an "economical mode" of expressing and determining the state of the "givens" of a theory; that is, the relevant facts in order to provide an empirical basis for the predictions; (b) "facilitate an indirect test" of a hypothesis of a theory by consideration of other hypotheses that are also implied; and (c) are a "convenient means of specifying the condition under which the theory is expected" to be applicable.

Friedman is not very careful about distinguishing between assumptions, hypotheses, or theories, and to make matters worse, in his Section IV he introduces the concept of a model. This can present some difficulty for the careful reader. Inductivist methodology posits significant differences between assumptions, hypotheses, theories, and some other things that are called "laws." The inductivist's distinctions are based on an alleged difference in the levels of inductive proofs of their truth. Assumptions are the least established and laws are the most. Without

514   *Journal of Economic Literature, Vol. XVII (June 1979)*

committing oneself to this inductivist tradition, one can easily see hypotheses as intermediate conjunctions formed by using only part of the assumptions of a theory. For example, the theory of the consumer entails certain hypotheses about the slope of the demand curve, but the assumptions of the theory of the consumer are only part of our market theory of prices. Moreover, the assumptions and hypotheses of consumer theory are independent of the theory of the firm.

Discussing models raises totally new issues. A model of a theory is a conventionalist concept. As Friedman correctly puts it, "the model is the logical embodiment of the half-truth" [4, p. 25]. Models in his sense correspond to the concept of models used in engineering. When one builds a model of something, one must simplify in order to emphasize the essential or significant features. Such simplification can always be seen to involve extra assumptions about the irrelevance of certain empirical considerations. These extra assumptions are usually descriptively false.

Most simplifying assumptions are designed to exclude certain real world complications or variables. Such exclusion also reduces the need for information concerning those variables when one wishes to apply the model. In this sense, assumptions are economical in terms of the amount of prior information required for empirical application.

Friedman notes that the problem of choosing models can be seen as a problem of explaining when the model is applicable. To solve the latter version of this problem, he says that to any model of a theory or hypothesis one must add "rules for using the model" [4, p. 25]. These required rules, however, are not mechanical. He says that "no matter how successful [one is in explicitly stating the rules] . . . there inevitably will remain room for judgement in applying the rules" [4, p. 25]. Unfortunately, the "capacity to judge" can-

not be *taught*, as each case is different (another instance of the problem of induction). However, it can be *learned*, "but only by experience and exposure in the 'right' scientific atmosphere" [4, p. 25] (this is a version of conventionalism). This seems to bring us back to the inductive problem that his version of instrumentalism was intended to solve.

In spite of all the discussion about "assumptions," Friedman cautions us not to put too much emphasis on that word. By saying there are problems concerning judgements about the applicability of certain assumptions of particular hypotheses or theories, we are not to be misled into thinking there is some special meaning to the term "assumption." The assumptions of one hypothesis may be the conclusions of a (logically) prior set of assumptions. In other words, when one says a statement is an assumption, one is not referring to any intrinsic property. A statement is called an assumption because that is how one chooses to use it. There is nothing that prevents one from attempting to explain the assumed "truth" of one's assumption by considering it to be a conclusion of another argument, which consists of yet another set of assumptions.[15] Moreover, the popular notion of a "crucial assumption" is likewise relative to the particular model in which it is being used.

In the last part of his Section IV, Friedman faces an alleged problem that may be created by the dismissal of the testability (*i.e.*, confirmability) of assumptions. The set of conclusions of any argument must contain the assumptions themselves. In some cases, within some subsets of assumptions and conclusions of a given theory there is interchangability. In these cases dismissing testability of assumptions can seem to mean that the testability of

[15] For example, the assumption of a negatively sloped demand curve may be an assumption for the market determination of price, but it is the conclusion of the theory of the consumer.

some conclusions has been dismissed as well. Recall, however, that testing for Friedman still means confirming. Thus, if one considers the testing of an assumption one can, in effect, be seen to be considering merely the confirming of one of the conclusions. Friedman's emphasis on true (successful) conclusions is seen to be playing a role here, too. Of course, there are other conclusions besides the assumptions themselves. However, someone may propose a set of assumptions only because *one* of the (true or observed) conclusions of interest is a logical consequence of that set. If one bothers to use the proposed assumptions to derive other conclusions from these assumptions, one can try to confirm the additional conclusions. In this sense, the assumptions used to derive one conclusion or hypothesis can be used to "indirectly test" the conclusion of interest. Nevertheless, logic does not permit one to see the confirmation of the secondary conclusion as a direct confirmation of the conclusion of interest. The significance of such an indirect test is also a matter of judgement [4, p. 28].

3.6 *"Economic Issues" or Some Examples of Instrumentalist Successes*

Finally, in his Section V, Friedman applies his methodological judgements to some specific examples, but here he does not raise any new questions of methodology. His objective seems merely to provide a demonstration of the success of instrumentalist methodology with several illustrations. Note that such a line of argument is quite consistent with instrumentalism and its compatibility with the disjunctive form of argument.

4. *The Critics*

Friedman's paper elicited a long series of critiques, none of which dealt with every aspect of his essay. The primary motivation for all of the critics seems to be that they disagree with particular things

Friedman said. I will argue here that the basis for each of the critiques is a misunderstanding and hence a false accusation.

4.1 *Testability vs. Refutability: Koopmans*

Most misunderstandings are the result of Friedman's "Introduction," where he seems to be saying that he is about to give another contribution to the traditional discussion about the methodology of inductivism and conventionalism. Such a discussion would usually be about issues, such as the verifiability or refutability of truely scientific theories. What Friedman actually gives is an alternative to that type of discussion. Unfortunately, most critics miss this point.

In regard to the traditional discussion, Tjalling Koopmans says that the object of our attempts to develop or analyze the "postulational structure of economic theory" is to obtain ". . . those implications that are verifiable or otherwise interesting" [5, 1957, p. 133]. In this light, Koopmans says that one must distinguish between the logical structure of a theory and the "interpretation" of its terms. He says that the logical structure's validity is considered to be independent of the interpretations (Koopmans is using the term "validity" correctly, but it does not correspond to Friedman's usage). He says, ". . . from the point of view of the logic of the reasoning, the interpretations are detachable. Only the logical contents of the postulates matter" [5, p. 133]. When any argument is logically valid, no interpretation can lead to a contradiction. (This is one interpretation of *modus ponens*.) One way to view the testing of an argument is to see a test as one interpretation of the terms such that a conjunction of the argument and the specific interpretation in question forms an empirical proposition about the real world, which does or does not correspond to our observations.

Koopmans also says a "distinction needs to be made here between *explanatory* and *normative* analysis" [5, p. 134]. Here Koopmans explicitly equates *positive* with *explanatory*. He adds that

> these two types of analysis do not necessarily differ in the interpretations placed on the terms. They differ *only* in the motivation of the search for conclusions. . . . In explanatory analysis, what one looks for in a conclusion or prediction is the possibility of testing, that is, of verification or refutation by observation. Of course, the interpretations of the terms used in the postulates form the connecting link through which observation is brought to bear on the statements that represent conclusions. Verification, or absence of refutation, lends support to the set of postulates taken as a whole. [5, p. 134, emphasis added.]

Now Friedman clearly does not agree with this distinction since he argues that how one views the parts of a theory depends on its use and that a theory cannot be analyzed independently of its use. Also, Koopmans's statement seems to suggest that priority should be given to testing conclusions. Friedman need not agree. Since Friedman's analysis begins with *successful* conclusions, testing is precluded because it is automatically implied by the usefulness and the logicality of the explanation.

Starting with a different concept of theorizing—that is, that theories are directly analyzable independently of their uses—Koopmans proceeds to criticize Friedman by restating Lionel Robbins's methodological position [8, 1935]. The basic concern for Koopmans (but not Friedman) is the sources of the basic premises or assumptions of economic theory. For the followers of Robbins, the assumptions of economic analysis are promulgated and used *because* they are (obviously) true. The truth of the assumptions is never in doubt. The only complaint Koopmans brings against Robbins is that his assumptions were a bit vague—a problem that Koopmans thinks can be solved with the use

of sophisticated mathematics. The primary virtue of Koopmans's work is that it does try to solve that problem. Implicitly, both Robbins and Koopmans see the process of economic theorizing as merely the task of applying exclusively *modus ponens* and *modus tollens*. In particular, the sole purpose of developing a theory is so that one can "pass" the obvious truth of the assumptions on to some conclusions.

Koopmans seems to object to Friedman's dismissal of the problem of clarifying the truth of the premises—the problem that Koopmans wishes to solve. Friedman's view is that (*a priori*) "realism" of assumptions does not matter (*i.e., modus ponens* is not applicable). The source of the disagreement is Koopmans's confusion of *explanatory* with *positive*. Koopmans is an inductivist, who defines successful explanation as being logically based on observably true premises, that is, ones that are in turn (inductively) based on observation. Friedman does not consider assumptions or theories to be the embodiment of truth but only as instruments for the generation of useful (because successful) predictions. Thus, for Friedman *positive* is not equivalent to *explanatory* because he does not use *modus ponens*. Explanation in Koopmans's sense is irrelevant in Friedman's instrumentalism.

In order to criticize Friedman's argument against the concern for the "realism" of assumptions, Koopmans offers an *interpretation* of his own theory of the logical structure of Friedman's view. Koopmans says,

> Since any statement is implied by itself, one *could* interpret Professor Friedman's position to mean that the validity or usefulness of any set of postulates depends on observations that confirm or at least fail to contradict (although they could have) *all* their implications, immediate and derived. [5, 1957, p. 138, first emphasis added.]

He then goes on to claim that this interpretation of Friedman's argument leads to some objectionable conclusions and thus claims to destroy Friedman's argument. The details of this line of argument do not matter here, since Koopmans's argument itself can be shown to be irrelevant and thus of no logical value.

Koopmans's interpretation contradicts Friedman's purpose (that *some* conclusions be successful—not necessarily *all*). Remember that Friedman is only concerned with the *sufficiency* of a theory or set of assumptions. He would allow any theory to be even more than "just" sufficient[16] so long as it is sufficient for the successful predictions at issue. On the other hand, Koopmans's interpretation falsely presumes a concern for *necessity*. In other words, Koopmans's theory of Friedman's view is itself void because (by his own rules) at least one of its assumptions is false. Or, also by Koopmans's own rules (*modus tollens*) his own theory of Friedman's view must be considered refuted, since the false assumption is also one of the conclusions. His theory is not "realistic" even though some of his conclusions may be. There is nothing in the application of *modus tollens* to a specific interpretation (which necessarily involves additional assumptions—*e.g.*, rule of correspondence) that would require the rejection of Friedman's view itself.[17]

4.2 *Necessity of Verifying Assumptions: Rotwein*

Some economists would accept the obviousness of the premises of economic theory. In this group would fall the self-proclaimed "empiricists." The basis of their philosophy is the view that the truth of one's conclusions (or predictions) rest

[16] That is, Friedman might argue that "Occam's Razor" need not be used, as it is a pure intellectual exercise, which serves no useful purpose.
[17] Specifically, with an argument consisting of a conjunction of many interdependent assumptions, a false conclusion does not necessarily implicate any particular assumption but only the conjunction of all of them.

solely (and firmly) on the demonstrable truth of the premises; and the prescription that one *must* so justify every claim for the truth of one's conclusions or predictions. Needless to say, empiricists do not see a problem of induction. Friedman clearly does, and in this sense he is not an orthodox empiricist (even though the term "positive" usually means "empirical"). Along these lines, Eugene Rotwein criticizes Friedman's view by claiming that it represents "a form of naive and misguided empiricism" [9, 1959, p. 555]. Thus Rotwein sees his criticism as a family dispute amongst empiricists. What is questioned is

> Friedman's contention . . . that the "validity" of a "theory" is to be tested *solely* by its "predictions" with respect to a given class of phenomena, or that the question of whether or to what extent the assumptions of the "theory" are "unreal" (i.e., falsify reality) is of no relevance to such a test. [9, p. 556.]

(Note that Friedman was not discussing the "validity of theories" but rather the validity of "hypotheses" used in a model of a theory.[18])

Now it seems to me there is "good" and "bad" naivety. Good naivety is exemplified by the little boy in Andersen's story "The Emperor's New Clothes." Good naivety exposes the dishonesty or ignorance of others. Friedman simply refuses to join in the pretence that there is an inductive logic that will serve as a foundation for Rotwein's verificationist-empiricism. Rotwein attempts to twist the meaning of "validity" into a matter of probabilities so that he can use something like *modus ponens* [9, p. 558]. But *modus ponens* will not work with statements whose truth status is a matter of probabilities, and thus Friedman is correct in rejecting this approach to empiricism. Rotwein's arguments are on a far weaker foundation than are Friedman's. It is, in

[18] Nor does he say "solely."

fact, Rotwein's view that is naive, since it is based on an unfounded belief that science is the embodiment of truths based (inductively) on true observations, which are beyond doubt, or on true hypotheses, which can be inductively proven.

4.3 *Testability as Refutability: Bear and Orr and Melitz*

Some sophisticated and friendly critics of Friedman choose to criticize only certain aspects while accepting others. This can lead to criticisms that are necessarily invalid. For example, Donald Bear and Daniel Orr dismiss Friedman's instrumentalism, yet they recommend what they call his "as if" principle [1, 1967]. They recommend "as if" because they too accept the view that the problem of induction is still unsolved. They are correct in appreciating that the principle is an adequate means of dealing with the problem of induction.

That it is possible to accept one part of Friedman's methodology while rejecting another does not necessarily create a contradiction. The appreciation of such a possibility is facilitated by recalling that each part of Friedman's argument is designed to be sufficient. In this vein, Bear and Orr claim that Friedman's arguments against the necessity of testing and against the necessity of "realism" of assumptions are both wrong. Bear and Orr (agreeing with Jack Melitz) say that Friedman erred by ". . . confounding . . . abstractness and unrealism" [1, p. 188, *fn.* 3]. And they further claim "all commentators except Friedman seem to agree that the testing of the whole theory (and not just the predictions of theory) is a constructive activity" [1, p. 194, *fn.* 15].

These criticisms are somewhat misleading because Friedman's concept of testing (*sc.* verifying) does not correspond to theirs. It is not always clear what various writers mean by "testing," mostly because its meaning is too often taken for granted.

One can identify implicitly three distinct meanings as used by the authors under consideration. Where Friedman sees testing only in terms of verification or "confirmation," Bear and Orr adopt Karl Popper's view that a successful test is a refutation [1, 1967, pp. 189 *ff*]. But Melitz sees testing as confirmation or disconfirmation [6, 1965, pp. 48 *ff*]. Unfortunately, one can only arrive at these distinctions by inference. Bear and Orr present, in one section, the logic of refuting theories, followed by a lengthy discussion of tests and the logic of testing. Melitz is more difficult to read. The word "testing," which figures prominently in the article's title, never appears anywhere in the introduction. Melitz never does directly discuss his own concept of testing.

In both critiques, the logic of their criticisms is an allegation of an inconsistency between *their* concepts of testing and Friedman's rejection of the necessity of testing assumptions. The logic of their critiques may be valid, but in each case it presumes a rejection of instrumentalism. But instrumentalism, I argue, is an absolutely essential part of Friedman's point of view. Consequently, contrary to the critics' views, the alleged inconsistency does not exist *within* Friedman's instrumentalist methodology.

As was argued above (*Sections* 2.4, 3.3, and 3.4), Friedman's concept of testing is quite consistent with his instrumentalism and *his* judgements about testing. Viewed from the standpoint of Friedman's concept of testing, Melitz and Bear and Orr present criticisms that are thus logically inadequate. This situation shows, I think, that one cannot understand the particular methodological judgements of Friedman unless one accepts or at least understands his instrumentalism.

Their suggestion that Friedman's view is based on an error of logic is simply wrong. And furthermore, it is unfair to make that suggestion only on the basis of an inconsistency between *their* concept of testing and his judgements, which were based on *his* concept. There is no reason why Friedman's view should be expected to be consistent with their view of what constitutes science or of what others think testability or testing really is.

4.4 *Errors of Omission: De Alessi*

Another even more friendly criticism is offered by Louis De Alessi. He meekly criticizes Friedman for seeing only *two* attributes of theories—namely, a theory can be viewed as a language and as a set of substantive hypotheses. On the other hand, De Alessi seems to think Friedman should have included a set of rules of correspondence or rules of interpretation. His criticism of Friedman is in the spirit that such rules of interpretation are necessary for a positive theory. He says, ". . . Unfortunately, Friedman's analysis has proved to be amenable to quite contradictory interpretations" [2, 1965, p. 477]. But as I said before, this is not necessarily a criticism for an instrumentalist who has rejected further applications of *modus tollens*.

De Alessi later raises another minor criticism [3, 1971]. He says Friedman leaves room for error by telling us that some assumptions and conclusions are "interchangeable." De Alessi correctly notes that such "reversability" of an argument may imply that the argument is tautological. When an argument is tautological, it cannot also be empirical, *i.e.*, positive. The logic of De Alessi's argument is correct. However, it is not clear that with Friedman's use of "interchangable" he was indicating "reversability" of (entire) arguments. The only point Friedman was attempting to make was that the status of being an "assumption" is not necessarily automatic. In any case, just because some of the conditions and assumptions are interchangable does not necessarily mean that the theory as a whole is tautological.

If Friedman were viewing assumptions as "necessary" conditions, then the problem that De Alessi raises would be more serious. But Friedman's instrumentalism does not require such a role for assumptions. Both of De Alessi's criticisms are founded on the view that *modus tollens* can be applied to Friedman's view. In particular, it is the view that was asserted by Koopmans, namely that if *any interpretation* of a view (or argument) is considered false then the view itself must be false. But this presumes that the assumptions were necessary conditions. As I have said, that is not the case with instrumentalism. Hence De Alessi's criticisms are irrelevant, even though one might find merit in the details of his argument.

4.5 *The "F-Twist": Samuelson*

The most celebrated criticism of Friedman's methodology was presented by Paul Samuelson [10, 1963] in his discussion of a paper by Ernest Nagel.[19] Samuelson explicitly attributes the following proposition to Friedman.

> A theory is vindicable if (some of) its consequences are empirically valid to a useful degree of approximation; the (empirical) unrealism of the theory "itself," or of its "assumptions," is quite irrelevant to its validity and worth. [10, 1963, p. 232.]

Samuelson calls this the "F-Twist." And about this he says, it is

> fundamentally wrong in thinking that unrealism in the sense of factual inaccuracy even to

[19] Nagel's paper [7, 1963] is often alleged to be a criticism of Friedman's essay. But Nagel's paper only tries to show that some of Friedman's definitions may not be universally accepted. Furthermore, a close reading will show that Nagel explicitly agrees with Friedman's methodological position. It is for this latter reason that Samuelson responds *to Nagel* by offering a criticism of Friedman's position. Also, it might be noted that Stanley Wong's paper [11, 1973] is likewise not very critical of Friedman's methodology, although Wong, like Nagel, does note that Friedman's methodology is an example of instrumentalism.

a tolerable degree of approximation is anything but a demerit for a theory or hypothesis (or set of hypotheses). [10, 1963, p. 233.]

However, Samuelson admits that his representation of Friedman's view may be "inaccurate" (that is supposedly why he called it the "F-Twist" rather than the "Friedman-Twist"). Nevertheless, Samuelson is willing to apply his potentially false assumption about Friedman to explain (should one say describe?) Friedman's view. His justification for using a false assumption is Friedman's own allegedly valid "as if" principle. Samuelson argues in this way on the basis of the theory that if he can discredit or otherwise refute Friedman's view by using Friedman's view, then followers of Friedman's methodology must concede defeat.

Samuelson's argument goes as follows. First he says:

> The motivation for the F-Twist, critics say, is to help the case for (1) the perfectly competitive laissez faire model of economics, . . . and (2), but of lesser moment, the "maximization-of-profit" hypotheses. [10, 1963, p. 233.]

Then he says,

> If Dr. Friedman tells us this was not so; if his psychoanalyst assures us that his testimony in this case is not vitiated by subconscious motivations; . . .—still it would seem a fair use of the F-Twist itself to say: "Our theory about the origin and purpose of the F-Twist may be 'unrealistic' . . . but what of that? The consequence of our theory agrees with the fact that Chicagoans use the methodology to explain away objections to their assertions." [10, 1963, p. 233.]

Samuelson admits that there is an element of "cheap humor" in this line of argument. But nevertheless, it is an attempt to criticize Friedman by using Friedman's own methodology.

I will argue here that Samuelson does not appear to understand the "as if" principle. In *Section* 3.4 above I argued that when using the "as if" principle, one must distinguish between the empirical *truth* of a behavioral assumption and the *va-*lidity of *using* that assumption, and I noted that the latter does not imply the former.

Perhaps Samuelson is correct in attributing a pattern of behavior to the followers of Friedman and that such a pattern can be shown to follow logically from his assumption concerning their motivation, but the "as if" principle still does not warrant the empirical claim that his assumption about Friedman's or his followers' motivation is true. More important, the "as if" principle is validly used *only* when explaining *true* conclusions. That is, one cannot validly use such an "as if" argument as a critical device similar to *modus tollens*. If the implications of using Samuelson's false assumption are undesirable, one cannot pass the undesirableness back to the assumption. Furthermore, there are infinitely many false arguments that can imply any given (true) conclusion. The question is whether Samuelson's assumption is necessary for his conclusion. Of course, it is not, and that is because Samuelson is imitating Friedman's mode of argument using sufficient assumptions.

The mode of argument in which Friedman accepts the "as if" principle is neither a case of *modus ponens* nor *modus tollens*. Yet when Samuelson proceeds to give a serious criticism of the "as if" principle, he assumes that both of them apply. But even worse, by Samuelson's own mode of argument, his assumption that attributes the F-Twist to Friedman is false and his attempts to apply this by means of *modus ponens* are thus invalid.

5. On Criticizing Instrumentalism

It would seem to me that it is pointless (and illogical) to criticize someone's view with an argument that gives different meanings to the essential terms.[20] Yet this is just what most of the critics do. Simi-

---

[20] Such an argument would at least involve a violation of the axiom of identity.

larly, using assumptions that are allowed to be false while relying on *modus ponens*, as Samuelson does, is also pointless. Any effective criticism must deal properly with Friedman's instrumentalism. Presenting a criticism that ignores his instrumentalism will always lead to irrelevant critiques such as those of Koopmans, Rotwein, and De Alessi. None of these critics seems willing to straightforwardly criticize instrumentalism.

Instrumentalism presents certain obstacles to every critic. When instrumentalists argue by offering a long series of reasons, each of which is sufficient for their conclusions, it puts the entire onus on the critic to refute each and every reason. Friedman makes this all the more difficult by giving us, likewise, an instrumentalist argument in support of instrumentalism itself. Thus, refuting or otherwise successfully criticizing only some of Friedman's reasons will never defeat his view. Since Friedman never explicitly claims that his argument is intended to be a logically sufficient defense of instrumentalism, one cannot expect to gain even by refuting its "sufficiency." Yet it would be fair to do so, since "sufficiency" is the only logical idea that instrumentalism uses. Such a refutation, however, is unlikely, since it would seem to require a solution to the problem of induction.

Finally, and most importantly, I think it essential to realize that instrumentalism is solely concerned with (immediate) practical success. In this light, one should ask, "What are the criteria of success? Who decides what they are?" Questions of this type, I think, must also be dealt with before one can ever begin—constructively or destructively—to criticize effectively the instrumentalism that constitutes the foundation of Friedman's methodology.

What then must one do to form an effective but fair and logical critique of Friedman's methodology? Whatever one does, one cannot violate the axioms of logic. It

does not matter to instrumentalists if others have different definitions of the words "testing," "validity," "assumptions," "hypothesis," *etc.* When criticizing an argument in which reasons are offered as sufficient conditions, it should be recognized that *modus tollens* is useless. And when *modus tollens* is useless, there is no way one can directly criticize.

Since, as I have argued here, the internal construction of Friedman's instrumentalism is logically sound, in any effective criticism of his view the only issue possibly at stake is the truth or falsity of instrumentalism itself. But no one has been able to criticize or refute instrumentalism. That no one has yet refuted it does not prove that instrumentalism is universally correct. To claim that it does is to argue from *reverse modus ponens.* Again, this is a matter of logic.

Any effective criticism of instrumentalism must at least explain the absence of refutations. There are, I think, three possible ways any given argument may avoid refutations. First, as a matter of logical form, an argument may merely be irrefutable.[21] Second, if an argument is of a logical form that is conceivably refutable, it may simply be that it is true, hence no one will ever find refutations because they will never exist. Third, the absence of refutations may not be the result of an intrinsic property of the argument itself, but the consequence of how one deals with all potential refutations. That is, the defense may be either circular or infinitely regressive.[22]

As a matter of logic alone, instrumental-

[21] Statements of the form "there will be a revolution" can never be proven false *even if they are false.* And tautological statements are true by virtue of the logical form alone, hence they cannot be refuted simply because one cannot conceive how they might be false.

[22] For example, if one were to argue that revolutions are never successful, and one supports this with the evidence that every revolution has failed, the revolutionary may respond by saying that those were not "genuine" revolutions.

ism need not be irrefutable. So, as an argument about how one should treat economic analysis, instrumentalism is either true or its proponents have been supporting it with a circularity or an infinite regress. And thus the first question is, is instrumentalism true? Repeated successes (or failed refutations) of instrumentalism is logically equivalent to repeated successful predictions or true conclusions. We still cannot conclude logically that the assumptions, *i.e.*, the bases of instrumentalism itself, are true. They could very well be false, and in the future someone may be able to find a refutation.

It has been argued in this paper that Friedman's essay is an instrumentalist defense of instrumentalism. That may be interpreted to mean that Friedman's methodology is based on an infinite regress, but if it is then at least it is not internally inconsistent or otherwise illogical. His success is still open to question. The repeated attempts to refute Friedman's methodology have failed, I think, because instrumentalism is its own defense and its *only* defense.

REFERENCES

1. BEAR, DONALD V. T. AND ORR, DANIEL. "Logic and Expediency in Economic Theorizing," *J. Polit. Econ.*, April 1967, *75*, pp. 188–96.
2. DE ALESSI, LOUIS. "Economic Theory as a Language," *Quart. J. Econ.*, August 1965, *79*, pp. 472–77.
3. ———. "Reversals of Assumptions and Implications," *J. Polit. Econ.*, July-August 1971, *79* (4), pp. 867–77.
4. FRIEDMAN, MILTON. "The Methodology of Positive Economics" in *Essays in positive economics*. Chicago: University of Chicago Press, 1953, pp. 3–43.
5. KOOPMANS, TJALLING. *Three essays on the state of economic science*. New York: McGraw-Hill, 1957.
6. MELITZ, JACK. "Friedman and Machlup on the Significance of Testing Economic Assumptions," *J. Polit. Econ.*, Feb. 1965, *73*, pp. 37–60.
7. NAGEL, ERNEST. "Assumptions in Economic Theory," *Amer. Econ. Rev.*, May 1963, *53*, pp. 211–19.
8. ROBBINS, LIONEL. *An essay on the nature and significance of economic science*. London: Macmillan, 1935.
9. ROTWEIN, EUGENE. "On 'The Methodology of Positive Economics,'" *Quart. J. Econ.*, Nov. 1959, *73*, pp. 554–75.
10. SAMUELSON, PAUL. "Problems of Methodology: Discussion," *Amer. Econ. Rev.*, May 1963, *53*, pp. 231–36.
11. WONG, STANLEY. "The 'F-Twist' and the Methodology of Paul Samuelson," *Amer. Econ. Rev.*, June 1973, *63*(3), pp. 313–25.

A Critique of Friedman's Methodological Instrumentalism*

BRUCE J. CALDWELL
University of North Carolina at Greensboro
Greensboro, North Carolina

I. Introduction

Milton Friedman's 1953 classic, "The Methodology of Positive Economics," is probably the best-known piece of methodological writing in the discipline [9]. It is also a marketing masterpiece. Never before has one short article on methodology been able to generate so much controversy. It was reviewed often, usually negatively. Yet ironically, the methodological prescriptions advanced in his essay have been accepted by many working economists. And this has happened without Friedman ever having directly responded to his critics!

The most recent contribution to the secondary literature is Lawrence Boland's piece, "A Critique of Friedman's Critics" [4, 503–22]. Boland argues that Friedman's methodology is best understood as a variant of the philosophical position known as instrumentalism, and that if Friedman is so interpreted, many critiques of his position existent in the economic literature miss their mark. While these points are well-taken, Boland states in his conclusion that "no one has been able to criticize or refute instrumentalism" [4, 521]. Such a statement leaves the reader with the impression that Friedman's position is not only untouched, but perhaps even vindicated. It is the purpose of this paper to challenge such a conclusion by critiquing Friedman's methodological instrumentalism.

In the next section, some brief comments on definitional and interpretive issues are followed by a restatement of Friedman's position. Sections III, IV, and V contain the core of the criticisms against Friedman's methodological instrumentalism, from both philosophical and methodological perspectives. A conclusion emphasizes the importance of this debate for the critical methodological question of how theory choice is effected in economics.

II. The Restatement of Friedman's Position in Philosophical Terms

Some Definitional and Interpretive Issues

To understand what follows, the philosophical positions of instrumentalism and conventionalism must first be defined.

* I would like to thank Professor Lawrence Boland for many helpful comments.

366

Instrumentalists claim that theories are best viewed as *nothing more* than instruments. So viewed, theories are neither true nor false (instruments are not true or false), but only more or less adequate, given a particular problem. Just as a hammer is an adequate instrument for certain tasks, and not for others, theories are evaluated for their adequacy, which is usually measured by predictive power.

The conventionalist view stresses the organizational function of theories: theory construction is undertaken to organize a complex of facts into a coherent whole. In the words of philosopher Joseph Agassi, theories are "mathematical systems which serve as pigeon-holes within which to store empirical information" [2, 29]. In this view, theories are again neither true or false, but are posited for a time as being true by convention, given consensus within a community of scholars. The primary conventionalist criterion of theory choice is simplicity: the simpler theory organizes the facts better. But only revolutionary conventionalists try to find ever simpler theories; conservative conventionalists attempt to preserve existent theories by building onto them ever more elaborate (critics would label them ad hoc) peripheral systems.[1]

As Boland emphasizes [4, 509–16], Friedman's methodology combines elements of both instrumentalism and conventionalism. However, Friedman's most controversial statements, that the purpose of science is prediction and that the "realism" of assumptions does not matter, are instrumentalist.

Two more observations are necessary before proceeding. First, it is clear that Friedman was not aware that he was advancing an instrumentalist position when he wrote his 1953 article. This poses no serious problems: Friedman, after all, should be the last to object to a reviewer treating him "as if" he were an instrumentalist. More to the point, in private correspondence with Boland, Friedman states that Boland's representation of him as an instrumentalist is "entirely correct."[2]

The second observation concerns Boland's characterization of instrumentalism, which this author feels is incomplete. Boland isolates the strictly methodological implications of the instrumentalist view: that theories and the theoretical terms contained in them are only instruments; that it is therefore meaningless or irrelevant to speak of them as either true or false; and that theories and their constituent parts can only be judged for their adequacy, which is usually measured by how well their implications (predictions) are confirmed by the data. Boland further characterizes instrumentalism as a methodological response to the problem of induction, and contrasts it favorably with inductivism and conventionalism [4, 506–509].

Within the philosophy of science, instrumentalism is much more than a response to the problem of induction. It is, for example, one side in the debate over the ontological status of the entities referred to by theories and theoretical terms. In that debate, instrumentalism is contrasted with realism: realists claim that theories and theoretical terms should make real references, instrumentalists deny it. Where one stands in such a debate determines one's perception of the role, status and function of theories and theoretical terms in science [28, 29–36]. Philosophers Joseph Agassi and Imre Lakatos claim that one's position on such issues even affects the way the history of science is written [2; 17, 91–136].

1. Popper defines and discusses instrumentalism in two works [24, section 12; 25, 97–119, 215–50]; a number of philosophers have addressed conventionalism [2, section 8; 17, 94–96; 24, sections 19, 20, 30, 46]. Latsis offers an interesting interpretation of Friedman as a conventionalist [18]; Stanley Wong, a student of Boland, was the first to label Friedman an instrumentalist [31, 314].
2. I would like to thank Professor Boland for sharing this information with me.

In his attacks against "realistic assumptions" Friedman was not advancing an argument concerning the ontological status of theoretical entities: he was concerned with methodology, not epistemology. For this reason, Friedman should be viewed as a "methodological instrumentalist," to emphasize that though his analysis is consistent with the methodological implications of instrumentalism, he never dealt with the epistemological issues associated with that philosophical position.

The Restatement of Friedman's Position

The salient features of Friedman's methodology may be summarized as follows:

1. The goal of science is to discover hypotheses that predict well. In Friedman's words, "The ultimate goal of a positive science is the development of a 'theory' or 'hypothesis' that yields valid and meaningful (i.e., not truistic) predictions about phenomena not yet observed" [9, 7].

2. Assumptions are not a locus of testing for theories; their "realism" does not matter. If Friedman is an instrumentalist, "realism" refers to truth-value. Realism is then unimportant because theories are not true or false, but only instruments.

Much confusion in the debates on Friedman's position is due to a sloppy usage by all participants of such key concepts as realism, testability, degree of confirmation, and truth. "Realistic" and its opposite are perhaps the most notorious in this group of ill-defined terms; philosopher Ernest Nagel [22, 214–15] scores Friedman for using at least three senses of the word unrealistic in his essay. No work has been done on how the word realistic has been used by economists, and that task will not be attempted here. Realistic is probably best defined as meaning "understandable," "intuitively plausible," or "reasonable" in the common-sense usages of those words. Testability refers to the *capability* of an assumption or hypothesis to be subjected to test; degree of confirmation refers to the extent to which an assumption or hypothesis is confirmed or disconfirmed by testing, hence, it focuses on the *results* of such testing. Finally, we may follow Popper's reading of Tarski in defining truth as "correspondence to facts" relative to a given background knowledge. In this way, essentialism is avoided [25, 97–119, 215–50].

In much of the literature, the concept "realistic" is conflated with the concepts testable, highly confirmed and true.[3] A few examples show that these are not interchangeable terms. If a Roman philosopher postulated a heliocentric theory of the solar system, he would be propounding a theory which was both untestable and unrealistic (given the state of knowledge at the time) yet true (given the present state of knowledge). Conversely, a theory can be realistic, testable, perfectly confirmed, and false: one could theorize that air pressure increases at high altitudes, and test it by throwing a ball in the air, with its dropping back to earth counting as a confirming instance. Descartes' vortex theory of planetary motion, which fit the data and had analogues in the earthly phenomenon of eddies, was testable, somewhat confirmed, more realistic than action at a distance, and false. The point is made: a realistic theory need not be testable, a testable theory need not be confirmed, and even a perfectly

---

3. In reply to a comment by Robert Piron, Eugene Rotwein states that if assumptions are to have explanatory power, they should be realistic or true [26, 666–68]. Jack Melitz uses the terms realistic, highly confirmed and true interchangeably in his article on Friedman and Machlup [20, 37–39]. D. V. T. Bear and Daniel Orr state that Friedman's position comes down to the proposition, "the truth of the assumptions is largely irrelevant" [3, 188].

confirmed theory need not be true.[4] Confusing these terms makes the evaluation of Friedman's position all the more difficult.

3. Simplicity is a methodological virtue; the most significant theories explain "much by little" [9, 14].

4. In most cases, a number of hypotheses will meet the criterion of predictive adequacy. In such cases, additional criteria of theory choice (which are "to some extent . . . arbitrary") must be invoked to choose among them. These include simplicity and fruitfulness, and to a lesser degree, logical completeness and consistency [9, 9–10].[5]

The first two propositions comprise the core of Friedman's methodological instrumentalism; they will be the focus of the critique which follows.

III. The Philosophical Rejection of Instrumentalism

The Goal of Science

Philosophers of science since the 1940's have been unanimous in their rejection of the notion that the only goal of science is prediction. Even such positivist philosophers as Carl Hempel have claimed that explanation, not prediction, is the goal of science; it was Hempel who with Paul Oppenheim developed the covering law models of scientific explanation [12; 13]. More recent models of the structure and nature of explanation in science admit to even broader definitions of the concept than did the covering law models.[6] Once one takes the position that explanation is the goal of science, the instrumentalist view of theories and theoretical terms is considerably weakened. If science seeks theories that have explanatory as well as predictive powers, then theories that merely predict well may not be satisfactory, and the view that theories are nothing more than instruments for prediction must be rejected.

The Truth-Value of Theories

Even if it is admitted that science seeks theories that explain as well as predict, the instrumentalist has a second line of defense. It is well known that for any set of empirical data, an infinite number of mutually incompatible theories exist that can explain the evidence at hand. Even a moderate skeptic must therefore despair over the possibilities of ever finding the "true" theory. Instrumentalism allows one to circumvent the entire issue by claiming that

---

4. Jim Murphy provides the air pressure example, and Rowan and Eckberg discuss Descartes's vortex theory [21, 473; 27, 224–34].

5. Friedman, like most writers in methodology, goes beyond predictive adequacy and simplicity in defining criteria of theory-choice; for this reason, categories like instrumentalism and conventionalism must be viewed as extreme versions of how one may view theories and their selection. In a recent paper, Vincent Tarascio and I enumerate a number of empirical and non-empirical criteria of theory-choice [29]. Using that more general schema, one can characterize particular methodological viewpoints as instrumentalist, conventionalist, falsificationist, etc., depending on which criteria of theory-choice are emphasized.

6. The relevant literature on explanation is extensively documented by Caldwell [5; 6]. A point of clarification: Hempel and Oppenheim state that "an explanation is not fully adequate unless its explanans, if taken account of in time, could have served as a basis for predicting the phenomena under question" [13, 138]. This is *not* the same as stating that explanation and prediction are equivalent; rather, it is a *logical* analysis of the structure of an explanation, as is emphasized in Hempel's later paper. That the covering law models cannot be used to justify Friedman's instrumentalism is clear once one notes that one of Hempel and Oppenheim's "conditions of adequacy," which all sound explanations must meet, states that "the sentences constituting the explanans must be true" [13, 138].

theories are only instruments and that as such it is meaningless to speak of them being either true or false; as Boland puts it, instrumentalists "think they have solved the problem of induction by ignoring truth" [4, 509].

But indeed, such an approach does *not* solve the problem. Instrumentalists fail to comprehend that though we may not know whether a theory is true or false, it in fact is true or false. An analogy from probability theory illustrates this point: when an estimate of a probability distribution is made, the estimate may be wrong, but the actual distribution exists if the population is finite. Even if we never know what the actual distribution is, we should still try to make the best estimate using all of the available information. In regards to theories, the philosophical realist (who is, in such discussions, the opposite of the instrumentalist) recognizes at all times that his theory may be wrong, but is still willing to accept that risk and seek for the true theory. The realist will support only those theories he believes may actually be true, and he will posit such theories for a time as being "true by convention." Realism thus contains elements of conventionalism. Instrumentalists refuse to take such a step, and philosopher Imre Lakatos views this as a gross error on their part.

> ... some conventionalists did not have sufficient logical education to realize that some propositions may be true whilst being unproven; and others false whilst having true consequences, and also some which are both false and approximately true. These people opted for 'instrumentalism': they came to regard theories as neither true nor false but merely as 'instruments' for prediction. Conventionalism, as here defined, is a philosophically sound position; instrumentalism is a degenerate version of it, based on a mere philosophical muddle caused by a lack of elementary logical competence [16, 95].

Whether instrumentalism arose due to "a lack of elementary logical competence" on the part of its supporters is doubtless an arguable point; however, most contemporary philosophers of science share with Lakatos misgivings about the adequacy of instrumentalism. Thus, Peter Achinstein states that if we are to consider a set of propositions T a theory, then the person who holds it "does not know that T is true, although he believes that T is true or that it is plausible to think that it is" [1, 122]. Karl Popper also rejects instrumentalism, primarily because it forces scientists to abandon the search for truth. When one seeks for truth, it does not mean that one is searching for the "essential nature" of things: that view Popper labels essentialism, and he rejects it because the scientific enterprise is constantly seeking fuller rather than ultimate explanations. Instrumentalism is untenable because it does not urge scientists to practice a critical methodology; it is satisfied with high correlation and does not push the scientist to seek out fuller explanations [24, 103–14]. Other philosophers who reject instrumentalism include most contemporary positivists, Grover Maxwell, and P. K. Feyerabend; the notable exception is Stephen Toulmin [7; 19; 28, 27–37, 128–35; 30].

Boland's defense of Friedman rests on the claim that his critics did not deal with that economist's instrumentalism. The arguments above indicate that instrumentalism finds few supporters in contemporary philosophy of science. This point is important in its own right, but also is crucial to the evaluation of instrumentalism on purely methodological grounds, as is shown next.

IV. The Methodological Critique of Instrumentalism

Instrumentalism could still be retained if it was shown to be a superior position on strictly methodological grounds. Methodological positions can only be evaluated *given* a certain view of the nature and purpose of science. If the goal of science is to find theories that are predictively adequate, instrumentalism is a viable methodological stance. However, if the goal of science is the discovery of true explanatory theories, instrumentalism fails.

If we assume that contemporary philosophers of science are right, and that their view is the better characterization of the scientific enterprise, the question may be asked: Will instrumentalist methodology aid us in our quest for true, explanatory theories? Clearly not. First, the instrumentalist preoccupation with predictive adequacy forces scientists to prefer statistical correlation over causal explanation if the former provides better predictions.[7] Next, as Bear and Orr show, false antecedents can generate true consequences; if we wish our theories to be true as well as predictively adequate, prediction must be supplemented with other criteria of theory-appraisal [3, 188–91]. Third, as argued by Popper and repeated by Bear and Orr, acceptance of instrumentalism rules out disconfirmation in science: a theory that is neither true or false can be found inadequate, but not disconfirmed [25, 113–14; 3, 189–192]. Finally, the poor predictive record of the economics profession challenges the belief that even discovering theories which are predictively adequate will be a simple task [29].

These arguments are not new; all have been made by critics of Friedman. The point is that they are appropriate criticisms of Friedman only if one asserts that the goal of science is to seek for true, explanatory theories.

Philosopher Jerzy Giedymin has highlighted the methodological advantages of instrumentalism, If that position is interpreted as saying that theories need not be eliminated for their unrealism (or because they do not meet some other criteria excepting predictive adequacy), instrumentalism becomes a liberal methodological position which encourages theoretical pluralism [11, 178–80].

As is emphasized in an early article by Klappholz and Agassi, however, Friedman did not interpret instrumentalism in this way. Instead of arguing for a liberal methodology which encourages pluralism, Friedman claimed that realism was a vice and not a virtue and that theories which exhibited greater realism should not even be considered theoretical advances. By this wholesale elimination of possible competitors to neoclassical theory, "Friedman adopts a position which impedes criticism in general" [14, 66]. Even had Friedman taken a more liberal stance, instrumentalism is sufficient but not necessary for one to support theoretical pluralism: Kuhn, Lakatos and Feyerabend all call for tolerance in the assessment of new theories without invoking instrumentalism. It seems, then, that a strictly methodological defense of instrumentalism in unsuccessful, given a non-instrumentalist view of the nature and goals of science.

V. A Recent Example of Inconsistency in Friedman's Position

Defenders of Friedman might claim that the epistemological and methodological criticisms above do not defeat Friedman's position because that economist's methodology goes beyond simple instrumentalism. Specifically, Friedman adds additional criteria of theory choice (the most important of which is simplicity) to predictive adequacy for the appraisal of theories. Such a defense would claim that Friedman's position must be evaluated as a totality, and not for its purely instrumentalist aspects.

7. Charles Nelson's study shows that statistical data can be used to generate adequate predictions of the behavior of aggregates in the U. S. economy [23].

I have argued with Vincent Tarascio elsewhere that the arbitrary selection of only certain criteria of theory choice to supplement predictive adequacy is suspect, since the selection of such criteria is not always independent of the characteristics of one's favored theory [29, 991–95]. For example, proponents of well-established theories might view logical consistency and theoretical support as important criteria of theory choice, while advocates of newer theories might select realism or fruitfulness as their preferred criteria. But it is sufficient to show that even Friedman himself is not always consistent in his choice of supplemental criteria of theory selection.

In his Nobel lecture, Friedman reviews some of the changes in thinking which have occurred in the profession in the last several decades on the relationship between inflation and unemployment. He views those changes as illustrative of "the classical process for the revision of a scientific hypothesis" since they were occasioned "primarily by the scientific response to experience that contradicted a tentatively accepted hypothesis" [10, 453]. There have been three stages in the profession's analysis of the unemployment-inflation relationship. The first consisted of the simple acceptance of a stable, downward-sloping Phillips Curve; the second involved the introduction of a long run, vertical Phillips Curve (whose position corresponds to the natural rate of unemployment) together with a body of short run downward sloping curves whose levels correspond to different sets of inflationary expectations. In the third stage, which we are now entering, economists concern themselves with explaining the apparent positive relationship between inflation and unemployment. Friedman believes that analytic progress in the second stage leaned heavily on pioneering work done in the areas of expectation formation and information and contract theory; he expects that similar progress in the third stage will rely on the investigations by Arrow, Buchanan, Tullock and others who have applied economic analysis to political behavior [10, 454–60].

It is Friedman's conviction that the changes described above were brought on by the failure of earlier hypotheses to offer predictions which were consistent with the empirical evidence. This is undoubtedly true and indicates the important role of predictive adequacy in this branch of economics; but in not one place does he state that the most significant theories "explain much by little." Instead, he praises the newer theories for their "richness," and for their ability to "rationalize a far broader range of experience" [10, 470]. But doesn't the concept of costly information, the inclusion of stochastically changing inflationary expectations, and the existence of long run implicit or explicit contracts in goods and labor markets, doesn't all of that fly in the face of Friedman's earlier methodological dictums? And what about the holistic attempt (which characterizes the third stage) to include political institutions in an economic analysis; is there any way to defend that addition as simpler, more economical, or less concerned with realism? Clearly, Friedman's invocation of simplicity is much more useful if one is defending the quantity theory of money or the profit maximization assumption than if one is discussing recent developments in Phillips Curve analysis.

VI. Conclusion

The arguments above show that instrumentalism can and has been criticized on both epistemological and methodological grounds; as such, Boland's statement that "no one has been able to criticize or refute instrumentalism" [4, 521] must be rejected. In addition, I argued that Friedman himself has not always followed the dictates of his own professed methodology.

Instrumentalists and their opponents hold starkly contrasting views of the scientific enterprise, of the nature of explanation in science, and of the status and function of scientific theories. Instrumentalism is the more skeptical view: theories are no more than instruments, scientists are urged to be content with correlation, and to abandon any attempts at explanation. Opponents of instrumentalism demand more from their science; they believe that the search for theories which are explanatory, plausible and possibly true is a worthwhile scientific activity. Opponents of instrumentalism are not naively optimistic that such search will always end in success. Indeed, much of contemporary philosophy of science is concerned with whether rational theory choice is even possible in science [8; 15; 16]. But the invocation to try is ever-present.

Choice between these two visions of science is ultimately a personal matter, and may crucially depend upon whether the discipline involved is in a skeptical or optimistic period. For this reason, no ultimate, axiomatic refutation of instrumentalism is possible, or even desirable.[8]

One point, however, is clear. The question of how scientists choose among competing theories has been much debated recently in the philosophy of science, and such discussions are now having an impact on economic methodology [18; 29]. The selection of predictive adequacy, supplemented by a few other arbitrarily chosen criteria, as the penultimate and invariant guarantors of rational theory choice does little to advance or illuminate these discussions. Perhaps the most damaging claim against Friedman's own particular brand of instrumentalism is not that it is incorrect, or even implausible, but that it must be viewed, in the light of more recent work, as anachronistic.

---

8. Boland seems to think that opponents of instrumentalism have failed because they have not delivered an axiomatic refutation of instrumentalism [4, 521–22]. But waiting for such an axiomatic refutation is like waiting for Godot! Consensus among philosophers does not *refute* instrumentalism, it only raises questions about the legitimacy and adequacy of that position and the instrumentalist must respond to these charges. My invocation of *consensus* among philosophers of science (that instrumentalism is an inadequate position) caused Professor Boland to quip that, just as his paper involves an instrumentalist defense of instrumentalism, mine is essentially "a conventionalist defense of conventionalism."

On a separate but related point, it should be stressed that my attack on instrumentalism does not deny its value in situations when economists are only interested in generating predictions. Because economists, like other scientists, are ultimately concerned with *explaining* economic phenomena, however, Friedman's instrumentalism must be regarded as a "special case" rather than as *the* methodology of positive economic science, as he claims.

References

1. Achinstein, Peter. *Concepts of Science: A Philosophical Analysis.* Baltimore: Johns Hopkins Press, 1968.
2. Agassi, Joseph. *Towards an Historiography of Science.* The Hague: Mouton and Co., 1963.
3. Bear, D. V. T. and Daniel Orr, "Logic and Expediency in Economic Theorizing." *Journal of Political Economy,* April 1967, 188–96.
4. Boland, Lawrence, "A Critique of Friedman's Critics." *Journal of Economic Literature,* June 1979, 503–22.
5. Caldwell, Bruce, "Two Suggestions for the Improvement of Methodological Work in Economics." *American Economist,* Fall 1979, 56–61.
6. ———, "Positivist Philosophy of Science and the Methodology of Economics." *Journal of Economic Issues,* March 1980, 53–76.
7. Feyerabend, Paul K. "Realism and Instrumentalism: Comments on the Logic of Factual Support," in *The Critical Approach to Science and Philosophy,* edited by M. Bunge. New York: The Free Press, 1964, pp. 280–308.
8. ———. *Against Method: Outline of an Anarchistic Theory of Knowledge.* London: New Left Review, 1975.
9. Friedman, Milton. "The Methodology of Positive Economics," in *Essays in Positive Economics.* Chicago: University of Chicago Press, 1953, pp. 3–43.

374 *Bruce J. Caldwell*

10. ———, "Nobel Lecture: Inflation and Unemployment." *Journal of Political Economy*, June 1977, 451–72.

11. Geidymin, Jerzy. "Instrumentalism and Its Critique: A Reappraisal," in *Boston Studies in the Philosophy of Science*, Vol. 39, *Essays in Memory of Imre Lakatos*, edited by R. Cohen, P. K. Feyerabend, and M. Wartofsky. Dordrecht, Holland: D. Reidel Publishing Co., 1976, pp. 179–207.

12. Hempel, Carl G. "Explanation and Prediction by Covering Laws," in *Philosophy of Science: The Delaware Seminar*, Vol. 1, edited by B. Baumrin. New York: John Wiley and Sons, 1963, pp. 107–33.

13. Hempel, Carl G. and Paul Oppenheim, "Studies in the Logic of Explanation." *Philosophy of Science*, April 1948, 135–75.

14. Klappholz, K. and J. Agassi, "Methodological Prescriptions in Economics." *Economica*, February 1959, 60–74.

15. Kuhn, Thomas. *The Structure of Scientific Revolutions*, 2nd ed., enlarged. Chicago: University of Chicago Press, 1970.

16. Lakatos, Imre. "Falsification and the Methodology of Scientific Research Programmes," in *Criticism and the Growth of Knowledge,* edited by I. Lakatos and A. Musgrave. Cambridge, Eng.: Cambridge University Press, 1970, pp. 91–196.

17. ———. "History of Science and Its Rational Reconstructions," in *Boston Studies in the Philosophy of Science*, Vol. 8, *PSA 1970: In Memory of Rudolph Carnap*, edited by R. Buck and R. Cohen. Dordrecht, Holland: D. Reidel Publishing Co., 1971, pp. 91–136.

18. Latsis, Spiro, ed. *Method and Appraisal in Economics.* Cambridge, Eng.: Cambridge University Press, 1976.

19. Maxwell, Grover, "Some Current Trends in the Philosophy of Science," in *Boston Studies in the Philosophy of Science*, Vol. 32, *PSA 1974*, edited by R. Cohen, C. Hooker, A. Michalos, and J. W. Van Evra. Dordrecht, Holland: D. Reidel Publishing Co., 1976, pp. 565–84.

20. Melitz, Jack, "Friedman and Machlup on the Significance of Testing Economic Assumptions." *Journal of Political Economy*, February 1965, pp. 37–60.

21. Murphy, James. *Introductory Econometrics.* Homewood, Ill.: Richard Irwin, Inc., 1973.

22. Nagel, Ernest, "Assumptions in Economic Theory." *American Economic Review Papers and Proceedings*, May 1963, 211–19.

23. Nelson, Charles R., "The Predictive Performance of the FRB-MIT-PENN Model of the U. S. Economy." *American Economic Review*, December 1972, 902–17.

24. Popper, Karl. *The Logic of Scientific Discovery.* Eng. ed. New York: Basic Books, 1961.

25. ———. *Conjectures and Refutations: The Growth of Scientific Knowledge.* 2nd ed. New York: Basic Books, 1965.

26. Rotwein, Eugene, "Reply." *Quarterly Journal of Economics*, November 1972, 666–68.

27. Rowan, Herbert and Carl Ekberg, eds. *Early Modern Europe: A Book of Source Readings.* Itasca, Ill.: F. E. Peacock Publishers, 1973.

28. Suppe, Frederick, ed. *The Structure of Scientific Theories.* 2nd ed. Urbana, Ill.: University of Illinois Press, 1977.

29. Tarascio, Vincent J. and Bruce Caldwell, "Theory Choice in Economics: Philosophy and Practice." *Journal of Economic Issues*, December 1979, 983–1006.

30. Toulmin, Stephen. *Human Understanding.* Vol. 1. Princeton, N.J.: Princeton University Press, 1972.

31. Wong, Stanley, "The F-Twist and the Methodology of Paul Samuelson," *American Economic Review*, June 1973, 312–25.

KYKLOS, Vol. 34 – 1981 – Fasc. 3, 377–387

'UNREAL ASSUMPTIONS' IN ECONOMIC THEORY: THE F-TWIST UNTWISTED

Alan Musgrave*

Economic theorists often make assumptions which seem to be quite obviously false. For example, an economist may assume that goods are infinitely divisible, that consumers have a perfect knowledge of them, that transport costs are nil, that the government's budget is balanced, even that there is no government – the list could be extended. Students of economics, faced with obviously false or 'unreal' assumptions like these, often complain that theories which contain them do not concern the real economic world at all, but rather some simple, imaginary world dreamt up by the economist. And some developments in economics have been inspired by a desire to eliminate 'unreal assumptions' from economic theory, or at any rate, to make it more realistic than it already is.

In a famous essay '*On the Methodology of Positive Economics*', published in 1953, MILTON FRIEDMAN defended the apparently absurd view that 'unreal assumptions' are not a vice but a virtue:

'Truly important and significant hypotheses will be found to have "assumptions" that are wildly inaccurate descriptive representations of reality, and, in general, the more significant the theory, the more unrealistic the assumptions (in this sense)[1].'

Friedman went on to claim that an economic theory should not be criticized for containing 'unreal assumptions': the only legitimate way to criticize an economic theory is to point out that its *predictions* are at variance with the facts. Friedman's argument, sometimes called 'the F-twist', sparked off a vigorous controversy, which has continued right up to the present day.

* Professor of Philosophy, University of Otago, Dunedin, New Zealand.
1. MILTON FRIEDMAN [1953, p. 14].

ALAN MUSGRAVE

I shall not review the extensive literature which now exists concerning the F-twist. Such an enterprise would be unfruitful, I think, because both FRIEDMAN's original article and the subsequent discussion are marred by unclarity about the status of 'assumptions' in economic theories (and in physical theories, for that matter). More precisely, there has been a failure to distinguish between three different types of 'assumption', each of which makes a different type of assertion and therefore plays a different role in the theory. My aim in this note is simply to explain these distinctions, and to evaluate FRIEDMAN's original position in the light of them.

I. NEGLIGIBILITY ASSUMPTIONS

Suppose a scientist is investigating some phenomenon and has the hypothesis that some factor F which might be expected to affect that phenomenon actually has no effect upon it, or at least no detectable effect. For example, suppose that when GALILEO investigated the motion of bodies falling through relatively short distances or rolling down inclined planes, he supposed that air-resistance had no effect, or no detectable effect, on such motions. We might express this supposition by saying that the effect of air-resistance is *negligible*, or by saying that such bodies move *as if* there were no air-resistance or *as if* they were in a vacuum. Or less perspicaciously, we might say that GALILEO 'assumes a vacuum' or 'assumes that there is no air resistance'. For obvious reasons, I will call assumptions like these *negligibility assumptions*[2].

2. In any empirical situation there will be countless factors about which we *might* formulate negligibility assumptions but do not: GALILEO did not explicitly state that the colour of the experimenter's eyes or the day of the week on which he performed the experiment would not affect its outcome. Negligibility assumptions are stated only for factors which might be *expected* to have some effect but which, we claim, will not. GALILEO knew that air-resistance *does* affect objects falling through great distances or feathers falling through small ones: hence he stated explicitly that its affect on the motion of the objects in his experiments was negligible. The logical situation can be represented as follows. GALILEO first develops a theory for 'freely-falling bodies' or bodies falling in a vacuum. He then renders this theory testable against bodies falling (or rather rolling) short distances through air by adding to it the assertion that here air-resistance is negligible. (One might

378

'UNREAL ASSUMPTIONS' IN ECONOMIC THEORY

Now some of the time FRIEDMAN is clearly talking about negligibility assumptions; and much of what he says about them is true. In particular, he is quite right to insist that a theory containing a negligibility assumption can only be evaluated by testing its consequences. It would be plain silly to object to GALILEO that the objects in his experiments fall through air and not through a vacuum. For properly understood, GALILEO is not denying this at all, but rather asserting that the effect of air-resistance is negligible. To find out whether this is true, we must test the consequences of the entire theory. Now suppose an economist 'assumes that there is no government', meaning thereby to assert that the existence of the government has negligible effects on the phenomena he is investigating. It would be plain silly to object that his assumption is 'unreal' because there is, in fact, a government[3].

Again, FRIEDMAN is quite right to say that in general:

'A hypothesis is important if it "explains" much by little, that is, if it abstracts the common and crucial elements from the mass of complex and detailed circumstances surrounding the phenomena to be explained and permits valid predictions on the basis of them alone. [Such a hypothesis] takes account of, and accounts for, none of the many other attendant circumstances, since its very success shows them to be irrelevant for the phenomena to be explained[4].'

But FRIEDMAN is wrong to conclude from this that 'the more significant the theory, the more unrealistic the assumptions'. He is wrong to conclude:

also render the theory testable against objects falling through air by adding to it an auxiliary theory about the *non*-negligible difference the air will make – in this case the initial 'assumption of a vacuum' is not a *negligibility* assumption at all, but what I shall be calling a 'heuristic assumption'.)

3. Such objections could only be justified by the general principle that every factor in a social situation has a non-negligible effect on every other factor. This principle is assumed when it is said that while in the natural sciences negligibility assumptions can be true, in the social sciences they cannot. But this involves a kind of Bradleyan social metaphysic which I see little reason to accept: does the colour of a consumer's or a businessman's eyes have a non-negligible effect on his economic behaviour? (If it is objected that eye-colour is not an *economic* factor and can therefore be discounted, then we can in turn reply that what is an economic factor and what is not can only be discovered by proposing and testing theories containing negligibility assumptions.)

4. FRIEDMAN [1953, p. 14].

379

ALAN MUSGRAVE

'To be important, therefore, a hypothesis must be descriptively false in its assumptions... To put this point less paradoxically, the relevant question to ask about the "assumptions" of a theory is not whether they are descriptively "realistic", for they never are,...[5]'

This error stems from unclarity about what is stated by a negligibility assumption (and it is obviously such assumptions that FRIEDMAN has in mind here). They are not necessarily 'descriptively false', for they do not assert that present factors are absent but rather that they are 'irrelevant for the phenomena to be explained'. The relevant question to ask of them is whether they are true (or 'descriptively realistic'): but we can only try to answer this question by examining the consequences of the theory in which they are embedded.

I labour these obvious points because FRIEDMAN's unclarity about them seems to have led him into an *instrumentalist* view of economic theory. (Some of FRIEDMAN's critics deplore his lapse into instrumentalism; other writers applaud it.) According to the instrumentalist view, theories do not even *aim* to be true descriptions of reality, and cannot therefore really explain the phenomena derivable from them. Instead, theories are merely more or less useful instruments or tools for analysing and predicting phenomena. (Instrumentalism might better be called 'The Toolkit Theory of Scientific Theory'.) The lapse into instrumentalism is unnecessary. Negligibility assumptions are true or false descriptions of reality which help to explain features of it. GALILEO's assumption that air-resistance was negligible for the phenomena he investigated was a true statement about reality, and an important part of the explanation GALILEO gave of those phenomena. So much for negligibility assumptions.

II. DOMAIN ASSUMPTIONS

The whole issue is complicated by the fact that negligibility assumptions are not the only type of assumption. Suppose a scientist makes a negligibility assumption, embeds it in a theory, tests that theory, and finds that its predictions are false. He may pin the blame on his negligibility assumption, and decide that the factor F whose effects

5. FRIEDMAN [1953, pp. 14–25] (italics mine).

380

'UNREAL ASSUMPTIONS' IN ECONOMIC THEORY

he had assumed to be negligible does have significant effects after all. And he may conclude that his theory will only work where factor F is absent, and restrict its applicability to cases of this kind. He may retain the 'assumption' that F is absent, but now use it to specify the *domain of applicability* of his theory. Let us call assumptions of this second kind *domain assumptions*.

What begins as a negligibility assumption may, when it gets refuted, turn into a domain assumption. And the interesting thing is that this quite radical change in the theory may go unnoticed because the same form of words is used to express both assumptions. An economist who says 'assume the government has a balanced budget' may mean that any actual budget imbalance can be ignored because its effects on the phenomena he is investigating are negligible. But he may *also* mean precisely the opposite: that budget imbalance would have significant effects, so that his theory will only *apply* where such an imbalance does not exist.

The switch from a negligibility assumption to a domain assumption is important: it replaces a stronger or more testable theory with a weaker or less testable one. It is therefore an *ad hoc* modification, in POPPER's sense[6]. But we cannot unreservedly condemn such modifications: we value strength but we also value truth, and the weaker theory might be true where its stronger ancestor was false. For we do not falsify a theory containing a domain assumption by showing that this assumption is not true of some situation (or is not 'descriptively realistic', as FRIEDMAN would say); we merely show that the theory is not applicable to that situation in the first place. (We do, if you like, refute the claim that it was applicable.) If a domain assumption is always false, then the theory containing it can be applied to no actual situ-

6. See K. R. POPPER [1959, section 20, pp. 81–84]. POPPER here seems to condemn *ad hoc* modifications out of hand: but we may make progress with respect to truth if introducing a domain assumption replaces a stronger falsehood by a weaker truth. It is also worth noting here that the presence of a domain assumption in a theory does not turn it into a mere *instrument*: it remains a true or false description of a restricted domain of phenomena. 'If a thing is a swan, then it is white' is not a mere instrument just because it applies only to swans and cannot be refuted by observations of non-swans. (A form of instrumentalism will arise, however, if we deny that this universal proposition is a statement about the world *at all*, and construe it rather as an 'inference-licence': see my 'Wittgensteinian Instrumentalism', forthcoming in *Theoria*.)

381

ALAN MUSGRAVE

ation and is in fact untestable. If governments never balance budgets, then a theory about what happens *if they do* cannot be tested[7]. So if we value testability, we must hope that our domain assumptions are not always false; indeed, we must hope that they are true of as many actual situations as possible. FRIEDMAN does value testability. But concerning domain assumptions his dictum that 'the more significant the theory, the more unrealistic the assumptions' is precisely the reverse of the truth. The more unrealistic domain assumptions are, the less testable and hence less significant is the theory. Contrariwise, the more significant the theory, the more widely applicable it will be.

This might lead us to suppose that when FRIEDMAN spoke of 'assumptions' he had in mind only what we have called 'negligibility assumptions'. But that is not so. He speaks of 'the entirely valid use of "assumptions" in *specifying* the circumstances for which a theory holds[8].' And later he says:

'So far as I can see, the "assumptions of a theory"... are sometimes a convenient way of specifying the conditions under which the theory is expected to be valid[9].'

FRIEDMAN obviously refers here to what I call 'domain assumptions'. The fact is that he has not seen the crucial differences between these two kinds of assumption. So much for domain assumptions.

III. HEURISTIC ASSUMPTIONS

We have not yet done with 'assumptions', for the situation is more complicated still. We have seen how a negligibility assumption may, after it has been refuted, turn into a domain assumption. Now suppose that a scientist finds that his domain assumption is never true, so that his theory can never be (directly) tested. Obviously, if he is to have a testable theory, he must take into account the factor F whose presence he took first to be negligible and then to limit the

7. Or at least, it cannot be tested *directly*. We may test it *indirectly* by adding an account of how budget imbalances will influence or disturb the conclusions we have reached. But now our assumption of a balanced budget is playing a *third* distinct role in our overall theory: it is what I will call a '*heuristic assumption*' (see *below*).

8. FRIEDMAN [1953, p. 19].

9. FRIEDMAN [1953, p. 23].

382

'UNREAL ASSUMPTIONS' IN ECONOMIC THEORY

domain of applicability of his theory. But he may wish to *develop* such a theory in two stages: in the first stage he takes no account of factor *F*, or 'assumes' that it is negligible; in the second stage he takes account of it and says what difference it makes to his results. Here the 'assumption' that factor *F* is negligible is merely a heuristic device, a way of simplifying the logical development of the theory. Let us call such assumptions *heuristic assumptions*.

Heuristic assumptions play an important role in developing any theory whose logico-mathematical machinery is so complicated that a *method of successive approximation* has to be used. Yet their status is often misunderstood. Consider an example from physics. When NEWTON sought to discover what his theory predicted about the solar system, he first neglected inter-planetary gravitational forces by 'assuming' that there was only one planet orbiting the sun. He proved that, if his theory was correct, the planet would move in an ellipse with the sun at one of its foci. This assumption was not a negligibility assumption: NEWTON knew that planets would sometimes have detectable gravitational effects on one another. Nor was it a domain assumption: NEWTON was not saying that his theory only applied to one-planet solar systems. You miss the point if you object that NEWTON's assumption is false, because our solar system has more than one planet. You also miss the point, though less obviously, if you object that the *consequence* of NEWTON's assumption was false, because planets do not move exactly in ellipses. The consequences drawn from heuristic assumptions do not represent the precise predictions of the theory in question; rather, they are steps towards such precise predictions[10].

---

10. It is instructive to see NEWTON grappling, in effect, with one of the distinctions I have drawn (and getting misunderstood in the process). Proposition XIII, Theorem XIII of Book III of his *Principia* begins with the categorical statement '*The planets move in ellipses which have their common focus in the centre of the sun; and by radii drawn to that centre, they describe areas proportional to the times of description.*' (NEWTON [1934, vol. II, p. 420].) As a result, EDMUND HALLEY in his review of the *Principia* said that in it 'the verity of the *Hypothesis* of KEPLER is demonstrated' (*cf.* I. NEWTON [1958, p. 410]. But in the next sentence but one NEWTON restates the theorem thus: 'if the sun were at rest, and the other planets did not act one upon another, their orbits would be ellipses, having the sun in their common focus; and they would describe areas proportional to the times *of description*'. What sort of assumptions are contained in the 'if' clause here? The next sentence suggests that

383

ALAN MUSGRAVE

Now FRIEDMAN may have had 'heuristic assumptions' in mind when he said that 'the "assumptions of a theory"'... are often an economical mode of describing or presenting a theory' (though his subsequent elaboration of the point does not really bear this out[11]).

they are negligibility assumptions: 'the actions of the planets one upon another are so very small, that they may be neglected; and ... they disturb the motions of the planets around the sun in motion, less than if these motions were performed about the sun at rest'. But the next two sentences deny this: 'It is true, that the action of Jupiter upon Saturn is not to be neglected ... [for it produces] a perturbation of the orbit of Saturn in every conjunction of this planet with Jupiter, so sensible, that astronomers are puzzled with it'. And NEWTON goes on to explain that 'the perturbation of the orbit of Jupiter is much less than that of Saturn's. The perturbations of the other orbits are yet far less, except that the orbit of the earth is sensibly disturbed by the moon'. Subsequently, under the pressure of more refined astronomical observation, even NEWTON's restricted negligibility assumptions were turned into heuristic ones: this is, in effect, what the theory of perturbations is about.

   11. In elaborating the point, FRIEDMAN considers 'assumptions' or hypotheses like the following: 'Consider the density of leaves around a tree. I suggest the hypothesis that the leaves are positioned as if each leaf deliberately sought to maximise the amount of sunlight it receives' [1953, p. 19]; '...an expert billiard player ...[makes] his shots *as if* he knew the complicated mathematical formulas that would give the optimum directions of travel, could estimate accurately by eye the angles, etc., ...' [1953, p. 21]; and finally, 'under a wide range of circumstances individual firms behave *as if* they were seeking rationally to maximize their expected returns' [1953, p. 21]. Now such hypotheses are not obviously 'assumptions' of any of the three types I have distinguished. FRIEDMAN is clearly *right* that they cannot be criticised by pointing out that leaves do not deliberately seek anything, that expert billiard players may be ignorant of mechanics, or that businessmen may not know that to maximize expected returns they must equate marginal cost with marginal revenue. Such criticism is misguided precisely because we say '*It is as if p*', and not simply '*p*', when we do *not* want to assert the truth of *p*.

   Are such hypotheses simply convenient mathematical devices for predicting leaf-distribution on trees, billiard shots, or industrial behaviour? Are they, in other words, mere instruments which do not really explain the facts which they predict? I do not think that we are forced to such instrumentalist conclusions. For we can give our three hypotheses descriptive and explanatory force by recasting them as follows (the paraphrases are about as rough as the originals): 'Leaf-growth on trees is governed by principles, presumably fixed by natural selection, which have the effect of maximising the amount of sunlight which each leaf receives'; 'an expert billiard player is able, by unconscious and extremely rapid neural processes, to assess optimum directions of travel, estimate accurately by eye the angles, etc.'; 'under a wide range of circumstances the conscious deliberations which

384

'UNREAL ASSUMPTIONS' IN ECONOMIC THEORY

At any rate, his central thesis that 'the more significant the theory, the more unrealistic the assumptions' is not true of 'heuristic assumptions' either.

I have claimed that the so-called 'assumptions' of economic theories (and of other scientific theories) play (at least) three different roles within those theories, and are assertions of (at least) three different types. I have argued that FRIEDMAN overlooked these distinctions, and was led thereby to the mistaken thesis that 'the more significant the theory, the more unrealistic the assumptions'. (I have not shown, though I think it true, that subsequent discussions of FRIEDMAN's views are also bedevilled by the failure to draw these distinctions.)

Finally, I have conjectured that criticism may change the status of an assumption: what in youth was a bold and adventurous negligibility assumption, may be reduced in middle-age to a sedate domain assumption, and decline in old-age into a mere heuristic assumption. Such changes can be almost imperceptible if the same form of words is employed for all three 'assumptions'. It is an interesting historical question whether this has actually happened in the development of economic theory, and in particular, whether it has happened in the development of the theories which FRIEDMAN invokes his methodology to defend. I have the impression that it has sometimes happened, and that this has gone unnoticed in the debate. If this is correct, then perhaps economists would do well to try to make it clear exactly which sort of assumption they are making at any point in their investigations. The English language has the resources to make this possible, and in several different ways. For example, 'Assume that the budget is balanced' might be written 'Whether or not the budget is balanced makes no detectable difference to the phenomena being

---

underlie business behaviour have the overall effect of maximising expected returns'. (Notice that while the three 'as if' statements are non a par, the three paraphrases are not. This is as it should be: leaves do not deliberate consciously or unconsciously, while billiard players *do* act on their assessment of the situation of the balls (which they cannot articulate in mechanical terms), and businessmen make *conscious* and articulable decisions.) I prefer the paraphrases. This is partly because I prefer scientific realism to instrumentalism. It is also because the paraphrases eliminate 'as if': for the *logic* of 'as if' statements (what follows from them and what does not follow from them) is terribly unclear.

385

ALAN MUSGRAVE

investigated' *(negligibility assumption)* or it might be written 'If the budget is balanced, then...' *(domain assumption)* or it might be written 'Assume for the moment that the budget is balanced (we will relax this assumption shortly)' *(heuristic assumption)*. Misunderstanding, misguided criticism, and methodological controversy, could be alleviated if this rather prosaic recommendation were to be followed.

REFERENCES

FRIEDMAN, MILTON: 'The Methodology of Positive Economics', in: *Essays in positive economics*, Chicago: University of Chicago Press, 1953, pp. 3–43.
NEWTON, ISAAC: *Sir Isaac Newton's Mathematical Principles of Natural Philosophy and his System of the World*, translated by A. MOTTE, revised by F. CAJORI, Berkeley/Los Angeles: University of California Press, 1934.
NEWTON, ISAAC: *Isaac Newton's Papers and Letters on Natural Philosophy*, edited by I. B. COHEN, London, Cambridge University Press, 1958.
POPPER, KARL R.: *The Logic of Scientific Discovery*, London, Hutchinson & Co., 1959.

SUMMARY

Economic theory is often criticized for the lack of 'realism' of its assumptions. MILTON FRIEDMAN rebutted such criticism with the famous dictum 'the more significant the theory, the more unrealistic the assumptions'. FRIEDMAN's position, often called the '*F-twist*', stems from his failure to distinguish three different types of assumption. *Negligibility assumptions* state that some factor has a negligible effect upon the phenomenon under investigation. *Domain assumptions* specify the domain of applicability of the theory. *Heuristic assumptions* are a means of simplifying the logical development of the theory. It is argued that FRIEDMAN's dictum is false of all three types of assumption. Finally, it is conjectured that what began as a negligibility assumption may be changed under the impact of criticism first into a domain assumption, then into a mere heuristic assumption; and that these important changes will go unnoticed if the different types of assumption are not clearly distinguished from one another.

ZUSAMMENFASSUNG

Die Wirtschaftswissenschaften werden oft wegen Mangels an Realismus in den Annahmen kritisiert. MILTON FRIEDMAN wies diesen Kritizismus mit seinem berühmten Ausspruch «je signifikanter die Theorie, desto unrealistischer die Annahmen» zurück. FRIEDMANS Standpunkt, oft « *F-Twist* » genannt, beruht auf dem Versäumnis, drei Typen von Annahmen zu unterscheiden: *Annahmen über Unerhebliches* behaupten, dass ein Faktor nur eine vernachlässigbare Wirkung auf den

386

'UNREAL ASSUMPTIONS' IN ECONOMIC THEORY

Untersuchungsgegenstand ausübt. *Domäne-Annahmen* grenzen den Anwendungs-
bereich für eine Theorie ein. *Heuristische Annahmen* sind ein Mittel, um die logische
Entwicklung einer Theorie zu vereinfachen. Schliesslich wird vermutet, dass, was
als Annahme über Unerhebliches begann, unter dem Druck der Kritik zuerst in
eine Domäne-Annahme und dann in eine bloss heuristische Annahme geändert
wird; und dass diese wichtigen Änderungen unbemerkt bleiben, weil die verschie-
denen Typen von Annahmen nicht klar voneinander unterschieden sind.

RÉSUMÉ

On critique souvent un manque de réalisme dans les suppositions de la théorie
économique. MILTON FRIEDMAN rejette cette critique avec le mot célèbre: «plus
la théorie est significative, moins les suppositions sont réalistes». Le point de vue
de FRIEDMAN, souvent appelé le «*F-twist*», provient du fait qu'il ne distingue pas
trois types différents de suppositions. Une *supposition d'influence négligeable* indique
que tel facteur n'a qu'une influence négligeable sur le phénomène étudié. Une
supposition relative à un domaine indique le domaine où telle théorie peut s'appliquer.
Une *supposition heuristique* permet de simplifier le développement logique d'une
théorie. Dans cet article, on soutient que le mot de FRIEDMAN est faux pour chacun
des trois types de suppositions. Enfin, on formule l'hypothèse suivante: ce qui à
l'origine a été une supposition d'influence négligeable peut, sous l'effet de la critique, se transformer en supposition relative à un domaine, ensuite en simple
supposition heuristique; de plus, ces transformations passeront inaperçues si l'on
ne distingue pas bien nettement les différents types de suppositions.

387

5

Criticism and the Neoclassical Maximization Hypothesis

Lawrence Boland, 'On the Futility of Criticizing the Neoclassical Maxim-
ization Hypothesis', *American Economic Review*, vol. 71, no. 5, Dece-
mber 1981, pp. 1031–6.
Bruce Caldwell, 'The Neoclassical Maximization Hypothesis: Comment',
American Economic Review, vol. 73, no. 4, September 1983, pp.
824–7.
Lawrence Boland, 'The Neoclassical Maximization Hypothesis: Reply',
American Economic Review, vol. 73, no. 4, pp. 828–30.

Editor's comments

On the following pages, Larry Boland and I disagree about the best
definition of the word 'criticism'. Perhaps more important than our
disagreement is that we both believe that the neoclassical maximization
hypothesis – Hutchison's 'fundamental assumption' – cannot be tested.
We come to this conclusion from different routes. Boland claims that the
logical form of the maximization assumption, that of an 'all-and-some'
statement, renders it untestable. I prefer to emphasize empirical problems
that arise when tests of the hypothesis are attempted. If Boland and I are
right, then those who claim that the assumption should be tested (or, even
stronger, that it has been tested and confirmed) are wrong.

Though we concur about the untestability of the maximization assumption, Boland thinks that attempts to criticize it are futile, whereas I
argue that it can be criticized and that past attempts at criticism have been
fruitful. Our real quarrel is about what types of criticism should count.
Broadly speaking, Boland thinks that only logically compelling criticism
is important, and I argue that other kinds of criticism should also be
considered.

By including two of my own articles in this reader, I am already open to
the charge of being immodest. I do not wish to be open to the additional
charge of being disingenuous. Therefore, I won't make any further comments on this debate.

On the Futility of Criticizing the Neoclassical Maximization Hypothesis

By Lawrence A. Boland*

The last few years have seen an intensification of methodological criticism of the foundations of neoclassical theory and in particular of the maximization hypothesis. Harvey Leibenstein argued for a "Micro-Micro Theory" on the grounds that profit maximization is not necessarily the objective of the actual decision makers in a firm and that a complete explanation would require an explanation of intrafirm behavior. He also gave arguments for why maximization of anything may not be realistic or is at best a special case. Herbert Simon's Nobel lecture argued that individuals do not actually maximize anything—they "satisfice." And of course, George Shackle has for many years argued that maximization is not even possible.

Some antineoclassical economists are very encouraged by these arguments, but I think these arguments are unsuccessful. For anyone opposed to neoclassical theory, a misdirected criticism which by its failure only adds apparent credibility to neoclassical theory will be worse than the absence of criticism The purpose of this paper is to explain why, although the neoclassical hypothesis is *not* a tautology, no criticism of that hypothesis will ever be successful. My arguments will be based first on the possible types of theoretical criticism and the logic of those criticisms, and second on the methodological status of the maximization hypothesis in neoclassical explanations.

I. Types of Criticism and the Maximization Hypothesis

There are only two types of criticism of any behavioral hypothesis once one has established its logical validity. One can argue against the *possibility* of the hypothesized behavior or one can argue against the empirical truth of the premise of the hypothesis. In the case of the neoclassical maximization hypothesis, virtually everyone accepts the logical validity of the hypothesis. For example, everyone can accept that *if* the consumer is a utility maximizer, then for the particular bundle of goods chosen: (a) the marginal utility is zero, and (b) the slope of the marginal utility curve at the point representing the chosen bundle is nonpositive and usually negative.[1] That is to say, necessarily the marginal increment to the objective must be zero and falling (or not rising) whenever (i.e., without exception) the maximization premise is actually true. Of course, one could substitute the word "profit" for the word "utility" and the logic of the hypothesis still holds. In either form (a) and (b) are the "necessary conditions" for maximization. Note that there are no "sufficient conditions" for maximization. Rather, the maximization premise is the sufficient condition for (a) and (b).

Parenthetically, I should note that economists often refer to (b), or more properly to the conjunction of (a) and (b), as a sufficient condition for maximization. This is a common error. Even if (a) and (b) are both true, only *local* maximization is assured. However, maximization in general (i.e., *global*) is what the premise explicitly asserts and is not assured by (a) and (b) alone. I will return to this in Section III when I discuss the methodological uses of the maximization hypothesis.

II. The Logical Basis for Criticism

As stated above, there are two types of criticism of the maximization hypothesis: the

*Professor of economics, Simon Fraser University. I thank Robert Clower, John Chant, Mahmood Khan, Shyam Kamath, James Dean, and John Richards for the helpful suggestions for improving an earlier draft.

[1] Note that any hypothesized utility function may already have the effects of constraints built in as is the case with the Lagrange multiplier technique.

1031

246

possibilities criticism and the *empirical* criticism. In this section I will examine the logical bases of these critiques, namely of the possibilities argument which concerns only the *necessary conditions* and of the empirical argument which concerns only the *sufficient conditions*. In each case I will also discuss the possible logical defense for these criticisms.

A. *The Possibilites Critique: Can the Necessary Conditions be Fulfilled?*

The possibilities critique builds on the difference between necessary and sufficient conditions. Specifically, what is criticized is the possibility of fulfilling *all* of the necessary conditions for maximization. Of course, this type of critique begs the question as to what are all the necessary conditions. Are there more conditions than the (a) and (b) listed above? Shackle, following Friedrich Hayek and John Maynard Keynes, argues that maximization also presumes that the knowledge necessary for the process of choosing the "best" alternative has been acquired.[2] That is to say, as a behavioral hypothesis (i.e., about the behavior of decision makers) if maximization is a deliberate act, Shackle argues that the actor must have acquired all of the information necessary to determine or calculate which alternative maximizes utility (or profit, etc.) and he argues that such acquisition is impossible hence deliberate maximization is an impossible act.

This argument appears to be quite strong although it is rather elementary. A closer examination will show it to be overly optimistic because it is epistemologically presumptive. One needs to ask: *Why* is the possession of the necessary knowledge impossible? This question clearly involves one's epistemology — that is, one's theory of knowledge. The answer, I think, is quite simple. Shackle's argument (also Hayek's and Keynes') presumes that the truth of one's knowledge requires an inductive proof (see my 1978 paper). And as everyone knows today, there is no inductive logic which could supply a proof whenever the amount of information is finite or it is otherwise incomplete (for example, about the future).

The strength of the Shackle-Hayek-Keynes argument is actually rather vulnerable. Inductive proofs (and hence inductive logic) are not necessary for true knowledge. One's knowledge (i.e., one's theory) can be true even though one does not know it to be true—that is, even if one does not have proof. But I think there is an even stronger objection to the "true knowledge is necessary for maximization" argument. *True* knowledge is not necessary for maximization! As I have argued elsewhere, the consumer, for example, only has to think that his theory of what is the shape of his utility function is true. Once the consumer picks the "best" option there is no reason to deviate or engage in "disequilibrium behavior" unless he is prone to testing his own theories.[3]

In summary, the Shackle-Hayek-Keynes inductivist argument against the possibility of a true maximization hypothesis is a failure. Inductive proofs are not necessary for true knowledge and true knowledge (by any means) is not necessary for successful or determinate decision making. Maximization behavior cannot be ruled out as a logical impossibility.

B. *The Empirical Critiques: Is the Sufficient Premise True?*

Simon and Leibenstein argue against the maximization hypothesis in a more straightforward way. While accepting the logical validity of the hypothesis, they simply deny the truth of the premise of the hypothesis. They would allow that *if* the consumer is actually a maximizer, the hypothesis would be a true explanation of the consumer's behavior but they say the premise is false;

---

[2]Although the Shackle-Hayek-Keynes argument applies to the assumption of either local or global maximization, it is most telling in the case of global maximization.

[3]Again this raises the question of the intended meaning of the maximization premise. If global maximization is the intended meaning, then the consumer must have a (theory of his) preference ordering over all conceivable alternative bundles. At a very minimum, he must be able to distinguish between local maxima all of which satisfy both necessary conditions, (a) and (b).

consumers are not necessarily maximizers hence their behavior (for example, their demand) would not necessarily be determinable on that basis. Leibenstein may allow that the consumer's behavior can be determined, but it is an open question as to what is the determining factor—utility, prestige, social convention, etc.? Simon seems to reject as well the necessity of determinate explanation although he does discuss alternate decision rules to substitute for the maximization rule.[4]

A denial of the maximization hypothesis on empirical grounds raises the obvious question: How do they know the premise is false? Certain methodological considerations would seem to give an advantage to the critics over those who argue in its favor. Recall that we distinguish between those statements which are verifiable (i.e., can be proven true) and those which are refutable (i.e., can be proven false) on purely logical grounds. As we know, (strictly) universal statements—those of the form "*all X*'s have property *Y*"—are refutable (if false) but not verifiable (even if true). On the other hand, (strictly) existential statements—those of the form "there are *some X*'s which have property *Y*"—are verifiable (if true) but not refutable (even if false). At first glance it would seem that the maximization hypothesis —"all decision makers are maximizers"—is straightforwardly a universal statement and hence is refutable but not verifiable. But the statistical problems of empirical refutation present many difficulties. Some of them are well known, but as I shall show a little later, the logical problems are insurmountable.

The methodological problems of empirical refutations of economic theories are widely accepted. In the case of utility maximization we realize that survey reports are suspect and direct observations of the decision-making process are difficult or impossible. In this sense behavioral maximization is not directly testable. The only objective part of the maximization hypothesis is the set of logical consequences such as the uniquely determinate choices. One might thus attempt an indirect test of maximization by examining the outcomes of maximization, namely, the implied pattern of observable choices based on a presumption that there is a utility function and that utility is being maximized by the choices made.

If one wishes to avoid errors in logic, an indirect test of any behavioral hypothesis which is based on a direct examination of its logical consequences must be limited to attempting refutations of one or more of the necessary conditions for the truth of the hypothesis. For example, in the case of consumer theory, whenever utility maximization is the basis of observed choices, a necessary condition is that for any given pattern of choices the "Slutsky Theorem" must hold (see William Baumol, pp. 336–39). It might appear then that the above methodological problems of observation could be easily overcome, since the Slutsky Theorem can in principle be made to involve only observable quantities and prices. And, if one could refute the Slutsky Theorem then one could indirectly refute the maximization hypothesis.[5] Unfortunately, even if from this perspective such an indirect refutation cannot be ruled out on logical grounds alone, the methodological problems concerning observations will remain.

The fundamental methodological problem of refuting any behavioral hypothesis indirectly is that of constructing a convincing refutation. Any indirect test of the utility maximization hypothesis will be futile if it is to be based on a test of any logically derived implication (such as the Slutsky Theorem). On the one hand, everyone—even critics of maximization—will accept the theorem's logical validity. On the other hand, given the numerous constraints involved in any concrete situation, the problems of observation

[4]Some people have interpreted Simon's view to be saying that the reason why decision makers merely satisfice is that it would be "too costly" to collect all the necessary information to determine the unique maximum. But this interpretation is inconsistent if it is a justification of assuming only "satisficing" as it would imply cost minimization which of course is just the dual of utility maximization!

[5]For example, if one could show that when the income effect is positive but the demand curve is positively sloped, then the Slutsky Theorem would be false or there is no utility maximization (see Cliff Lloyd).

will be far more complex than those outlined by the standard theory. Thus, it is not difficult to see that there are numerous obstacles in the way of constructing any convincing refutation of maximization, one which would be beyond question.

I now wish to offer some new considerations about the potential refutations of the neoclassical behavioral hypothesis. I will argue here that even if one could prove that a consumer is not maximizing utility or a producer is not maximizing profit, this would not constitute a refutation of the neoclassical hypothesis. The reason why is that the actual form of the neoclassical premise is not a strictly universal statement. Properly stated, the neoclassical premise is: "For all decision makers there is something they maximize." This statement has the form which is called an "All-and-some statement." All-and-some statements are neither verifiable nor refutable! As a universal statement claiming to be true for all decision makers, it is unverifiable. But, although it is a universal statement and it should be logically possible to prove it is false when it is false (viz., by providing a counterexample) this form of universal statement cannot be so easily rejected. Any alleged counterexample is unverifiable *even if the counterexample is true*!

Let me be specific. Given the premise— "All consumers maximize something"—the critic can claim he has found a consumer who is not maximizing anything. The person who assumed the premise is true can respond: "You claim you have found a consumer who is not a maximizer but how do you know there is not something which he is maximizing?" In other words, the verification of the counterexample requires the refutation of a strictly existential statement; and as stated above, we all agree that one cannot refute existential statements.

In summary, empirical arguments such as Simon's or Leibenstein's that deny the truth of the maximization hypothesis are no more testable than the hypothesis itself. Note well, the logical impossibility of proving or disproving the truth of any statement does not indicate anything about the truth of that statement. The neoclassical assumption of universal maximization could very well be

false, but as a matter of logic we cannot expect ever to be able to prove that it is.

III. The Importance of Distinguishing between Tautologies and Metaphysics

Some economists have charged that the maximization hypothesis should be rejected because, they argue, since the hypothesis is not testable it must then be a tautology hence it is "meaningless" or "unscientific." Although they may be correct about its testability, they are wrong about its being necessarily a tautology. Statements which are untestable are not necessarily tautologies because they may merely be metaphysical.

A. *Distinguishing between Tautologies and Metaphysics*

Tautologies are statements which are true by virtue of their logical form alone—that is, one cannot even conceive of how they could ever be false. For example, the statement "I am here or I am not here" is true regardless of the meaning of the nonlogical words "I" or "here." There is no conceivable counterexample for this tautological statement. But, the maximization hypothesis is not a tautology. It is conceivably false. Its truth or falsity is not a matter of logical form. The problem with the hypothesis is that it is metaphysical.

A statement which is a tautology is intrinsically a tautology. One cannot make it a nontautology merely by being careful about how it is being used. A statement which is metaphysical is *not* intrinsically metaphysical. Its metaphysical status is a result of *how* it is used in a research program. Metaphysical statements can be false but we may never know because they are the assumptions of a research program which are *deliberately put beyond question*. Of course, a metaphysical assumption may be a tautology but that is not a necessity.

Typically, a metaphysical statement has the form of an existential statement (for example, there is class conflict; there is a price system; there is an invisible hand; there will be a revolution; etc.). It would be an error to think that because a metaphysical existential statement is irrefutable that it must also be a tautology. More importantly, a unanimous acceptance of the truth of any existential statement still does not mean it is a tautology.

Some theorists inadvertently create tautologies with their *ad hoc* attempts to overcome any possible informational incompleteness of their theories. For example, as an explanation, global maximization implies the adequacy of the consumer's preferences or his theory of all conceivable bundles which in turn implies his acceptance of an unverifiable universal statement. Some theorists thus find global maximization uncomfortable as it expects too much of any decision maker—but the usual reaction only makes matters worse. The maximization hypothesis is easily transformed into a tautology by limiting the premise to local maximization. Specifically, while the necessary conditions (a) and (b) are not sufficient for global maximization, they are sufficient for local maximization. If one then changes the premise to say, "if the consumer is maximizing over the neighborhood of the chosen bundle," one is only begging the question as to how the neighborhood was chosen. If the neighborhood is defined as that domain over which the rate of change of the slope of the marginal utility curve is monotonically increasing or decreasing, then at best the hypothesis is circular. But what is more important here, if one limits the premise to local maximization, one would severely limit the explanatory power or generality of the allegedly explained behavior.[6] One would be better off maintaining one's metaphysics rather than creating tautologies to seal their defense.

B. *Metaphysics vs. Methodology*

Fifty years ago metaphysics was considered a dirty word but today most people realize that every explanation has its metaphysics. Every model or theory is merely another attempted test of the "robustness" of a given metaphysics. Every research program has a foundation of given behavioral or structural assumptions. Those assumptions are implicitly ranked according to their questionability. The last assumptions on such a rank-ordered list are the metaphysics of that research program. They can even be used to define that research program. In the case of neoclassical economics, the maximization hypothesis plays this methodological role. Maximization is considered fundamental to everything; even an assumed equilibrium need not actually be put beyond question as disequilibrium in a market is merely a consequence of the failure of all decision makers to maximize. Thus, those economists who put maximization beyond question cannot "see" any disequilibria (for example, the Coase theorem).

The research program of neoclassical economics is the challenge of finding a neoclassical explanation for any given phenomenon—that is, whether it is possible to show that the phenomenon can be seen as a logical consequence of maximizing behavior—thus, maximization is beyond question for the purpose of accepting the challenge.[7] The only question of substance is whether a theorist is willing to say what it would take to convince him or her that the metaphysics used failed the test. For the reasons I have given in Section II, no logical criticism of maximization can ever convince a neoclassical theorist that there is something intrinsically wrong with the maximization hypothesis.

Whether maximization should be part of anyone's metaphysics is a methodological problem. Since maximization is part of the metaphysics, neoclassical theorists too often employ *ad hoc* methodology in order to deflect possible criticism; thus any criticism or defense of neoclassical maximization must

---

[6] See fn. 3 above. If one interprets maximization to mean only local maximization, then the question is begged as to how a consumer has chosen between competing local maxima.

[7] For these reasons the maximization hypothesis might be called the "paradigm" according to Thomas Kuhn's view of science. But note that the existence of a paradigm or of a metaphysical statement in any research program is not a psychological quirk of the researcher. Metaphysical statements are necessary because we cannot simultaneously explain everything. There must be some exogenous variables or some assumptions (for example, universal statements) in every explanation whether it is scientific or not.

deal with neoclassical methodology rather than the truth of the assumption. Specifically, when criticizing any given assumption of maximization it would seem that critics need only be careful to determine whether or not the truth of the assumption matters. It is true that for followers of Friedman's instrumentalism, the truth of the assumption does not matter hence for strictly methodological reasons it is futile to criticize maximization. And the reasons are quite simple. Practical success does not require true knowledge and instrumentalism presumes that the sole objective of research in economic theory is immediate solutions to practical problems. The truth of assumptions supposedly matters to those economists who reject Friedman's instrumentalism, but for those economists interested in developing economic theory for its own sake, I have argued here that it is still futile to criticize the maximization hypothesis. There is nothing intrinsically wrong with the maximization hypothesis. The only problem, if there is a problem, resides in the methodological attitude of most neoclassical economists.

REFERENCES

William Baumol, *Economic Theory and Operations Analysis*, Englewood Cliffs: Prentice-Hall, 1977.

L. Boland, "Time in Economics vs. Economics in Time," *Canadian J. Econ.*, May 1978, *11*, 240–62.

F. Hayek, "Economics and Knowledge," *Economica*, Feb. 1937, *4*, 33–54.

J. M. Keynes, "The General Theory of Employment," *Quart. J. Econ.*, Feb. 1937, *51*, 209–23.

H. Leibenstein, "A Branch of Economics is Missing: Micro-Micro Theory," *J. Econ. Lit.*, June 1979, *17*, 477–502.

C. Lloyd, "On the Falsifiability of Traditional Demand Theory," *Metroeconomica*, Aug. 1965, *17*, 17–23.

George Shackle, *Epistemics and Economics*, Cambridge: Cambridge University Press, 1973.

H. Simon, "Rational Decision Making in Business Organizations," *Amer. Econ. Rev.*, Sept. 1979, *69*, 493–513.

The Neoclassical Maximization Hypothesis: Comment

By BRUCE J. CALDWELL*

In a recent paper in this *Review*, Lawrence Boland argues it is "futile" to criticize the neoclassical maximization hypothesis. His argument is summarized as follows.

1) "There are only two types of criticism of any behavioral hypothesis once one has established its logical validity. One can argue against the *possibility* of the hypothesized behavior or one can argue against the empirical truth of the premise of the hypothesis" (p. 1031). Boland hopes to show that neither of the two forms of criticism works against the maximization hypothesis.

2) One cannot *prove* the *logical impossibility* of the maximization hypothesis. Attempts to do so fail for one of two reasons: either one must assume that inductive proofs are necessary for true knowledge, or one must assume that true knowledge is necessary for maximization (see pp. 1032–33). Boland argues that neither assumption can be maintained.

3) Regarding empirical criticism, "The methodological problems of empirical refutations of economic theories are widely accepted" (p. 1033).

4) Even were this not true, the logical form of the maximization hypothesis (an "all-and-some statement") makes it neither verifiable nor refutable. "[E]ven if one could prove that a consumer is not maximizing utility...this would not constitute a refutation of the neoclassical hypothesis" (p. 1034), because one can always claim that the consumer was maximizing *some*thing, that is, something *other* than utility.

5) Finally, this does not imply that the hypothesis is necessarily a tautology. The

hypothesis is best considered an untestable "metaphysical statement" which is an essential component of the neoclassical research program.

Points 3 and 5 above attributed to Boland are acceptable as stated. They are related points: the empirical problems mentioned in point 3 are sufficient to establish the untestability of the maximization hypothesis, which supports the conclusion in point 5. The purpose of this comment is to criticize points 1, 2, and 4. Specifically, it is shown that though there are only two forms of *logically compelling* criticism, many other forms of criticism that are useful exist; and that given a broader interpretation of the term criticism, Boland's remarks about proofs of logical impossibility, though correct, miss the point of what critics of the maximization hypothesis tried to do. An alternative to Boland's characterization of the maximization hypothesis as an all-and-some statement, one more consistent with well-known developments in philosophy of science, is also presented. In the final section, it is shown that Boland's approach of necessity neglects some widely known and relevant developments in the methodological literature.

I. The Untestability of the Maximization Hypothesis

An area of agreement can be noted first: Boland is on firm ground when he states that the maximization hypothesis is untestable. (Metaphysical seems a rather loaded word, but it is acceptable.) There are a number of problems associated with testing the hypothesis; perhaps the most telling is that any direct test, including the revealed preference approach, requires that assumptions be made concerning the stability of preferences of the choosing agent, as well as the states of information confronting him. Since the content of these assumptions (properly called initial

*Associate Professor of Economics, University of North Carolina, Greensboro, NC 27412. I would like to thank Lawrence Boland and members of the New York University Colloquium in Austrian Economics, 1981–82, for many valuable comments on earlier drafts. Any remaining errors are my own.

conditions) are subject to change but are not themselves directly testable, test results (whether confirming or disconfirming) are not unambiguously interpretable. Whether we interpret this to mean that the hypothesis is untestable, or that it is conceivably testable but that test results are not unambiguously interpretable, is a matter of semantic preference. The point is that the maximization hypothesis is neither directly (since preferences are nonobservable, and introspection and surveys are ruled out as unreliable) nor indirectly testable, in the usual senses of these terms.

II. Forms of Criticism

Boland's assertion that there are only two forms of criticism of a logically valid behavioral hypothesis is true if one counts only logically compelling criticism as legitimate or important. But such a narrow definition of criticism is of little use when one considers the appraisal of scientific theories, all of which (if we take Kuhn and Lakatos seriously) contain untestable, "metaphysical" hard cores, theoretical terms which do not make reference to observable entities, and the like. In the evaluation and criticism of scientific theories, a number of criteria of appraisal may be employed, depending on the purposes of the theory in question: predictive adequacy, simplicity, generality, heuristic value, mathematical elegance, plausibility, and extensibility are among the criteria commonly mentioned. The definitions of, and the relative weights that should be attached to, such criteria have provided the grist for numerous debates in economic methodology. Criticism can also take place on another level —Karl Popper's distinction between internal and external criticism comes to mind.[1] In short, there are many routes to criticism in the appraisal of scientific theories; Boland's definition of criticism is overly narrow. His

[1] Criteria of theory appraisal are discussed in Vincent Tarascio and myself. See Stanley Wong for an application of the internal-external criticism framework to a research program in economics.

restricted definition causes Boland to misinterpret the writings of other economists, as is shown next.

III. Proofs of Logical Impossibility

Boland is correct in asserting that no one has thus far *proven* the *logical impossibility* of the maximization hypothesis: after all, even if an agent has *zero* information, he still may choose the "best" option, or think that he has. But Boland's point is trivial: no one has ever attempted to prove the logical impossibility of the maximization hypothesis!

Boland is blinded by constructs which are of his own making. *If* one believes that there are only two forms of criticism, then one might believe that the works of Keynes, Hayek, and Shackle are attempts to prove logical impossibility. But a far more reasonable interpretation of these economists' efforts is that they all questioned the *usefulness* of a research program that either ignores the question of information, or posits agents with full information over all past, present, and future states of the world. Both Hayek and Shackle are subjectivists (as was Keynes on some readings), and *that* fact explains the emphasis on decision making under uncertainty, on the formation of expectations, and on the process of knowledge acquisition and dissemination that figures so prominently in their works. By focusing on proofs of logical impossibility, Boland misses both the intent, and worse, the significance of these economists' contributions.

In recent years, economists outside of the subjectivist camp (and this includes both advocates and critics of the neoclassical program) have asked similar questions. Indeed, even if one focuses only on the present "orthodoxy" in economics, such questioning has led to some of the most important recent work in economic theory-decision theory; various approaches to the modelling of expectations formation; the rationale for a monetary economy; search, contract, and optimal control theory; and so on. It is a telling indictment of Boland's definition of "criticism" that the sorts of questions that have led to these developments either would not count as criticism, or would be lumped with the straw man of "proofs of logical impossibility," and thereby dismissed as unfounded.

IV. The Logical Form of the Maximization Hypothesis

Boland notes that affirmative universal statements are not verifiable, even if true, and that affirmative existential statements are not refutable, even if false. He then argues that the maximization hypothesis, restated as "*All* consumers maximize *some* thing," is a hybrid all-and-some statement that is neither verifiable nor refutable, hence untestable. Though Boland's conclusion that the hypothesis is untestable is correct, it only works because the term "utility" has been replaced by the term "something" in the hypothesis. A more direct approach, offered below, demonstrates that the hypothesis "All consumers maximize utility" is untestable, *not* because of its logical form, but due to the presence of an undefined theoretical term, utility, in the sentence. This more direct approach has the added advantage of being consistent with well-known results in philosophy of science. The argument is by analogy.

Take the sentence, "All consumers maximize glitch." It has the logical form of an affirmative universal statement, so should be refutable, but not verifiable, according to Boland. But because "glitch" has been left undefined in the protocol language, the statement is neither verifiable nor refutable.

If the undefined term "utility" is substituted for "glitch," the same problem exists, *not* because the form of the sentence has changed, but because (in many formulations by economists) utility is undefined. Boland's logical objection, which holds when "utility" is taken to mean "something," can also be viewed as an empirical problem: a sentence containing an undefined theoretical term is not directly testable. (In their attempts to "operationalize" the concept of utility, revealed preference theorists avoid this problem. Unfortunately, they are still faced with the other empirical problems mentioned earlier.)

Boland's argument provides a textbook example of why logical empiricists since the mid-1930's have avoided discussing scientific theories in terms of the cognitive significance of individual sentences. Their predecessors, the logical positivists, tried to rid scientific discourse of the metaphysical by insisting that only analytic and synthetic sentences be accepted as cognitively significant. Identifying analytic sentences seemed to pose no problems (until Quine raised some questions), but it was necessary to find some criterion by which legitimate synthetic statements could be separated from metaphysical ones. Testability was the criterion chosen, but making that notion concrete proved difficult. Neither verifiability nor falsifiability were acceptable criteria because sentences expressed in certain common forms (affirmative universal and affirmative existential) would have to be ruled out as "metaphysical," even though they are widely used in scientific discourse.

An additional problem, independent of the notion of sentence forms, existed. Sentences making reference to unobservable theoretical entities (atoms, magnetic fields) often cannot be directly tested. Some philosophers and scientists (following Bridgman and Mach) recommended that all such theoretical terms be replaced by operational ones, but most recognized the important role played by theoretical terms in scientific theories.[2]

Both problems were resolved when strength of confirmation became the criterion of cognitive significance embraced by logical empiricists like Carnap, Hempel, and Nagel. Rather than check each sentence for cognitive significance, entire theories would be tested. Not every term would be required to have an empirical counterpart, but such undefined "theoretical terms" would gain meaning indirectly when the theories in which they were embedded survived numerous test instances. The logical empiricist solution has been challenged by both Popperian falsificationists and growth of knowledge theorists like Kuhn, but that is another story.[3] What is

---

[2] The necessity of retaining theoretical terms in scientific discourse is discussed in Carl Hempel.

[3] For a more thorough development of these themes, see my earlier article.

important for our purposes is that when utility is viewed as an undefined theoretical term, the hypothesis is rendered untestable, and that this approach avoids the circumlocution of transforming the hypothesis into an all-and-some statement.

V. The Ingenuity of Economists

It can finally be noted that many (though not all) economists have recognized that the maximization hypothesis is untestable, and that their responses to this apparent dilemma have been varied and, at times, ingenious.

Empiricists of all stripes try to reformulate the problem in operational terms. Certain Austrians, on the other hand, insist that the hypothesis (albeit expressed in slightly different form) is the fundamental axiom of human action which is known to be true a priori but which nonetheless has empirical content. (This is perhaps the most radical interpretation in that it presupposes an alternative epistemology.) Fritz Machlup views "homunculus oeconomicus" as an ideal type, an artificial device whose acceptability as a theoretical construct depends on the range of applicability of the theories in which he is used. James Buchanan distinguishes between a nonpredictive logic of choice, in which choices are based on the subjective perceptions of individual agents, and a predictive science of choice, in which specific, falsifiable predictions about choice behavior are made. Milton Friedman argues that the assumption should be ignored altogether, and that economists should focus instead on the predictive adequacy and simplicity of theories. Gary Becker and Armen Alchian insist that market behavior, not individual behavior, reveals rationality. And for those who believe that the individual agent should still receive attention, Becker joins with George Stigler to argue that alleged differences in tastes and preferences, usually viewed as exogenously determined by economists, can

themselves be explained as responses to changes in incomes and relative prices.

Thus both advocates and opponents of the hypothesis have discussed at length the status of the maximization postulate. Sometimes the hypothesis is viewed as possessing empirical content, and sometimes it is expressed as a tautology; sometimes it is the centerpiece of a theoretical system, and sometimes a barely noticed artifact. Boland's contribution, though it sounds quite controversial, actually adds little to this well-developed literature. Only if one accepts his exceedingly narrow definition of the term criticism does it make sense to say that it is futile to criticize the hypothesis. Significantly, even in the absence of logically compelling criticism, debate over the merits of the hypothesis have yielded many important contributions, both in the methodological literature and in economics generally.

REFERENCES

Boland, Lawrence, "On the Futility of Criticizing the Neoclassical Maximization Hypothesis," *American Economic Review*, December 1981, *71*, 1031–36.

Caldwell, Bruce, "Positivist Philosophy of Science and the Methodology of Economics," *Journal of Economic Issues*, March 1980, *14*, 53–76.

Hempel, Carl, "The Theoretician's Dilemma," in H. Feigl et al., eds., *Minnesota Studies in the Philosophy of Science*, Vol. 2, Minneapolis: University of Minnesota Press, 1958, 37–98.

Tarascio, Vincent and Caldwell, Bruce, "Theory Choice in Economics: Philosophy and Practice," *Journal of Economic Issues*, December 1979, *13*, 983–1006.

Wong, Stanley, *The Foundations of Paul Samuelson's Revealed Preference Theory: A Study by Method of Rational Reconstruction,* London: Routledge & Kegan Paul, 1978.

Reprinted from

THE AMERICAN ECONOMIC REVIEW
© The American Economic Association

The Neoclassical Maximization Hypothesis: Reply

By Lawrence A. Boland*

Bruce Caldwell has chided me for ignoring the contributions of modern philosophers in my 1981 article. Supposedly, if I were to appreciate the contributions of the "logical empiricists since the mid-1930's" I would see the error of my ways. Caldwell chooses to focus on my view of criticism—namely, that for any criticism to be successful it must be decisive, or as he says, "logically compelling." He feels this concept is "overly narrow."[1] I understand him to be saying that there are other concepts which are "less" narrow and thus my concept is only a special case. He recommends a more liberal concept of criticism which he calls "appraisal."

My reply is that he is exactly wrong. The idea that criticism must be logically compelling is not narrow but, instead, the broadest possible. And worse, his concept of criticism is completely inadequate. The implication that we should avoid logically compelling criticism in favor of a weaker line of argument (which he calls appraisal) is merely an expression of Caldwell's advocacy of the commonly promoted, but logically inadequate, methodology which philosophers today call "conventionalism."

I. Appraisal as Criticism

From the standpoint of logic, it would seem to many of us that there is only one form of logically compelling criticism—namely, the demonstration that the argument being criticized leads to a contradiction and thus is logically invalid. Note that this was not the basis of my argument in my earlier paper. My paper was about arguments about the neoclassical maximization hypothesis that arise *after* "one has established its logical validity." That is, the maximization hypothesis, like any hypothesis, asserts that if certain prior conditions are met, then, *necessarily* particular subsequent conditions will be met. In short, if the prior conditions are all true then the subsequent conditions will also be true (see further, my 1979 article). Logical validity concerns the term "necessarily," and thus if logical validity has been established, the hypothesis can only fail to explain the truth of the subsequent condition because one or more of the prior conditions cannot or are not met. The former is about the possibility of the hypothesis being employed in a successful explanation and the latter is about the empirical truth of an explanation based on the hypothesis.

I will have to agree that even these two forms of criticism can be seen to be invocations of logically compelling criticism. Any condition is truly impossible only if it leads to a necessary contradiction (a classic example is Kenneth Arrow's Possibility Theorem), and a condition is empirically false whenever the conjunction of it with an observation statement necessarily yields a contradiction. So, if Caldwell is correct, there must be some other form of criticism which can never be reduced to a claim that there exists a contradiction.

What alternative does Caldwell offer? First, he gives us a list of conventionalist criteria—simplicity, generality, mathematical elegance, plausibility, and so forth. Presumably, such criteria are to be used to "appraise" economic explanations in the same way a welfare function is used to appraise alternative economic policy recommendations.[2] But how are such criteria used to form a criticism? Perhaps one is supposed to

---

*Department of Economics, Simon Fraser University, Burnaby, B.C., Canada V5A 1S6.

[1] This kind of discussion can get quite awkward. Is his criticism of my paper intended to be logically compelling, or something else? For my purposes I will assume that he is intending to convince us of something —in this case, it is that my concept of criticism is too narrow.

[2] In effect, the methodology of appraisal is a variation on neoclassical analysis and it is for this reason I examined methodology in these terms (see my 1971 article). The difficulty is that the use of such criteria in the appraisal of theories or models fails to fulfill its objective for the very same reason that plagues welfare economics—there does not exist a universal criterion

adopt a criterion and use it to measure a given model or theory. Now the only possibility of a criticism that can be advanced against the given theory is that *if* one's aim is to maximize according to the accepted criterion, then the criticized theory somehow fails to achieve the maximum. But failure to achieve one's aim can easily be reduced to a failure to avoid a contradiction between one's aim and one's achievement. In other words, Caldwell's first alternative form of criticism, the use of conventionalist criteria, does not avoid the use of logically compelling criticism.

His second alternative, "Popper's distinction between internal and external criticism," fares the same fate. Internal criticism is merely based on the theorist's acceptance of his or her aims and failure to achieve them. External criticism centers on criticism of the theorist's aim by measuring it against some externally given criterion. In either case, my above discussion of aims applies, but with a more general view of what constitutes an aim. Namely, his second alternative involves criticism that a given explanation fails to solve some particular theoretical problem (Stanley Wong, 1978, pp. 23–24), and thus does not avoid being reducible to logically compelling criticism.

All forms of criticism depend on aims, criteria, testing conventions, and so forth, which are put beyond question *for the purposes of the criticism.* Any criticism succeeds only by showing that to remain consistent, the only alternative is to give up one's aims, criteria, and the like, to avoid being inconsistent. So, contrary to Caldwell's arguments, my concept of criticism is not narrow, but rather it is the most general, since all forms of criticism can be reduced to matters of logical consistency.

II. The Poverty of Conventionalist Methodology in Economics

The only contribution of "logical empiricists [of] the mid-1930's" was to deflect interest from the difficult question of the empiri-

cal truth or falsity of explanations to the more convenient question of the logical validity of argument formed by any explanation. Rather than arguing about whether a theory is true or false, we are supposed to choose between the available theories by some criterion such as "simplicity" or "mathematical elegance." Instead of claiming that a theory is true or false, we are supposed to judge it as being better or worse than any other theory according to the accepted criterion. Obviously, this approach to methodology leads to an infinite regress (see further, my 1974 paper). By what supercriterion do we choose the best criterion?

Each of the criteria listed by Caldwell has its advocates and critics. No logical empiricist would ever claim that his or her employment of a supercriterion to choose a particular theory constitutes a proof that the theory is actually true. But if it is not intended to be a proof, what is accomplished? Or better still, how do we know when any critical appraisal is successful and when it is not?

The idea that we should appraise rather than criticize the theories of economists is promoted because most people feel that decisive criticism fosters unproductive fights and controversies over the truth or falsity of theories. Supposedly, reasonable people would see that theories cannot be proven absolutely true or false. And thus, to be productive we should be more tolerant. The difficulty with this "reasonable" view is that it fails on its own terms. The statement that theories are not true or false is itself a statement—one which is claimed to be true!

Some economists may feel better by advocating appraisal rather than logically compelling criticism, but it only postpones the arguments as we would still have to decide which appraisal criteria are true in order to make our appraisals. The room for differences of opinion and controversy is even greater when it comes to choosing one's criteria.

REFERENCES

Boland, Lawrence A., "Methodology as an Exercise in Economic Analysis," *Philosopy of Science*, March 1971, *38*, 105–17.

_____, "Lexicographic Orderings, Multiple

that will work in all cases. A more general criticism of conventionalist theory-choice criteria—namely, that it is self-contradictory—is offered in my book (1982).

Criteria, and 'ad hocery'," *Australian Economic Papers*, June 1974, *13*, 152–57.

_____, "A Critique of Friedman's Critics," *Journal of Economic Literature*, June 1979, *17*, 503–22.

_____, "On the Futility of Criticizing the Neoclassical Maximization Hypothesis," *American Economic Review*, December 1981, *71*, 1031–36.

_____, *Foundations of Economic Method* London: Allen & Unwin, 1982.

Caldwell, Bruce J., "The Neoclassical Maximization Hypothesis: Comment," *American Economic Review*, September 1983, *73* 824–27.

Wong, Stanley, *The Foundations of Pau Samuelson's Revealed Preference Theory* London: Routledge & Kegan Paul, 1978.

6

Philosophy and the Appraisal of Economic Research Programs

Brian Loasby, 'Hypothesis and Paradigm in the Theory of the Firm',
Economic Journal, vol. 81, December 1971, pp. 863−85.
Rod Cross, 'The Duhem−Quine Thesis, Lakatos and the Appraisal of
Theories in Macroeconomics', *Economic Journal*, vol. 92, June 1982,
pp. 320−40.

Editor's comments

In 1965, the work of Thomas Kuhn was mentioned for the first time by an
economist in an article by D. F. Gordon entitled 'The Role of the History
of Economic Thought in the Understanding of Modern Economic Theory'.
Since then, dozens of articles have been published that apply Kuhn's
categories of 'normal science', 'paradigm', and 'scientific revolution' to
episodes in the development of economics. Kuhn has been joined on the
dais by Imre Lakatos, and the latter's terminology − 'research programmes', 'hard core', and 'protective belt' − has become similarly
ubiquitous. What accounts for our profession's continuing love affair
with the pronouncements of these two men, one an historian of science
and the other a philosopher of mathematics and physical science?

Economists are not unique; many other disciplines have been attracted
to their analyses. What Kuhn and Lakatos provide are two wide-ranging,
general accounts of how scientific activity takes place, and how sciences
grow and change. If one prefers a cataclysmic vision of periods of change,
Kuhn's model provides it, whereas Lakatos offers a picture of a more
gradual transformation. Both offer the sort of descriptive vehicle that
historians find attractive, so it is understandable that historians of economic thought were the first to adapt the Kuhnian and Lakatosian frameworks to their discipline. Both models also contain prescriptive elements,
and this was not lost on critics of mainstream economics. Thus advocates
of alternative approaches to economics found Kuhnian 'anomalies' every
where; economics was in the middle of a 'revolutionary crisis', and, once
this was widely recognized, a 'paradigm-switch' (to the views propagated
by whichever group was doing the talking) would occur. The Lakatosian
idea of a non-testable hard core also appealed to critics, especially those
whose own programs contained untestable elements. So we find that,
much in the way that earlier generations had turned towards the analyses

of positivist philosophy of science, contemporary economic methodologists have incorporated the ideas of men like Kuhn and Lakatos into their writings.

Very recently this has begun to change. Some economists have expressed doubts about the usefulness of applying these broad, externally produced visions of scientific evolution to their field (Leijonhufvud, 1976; Hutchison, 1978; Hands, 1985). The individuality of economics is now being explored. Perhaps unsurprisingly, similar notions can be found in the writings of some philosophers, so it seems we are still following their lead. We have all heard of the imperialism of economics, maybe it is time to speak of the imperialism of philosophers!

Having said all of that, the next two articles demonstrate that ideas borrowed from the works of Kuhn and Lakatos (and others) can be used, and used very effectively, in methodological treatments of subjects in economics. Like master chefs with strong spices, the authors use the borrowed concepts sparingly, judiciously and always with an eye towards enhancing rather than dominating the main course. Perhaps most noteworthy, in the course of accomplishing their stated goals, the authors raise a number of fascinating subsidiary issues.

Loasby's piece is nominally a discussion of the development of the theory of the firm from Sraffa's 1926 challenge to the emergence of organizational theories some three decades later. He does a good job, but there are so many other things going on, too. He argues that it is better to speak of the sufficiency of theories, rather than of their realism. He states that, in their widest interpretation, paradigms are untestable, and that that is *good*. Broadly defined paradigms are richer because they are consistent with many derived testable hypotheses. By inference, complaints against the untestability of the profit maximization hypothesis are misguided. He slips easily back and forth in his comparisons of the roles played by laboratory scientists, research scientists, economists and businessmen, and some of his analogies are thought-provoking. In his brilliant discussion of Hicks versus Sraffa, he argues that the choice of paradigms seldom depends on the results of empirical work. And what could be more provocative than his claim that internal consistency in paradigms may be as much of a vice as a virtue? (Shades of Feyerabend!)

Rod Cross brings to his essay a superb understanding of the philosophical issues combined with a thorough knowledge of a particular research program in economics. Too often in the past, economists who have cast doubt on the profession's ability to undertake meaningful tests of hypotheses have argued their case in general terms. (I know, I am one of them.) Cross makes the argument concretely and forcefully, and in this he resembles Machlup. In addition, he raises a number of interesting philosophical issues. What are the interrelationships among the Duhem-Quine thesis, Popper's work and the methodology of scientific research programs? Does Cross's modification of the MSRP, in which the negative heuristic is pushed aside and attention is focused on the positive heuristic, make it more applicable to economics? How can one walk the line between prescription and description in appraisal? Cross accomplishes much in this article, not the least of which is to raise questions worthy of further attention.

HYPOTHESIS AND PARADIGM IN THE THEORY OF THE FIRM[1]

THOUGH here applied to a particular subject area, the arguments presented in this article have a much wider significance. The article begins with an emphasis on the kinds of abstraction which are necessary in a study of complex systems, and an exposition, in the context of economics, of the ideas developed by T. S. Kuhn to analyse theoretical innovation in the physical sciences.[2] This apparatus is then used to illuminate some critical developments in the theory of value, leading up to an examination of the credentials of behavioural theories of the firm. In the process, it reveals some widespread misconceptions among economists about the nature of economic science, and shows how these misconceptions have not only been responsible for much confusion but have also critically influenced the development of economic theory.

SYSTEMS

Logically, as well as historically, the development of economics as an important and distinctive discipline derives from the increasing extent and complexity of the division of labour. It is true that an allocation problem exists whenever an individual's resources are not sufficient for the satisfaction of all his wants; but although the economic problems of Robinson Crusoe are very convenient for elucidating some features of the elementary analysis of choice, they are scarcely adequate material for a major field of study. That material is to be found in the interdependent choices which result from an elaborate division of labour—between individuals, between firms, between regions and between countries.

Because interdependence is its basis, economics is necessarily a study of systems; because it is concerned with the allocation of resources by human beings, it is a study of decision-making systems. (As we shall see, this does not necessarily imply a study of the process of decision-making; microeconomists have generally been concerned with consequences rather than processes.) Economists have therefore to cope with two intrinsic difficulties of system analysis—the definition of system boundaries and the specification of system structure. On the one hand, all economic systems are sub-systems—sub-systems both of larger economic systems (unless one is explicitly dealing with the world economy) and also of more broadly defined human and ecological systems; thus interdependencies transcend the bounds of the

---

[1] A version of this paper was presented at the Annual Conference of the Association of University Teachers of Economics at Canterbury on April 6, 1971.

[2] T. S. Kuhn, *The Structure of Scientific Revolutions* (Chicago: University of Chicago Press, 1962).

system being studied.   On the other hand, some abstraction from detail is essential, and this involves not only the omission of variables, but also distortion of the relationships which are included.   Thus the economist has no option but to construct models which fall short—usually far short— of a complete specification of the system which he wishes to analyse; he must choose where to make his approximations, some of which must normally be very drastic.   It follows, first, that no economic model can be finally judged by the resemblance between its specification and the real-life system which it claims to represent; and, second, that the choice of different speci- fications by different economists for their models of the same system carries no presumption that one of them must be in error.   For these reasons, it is safer to talk of the " sufficiency " of models than of their " realism."

Though approximations in both directions are necessary, economists tend either to jettison detail in order to concentrate on major interactions, or to ignore interdependencies in order to concentrate on relative detail.   This, of course, is the basis of the distinction between macro-economics and micro- economics.   Macro-economics explores the system known as the national economy, defined into such sectors as consumption, investment, government expenditure and exports, each of which is a highly complex sub-system. The export sector necessarily implies interdependence with other national economies: this interdependence may be handled very crudely—even ignored—or analysis may concentrate, in international trade theory, on the intersections of these national economy sets.   Sometimes the components of the national economy will be defined, for the purposes of input–output analysis, as industry groups—which are not proper sub-sets of the major sectors normally used in macro-economic analysis.   Whatever the form of the macro-level analysis, the sub-systems of which it is composed are treated very simply by the use of assumptions which may be rejected in the analysis of the sub-systems themselves.   (For example, theoretical international trade usually appears to be carried on under conditions of universal perfect compe- tition, while the industries analysed in input–output analysis may operate with both constant marginal costs and constant returns to scale.)   But, be- cause of the fundamental difficulties of system analysis, such a conflict of assumptions at different levels cannot invalidate the arguments which rest on them.

Micro-economics, on the other hand, simply assumes away some of the interdependencies which form the subject-matter of macro-system analysis. But this obvious contrast with macro-economics should not be allowed to obscure the fact that micro-economics makes its sacrifices of detail too; and they can be very large.   For, although it claims to include within its scope the allocation of a firm's internal resources, it regards the firm itself as the basic decision-making unit.   Since, however, the greater part of resource allocation within industry is determined nowadays by firms which are them- selves decision-making systems, a third level of analysis is possible, which is likely to require further sacrifice of interdependencies in order to explore the details of sub-system behaviour.   The economics of organisational behaviour not only illuminates the affinities between economics and organisation theory; it is a natural extension of the scope of the subject, being characteristically concerned with the relationship between structure and performance—the ways in which the system being studied responds to and regulates choice.

Theory and Experiment

This emphasis on a systems study necessarily implies some qualifications to the view sometimes expressed that economists should seek to emulate as closely as possible the methodology of the experimental sciences.[1]   Since this methodology has traditionally rested on the isolation and manipulation of closely-specified relationships, it presents difficulties for the economist, whose manipulation must usually be statistical (possibly with the number of trials outside his control), and who frequently cannot isolate the phenomena which he wishes to study.   But not only is narrow isolation difficult; it is often inappropriate.   For it is characteristic of system behaviour that it may not be explicable as a simple—or even weighted—sum of separate effects.   From this point of view, it is the contrast, not the comparison, between economics and experimental science which is illuminating.

There are greater similarities between economics and applied science, especially science directed towards the development and operation of industrial processes.   For these are systems too, and systems normally too large to be modelled in full.   So the scientist is here faced with a problem akin to that of the economist: to choose a degree of abstraction in his experimentation which is drastic enough to simplify his analysis and yet robust enough to give value to his conclusions.   For such choices his academic training in experimental method does not prepare him very well.   " The transition from the laboratory to plant implies a change of scale from what can, in most cases, be handled and controlled manually by one scientist, to a system which is far outside the capacity of one man, unaided by automation and instrumentation, to control.   Many scientists, we find, have a very hazy idea of the sort of problems that arise on transferring operations from laboratory to plant." [2]   But awareness of such problems is necessary if the laboratory experiments performed are to be those which are most relevant.

However, although the unrealistic assumptions of the economist may be fairly compared with the artificial environment of the laboratory as a means of abstracting from complex systems, yet it should not be overlooked that the

---

[1] E.g., R. G. Lipsey, *An Introduction to Positive Economics*, Second edition (London: Weidenfeld & Nicolson, 1966), Chapter 1.

[2] A. Baines, F. R. Bradbury and C. W. Suckling, *Research in the Chemical Industry* (London: Elsevier, 1969), p. 165.   Their example of filtration suggests some analogies in economic policy-making.

character of the abstraction is different. The scientist abstracts from complexities towards the detail of real phenomena; the economist tends to abstract from detail into terms which have only economic meaning.[1]

PARADIGM

There is a further difficulty in the way of general reliance on experimental or statistical-experimental method in economics. Not only may hypotheses be difficult to test, or relate to system behaviour to which closely restricted analysis is not appropriate; some economic hypotheses turn out not to be hypotheses at all, but paradigms.

A paradigm, in the natural sciences as well as in economics, defines the type of relationships to be investigated and the methods and abstractions to be regarded as legitimate within a particular problem area.[2] Once such terms of reference are generally accepted by practitioners within that area, research becomes " a strenuous and devoted effort to force nature into the conceptual boxes supplied by professional education." [3] (All boxes are empty until the work of filling them begins.) A paradigm must therefore be both comprehensive and open-ended; it leaves many problems to be solved and holds out the prospect of successful solutions to those who formulate and test with skill and care particular hypotheses consistent with the paradigm. For the natural scientist, at least, therefore, it offers " a criterion for choosing problems that, while the paradigm is taken for granted, can be assumed to have solutions." [4] That such criteria are indispensable for the natural scientist is emphasised by P. B. Medawar, explaining " why scientists seem so often to shirk the study of really fundamental or challenging problems. . . . No scientist is admired for failing in the attempt to solve problems that lie beyond his competence. The most he can hope for is the kindly contempt earned by the Utopian politician. If politics is the art of the possible, research is surely the art of the soluble. Both are immensely practical-minded affairs." [5]

H. A. Simon applies a similar argument more widely. " People (and rats) find the most interest in situations that are neither completely strange nor entirely known—where there is novelty to be explored, but where similarities and programs remembered from past experience help guide the exploration. Nor does creativity flourish in completely unstructured situations. The almost unanimous testimony of creative artists and scientists is that the first task is to impose limits on the situation if the limits are not already

---

[1] Cf. R. M. Cyert and E. Grunberg, " Assumption, Prediction and Explanation in Economics," in R. M. Cyert and J. G. March, *A Behavioural Theory of the Firm* (Englewood Cliffs, N. J.: Prentice-Hall, 1963), pp. 301–2.

[2] Kuhn, *op. cit.*, pp. 10, 11.

[3] Kuhn, *op. cit.*, p. 5.

[4] Kuhn, *op. cit.*, p. 37.

[5] P. B. Medawar, *The Art of the Soluble* (London: Methuen, 1967), pp. 86–7.

given." [1] It is the role of the paradigm to provide such limitations to the agenda for inquiry.

Because a paradigm defines a set—often a very large set—of possible hypotheses, but makes no claims for the validity of any particular members of that set (some of which, indeed, will be mutually exclusive alternatives), it follows that paradigms, unlike the hypotheses to which they give rise, cannot be validated by experimental or statistical methods.   Failure to recognise this distinction has led to much unnecessary argument, of which the disputes over profit-maximisation provide a notorious example.   For profit-maximisation is not a hypothesis but a paradigm; and whereas a specific hypothesis embodying some version of profit-maximisation can, in principle, be tested, the paradigm of profit-maximisation cannot.   Only in long-period static equilibrium with perfect knowledge is its formulation unique; and no such experimental conditions can be found.   One common form of criticism is, in fact, a tribute to its virtue.   With a little ingenuity, it is possible to explain almost any kind of business behaviour as profit-maximisation.   The retort that, " if it can explain everything, it explains nothing " would be conclusive against a loosely formulated hypothesis; but it is precisely this ability to generate a variety of hypotheses to explain, if not everything, yet a large body of important phenomena, which is the essential virtue of a paradigm.   Lipsey's attempt to emphasise the testing of economic predictions suffers from a similar confusion: the theory expounded in his text-book is necessarily a paradigm, to which his proposed tests, being designed for hypotheses, cannot properly be applied.[2]

The obverse of a paradigm's continued fertility is the continued existence of unsolved problems.   A paradigm which left no issues unresolved would be useless as a guide to further work.   Thus " a thousand difficulties do not make one doubt " [3] concerning the acceptability of a paradigm; on the contrary they offer a thousand opportunities for the deployment of professional skill.   Provided that they are being steadily resolved, the existence of difficulties is a symptom, not of a paradigm's weakness, but of its continuing strength.   This remains true even when some major difficulties prove recalcitrant.   For example, attempts to explain the path of the moon by the application of Newtonian theory failed consistently for sixty years; yet there were no serious proposals for the rejection of Newtonian theory.   What was in question was not the paradigm, but the professional skill of the scientists who had failed to derive an appropriate hypothesis from it; and, in the event, confidence in Newtonian theory was justified.[4]

[1] H. A. Simon, *The Shape of Automation for Men and Management* (New York: Harper & Row, 1965), pp. 97–8.
[2] Lipsey, *op. cit., e.g.,* Chapter 29.
[3] J. H. Newman, *Apologia Pro Vita Sua.*
[4] Kuhn, *op. cit.,* pp. 39, 81.

Paradigm Change

It is not, therefore, surprising, that a paradigm, once established, should prove difficult to overthrow. Since its continued usefulness depends on the double condition of unresolved problems and good prospects of their eventual solution by the application of the paradigm, there can be no unequivocal standard by which a paradigm can be judged to have failed. Those who attack a paradigm may simply be confessing their inability to use the tools of their trade as effectively as their fellows. Even if this is not an effective deterrent, to discard a well-established paradigm is to discard an important part of one's apparatus for recognising and solving problems. Furthermore, since a paradigm, like a management control system, provides the basis for selecting both problems and the relevant variables to be investigated, it may condition its users against even the perception of some of the more fundamental threats. An experiment in which subjects readily identified as normal wrongly coloured playing cards inserted into an otherwise normal pack provides some formal confirmation of the common experience in all manner of contexts that observations are " fitted to one of the conceptual categories prepared by prior experience." [1] A paradigm produces intellectual tunnel vision.

Thus something quite exceptional in the way of difficulties must become apparent before an established paradigm can be seriously challenged. As Shackle says, " Theoretical advance can spring only from theoretical crisis." [2] In the natural sciences, at least, the existence of a rival paradigm is a necessary condition for a challenge—no paradigm which offers some answers is going to be abandoned unless alternative answers are on offer. But it is certainly not sufficient. The clearest evidence for this statement is provided by the anticipations of later major developments to be found, not in the underworld of economics, but in the intendedly definitive text of Marshall's *Principles*.[3] Until the definitiveness of Marshall was challenged, these anticipations lay not only undeveloped but often unnoticed.

Shackle's own explanation of the persistence of paradigms can be summarised in his own words. " The chief service rendered by a theory "—by which he clearly means a paradigm, not a hypothesis—" is the setting of minds at rest. So long as we have a satisfying conceptual structure, a model or a taxonomy which provides for the filing of all facts in a scheme or order, we are absolved from the tiresome labour of thought, and the uneasy consciousness of mystery and a threatening unknown." [4] This explanation is

---

[1] Kuhn, *op. cit.*, pp. 62–4; the experiment is reported in J. S. Bruner and L. Postman, " On the Perception of Incongruity: A Paradigm," *Journal of Personality*, Vol. XVIII, 1949, pp. 206–23.

[2] G. L. S. Shackle, *The Years of High Theory* (Cambridge: Cambridge University Press, 1967), p. 288.

[3] A convenient selection of examples may be found in D. H. Robertson, " A Revolutionist's Handbook," reprinted in *Utility and All That and Other Essays* (London, Allen and Unwin, 1952), pp. 66–80.

[4] Shackle, *op. cit.*, p. 288.

in part misleading.   To see why, it is necessary to distinguish between un-ease and hard thought.   Paradigms, far from avoiding the labour of thought, may call for both intense and protracted effort if they are to be expressed in viable hypotheses.[1]   Their virtue, in this respect, lies in permitting that effort to be deployed within a well-defined structure, instead of having to be applied to the definition of that structure; they permit a concentration on short-run questions.   But in academic work, as in business, long-run questions, even if no more intellectually taxing, are much less comfortable, because they tend to open up an unpalatable range of options.   They require the managing director to consider what business he should be in, or the academic the proper scope of his subject.   An acceptable paradigm affords protection from such disturbing speculations.

> " Theory . . . imposes a beautiful simplicity on the unbearable multiplicity of fact, gives comfort in face of the unknown and un-experienced, stops the teasing of mystery and doubt which, though salutory and life-preserving, is uncomfortable, so that we seek by theory to sort out the justified from the unjustified fear.   Theories by their nature and purpose, their role of administering to a ' good state of mind,' are things to be held and cherished.   Theories are altered or discarded only when they fail us." [2]

Intellectual retooling is uncomfortable, as well as expensive.

This argument needs to be taken just one stage further, in order to ex-plain the tenacity with which people cling to old paradigms even in crisis, and even when alternatives are available.   Often the new contender is not a perfect substitute for the old: while offering solutions to some difficulties which appear insoluble within the established paradigm, it may offer in-ferior solutions to others; and, indeed, to some questions hitherto satis-factorily handled it may offer no solution at all.   For example, Lavoisier, in offering a solution to the critical issues which the phlogiston theory seemed unable to resolve, could provide no explanation whatever for the similarities between metals, which phlogiston theory had readily accounted for.[3]

Thus the competition between paradigms turns not simply on their relative merits in explaining certain important phenomena, but on judgments about which are the important phenomena to explain.   For these judgments there are no generally acceptable criteria; indeed they cannot be made without excursions into those regions of mystery and doubt from which paradigms, once accepted, serve to protect us.   A change of paradigm re-defines the set of relevant problems, and the criteria for selecting problems and evaluating solutions: it changes to some degree—occasionally to a large degree—the accepted definition of the scope of a subject.   With its com-bination of the threatened obsolescence of some established methodology,

---

[1] Kuhn, *op. cit.*, pp. 26, 30.   [2] Shackle, *op. cit.*, pp. 288-9.
[3] Kuhn, *op. cit.*, p. 147.

and the posing of awkward, sometimes fundamental, questions about the nature of a subject, a time of paradigm change is a time of upheaval that for many may be more disturbing than exhilarating. A subject in which paradigms are often not firmly-established, like economics, offers much less security to its practitioners than one, like chemistry, in which they are relatively secure. (Graduate chemists turning to economics for the first time are liable to be disconcerted by this loss of security.) But even apparently-assured security can prove illusory, as atomic physicists have painfully realised in recent years.

Whether economics (or any other social science) has yet succeeded in establishing any paradigms as widely accepted, even for a short time, as those associated with Copernicus, Newton or Lavoisier, may be doubted. Nevertheless, the concept of paradigm change seems capable of extension to illuminate some major innovations in economic theory. It has, indeed, recently been effectively used by Axel Leijonhufvud in his examination of the Keynesian revolution.[1] Leijonhufvud argues that the neo-classical synthesis has been achieved by forcing Keynes' ideas within the traditional general equilibrium paradigm of a static system of simultaneous equations; and that Keynes' attempt to construct a new paradigm, emphasising processes and information flows within the system, has been rejected, or even unrecognised. This argument will not be further considered in this paper, except for drawing a later analogy with behavioural theory; attention will be concentrated on micro-economics, beginning with the emergence of the theory of the firm.

THE PARADIGM OF PERFECT COMPETITION

The Marshallian synthesis on the theory of value was constructed with almost incredible care and subtlety; indeed some of the sharpest minds of the 'twenties and 'thirties simply failed to appreciate what Marshall had done, and construed his caution as hesitancy and his subtlety as confusion. But Marshall was facing methodological difficulties which could not be solved, only lived with. Shackle partially explains the situation. "Marshall's self-imposed endeavour was an intensely difficult one. He sought to describe a mechanism of evolution of the firm and industry; to derive the principles of this mechanism from the detailed and wide observation of a segment of British economic and social history, . . . and to make his account of this observable productive evolution the vehicle of laws which should be in some degree general and permanent." [2]

Shackle places the emphasis on the problem of explaining a great variety of specific facts by a single body of theory—the achievement of a high level

---

[1] Axel Leijonhufvud, *On Keynesian Economics and the Economics of Keynes* (New York and London: Oxford University Press, 1968). I am indebted to Professor A. D. Bain for drawing my attention to the significance of this work.

[2] Shackle, *op. cit.*, p. 44.

of abstraction without significant loss of sufficiency.   This type of problem, as was pointed out earlier, is characteristic of all science, though of peculiar difficulty in this particular instance.   But the way Marshall tackled the problem evoked a difficulty of a special sort.   The key lies in Shackle's phrase "a mechanism of evolution."   Mechanism suggests mathematics; and it was not surprising that Marshall, a mathematician himself, should turn to mathematics for a formal exposition of "general and permanent laws."   If a formal mathematical model was to be produced, then the obvious—perhaps the only possible—body of theory to use was the differential calculus, the value of which in economics had first been effectively demonstrated by Cournot.   But an analytical method based on differential calculus, though the best available, was hardly ideal as a paradigm of growth and change.   Marshall consistently emphasised biological analogies, but there was simply no "biological mathematics" adequate for his purpose; and so evolution had to be explained in terms of static equilibrium.   The use of a strictly timeless theory by one who was so conscious of the importance of time represents a heroic—and highly successful—use of abstraction; but only by the use of all Marshall's care and subtlety could it be made to appear convincing.   It may, indeed, be judged too successful and too convincing; for whereas Marshall was keenly aware that his mathematical abstractions would lose sufficiency if pressed much further, some of his successors, being young and bold, were less inhibited.   By revealing the inherent contradictions between the model and the real world, which Marshall had so skilfully concealed, they helped to precipitate a crisis in value theory.

The theoretical argument was forcefully summarised by Sraffa in his famous article of 1926, in which he demonstrated that increasing and decreasing returns were both strictly incompatible with other assumptions of the standard formal analysis, that the size of the firm was therefore left indeterminate by this analysis, and that there was thus no adequate justification for casting that analysis in terms of perfect competition.[1]   The logic of Sraffa's criticism and of his proposed solution are worth examining.   The key sentences run as follows.

> "If diminishing returns arising from a 'constant factor' are taken into consideration, it becomes necessary to extend the field of investigation so as to examine the conditions of simultaneous equilibrium in numerous industries: a well-known conception, whose complexity, however, prevents it from bearing fruit, at least in the present state of our knowledge, which does not permit of even much simpler schemata being applied to the study of real situations.   If we pass to external economies, we find ourselves confronted by the same obstacle, and there is also the impossibility of confining within statical conditions the circumstances from which they originate.

[1] P. Sraffa, "The Laws of Returns under Competitive Conditions," ECONOMIC JOURNAL, Vol. XXXVI 1926, reprinted in G. J. Stigler and K. E. Boulding (eds.), *Readings in Price Theory* (London: Allen and Unwin, 1953), pp. 180–97.

It is necessary, therefore, to abandon the path of free competition and turn in the opposite direction, namely towards monopoly. Here we find a well-defined theory in which variations of cost connected with changes in the dimensions of the individual undertaking play an important part." [1]

These sentences are perhaps so familiar that it will be easier to analyse the argument if they are paraphrased. The strict formal requirements of static partial equilibrium analysis do not permit the conditions which are logically necessary for the existence of perfect competition. Therefore something must go. The cost conditions which make perfect competition possible are indeed compatible with dynamic general equilibrium; but general equilibrium is a much less usable paradigm than partial equilibrium, and dynamic analysis is still more hopeless. On the other hand, the theory of monopoly offers a readily-available alternative to perfect competition, while still retaining all the usual conditions of static partial equilibrium.

Thus the argument turns, not on the existence of perfect competition as a recognisable state of affairs, but on first, the internal consistency, and second, the relative usefulness, of competing paradigms. It is important to take these two criteria, of internal consistency and relative usefulness, separately; and it is convenient to begin with the latter.

IMPERFECT COMPETITION OR GENERAL EQUILIBRIUM?

Let us accept for the moment Kaldor's conclusion that "long-period static equilibrium and perfect competition are incompatible assumptions." [2] Marshall's theory made room for monopoly; the new theory had no room for perfect competition, as Joan Robinson forcefully made clear. When we see some situations approximating to perfect competition, but none, in developed economies, approximating to long-period static equilibrium, what are we to think of a choice of paradigm in which perfect competition becomes an inadmissible market form? Surely the answer is that the choice was soundly based on good scientific practice, which exemplifies at this point the economic doctrine of opportunity cost. Usefulness, rather than immediate realism, is the proper ground for choosing between paradigms. The cost of giving up static partial equilibrium analysis, in terms of existing theory to be discarded, was far higher than the cost of giving up perfect competition, and the gains, in terms of alternative theory lying ready for exploitation, were far less.

That this is the relevant basis for choice is confirmed by the reasoning of the most distinguished economist who made the opposite choice, in favour of general equilibrium theory—J. R. Hicks. He stood Sraffa's conclusion

---

[1] Sraffa, op. cit., p. 187.
[2] N. Kaldor, "The Equilibrium of the Firm," ECONOMIC JOURNAL, Vol. XLIV (1934); reprinted in N. Kaldor, Essays on Value and Distribution (London: Duckworth, 1969), p. 46.

on its head: if perfect competition was incompatible with partial equilibrium, general equilibrium was incompatible with anything other than perfect competition.   The essentials of Hicks' argument, too, are worth quoting in his own words.[1]

> " It has to be recognised that a general abandonment of the assumption of perfect competition, a universal adoption of the assumption of monopoly, must have very destructive consequences for economic theory. Under monopoly the stability conditions become indeterminate; and the basis on which economic laws can be constructed is therefore shorn away. . . .
>
> " It is, I believe, only possible to save anything from this wreck— and it must be remembered that the threatened wreckage is that of the greater part of general equilibrium theory—if we can assume that the markets confronting most of the firms with which we shall be dealing do not differ very greatly from perfectly competitive markets. . . . At least, this get-away seems well worth trying. We must be aware, however, that we are taking a dangerous step, and probably limiting to a serious extent the problems with which our subsequent analysis will be fitted to deal.   Personally, however, I doubt if most of the problems we shall have to exclude for this reason are capable of much useful analysis by the methods of economic theory."

No more than Sraffa, Kaldor, and the others who argued the opposite case, does Hicks appeal to facts.   Indeed, he admits that the facts may well be against him.   Neither party follows Beveridge's prescription, endorsed by Lipsey, to seek empirical verification.[2]   And on this issue they are right, and Beveridge and Lipsey are wrong.   For the argument is not about hypotheses—concerning which Beveridge and Lipsey are of course quite correct— but about the kinds of hypotheses and the kinds of data that might be presented for verification; and here the empiricist's prescription is not only inappropriate but often impossible.

The readiness with which Hicks is prepared to accept the exclusion of important problems from consideration as the price of using the paradigm of perfect competition should also be noted.   The availability of a paradigm is more relevant than the importance of a problem.   Here again Hicks is following scientific principles, as explained by Medawar.   " Good scientists study the most important problems they think they can solve.   It is, after all, their professional business to solve problems, not to grapple with them.   The spectacle of a scientist locked in combat with the forces of ignorance is not an inspiring one if, in the outcome, the scientist is routed." [3] Economists are perhaps in general readier than natural scientists to tackle ignorance with inadequate weapons; but this readiness springs from inferior armament rather than superior virtue.   And it is, after all, only relative; it would be difficult to maintain that the distribution of economic effort

[1] J. R. Hicks, *Value and Capital* (Oxford: Oxford University Press, 1939), pp. 83–5.

[2] Lipsey, *op. cit.*, pp. xi–xii, 3–18.

[3] Medawar, *op. cit.*, p. 7.

reflects at all closely the importance of economic issues; much less difficult to relate it to the availability of usable paradigms. Nor is this necessarily wrong, for it can be argued that a discipline will make faster progress if its practitioners are insulated from pressures to " choose problems because they urgently need solution and without regard for the tools available to solve them." [1]

The Illusory Crisis and Its Consequences

So far we have argued that, given the existence of a crisis in value theory, the solution of abandoning perfect competition, though apparently odd, was justified. But we still have to ask, was there a real theoretical crisis? If one accepts the earlier argument about the significance of paradigms, and, particularly, the argument about the degree of abstraction—in structure as well as in the choice of variables—required to create a usable paradigm in a study of such complex systems, the answer must surely be no. The theoretical crisis arose out of a misconception about the nature of the subject, and therefore of the way it should develop. Any usable model must be a mis-specification of the reality to which it refers; in economics this mis-specification must often be so great as to show little apparent resemblance to that reality. To refine the abstractions in a workable paradigm is often to refine away the reality that remains; consistency must often be sacrificed in order to retain adequate sufficiency. When the conditions requisite for static partial equilibrium analysis are carefully spelt out, as they were for example by Kaldor in 1934,[2] it should become obvious that long-period static equi- librium is formally incompatible not merely with perfect competition, but with any of the real-world phenomena which we habitually use it to explain. Not even the simplest curve shifting is logically permissible: as Mrs. Robin-son has sardonically observed, equilibrium is not a position at which one can arrive; one must be in it already.[3]

Thus " a more rigorous formulation of the conditions under which it is possible to make generalisations about the factors determining economic equilibrium " [4] must be no more than a subsidiary concern, since it is obvious that the conditions will never be met. What matters is how extensively they can be violated without seriously impugning the result to which they lead. A strict regard for internal consistency in economic theory is as likely to be a vice as a virtue.

Therefore before deciding whether she took the " wrong turning " in writing *The Economics of Imperfect Competition* instead of " abandoning static

---

[1] Kuhn, *op. cit.*, p. 163.

[2] N. Kaldor, " The Determinateness of Static Equilibrium," *Review of Economic Studies*, February 1934; reprinted in *Essays on Value and Distribution*, pp. 13–33.

[3] J. Robinson, *Collected Economic Papers, Vol. II* (Oxford: Blackwell, 1966), p. 120.

[4] Kaldor, *Essays*, p. 13.

analysis and trying to come to terms with Marshall's theory of development,"
Mrs. Robinson ought first to have enquired a little more carefully whether any
turning was needed at all.   Simply to state that " the profound inconsistency
between the static base and the dynamic superstructure had become too
obvious " just will not do.[1]   Nor will the more recent argument that " imperfect competition came in to explain the fact, in the world around us, that
more or less all plants were working part time: "[2] the phenomena of short-
run general disequilibrium cannot be explained in terms of long-run partial
equilibrium.

Are we then, as D. H. Robertson suggested, no more than half in jest,
" to regard all that has happened since (Marshall) in this field as a vast crime
wave "?[3]   Surely not; for two reasons.   The less important reason is that
the changing structure of industry did pose problems of fact which appeared
to reinforce the problems of theory; any commentary on the arguments of
the time which ignores the contemporary concern with these problems must
appear unfair to some of the protagonists of change, even though one may
doubt the completeness of their success in explaining the new structure by the
new theory.   The more important reason is that, as is likely to happen when
a paradigm changes, the new theory redefined the scope of this branch of
economics.   As Shackle observes, " not only the answers, but the questions,
were new.   The whole notion of what value theory sought to do and the way
its aim should be accomplished had been changed . . . Primacy had passed
from the autonomously self-subsisting technical commodity to the firm considered as a profit-maximising policy-maker."[4]   The creation of the theory
of the firm brought the analysis of decision-making within the accepted scope
of the subject; it thus not only made possible the development of managerial
economics, but determined its characteristic virtues and defects.

Imperfect and Monopolistic Competition: One Theory or Two?

The almost simultaneous appearance of two full-length presentations of
the new theory of the firm by E. H. Chamberlin and Mrs. Robinson necessarily raised the question whether it was indeed one theory or two.   But the
question was apparently soon disposed of: although Chamberlin continued
to insist, to the end of his life, on the fundamental differences between the
concepts of monopolistic and of imperfect competition, very few economists
of importance, even among those most sympathetic to Chamberlin's formulation, took the claim seriously.[5]   This was unfortunate, because Chamberlin
was quite right.

[1] J. Robinson, *Collected Economic Papers, Vol. 1* (Oxford: Blackwell, 1951), pp. vii–viii.
[2] J. Robinson, *The Economics of Imperfect Competition*, Second Edition (London: Macmillan, 1969), p. vi.
[3] Robertson, *op. cit.*, p. 73.
[4] Shackle, *op. cit.*, p. 65.
[5] Shackle, *op. cit.*, p. 62.

The trouble may be explained as a confusion between hypothesis and theory.   Much of the formal analysis, notably the tangency solution which reconciles monopolistic discretion over price with normal competitive profits, can indeed be regarded as common to both.   But these similarities can be explained by the natural inclination to use and develop familiar tools of analysis within the accepted framework of partial equilibrium and profit-maximisation; the function of the analysis, in relation to both theoretical issues and their views of the world, is very different for the two authors.

Imperfect competition was created to escape from the dilemma propounded by Sraffa.   Since rising costs were excluded by the formal conditions of perfectly competitive partial equilibrium (as well as apparently absent from many firms), and yet the method of partial equilibrium analysis seemed indispensable, the only escape seemed to lie in a falling demand curve for the individual firm.   This falling demand curve was not an observed fact, but—most compelling of arguments—a methodological necessity.   As P. W. S. Andrews observed, " Seen from this methodological point of view, Joan Robinson's demand functions have no analytical roots.   Her demand curves fall simply because she tells them to do so." [1]   Indeed, she was inhibited from looking for analytical roots by her concern to preserve the concept of the industry, which led her to regard the products of competing firms as virtually identical in all respects save the attitudes of individual customers towards them, and thus eliminated any rational basis for the falling demand curves which her theory required.

Such abstractions may well be justified by the usefulness of the theoretical structure which they make possible (and some such concept as the industry is essential to partial equilibrium analysis); but there is a danger that inferences about the real world may be drawn from theoretical assumptions, instead of the reverse.   And of course in this instance such inferences were drawn, most conspicuously by Mrs. Robinson herself.   For example, the section headed " Forms of Competition " in her article " Imperfect Competition Revisited " lays overwhelming emphasis on competitive waste.[2]   In addition, the excess capacity and unexhausted economies of scale which were presented as such notable consequences of the theory were already explicit in the assumption of falling costs on which it was founded.   The moral of imperfect competition is that potential economies of large-scale production are frustrated by producers' iniquity and consumers' gullibility or perversity; the situation therefore seems to demand, rather than permit, " almost unlimited pushing around." [3]   But this is not the only theory which fits the formal analysis.

---

[1] P. W. S. Andrews, *On Competition in Economic Theory* (London: Macmillan, 1964), p. 22.

[2] J. Robinson, "Imperfect Competition Revisited," ECONOMIC JOURNAL, September 1953, reprinted in *Collected Economic Papers, Vol. II* (Oxford: Blackwell, 1960), pp. 228–9.

[3] Robertson, *op. cit.*, p. 75.

Chamberlin, by contrast, started not with costs but with demand, which reflected differences in consumers' preferences and between competitive products. His assumption of uniform demand and cost curves is much more obviously a temporary expedient to aid exposition than it is in Mrs. Robinson's analysis, and the tangency equilibrium is not presented as a general solution. Because products and consumers do differ, even in equilibrium " some (or all) of the demand curves may lie at various distances to the right of the point of tangency, leaving monopoly profits scattered throughout the group—and throughout the price system." [1] We should therefore be much less surprised than even the sympathetic D. H. Robertson to find Chamberlin speaking of his equilibrium—monopoly profits and all—as a sort of ideal.[2] If economies of scale are frustrated in this paradigm, it is largely because the alternative is to frustrate the need for variety which flows from " differences in tastes, desires, incomes, and locations of buyers, and differences in the uses which they wish to make of commodities." [3] But perhaps Chamberlin did not take his falling cost curves too seriously. After all, they were a methodological necessity, given a falling demand curve, for equilibrium with normal profits, just as falling demand curves were a methodological necessity, given falling costs, for Mrs. Robinson.

The distinction between imperfect and monopolistic competition is perhaps especially marked in the area of managerial economics. The concepts of monopolistic competition harmonise readily with the emphasis in marketing theory on the profit opportunities in offering distinctive consumer satisfactions, as evaluated by the consumer. To the marketer, as once to the economist, the customer buys, not a product, but the expectation of benefits: the variety of ways to consumer satisfaction, and the importance of consumer satisfaction, both submerged by the tendency of imperfect competition theory to regard every means by which a firm may aim to give added value as a wasteful device for bamboozling the ignorant customer, are fundamental assumptions of monopolistic competition. In the current management jargon, imperfect competition is producer-oriented, monopolistic competition is consumer-oriented.

Furthermore, monopolistic competition theory, though formulated in terms of static partial equilibrium for the single-product firm, has adequate sufficiency to handle in a modest way questions of product-line policy, new-product pricing, and the exploitation of the product life cycle. Even innovation can be treated in terms of competitive strategy—but not if one confuses monopolistic with imperfect competition. B. R. Williams' complaint against economists' treatment of competitive pressure is justified, but his

---

[1] E. H. Chamberlin, *The Theory of Monopolistic Competition* (Cambridge, Mass.: Harvard University Press, 1933), p. 113.

[2] Robertson, *ibid.*

[3] Chamberlin, *op. cit.*, p. 214.

explanation is not quite right. " Whether, and in what way, competition stimulates . . . innovation," writes Williams:

> " is a problem foreign to static theory, though in fact static theory has exercised a very strong influence on economists' approach to dynamic problems. Thus, examples of product differentiation are generally drawn from the market for consumer goods and stress brand differences in fields like cereals and cosmetics. When, however, we take examples such as aircraft engines, electronics, man-made fibres, and pharmaceuticals, we face the significant possibility that product differentiations may not be ' market imperfections ' in the static sense, but an inevitable part of the process of man-made innovations required for the efficient pursuit of economic growth." [1]

Of course static theory is strictly inconsistent with change of any kind, even the introduction of a different packet for an unchanged product. But once we reject the hobgoblin of consistency,[2] we find comparative statics a useful method of handling change. The cause of the trouble is less the static formulation of the models than the assumption of imperfect competition theory that product differentiation produces waste, not progress. Novelty is undesirable because it impedes mass-production. Monopolistic competition, on the other hand, does allow us to ask whether mass-production may be undesirable because it impedes novelty.

If monopolistic competition is both so different and in some ways so superior to imperfect competition, why have the two been treated as so nearly synonymous? Part of the explanation, as given before, is that the central analysis appeared so similar that almost everyone assumed the theories to be similar also. It is still necessary to explain why the assimilated theory looks so distinctly Robinsonian; but that is easy. The theory of value was apparently in a state of crisis, and Mrs. Robinson's book appeared as the culmination of a painful and difficult struggle to resolve it, in which many of the keenest economic minds had publicly engaged. The urgency and difficulty of that struggle made impossible the perception of Chamberlin's work in any other way than as a solution to the crisis. Its entirely different origins, being neither a common concern nor well-publicised, aroused no interest whatsoever. The saddest part of this paradox is that, had there been no crisis, Chamberlin's book would have received far less attention, because it would have met no apparent need. The tragedy of Chamberlin's professional life is that if he had not spent so much of his time and energy protesting the distinctiveness of his theory, he would probably have spent that time and energy protesting its importance.

---

[1] B. R. Williams, *Technology, Investment and Growth* (London: Chapman & Hall, 1967), p. 83.
[2] " A foolish consistency is the hobgoblin of little minds, adored by little statesmen and philosophers and divines." R. W. Emerson, *Essays*.

The Defence of the Revolution

By setting out to show that " the analysis of the output and price of a single commodity can be conducted by a technique based upon the study of individual decisions," [1] Mrs. Robinson for the first time appeared to bring decision-making by the competitive firm within the ambit of empirical economic research.   That the definition of such an important new field failed to precipitate a flood of investigations, as one would expect in the experimental sciences, was probably largely due to the feeling that research was unnecessary since facts could apparently be deduced from purely geometrical arguments.   There certainly do not seem to have been any immediate doubts that the new theory offered an adequate description—or prescription: it was not always clear which—of actual business behaviour. Thus the report of the first serious investigation (the Oxford inquiry) [2] that businesses did not behave in this way inevitably caused some consternation; the paradigm has been in a kind of crisis ever since.

Many typical features of a paradigm crisis have been visible.   There has been no general agreement on the terms of reference for the debate, nor indeed on the precise scope of paradigm under attack.   Nor has the attack been well co-ordinated: P. W. S. Andrews, the only economist to develop both a full-scale critique and an alternative paradigm, published the two halves of his argument fifteen years apart, and in the wrong sequence for maximum effect.[3]   On the opposing side, many of the successful revolutionaries, quite properly, turned conservative to protect the newly-established paradigm; and their defence owed little to empirical evidence about firms' pricing behaviour.

Such disregard for empirical evidence, it was argued earlier, is generally appropriate in a conflict of paradigms; and it is particularly appropriate in this instance.   For Mrs. Robinson's theory was based not, as she claimed, on " the study of individual decisions," but on the conditions of individual equilibrium, just as perfect competition had been; and both perfect and imperfect competition are empty of predictions about the ways in which firms actually fix prices.   Andrews saw more clearly than most that the dispute turned on questions not of behaviour but of structure: whether the model should assume atomistic competition or oligopoly, and whether it should be formulated in terms of equilibrium.   Part of Andrews' critique offers a remarkable parallel to Sraffa's earlier argument; whereas Sraffa had shown that a strict interpretation of the conditions of long-period static partial equilibrium virtually excluded increasing costs for the individual firm, Andrews now argued that these conditions also excluded falling demand

[1] J. Robinson, *The Economics of Imperfect Competition* (London: Macmillan, 1933), p. 15.

[2] R. L. Hall and C. J. Hitch, " Price Theory and Business Behaviour," *Oxford Economic Papers*, No. 2, 1939.

[3] P. W. S. Andrews, *Manufacturing Business* (London: Macmillan, 1949), and *On Competition in Economic Theory* (London: Macmillan, 1964).

curves for the individual firm.[1] Thus we reach the final condemnation of long-period static partial equilibrium: it is incompatible first, with perfect competition, second, with real-world phenomena, and finally, even with itself.

This rejection of equilibrium theory did not worry Andrews, who had previously developed an alternative paradigm, in which a " steady state " of uniform prices is determined by competition within an industry, and each firm's market share depends on dynamic considerations of goodwill; but, as he acknowledged, it worried other people.[2] For it is the concept of equilibrium which is at the heart of the crisis; and the abandonment of equilibrium is a much more fundamental change than that implied by the creation of the theory of the firm, which was developed, in accordance with Sraffa's advice, precisely in order to preserve the static equilibrium method of analysis. Micro-economists need a theory of the firm; and for some purposes the marginalist equilibrium theory is the best theory we have.

How, then, is the paradigm defended? Andrews' critique, though in its own terms irrefutable, is unacceptable; it has therefore apparently been ignored. Perhaps economists have learned to be less impressed by revelations of inconsistency in their theoretical assumptions, and accept that Andrews' criticisms are no more valid than were Sraffa's. Expositions and explanations of business behaviour which conflict with micro-equilibrium theory, however, have met with vigorous onslaughts, in which the terms of the argument, as is usual in controversies over paradigms, have been defined in a way that comes near to ensuring success. Equilibrium theory is justified by assuming its validity. Rationality is equated with profit maximisation, which in static equilibrium implies mathematically the equality of marginal cost and marginal revenue; therefore any business observed violating the theory is behaving irrationally, and any alternative theory must assume irrationality, which, as we all know, makes theorising impossible—unless, of course, it be the consumer irrationality which is the not-quite-explicit basis of imperfect competition. Even Cohen and Cyert, who might be expected to be particularly sensitive to this issue, discuss decision-making by marginal analysis as if this were synonymous with rationality.[3] Andrews' own theory has inevitably come in for particularly harsh treatment, and it has unfortunately been too easy to assume that the obscurity of his style reflects confusion in his thought; but the standard accusation that he is rejecting profit-maximisation, rather than equilibrium (which persists even in Silberston's recent survey)[4] simply indicates the confusion of his critics.

Nevertheless, some progress has been made. The exercise of construing reported business behaviour in terms of accepted theory has revealed much

[1] Andrews, *On Competition*, pp. 73–80.
[2] Andrews, *op. cit.*, pp. 90–93.
[3] K. J. Cohen & R. M. Cyert, *Theory of the Firm* (New Jersey: Prentice-Hall, 1965), Chapter 3.
[4] A. Silberston, " Surveys of Applied Economics: Price Behaviour of Firms," ECONOMIC JOURNAL, September, 1970. Professor Andrews' death this year has deprived the profession of a widely-underrated, because misunderstood, economist.

more clearly than before the level of abstraction involved in that theory. One result is that micro-economists now have a somewhat better appreciation of the nature of their subject.   Another is that the partial withdrawal of pretensions to describe the processes of decision-making by the use of the theory of the firm has facilitated the emergence of a very different paradigm for that purpose.

Organisational Behaviour

The logical justification for a separate paradigm of organisational decision-making was clearly set out for any one to see in Coase's article " The Nature of the Firm." [1]   This article was presented as a skilful and wholly satisfying resolution of a very awkward anomaly in the theory of the firm—its failure, until that time, to account for the existence of firms at all in a specialised exchange economy.   In explaining the allocation of economic decision-making between the market and a directing authority by applying marginal analysis to the cost of each kind of decision-process, Coase significantly reinforced the marginalist paradigm.   But in basing his argument on the premise that decision-making within firms was different from decisions in the market, he excluded any detailed study of decision-making within firms from the fields of application of that paradigm.   The theory of the firm might still be used as a highly-abstract model for predicting the overall results of the decisions of individual firms; but since bringing a decision within a firm implied, by definition, a rejection of the market mechanism, it now had a very limited sufficiency as a working model of the decision-making process.

The failure to notice this obvious implication of Coase's work has resulted in much unnecessary expenditure of ink, time and temper.   But though it may be thought unfortunate, it is not at all surprising that the article should be interpreted solely in terms of the paradigm which it employed, and that a new paradigm of business behaviour should have been created with small help from economists.   That paradigm emerged primarily from concern with two organisational problems.   On the one hand there was the question of organisational relationships, which was attracting increasing attention (primarily in the United States) from some psychologists and sociologists. On the other hand there was the need (implied in Coase's analysis) for selective attention to problems and for economy in the search for solutions, which long remained the pragmatic concern of accountants establishing management control systems.

At first quite distinct, gradually these two areas of inquiry began to overlap, as increasing attention was given to behavioural aspects of control systems, and the inter-relationships of management structure and manage-

[1] R. H. Coase, " The Nature of the Firm," *Economica*, N S 1937; reprinted in *Readings in Price Theory*, pp. 331–51.

ment perception were more deeply explored.   The major credit for evolving a new paradigm of organisational decision-making must go to H. A. Simon; and perhaps Simon's critical contribution was the introduction of the concepts of limited knowledge and bounded rationality into his explanation of organisational cohesion, which made the identification of occasions for decision as crucial for him as for the designers of control systems.   The new paradigm was introduced to economics by the work of Cyert and March.

Yet its impact has been very slight.   To anyone accepting the argument hitherto, this should not be surprising.   The failure to visualise economics explicitly as a systems study, and the dominance of market paradigms, conditioned economists to think of the firm as a basic element rather than as an economic system worthy of study in its own right.   The widespread contempt exhibited by economists for accounting (the more scandalous for not being recognised as a scandal) prevented them from appreciating either the real difficulties or the practical importance of management control.   Above all, the criteria employed in the existing paradigm were inevitably used in judging between it and the new; and on those criteria behavioural theory does rather badly.   It has no answer to the questions of efficiency or stability as those questions are traditionally posed.   It has no use for traditional basic concepts: optimisation has no usable meaning; economists' heavy investment in calculus becomes redundant; equilibrium is not defined; and there are no general analytical solutions.

A Comparison of Paradigms

But the characteristics of one paradigm should not be used as the criteria by which a rival is judged.   It is more helpful to compare the abstractions and the methods of analysis which are legitimised by each, the kinds of answer which each can give, and the questions which each permits to be asked.   The critical distinction, which is a condition of all the others, is that between the definition of positions of rest and the specification of an ongoing process.   (This is very like the distinction which Leijonhufvud regards as critical to an understanding of Keynes' thought.)[1]   As a consequence, instead of a defined goal, we have a defined origin.   Thus, for example, a firm's history and financial position become elements of the analysis, whereas in micro-equilibrium theory they are quite properly excluded as irrelevant.   (Silberston's criticism of standard theories of the firm on this score is misplaced.)[2]

Such a shift of focus, from destination to origin, has been a central feature of some major paradigm changes in other fields.   It was, indeed, precisely such a shift, in the study of falling bodies, which gave rise to the concept of

---

[1] Axel Leijonhufvud, *Keynes and the Classics* (London: Institute of Economic Affairs, 1969), p. 29.
[2] Silberston, *op. cit.*, p. 525.

instantaneous, as distinct from average, speed,[1] and thus in due course led to the development of differential calculus, which the equivalent shift in the theory of the firm now threatens to dethrone.   It was precisely such a shift in the study of evolution which made Darwin's ideas so disturbing; and it is apparently this absence of finality which most disturbs some critics of behavioural theory—not surprisingly, because it leaves us exposed forever to the " mystery and doubt " from which, as Shackle observes, we seek protection in theory.[2]

But exposure brings greater freedom.   A process with no definable end does not lend itself to optimisation techniques of analysis, and so there is no pressure to build only optimising models.   Instead, therefore, of being confined to studying the response of a system to changes in its parameters, one can develop a model in which these parameters become variables, and which therefore may initiate the changes to which it later responds.   There is no need for the system to be dominated by negative feedback, as must necessarily be assumed—albeit unconsciously—in equilibrium models: the " cobweb theorem," for instance, so anomalous in traditional micro-theory, fits easily into this type of analysis.

Another gain of freedom is in the handling of uncertainty.   It is now possible to admit that in our world uncertainty is often a euphemism for ignorance, which cannot often be adequately represented by the use of certainty equivalents.   It is the unknown, rather than the uncertain, which leads to the behaviour that Cyert and March categorise as uncertainty-avoidance,[3] and to the emphasis on flexibility as an objective in corporate strategy.[4]   It is the unknown, rather than the uncertain, which makes satisficing rational.   Satisficing is not equivalent to what Baumol and Quant call " optimally imperfect decision-making," [5] not because it is " constrained maximisation with only constraints and no maximisation," [6] but because it is embedded in a paradigm in which optimality has no definable meaning.   Vickers' model of long-run profit-maximisation, for example, relies on a series of conceptual production, investment and financing plans, of a precision which is irrational (which does not mean non-optimal) within the assumptions of the behavioural paradigm.[7]

Where there is neither finality nor optimality, there can hardly be general determinate solutions.   It is the abandonment of the search for such solutions

[1] Kuhn, *op. cit.*, pp. 123–4.
[2] Shackle, *op. cit.*, pp. 288–9.
[3] Cyert and March, *op. cit.*, pp. 118–20.
[4] H. I. Ansoff, *Corporate Strategy* (New York: McGraw-Hill, 1965), Chapter 4.
[5] " which requires that the marginal cost of additional information gathering or more refined calculation be equal to its marginal (expected) gross yield." W. J. Baumol and R. E. Quant, " Rules of Thumb and Optimally Imperfect Decisions," *American Economic Review*, March 1964, p. 23.
[6] *Ibid.*, p. 24.
[7] D. Vickers, *The Theory of the Firm: Production, Capital and Finance* (New York: McGraw-Hill, 1968).

that permits the use of behavioural variables in the way which gives behavioural theory its name. A fully determinate solution requires the behaviour, at least of relevant aggregates, to be fully constrained by the system. But if constraints are obligatory, objectives are optional, and the dilemma of micro-equilibrium theory is to reconcile the element of choice in the assumptions with the absence of choice in the results. This dilemma is brilliantly resolved in the theory of perfect competition, which combines completely independent decisions into a fully-determined system. Although normally employed in the exposition, the assumption of profit maximisation is redundant in this theory, at least in the long-run version: the behavioural assumptions are almost irrelevant, as a wide range of plausible assumptions all lead to the same result. Every objective turns out to be a constraint. The theory of imperfect competition with normal profits shares this highly desirable attribute; thus as long as free entry can be assumed, the behaviour of firms cannot affect the long-run equilibrium solution, and is not therefore a sensible subject for research. Within these limits, pricing behaviour is irrelevant to price theory. This essential point is thoroughly obscured in Silberston's survey—not least effectively in its title.

The introduction of elements of monopoly destroys this happy conjuncture, for, in the absence of a perfect capital market and effective shareholder control of management, monopoly profits represent an area of discretion. Profit-maximisation does now become a necessary assumption for the unique determination of price and output; but for precisely the same reason, it is not the inevitable assumption: Baumol[1] and Williamson[2] have proferred plausible alternatives. If product differentiation is also allowed, one has a conceptual framework with very few general properties, but potentially rich in highly-specific hypotheses: in short, what economists call an empty model.

It does not, however, follow that elements of monopoly are necessary to behavioural theory, as seems to be generally believed (even by Cyert and March).[3] There is no reason why behavioural theory should not be applied to a firm which is a determined profit-seeker in a highly-competitive industry; it is not another version of monopoly or oligopoly theory, but a different paradigm, embodying a much lower degree of abstraction. Let us take three of the features which are normally regarded as evidence of some degree of monopoly. First, no organisation which delegates decision-making can avoid multiple objectives; and even if its objective function is well-defined, to distribute its components among managers in such a way as to produce organisationally-optimal decisions is hardly conceivable. Second, the need to allocate responsibility for sub-objectives, together with partial ignorance, makes the definition of objectives in terms of target levels,

---

[1] W. J. Baumol, *Business Behaviour, Value and Growth* (New York: Macmillan, 1959).

[2] O. E. Williamson, *The Economics of Discretionary Behaviour: Managerial Objectives in a Theory of the Firm* (Chicago: Markham Publishing Co., 1967).

[3] *E.g.*, Silberston, *op. cit.*, p. 536.

which are more often derived from experience than from optimising procedures, a rational policy. Third, there are many items of " managed costs," which, by definition, represent an area of discretion, but which also enter as arguments into the profit function in ways which are often very poorly understood. In an equilibrium model, expenditures on such items as advertising, research, management training and management information and control systems, would appear as elements of long-run cost, each with an appropriate pay-off (no doubt including a stochastic term); but if neither equilibrium nor pay-offs can be specified, then these costs are most plausibly treated as discretionary, even apparently slack, payments: they are certainly likely to be cut in a cash squeeze—which might be non-optimal behaviour, if optimal behaviour could be defined.

Conclusion

The purpose of the previous section has been to demonstrate how different is the behavioural paradigm from any of the micro-equilibrium paradigms discussed earlier. It was not intended to demonstrate its superiority—indeed an important part of the argument of this paper has been that it is hard to find criteria for judging between paradigms that are not products of the paradigms themselves: rationality for example, apparently so objective, is in fact very heavily paradigm-dependent. Indeed, observant readers will have noticed that, like Kuhn's view of scientific progress, the development of the theory of the firm, as presented in this article, falls entirely within the behavioural paradigm: problemistic search is evoked by a disparity between aspiration and the apparent performance of existing theories, and neither equilibrium nor optimality have any part to play in explaining the course of events.

If the new paradigm were to replace the old, much would be lost. But if it were to be finally rejected by economists, perhaps even more would be lost. For there are many areas of interest and issues of public policy in which the new has the advantage—for example, in questions of efficiency in the popular sense, and in analysing the character and the timing of responses to new situations (such as the introduction of S.E.T.). Fortunately, this is not, as it has sometimes been presented, a conflict for the title of the theory of the firm. For the most part, these paradigms operate at different system levels: once the effort has been made to view both of them with equal bias, there is nothing but an excessive and unscientific regard for consistency to prevent both being used, either separately or together as convenient, until the emergence of a new crisis and the rise of a new challenger. Perhaps next time, given a rather better appreciation of what is happening, the process will be rather less wasteful of time and energy; though it can never be either easy or comfortable.

University of Stirling.   Brian J. Loasby

The Economic Journal, **92** (*June* 1982), 320–340
Printed in Great Britain

THE DUHEM–QUINE THESIS, LAKATOS
AND THE APPRAISAL OF THEORIES
IN MACROECONOMICS*

Rod Cross

The point of this paper is to outline the implications of the Duhem–Quine thesis for the task of appraising theories in economics. The Duhem–Quine thesis (DQ from now on) states that it is not possible to falsify single hypotheses because it is invariably conjunctions of hypotheses which are being tested. Thus if a particular hypothesis is found to be in conflict with some piece of empirical evidence all that we can say is that the conjunction of the particular hypothesis with a set of auxiliary hypotheses is false. We can never be sure that it is not one or more of the auxiliary hypotheses which is responsible for the anomalous empirical evidence, rather than the particular hypothesis in which we are most interested. Expressed in symbols, this means that arguments of the form $[H_0 \to O . \sim O] \to \sim H_0$ are not justified, where H_0 is a particular hypothesis, O is the observational evidence and the symbols $\to$, . and $\sim$ mean 'imply', 'conjoined with', and 'not'. Instead our arguments can only justifiably be phrased in the form $[G_1 \to O . \sim O] \to \sim G_1$, where G_1 is a conjunction of hypotheses which contains H_0: there could well be some different conjunction of hypotheses G_N which contains H_0 which is consistent with the empirical evidence.

The contention of this paper is that many of the debates in macroeconomics have been misguided in that the jointness of hypothesis testing has been ignored by participants in the debates. Instead the focus of attention has been on the appraisal of single target hypotheses considered in isolation from supportive auxiliary hypotheses, the implicit assumption being that it is possible to falsify single target hypotheses. The latter assumption is wrong. Following the logic of the DQ thesis we are obliged to conduct our appraisal at the level of groupings of hypotheses, that is to appraise any target hypothesis *in conjunction with* its supportive auxiliary hypotheses.

The implications of this line of reasoning are perhaps best unravelled in the context of concrete examples from debates in macroeconomics over the last two decades. Before moving to this task we will, in Section I, provide a brief outline of the history of the DQ thesis. Section II will then illustrate the misguidedness of appraising target hypotheses in isolation from their supportive auxiliary hypotheses with reference to the often heated and continuing debate regarding the stability of the demand for money function. The question of how to appraise groupings of hypotheses is considered in Section III. Here we will centre the

* I would like to thank two anonymous referees, Mark Blaug, Jeremy Bray and Alan Coddington for helpful comments on an earlier draft of this paper. None of the above are responsible for the errors that remain.

[320]

discussion on an appraisal of the late Imre Lakatos' theory of the methodology of scientific research programmes. The argument will be that the Lakatosian notions of progressivity and degeneracy in the problem shifts associated with amendments made to groupings of hypotheses can be usefully applied to debates in macroeconomics. Section IV will illustrate this claim by sketching an appraisal of monetarism which makes use of the method of appraisal suggested in this paper.

I. THE DUHEM–QUINE THESIS

The DQ thesis derives from the work of the French physicist Duhem (1906) and the American philosopher Quine (1951). An excellent selection of papers regarding the thesis is available in Harding (1976), which is the source for much of the following exposition.

Duhem pointed out that 'an experiment in physics can never condemn an isolated hypothesis but only a whole theoretical group . . .' (in Harding, p. 4). The idea that it is only the isolated hypothesis which is being tested stems from the unjustifiable belief that the supportive hypotheses and ceteris paribus clauses hold with certainty. Duhem then provides historical examples of supportive hypotheses not holding to support his point. This line of reasoning is then used to argue that 'a "crucial experiment" is impossible in physics' because to uphold such an experiment would require that we were able 'to enumerate completely the various hypotheses which may cover a determinate group of phenomena' (in Harding, pp. 9–11). Thus 'crucial experiments' can neither confirm the target hypothesis, because of the jointness of testing; nor serve to confirm alternative hypotheses, since the only truth established by a falsification is the denial of the hypothesis, and a denial does not imply any single 'opposite' hypothesis, but rather, entails various alternative conjunctions of hypotheses, some of which may contain the target hypothesis.

Quine refers approvingly to Duhem when arguing that 'our statements about the external world face the tribunal of sense experience not individually but only as a corporate body' (Quine, 1980, p. 41): 'total science is like a field of force whose boundary conditions are experience. A conflict with experience at the periphery occasions readjustments in the interior of the field. Truth values have to be re-distributed over some of our statements. Re-evaluation of some statements entails re-evaluation of others because of their logical interconnections . . . there is much latitude as to what statements to re-evaluate in the light of any single contrary experience. No particular experiences are linked with any particular statements in the interior of the field, except indirectly through considerations of equilibrium affecting the field as a whole' (Quine, 1980, p. 43). This 'holistic' view might be taken to imply that a large part of the whole of scientific knowledge is contained in the conjunctions of hypotheses with which we confront the empirical world. In the foreword to a recent edition containing his 1951 paper, Quine admits that this 'holism' 'has put many readers off . . . [the] fault is one of emphasis. All we really need to say in the way of holism . . . is that empirical content is shared by the statements of science in clusters and cannot for the most part be sorted out among them.

Practically the relevant cluster is indeed never the whole of science; there is a grading off . . ..' For further discussion of the Quine version of the DQ thesis, see Harding (1976), Orenstein (1977) and Shahan and Swoyer (1979).

The DQ thesis was criticised by Popper in his *Logic of Scientific Discovery* (1959). Popper did not so much deny the problem of theory appraisal raised by the DQ thesis as object to the argument that the DQ thesis destroys the possibility of subjecting hypotheses to vigorous empirical criticism. Popper argues that scientists *should* exclude in advance of testing defensive strategems for evading refutations of hypotheses: 'the empirical method shall be characterised as a method which excludes precisely those ways of evading falsification . . . which are logically admissible' (in Harding, p. xiv). A problem with this normative prescription as to how scientists should behave is that we do not have any sure way of knowing which constituent hypothesis of a theory or conjunction of hypotheses is at fault in the event of falsification of the empirical content of the theory. In *Conjectures and Refutations* (1963) Popper admits this: 'we can often test only a large chunk of a theoretical system, and sometimes perhaps only the whole system . . . in these cases it is sheer guesswork which of the ingredients should be held responsible for [the] falsification . . .' (in Harding, p. xv); but proceeds to argue that it is possible 'in quite a few cases to find which hypothesis is responsible for the refutation . . .' (in Harding, p. xv). Here, however, we can *never be sure* which hypothesis is responsible for the refutation. The fact that scientists may reach some intersubjective agreement about which part of their theoretical system to revise in response to a refutation merely masks the problem of theory appraisal raised by the DQ thesis. In Section III of this paper we will discuss a method of appraisal which addresses rather than attempts to avoid the appraisal problem raised by the DQ thesis.

Grünbaum, in a series of papers beginning in 1960, has attacked a version of the DQ thesis which asserts that we can *always* rescue a particular hypothesis from refutation by amending auxiliary hypotheses (see Harding, 1976). To uphold the DQ thesis, however, all we need to say is that we can *never be sure* which constituent hypothesis in a theory is responsible for a refutation. Thus we can *never be sure* that anomalous empirical evidence serves to refute a particular hypothesis. In a sense the issue here is one of the burden of proof. Is the scientist who refuses to drop a particular hypothesis which has been 'refuted' obliged to demonstrate precisely how the particular hypothesis can be saved by the amendment of auxiliary hypotheses? Or is the burden of proof on those who would drop the particular hypothesis to demonstrate that a set of amendments to auxiliary hypotheses *cannot* be made to save the particular hypothesis from refutation? It is in the latter sense – that it is impossible to demonstrate that saving auxiliary hypotheses do not exist – that the DQ thesis has, to date, withstood criticism.

II. THE STABILITY OF THE DEMAND FOR MONEY HYPOTHESIS

The task of this section is to illustrate our argument that it is misguided to appraise single target hypotheses in isolation from their supportive auxiliary hypotheses. The example chosen is the hypothesis that the demand for money is a 'stable' function of a vector of 'relevant' explanatory variables: stability and relevance are defined below. We could equally well have illustrated our argument with regard to other hypotheses regarding the demand for money; hypotheses regarding the demand for consumption and investment goods and non-money assets; hypotheses regarding the supply of goods and assets; or with regard to hypotheses regarding the rate of inflation, interest rates and the other main price variables in macroeconomics.

Much effort has been expended in testing the target hypothesis of stability in the demand for money function, most studies up until the 1970s publishing results to the effect that the hypothesis stood unrefuted by a wide set of data thrown up during different historical episodes in different countries[1] (for a review of such evidence, see Laidler, 1977). The 1970s produced observations of actual money holdings in countries such as the United Kingdom and United States which were significantly higher than predicted by the then received demand for money equations. Such evidence has been seen, particularly by anti-monetarists, as refuting the hypothesis of stability in the demand for money function (see Kaldor, 1980, paras. 22, 63–66 and 72–78, for example). Laidler (1980, 1981) provides a useful discussion of the inferences that can be drawn from the higher than predicted holdings of money balances in the 1970s. A distinction is drawn between those who argue that the anomalously high money balance holdings reflect a mis-specification of an otherwise stable demand for money function, and those who argue that once-off shifts in the demand for money function occurred.

Overall the tendency has been to see: (1) the stability of the demand for money function as a key target hypothesis which can be appraised in isolation from other hypotheses; (2) the empirical performance of this hypothesis as playing a key role in the task of stating rational grounds for preferring monetarist to non-monetarist ideas and vice-versa; and (3) tests of the stability of the demand for money function as having the character of 'crucial test' experiments, anomalous empirical evidence implying not only a refutation of the hypothesis but also grounds for preferring the competing hypothesis of instability in the demand for money function.

The above position is seen as sadly misguided once we accept the logic of the DQ thesis: (1a) when testing for stability in the demand for money function we are not only testing this target hypothesis (H_0) but also a large number of other hypotheses; (2a) given this jointness of testing, a grouping of hypotheses in which the hypothesis of stability is embedded can only justifiably be appraised by using methods for assessing groupings of hypotheses rather than single hypotheses; and (3a) the denial of the H_0 stability hypothesis does not imply the opposite $\sim H_0$ of instability but rather, alternative conjunctions of hypotheses some of which might contain the H_0 stability hypothesis. Thus the claim made here is that the debate regarding the stability of the demand for money hypo-

---

[1] Here we neglect the important issue of the extent to which such published results represent biased tests of the stability hypothesis because they were arrived at by mining data to produce 'best fitting' equations. Such malpractice is cogently analysed by Leamer (1974, 1975, 1978).

thesis has been methodologically misguided in that little or no attention has been paid to the appraisal of the auxiliary hypotheses being tested jointly with the stability hypothesis.

In the rest of this section we will attempt to illustrate this DQ line of reasoning by spelling out the types of auxiliary hypotheses which are being tested[1] along with the H_0 hypothesis of stability. The method of 'proof' adopted here might be termed *reductio ad taedium*. The following is an attempt to set out a taxonomy of some of the more obvious sets of auxiliary hypotheses being jointly tested:

H_0 — the target hypothesis of stability;

H_1 — the hypotheses used to define a relevant set of explanatory variables, $M^D = M^D(...)$;

H_2 — the functional form $M^D = ...$;

$H_3, H_4, ..., H_x$ — auxiliary hypotheses from the rest of economic theory;

$O_1, O_2, ..., O_M$ — the hypotheses adopted regarding the measurement of the variables involved in the theory;

$T_1, T_2, ..., T_M$ — hypotheses regarding the appropriate time lag structures involved in the H_2 relationship;

$I_1, I_2, ..., I_N$ — the hypotheses sufficient for the identification of H_2 from the observations;

$C_1, C_2, ..., C_P$ — the hypotheses underlying the *ceteris paribus* clause;

$E_1, E_2, ..., E_Q$ — hypotheses regarding the generation of the error terms in H_2;

S — the statistical inference rule adopted;

D — boundary conditions which delineate the range of empirical observations commensurate with the H_0 hypothesis.

Readers who are already persuaded that for any form of the demand for money function a very large number of auxiliary hypotheses must be tested along with the target hypothesis of stability, may prefer to skip the remainder of this section and proceed to page 327.

The hypotheses involved can be elaborated as follows:

H_0: here stability needs to be more precisely defined in terms of, for example, observations lying within certain bounds around predicted values; or in terms of parametric estimates for some time period $t_1 ... t_m$ not being significantly different from estimates for some other time period $t_n ... t_x$. Different definitions of stability can, of course, lead to different answers to the question as to whether the demand for money function is stable.

H_1: here a 'relevant' vector of explanatory variables needs to be defined. It has usually been thought desirable to define the relevant vector by analysing the constrained optimisation behaviour of economic agents: several such analyses are available, the inventory, direct utility, indirect utility, expected utility and asset price uncertainty approaches being obvious examples (see

---

[1] The question of whether all the hypotheses considered below are *necessary* to produce a given test statement regarding the stability of the demand for money function is not considered in this paper. The issues involved here are similar to those considered by Archibald (1961) when assessing whether the postulates of imperfect competition imply different predictions regarding market behaviour to those generated under the postulates of perfect competition.

Laidler, 1977, and Fisher, 1978, for surveys of such literature). At this stage the hypotheses underlying the chosen model of constrained optimisation are brought into the picture. In the case of the inventory approach, for example, the model of behaviour is constituted from hypotheses regarding: the time profile of payments and receipts; the information available to individuals regarding such flows; how expectations are formed regarding such flows; the costs of switching between money and non-money assets; the non-pecuniary or implicit yield on money balances; behaviour in the face of uncertainty; and so on (see Akerlof, 1979, and Akerlof and Milbourne, 1980, for example). The next step of moving from individual to aggregate behaviour involves the implicit introduction of aggregation hypotheses, the strongest hypothesis being that all individuals react in the same way to changes in the explanatory variables. A difficulty here is that some of the models of money holding behaviour imply the same vector of explanatory variables. Most of the models involve transactions, income or wealth, interest rates and the price level as explanatory variables – save the 'general equilibrium' models (e.g. Dutton and Gramm, 1973) which exclude the quantity constraints involved in the transactions, income or wealth variable. In addition to such variables, the models that deal with behaviour in the face of uncertainty imply parameters describing probability distributions and/or utility functions as explanatory variables. In what follows we will take the 'relevant' vector of explanatory variables to be:

$$M^D = M^D (Y, \mathbf{i}, P),$$

where Y is an index of the scale of transactions, $\mathbf{i}$ is a vector of opportunity cost variables measuring the differences between the yields on non-money assets and the implicit yield on money, and P is the purchasing power of money.

H_2: here a hypothesis regarding the appropriate functional form for M^D needs to be chosen, such as

$$M^D = \alpha_0 Y^{\alpha_1} \mathbf{i}^{\alpha_2} P^{\alpha_3}.$$

There is an infinite number of hypotheses from which to choose (see Courakis, 1978, for example). At this stage further hypotheses can be introduced to place restrictions on the size as well as signs of parameters: the homogeneity postulate would imply $\alpha_3 = 1$, for example. For discussion of the problems arising from specification searches, see Leamer (1978).

$H_3, H_4, ..., H_\infty$: a first issue here is whether we specify M^D as pertaining to equilibrium states of the economy in which case $M^D = M^D (w, \mathbf{i}, P)$ where w is the real wage rate, might be relevant given that only relative prices influence behaviour in full equilibrium; or whether we choose a disequilibrium or temporary equilibrium specification such as $M^D = M^D (Y, P, \mathbf{i})$, where the Y quantity variable enters to reflect quantity constraints on optimisation. Secondly, a hypothesis regarding adjustment to equilibrium is often required, such as

$$\dot{M} = \lambda[M^D - M],$$

there again being a infinite number of possibilities to choose from. Thirdly, hypotheses regarding any factors which are suspected of influencing M^D but which are not explicitly incorporated in H_1, are called into play, at least implicitly. As far as risk is concerned a hypothesis $\delta R_R(Y)/\delta Y = 0$ is maintained in the absence of an explicit incorporation of the $\delta R_R(Y)/\delta Y > 0$ hypothesis, where $R_R(Y)$ is the coefficient of relative risk aversion (see Arrow, 1965). The hypothesis that the α terms in H_2 are fixed parameters is maintained in the absence of an explicit treatment of, say, structural changes in financial markets which would imply such as $\alpha_{i,t} = \gamma\alpha_{i,t-1}, \gamma \neq 0$. In the case of transactions costs for money, an implicit hypothesis of constant marginal transactions costs is introduced in the absence of an explicit treatment of variable transactions costs. Similarly, in the case of uncertainty, the implicit hypothesis that unknown states of the world can be described in terms of probability concepts is being upheld in the absence of an explicit treatment of uncertainty. Fourthly but by no means exhaustively, the implicit hypothesis that a stable unique equilibrium exists in the economy as a whole might be maintained in order to make general equilibrium sense of an equilibrium formulation of an M^D function when it is considered in the context of an interactive economic system.

$O_1, O_2, ..., O_M$: here hypotheses are formulated as to how to measure the money stock (M), purchasing power of money (P), opportunity cost $(\mathbf{i})$ and transactions scale (Y) variables involved in M^D. The number of possible measures for M exceeds the number of motorways in the United Kingdom. As far as P is concerned, the conventional use of the GDP deflator measure implies the use of a hypothesis of myopic utility maximisation given that existing asset prices, such assets being held to yield (*inter alia*) future utility, are not captured in a GDP deflator (see Alchian and Klein, 1973). Concerning $\mathbf{i}$, hypotheses are upheld as to the relevant set of interest differentials which in turn involve implicit hypotheses regarding portfolio substitution possibilities. The Y variable measure involves the hypothesis that, say, domestic output rather than, say, domestic and foreign expenditure is the relevant scale variable constraining monetary transactions; involves the implicit hypothesis that the 'black economy' is not growing in importance and so is not leading to an increased transactions demand for cash not directly related to recorded Y; and so on.

$T_1, T_2, ..., T_M$: here auxiliary hypotheses regarding the time lag structures involved in the relationship between regressor and regressand are introduced, the contemporaneous relationship specification being the most primitive. The specification of the real time periods commensurate with the M^D hypothesis is of major importance to theories which distinguish between short and long run forms of the M^D function. In one version of the inventory model, for example, the short run elasticity of M^D with respect to Y is close to zero, whereas the long run elasticity is close to unity (see Akerlof, 1979, and Akerlof and Milbourne, 1980).

$I_1, I_2, ..., I_N$: here the hypothesis that the money stock is demand determined is being maintained if the parameters of M^D are estimated using M only as a regressand. Otherwise a potentially infinite number of identifying hypotheses can be chosen to maintain the hypothesis of identification in the face of exogeneity in M^S, the remaining hypothesis being that it is not possible to identify M^D. Such hypotheses will involve M^S being used as a regressor, and involve the introduction of auxiliary hypotheses concerning the determinants of P, $\mathbf{i}$ and/or Y (see Artis and Lewis, 1976).

$C_1, C_2, \ldots, C_P$: here hypotheses such as 'there is not a war', 'governments do not pay a competitive rate of interest on money holdings', 'M is freely convertible into gold or other currencies', are introduced, the *ceteris paribus* clause being a catch-all for a potentially infinite number of excluded changes in the state of the world.

$E_1, E_2, \ldots, E_Q$: here hypotheses regarding the ϵ error term in

$$M^D = \alpha_0 + \alpha_1 Y + \alpha_2 \mathbf{i} + \alpha_3 P + \epsilon$$

are introduced. The $\epsilon = N(0, \sigma_\epsilon^2)$ and $\rho = 0$ in $\epsilon_t = \rho \epsilon_{t-i}$ $(i = 1, 2, \ldots, n)$, 'standard' hypotheses are again merely the most primitive of a wide set of hypotheses which could be chosen (see Hendry and Mizon, 1978).

S: here some hypothesis regarding statistical inference is introduced to define a decision rule for accepting or rejecting the H_0 hypothesis of stability. Again an infinite number of hypotheses are potentially available from such as classical or Bayesian theories, there also being a choice as to how stringent a decision rule to adopt (see Giere, 1979, for further discussion).

D: here a hypothesis is used to delineate the boundary conditions or the range of empirical observations over which the H_0 hypothesis is to be appraised. Such a hypothesis will partly reflect the desire to protect H_0 from absurd refutations, such as might arise if H_0 were tested, say, in relation to squirrels' nut holdings: but will also partly reflect the aggressive or defensive stance of those maintaining the H_0 hypothesis. An amendment to D which involved an extension of H_0's applicability to Third World and Eastern European economies, or to longer periods of historical experience would reflect an aggressive strategy. An amendment to D_0 which placed an embargo on testing the H_0 hypothesis on 1971–3 United Kingdom data because of the changes in financial market behaviour associated with Competition and Credit Control would reflect a defensive strategy.

If the above *reductio ad taedium* 'proof' has worked it will have become apparent that tests of the hypothesis of stability in the demand for money function inevitably involve the testing of a substantial baggage of auxiliary hypotheses. Given this it is absurd to appraise the stability hypothesis in isolation from the auxiliary hypotheses. Rather it is necessary to appraise such as the stability hypothesis *in conjunction with* the auxiliary hypotheses. To do this we require methods of appraising groupings of hypotheses. It is to this issue that we now turn.

III. APPRAISAL OF GROUPINGS OF HYPOTHESES

Given that we are consciously or unconsciously testing a potentially infinite number of hypotheses when confronting a target hypothesis with the empirical world, are there criteria we can use to state rational grounds for preferring one grouping of hypotheses to another? The search for such criteria arises given that our interest in appraising hypotheses is not likely to be diminished over-much by the epistemological problems raised by the DQ thesis. If such criteria do not exist, the outlook for rational argument amongst macroeconomists is bleak. In what follows in this section we outline and appraise the Lakatos method of appraisal which has stimulated much interest over the last decade. Where relevant we will illustrate the argument by making reference to debates in macroeconomics over the last two decades.

Lakatos on Appraisal

The starting point for Lakatos is to see the groupings of hypotheses being tested as structured wholes. One subgroup of hypotheses is termed the *hard core*. This hard core is by agreement protected from empirical challenge by a *negative heuristic*, that is a method by which problems are *not* solved, which states that the hard core shall be protected from *modus tollens*[1] arguments. An example of a hard core hypothesis in monetarism might be the hypothesis that, in the absence of destabilising government behaviour, the equilibrium levels of output and unemployment are independent of aggregate demand. The rest of the hypotheses constituting a research programme are termed the *protective belt*, protecting the hard core hypotheses from challenge. Protective belt hypotheses are subjected to *modus tollens* arguments, such hypotheses being modified in the face of anomalous empirical observations or logical difficulties. An example of a protective belt hypothesis in monetarism might be an adaptive expectations hypothesis regarding how inflation expectations are formed.

The dynamic force underlying the research programme is termed the *positive heuristic*, that is the method by which problems *are* solved, which states how the protective belt of the research programme is to be modified in the face of empirical and logical challenge. One component in the *positive heuristic* under-lying monetarism might be an injunction to explain all sustained variations in the rate of inflation by prior variations in the rate of expansion of the money supply. Such an injunction would place restrictions on the protective belt changes that could be made in the face of logical or empirical challenges to the research programme.

The next step is to see a research programme as evolving over time in re-sponse to challenge. The appraisal procedure derives from observation of the evolution path. *Progressive research programmes* are characterised by progressive shifts in the problems with which the programmes deal, i.e. increases in the range of empirical phenomena for which the research programme gives refut-able predictions. The argument here is that a research programme giving a wider set of refutable predictions is to be preferred, there being greater scope

---

[1] *Modus tollens* is the destructive form of argument. The logical relations involved are such that if the conclusion of an argument is shown to be false, then at least one of the premises on which the argument is based is false. We cannot, however, read falsity forwards from the premises to the conclusion of an argument: false premises can entail conclusions which are true. Thus a conclusion that 'this journal is called *Econometrica*', which we know to be false, would be based on at least one false premise such as 'Professor C. H. Feinstein is the current editor of *Econometrica*'. False premises, however, such as 'the ECONOMIC JOURNAL only publishes articles by U.K. residents' can help generate true conclusions such as 'the ECONOMIC JOURNAL is prepared to publish articles by residents of Scotland'.

for destructive challenge of the *modus tollens* type. An example of a progressive problem shift occurred in monetarism in the early 1970s when amendments to *protective belt* hypotheses associated with the monetary theory of the balance of payments (see Frenkel and Johnson, 1976) generated new, additional predictions regarding international differences in inflation rates – the earlier versions of 'closed economy' monetarism having been silent on this issue. The above *theoretical* aspect of appraisal is complemented by an appraisal of the empirical performance of the research programme. Here the criterion is one of whether the changes in the field over which predictions are given are associated with empirical corroboration. Thus it is arguably the case that in the early 1970s monetarism was *empirically progressive* in the light of corroboratory studies of such as the convergence of inflation rates under the Bretton Woods system (see Genberg, 1976, for example). Research programmes are considered to be *theoretically degenerate* if protective belt amendments reduce the empirical content in terms of predictions given, and *empirically degenerate* if the predictions do not meet with empirical corroboration. An example of theoretical degeneracy occurred in Keynesian economics in the late 1960s when inflation was deemed to be determined by sociological or other factors outwith the remit of Keynesian economics, this following the breakdown of the simple Phillips relationship which had earlier been incorporated into Keynesian economics (see Laidler and Parkin, 1975).

Thus groupings of hypotheses are seen as being linked together into a series by the hard core and the set of *positive heuristics* which serve to define a research programme. This linked series of groupings of hypotheses which constitutes a research programme is to be appraised in terms of whether the evolution path generates extra empirical content; and in terms of whether this extra empirical content is corroborated. Appraisal is always relative: the appraisal of a particular research programme would be of little interest unless there were competing research programmes which make rival claims about the phenomena in which we are interested. The task here is one of comparing the corroborated empirical content of the rival research programmes, the preferred research programme being that with the greater corroborated content. One possibility here is that although a research programme may degenerate over time, it may still retain a greater corroborated content than its rivals. Thus a *degenerating* research programme may still be preferred to a *progressive* research programme if the *progressive* research programme has not of yet succeeded in generating greater corroborated content than the *degenerating* research programme. Thus, for example, although the corroborated empirical content of monetarism may have declined in the 1970s and early 1980s (see Laidler, 1981 for discussion of this), monetarism may still retain a greater empirical content than its rival research programmes.

One major problem with the Lakatos appraisal criterion is the commensurability of the empirical content of different research programmes, and of the content of a research programme during its own evolution path. We can think of a research programme as (*a*) having true implications about the phenomena in which we are interested, (*b*) having false implications, and (*c*) being silent regarding such phenomena. The problem is then one of trading off proficient performance as regards category (*a*) against deficient performance regarding categories (*b*) and (*c*). Our account of the evolution path of a particular research programme will partly depend on the comparative weights we attach to (*a*) true implications, (*b*) false implications and (*c*) silence. Similarly, our comparisons of the empirical content of rival research programmes will in part depend on the weights we attach to (*a*), (*b*) and (*c*). The problem here is one of comparing like with like. Most if not all methods of appraisal will be faced with such a problem (see Koertge, 1979, for further discussion).

An Appraisal of the Lakatosian Method of Appraisal

The Lakatosian method of appraisal stresses the dual task of seeing whether the methodology of appraisal postulated can be used successfully to *reconstruct rationally* the evolution of a putatively scientific body of knowledge on the basis of the Lakatos theory of the methodology of scientific research programmes; and of seeing whether the histories of particular bodies of knowledge are consistent with the *theory of* methodology postulated. Thus the idea is not to apply slavishly to economics a theory of methodology derived, in the first instance, from an examination of the history of physics. Rather, the idea is to allow the history of, in this case, macroeconomics to challenge the theory of appraisal postulated. In what follows we examine some of the problems which arise in applying the Lakatosian method of appraisal to macroeconomics.

The Hard-Core Distinction

To conduct a Lakatosian appraisal of research programmes we first need to specify the *hard cores* of the research programmes. This involves us in not only testing the Lakatos theory of methodology, when appraising a research programme such as monetarism, but also our characterisation of the division between *hard core* and *protective belt* hypotheses in monetarism. To take an example, we could specify the hypothesis that 'unemployment is independent of aggregate demand in the long run' – in the absence of destabilising government behaviour, given some real time measure for the long run, and so on – as being a *hard core* hypothesis of monetarism. As such, this hypothesis would be postulated to be one that monetarists would hold onto come what may in the face of empirical or logical difficulties with their research programme. Alternatively we could characterise this hypothesis as belonging to the *protective belt* of monetarism, that is as having the status of defending more elemental monetarist hypotheses, i.e. the *hard core*, from challenge during particular periods of evolution of monetarism. As such the hypothesis would be seen as dispensable in the face of challenges to the research programme.

Seen as part of the *hard core*, the hypothesis would require what might be regarded as remarkable leaps of the imagination in the formulation of protective belt hypotheses to explain such facts as the sustained high unemployment in the United Kingdom in the interwar period. Benjamin and Kochin (1979) provide such protective belt hypotheses in arguing that the sustained high unemployment can be explained by unemployment insurance induced increases in voluntary unemployment (though see the papers by Metcalf *et al.* (1982) and Cross (1982*a*), for critical evaluation of the Benjamin and Kochin thesis). If seen as part of the *protective belt*, however, the hypothesis could be replaced with hypotheses such as 'long run unemployment is an increasing function of the variance in aggregate demand'; or 'long run unemployment is an increasing function of the number of long-term unemployed[1] in the labour force' in order to attempt to explain the United Kingdom unemployment experience of the interwar period. Such hypotheses would arguably be consistent with the *positive heuristic* underlying monetarism.

Similar problems with the notion of a *hard core* have been raised by Berkson (1976, p. 52) who argues that in the beginning it is individual scientists who have ideas as to which hypotheses are fundamental to research programmes. Such ideas as to what is fundamental not only differ between scientists, but also the same scientist has often changed his or her ideas as to what is fundamental while continuing to work in the same research programme. Similar lines of criticism are to be found in Feyerabend (1976, p. 115) who argues that commonly held scientific wisdom is not very common; Musgrave (1976, p. 459) who argues that even such as the theory of gravitation had not attained *hard core* status in the Newtonian research programme by 1800; and that the application of a *negative heuristic* to the *hard core* 'gives *carte blanche* to any group who want to erect some pet notion into dogma' (p. 465).

It is no doubt the case that at certain times particular scientists have seen certain propositions as being more fundamental to their research programmes than others. We would argue, however, that views as to which propositions are more fundamental have not been widely accepted or time-invariate enough for us to be able to draw a clear distinction between hard core and protective belt propositions in economics. One way out of this problem would be to distinguish between *ex ante* and *ex post* hard core propositions.[2] *Ex ante* the members of a research programme may take most if not all of their propositions as being open to challenge. *Ex post*, however, certain propositions may be revealed to be ones which the research programme has held on to in the face of logical and empirical criticism. There is here, however, an economy of reason consideration that the drawing of a distinction between hard core and protective belt propositions increases the speculative baggage which we introduce into theory appraisal. In light of this we would argue that it is better to drop the hard core-protective belt distinction. This will make sense provided that we still have some sensible criterion for identifying linked series of hypothesis groupings for appraisal. In the next section we argue that linked series of hypothesis groupings, or research programmes, can be suitably identified for appraisal by way of their *positive heuristics*.

Identifying Research Programmes

Lakatosian appraisals of research programmes in physics have been criticised as being 'arbitrary because they rest on an arbitrary choice of rival research

---

[1] That is those with uncompleted spells of unemployment in excess of six months.
[2] I am grateful to an anonymous referee for this point.

programmes' (Feyerabend, 1976, p. 134). Somewhat milder misgivings have been expressed regarding the identification of research programmes in economics: 'A necessary condition for the transfer of Lakatosian methodology to other disciplines is that programmes be well defined or at least easily recognisable. I doubt if this is the case' (Archibald, 1979, p. 308). A wide variety of characterisations of research programmes in economics has been suggested. At one extreme, it is possible to characterise the whole of orthodox economics in the last 200 years since Adam Smith as one research programme. At the other extreme, the theory of the firm under perfect competition (Latsis, 1976a) and the theory of comparative advantage (de Marchi, 1976) have been identified as separate research programmes. For an excellent review of attempts to identify research programmes in economics, see Blaug (1981).

Given the abandonment of the *hard core – protective belt* distinction suggested above, it might be thought that we have also thrown out the only criteria which could be used to arrive at useful distinctions between groupings of hypotheses, and the only useful means of identifying the links which unify groupings of hypotheses over time into a research programme. This is not the case. The *negative heuristic* aspect of a research programme has been abandoned, but not the *positive heuristic*. The position taken here follows Archibald (1979) in arguing that it is only sensible to distinguish particular groupings of hypotheses for appraisal if such groupings are easily recognisable. The further argument is that certain groupings are so identifiable by way of the *positive heuristics* used, that is by way of the methods which are used to solve problems. This amounts to taking up a pragmatic position whereby the 'proof' of the relevance of particular groupings of hypotheses identified for appraisal lies in the ease with which such groupings are recognisable as capturing the positions taken up by participants in debates in macroeconomics.

Two examples of *positive heuristics* in macroeconomics are now provided. These are injunctions to: (a) 'explain fluctuations in output and employment by analysing trading sequences taking place at disequilibrium prices'; and (b) 'explain fluctuations in output and employment by analysing errors in rational expectations regarding the rate of inflation'. If the claim made above regarding the identification of groupings of hypotheses holds water, injunction (a) will be recognisable as identifying the grouping of Keynesian hypotheses termed 'reconstituted reductionism' by Coddington (1976), that is the research programme formalised by Clower (1965). Similarly, injunction (b) would be recognisable as identifying the grouping of 'new classical macroeconomics' hypotheses, that is the research programme initiated in Lucas (1972). Given some measure of agreement that such hypothesis groupings are recognisable, the way is then open to compare the paths of evolution in terms of degrees of *progressivity* and *degeneracy* in problem shifts.

Appraisal Time Period

Identified by its *positive heuristic*, a research programme will throw up a series of groupings of hypotheses $G_1, G_2, G_3, \ldots$, 'where each subsequent theory results from adding auxiliary clauses to (or from semantical reinterpretations of) the previous theory in order to accommodate some anomaly, each theory having at least as much content as the unrefuted content of its predecessor' (Lakatos, 1978, vol. 1, p. 33). A version of the research programme G_N which has excess empirical content over its predecessor G_{N-1} will be appraised as *theoretically progressive*, a version which has less empirical content than its predecessor *theoretically degenerate*. The contention then is that there are rational grounds, other things being equal, for preferring research programmes generating the former type of problem shifts. The main thing to be kept equal here, of course, is that the *progressive* research programme develops at least as much corroborated content as its rivals. The problem with this procedure is that some time limit needs to be applied in order to judge the degree of *progressivity/degeneracy* in problem shifts. A programme may degenerate consistently over a period of years only to more than recoup the loss of content in some future period of progression, and vice-versa: 'the butterfly emerges when the caterpillar has reached its lowest state of degeneration' (Feyerabend, 1976, p. 121). The question here is whether appraisal of the past performance of research programmes is worthwhile given that the past performance might be reversed in the future.

The commonsense answer to this question is that any method of appraisal can only state rational grounds for preferring one research programme to another on the basis of the information available at the time. It is not the lot of humans to know the future, and the question of whether past performance is a reliable guide to the future may be addressed to all methods of appraisal. The more interesting issue is of how the information derived from the appraisal method is used. The question is one of whether our method of appraisal should be used to give *prescriptive* advice as to which research programme should be preferred, or merely purport to describe the evolution paths of different research programmes.

Should a Method of Appraisal be also Prescriptive?

Lakatos argued that methods of appraisal should not be used to give advice to practising scientists: '. . . my "methodology", older connotations of the word notwithstanding . . . presumes to give advice to the scientist neither about how to *arrive* at good theories nor even about which of two rival programmes he should work on' (Lakatos, 1971, p. 174). There is, however, a schizophrenic air about the Lakatos position here given that he also affirmed that: 'Editors of scientific journals should refuse to publish *the papers of those who stick to a degenerating programme*' (Lakatos, 1978, vol. 1, p. 117 – italics indicate a re-arrangement of the quotation).

The Lakatos position on this issue has been criticised by Musgrave (1976), who argues that although appraisal does not logically imply a piece of advice, appraisal certainly suggests grounds for preferring one course of action to another. It can also be argued that 'in the social sciences we have a use for some litmus paper to detect the pretentious, the bogus, and the unscientific' (Archibald, 1979, p. 132). In the context of the present paper, the litmus paper would be one that indicates some shade of red if a grouping of theories has increased its empirical content, and some shade of blue if the empirical content has been reduced. Given that the problems raised by the DQ thesis do not go away if we do not look at them, and neither do the problems of choosing between different theories in macroeconomics, there is a prima facie case that the use of some such test would be of assistance in appraising theories in macroeconomics. If such tests suggest certain courses of action rather than others to macroeconomists, this is all well and good provided that we are clear that no method of appraisal by itself can hasten the progress of knowledge in macroeconomics. Also, of course, macroeconomists can take or leave any such advice which might seem to be offered, preferably after considering the set of considerations discussed in this paper.

To summarise here, the method of appraisal considered in this paper does not logically *entail* any specific prescriptive advice, but it does *suggest* certain courses of action, such as: 'appraise target hypotheses in conjunction with their supportive auxiliary hypotheses'; 'consider the comparative degree of *progressivity/degeneracy* in problem shifts when choosing between the statements made about the world by rival theories'; 'compare the corroborated empirical content when assessing the merits of rival theories'; and even, to avoid methodology madness, 'do not overlook the possibility that a degenerate grouping of hypotheses will re-emerge as progressive in the future'.

Against Method

The title of this section is that of a book by Feyerabend (1975), who argues that the only good method is no method. This argument is more specifically directed towards the Lakatos method of appraisal in Feyerabend (1976). In broad summary the argument runs as follows: the Lakatos method derives its standards of exemplary knowledge from an analysis of modern science, especially physics; the excellence of such standards is assumed not argued for, there not being 'a single argument to show that they are better than the standards that underlie the practice of magic' (Feyerabend, 1976, p. 112); such standards are not strong enough to yield rational criteria for choosing between theories (*op. cit.*, pp. 120–5); Lakatosian rational reconstructions of the histories of theories do not explain how some scientists managed to behave 'rationally' whilst upholding misguided principles of methodology (*op. cit.*, pp. 129–31); appraisals of theories are arbitrary in that they depend on arbitrary designations of research programmes and arbitrary choices of time periods over which to evaluate progression and degeneration (*op. cit.*, pp. 131–6). Overall, the assessment is: 'The methodology of research programmes most certainly has led to some interesting historical discoveries. This is not surprising. Any hypothesis, however implausible, can widen our horizon. It has not led to a better understanding of science and it is even a hindrance to such a better understanding because of its habit of beclouding facts with sermons and moralising phrases' (Feyerabend, *op. cit.*, p. 136).

Feyerabend's strictures would imply that the method of appraisal considered in this paper might produce some interesting insights into past debates in macroeconomics but at the expense of muddying the debates with 'sermons and moralising phrases'. The latter implication can be countered on several levels. First, although attempts to define and use standards of 'science' and 'rationality' may face substantial difficulties and encounter severe problems this does not logically imply that we should abandon such standards. Similar difficulties and problems arise with regard to attempts to define and use standards of 'democracy' and 'rights' – not to mention the 'anarchism' advocated by Feyerabend! Should we then abjure from using concepts of 'democracy' and 'rights' in political discussion? For further discussion here, see Gellner (1975). Secondly, although fish (macroeconomists) seem to be able to swim (argue about the relative merits of theories) without knowing about hydrodynamics (theories of appraisal), we cannot infer from this that an awareness of hydrodynamics would not allow fish to use their energies more constructively when swimming. Thirdly, the method of appraisal suggested in this paper rests on a component of the Lakatos theory which can be evaluated in its own right. In the words of a vehement critic of the Lakatos theory of the methodology of scientific research programmes: 'Lakatos' idea of progressiveness stands in its own right and is interesting' (Agassi, 1979, p. 323). Feyerabend's criticisms of the Lakatos ideas of progression and degeneration have been considered earlier in this section. Fourth, we do not have the knowledge of the future required to *deny* that there are methods of appraisal which would alleviate the problems raised by the DQ thesis. Finally, judgement on whether the use of a particular method of appraisal to augment the existing ways of arguing about theories in macroeconomics is an aid or a hindrance is best suspended until such a method has been tried.

IV. AN ILLUSTRATION OF THE METHOD OF APPRAISAL

The method of appraisal suggested in this paper involves assessing the progression or degeneration in empirical content associated with the amendments that are made to groupings of hypotheses, the latter groupings to be identified for appraisal by their *positive heuristics*. A full examination of groupings of hypotheses in macroeconomics, or even of a specific grouping, is beyond the scope of the present paper. Instead we attempt to illustrate the approach by suggesting some of the conclusions that *might* emerge from a more detailed application of our method of appraisal to the evolution of a particular grouping of hypotheses, monetarism.[1]

A Sketch of Monetarism

Starting from scratch, we can attempt to identify a grouping of hypotheses with regard to the *positive heuristics* which are applied to the explanation of some variable of major interest to those concerned. The injunction, 'explain sustained variations in the rate of inflation by sustained prior variations in the rate of monetary expansion' would seem to be a promising candidate with which to

---

[1] The term 'monetarism' was coined by Brunner (1968) to describe the set of ideas which claims that changes in the stock of money are the major sources of changes in nominal income.

identify monetarist hypotheses. The way would then be clear to conduct an appraisal of the evolution of empirical content in monetarist hypotheses regarding the rate of inflation. At this juncture it would become apparent that monetarist hypotheses specify certain variables as being co-determined with the rate of inflation. Thus monetarism would have additional empirical content with regard to such variables as the level of interest rates, output, unemployment, foreign exchange rates, economic agents' expectations and so on to the extent to which such variables were co-determined with the rate of inflation, and so explained by a common *positive heuristic*. Such content would then need to be appraised alongside the content with regard to the rate of inflation. Indeed we could re-phrase the scientific maxim of 'explaining a lot from a little' as 'explaining a lot from a simple *positive heuristic*'.

Ab initio we could identify the grouping of hypotheses contained in Friedman (1956) as our point of departure. This 1956 version of monetarism, M_{1956} – this and subsequent dates are suggestive rather than definitive – had content with regard to the level of nominal income, the level of money interest rates and little else. Early revisions of M_{1956} saw the content extended to the rate of change of nominal income, the rate of inflation sometimes being substituted for the latter on the assumption of full-employment. The first major change in content, however, comes with Friedman (1968). Here unemployment is introduced into the range of phenomena for which explanations are offered. M_{1956} has variations in the rate of monetary expansion affecting actual unemployment, deviations between the latter and the natural unemployment rate inducing changes in the actual compared to the expected rate of inflation. Subsequently refutable empirical content was added by way of auxiliary hypotheses regarding the determination of inflation expectations, the adaptive expectations hypothesis for example; and by way of auxiliary hypotheses concerning the determinants of the natural rate of unemployment, the 'replacement ratio'[1] hypothesis for example (see Laidler (1981) for an account of this development). The second major change in content occurs with the introduction of hypotheses regarding open economies, the Johnson (1973) paper on the monetary theory of the balance of payments – which circulated widely before this – being particularly influential.[2] This M_{1973} has additional content with regard to international differences in inflation rates under a fixed exchange rate regime, convergence in such inflation rates being predicted in the face of endogeneity in national money stocks; and with regard to variations in foreign exchange rates under a flexible exchange rate system, such divergences being postulated to reflect differences between countries' rates of monetary expansion (again see Laidler (1981) for references and an account of this development).

As far as appraisal is concerned it is possible to detect a more or less uninterrupted increase in empirical content on the path $M_{1956} \ldots M_{1968} \ldots M_{1973}$. This increase in content arose from a pre-stated *positive heuristic*, and much of

---

[1] This is the ratio between unemployment benefits and wages net of tax.

[2] The monetary theory of the balance of payments or exchange rate was, of course, invented long before this – see Frenkel and Johnson (1976). It was, however, only in the early 1970's that this theory came to be fully incorporated into monetarism.

this content was corroborated. Thus, for example, the simultaneous increases in inflation rates in Western industrial countries in the late 1960s were successfully explained; and an explanation of the rise in United Kingdom unemployment in the late 1960s was given by way of the rise in the United Kingdom 'replacement ratio', the latter being the first auxiliary hypothesis to be employed regarding the determinants of the natural rate of unemployment. Thus while still retaining as corroborated the content of M_{1965} regarding the rate of change in nominal income, the M_{1968} and M_{1973} hypothesis groupings succeeded in generating excess empirical content regarding the rate of inflation, actual unemployment and natural or equilibrium unemployment. Further, at least one new fact was predicted, that of convergence of inflation rates under the Bretton Woods fixed exchange rate system. Arguably, most of this empirical content was corroborated. Another aspect of progression was the willingness to apply the M_{1973} theory to episodes in pre-war macroeconomic history and to Third World countries.

After 1973, however, several instances can be cited where the content of M_{1973} has not been corroborated. Thus the unusually high holdings of money balances in the United Kingdom in 1972–4 and 1980–1 are not explained by M_{1973}. Several major movements in foreign exchange rates, such as in sterling in 1976 and 1980–1 are not explained by M_{1973}. Similarly the trebling of United Kingdom unemployment in 1977–81 cannot be explained by the auxiliary hypotheses invoked in M_{1973} to explain the natural rate of unemployment, the 'replacement ratio', for example, having fallen during the period. The reaction to such anomalies has largely involved amendments to M_{1973} which have reduced the empirical content of monetarism. Thus 'structural change', 'mismanagement of monetary policy' and 'increased uncertainty' have been invoked as *ad hoc* auxiliary hypotheses to explain the excess money holdings of 1972–4 and 1980–1. Auxiliary hypotheses involving 'confidence' and 'North Sea Oil' effects not derived from a pre-planned *positive heuristic* have been introduced to explain movements in the sterling exchange rate in 1976 and 1980–1. Similarly *ad hoc* auxiliary hypotheses such as 'oil price shocks', 'the emergence of new industrial economies in the Third World', and 'real wages being too high' have been invoked to explain the rise in the United Kingdom natural rate of unemployment in the 1976–81 period (see Cross, 1982*b*, for further discussion and references here).

Thus the path from M_{1973} to M_{1981} has not only been characterised by empirical degeneration, but also by amendments to hypotheses which have reduced the empirical content of monetarism, i.e. theoretical degeneration. At this point it is worth quoting Lakatos: '. . . I define a research programme as degenerating even if it anticipates novel facts but does so in a patched-up development rather than by a coherent pre-planned positive heuristic. I distinguish three types of *ad hoc* auxiliary hypotheses: those which have no excess empirical content over their predecessor (*ad hoc*$_1$), those which do have such content but none of which is corroborated (*ad hoc*$_2$) and finally those which are not *ad hoc* in these two senses but do not form part of the positive heuristic (*ad hoc*$_3$) . . .' (Lakatos, 1978, vol. I, p. 112, footnote 2). The invocation of *ad hoc*$_3$ type auxiliary hypotheses is tantamount to declaring phenomena to be determined outwith the scope of the theory. Several such instances have occurred on the path $M_{1973} ... M_{1981}$.

Limitations of this Sketch of Monetarism

Given that we have only had the time in this paper to present a cursory appraisal of the complex webs of ideas that have constituted different vintages of monetarism, it is advisable to list some of the limitations of the sketch provided. First we have not *compared* the evolution path of the identified monetarist research programme with the paths of rival research programmes. Of particular interest here is the emergence of the 'new classical macroeconomics' (see Lucas, 1980) as a rival to orthodox monetarism. This research programme postulates that: economies are in a continuous state of market-clearing equilibrium, in contrast to orthodox monetarism where economies are postulated to be in such a state only in the long-run 'natural' rate equilibrium; and that business cycle fluctuations reflect errors in rational expectations regarding the rate of inflation, whereas orthodox monetarism contains no such account of the propagation of the impulses underlying cyclical fluctuations (see Cross (1982 *b*) for an appraisal of the 'new classical macroeconomics'). Similarly we have not appraised orthodox monetarism alongside Keynesian research programmes such as the 'hydraulic', 'fundamentalist' and 'reconstituted reductionist' programmes identified by Coddington (1976). Thus although our appraisal suggests that orthodox monetarism has degenerated since the mid-1970s, we have not addressed the question of whether the rival research programmes have greater empirical content. It is not obvious that a comparative appraisal would reveal orthodox monetarism to have less corroborated content than its rivals.

Second, we have not considered the commensurability of problem shifts. Are progressions in content in a monetarist research programme with regard to the rate of inflation to be weighed equally with similar progressions in content in Keynesian research programmes with regard to the level of unemployment? Or, inside a particular research programme, is progression in one direction to be weighed equally with degeneration in another direction?

Third, is not the period 1956–81 too short, and the 1973–81 period too recent to conduct a satisfactory appraisal of monetarism? Of course it is possible, given the arguments in Section III of this paper, that an appraisal of M_{2000} will reveal $M_{1973} ... M_{1981}$ as a local period of degeneration on a globally progressive path.

Fourth, has our broad brush appraisal of monetarism not missed important differences between individuals, and between different countries as far as monetarist research programmes are concerned? In the United Kingdom, for example, monetarists tend to lay greater stress on the open economy aspects of monetarism than do United States monetarists.

Finally, but by no means exhaustively, how does our sketch of monetarism compare with those derived from other means of appraisal? Here we would argue that the above sketch adds insights to those to be found in work such as Mayer (1978) and Purvis (1980) in terms of: (*a*) the identification of monetarist hypotheses by a *positive heuristic*; (*b*) the account given of the evolution of different vintages of monetarism; and (*c*) the appraisal criteria suggested.

V. CONCLUSION

This paper started by outlining the problems raised for theory appraisal in macroeconomics by the DQ thesis. Such problems exist whether or not the approach to the appraisal of theories outlined in this paper is thought to be a productive one to pursue. So do the difficulties in comparing the statements made about the world by different macroeconomic theories. We would argue that there is a *prima facie* case for introducing a method of appraisal which at least attempts to capture the conjointness of hypothesis testing.

University of St Andrews

Date of receipt of final typescript: November 1981

REFERENCES

Agassi, J. (1979). 'The legacy of Lakatos.' *Philosophy of the Social Sciences*, vol. 9, pp. 316–26.
Akerlof, G. (1979). 'Irving Fisher on his head: the consequences of constant target-threshold monitoring of money holdings.' *Quarterly Journal of Economics*, vol. 93 (May), pp. 169–88.
—— and Milbourne, R. D. (1980). 'The short run demand for money.' ECONOMIC JOURNAL, vol. 90 (December), pp. 885–900.
Alchian, A. A. and Klein, B. (1973). 'On a correct measure of inflation.' *Journal of Money and Credit Banking*, vol. 5 (February), pp. 173–91.
Archibald, G. C. (1961). 'Chamberlain versus Chicago.' *Review of Economic Studies*, vol. 29, pp. 1–28.
—— (1979). 'Method and appraisal in economics.' *Philosophy of the Social Sciences*, vol. 9, pp. 304–15.
Arrow, K. J. (1965). *Aspects of the Theory of Risk-Bearing*. Helsinki: Yrjö Jahnssonin Säätiö.
Artis, M. J. and Lewis, M. K. (1976). 'The demand for money in the United Kingdom 1963–1973.' *Manchester School*, vol. 44 (June), pp. 147–81.
Benjamin, D. K. and Kochin, L. A. (1979). 'Unemployment in Interwar Britain.' *Journal of Political Economy*, vol. 87 (June), pp. 441–78.
Berkson, W. (1976). 'Lakatos One and Lakatos Two: an appreciation.' In *Essays in Memory of Imre Lakatos* (ed. R. S. Cohen), pp. 39–54. Reidel.
Blaug, M. (1981). *The Methodology of Economics: How Economists Explain*. Cambridge University Press.
Brunner, K. (1968). 'The role of money and monetary policy.' *Federal Reserve Bank of St Louis Review*, vol. 50 (July), pp. 8–24.
Clower, R. W. (1965). 'The Keynesian counter-revolution: a theoretical appraisal.' In *The Theory of Interest Rates* (ed. F. Hahn and F. Brechling). Macmillan.
Courakis, A. S. (1978). 'Serial correlation and a Bank of England study of the demand for money: an exercise in measurement without theory.' ECONOMIC JOURNAL, vol. 88 (September), pp. 537–48.
Cross, R. (1982a). 'How much voluntary unemployment in interwar Britain?' *Journal of Political Economy*, vol. 90, no. 2 (April), pp. 61–6.
—— (1982b). *Economic Theory and Policy in the U.K.: An Outline and Assessment of the Controversies*. Martin Robertson.
Coddington, A. (1976). 'Keynesian economics: the search for first principles.' *Journal of Economic Literature*, vol. 14, no. 4 (December), pp. 1258–73.
Cohen, R. S., Feyerabend, P. K. and Wartofsky, M. W. eds. (1976). *Essays in Memory of Imre Lakatos*. Reidel.
De Marchi, N. (1976). 'Anomaly and the development of economics: the case of the Leontief paradox.' In *Method and Appraisal in Economics* (ed. S. J. Latsis). Cambridge University Press.
Duhem, P. (1906). *The Aim and Structure of Physical Theory*, transl. P. Wiener. Princeton University Press, 1954.
Dutton, D. S. and Gramm, W. P. (1973). 'Transactions costs, the wage rate and the demand for money.' *American Economic Review*, vol. 63 (September), pp. 652–65.
Feyerabend, P. K. (1975). *Against Method*. New Left Books.

340 THE ECONOMICAL JOURNAL [JUNE 1982]

—— (1976). 'On the critique of scientific reason.' In *Essays in Memory of Imre Lakatos* (ed. R. S. Cohen *et al.*), pp. 109–43, Reidel.

Fisher, D. (1978). *Monetary Theory and the Demand for Money*. Martin Robertson.

Frenkel, J. and Johnson, H. G. (1976). *The Monetary Approach to Balance of Payments Theory*. Allen and Unwin.

Friedman, M. (1956). 'The quantity theory of money – a restatement.' In *Studies in the Quantity Theory of Money* (ed. M. Friedman). University of Chicago Press.

—— (1968). 'The role of monetary policy.' *American Economic Review*, vol. 58 (March), pp. 1–17.

Gellner, E. (1975). 'Beyond truth and falsehood.' *British Journal for the Philosophy of Science*, vol. 26, pp. 331–42.

Genberg, H. (1976). 'A note on inflation rates under fixed exchange rate open economies.' In *Inflation in the World Economy* (ed. M. Parkin and G. Zis). Manchester University Press.

Giere, R. N. (1979). 'Foundations of probability and statistical inference.' In *Current Research in the Philosophy of Science* (ed. P. D. Asquith and H. E. Kyburg Jr). Philosophy of Science Association, Michigan.

Grünbaum, A. (1960). 'The Duhemian argument.' *Philosophy of Science*, vol. 2, pp. 75–87.

Harding, S. G. (ed.) (1976). *Can Theories be Refuted?* Reidel.

Hendry, D. F. and Mizon, G. E. (1978). 'Serial correlation as a convenient simplification, not a nuisance . . .' ECONOMIC JOURNAL, vol. 88 (September), pp. 549–68.

Johnson, H. G. (1973). 'The monetary approach to balance of payments theory.' In H. G. Johnson, *Further Essays in Monetary Economics*. London.

Kaldor, N. (1980). 'Memorandum of evidence on monetary policy to the Select Committee on the Treasury and the Civil Service.' *Memoranda on Monetary Policy*, pp. 86–130. Treasury and Civil Service Committee, HC720, July.

Koertge, N. (1979). 'The problem of appraising scientific theories.' In *Current Research in the Philosophy of Science* (ed. P. D. Asquith and H. E. Kyburg). Philosophy of Science Association, Michigan.

Laidler, D. E. W. (1977). *The Demand for Money*, 2nd ed. Dun-Donnelley.

—— (1980). 'The demand for money in the United States – yet again.' In *On the State of Macroeconomics* (ed. K. Brunner and A. H. Meltzer). Vol. 12 of Carnegie-Rochester Conference Series on Public Policy. North Holland.

—— (1981). 'Monetarism: an interpretation and assessment.' ECONOMIC JOURNAL, vol. 91 (March), pp. 1–28.

—— and Parkin, J. M. (1975). 'Inflation: a survey.' ECONOMIC JOURNAL, vol. 85 (December), pp. 741–809.

Latsis, S. J. (ed.) (1976a). *Method and Appraisal in Economics*. Cambridge University Press.

—— (1976b). 'A research programme in economics.' In *Method and Appraisal in Economics*. Cambridge University Press.

Lakatos, I. (1971). 'Replies to critics.' In *Boston Studies in the Philosophy of Science*, vol. 8 (ed. R. C. Buck and R. S. Cohen), pp. 174–82. Reidel.

—— *Philosophical Papers*. Vol. 1: *The Methodology of Scientific Research Programmes*. Vol. 2: *Mathematics Science and Epistemology* (ed. J. Worrall and G. Currie). Cambridge University Press.

Leamer, E. A. (1974). 'False models and post-data model construction.' *Journal of American Statistical Association*, vol. 69 (March), pp. 122–31.

—— (1975). '"Explaining your results" as access-biased memory.' *Journal of American Statistical Association*, vol. 70 (March), pp. 88–93.

—— (1978). *Specification Searches: Ad Hoc Inference with Non-Experimental Data*. John Wiley.

Lucas, R. E., Jr. (1972). 'Expectations and the neutrality of money.' *Journal of Economic Theory*, vol. 4, pp. 103–24.

—— (1980). 'Methods and problems in business cycle theory.' *Journal of Money Credit and Banking*, Supplement, vol. 12 (November), pp. 788–99.

Mayer, T. (ed.) (1978). *The Structure of Monetarism*. W. W. Norton.

Metcalf, D., Nickell, S. and Floros, N. (1982). 'Still searching for an explanation of unemployment in interwar Britain.' *Journal of Political Economy*, vol. 90. no. 2 (April).

Musgrave, A. (1976). 'Method or madness?' In *Essays in Memory of Imre Lakatos* (ed. R. S. Cohen *et al.*), pp. 457–91, Reidel.

Orenstein, A. (1977). *Willard van Orman Quine*. Boston: Twayne.

Popper, K. R. (1959). *The Logic of Scientific Discovery*. Hutchinson.

—— (1963). *Conjectures and Refutations*. Routledge and Kegan Paul.

Purvis, D. D. (1980). 'Monetarism: a review.' *Canadian Journal of Economics*, vol. 13 (February), pp. 96–122.

Shahan, R. W. and Swoyer, C. (eds.) (1979). *Essays on The Philosophy of W. V. Quine*. Harvester Press.

Quine, W. van O. (1951). 'Two dogmas of empiricism.' *Philosophical Review*, reprinted in W. van O. Quine, *From a Logical Point of View*, pp. 20–46. Harper and Row, 1961.

—— (1980). *From a Logical Point of View*, 2nd ed., revised. Harvard University Press.

7

Meta-Methodology-Falsificationism and the Rhetoric of Economics

Mark Blaug, *The Methodology of Economics*, Cambridge: Cambridge University Press, 1980, Chapter 15.

Donald McCloskey, 'The Rhetoric of Economics', *Journal of Economic Literature*, vol. 21, June 1983, pp. 481–517.

Editor's comments

In the preface I remarked that, in the course of studying methodology, one encounters more questions than answers. There are a set of questions raised by the demise of positivism that I have found to be both persistent and perplexing. Though many have tried their hand at answering them, none of the answers have been completely satisfactory. This is not meant as a counsel of despair, but rather as a call to arms. Those who join the melee, however, should be aware that the enemy is formidable.

In their most general formulations, the questions are about what, if anything, should replace positivism. In this sense they are meta-methodological, for they involve assessing the direction of methodological inquiry in the post-positivist era. When more narrowly defined, the problems of theory appraisal and theory choice are encountered. Is there a best, or perhaps a least harmful, general set of procedures that may be used to assess the merits of individual or competing hypotheses, theories and research programs? If it exists, what is the 'scientific method', and how does it differ from other attempts at knowledge acquisition by humans?

Both logical positivism and logical empiricism tried to answer these questions; and both encountered fatal problems, in the form of unresolved dichotomies. Logical positivists tried and failed to discover a criterion of cognitive significance with which to distinguish between analytic and synthetic statements. Logical empiricists similarly foundered in their attempts to distinguish between theoretical and observational statements. In the post-positivist era, the question has been called: perhaps it is quixotic even to search for a general set of criteria of theory appraisal. Does that mean there is *no* scientific method? Are there no prescriptions in science? Is methodology really only a descriptive field, describing past episodes of scientific change? In coming up with answers to these and other meta-methodological questions, economic methodologists have divided themselves into a number of different groups.

Even though they admit that the theory choice problem is unsolvable, some economists nonetheless insist that there is a least harmful set of general procedures for evaluating theories that we should try, whenever possible, to follow. (It should be noted that all methodologists agree that certain general prescriptions – don't shout, don't use physical force, etc. – are commonly followed in science. This group goes beyond that to say that certain criteria for identifying the best theories exist and should be used.) Both Terence Hutchison and Mark Blaug are in this camp, and both endorse Karl Popper's falsificationism. To represent this view, I have selected the final chapter of Blaug's admirable 1980 survey, *The Methodology of Economics*, for the first reading.

The book is a remarkable one: the philosophy of science is surveyed, the major methodological works of the past two centuries are carefully and critically reviewed, and nine contemporary research programs are methodologically assessed. It is also a polemic, for throughout its pages Blaug pleads that economists start taking falsification seriously. His argument reaches its culmination in this final chapter, and rarely has the case for prescriptive methodology been put more eloquently. For Blaug and other advocates of prescriptive methodology, the demarcation problem (How can we tell science from non-science?) is an essential one. In the post-positivist era, it is clear that there are no easy answers to such questions, but Blaug and others insist we still must *try* to answer them.

Another response to the theory appraisal dilemma is to eschew any single methodological approach. This is methodological pluralism, and both Lawrence Boland and I are in its camp. If one is a pluralist, one is less interested in specific prescriptions about 'proper' behavior than are methodological monists. There are other items on the pluralist's agenda. One major task is to show what kinds of criticism, if any, are possible in a pluralist environment. This is the problem that Boland and I grappled with in our earlier exchange on the maximization hypothesis. Since pluralists are well represented in this volume, we shall move on to other views.

For some contemporary methodologists, the grand issues of pluralism versus monism are uninteresting. They believe that a primary goal for contemporary methodology is to describe scientific behavior, which is accomplished by carefully examining theory growth and change in past and present research programs. Some think that such studies will someday reveal a common methodology in economics, and others believe that such studies will reveal that science is an amalgam of diverse procedures. So far, most of these descriptive exercises have looked at theory change from the perspective of the philosophy of science. This approach is exemplified by the pieces by Loasby and Cross in the last chapter. But there have been other vantage points (descriptions are always from a particular perspective). The sociology of science has been tried, but much more work is needed here, since early attempts have been crude. Oral history has been tried, and tried successfully (see Reder's piece in the next chapter). And, most recently, methodology has been compared to rhetoric.

It might seem that my second selection by Donald McCloskey is simply another attempt to describe economic methodology and the methodological tools of theory appraisal, one that emphasizes their similarity with various rhetorical devices. But much more is going on here, for McCloskey is making a case against the study of Methodology altogether. He likes the methodology (little m) that is employed by the working economist; that methodology is nothing more than rhetoric, and McCloskey says we should study it more carefully. We should not waste our time talking about Methodology (big M), which is the arrogant and pretentious effort by some economists to prescribe behavior. Methodologists familiar with philosopher Paul Feyerabend's ideas will note some similar themes in McCloskey's piece, but his major source of inspiration is the work of philosopher Richard Rorty. One conclusion of this line of argument is that there is no meaningful way to separate science from non-science, so that the demarcation problem, so important to a monist like Blaug, is a pseudo-problem for McCloskey.

15

Conclusions

The crisis of modern economics

The 1960s was a decade in which the public esteem of economics and the professional euphoria of economists rose to an all-time pitch. The 1970s, on the other hand, have been full of talk of "crisis," "revolution," and "counterrevolution," amounting at times to a veritable orgy of self-criticism on the part of some of the leading spokesmen of the economics profession. According to Wassily Leontief (1971, p. 3), "Continued preoccupation with imaginary, hypothetic, rather than with observable reality has gradually led to a distortion of the informal valuation scale used in our academic community to assess and to rank the scientific performance of its members. Empirical analysis, according to this scale, gets a lower rating than formal mathematical reasoning." Furthermore, he charged, economists care too little about the quality of the data with which they work, and he blamed this attitude on the baleful influence of the methodology of instrumentalism or as-if theorizing (p. 5). Henry Phelps Brown (1972, p. 3), however, went much further: what is basically wrong with modern economics, he argued, is that its assumptions about human behavior are totally arbitrary, being literally "plucked from the air," and he blamed this habit of building make-believe worlds on the failure to train economists in the study of history. David Worswick (1972, p. 78) voiced similar sentiments, adding that "there now exist whole branches of abstract economic theory which

253

have no links with concrete facts and are almost indistinguishable from pure mathematics."[1]

Benjamin Ward devoted an entire book to the question *What's Wrong With Economics?* and his answer in brief is that economics is basically a normative policy science adorning itself with the fig leaf of hard-headed positivism. In so far as economics is a positive science, Ward (1972, p. 173) concluded, "the desire systematically to confront the theory with fact has not been a notable feature of the discipline." For him, however, this failure consistently to pursue the task of empirical testing "is not the central difficulty with modern economics" (p. 173). My own contention, by way of contrast, is that the central weakness of modern economics is, indeed, the reluctance to produce the theories that yield unambiguously refutable implications, followed by a general un-willingness to confront those implications with the facts.

Consider, for example, the preoccupation since 1945 of some of the best brains in modern economics with the esoterica of growth theory, when even practitioners of the art admit that modern growth theory is not as yet capable of casting any light on actual economies growing over time.[2] The essence of modern growth theory is simply old-style station-ary state analysis in which an element of compound growth is introduced by adding factor-augmenting technical change and exogenous increases in labor supply to an otherwise static, one-period, general equilibrium model of the economy. In view of the enormous difficulties of handling anything but steady-state growth (equiproportionate increases in all the relevant economic variables), the literature has been almost solely taken up with arid brain-twisters about "golden rules" of capital accumulation. To put it bluntly: no economy has ever been observed in steady-state

---

[1] Two government economists, Macdougall (1974) and Heller (1975), have sup-plied more cheerful assessments, while nevertheless conceding most of the points made by Leontief, Phelps, Brown, and Worswick. For these and other expressions of, and reactions to, the "crisis" in modern economics, see Hutch-ison (1977, chap. 4), O'Brien (1974), and Coats (1977).

[2] As even Hicks (1965, p. 183), a leading modern growth theorist, admits: mod-ern growth theory "has been fertile in the generation of class-room exercises; but so far as we can yet see, they are exercises, not real problems. They are not even hypothetical real problems, of the type 'what would happen if?' where the 'if' is something that could conceivably happen. They are shadows of real problems, dressed up in such a way that by pure logic we can find solutions for them."

growth and, besides, there are deep, inherent reasons why actual growth is always unsteady and always unbalanced.

Growth theory is usually defended as an abstract formulation of the conditions required for the economy to reproduce itself unchanged in all essential respects from one period to another, which formulation is then supposed to serve as a reference point against which various patterns of unbalanced growth can be studied. But if there is no correspondence whatever between the steady-state path and the actual historical experience of economic development, it is not easy to see how growth theory can be expected to throw light on the causes of unbalanced growth, or on the policies that may be required to manage the economy.[3] This is not to say, therefore, that growth theory is simply a waste of time but, given its extremely limited practical implications, we may question the magnitude of the intellectual resources that have been devoted to growth theory in recent years. Certainly, it smacks of a subject more devoted to solving logical puzzles than to furthering positive science.

But perhaps the example of growth theory is too easy. Consider instead that part of the neoclassical research program that comes closest in matching the rigor and elegance of quantum physics, the modern theory of consumer behavior based on the axioms of revealed preference, to which a which a long line of great economists have devoted their most intense efforts. There is little sign, as we have seen, that these prodigious labors have had much impact on the estimation of statistical demand curves. Even if this much is denied, it can hardly be argued that the quantity and quality of intellectual effort devoted to rationalizing the negative slope of the demand curve over the last ninety years has been in due proportion to its practical fruits in empirical work.

Or, to switch topics, consider the endless arguments in textbooks on labor economics about the assumptions that underlie the misnamed "marginal productivity theory of wages" at the expense of space devoted to considering what the theory actually predicts about the workings of the labor market. If this is not misplaced emphasis, what is? Consider

---

[3] Hollis and Nell, it will be remembered (see Chapter 4) regarded the study of the conditions for an economy to reproduce itself to be the "essence" of any proper science of economics. Alas, economic systems never reproduce themselves in an unaltered state: the children, so to speak, never completely resemble the parents.

next the decisively refuted Heckscher–Ohlin theorem in all its $2 \times 2 \times 2$ box-diagram varieties, taught in all textbooks on international trade, not so much as a parable for purposes of limbering up but, on the contrary, as a simplified but nevertheless valid explanation of the pattern of goods traded between countries. Once again, all the emphasis falls on teaching the analytical subtleties of the Heckscher–Ohlin theorem at the expense of time devoted to considering the simply overwhelming evidence against the theorem.

Take, finally, the infinite refinements that have been achieved by Arrow, Debreu, McKenzie, and many others in the formulation of existence proofs of general equilibrium (GE). It cannot be denied that such work has generated some deep insights into the logical characteristics of economic theories – the role of money in perfect-certainty models, the requirement of forward markets in all goods to secure competitive equilibrium, the need for noncompetitive disequilibrium transactions to keep competitive equilibria stable, etcetera – but what may be doubted is that GE theory has contributed much to increasing the predictive powers of modern economics. Even this would not constitute a serious criticism of GE theorizing were it not for the fact that the work in the area of GE theory is generally regarded as ranking high in the intellectual pecking order of the economic profession and deemed to be an absolutely essential part of the training of professional economists. And yet GE theory is at best a species of "solving the puzzles that we have ourselves created," and time spent in mastering it is time taken away from learning the empirical methods of economics.

Measurement without theory

But, surely, economists engage massively in empirical research? Clearly they do but, unfortunately, much of it is like playing tennis with the net down: instead of attempting to refute testable predictions, modern economists all too frequently are satisfied to demonstrate that the real world conforms to their predictions, thus replacing falsification, which is difficult, with verification, which is easy. We have seen some striking examples of this attitude in the sources-of-growth literature and in the new economics of the family. The journals abound with papers that apply regression analysis to every conceivable economic problem, but it is no secret that success in such endeavors frequently relies on "cookbook econometrics": express a hypothesis in terms of an equation, estimate a variety of forms for that equation, select the best fit, discard the rest, and then adjust the theoretical argument to rationalize the hypothesis that is being tested (Ward, 1972, pp. 146–52). Marshall used to say that scientific explanation is simply "prediction written backwards." But the reverse proposition is false: prediction is not necessarily explanation written forwards. Empirical work that fails utterly to discriminate between competing explanations quickly degenerates into a sort of mindless instrumentalism and it is not too much to say that the bulk of empirical work in modern economics is guilty on that score.

A wild exaggeration? Perhaps, but there are many others who have' said as much. Peter Kenen (1975, p. xvi) expresses the same thought in forceful language:

> I detect a dangerous ambiguity in our quantitative work. We do not distinguish carefully enough between the *testing* of hypotheses and the estimation of structural relationships. The ambiguity is rampant in economics. . . . We should be spending more time and thought on the construction of tests that will help us to discriminate between hypotheses having different economic implications. It is not enough to show that our favourite theory does as well as – or better than – some other theory when it comes to accounting retrospectively for the available evidence.

Those who explicitly revolt against orthodoxy are often infected by the same disease. So-called Cambridge controversies in the theory of capital, which would be better described as controversies in the theory of functional income distribution, have raged on for twenty years without so much as a reference to anything but "stylized facts," such as the constancy of the capital–output ratio and the constancy of labor's relative share, which turn out on closer examination not to be facts at all. The fundamental issue at stake between Cambridge, United Kingdom **and Cambridge**, United States, we are told by no less an authority on the debate than Joan Robinson (1973, p. xii), is not so much the famous problem of measuring capital as the question of whether it is saving that

Conclusions 258

determines investment by means of variations in prices or investment that determine saving via changes in the wage–profit ratio. It is clear that a Keynesian-type growth model, assigning a key role to autonomous investment, makes perfectly good sense when there is a situation of less than full employment. On the other hand, if fiscal and monetary policies succeed in maintaining full employment, it would appear that growth depends critically on saving rather than investment, in which case anti-Keynesian, neoclassical growth models appear to be appropriate. The issue of the respective primacy of investment and saving is, therefore, a matter of deciding whether the world is better described by full-employment or by underemployment equilibrium.

However, inasmuch as the entire debate is carried out in the context of steady-state growth theory, and as both sides agree that steady-state growth is never even approximated in the real world, Cambridge controversies, as they are currently formulated are incapable of being resolved by empirical research. But this has not prevented either side from battling over the issues with redoubled fury. Protagonists in both camps have described the controversy as a war of "paradigms," but in fact the two paradigms intersect and indeed overlap entirely. Rhetoric apart, there is nothing to choose between the styles of theorizing of the two Cambridges.[4]

Even radical political economists, a growing breed in the United States, have devoted most of their efforts to "telling a new story": the same old facts are given a different interpretation in terms of the paradigm of power conflict rather than the paradigm of utility maximization, as if social science were reducible to "hard cores" selected according to taste (see Worland, 1972; Applebaum, 1977). What little empirical work has appeared in the *Review of Radical Political Economics* on economic imperialism, race and sex discrimination, the financial returns to education, and the patterns of social mobility has lacked discriminating, well-articulated hypotheses that could distinguish between mainstream and radical predictions (Bronfenbrenner, 1970; Lindbeck, 1971). But

---

[4] For sympathetic surveys of Cambridge United Kingdom theories, sometimes labeled "post-Keynesian economics" (there is an American wing that has just founded a new *Journal of Post-Keynesian Economics*), see Asimakopulos (1977) and Kregel (1977). For an unsympathetic survey, see Blaug (1975, chap. 6).

313

radical economists do at least have the excuse of explicitly announcing their preference on methodological grounds for social and political relevance over empirical reliability as the acid test of "good" theory.[5] Indeed, if radical economists can be said to share a common methodology, it seems to be that of voluntarism or "thinking makes it so."

Similarly, latter-day Austrians claim to derive their economic insights from a priori reasoning unaided by experience and hence repudiate empirical testing as a method for establishing the validity of their conclusions. Likewise, institutionalists purport to model economic behavior in terms of definite patterns and are satisfied to "understand" the workings of an economy even if this implies little power to predict the actual course of economic events. Lastly, Marxists are too deeply committed to the philosophy of essentialism to be willing to run the gauntlet of empirical testing: they hope of course to prophesy correctly, but they have developed an ample store of immunizing stratagems to protect Marxism against any prophecies that have failed to materialize. In short, radicals, modern Austrians, institutionalists, and Marxists all have very good excuses for not paying much heed to the methodological imperatives of falsificationism.

Falsificationism once again

Mainstream neoclassical economists do not have the same excuse. They preach the importance of submitting theories to empirical tests, but they rarely live up to their declared methodological canons. Analytical elegance, economy of theoretical means, and the widest possible scope obtained by ever more heroic simplification have been too often prized above predictability and significance for policy questions. The working philosophy of science of modern economics may indeed be characterized as "innocuous falsificationism."

To be sure, there are still some, like Shackle or the modern Austrians, who will argue that prediction is absolutely impossible in a subject like

---

[5] Franklin and Resnik (1973, pp. 73–4) provide a typical radical methodological pronouncement: "From a radical perspective, in which analysis is closely linked to advocacy of fundamental changes in the social order, an abstract model or category is not simply an aesthetic device [sic]. It is purposely designed to assist in the changes advocated, or in describing the nature of the barriers that must be broken down if the advocated changes are to occur."

economics because economic behavior, being forward-looking, is inherently unpredictable. But these economists are in a minority. For the most part, the battle for falsificationism has been won in modern economics (would that we could say as much about some of the other social sciences). The problem now is to persuade economists to take falsificationism seriously.

Applied econometrics

It is not difficult to think of many good reasons why economists fail to practice the methodology that they preach: all scientists sometimes cling tenaciously to "degenerating" research programs in the presence of "progressive" rivals, but economists are particularly prone to this tendency if only because an economic system, unlike the state of nature, cries out to be evaluated and not just to be studied with Olympian detachment. Furthermore, economics continually touches on questions that are subject to government policy, so that major economic doctrines are not only scientific research programs (SRP) in the sense of Lakatos but also political action programs (PAP). This dual function of economic theories allows for situations in which a particular theory is simultaneously a "degenerating" SRP and a "progressive" PAP, that is, one that offers governments an expanding agenda of policy measures. (Marxian economics may be a case in point, and monetarism in its latest phase is perhaps an example of exactly the opposite conjunction.) It is only when a theory defines both a "progressive" SRP and a "progressive" PAP that we talk of a "revolution" in economic thought; (the obvious example is Keynesian economics in the 1930s).[6]

Be that as it may, the fact that economics is, among other things, a policy science is at least one major reason why Lakatos's methodology of SRP does not fit the history of economics perfectly, or at any rate fits it much less perfectly than it does the history of physics. It is precisely for that reason that the attempt to separate positive from normative propositions in economics, and clearly to specify the conditions for submitting positive propositions to the text of experience, remains a task which is as important to the progress of economics today as it ever was.

Unfortunately, we lack both reliable data and powerful techniques for

[6] I owe this point to R. G. Lipsey.

distinguishing sharply between valid and invalid propositions in positive economics, and the professional pressures to "publish or perish" continually encourage a "game playing" approach to econometric work that does nothing to improve the data base or the standard techniques that are regularly employed for testing economic hypotheses. These weaknesses, not so much of theoretical econometrics as of the actual procedures followed by applied econometricians, go a long way toward explaining why economists are frequently reluctant to follow their avowed falsificationist precepts. In many areas of economics, different econometric studies reach conflicting conclusions and, given the available data, there are frequently no effective methods for deciding which conclusion is correct. In consequence, contradictory hypotheses continue to coexist sometimes for decades or more.

For some, this is a good reason for abandoning applied economics altogether. But that is not an attractive alternative because it would leave economics with almost no way of selecting from among a plethora of possible explanations the one that best explains economic events. Even if we argue that there are other methods for testing economic hypotheses, such as the looser methods of "colligation" practiced by economic historians, or the ethnographic methods favored by some institutionalists, the demands of economic policy makers will nevertheless drive us back to the use of econometrics, which alone can provide a quantitative as well as a qualitative calculus. Our only hope, therefore, is to improve both theoretical and applied econometrics, and indeed it is the latter where improvements could come fairly rapidly if only better workaday practices were adopted.

Thomas Mayer (1980) has a number of concrete suggestions to make that would do much to strengthen the claim of economics as a "hard science." First, he echoes Leontief in urging us to place far more emphasis on the problem of data collection. Second, he deplores the tendency to treat econometric results as evidence from a "crucial experiment," which is never to be repeated; on the contrary, most applied econometrics should seek to replicate previous results using a different data set; as we come to rely increasingly on the weight of many pieces of evidence, rather than a single crucial experiment, periodic surveys should pull the evidence together with a view to resolving contradictions between them. Third, he argues that it would help to raise the standards for assessing econometric work if the journals could encourage work on the basis of the likely validity of the results reported and not on the basis of the technical sophistication of the techniques employed. Fourth, he recommends that we guard against data mining by requiring authors to present all the regressions they ran, and not just the particular regression that happened to support their hypothesis. Fifth, he proposes that authors should not use up all their data in fitting their regressions, but leave some as a reserve sample against which to test the regressions; this harks back to the early distinction we drew between estimating a structural relationship and testing an economic hypothesis. Sixth, he urges journals to publish papers that report insignificant results and to require authors to submit their unpublished data so that their work can be easily verified by others. Finally, he adds that "given all the weaknesses of econometric techniques, we should be open minded enough to accept that truth does not always wear the garb of equations, and is not always born inside a computer. Other ways of testing, such as appeals to economic history, should not be treated as archaic" (Mayer, 1980, p. 18).

The best way forward

I have argued throughout this book that the central aim of economics is to predict and not merely to explain and I have implied that of all the contending economic doctrines of the past, it is only orthodox, timeless equilibrium theory – in short, the neoclassical SRP – that has shown itself to be willing to be judged in terms of its predictions. Orthodox economics can indeed boast that it has increased the economist's capacity for making predictions. At the same time, it must be emphasized how limited this capacity is even now. We cannot accurately predict the growth of GNP in an economy more than a year ahead, and we cannot even predict the growth of NNP in individual sectors of the economy beyond two or three years.[7] This is an improvement over what

---

[7] Thus, Victor Zarnowitz (1968, pp. 435–6) sums up present-day achievements in GNP forecasting in the United States in these words: "The record of economic forecasters in general leaves a great deal to be desired, although it also includes some significant achievements and may be capable of further improvements. According to the current NBER study, the annual GNP predictions for 1953–63 made by some three hundred to four hundred forecasters (company

The best way forward 263

can be obtained by mere mechanical extrapolation of past trends, but nevertheless it is insufficient to support complacency about the state of modern, orthodox economics. Similarly, for a wide variety of problems – demand functions for consumer goods, investment functions, money demand and supply functions, and large-scale econometric models of the entire economy – it turns out that goodness of fit of a regression equation during the sample period invariably proves to be an unreliable guide to what happens subsequently in the postsample period (Shupak, 1962; Streissler, 1970; Mayer, 1975, 1980; Armstrong, 1978, chap. 13). Clearly, there are still serious limitations in the capacity of economists to predict the actual course of economic events and hence ample room for skepticism about mainstream economics.

There are now a number of alternative research programs in economics that express this sense of disillusionment with the past accomplishments of received economic doctrines. The radical economists have their own house organ, *The Review of Radical Political Economics,* and so do the institutionalists (*The Journal of Economic Issues,* published by the Association of Evolutionary Economics). A new *Journal of Post-Keynesian Economics* seeks to unite those who hope to develop Keynesian economics in new directions to attack the problems of inflation and income distribution. Likewise, another group of economists are determined to focus their research program on Herbert Simon's concept of "bounded rationality," denoting a central concern with the underlying motivational assumptions of economic theory, and they are about to launch a new *Journal of Economic Behavior and Organization* to give expression to their sense of dissatisfaction with contemporary economic theory. In other words, we seem to be entering an era in which there will

staffs and groups of economists from various industries, government, and academic institutions) had errors averaging $10 billion. Although this amounts to about 2 per cent of the average level of GNP, the errors were big enough to make the difference between a good and bad business year. . . . Had the forecasters assumed that GNP would advance next year by the average amount it had advanced in the preceding postwar years, the resulting average error would not have been greater than $12 billion." Similarly, Hans Theil (1966, chaps. 6, 7) has shown that the use of an input-output model to forecast value added in twenty-seven sectors of the Dutch economy over a ten-year period, given observed final demand in the economy as a whole, predicted better than a simple extrapolation of past trends for periods up to two or three years, but it predicted much worse for periods longer than three years.

be too many, rather than too few, competing economic research programs.

It would be very convenient if all of these alternative research programs were addressed to the same set of questions that preoccupy the neoclassical SRP, because then we could choose among them solely, or at any rate largely, on the basis of the empirical evidence. Alas, it is a characteristic feature of many of the rival SRPs that they ask different questions about the real world from those posed by the neoclassical SRP, so that choice among them involves difficult judgments of fruitfulness, that is, promises of empirical evidence to be delivered in the future. Economic methodology, therefore, is unlikely to tell us which of these competing programs is likely most to contribute in the years ahead to substantive knowledge of the workings of economic systems.

What methodology can do is to provide criteria for the acceptance and rejections of research programs, setting standards that will help us to discriminate between wheat and chaff. These standards, we have seen, are hierarchical, relative, dynamic, and by no means unambiguous in terms of the practical advice they offer to working economists. Nevertheless, the ultimate question we can and indeed must pose about any research program is the one made familiar by Popper: what events, if they materialized, would lead us to reject that program? A program that cannot meet that question has fallen short of the highest standards that scientific knowledge can attain.

Journal of Economic Literature
Vol. XXI (June 1983), pp. 481–517

The Rhetoric of Economics

By DONALD N. MCCLOSKEY

The University of Iowa

The length of the acknowledgments here testifies to an unexplored feature of the rhetoric of economics, the role of the audience: like oratory, scholarship depends for its virtues on the virtues of its audience. I have been fortunate in mine. I must apologize for my amateurish understanding of what is happening in philosophy, mathematics, literary criticism, rhetorical studies, and other places beyond my competence, and ask that practitioners in these fields assist in my further education. For their early attempts I thank Evan Fales, Paul Hernadi, John Lyne, Michael McGee, Allan Megill, John Nelson, and Jay Semel of the Colloquium on Applied Rhetoric at The University of Iowa; Wayne Booth, Ira Katznelson, and others at the University of Chicago in the program in Politics, Rhetoric and Law, before which the earliest version was delivered; Robert Boynton, Bernard Cohn, John Comaroff, Otis Dudley Duncan, James O. Freedman, Clifford Geertz, William Kruskal, Donald Levine, Laura McCloskey, Richard Rorty, Renato Rosaldo; and the Humanities Society at the University of Iowa. That the economists on whom I have inflicted the argument have reacted with such intelligent skepticism and generous encouragement suggests, as the paper does, that we are better scholars than our methodology would allow. I thank my colleagues in economics at Iowa, especially the Sanctuary Seminar in Economic Argument; Seminars at the World Bank and the National Science Foundation; my colleagues at the Institute of Advanced Studies and the Faculty of Economics at the Australian National University; seminars at the universities of Adelaide, Auckland, Melbourne, New South Wales, Tasmania and Western Australia; at Monash, and Iowa State universities; Victoria University of Wellington; and an assemblage of economists elsewhere: William Breit, Ronald Coase, Arthur Diamond, Stanley Engerman, J. M. Finger, Milton Friedman, Allan Gibbard, Robert Goodin, Gary Hawke, Robert Higgs, Albert Hirschman, Eric Jones, Arjo Klamer, Harvey Leibenstein, David Levy, Peter Lindert, Neil de Marchi, Michael McPherson, Amartya Sen, Robert Solow, Larry Westphal, Gordon Winston, and Gavin Wright. Thomas Mayer's encouragement at an early stage and his detailed comments as referee for this Journal *at a later stage were exceptionally heartening and useful.*

481

ECONOMISTS DO NOT FOLLOW the laws of enquiry their methodologies lay down. A good thing, too. If they did they would stand silent on human capital, the law of demand, random walks down Wall Street, the elasticity of demand for gasoline, and most other matters about which they commonly speak. In view of the volubility of economists the many official methodologies are apparently not the grounds for their scientific conviction.

Economists in fact argue on wider grounds, and should. Their genuine, workaday rhetoric, the way they argue inside their heads or their seminar rooms, diverges from the official rhetoric. Economists should become more self-conscious about their rhetoric, because they will then better know why they agree or disagree, and will find it less easy to dismiss contrary arguments on merely methodological grounds. Philosophy as a set of narrowing rules of evidence should be set aside in scientific argument, as even many philosophers have been saying now for fifty years.

Economics will not change much in substance, of course, when economists recognize that the economic emperor has positively no clothes. He is the same fellow whether philosophically naked or clothed, in reasonably good health aside from his sartorial delusion. But the temper of argument among economists would improve if they recognized on what grounds they were arguing. They claim to be arguing on grounds of certain limited matters of statistical inference, on grounds of positive economics, operationalism, behaviorism, and other positivistic enthusiasms of the 1930s and 1940s. They believe that these are the only grounds for science. But in their actual scientific work they argue about the aptness of economic metaphors, the relevance of historical precedents, the persuasiveness of introspections, the power of authority, the charm of symmetry, the claims of morality. Crude positivism labels such issues "meaningless" or "nonscientific" or "just matters of opinion." Yet even positivists actually behave as though the matters are discussable. In fact, most discussion in most sciences, and especially in economics, arises from them. Nothing is gained from clinging to the Scientific Method, or to any methodology except honesty, clarity, and tolerance. Nothing is gained because the methodology does not describe the sciences it was once thought to describe, such as physics or mathematics; and because physics and mathematics are not good models for economics anyway; and because the methodology is now seen by many philosophers themselves to be uncompelling; and because economic science would stop progressing if the methodology were in fact used; and, most important, because economics, like any field, should get its standards of argument from itself, not from the legislation of philosopher kings. The real arguments would then be joined.

I. *Rhetoric Is Disciplined Conversation*

These points, elaborated below, amount to an appeal to examine the rhetoric of economics. By "rhetoric" is not meant a verbal shell game, as in "empty rhetoric" or "mere rhetoric" (although form is not trivial, either: disdain for the form of words is evidence of a mind closed to the varieties of argument). In *Modern Dogma and the Rhetoric of Assent* Wayne Booth gives many useful definitions. Rhetoric is "the art of probing what men believe they ought to believe, rather than proving what is true according to abstract methods"; it is "the art of discovering good reasons, finding what really warrants assent, because any reasonable person ought to be persuaded"; it is "careful weighing of more-or-less good reasons to arrive at more-or-less probable or plausible conclusions—none too secure but better than would be arrived at by chance or unthink-

McCloskey: The Rhetoric of Economics   483

ing impulse"; it is the "art of discovering warrantable beliefs and improving those beliefs in shared discourse"; its purpose must not be "to talk someone else into a preconceived view; rather, it must be to engage in mutual inquiry" (Booth, 1974, pp. xiii, xiv, 59, 137). It is what economists, like other dealers in ideas, do anyway: as Booth says elsewhere, "We believe in mutual persuasion as a way of life; we live from conference to conference" (Booth, 1967, p. 13). Rhetoric is exploring thought by conversation.

The word "rhetoric" is doubtless an obstacle to understanding the point, so debased has it become in common parlance. If "pragmatism" and "anarchism" had not already suffered as much, unable to keep clear of irrelevant associations with the bottom line or the bomb, the title might better have been "Pragmatism's Conception of Truth in Economics" or "Outline of an Anarchistic Theory of Knowledge in Economics" (William James, 1907; Paul Feyerabend, 1975). But the enemies of sophisticated pragmatism and gentle anarchism, as of honest rhetoric, have used the weapons at hand. The results discourage onlookers from satisfying the curiosity they might have had about alternatives to coercion in philosophy, politics, or method. A title such as "How Economists Explain" (Mark Blaug, 1980; but see below) or "Why Methodology Is a Bad" would perhaps have been meeker and more persuasive.[1] Still, "rhetoric" like the others is a fine and ancient word, whose proper use ought to be more widely known among economists and calculators.

The rhetoric here is that of Aristotle, Cicero, and Quintilian among the ancients, reincarnated in the Renaissance, crucified by the Cartesian dogma that only the indubitable is true; which in the third

century after Descartes rose from the dead. The faith built on these miracles is known in literary studies as the New Rhetoric, new in the 1930s and 1940s from the hands of I. A. Richards in Britain and Kenneth Burke in America (Richards, 1936; Burke, 1950). In philosophy John Dewey and Ludwig Wittgenstein had already begun to criticize Descartes' program of erecting belief on a foundation of skepticism. More recently Karl Popper, Thomas Kuhn, and Imre Lakatos among others have undermined the positivist supposition that scientific progress does in fact follow Descartes' doubting rules of method. The literary, epistemological, and methodological strands have not yet wound into one cord, but they belong together. On the eve of the Cartesian revolution the French philosopher and educational reformer, Peter Ramus (*fl.* 1550), brought to completion a medieval tendency to relegate rhetoric to mere eloquence, leaving logic in charge of reason. In the textbooks that Descartes himself read as a boy probable argument was made thus for the first time wholly subservient to indubitable argument. Hostile to classical rhetoric, such a reorganization of the liberal arts was well suited for the Cartesian program extending over the next three centuries to put knowledge on foundations built by philosophy and mathematics. The program failed, and in the meantime probable argument languished. In Richard Rorty's words, following Dewey, the search for the foundations of knowledge by Descartes, Locke, Hume, Kant, Russell, and Carnap was "the triumph of the quest for certainty over the quest for wisdom" (Rorty, 1979, p. 61; *cf.* John Dewey, 1929, pp. 33, 227). To reinstate rhetoric properly understood is to reinstate wider and wiser reasoning.

The reaction to the narrowing of argument by the Cartesian program is by now broad. Its leading figures range from professional philosophers (Stephen Toulmin,

---

[1] After recognizing the intent, Colin Forster of Australian National University suggested the title "The Last Paper on Methodology." But ambition must have limits.

484   *Journal of Economic Literature, Vol. XXI (June 1983)*

Paul Feyerabend, Richard Rorty) to a miscellany of practitioners-turned-philosophers in chemistry (Michael Polanyi), law (Chaim Perelman), and literary criticism (Wayne Booth). The reach of the idea nowadays that argument is more than syllogism is illustrated well by the lucid treatment of it in what would seem an unlikely place, by Glenn Webster, Ada Jacox, and Beverly Baldwin in "Nursing Theory and the Ghost of the Received View" (1981, pp. 25–35). The reach, however, has not extended to economics. Austrian, institutionalist, and Marxist economists, to be sure, have for a century been attacking certain parts of positivism as the basis for economic knowledge. But they have seized on other parts with redoubled fervor, and have so expressed their remaining doubts as to make them unintelligible to anyone but themselves. In their own way they have been as narrowing as thoroughgoing positivists—the rejection of econometrics, for instance, would be reasonable only if its more naive claims were taken seriously. For the rest, economists have let philosophical scribblers of a few years back supply their official thinking about what a good argument is.

II. *The Official Methodology of Economics Is Modernist*

Economists have two attitudes towards discourse, the official and unofficial, the explicit and the implicit. The official rhetoric, to which they subscribe in the abstract and in methodological ruminations, declares them to be scientists in the modern mode. The credo of Scientific Method, known mockingly among its many critics as the Received View, is an amalgam of logical positivism, behaviorism, operationalism, and the hypothetico-deductive model of science. Its leading idea is that all sure knowledge is modeled on the early 20th century's understanding of certain pieces of 19th century physics. To empha-

size its pervasiveness in modern thinking well beyond scholarship it is best labeled simply "modernism," that is, the notion (as Booth puts it) that we know only what we cannot doubt and cannot really know what we can merely assent to.

Among the precepts of modernism are:

(1) Prediction (and control) is the goal of science.

(2) Only the observable implications (or predictions) of a theory matter to its truth.

(3) Observability entails objective, reproducible experiments.

(4) If (and only if) an experimental implication of a theory proves false is the theory proved false.

(5) Objectivity is to be treasured; subjective "observation" (introspection) is not scientific knowledge.

(6) Kelvin's Dictum: "When you cannot express it in numbers, your knowledge is of a meagre and unsatisfactory kind."[2]

(7) Introspection, metaphysical belief, aesthetics, and the like may well figure in the discovery of an hypothesis but cannot figure in its justification.

(8) It is the business of methodology to demarcate scientific reasoning from non-scientific, positive from normative.

(9) A scientific explanation of an event brings the event under a covering law.

(10) Scientists, for instance economic scientists, have nothing to say as scientists about values, whether of morality or art.

---

[2] From Sir William Thomson (Lord Kelvin), *Popular Addresses*, edition of 1888–1889, quoted in Kuhn, 1977, p. 178n. An approximation to this version is inscribed on the front of the Social Science Research Building at the University of Chicago. Frank Knight, the famous University of Iowa economist, is said to have remarked on it one day: "Yes, and when you *can* express it in numbers your knowledge is of a meagre and unsatisfactory kind."

McCloskey: The Rhetoric of Economics 485

(11) Hume's Fork: "When we run over libraries, persuaded of these principles, what havoc must we make? If we take in our hand any volume—of divinity or school metaphysics, for instance—let us ask, *Does it contain any abstract reasoning concerning quantity or number?* No. *Does it contain any experimental reasoning concerning matter of fact and existence?* No. Commit it then to the flames, for it can contain nothing but sophistry and illusion" (italics his [1748], 1955, p. 173).

Few in philosophy now believe as many as half of these propositions. A substantial, respectable, and growing minority believes none of them. But a large majority in economics believes them all.

For instance, the leading methodologists in economics do. It is odd but true that modernism in economic methodology is associated with the Chicago School.[3] The main texts of economic modernism, such as Milton Friedman's "The Methodology of Positive Economics" (1953) or Gary Becker and George Stigler's *"De Gustibus Non Est Disputandum"* (1977), bear a Chicago postmark; and the more extreme interpretations of the texts flourish among economists bearing a Chicago degree. What is odd about it is that a group so annoying to other economists in most of its activities should have their assent in the matter of official method: Oddly, a watered down version of Friedman's es-

---

[3] Nothing in this essay is meant to give comfort to the enemies of Chicago. Having long been a victim of their anti-Chicago dogmatism, I am not impressed by the assertion that Chicago economics is peculiarly dogmatic. Chicago is merely a particularly clear and candid version of a dogmatic impulse common to all economics, expressing itself in methodological imperatives. Economists appear to believe that economics is too important to be left to the open-minded, and especially must never be left to anyone lacking faith in some approved formula for achieving knowledge. Chicago is no worse than the rest. *Immo, civis Chicagonus sum, subspecies TP* (*cf.* Melvin Reder, 1982).

say is part of the intellectual equipment of most economists, and its arguments come readily to their lips.

Premeditated writings on method, not excluding Chicago's own, are more careful than the remark in the course of other business that reveals modernism in its rawer form. In precept one can be vague enough to earn the assent of everyone; in practice one must make enemies. Kalman Cohen and Richard Cyert, to take one among many examples of first-chapter methodology in economics texts, present in their book an outline of modernism, which they assert is the method "used in all scientific analyses" (1975, p. 17). The "method" they then outline, with a bibliography heavily weighted towards logical positivism and its allies, reduces to an appeal to be honest and thoughtful. Only when such a phrase as "at least in principle testable by experiment and observation" (p. 23) is given content by practice do we know what is at stake. To be sure, vague precepts are not without their uses. When Friedman wrote, for instance, the practice of economics was split into theory without fact and fact without theory. His modernist incantations, supported by choruses of philosophers, were at the time probably good for the souls of all concerned.

Friedman's essay was even then more post-modernist than one might suppose from slight acquaintance with its ideas. He did, for example, mention with approval the aesthetic criteria of simplicity and fruitfulness that an economist might use to select among a multiplicity of theories with the same predictions, though in the next sentence he attempted to reduce them to objective matters of prediction (p. 10). He accepted that questionnaires, forbidden to the modernist in economics, are useful for suggesting hypotheses, though in the next sentence he asserted that they are "almost entirely useless as a means of *testing* the validity of eco-

nomic hypotheses" (p. 31n). He emphasized the role of the rhetorical community
to which the scientist speaks in producing
conviction—whether made up of sociologists, say, or of economists—though in the
next sentence he returned to an "objective" theory of testing. Like Karl Popper,
Friedman appeared to be struggling to escape the grip of positivism and its intellectual traditions, though with only sporadic
success. Perhaps that the *locus classicus*
of economic modernism contains so much
that is anti-modernist indicates that modernism cannot survive intelligent discussion even by its best advocates.

The unpremeditated remark in the heat
of economic argument, however, usually
has a crudely modernist content, often in
Friedman's very words. An article by
Richard Roll and Stephen Ross on finance,
for instance, asserts that "the theory
should be tested by its conclusions, not
by its assumptions" and that "similarly,
one should not reject the conclusions derived from firm profit maximization on the
basis of sample surveys in which managers
claim that they trade off profit for social
good" (1980, p. 1093 and footnote). The
same can be found elsewhere, in nearly
identical terms, all dating back to Friedman's essay: William Sharpe (1970, p. 77),
for instance, writing on the same matter
as Roll and Ross, takes it as a rule of polite
scientific behavior that "the realism of the
assumptions matters little. If the implications are reasonably consistent with observed phenomena, the theory can be said
to 'explain' reality" (1970, p. 77). Repeated
often, and exhibiting modernism as well
in their devotion to objective evidence,
quantifiable tests, positive analysis, and
other articles of the faith, such phrases
have the ring of incantation. Modernism
is influential in economics, but not because its premises have been examined
carefully and found good. It is a revealed,
not a reasoned, religion.

III. *Modernism Is a Poor Method*

Modernism Is Obsolete in Philosophy

There are a great many things wrong
with modernism as a methodology for science or for economic science.[4] Even when
philosophically inclined, economists appear to read about as much in professional
philosophy as philosophers do in professional economics. It is unsurprising, then,
that the news of the decline of modernism
has not reached all ears. From a philosopher's point of view the worst flaw in the
hostility to the "metaphysics" that modernism sees everywhere is that the hostility is itself metaphysical. If metaphysics
is to be cast into the flames, then the methodological declarations of the modernist
family from Descartes through Hume and
Comte to Russell and Hempel and Popper
will be the first to go. For this and other
good reasons philosophers agree that strict
logical positivism is dead, raising the question whether economists are wise to carry
on with their necrophilia.[5]

In the economic case the metaphysical
position akin to logical positivism is not
well argued, probably because its roots lie
more in the philosophizing of physicists
from Mach to Bridgeman than in the parallel thinking of professional philosophers.
It is at least obscure what might be the
appeal of "operationally meaningful statements" (Paul Samuelson, 1947, p. 3 and

---

[4] The overdiscussed question of whether there can
be a value-free social science will not be much discussed here, but it must be accounted one of the
chief failings of modernism that it places moral argument outside the pale of rational discussion. In this
connection it should be more widely known that
Morris Schlick, the founder of the Vienna Circle of
logical positivism and a vigorous lecturer on the
theme that moral knowledge is no knowledge at all,
was murdered in 1936 by one of his students.

[5] See John Passmore, 1967. Karl Popper quotes
Passmore with approval for the motto of a chapter
of his own entitled "Who Killed Logical Positivism?"
(Popper, 1976, pp. 87–90), in which he confesses to
the murder.

McCloskey: The Rhetoric of Economics 487

throughout) or "valid and meaningful predictions about phenomena not yet observed" (Friedman, p. 7) as standards against which all but mathematical assertions are to be judged. Samuelson, Friedman, or their followers do not present reasons for adopting such metaphysical positions, except for confident assertions, at the time correct, that they were the received views of philosophers on the method of science. The trust in philosophy was a tactical error, for the philosophy itself has since changed. Some philosophers now doubt the entire enterprise of epistemology and its claim to provide foundations for knowledge (Richard Rorty, 1982b). A great many doubt the prescriptions of modernist methodology.

Falsification Is Not Cogent

A prescription that economic methodologists have in common, for instance, is an emphasis on the crucial falsifying test, supposedly the hallmark of scientific reasoning. But philosophers have recognized for many decades that falsification runs afoul of a criticism made by the physicist and philosopher Pierre Duhem in 1906, evident at once without philosophical reading to an economist who has tried to use falsification for science. Suppose that the hypothesis H ("British businessmen performed very poorly relative to Americans and Germans in the late 19th century") implies a testing observation O ("Measures of total factor productivity in iron and steel show a large difference between British and foreign steelmaking"); it implies it, that is, not by itself, but only with the addition of ancillary hypotheses H_1, H_2, and so forth that make the measurement possible ("Marginal productivity theory applies to Britain 1870–1913"; "British steel had no hidden inputs offsetting poor business leaderships"; and so forth). Then of course not-O implies not-H—or not-H_1 or not-H_2 or any number

of failures of premises irrelevant to the main hypothesis in question. The hypothesis in question is insulated from crucial test by the ancillary hypotheses necessary to bring it to a test. This is no mere possibility but the substance of most scientific disagreement: "Your experiment was not properly controlled"; "You have not solved the identification problem"; "You have used an equilibrium (competitive, single-equation) model when a disequilibrium (monopolistic, 500-equation) model is relevant." And even if the one hypothesis in question could be isolated, the probabilistic nature of hypotheses, most especially in economics, makes crucial experiments non-crucial: chance is the ever present alternative, the H_n that spoils falsificationism.

Prediction Is Impossible in Economics

The common claim that prediction is the defining feature of a real science, and that economics possesses the feature, is equally open to doubt. It is a cliché among philosophers and historians of science, for instance, that one of the most successful of all scientific theories, the theory of evolution, has no predictions in the normal sense, and is therefore unfalsifiable by prediction. It is at least suggestive of something odd in prediction as a criterion for useful economics that Darwin's theory was inspired by classical economics, a system as it happens erroneous in most of the predictions it made. With no apparent awareness of the incongruity, Friedman quoted Alchian's revival of the connection (Armen Alchian, 1950) in the midst of his most famous piece of predictionist metaphysics ("the leaves are positioned as if each leaf deliberately sought to maximize the amount of sunlight it receives").

In any event, predicting the economic future is, as Ludwig von Mises put it, "beyond the power of any mortal man" (1949, p. 867). What puts it beyond his power is the very economics he uses to make the prediction. When the economist for a big bank predicts lower interest rates after Christmas, and has not before the prediction placed his net worth in margin loans on bonds, properly hedged and insured against variance, he is behaving either irrationally or self-deceivingly. If he knows the expected value of the future, he for some reason chooses not to take the unlimited wealth that such Faustian knowledge can surely bring, and is willing for some reason instead to dissipate the opportunity by the act of telling others about it. If he does not really know, then he faces no such unexploited opportunity. But then he has perhaps no business talking as though he does. Predictionism cannot be rescued by remarking that the big bank economist makes only conditional predictions. Conditional predictions sell for their value in a soft market: if the sea were to disappear, a rock would accelerate in falling from sea level to the sea floor at about 32.17 feet per second per second. But a serious prediction has serious boundary conditions. If it does it must answer again the American Question: If you're so smart why aren't you rich? At the margin (because that is where economics works) and on average (because some people are lucky) the industry of making economic predictions, which includes universities, earns only normal returns.

Modernism Itself Is Impossible, and Is Not Followed

The most damaging, however, of these lesser criticisms of the modernist methodology is that if taken at its word it is narrow to absurdity. Consider again the steps to modernist knowledge, from predictionism through Kelvin's Dictum to Hume's Fork. If economists (or physicists) confined themselves to economic (or physical) propositions that literally conformed to such steps they would have nothing to say. Cartesian or Humean skepticism is too

corrosive a standard of belief for a real human. As the chemist and philosopher Michael Polanyi put it, the methodology of modernism sets up "quixotic standards of valid meaning which, if rigorously practiced, would reduce us all to voluntary imbecility" (1962, p. 88). Modernism promises knowledge free from doubt, metaphysics, morals, and personal conviction; what it delivers merely renames as Scientific Method the scientist's and especially the economic scientist's metaphysics, morals, and personal convictions. It cannot, and should not, deliver what it promises. Scientific knowledge is no different from other personal knowledge (Polanyi, 1962). Trying to make it different, instead of simply better, is the death of science.

In other words, the literal application of modernist methodology cannot give a useful economics. The best proofs are historical. In his *Against Method* (1975) Paul Feyerabend uses an interpretation of Galileo's career to attack the claims of prescriptive methodology in physics; the same point can be made about economics. Had the modernist criterion of persuasion been adopted by Galileo's contemporaries, he argues, the Galilean case would have failed. A grant proposal to use the strange premise that terrestrial optics applied also to the celestial sphere, to assert that the tides were the sloshing of water on a mobile earth, and to suppose that the fuzzy views of Jupiter's alleged moons would prove, by a wild analogy, that the planets, too, went around the sun as did the moons around Jupiter would not have survived the first round of peer review in a National Science Foundation of 1632, at any rate if that one (unlike ours) were wedded to modernist ideology. The argument applies widely to the history of physics: observational anomalies in the experiments testing Einstein's theories were ignored for many years, to be revealed as errors of measurement long after the

McCloskey: The Rhetoric of Economics 489

theories had been embraced, embraced on grounds of "the reason of the matter," as Einstein was fond of saying (Feyerabend, 1975, pp. 56–57).

Historians of biology have uncovered one after another case of cooking the statistical results to fit modernist precepts of what counts as evidence, from Pasteur and Mendel down to the present. The measurement of IQ has been a scandal of self-deception and bold fraud in the name of scientific method from its beginning (Stephen Jay Gould, 1981). Perhaps modernism fits poorly the complexities of biology and psychology: straining after evidence of a sort typically available only in the simplest experiments in physics may not suit their frontiers. It suits the frontiers of economics poorly enough. For better or worse the Keynesian revolution in economics would not have happened under the modernist legislation recommended for the method of science. The Keynesian insights were not formulated as statistical propositions until the early 1950s, well after the bulk of younger economists had become persuaded they were true. By the early 1960s liquidity traps and accelerator models of investment, despite failures in their statistical implementations, were taught to first-year students of economics as matters of scientific routine. Modernist methodology would have stopped all this in 1936: where was the evidence of an objective, statistical, controlled kind?

Nor was the monetarist counterrevolution a success for modernist methodology, though so powerful had the methodology become by the 1960s in the minds of economists and especially of monetarist economists that most of the explicit debate took place in its terms. Yet in truth crude experiments and big books won the day, by their very crudeness and bigness. The Kennedy tax cut boosted the Keynesians to their peak of prestige; the inflation of the 1970s brought them down again, leaving the monetarists as temporary kings of

the castle. An important blow for monetarism was Friedman and Schwartz' big book, A Monetary History of the United States, 1867–1960. It established a correlation, which Keynesians would not deny, between money and money income. The significance of the correlation, however, depended on the assumption that money caused prices and that money was determinable by the monetary authority (in 1929–1933, for example) despite the openness of the American economy to trade in both goods and money itself. Nonetheless, what was telling in the debate was the sheer bulk of the book—the richness and intelligence of its arguments, however irrelevant most of the arguments were to the main point.

A modernist method thoroughly applied, in other words, would probably stop advances in economics. What empirical anomaly in the traditional tale inspired the new labor economics or the new economic history? None: they were merely realizations that the logic of economics had not exhausted its applicability at conventional borders. What observable implications justify the investment of intellect since 1950 in general equilibrium theory? For all the modernist talk common among its theorists, none; but so what? Could applications of economics to legal questions rely entirely on objective evidence? No; but why would one wish to limit the play of understanding? And so forth. There is nothing to be gained and a great deal to be lost by adopting modernism in economic methodology.

The very point is economic. In order for an economic theory to be tested, Ronald Coase points out, some economists must care enough about it to bother. They care only when it is believed by some investigators—they and their allies or some significant group of opponents. Only when many believe is there a demand for tests. Fortunately, "economists, or at any rate enough of them, do not wait to discover whether a theory's predictions are accurate before making up their minds"; to wait in proper modernist style "would result in the paralysis of scientific activity" (Coase, 1982, p. 14) because no one would have an incentive to choose one out of the infinite number of hypotheses for test. Even quantitative studies, he argues, rely heavily on pre-quantitative arguments founding belief, and he quotes with approval T. S. Kuhn's remark that "the road from scientific law to scientific measurement can rarely be traveled in the reverse direction" (Coase, p. 18, quoting Kuhn, 1977, p. 219). The laws come from a rhetoric of tradition or introspection, and in physics as in economics "quantitative studies . . . are explorations with the aid of a theory" (Coase, p. 17), searches for numbers with which to make specific a theory already believed on other grounds (see Edward Leamer, 1978, and the discussion below). Modernism is impractical.

Any Method Is Arrogant and Pretentious

The objections to modernist method so far, however, are lesser ones. The greater objection is simply that modernism *is* a method. It sets up laws of argument drawn from an ideal science or the underlying history of science or the essence of knowledge. The claim is that the philosopher of science can tell what makes for good, useful, fruitful, progressive science. He knows this so confidently that he can limit arguments that worthy scientists make spontaneously, casting out some as unscientific, or at best placing them firmly in the "context of discovery." The philosopher undertakes to second-guess the scientific community. In economics the claim of methodological legislation is that the legislator is not merely expert in all branches of economic knowledge within sound of his proclamations but expert in all possible future economics, limiting the growth of economics now in order to

make it fit a philosopher's idea of the ultimate good.

It is hard to take such claims seriously. Einstein remarked that "Whoever undertakes to set himself up as a judge in the field of Truth and Knowledge is shipwrecked by the laughter of the gods" (Einstein, 1953, p. 38). Modernism sets up a court of the Red Queen ("Normative argument," she says, "off with his head"), and the gods laugh merrily. Any methodology that is law-making and limiting will do so. It will do so with the noblest intentions, but economists are fond of pointing out in like cases that noble intentions can have bad consequences. The methodologist fancies himself the judge of the practitioner. His proper business, though, is an anarchistic one, resisting the rigidity and pretension of rules. I. A. Richards applied the point to the theory of metaphor: "Its business is not to replace practice, or to tell us how to do what we cannot do already; but to protect our natural skill from the interference of unnecessarily crude views about it" (1936, p. 116).

The crudeness of modernist methodology, or of any methodology reducible to rigid precept, is bad; but that it is allowed to interfere with practice is worse. The custom of methodological papers in economics is to scold economists for not allowing it to interfere more. Mark Blaug's useful book summarizing the state of play of economic methodology in 1980, *The Methodology of Economics: Or How Economists Explain,* is a recent case in point. It would be better subtitled "How the Young Karl Popper Explained," since it repeatedly attacks extant arguments in economics for failing to comply with the rules Popper laid down in *Logik der Forschung* in 1934. Blaug's exordium is typical of the best of the methodologists in economics: "Economists have long been aware of the need to defend 'correct' principles of reasoning in their subject; although actual practice may bear little relationship to what is preached, the preaching is worth considering on its own ground" (Blaug, p. xii). Words like these flow easily from a modernist's pen. But why would preaching unrelated to actual practice be worth considering at all? Why do economists have to defend in the abstract their principles of reasoning, and before what tribunal? A case for having a methodology—whether logical positivist or Popperian or Austrian or Marxist— would be expected to give answers to the questions of why, but commonly does not. Recent philosophy of science and ordinary good sense suggest that it cannot. Blaug's peroration is frankly prescriptive, taking economic rhetoric directly from philosophy:

> What methodology can do is to provide criteria for the acceptance and rejection of research programs, setting standards that will help us to discriminate between wheat and chaff. The ultimate question we can and indeed must pose about any research program is the one made familiar by Popper: what events, if they materialize, would lead us to reject that program? A program that cannot meet that question has fallen short of the highest standards that scientific knowledge can attain [1980, p. 264].

It sounds grand, but Einstein's gods are rolling in the aisles. Why should a dubious epistemological principle be any test of practice, much less the ultimate test? And doesn't science take place most of the time well short of the ultimate?

Anyone would commend the vision of science that Popper and his followers have—of science as a self-correcting exploration verging on the dialectic otherwise so foreign to the analytic tradition in philosophy. For an economic scientist to adopt an obdurate refusal to consider objections and to resist offering hostages to evidence, though as common in modernist as in nonmodernist circles, is not merely unscientific; it is cowardly. So much one can take from the idea of falsification by evidence. The problem comes, and the modernist preaching begins, with

the word "evidence." Should it all be "objective," "experimental," "positive," "observable"? Can it be? In *The Open Society and Its Enemies* (1945) Popper closes the borders of his society to psychoanalysts and Marxists on the grounds that they do not conform to the modernist notion of evidence prevalent there. He would also have to close it to physicists from Galileo Galilei to particle charmers. An economist bracero, surely, would be deported on the next truck from such an open intellectual society.

Other Sciences Do Not Follow Modernist Methods

For all its claims to the scientific priesthood, then, economics is different from the man-in-the-street's image of Science. Economists should be glad that their subject fits poorly with this image and well with the New Rhetoric, as do studies long foreign to economics such as the study of literature or law or politics. Economics, in other words, is not a Science in the way we came to understand that word in high school.

But neither, really, are other sciences. Other sciences, even the other mathematical sciences, even the Queen herself, are rhetorical. Mathematics appears to an *incognoscento* to be the limiting example of objectivity, explicitness, and demonstrability. Surely here is bedrock for belief. Yet standards of mathematical demonstration change. The last fifty years have been a disappointment to followers of David Hilbert and his program to put mathematics on indubitable foundations. The historian of mathematics, Morris Kline, wrote recently that "it is now apparent that the concept of a universally accepted, infallible body of reasoning—the majestic mathematics of 1800 and the pride of man—is a grand illusion." Or again:

> There is no rigorous definition of rigor. A proof is accepted if it obtains the endorsement of the leading specialists of the time and employs

the principles that are fashionable at the moment. But no standard is universally acceptable today [1980, pp. 6, 315].

The recent flap over a computerized proof of the four-color proposition is one example. The more fundamental example is said to be Kurt Gödel's proof fifty years ago that some true and statable propositions in mathematics are unprovable. The point is controversial. John van Heijenoort writes that "the bearing of Gödel's results on epistemological problems remains uncertain. . . . [T]hey should not be rashly called upon to establish the primacy of some act of intuition that would dispense with formalization" (1967, p. 357). To be sure. But one need not dispense with formalization and flee to an unexamined act of intuition to think that formalization has limits.

Kline's opinions are somewhat loosely expressed, and unpopular among mathematicians. Apparently less so are those of Philip J. Davis and Reuben Hersh, whose recent book *The Mathematical Experience* (1981) was described in the *American Mathematical Monthly* as "one of the masterpieces of our age." Davis and Hersh speak of the crisis of confidence in modern mathematical philosophy, however, in terms nearly identical with Kline's. In the work of The Ideal Mathematician "the line between complete and incomplete proof is always somewhat fuzzy, and often controversial" (p. 34; cf. p. 40). They quote a living Ideal Mathematician, Solomon Feferman, who writes "it is also clear that the search for ultimate foundations via formal systems has failed to arrive at any convincing conclusion" (p. 357). Without using the word, Davis and Hersh argue that what is required is a rhetoric of mathematics:

> The dominant style of Anglo-American philosophy . . . tends to perpetuate identification of the philosophy of mathematics with logic and the study of formal systems. From this standpoint, a problem of principal concern to the mathematician becomes totally invisible. This is the problem of giving a philosophical account . . . of preformal mathematics. . . , including an examination of how [it] relates to and is affected by formalization [1981, p. 344].

They assert that "informal mathematics *is* mathematics. Formalization is only an abstract possibility which no one would want or be able actually to carry out" (p. 349). Real proofs "are established by 'consensus of the qualified' " and are "not checkable . . . by any mathematician not privy to the gestalt, the mode of thought in the particular field. . . . It may take generations to detect an error" (p. 354). They conclude:

> The actual experience of all schools—and the actual daily experience of mathematicians—shows that mathematical truth, like other kinds of truth, is fallible and corrigible. . . . It is reasonable to propose a different task for mathematical philosophy, not to seek indubitable truth, but to give an account of mathematical knowledge as it really is—fallible, corrigible, tentative, and evolving, as is every other kind of human knowledge [p. 406].

Not much in this line has been done, though one astounding piece has shown what can be: Imre Lakatos' *Proofs and Refutations: The Logic of Mathematical Discovery* gives an account for a theorem in topology of the rhetoric of mathematics.

It appears, then, that some deep problems facing mathematics are problems of rhetoric, problems in "the art of probing what men believe they ought to believe." Similar points can be made about other sciences, such as paleontology. The sudden proliferation of species at the beginning of the Cambrian period, one of the great puzzles in evolution, was explained by Steven Stanley in 1973 by supposing the sudden arrival of forms of life that fed on other forms of life, single-celled herbivores, as it were, in a grassy sea. Their grazing on the dominant forms allowed new forms to survive the competition from the previously dominant ones, which in turn resulted in new grazers. Stephen Jay Gould remarks of the arguments offered in support of this brilliant and persuasive theory that:

> . . . they do not correspond to the simplistic notions about scientific progress that are taught in most high schools and advanced by most media. Stanley does not invoke proof by new information obtained from rigorous experiment. His second criterion is a methodological presumption, the third a philosophical preference, the fourth an application of prior theory. . . . Science, at its best, interposes human judgment and ingenuity upon all its proceedings. It is, after all (although we sometimes forget it), practiced by human beings [Gould, 1977, p. 125].

One can even say the same of physics, that favorite of outsiders seeking a prescription for real, objective, positive, predictive science. The sequence Carnap-Popper-Lakatos-Kuhn-Feyerabend represents in the history and philosophy of physics a descent, accelerating recently, from the frigid peaks of scientific absolutism to the sweet valleys of anarchic rhetoric (see Popper, 1934, 1976; Lakatos, 1970; Kuhn, 1970; Feyerabend, 1975, 1978). If economics should imitate other sciences, imitate even the majesty of physics and mathematics (there is, to be sure, considerable doubt that it should), then it should officially open itself to a wider range of discourse.

IV. *The Unofficial Rhetoric Is Honorable But Unexamined*

Econometric Rhetoric Is Too Narrow

But unofficially it does. The second attitude towards discourse is that adopted in actual scientific work in economics. It is different from the official, modernist rhetoric. What is alarming about the workaday rhetoric is not its content but that it is unexamined, and that in consequence the official rhetoric pops up in mischievous ways. Economists agree or disagree—their disagreements are exaggerated—but they

do not know why. Any economist believes more than his evidence of a suitably modernist and objective sort implies. A recent poll of economists, for example, found that only three percent of those surveyed flatly disagreed with the assertion that "tariffs and import quotas reduce general economic welfare." Only two percent disagreed with the assertion that "a ceiling on rents reduces the quantity and quality of housing available." Only eight percent disagreed with the assertion that "the taxing and spending of government has a significant impact on the income of a partly idle economy" (J. R. Kearl, Clayne Pope, Gordon Whiting, and Larry Wimmer, 1979). You probably fall into the 97, 98, and 92 percent majorities. The evidence for the assertions, however, is obscure. How do economists know these statements are true? Where did they acquire such confidence? The usual answer is that "theory tells us." But great social questions are not answered by looking at a diagram on a blackboard, because it is trivially easy to draw a diagram that yields the opposite answer. The factual experience of the economy, certainly, has little to do with their confidence. No study has shown in ways that would satisfy a consistent modernist, for example, that high tariffs in America during the 19th century, on balance, hurt Americans. Yet it is believed that tariffs hurt then and now.[6] No study has shown that an inadvertent policy of fiscal ease brought unemployment down during the War. Yet it is believed on all sides. Economists have not considered their rhetoric.

Everywhere in the literature of economics one is met with premises that are unargued, tricks of style masquerading as reason ("it is evident that"), forms of evidence that ignore the concerns of the au-

---

[6] Charles Peirce, the founder of pragmatism, related in 1877 how he had been "entreated not to read a certain newspaper lest it might change my opinion upon free-trade" (p. 101).

dience, and other symptoms of a lack of self-consciousness in rhetoric. The lack is most evident in quarrels across research paradigms. Some economists (I am one) believe that peasants are rational. The mass of modernist proofs, originating largely from Chicago, that resistance to the "Green Revolution" or persistence in scattering plots of land are rational leave many other economists cold. Some economists (I am one) believe that competition is a robust characterization of the modern American economy. The mass of modernist proofs, originating largely from Chicago, that, for instance, advertising has small effects on profits leaves the others cold. Why? Why do Chicago proofs leave Texas institutionalists or NYU Austrians or Massachusetts Marxists or even Berkeley neoclassicists cold? The non-Chicago economists, of course, believe they have modernist evidence of their own. But part of the problem is that they also believe, without thinking about it much, that they have evidence of a non-modernist sort: stories of peasants and their lumpish character in the flesh; self-awareness of the force of advertising. A good part of the disagreement is over evidence that is not brought openly into the discussion, though it is used.

Even in the most narrowly technical matters of scientific discussion economists have a shared set of convictions about what makes an argument strong, but a set which they have not examined, which they can communicate to graduate students only tacitly, and which contains many elements embarrassing to the official rhetoric. A good example is the typical procedure in econometrics. From economic theory, politics, and the workings of the economist's psyche, all of which are in the rhetorical sense unexamined, come hypotheses about some bit of the economy. The hypotheses are then specified as straight lines, linear models being those most easily manipulated. The straight

lines are fitted to someone else's collection of facts. So far the official and workaday rhetoric correspond, and the one might with justice be called a guide to the other. Presently, however, they diverge. If the results of the fitting to the data are reasonable, on grounds that are not themselves subject to examination, the article is sent off to a journal. If the results are unreasonable, the hypothesis is consigned to a do loop: the economic scientist returns to the hypotheses or the specifications, altering them until a publishable article emerges. The product may or may not have value, but it does not acquire its value from its adherence to the official rhetoric. It violates the official rhetoric blatantly.

But why shouldn't it? Even at the level of tests of statistical significance the workaday rhetoric violates the philosopher's law. But so what? It is a cliché of cynicism in economics and related statistical fields to point out that a result significantly different from one that may have been gotten by chance does not have the significance it claims if the hypothesis has been manipulated to fit the data. That only significant results get published has long been a scandal among statistical purists: they fear with some reason that at the five percent level of significance something like five percent of the computer runs will be successful. The scandal is not, however, the failure to achieve modernist standards of scientific purity. The scandal is the failure to articulate reasons why one might want to ignore them.

It would be arrogant to suppose that one knew better than thousands of intelligent and honest economic scholars what the proper form of argument was. The Received View is arrogant in this way, laying down legislation for science on the basis of epistemological convictions held with vehemence inversely proportional to the amount of evidence that they work. Better to look hard at what is in fact done. In an important book that is an exception

McCloskey: The Rhetoric of Economics 495

to the general neglect of rhetorical considerations in economics Edward Leamer
asks what purpose the workaday procedures in econometrics may be serving
(Leamer, 1978, esp. p. 17). Instead of comparing them with a doctrine in the philosophy of science he compares them with
reasons that ought to persuade a reasonable person, with what really warrants assent, with, in short, economic rhetoric. As
Christopher Sims points out in a review,
"there is a myth that there are only two
categories of knowledge about the
world—'the' model, given to us by 'economic theory,' without uncertainty, and
the parameters, about which we know
nothing except what the data, via objectively specified econometric methods,
tells us. . . . The sooner Leamer's cogent
writings can lead us to abandon this myth,
to recognize that nearly all applied work
is shot through with applications of uncertain, subjective knowledge, and to make
the role of such knowledge more explicit
and more effective, the better" (Sims,
1979, p. 567). Yes. The very title of Leamer's book is an outline of rhetoric in
econometrics: *Specification Searches: Ad
Hoc Inference with Nonexperimental
Data.*

Examples of the search abound. It is
common in a seminar in economics for
the speaker to present a statistical result,
apparently irrefutable by the rules of positive economics, and to be met by a chorus
of "I can't believe it" or "It doesn't make
sense." Milton Friedman's own Money
Workshop at Chicago in the late 1960s and
the early 1970s was a case in point. Put
in statistical language, the rhetorical context that creates such skepticism can be
called a priori beliefs and can be analyzed
in Bayesian terms. It seldom is, but such
a step would not be enough even if it were
taken. That the rhetorical community in
economics might reject "solid" results, for
instance that oil prices appear in a regression explaining inflation, and accept

"flimsy" ones, for instance that money
causes inflation, shows the strength of
prior beliefs. (The beliefs can be reversed
without changing the example.) To leave
the discussion at prior beliefs, however,
perhaps formalizing them as prior probability distributions, is to perpetuate the
fact-value split of modernism, leaving
most of what matters in science to squeals
of pleasure or pain. What is required is
an examination of the workaday rhetoric
that leads to the prior beliefs. It is not
enough, as Thomas F. Cooley and Stephen
F. LeRoy do in their recent, penetrating
paper on "Identification and Estimation
of Money Demand" (1981) to merely
stand appalled at the infection of econometric conclusions by prior beliefs. If
econometric argument does not persuade
it is because the field of argument is too
narrow, not because the impulse towards
thoughtfulness and explicitness which it
embodies is wrong. The arguments need
to be broadened, not merely dismissed.

The Controversy Over Purchasing Power Parity Is an Example of Unexamined Rhetoric

A good example of how the official rhetoric—in the absence of an examination of
the workaday rhetoric—can lead a literature in economics astray, especially in
econometric matters, is the debate about
purchasing power parity. It is worth examining in detail as a case study in unexamined rhetoric and the need to broaden
it (Donald McCloskey and J. Richard
Zecher, 1982). The question is: is the international economy more like the economy
of the Midwest, in which Iowa City and
Madison and Champaign all face given
prices for goods; or is it more like the solar
system, in which each planet's economy
is properly thought of in isolation? If the
Iowa City view is correct, then the prices
of all goods will move together everywhere, allowing for exchange rates. If the
Martian view is correct they will move

differently. If the Iowa City view is correct, then all closed models of economies, whether Keynesian or monetarist or rationally expecting, are wrong; if the Martian view is correct, then economists can (as they do) go on testing macroeconomic faiths against American experience since the War.

The question of whether prices are closely connected internationally, then, is important. The official rhetoric does not leave much doubt as to what is required to answer it: collect facts on prices in, say, the United States and Canada and . . . well . . . test the hypothesis (derived in orthodox fashion from a higher order hypothesis, using objective data, looking only at observable facts, controlling the experiment as much as possible, and so forth, according to the received view). A large number of economists have done this. Half of them conclude that purchasing power parity works; the other half conclude that it fails. A misleading but nonetheless superb paper by Irving Kravis and Robert Lipsey on the subject concludes that it fails, in terms that are worth repeating:

> We think it *unlikely* that the *high* degree of national and international commodity arbitrage that many versions of the monetarist [sic] theory of the balance of payments contemplate is *typical* of the real world. This is not to deny that the price structures of the advanced industrial countries *are linked* together, but it is to suggest that the links are *loose* rather than *rigid* [1978, p. 243, italics added].

Every italicized word involves a comparison against some standard of what constitutes unlikelihood or highness or typicality or being linked or looseness or rigidity. Yet here and elsewhere in the tortured literature of purchasing power parity no standard is proposed.

The narrowest test of purchasing power parity, and the one that springs most readily to a mind trained in the official rhetoric, is to regress the price in the United States (of steel or of goods-in-general, in levels or in differences) against the corresponding price abroad, allowing for the exchange rate. If the slope coefficient is 1.00 the hypothesis of purchasing power parity is said to be confirmed; if not, not. Kravis and Lipsey perform such a test. Being good economists they are evidently made a little uncomfortable by the rhetoric involved. They admit that "Each analyst will have to decide in the light of his purposes whether the purchasing power parity relationships fall close enough to 1.00 to satisfy the theories" (p. 214). Precisely. In the next sentence, however, they lose sight of the need for an explicit standard if their argument is to be cogent: "As a matter of general judgment we express our opinion that the results do not support the notion of a tightly integrated international price structure." They do not say what a "general judgment" is or how one might recognize it. The purpose of an explicit economic rhetoric would be to provide guidance. The guidance Kravis and Lipsey provide for evaluating their general judgment is a footnote (p. 214) reporting the general judgments of Houthakker, Haberler, and Johnson that deviations from parity of anything under 10 to 20 percent are acceptable to the hypothesis. It happens, incidentally, that the bulk of the evidence offered by Kravis and Lipsey passes rather than fails such a test, belying their conclusions. But accepting or rejecting one unargued standard by comparing it with another unargued standard does not much advance the art of argument in economics.

Kravis and Lipsey, to be fair, are unusually sensitive to the case for having some standard, more sensitive than are most economists working the field. They return repeatedly to the question of a standard, though without resolving it. On page 204 they reject in one irrelevant sentence the only standard proposed in the literature so far, the Genberg-Zecher criterion, described below. On pages 204–05 and on 235 and again on 242 they draw a distinction between the statistical and the economic significance of their results. So frequently do they make the point that it must be counted one of the major ones in the paper. On page 205 they remark, for example, that even small differences between domestic and export prices can make a big difference to the incentive to export: "this is a case in which statistical significance [that is, a correlation of the two prices near 1.0, which one might mistakenly suppose to imply that they were insignificantly different] does not necessarily connote economic significance." Yet they do not turn the sword on themselves. No wonder: without a rhetoric of *economic* significance, and in the face of a modernist rhetoric of statistical significance with the prestige of alleged science behind it, they are unaware they are wielding it.

The abuse of the word "significant" in connection with statistical arguments in economics is universal. Statistical significance seems to give a standard by which to judge whether a hypothesis is true or false that is independent of any tiresome consideration of how true a hypothesis must be to be true enough. The point in the present case is that the "failure" of purchasing power parity in a regression of the usual type is not measured against a standard. How close does the slope have to be to the ideal of 1.00 to say that purchasing power parity succeeds? The literature is silent. The standard used is the irrelevant one of statistical significance. A sample size of a million yielding a tight estimate that the slope was .9999, "significantly" different from 1.00000, could be produced as evidence that purchasing power parity had "failed," at least if the logic of the usual method were to be followed consistently. Common sense, presumably, would rescue the scholar from asserting that an estimate of .9999 with

a standard error of .0000001 was significantly different from unity in a significant meaning of significance. Such common sense should be applied to findings of slopes of .90 or 1.20. It is not.[7]

The irrelevance of the merely statistical standard of fit does not undermine only that half of the empirical literature that finds purchasing power parity to be wrong. Towards the end of a fine article favorable to purchasing power parity, Paul Krugman writes:

> There are several ways in which we might try to evaluate purchasing power parity as a theory. We can ask how much it explains [that is, R-square]; we can ask how large the deviations from purchasing power parity are in some absolute sense; and we can ask whether deviations from purchasing power parity are in some sense systematic [1978, p. 405].

The defensive usage "in some absolute sense" and "in some sense" betrays his unease, which is in the event justified. There is no "absolute sense" in which a description is good or bad. The sense must be comparative to a standard, and the standard must be argued.

Similarly, Jacob Frenkel, an enthusiast for purchasing power parity as such things go among economists but momentarily bewitched by the ceremony of regression, says that "if the market is efficient and if the forward exchange rate is an unbiased forecast of the future spot exchange rate, the constant [in a regression of the spot rate today on the future rate for today quoted yesterday] . . . should not differ *significantly* from unity." In a footnote on the next page, speaking of the standard

---

[7] An example is J. D. Richardson's paper, "Some Empirical Evidence on Commodity Arbitrage and the Law of One Price" (1978). He regresses Canadian on American prices multiplied by the exchange rate for a number of industries and concludes: "It is notable that the 'law of one price' fails uniformly. The hypothesis of *perfect* commodity arbitrage is rejected with 95 percent confidence for every commodity group" (p. 347, italics added). The question is, why in an imperfect world would it matter that *perfect* arbitrage is rejected?

errors of the estimates for such an equation in the 1920s, he argues that "while
these results indicate that markets were
efficient and that on average forward rates
were unbiased forecasts of future spot
rates, the 2–8 percent errors were *significant*"(1978, pp. 175–76, italics added). He
evidently has forgotten his usage of "significant" in another signification. What he
appears to mean is that he judges a 2–8
percent error to be large in some unspeci-
fied economic sense, perhaps as offering
significant profits for lucky guessers of the
correct spot rate. In any event, it is unclear what his results imply about their
subject, purchasing power parity, because
significance in statistics, however useful
it is as an input into economic significance,
is not the same thing as economic significance.

The point is not that levels of significance are arbitrary. Of course they are.
The point is that it is not known whether
the range picked out by the level of significance affirms or denies the hypothesis.
Nor is the point that econometric tests are
to be disdained. Quite the contrary. The
point is that the econometric tests have
not followed their own rhetoric of hypothesis testing. Nowhere in the literature of
tests of purchasing power parity does
there appear a loss function. We do not
know how much it will cost in policy
wrecked or analysis misapplied or reputation ruined if purchasing power parity is
said to be true when by the measure of
the slope coefficient it is only, say, 85 percent true. That is, the argument due to
Neyman and Pearson that undergirds
modern econometrics has been set aside
here as elsewhere in favor of a merely
statistical standard, and an irrelevant one
related to sampling error at that. We are
told how improbable it is that a slope coefficient of .90 came from a distribution cen-
tered on 1.00 in view of the one kind of
error we claim we know about (unbiased
sampling error with finite variance), but

we are not told whether it matters to the
truth of purchasing power parity where
such limits of confidence are placed.

Silence on the matter is not confined
to the literature of purchasing power parity. Most texts on econometrics do not
mention that the goodness or badness of
a hypothesis is not ascertainable on merely
statistical grounds. Statisticians themselves are more self-conscious, although
the transition from principle to practice
is sometimes awkward. A practical difficulty in the way of using the Neyman and
Pearson theory in pure form, A. F. Mood
and F. A. Graybill say, is that

> the loss function is not known at all or else it
> is not known accurately enough to warrant its
> use. If the loss function is not known, it seems
> that a decision function that in some sense min-
> imizes the error probabilities will be a reason-
> able procedure [1963, p. 278].

The phrase "in some sense" appears to
be a marker of unexplored rhetoric in the
works of intellectually honest scholars. In
any event, the procedure they suggest
might be reasonable for a general statisti-
cian, who makes no claim to know what
is a good or bad approximation to truth
in fields outside statistics. It is not reasonable for a specialist in international trade
or macroeconomics. If the loss function
is not known it should be discovered. And
that will entail a study of the question's
rhetoric.

One standard of economic significance
in questions of parity, for example, might
be the degree to which the customary regressions between countries resembled
similar regressions within a single country.
We agree, for purposes of argument, that
the United States is to be treated as a single point in space, as one economy across
which distances are said not to matter for
the purposes of thinking about inflation
or the balance of payments. Having done
so we have a standard: is Canada economically speaking just as closely integrated
with the United States as is California with

Massachusetts? Is the Atlantic Economy as closely integrated as the American Economy? The standard is called the Genberg-Zecher criterion, after its inventors (Hans Genberg, 1976; McCloskey and Zecher, 1976). It is not the only conceivable one. The degree of market integration in some golden age (1880–1913 perhaps; or 1950–1970) might be a standard; the profits from arbitrage above normal profits might be another standard; the degree to which an X percentage deviation from purchasing power parity does or does not disturb some assertion about the causes of inflation might be still another. The point is to have standards of argument, to go beyond the inconclusive rhetoric provided by the pseudo-scientific ceremony of hypothesis-regression-test-publish in most of modern economics.

V. *The Rhetoric of Economics Is a Literary Matter*

Even a Modernist Uses, and Must Use, Literary Devices

The mere recognition that the official rhetoric might be dubious, then, frees the reason to examine how economists really argue. Obscured by the official rhetoric the workaday rhetoric has not received the attention it deserves, and the knowledge of it is therefore contained only in seminar traditions, advice to assistant professors, referee reports (a promising primary source for its study), and jokes. It is significant that George Stigler, a leader of modernism in economics, chose to express his observations about the rhetoric of economics in a brilliantly funny "The Conference Handbook" ("Introductory Remark number E: 'I can be very sympathetic with the author; until 2 years ago I was thinking along similar lines' ") rather than as a serious study in one of the several fields he has mastered, the history of economic thought (1977). The attitude of the Handbook is that rhetoric is mere rhetoric, mere game playing in aid of ego gratification; the serious business of Science will come on that happy day when the information theory of oligopoly or the vulgar Marxist theory of the state is brought to a critical test under the auspices of naive falsificationism.

Economists can do better if they will look soberly at the varieties of their arguments. The varieties examined here can only be crude preliminaries to a fuller study, a study that might dissect samples of economic argument, noting in the manner of a literary or philosophical exegesis exactly how the arguments sought to convince the reader. It is not obvious a priori what the categories might be; in view of the methodological range of modern economics they doubtless would vary much from author to author. A good place to start might be the categories of classical rhetoric, Aristotle's divisions into invention, arrangement, delivery, and style, for instance, with his paired sub-headings of artificial (i.e., argumentative) and inartificial (i.e., factual) proofs, syllogism and example, and the like. A good place to continue would be the procedures of modern literary critics, bright people who make their living thinking about the rhetoric of texts.

The purpose would not be to make the author look foolish or to uncover fallacies for punishment by ridicule—fallacymongering is evidence of a legislative attitude towards method, and it is no surprise that Jeremy Bentham, confident of his ability to legislate for others in matters of method as in education, prisons, and government, had compiled from his notes *The Book of Fallacies* (1824). David Hackett Fischer's book, *Historians' Fallacies* (1970), has this flaw: that it takes as fallacious what may be merely probable and supporting argument.

The purpose of literary scrutiny of economic argument would be to see beyond the received view on its content. Two

500   *Journal of Economic Literature, Vol. XXI (June 1983)*

pages (pp. 122–23) chosen literally at random from that premier text of the received view, and a local maximum in economic scholarship, Samuelson's *Foundations*, will suffice for illustration:

(1) To begin with he gives a general mathematical form from which detailed results in comparative statics can be obtained by reading across a line. The implication of the lack of elaboration of the mathematics is that the details are trivial (leading one to wonder why they are mentioned at all). An "interesting" special case is left "as an exercise to the interested reader," drawing on the rhetorical traditions of applied mathematics to direct the reader's mind in the right directions. The mathematics is presented in an offhand way, with an assumption that we all can read off partitioned matrices at a glance, inconsistent with the level of mathematics in other passages. The air of easy mathematical mastery was important to the influence of the book, by contrast with the embarrassed modesty with which British writers at the time (Hicks most notably) pushed mathematics off into appendices.

Samuelson's skill at mathematics in the eyes of his readers, an impression nurtured at every turn, is itself an important and persuasive argument. He presents himself as an authority, with good reason. That the mathematics is so often pointless, as here, is beside the point. Being able to do such a difficult thing (so it would have seemed to the typical economist reading in 1947) is warrant of expertise. The argument is similar in force to that of a classical education conspicuously displayed. To read Latin like one's mother tongue and Greek like one's aunt's tongue is extremely difficult, requiring application well beyond the ordinary; therefore— or so it seemed to Englishmen around 1900—men who have acquired such a skill should have charge of a great empire. Likewise—or so it seemed to economists

around 1983—those who have acquired a skill at partitioned matrices and eigenvalues should have charge of a great economy. The argument is not absurd or a "fallacy" or "mere rhetoric." Virtuosity *is* some evidence of virtue.[8]

(2) There are six instances of appeal to authority (C. E. V. Leser, Keynes, Hicks, Aristotle, Knight, and Samuelson; appeal to authorities is something of a Samuelsonian specialty). Appeal to authority is often reckoned as the worst kind of "mere" rhetoric. Yet it is a common and often legitimate argument, as here. No science would advance without it, because no scientist can redo every previous argument. We stand on the shoulders of giants, and it is a perfectly legitimate and persuasive argument to point this out from time to time.

(3) There are several appeals to relaxation of assumptions. The demand for money is "really interesting . . . when uncertainty . . . is admitted." Again, the implicit assumption in Hicks that money bears no interest is relaxed, unhitching the interest rate from the zero return on money. Relaxation of assumptions is the literature generating function of modern economics. In the absence of quantitative evidence on the importance of the assumption relaxed it is no modernist evidence at all. Samuelson is careful to stick to the subjunctive mood of theory (money *"would* pass out of use"), but no doubt wants his strictures on a theory of the interest rate based merely on liquidity preference (that is, on risk) to be taken seriously as comments on the actual world. They are, surely, but not on the operationalist grounds he articulates when preaching methodology.

(4) There are several appeals to hypo-

---

[8] The limiting case is spelling. Most college teachers will agree that those who do not know how to spell "consensus" lose some of their authority to speak on it.

McCloskey: The Rhetoric of Economics 501

thetical toy economies, constrained to one or two sectors, from which practical results are derived. This has since Ricardo been among the commonest forms of economic argument, the Ricardian vice. It is no vice if done reasonably. "It would be quite possible to have an economy in which money did not exist, and in which there was still a substantial rate of interest." Yes, of course.

(5) There is, finally, one explicit appeal to analogy, which is said to be "not . . . superficial." Analogy, as will be shown in detail in a moment, pervades economic thinking, even when it is not openly analogical: transaction "friction," yield "spread," securities "circulating," money "withering away" are inexplicit examples here from one paragraph of live or only half-dead metaphors. Yet analogy and metaphor, like most of the other pieces of Samuelson's rhetoric, have no standing in the official canon.

Most of the Devices Are Only Dimly Recognized

The range of persuasive discourse in economics is wide, ignored in precept while potent in practice. At the broadest level it is worth noting that the practice of economic debate often takes the form of legal reasoning, for, as Booth put it, "the processes developed in the law are codifications of reasonable processes that we follow in every part of our lives, even the scientific" (1974, p. 157). Economists would do well to study jurisprudence, then, with some other aim than subordinating it to economic theory. For instance, economists, like jurists, argue by example, by what Edward Levi calls "the controlling similarity between the present and prior case" (1967, p. 7).

The details of the pleading of cases at economic law have little to do with the official scientific method. Without self-consciousness about workaday rhetoric

they are easily misclassified. A common argument in economics, for example, is one from verbal suggestiveness. The proposition that "the economy is basically competitive" may well be simply an invitation to look at it this way, on the assurance that to do so will be illuminating. In the same way a psychologist might say "we are all neurotic"—it does not mean that 95 percent of a randomly selected sample of us will exhibit compulsive handwashing; rather, it is merely a recommendation that we focus attention on the neurotic ingredient "in us all" (Passmore, 1966, p. 438). To misunderstand the expression as a properly modernist hypothesis would be to invite much useless testing. The case is similar to $MV=PT$ understood as an identity. The equation is the same term-for-term as the equation of state of an ideal gas, and has the same status as an irrefutable but useful notion in chemistry as it has in economics. The identity *can* be argued against, but not on grounds of "failing a test." The arguments against it will deny its capacity to illuminate, not its modernist truth.

Another common argument in economics with no status in the official rhetoric is philosophical consistency: "If you assume the firm knows its own cost curve you might as well assume it knows its production function, too: it is no more dubious that it knows one than the other." The argument, usually inexplicit though signalled by such a phrase as "it is natural to assume," is in fact characteristic of philosophical discourse (Passmore, 1970). It is analogous to symmetry as a criterion of plausibility, which appears in many forms and forums. A labor economist tells a seminar about compensating differentials for the risk of unemployment, referring only to the utility functions of the workers. An auditor remarks that the value of unemployment on the demand side (that is, to the firm) is not included.

502   *Journal of Economic Literature, Vol. XXI (June 1983)*

The remark is felt to be powerful, and a long discussion ensues of how the demand side might alter the conclusions. The argument from the-other-side-is-empty is persuasive in economics, but economists are unaware of how persuasive it is.

Likewise (and here we reach the border of self-consciousness in rhetoric), "ad hoccery" is universally condemned by seminar audiences. An economist will cheerfully accept a poor R^2 and terrible and understated standard errors if only she "has a theory" for the inclusion of such-and-such a variable in the regressions. "Having a theory" is not so open and shut as it might seem, depending for instance on what reasoning is prestigious at the moment. Anyone who threw accumulated past output into an equation explaining productivity change before 1962 would have been accused of ad hoccery. But after Arrow's essay on "The Economics of Learning By Doing" (which as it happened had little connection with maximizing behavior or other higher order hypotheses in economics), there was suddenly a warrant for doing it.

An example of the rhetoric of economics which falls well within the border of self-consciousness is simulation. Economists will commonly make an argument for the importance of this or that variable by showing its potency in a model with back-of-the-envelope estimates of the parameters. Common though it is, few books or articles are devoted to its explication (but, see Richard Zeckhauser and Edith Stokey, 1978). It would be as though students learned econometrics entirely by studying examples of it—no bad way to learn, but not self-conscious in grounding the arguments. What is legitimate simulation? Between A. C. Harberger's modest little triangles of distortion and Jeffrey Williamson's immense multiequation models of the American or Japanese economies since 1870 is a broad range. Economists have no vocabulary for criticizing any part of the range. They can deliver summary grunts of belief or disbelief but find it difficult to articulate their reasons in a disciplined way.

VI. *Economics Is Heavily Metaphorical*

Models Are Metaphors

The most important example of economic rhetoric, however, falls well outside the border of self-consciousness. It is the language economists use, and in particular its metaphors. To say that markets can be represented by supply and demand "curves" is no less a metaphor than to say that the west wind is "the breath of autumn's being." A more obvious example is "game theory," the very name being a metaphor. It is obviously useful to have in one's head the notion that the arms race is a two-person, negative-sum cooperative "game." Its persuasiveness is instantly obvious, as are some of its limitations. Each step in economic reasoning, even the reasoning of the official rhetoric, is metaphor. The world is said to be "like" a complex model, and its measurements are said to be like the easily measured proxy variable to hand. The complex model is said to be like a simpler model for actual thinking, which is in turn like an even simpler model for calculation. For purposes of persuading doubters the model is said to be like a toy model that can be manipulated quickly inside the doubter's head while listening to the seminar. John Gardner wrote:

> There is a game—in the 1950s it used to be played by the members of the Iowa Writers' Workshop—called 'Smoke.' The player who is 'it' [thinks of] some famous person . . . and then each of the other players in turn asks one question . . . such as 'What kind of weather are you?' . . . Marlon Brando, if weather, would be sultry and uncertain. . . . To understand that Marlon Brando is a certain kind of weather is to discover something (though something neither useful nor demonstrable) and in

the same instant to communicate something [Gardner, 1978, pp. 118–19].

On the contrary, in economics the comparable discovery is useful and by recourse to rhetorical standards demonstrable.

Metaphors in Economics Are Not Ornamental

Metaphor, though, is commonly viewed as mere ornament. From Aristotle until the 1930s even literary critics viewed it this way, as an amusing comparison able to affect the emotions but inessential for thought. "Men are beasts": if we cared to be flat-footed about it, the notion was, we could say in what literal way we thought them beastly, removing the ornament to reveal the core of plain meaning underneath. The notion was in 1958 common in philosophy, too:

> With the decline of metaphysics, philosophers have grown less and less concerned about Godliness and more and more obsessed with cleanliness, aspiring to ever higher levels of linguistic hygiene. In consequence, there has been a tendency for metaphors to fall into disfavour, the common opinion being that they are a frequent source of infection [H. J. N. Horsburgh, 1958, p. 231].

Such suspicion toward metaphor is widely recognized by now to be unnecessary, even harmful. That the very idea of "removing" an "ornament" to "reveal" a "plain" meaning is itself a metaphor suggests why. Perhaps thinking is metaphorical. Perhaps to remove metaphor is to remove thought. The operation on the metaphoric growth would in this case be worse than the disease.

The question is whether economic thought is metaphorical in some nonornamental sense. The more obvious metaphors in economics are those used to convey novel thoughts, one sort of novelty being to compare economic with noneconomic matters. "Elasticity" was once a

mind-stretching fancy; "depression" was depressing; "equilibrium" compared an economy to an apple in a bowl, a settling idea; "competition" once induced thoughts of horseraces; money's "velocity" thoughts of swirling bits of paper. Much of the vocabulary of economics consists of dead metaphors taken from noneconomic spheres.

Comparing noneconomic with economic matters is another sort of novelty, apparent in the imperialism of the new economics of law, history, politics, crime, and the rest, and most apparent in the work of that Kipling of the economic empire, Gary Becker. Among the least bizarre of his many metaphors, for instance, is that children are durable goods. The philosopher Max Black pointed out that "a memorable metaphor has the power to bring two separate domains into cognitive and emotional relation by using language directly appropriate to the one as a lens for seeing the other" (1962, p. 236). So here: the subject (a child) is viewed through the lens of the modifier (a durable good). A beginning at literal translation would say, "A child is costly to acquire initially, lasts for a long time, gives flows of pleasure during that time, is expensive to maintain and repair, has an imperfect second-hand market. . . . Likewise, a durable good, such as a refrigerator. . . ." That the list of similarities could be extended further and further, gradually revealing the differences as well—"children, like durable goods, are not objects of affection and concern"; "children, like durable goods, do not have their own opinions"— is one reason that, as Black says, "metaphorical thought is a distinctive mode of achieving insight, not to be construed as an ornamental substitute for plain thought" (p. 237). The literal translation of an important metaphor is never finished. In this respect and in others an important metaphor in economics has the quality admired in a successful scientific

504   *Journal of Economic Literature, Vol. XXI (June 1983)*

theory, a capacity to astonish us with implications yet unseen.[9]

But it is not merely the pregnant quality of economic metaphors that makes them important for economic thinking. The literary critic I. A. Richards was among the first to make the point, in 1936, that metaphor is "two thoughts of different things *active together, . . . whose meaning is a resultant of their interaction*" (Richards, 1936, p. 93, my italics; Black, 1962, p. 46; Owen Barfield, 1947, p. 54). A metaphor is not merely a verbal trick, Richards continues, but "a borrowing between and intercourse of *thoughts*, a transaction between contexts" (p. 94, his italics). Economists will have no trouble seeing the point of his economic metaphor, one of mutually advantageous exchange. The opposite notion, that ideas and their words are invariant lumps unaltered by combination, like bricks (Richards, p. 97), is analogous to believing that an economy is a mere aggregation of Robinson Crusoes. But the point of economics since Smith has been that an island-full of Crusoes trading is different from and often better off than the mere aggregation.

Another of Becker's favorite metaphors, "human capital," illustrates how two sets of ideas, in this case both drawn from inside economics, can thus mutually illuminate each other by exchanging connotations. In the phrase "human capital" the field in economics treating human skills was at a stroke unified with the field treating investment in machines. Thought in

both fields was improved, labor economics by recognizing that skills, for all their intangibility, arise from abstention from consumption; capital theory by recognizing that skills, for all their lack of capitalization, compete with other investments for a claim to abstention. Notice by contrast that because economists are experts only in durable goods and have few (or at any rate conventional) thoughts about children, the metaphor that children are durable goods has so to speak only one direction of flow. The gains from the trade were earned mostly by the theory of children (fertility, nuptiality, inheritance), gaining from the theory of durable goods, not the other way around.

Economic Metaphors Constitute a Poetics of Economics

What is successful in economic metaphor is what is successful in poetry, and is analyzable in similar terms. Concerning the best metaphors in the best poetry, comparing thee to a summer's day or comparing *A* to *B*, argued Owen Barfield,

> We feel that *B*, which is actually said, ought to be necessary, even inevitable in some way. It ought to be in some sense the best, if not the only way, of expressing *A* satisfactorily. The mind should dwell on it as well as on *A* and thus the two should be somehow inevitably fused together into one simple meaning [Barfield, 1947, p. 54].

If the modifier *B* (a summer's day, a refrigerator, a piece of capital) were trite—in these cases it is not, although in the poem Shakespeare was more self-critical of his simile than economists usually are of theirs—it would become as it were detached from *A*, a mechanical and unilluminating correspondence. If essential, it fuses with *A*, to become a master metaphor of the science, the idea of "human capital," the idea of "equilibrium," the idea of "entry and exit," the idea of "competition." The metaphor, quoth the poet, is the "consummation of identity."

---

[9] A good metaphor depends on the ability of its audience to suppress incongruities, or to wish to. Booth gives the example of:

> 'All the world's a stage' . . . [The reader must make a choice only if the incongruities—failures of fit—come too soon]. Usually they arrive late and without much strength. . . . [W]e have no difficulty ruling from our attention, in the life-stage metaphor, the selling of tickets, fire insurance laws, the necessity for footlights [1961, p. 22f].

The appreciation of "human capital" requires the same suspension of disbelief.

McCloskey: The Rhetoric of Economics   505

Explicit-ness	Extent	
	Short	Long
Explicit	simile (The firm behaves as if it were one mind maximizing its discounted value.)	tiresome caution (repeat the simile)
Middling	metaphor (human capital)	allegory (economics of education using human capital)
Implicit	symbol (income) (demand curve)	a symbol system: a mathematics; a theory (Keynesian theory of income determination) (supply and demand analysis)

Figure 1. Analogical Thinking Has Two Dimensions (And Economic Cases in Point)

Few would deny, then, that economists frequently use figurative language. Much of the pitiful humor available in a science devoted to calculations of profit and loss comes from talking about "islands" in the labor market or "putty-clay" in the capital market or "lemons" in the commodity market. The more austere the subject the more fanciful the language. We have "turnpikes" and "golden rules" in growth theory, for instance, and long disquisitions on what to do with the "auctioneer" in general equilibrium theory. A literary man with advanced training in mathematics and statistics stumbling into *Econometrica* would be astonished at the metaphors surrounding him, lost in a land of allegory.

Allegory is merely long-winded metaphor, and all such figures are analogies. Analogies can be arrayed in terms of explicitness, with simile ("as if") the most explicit and symbol ("the demand curve") the least explicit; and they can be arrayed by extent.

Economists, especially theorists, are for-

ever spinning "parables" or telling "stories." The word "story" has in fact come to have a technical meaning in mathematical economics, though usually spoken in seminars rather than written in papers. It means an extended example of the economic reasoning underlying the mathematics, often a simplified version of the situation in the real world that the mathematics is meant to characterize. It is an allegory, shading into extended symbolism. The literary theories of narrative could make economists self-conscious about what use the story serves. Here the story is the modifier, the mathematics the subject. A tale of market days, traders with bins of shmoos, and customers with costs of travel between bins illuminates a fixed point theorem.

Even Mathematical Reasoning Is Metaphorical

The critical question is whether the opposite trick, modifying human behavior with mathematics, is also metaphorical. If it were not, one might acknowledge the metaphorical element in verbal economics about the "entrepreneur," for instance, or more plainly of the "invisible hand," yet argue that the linguistic hygiene of mathematics leaves behind such fancies. This indeed was the belief of the advanced thinkers of the 1920s and 1930s who inspired the now-received view in economic method. Most economists subscribe to the belief without doubt or comment or thought. When engaging in verbal economics we are more or less loose, it is said, taking literary license with our "story"; but when we do mathematics we put away childish things.

But mathematical theorizing in economics is metaphorical, and literary. Consider, for example, a relatively simple case, the theory of production functions. Its vocabulary is intrinsically metaphorical. "Aggregate capital" involves an analogy of "capital" (itself analogical) with

506   *Journal of Economic Literature, Vol. XXI (June 1983)*

something—sand, bricks, shmoos—that can be "added" in a meaningful way; so does "aggregate labor," with the additional peculiarity that the thing added is no thing, but hours of conscientious attentiveness; the very idea of a "production function" involves the astonishing analogy of the subject, the fabrication of things, about which it is appropriate to think in terms of ingenuity, discipline, and planning, with the modifier, a mathematical function, about which it is appropriate to think in terms of height, shape, and single valuedness.

The metaphorical content of these ideas was alive to its inventors in the 19th century. It is largely dead to 20th-century economists, but deadness does not eliminate the metaphorical element. The metaphor got out of its coffin in an alarming fashion in the Debate of the Two Cambridges in the 1960s. The debate is testament, which could be multiplied, to the importance of metaphorical questions to economics. The very violence of the combat suggests that it was about something beyond mathematics or fact. The combatants hurled mathematical reasoning and institutional facts at each other, but the important questions were those one would ask of a metaphor—is it illuminating, is it satisfying, is it apt? How do you know? How does it compare with other economic poetry? After some tactical retreats by Cambridge, Massachusetts on points of ultimate metaphysics irrelevant to these important questions, mutual exhaustion set in, without decision. The reason there was no decision was that the important questions were literary, not mathematical or statistical. The continued vitality of the idea of an aggregate production function in the face of mathematical proofs of its impossibility and the equal vitality of the idea of aggregate economics as practiced in parts of Cambridge, England in the face of statistical proofs of its impracticality would otherwise be a great mystery.

Even when the metaphors of one's economics appear to stay well and truly dead there is no escape from literary questions. The literary man C. S. Lewis pointed out in 1939 that any talk beyond the level of the-cow-standing-here-is-in-fact-purple, any talk of "causes, relations, of mental states or acts . . . [is] incurably metaphorical" (1962, p. 47). For such talk he enunciated what may be called Screwtape's Theorem on Metaphor, the first corollary of which is that the escape from verbal into mathematical metaphor is not an escape:

> when a man claims to think independently of the buried metaphor in one of his words, his claim may . . . [be] allowed only in so far as he could really supply the place of that buried metaphor. . . . [T]his new apprehension will usually turn out to be itself metaphorical [p. 46].

If economists forget and then stoutly deny that the production function is a metaphor, yet continue talking about it, the result is mere verbiage. The word "production function" will be used in ways satisfying grammatical rules, but will not signify anything. The charge of meaninglessness applied so freely by modernists to forms of argument they do not understand or like sticks in this way to themselves. Lewis' second corollary is that "the meaning in any given composition is in inverse ratio to the author's belief in his own literalness" (p. 27). An economist speaking "literally" about the demand curve, the national income, or the stability of the economy is engaging in mere syntax. Lewis cuts close to the bone here, though sparing himself from the carnage:

> The percentage of mere syntax masquerading as meaning may vary from something like 100 percent in political writers, journalists, psychologists, and economists, to something like forty percent in the writers of children's stories. . . . The mathematician, who seldom forgets that his symbols are symbolic, may often rise for short stretches to ninety percent of meaning and ten of verbiage [p. 49].

If economists are not comparing a social fact to a one-to-one mapping, thus bringing two separate domains into cognitive and emotional relation, they are not thinking:

I've never slapped a curved demand;
I never hope to slap one.
But this thing I can tell you now:
I'd rather slap than map one.

Literary Thinking Reunifies the Two Cultures

Metaphor, then, is essential to economic thinking, even to economic thinking of the most formal kind. One may still doubt, though, whether the fact matters. For it is possible for rhetoricians as well as unreconstructed modernists to commit the Philosophizing Sin, to bring high-brow considerations of the ultimate into discussions about how to fix a flat tire. Pushkin's poetry may be ultimately untranslatable, in view of the difference in language, to be sure, but also the difference in situation between a Pushkin in Russia in the early 19th century and a bilingual translator in New York in the late 20th century. Because he was a different man speaking to a different audience even Nabokov's brilliant translation, in the words of the economist and litterateur, Alexander Gerschenkron, "can and indeed should be studied but . . . cannot be read" (in Steiner, 1975, p. 315). Our intrinsic loneliness will make some nuance dark. Yet crude translation, even by machine, is useful for the workaday purposes of informing the Central Intelligence Agency (for instance, "out of sight, out of mind" = "blind madman"). Likewise, the intrinsic metaphors of language may make it ultimately impossible to communicate plain meaning without flourishes—the flourishes *are* the meaning. But the economist may be able to get along without full awareness of his meaning for the workaday purposes of advising the Central Intelligence Agency.

So it might be argued. But it should be argued cautiously. Self-consciousness about metaphor in economics would be an improvement on many counts. Most obviously, unexamined metaphor is a substitute for thinking—which is a recommendation to examine the metaphors, not to attempt the impossible by banishing them.[10] Richard Whately, D.D., Archbishop of Dublin, publicist for free trade as for other pieces of classical political economy, and author of the standard work in the 19th century on *The Elements of Rhetoric*, drew attention to the metaphor of a state being like an individual, and therefore benefiting like an individual from free trade. But he devoted some attention, not all of it ironic, to the question of the aptness of the figure:

To this is it replied, that there is a great difference between a Nation and an Individual. And so there is, in many circumstances . . . [he enumerates them, mentioning for instance the unlimited duration of a Nation] and, moreover, the transactions of each man, as far as he is left free, are regulated by the very person who is to be a gainer or loser by each,—the individual himself; who, though his vigilance is sharpened by interest, and his judgment by exercise in his own department, may chance to be a man of confined education, possessed of no general principles, and not pretending to be versed in philosophical theories; whereas the affairs of a State are regulated by a Congress, Chamber of Deputies, etc., consisting perhaps of men of extensive reading and speculative minds [1894, p. 63].

The case for intervention cannot be put better. And the metaphor is here an occasion for and instrument of thought, not a substitute.

Metaphors, further, evoke attitudes that are better kept in the open and under the control of reasoning. This is plain in the ideological metaphors popular with parties: the invisible hand is so very discrete, so soothing, that we might be inclined to accept its touch without protest;

[10] An example of a naïve attack on economic metaphors, and of a failure to realize that economic theory is itself armed with metaphor, is the first page of McCloskey (1981).

the contradictions of capitalism are so very portentous, so scientifically precise, that we might be inclined to accept their existence without inquiry. But it is true even of metaphors of the middling sort. The metaphors of economics convey the authority of Science, and often convey, too, its claims to ethical neutrality. It is no use complaining that we didn't *mean* to introduce moral premises. We do. "Marginal productivity" is a fine, round phrase, a precise mathematical metaphor that encapsulates a most powerful piece of social description. Yet it brings with it an air of having solved the moral problem of distribution facing a society in which people cooperate to produce things together instead of producing things alone. It is irritating that it carries this message, because it may be far from the purpose of the economist who uses it to show approval for the distribution arising from competition. It is better, though, to admit that metaphors in economics can contain such a political message than to use the jargon innocent of its potential.

A metaphor, finally, selects certain respects in which the subject is to be compared with the modifier; in particular, it leaves out the other respects. Max Black, speaking of the metaphor "men are wolves," notes that "any human traits that can without undue strain be talked about in 'wolf-language' will be rendered prominent, and any that cannot will be pushed into the background" (1962, p. 41). Economists will recognize this as the source of the annoying complaints from non-mathematical economists that mathematics "leaves out" some feature of the truth or from non-economists that economics "leaves out" some feature of the truth. Such complaints are often trite and ill-formed. The usual responses to them, however, are hardly less so. The response that the metaphor leaves out things in order to simplify the story temporarily is disingenuous, occurring as it often does

in contexts where the economist is simultaneously fitting 50 other equations. The response that the metaphor will be tested eventually by the facts is a stirring promise, but seldom fulfilled (see again Leamer, throughout). A better response would be that we like the metaphor of, say, the selfishly economic person as calculating machine on grounds of its prominence in earlier economic poetry plainly successful or on grounds of its greater congruence with introspection than alternative metaphors (of people as religious dervishes, say, or as sober citizens). In *The New Rhetoric: A Treatise on Argumentation* (1967), Chaim Perelman and L. Olbrechts-Tyteca note that "acceptance of an analogy . . . is often equivalent to a judgment as to the importance of the characteristics that the analogy brings to the fore" (p. 390). What is remarkable about this unremarkable assertion is that it occurs in a discussion of purely literary matters, yet fits so easily the matters of economic science.

This is in the end the significance of metaphors and of the other rhetorical machinery of argument in economics: economists and other scientists are less separate from the concerns of civilization than many think. Their modes of argument and the sources of their conviction—for instance, their uses of metaphor—are not very different from Cicero's speeches or Hardy's novels. This is a good thing. As Black wrote, discussing "archetypes" as extended metaphors in science: "When the understanding of scientific models and archetypes comes to be regarded as a reputable part of scientific culture, the gap between the sciences and the humanities will have been partly filled" (p. 243).

VII. *Be Not Afraid*

The Alternative to Modernism Is Not Irrationalism

It will be apparent by now that the objectivity of economics is overstated and, what is more important, overrated. Pregnant economic knowledge depends little on, as Michael Polanyi put it, "a scientific rationalism that would permit us to believe only explicit statements based on tangible data and derived from these by a formal inference, open to repeated testing" (1966, p. 62). A rhetoric of economics makes plain what most economists know anyway about the richness and complexity of economic argument but will not state openly and will not examine explicitly.

The invitation to rhetoric, however, is not an invitation to irrationality in argument. Quite the contrary. It is an invitation to leave the irrationality of an artificially narrowed range of arguments and to move to the rationality of arguing like human beings. It brings out into the open the arguing that economists do anyway—in the dark, for they must do it somewhere and the various official rhetorics leave them benighted.

The charge of irrationalism comes easily to the lips of methodological authoritarians. The notion is that reasoning outside the constricted epistemology of modernism is no reasoning at all. Mark Blaug, for instance, charges that Paul Feyerabend's book *Against Method* "amounts to replacing the philosophy of science by the philosophy of flower power" (1980, p. 44). Feyerabend commonly attracts such dismissive remarks by his flamboyance. But Stephen Toulmin and Michael Polanyi are nothing if not sweetly reasonable; Blaug lumps them with Feyerabend and attacks the Feyerabend-flavored whole. On a higher level of philosophical sophistication Imre Lakatos' *Methodology of Scientific Research Programmes* (1978, from articles published from 1963 to 1976) repeatedly tars Polanyi, Kuhn, and Feyerabend with "irrationalism" (e.g., Vol. 1, pp. 9n1, 76n6, 91n1, 130 and 130n3), emphasizing their sometimes aggressively expressed case against rigid rationalism and ignoring their moderately expressed case

for wider rationality. The tactic is an old one. Richard Rorty notes that "the charges of 'relativism' and 'irrationalism' once leveled against Dewey [were] merely the mindless defensive reflexes of the philosophical tradition which he attacked" (1979, p. 13; Rorty, 1982a, Ch. 9). The position taken by the opponents of Dewey, Polanyi, Kuhn, and the rest is "if the choice is between Science and irrationality, I'm for Science." But that's not the choice.

The Barbarians Are Not at the Gates

Yet still the doubt remains. If we abandon the notion that econometrics is by itself a method of science in economics, if we admit that our arguments require comparative standards, if we agree that personal knowledge of various sorts plays a part in economic knowledge, if we look at economic argument with a literary eye, will we not be abandoning science to its enemies? Will not scientific questions come to be decided by politics or whim? Is the routine of Scientific Method not a wall against irrational and authoritarian threats to inquiry? Are not the barbarians at the gates?

The fear is a surprisingly old and persistent one. In classical times it was part of the debate between philosophy and rhetoric, evident in the unsympathetic way in which the sophists are portrayed in Plato's dialogues. Cicero viewed himself as bringing the two together, disciplining rhetoric's tendency to become empty advocacy and trope on the one hand and disciplining philosophy's tendency to become useless and inhuman speculation on the other. The classical problem was that rhetoric was a powerful device easily misused for evil ends, the atomic power of the classical world, and like it the subject of worrying about its proliferation. The solution was to insist that the orator be good as well as clever: Cato defined him as *"vir bonus dicendi peritus,"* the good man skilled at speaking, a Ciceronian ideal as well. Quintilian, a century and a half after Cicero, said that "he who would be an orator must not only *appear* to be a good man, but cannot *be* an orator unless he *is* a good man" (*Institutio* XII, 1, 3). The classical problem looks quaint to moderns, who know well that regressions, radios, computers, experiments, or any of the now canonized methods of persuasion can be and have been used as methods of deceit. There is nothing about anaphora, chiasmus, metonymy, or other pieces of classical rhetoric that make them more subject to evil misuse than the modern methods. One can only note with regret that the Greeks and Romans were more sensitive to the possibility, and less hypnotized by the claims of method to moral neutrality.

The 20th century's attachment to limiting rules of inquiry solves a German problem. In the German Empire and Reich it was of course necessary to propound a split of fact from values in the social sciences if anything was to be accomplished free of political interference. And German speculative philosophy, one hears it said, warranted a logical positivist cure. The German habits, however, have spilled over into a quite different world. It is said that if we are to avoid dread anarchy we cannot trust each scientist to be his own methodologist. We must legislate a uniform though narrowing method to keep scholars from resorting to figurative and literal murder in aid of their ideas. We ourselves could be trusted with methodological freedom, of course, but the others cannot. The argument is a strange and authoritarian one, uncomfortably similar to the argument of, say, the Polish authorities against Solidarity or of the Chilean authorities against free politics. It is odd to hear intellectuals making it. Perhaps their low opinion of the free play of ideas comes from experiences in the faculty senate: the results of academic democracy,

it must be admitted, are not so bad an argument for authoritarianism, at least until one looks more closely at the results of authoritarianism. Surely, though, the alternative to blindered rules of modernism is not an irrational mob but a body of enlightened scholars, perhaps more enlightened when freed to make arguments that actually bear on the questions at issue.

There Is No Good Reason to Wish to Make "Scientific" As Against Plausible Statements

The other main objection to an openly rhetorical economics is not so pessimistic. It is the sunny view that scientific knowledge of a modernist sort may be hard to achieve, even impossible, but all will be well on earth and in heaven if we strive in our poor way to reach it. We should have a standard of Truth beyond persuasive rhetoric to which to aspire. In Figure 2 all possible propositions about the world are divided into objective and subjective, positive and normative, scientific and humanistic, hard and soft. The modernist supposes that the world comes divided nicely along such lines.

scientific	humanistic
fact	opinion
objective	subjective
positive	normative
vigorous	sloppy
precise	vague
things	words
cognition	intuition
hard	soft

Figure 2. The Task of Science Is to Move the Line

According to the modernist methodologist the scientist's job is not to decide whether propositions are useful for understanding and changing the world but to classify them into one or the other half, scientific or nonscientific, and to bring as many as possible into the scientific por-

McCloskey: The Rhetoric of Economics 511

tion. But why? Whole teams of philosophical surveyors have sweated long over the placing of the demarcation line between scientific and other propositions, worrying for instance about whether astrology can be demarcated from astronomy; it was the chief activity of the positivist movement for a century. It is not clear why anyone troubled to do so. People are persuaded of things in many ways, as has been shown for economic persuasion. It is not clear why they should labor at drawing lines on mental maps between one way and another.

The modernists have long dealt with the embarrassment that metaphor, case study, upbringing, authority, introspection, simplicity, symmetry, fashion, theology, and politics serve to convince scientists as they do other folk by labeling these the "context of discovery." The way scientists discover hypotheses has been held to be distinct from the "context of justification," namely, proofs of a modernist sort. Thomas Kuhn's autobiographical reflections on the matter can stand for puzzlement in recent years about this ploy:

> Having been weaned intellectually on these distinctions and others like them, I could scarcely be more aware of their import and force. For many years I took them to be about the nature of knowledge, and . . . yet my attempts to apply them, even *grosso modo*, to the actual situations in which knowledge is gained, accepted, and assimilated have made them seem extraordinarily problematic [Kuhn, 1970, p. 9].

The methodologist's claim is that "ultimately" all knowledge in science can be brought into the hard and objective side of Figure 2. Consequently, in certifying propositions as really scientific there is great emphasis placed on *"conceivable falsification"* and *"some future"* test." The apparent standard is the Cartesian one that we can find plausible only the things we cannot possibly doubt. But even this curious standard is not in fact applied: a

conceivable but practically impossible test takes over the prestige of the real test, but free of its labor. Such a step needs to be challenged. It is identical to the one involved in equating as morally similar the actual compensation of those hurt during a Pareto optimal move with a hypothetical compensation not actually paid, as in the Hicks-Kaldor test; and it is identically dubious. A properly identified econometric measurement of the out-of-sample properties of macroeconomic policy is "operational," that is, conceivable, but for all the scientific prestige the conceivability lends to talk about it, there are grave doubts whether it is practically possible. While economists are waiting for the ultimate they might better seek wisdom in the humanism of historical evidence on régime changes or of introspection about how investors might react to announcements of new monetary policies. And of course they do.

The point is that one cannot tell whether an assertion is persuasive by knowing at which portion of the scientific/humanistic circle it came from. One can tell whether it is persuasive only by thinking about it. Not all regression analyses are more persuasive than all moral arguments; not all controlled experiments are more persuasive than all introspections. Economic intellectuals should not discriminate against propositions on the basis of race, creed, or epistemological origin. There are some subjective, soft, vague propositions that are more persuasive than some objective, hard, precise propositions.

Take, for instance, the law of demand. The economist is persuaded that he will buy less oil when its price doubles better than he or anyone else is persuaded of the age of the universe. He may reasonably be persuaded of it better than he is that the earth goes around the sun, because not being an astronomer with direct knowledge of the experiments involved he has the astronomical facts only from the testimony of people he trusts, a reliable though not of course infallible source of knowledge.[11] The economic fact he has mostly from looking into himself and seeing it sitting there. The ceremony of the official rhetoric to the contrary, it is not because the law of demand has predicted well or has passed some statistical test that it is believed—although such further tests are not to be scorned. The "scientific" character of the tests is irrelevant. It may be claimed in reply that people can agree on precisely what a regression coefficient means but cannot agree precisely on the character of their introspection. Even if true (it is not) this is a poor argument for ignoring introspection if the introspection is persuasive and the regression coefficient, infected with identification problems and errors in variables, is not. Precision means low variance of estimation; but if the estimate is greatly biased it will tell precisely nothing.

An extreme case unnecessary for the argument here will make the point clear. You are persuaded that it is wrong to murder better than you are persuaded that inflation is always and everywhere a monetary phenomenon. This is not to say that similar techniques of persuasion will be applicable to both propositions. It says merely that each within its field, and each therefore subject to the methods of honest persuasion appropriate to the field, the one achieves a greater certainty than the other. To deny the comparison is to deny that reason and the partial certitude it can bring applies to nonscientific subjects, a common but unreasonable position. There is no reason why specifically scientific persuasiveness ("at the .05 level the coeffi-

cient on M in a regression of prices in 30 countries over 30 years is insignificantly different from 1.0") should take over the whole of persuasiveness, leaving moral persuasiveness incomparably inferior to it. Arguments such as that "murder violates the reasonable moral premise that we should not force other people to be means to our ends" or that "from behind a prenatal veil of ignorance of which side of the murderer's revolver we would be after birth we would enact laws against murder" are persuasive in comparable units. Not always, but sometimes, they are, indeed, more persuasive, better, more probable (Toulmin, 1958, p. 34). We believe and act on what persuades us—not what persuades a majority of a badly chosen jury, but what persuades well educated participants in our civilization and justly influential people in our field. To attempt to go beyond persuasive reasoning is to let epistemology limit reasonable persuasion.

VIII. *The Good of Rhetoric*

Better Writing

Well, what of it? What is to be gained by taking the rhetoric of economics seriously? The question can be answered by noting the burdens imposed by an unexamined rhetoric.

First of all, economics is badly written, written by a formula for scientific prose. The situation is not so bad as it is in, say, psychology, where papers that do not conform to the formula (introduction, survey of literature, experiment, discussion, and so forth) are in some journals not accepted. But economists are stumbling towards conventions of prose that are bad for clarity and honesty. The study of rhetoric, it must be said, does not guarantee the student a good English style. But at least it makes him blush at the disdain for the reader that some economics exhibits (Walter Salant, 1969).

[11] The astronomical "fact" that the earth goes around the sun, of course, is not even a properly modernist fact, though it is commonly treated as one in such discussions. Which goes around which is a matter of the point of view one chooses. It is the aesthetics of the simpler theory, not the "facts," that leads to heliocentrism.

McCloskey: The Rhetoric of Economics 513

The economist's English contains a message, usually that "I am a Scientist: give way." Occasionally the message is more genial: Zvi Griliches' irony says "Do not make a fetish out of these methods I am expounding: they are mere human artifices." Milton Friedman's style, so careful and clear, has to an exceptional degree the character of the Inquirer. We will not raise up a race of Dennis Robertsons, Robert Solows, George Stiglers, or Robert Lucases by becoming more sensitive to the real messages in scientific procedure and prose, but maybe we will stunt the growth of the other kind.

Better Teaching

A second burden is that economics is badly taught, not because its teachers are boring or stupid, but because they often do not recognize the tacitness of economic knowledge, and therefore teach by axiom and proof instead of by problem-solving and practice. To quote Polanyi yet again:

> . . . the transmission of knowledge from one generation to the other must be predominantly tacit. . . . The pupil must assume that a teaching which appears meaningless to start with has in fact a meaning that can be discovered by hitting on the same kind of indwelling [a favorite Polanyi expression] as the teacher is practicing [1966, p. 61].

It is frustrating for students to be told that economics is not primarily a matter of memorizing formulas, but a matter of feeling the applicability of arguments, of seeing analogies between one application and a superficially different one, of knowing when to reason verbally and when mathematically, and of what implicit characterization of the world is most useful for correct economics. Life is hard. As a blind man uses his stick as an extension of his body, so whenever we use a theory "we incorporate it in our body—or extend our body to include it—so that we come to dwell in it." Problem-solving in economics

is the tacit knowledge of the sort Polanyi describes.[12] We know the economics, but cannot say it, in the same way a musician knows the note he plays without consciously recalling the technique for executing it. A singer is a prime example, for there is no set of mechanical instructions one can give to a singer on how to hit a high C. Al Harberger often speaks of so-and-so being able to make an economic argument "sing." Like the directions to Carnegie Hall, the answer to the question "how do you get to the Council of Economic Advisors?" is "practice, practice."

Better Foreign Relations

A third burden placed on economics by its modernist methodology is that economics is misunderstood and, when regarded at all, disliked by both humanists and scientists. The humanists dislike it for its baggage of antihumanist methodology. The scientists dislike it because it does not in reality attain the rigor that its methodology claims to achieve. The bad foreign relations have many costs. For instance, as was noted above, economics has recently become imperialistic. There is now an economics of history, of sociology, of law, of anthropology, of politics, of political philosophy, of ethics. The flabby methodology of modernist economics simply makes this colonization more difficult, raising irrelevant methodological doubts in the minds of the colonized folk.

Better Science

A fourth burden is that economists pointlessly limit themselves to "objective" facts, admitting the capabilities of one's own or others' minds as merely sources of hypotheses to be tested, not as themselves arguments for assenting to hypotheses. The modernist notion is that common sense is nonsense, that knowledge must somehow be objective, not *verstehen* or

[12] On this score, and some others, I can heartily recommend McCloskey, 1982.

514   *Journal of Economic Literature, Vol. XXI (June 1983)*

introspection. But, to repeat, we have much information immediately at our disposal about our own behavior as economic molecules, if we would only examine the grounds of our beliefs. The idea that observational proofs of the law of demand, such as the Rotterdam School's multi-equation approach, are more compelling than introspection is especially odd. Even the econometrics itself would be better, as Christopher Sims has recently argued:

> If we think carefully about what we are doing, we will emerge, I think, both more confident that much of applied econometrics is useful, despite its differences from physical science, and more ready to adapt our language and methods to reflect what we are actually doing. The result will be econometrics which is more scientific [by which he means "good"] if less superficially similar to statistical methods used in experimental sciences [Sims, 1982, p. 25].

The curious status of survey research in modern economics is a case in point. Unlike other social scientists, economists are extremely hostile towards questionnaires and other self-descriptions. Secondhand knowledge of a famous debate among economists in the late 1930s is part of an economist's formal education. The debate concerned the case of asking businessmen if they equalized marginal cost to marginal revenue. It is revealing that the failure of such a study—never mind whether that was indeed the study—is supposed to convince economists to abandon all self-testimony. One can literally get an audience of economists to laugh out loud by proposing ironically to send out a questionnaire on some disputed economic point. Economists are so impressed by the confusions that might possibly result from questionnaires that they abandon them entirely, in favor of the confusions resulting from external observation. They are unthinkingly committed to the notion that only the externally observable behavior of economic actors is admissable evidence in arguments concerning eco-

nomics. But self-testimony is not useless, even for the purpose of resolving the marginal cost-average cost debate of the 1930s. One could have asked "Has your profit margin always been the same?" "What do you think when you find sales lagging?" (Lower profit margin? Wait it out?) Foolish inquiries into motives and foolish use of human informants will produce nonsense. But this is also true of foolish use of the evidence more commonly admitted into the economist's study.

Better Dispositions

A fifth and final burden is that scientific debates in economics are long-lasting and ill-tempered. Journals in geology are not filled with articles impugning the character of other geologists. They are not filled with bitter controversies that drone on from one century to the next. No wonder. Economists do not have an official rhetoric that persuasively describes what economists find persuasive. The mathematical and statistical tools that gave promise in the bright dawn of the 1930s and 1940s of ending economic dispute have not succeeded, because too much has been asked of them. Believing mistakenly that operationalism is enough to end all dispute, the economist assumes his opponent is dishonest when he does not concede the point, that he is motivated by some ideological passion or by self-interest, or that he is simply stupid. It fits the naive fact-value split of modernism to attribute all disagreements to political differences, since facts are alleged to be, unlike values, impossible to dispute. The extent of disagreement among economists, as was mentioned, is in fact exaggerated. The amount of their agreement, however, makes all the more puzzling the venom they bring to relatively minor disputes. The assaults on Milton Friedman or on John Kenneth Galbraith, for example, have a bitterness that is quite unreasonable. If one cannot reason about values, and if most of what

McCloskey: The Rhetoric of Economics 515

matters is placed in the value half of the fact-value split, then it follows that one will embrace unreason when talking about things that matter. The claims of an overblown methodology of Science merely end conversation.[13]

A rhetorical cure for such disabilities would reject philosophy as a guide to science, or would reject at least a philosophy that pretended to legislate the knowable. The cure would not throw away the illuminating regression, the crucial experiment, the unexpected implication unexpectedly falsified. These too persuade reasonable scholars. Non-argument is the necessary alternative to narrow argument only if one accepts the dichotomies of modernism. The cure would merely recognize the good health of economics, disguised now under the neurotic inhibitions of an artificial methodology of Science.

REFERENCES

ALCHIAN, ARMEN. "Uncertainty, Evolution, and Economic Theory," *J. Polit. Econ.*, June 1950, *58*(3), pp. 211–21.

BARFIELD, OWEN. "Poetic Diction and Legal Fiction," in *Essays presented to Charles Williams.* London: Oxford U. Press, 1947; reprinted in *The importance of language.* Ed.: MAX BLACK, Englewood Cliffs, NJ: Prentice-Hall, 1962, pp. 51–71.

BECKER, GARY S. AND STIGLER, GEORGE J. "De Gustibus Non Est Disputandum," *Amer. Econ. Rev.*, Mar. 1977, *67*(2), pp. 76–90.

BENTHAM, JEREMY. *The book of fallacies from unfinished papers.* London: Hunt, 1824.

BLACK, MAX. *Models and metaphors: Studies in language and philosophy.* Ithaca, NY: Cornell U. Press, 1962.

BLAUG, MARK. *The methodology of economics: Or how economists explain.* Cambridge, U.K.: Cambridge U. Press, 1980.

BOOTH, WAYNE C. *The rhetoric of fiction.* Chicago, IL: U. of Chicago Press, 1961.

_____. "The Revival of Rhetoric," in *New rhetorics.*

[13] Listen to Harry Johnson: "The methodology of positive economics was an ideal methodology for justifying work that produced apparently surprising results without feeling obliged to explain why they occurred" (Johnson, 1971, p. 13). I do not need to think about your evidence for widespread monopolistic competition because my methodology tells me the evidence is irrelevant.

Ed.: MARTIN STEINMANN, JR. NY: Scribner's, 1967.

_____. *Modern dogma and the rhetoric of assent.* Chicago, IL: U. of Chicago Press, 1974.

BURKE, KENNETH. *A rhetoric of motives.* Berkeley: U. of California Press, 1950.

COASE, RONALD. "How Should Economists Choose?" The G. Warren Nutter Lectures in Political Economy. Washington, DC: American Enterprise Institute, 1982.

COHEN, KALMAN AND CYERT, RICHARD. *Theory of the firm.* 2nd ed. Englewood Cliffs, NJ: Prentice-Hall, 1975.

COOLEY, T. F. AND LEROY, S. F. "Identification and Estimation of Money Demand," *Amer. Econ. Rev.*, Dec. 1981, *71*(5), pp. 825–44.

DAVIS, PHILIP J. AND HERSH, REUBEN. *The mathematical experience.* Boston, MA: Houghton Mifflin, 1981.

DEWEY, JOHN. *The quest for certainty.* NY: Putnam, [1929] 1960.

EINSTEIN, ALBERT. "Aphorisms for Leo Baeck," reprinted in *Ideas and opinions.* NY: Dell, [1953] 1973.

FEYERABEND, PAUL. *Against method: Outline of an anarchistic theory of knowledge.* London: Verso, [1975] 1978.

_____. *Science in a free society.* London: New Left Books, 1978.

FISCHER, DAVID HACKETT. *Historians' fallacies.* NY: Harper & Row, 1970.

FRENKEL, JACOB. "Purchasing Power Parity: Doctrinal Perspectives and Evidence from the 1920s," *J. Int. Econ.*, May 1978, *8*(2), pp. 169–91.

FRIEDMAN, MILTON. "The Methodology of Positive Economics," in *Essays in positive economics.* Chicago, IL: U. of Chicago Press, 1953.

FRIEDMAN, MILTON AND SCHWARTZ, ANNA J. *A monetary history of the United States.* Princeton, NJ: Princeton U. Press, 1963.

GARDNER, JOHN. *On moral fiction.* NY: Basic Books, 1978.

GENBERG, A. HANS. "Aspects of the Monetary Approach to Balance-of-Payments Theory: An Empirical Study of Sweden," in *The monetary approach to the balance of payments.* Eds.: JACOB A. FRENKEL AND HARRY G. JOHNSON. London: Allen & Unwin, 1976.

GOULD, STEPHEN JAY. *Ever since Darwin.* NY: Norton, 1977.

_____. *The mismeasure of man.* NY: Norton, 1981.

VAN HEIJENOORT, JOHN. "Gödel's Proof," in *The encyclopedia of philosophy.* NY: Macmillan & Free Press, 1967.

HORSBURGH, H. J. N. "Philosophers Against Metaphor," *Philosophical Quart.*, July 1958, *8*(32), pp. 231–45.

HUME, DAVID. *An inquiry concerning human understanding.* Ed.: CHARLES W. HENDEL. Indianapolis: Bobbs & Merrill, [1748] 1955.

JAMES, WILLIAM. "Pragmatism's Conception of Truth" reprinted in *Essays in pragmatism by William James.* Ed.: CASTELL ALBUREY. NY: Hafner, [1907] 1948.

JOHNSON, HARRY G. "The Keynesian Revolution and

the Monetarist Counterrevolution," *Amer. Econ. Rev.*, May 1971, *61*(2), pp. 1–14.

KEARL, J. R.; POPE, CLAYNE; WHITING, GORDON AND WIMMER, LARRY. "A Confusion of Economists?" *Amer. Econ. Rev.*, May 1979, *69*(2), pp. 28–37.

KLINE, MORRIS. *Mathematics: The loss of certainty.* NY: Oxford, 1980.

KRAVIS, IRVING B. AND LIPSEY, ROBERT E. "Price Behavior in the Light of Balance of Payments Theories," *J. Int. Econ.*, May 1978, *8*(2), pp. 193–246.

KRUGMAN, PAUL R., "Purchasing Power Parity and Exchange Rates: Another Look at the Evidence," *J. Int. Econ.*, Aug. 1978, *8*(3), pp. 397–407.

KUHN, THOMAS. *The structure of scientific revolutions.* 2nd ed. Chicago: U. of Chicago Press, 1970.

──────. *The essential tradition: Selected studies in scientific tradition and change.* Chicago: U. of Chicago Press, 1977.

LAKATOS, IMRE. *Proofs and refutations: The logic of mathematical discovery.* Cambridge: Cambridge U. Press, 1976.

──────. *The methodology of scientific research programmes. From articles 1963–1976.* Cambridge, NY and London: Cambridge U. Press, 1978.

────── AND MUSGRAVE, ALAN. *Criticism and the growth of knowledge.* Cambridge: Cambridge U. Press, 1970.

LEAMER, EDWARD. *Specification searches. Ad hoc inferences with nonexperimental data.* NY: Wiley, 1978.

LEVI, EDWARD. *An introduction to legal reasoning.* Chicago, IL: U. of Chicago Press, [1948] 1967.

LEWIS, C. S. "Buspels and Flansferes," in *Rehabilitations and other essays.* London: Oxford U. Press, 1939; reprinted in *The importance of language.* Ed.: MAX BLACK. Englewood Cliffs, NJ: Prentice-Hall, 1962.

MCCLOSKEY, DONALD N. "The Loss to Britain from Foreign Industrialization," reprinted in his *Enterprise and trade in Victorian Britain.* London: Allen & Unwin, [1970] 1981.

──────. *The applied theory of price.* NY: Macmillan, 1982.

────── AND ZECHER, J. RICHARD. "How the Gold Standard Worked, 1880–1913," in *The monetary approach to the balance of payments.* Eds.: J. FRENKEL AND H. G. JOHNSON. London: Allen & Unwin, 1976.

────── AND ZECHER, J. R. "The Success of Purchasing Power Parity," in *A retrospective on the classical gold standard.* Eds.: MICHAEL BORDO AND ANNA J. SCHWARTZ. NBER conference, 1982. Forthcoming.

MISES, LUDWIG VON. *Human action.* New Haven, CT: Yale U. Press, 1949.

MOOD, A. F. AND GRAYBILL, F. A. *Introduction to the theory of statistics.* 2nd ed. NY: McGraw Hill, 1963.

PASSMORE, JOHN. *A hundred years of philosophy,* 2nd ed. London: Penguin, 1966.

──────. "Logical Positivism," in *The encyclopedia of philosophy.* NY: Macmillan, 1967.

──────. *Philosophical reasoning.* 2nd ed. London: Duckworth, 1970.

PEIRCE, CHARLES. "The Fixation of Belief," reprinted in *Values in a universe of chance: Selected writings of Charles S. Peirce.* Ed.: P. P. WIENER. Garden City, NJ: Doubleday, [1877] 1958.

PERELMAN, CHAIM AND OLBRECHTS-TYTECA, L. *The new rhetoric: A treatise on argumentation.* Eng. trans. Notre Dame: Notre Dame U. Press, [1958] 1967.

POLANYI, MICHAEL. *Personal knowledge: Towards a post-critical philosophy* Chicago, IL: U. of Chicago Press, 1962.

──────. *The tacit dimension.* Garden City, NY: Doubleday, 1966.

POPPER, KARL. *The logic of scientific discovery.* Eng. trans. NY: Harper, [1934] 1959.

──────. *The open society and its enemies.* London: Routledge, 1945.

──────. *Unended quest: An intellectual autobiography.* London: Collins, 1976.

QUINTILIAN, MARCUS F. *Institutio oratoria.* Cambridge, MA: Harvard U. Press, [c. 100 AD] 1920.

REDER, MELVIN. "Chicago Economics: Permanence and Change," *J. Econ. Lit.*, Mar. 1982, *20*(1), pp. 1–38.

RICHARDS, I. A. *The philosophy of rhetoric.* NY: Oxford U. Press, 1936.

RICHARDSON, J. D. "Some Empirical Evidence on Commodity Arbitrage and the Law of One Price," *J. Inter. Econ.*, May 1978, *8*(2), pp. 341–51.

ROLL, RICHARD AND ROSS, STEPHEN. "An Empirical Investigation of the Arbitrage Pricing Theory," *J. Finance*, Dec. 1980, *35*, pp. 1073–1103.

RORTY, RICHARD. *Philosophy and the mirror of nature.* Princeton NJ: Princeton U. Press, 1979.

──────. *Consequences of pragmatism (Essays: 1972–1980).* Minneapolis: U. of Minnesota Press, 1982a.

──────. "The Fate of Philosophy," *The New Republic,* Oct. 18, 1982b, *187*(16), pp. 28–34.

SALANT, WALTER. "Writing and Reading in Economics," *J. Polit. Econ.*, July-Aug. 1969, *77*(4, Pt. I), pp. 545–58.

SAMUELSON, P. A. *The foundations of economic analysis.* Cambridge, MA: Harvard U. Press, 1947.

SEN, AMARTYA. "Behaviour and the Concept of Preference," Inaugural Lecture. London School of Economics and Political Science, 1973.

SHARPE, WILLIAM. *Portfolio theory and capital markets.* NY: McGraw Hill, 1970.

SIMS, CHRISTOPHER. "Review of *Specification searches: Ad hoc interference with nonexperimental data.* By Edward E. Leamer." *J. Econ. Lit.*, June 1979, *17*(2), pp. 566–68.

──────. "Scientific Standards in Econometric Modeling," Unpub. paper for the 25th anniversary of the Rotterdam Econometrics Institute, Apr. 1982.

STEINER, GEORGE. *After Babel: Aspects of language.* London: Oxford U. Press, 1975.

STIGLER, GEORGE J. "The Conference Handbook," *J. Polit. Econ.*, Apr. 1977, *85*(2), pp. 441–43.

TOULMIN, STEPHEN. *The uses of argument.* Cambridge: Cambridge U. Press, 1958.

──────. "The Construal of Reality: Criticism in Modern and Postmodern Science," *Critical Inquiry*, Autumn 1982, *9*(1), pp. 93–110.

WEBSTER, GLENN; JACOX, ADA AND BALDWIN, BEVERLY. "Nursing Theory and the Ghost of the Received View," in *Current issues in nursing*. Eds.: JOANNE MCCLOSKEY AND HELEN GRACE.

Boston, MA: Blackwell Scientific, 1981, pp. 16–35.

WHATELY, RICHARD. *Elements of rhetoric*. 7th ed. London: [1846] 1894.

ZECKHAUSER, RICHARD AND STOKEY, EDITH. *A primer for policy analysis*. NY: Norton, 1978.

8

A Diversity of Themes in Contemporary Methodology

Melvin Reder, 'Chicago Economics: Permanence and Change', *Journal of Economic Literature*, vol. 20, March 1982, pp. 1−38.

Harvey Leibenstein, 'A Branch of Economics is Missing: Micro-Micro Theory', *Journal of Economic Literature*, vol. 17, June 1979, pp. 477−502.

E. Roy Weintraub, 'Substantive Mountains and Methodological Molehills', *Journal of Post-Keynesian Economics*, vol. 5, no. 2, Winter 1982−83, pp. 295−303.

Sheila Dow, 'Substantive Mountains and Methodological Molehills: A Rejoinder', *Journal of Post-Keynesian Economics*, vol. 5, no. 2, Winter 1982−83, pp. 304−8.

Elba Brown, 'The Neoclassical and Post-Keynesian Research Programs: The Methodological Issues', *Review of Social Economy*, vol. 39, no. 2, October 1981, pp. 111−32.

Edward E. Leamer, 'Let's Take the Con Out of Econometrics', *American Economic Review*, vol. 73, no. 1, March 1983, pp. 31−43.

Editor's comments

As the chapter title suggests, a variety of approaches to methodology are demonstrated in the readings to follow.

The front piece is Melvin Reder's superb essay on Chicago economics. The subject of Reder's article is not a new one: Martin Bronfenbrenner (1962), A. W. Coats (1963), Henry Miller (1962) and George Stigler (1962) tried their hands at describing the 'Chicago School(s)' in the early 1960s, and Warren Samuels (1976) edited a thick collection of essays on the subject in the mid-1970s. There are three reasons why I found Reder's article especially appealing. First, there are no histrionics, but quite a bit of history. Reder is close enough to Chicago to provide the insights of an insider, but far enough to be an impartial observer. Next, Reder focuses on the economic work of Chicago economists rather than on their methodological pronouncements. By looking at what Chicago economists do instead of what they say they do, Reder has advanced the discussion in a manner that would be applauded by most contemporary methodologists. Finally, his distinction between the 'tight prior' and 'diffuse prior' approaches is a useful (and catchy!) way to specify different sorts of equilibrium theorizing in economics. Heterodox economists are often imprecise in their attacks on what is variously labeled neoclassical, or orthodox, or mainstream economics. As further gradations are added to Reder's fruitful categorization, the level of debate should improve.

Since x-efficiency theory has been challenged by no less of a Chicago economist than George Stigler, what better counterpoint exists to Reder's piece than a recent contribution by Harvey Leibenstein? X-efficiency theory is by now a fairly well-established alternative in the theory of the firm, and Leibenstein does an admirable job of contrasting his approach with both the standard as well as other heterodox visions of firm behavior. Leibenstein's article also nicely complements and extends Brian Loasby's earlier contribution.

Though many branches of 'the orthodoxy' have been impugned by its critics, few areas have proved to be more attractive as a target than general equilibrium theory. Austrians and Marxists, Institutionalists and post-Keynesians, and even some empirically minded members of the mainstream, all seem to agree (though for decidedly different reasons) that its mathematical formalism is little more than a transparent mask for a theory bereft of realism, substance and meaning. In 1979, Roy Weintraub entered the lion's den with the publication of his survey, *Microfoundations: The Compatibility of Microeconomics and Macroeconomics*. No defensive apologist, Weintraub advances the thesis that the 'neo-Walrasian' program is best described as a progressive Lakatosian research program.

The exchange with Sheila Dow reprinted here is the last in a series. About the only things that the authors agree on is that they disagree, and that communication across paradigms is difficult. Weintraub would rather argue about 'real issues' instead of methodology (a devil's distinction in this collection of essays, some might add); Dow thinks clarity about methodological differences is the best way to move the debate forward. For readers who might not know how the post-Keynesian program differs from more standard approaches, I have also included Elba Brown's informative and even-handed assessment of the issues.

If you are not already one, imagine yourself as a disinterested observer of this debate. Has either side won? Have the authors had a meaningful exchange, or have they talked beyond one another? If you do think there is a winner, how did you come to your decision; what criteria of assessment did you use? If you are a scientist, you know that neither the author's rhetoric nor your own prior beliefs should interfere with your objective judgement. But then, what does count in such a debate? Must we agree with Brown that 'no *objective* way to choose between these alternative programs may exist', and what implications follow from such an agreement?

Positivism was a radically empirical philosophy of science, and econometrics is the field in which the empirical methods of economics are developed. Given that this is the post-positivist era, one might reasonably expect that the current methodological literature would be filled with studies of the uses and limitations of econometric technique. Remarkably, there is a void; the interaction between methodologists and econometricians is very nearly non-existent. How can this be? It is not the fault of econometricians, who have their own interests to pursue. Methodologists cannot be so sanguine, yet we have repeatedly focused on *theories* rather than techniques, and the field is all the weaker for the emphasis.

It has taken an econometrician to reverse the trend. And, happily, the one who has done it is also known for his wit and clarity. There are many lessons in E. E. Leamer's excellent little piece. Few economists can get through it without wondering about their own 'priors'. Other econometricians who have raised similar queries are listed in his conclusion, and his comparison between methodology and sex is too accurate to warrant further comment. Most important, a new research path has been started, and it is to be hoped that both methodology and econometrics will benefit.

Journal of Economic Literature
Vol. XX (March 1982), pp. 1–38

Chicago Economics:
Permanence and Change

By Melvin W. Reder

University of Chicago

M Y PERCEPTION of Chicago economics is that of participant-observer. As a working economist at Chicago, I have observed other members of the tribe at close hand, and have obtained their critical reactions to this description of their intellectual outlook and styles of work.[1] The perceptions of any participant-observer are conditioned, however, by his position in time and in the institutional configuration. My vantage points have been those of a graduate student in the Economics De-

partment, of an assistant and personal friend of Oscar Lange from 1939–41, and of a Professor in the Graduate School of Business since 1974.

Yet another source of perspective bias is field of specialization. As a graduate student, my primary interests were Pure Theory, Welfare Economics and Macroeconomics; my present focus is upon Labor Economics, with Industrial Organization a secondary interest. This pattern of specialization determines the workshops that I regularly attend, the manuscripts that I read and the individuals with whom I am in close contact. The influence of specialty upon one's perspective of Chicago economics is not trivial. In preparing this essay, I have found that our Chicago corner of the economics profession can look quite different to someone in Monetary Theory or International Trade than to a specialist in Labor, Industrial Organization or Law and Economics.

This essay does not pretend to be an exhaustive account of Chicago economics during the past half century. It is primarily an attempt to describe the evolution of a few basic ideas associated with a particular institution. The focus is upon ideas rather than their protagonists or the institution whose name is their generic label.

Describing these ideas is not easy because their central tendency has changed

---

[1] Manifestly, this paper is a personal statement for which no one but the author is responsible. However, I have had far more than normal critical input from friends and colleagues at Chicago and elsewhere. My Chicago associates have served in the dual capacity of information sources and critics: George Stigler's contributions are acknowledged in footnotes, though inadequately, and I have also benefitted from the comments of Jacob Frenkel, David Galenson, Robert Lucas, Merton Miller, George Neumann, Peter Pashigian, Sam Peltzman, and T. W. Schultz. Among the non-Chicago friends who have made especially helpful suggestions are: Kenneth Arrow, Martin Bronfenbrenner, Albert Rees, and the editor.

My readers have been unanimous in urging reduction in over-all length, but virtually all of them also suggested "small additions." Of course, most of their suggestions would have improved the final product, if only I had had the skill to implement them. Lacking this, I have been compelled to omit discussion of many important ideas and persons. Also, I have not had space to relate the discussion of this paper to previous discussions of Chicago economics such as Warren J. Samuels (1976), Bronfenbrenner (1962), A. W. Coats (1963), Miller (1962), and Stigler (1962a). My only defense for these sins of omission is lack of space and inability to organize better.

1

over time, and because there has always been appreciable variation in the views of different individuals at any given moment. Nevertheless, I believe that within the economics profession there is a "subculture" characterized by a viewpoint that can be described as "Chicago." I attempt to describe the generic features of this outlook in Section III. Sections I, II and IV are attempts to relate the Chicago view to its history and institutional locus.

I. *The University of Chicago*

Both in the late 1930s and forty years later, the dominant characteristic of a Chicago economist's professional environment is the frequency and intensity with which he engages in substantive discussion about on-going research. Seminars, workshops, and discussion groups exist elsewhere, but at Chicago the number is very large,[2] and the discussion intense. While students attend them (dissertation students are required to present their research to a session of the relevant workshop), workshops are not student discussion groups. Rather they are places where faculty members of all ranks, and visitors, discuss current research and debate new results. The tone of workshop discussion is greatly influenced by the fact that senior faculty members attend, and participate actively. The senior faculty is not confined to the workshop's directors, but normally include others. Workshops, therefore, are places where issues in current research are debated by leaders of the field immediately concerned and of adjacent fields as well.

Workshop or seminar participation by junior faculty is quite common, for obvious reasons, and not distinctive of Chicago. Neither is the participation of a minority of senior faculty who maintain an active research interest. What is unusual

is the very high percentage of senior faculty members who maintain such interest. At Chicago diligent teaching, service in university administration, great distinction—even fame—in government service are at best partial substitutes for continuing research productivity. Therefore it is not surprising that, disproportionately, long-service Chicago economists are both research oriented and active workshop participants.[3]

The Chicago emphasis upon research promise and continuing performance as a criterion for faculty recruitment and preferment has not been confined to economics, but has been characteristic of the University. As Milton Friedman put it, with a credit to Edward Shils:

> The University of Chicago . . . was the first major university, with the possible exception of Johns Hopkins, that was not established primarily as either a finishing school for the children of the upper classes, or as a seminary for training clerics. From the very beginning, Chicago was established as a center of learning, devoted to advancing and transmitting knowledge. Harper's vision led to the assembling at the University of Chicago of an exceptionally able and dedicated faculty . . . and for our purposes, the critical feature is that they were dedicated not to training gentlemen for gentlemanly pursuits, not to spreading particular religious or ethical or social doctrines, but to the objective pursuit of knowledge . . . to science in the broadest sense. [1974, p. 9-10]

II. *Chicago Economics: Circa 1940*

Prewar Diversity

In retrospect, the Chicago economics of the 1930s may appear as the precursor of what it was to become in the 1960s and 1970s. But in prospect this did not seem the only possible course of development, or even the most likely. In the late 1930s, Chicago economics was a mixed

---

[2] Varying from year to year, the number was about 15 (circa 1980).

[3] This statement applies to the middle and late 1970s. It may have been less widely applicable in the 1930s.

bag: Frank Knight, Jacob Viner, Henry Simons and Lloyd Mints can be considered precursors of Friedman, George Stigler, Gary Becker and Robert Lucas. But there were also John U. Nef, Chester Wright, Simeon Leland, and H. A. Millis.

This second group, some of whom were men of great distinction, were hardly Chicago economists—or economists at all—in the current sense of the term.[4] They represented the institutionalist tradition in American economics which was still very strong in 1940. Their students constituted a substantial part of the graduate student body and could not have been sharply distinguished from their counterparts at other institutions.

There was yet a third group, small but highly influential; the quantitative economists or pioneer econometricians, Paul Douglas, Henry Schultz, and Oscar Lange. These men had a very important impact on the development of Chicago economics.

Douglas

Douglas was a man of tremendous energy with at least two separate careers, and an appropriate compartmentalization of mind. The views of one Douglas were those of a more or less conventional institutional economist. He wrote non-quantitative descriptions of wage earners' living and working conditions, freely blended with advocacy of various reforms to be achieved by appropriate governmental intervention in economic activity. Like others of this genre, Douglas was a participant in, as well as an analyst of, the reform process. In his late forties he abandoned academic life for a political career.[5]

A second Douglas was a pioneer of quantitative labor economics, making

measurements of labor supply, of the cost of living, of real wage rates and, most of all, initiating the estimation of production functions (Albert Rees, 1979; Paul A. Samuelson, 1979). This Douglas exemplified the enthusiasm of his generation for making the study of society scientific through quantification.

While Douglas was anxious to give theoretical interpretation to his statistical calculations, he was not fully aware of, or greatly concerned with, the analytical problems that such interpretation involved. Attempts to interpret the properties of estimated production functions have inspired major developments in econometric technique, but Douglas took little part in the technical development that stemmed from his research.

The tradition of empirical labor economics at Chicago that Douglas founded was carried on for over 30 years by one of his research assistants, H. Gregg Lewis. Lewis' many students have transformed the subject into a major field of applied quantitative research. Comparison of their (and Lewis') style of research with that of Douglas, provides an excellent illustration of what is permanent, and what has changed, in Chicago economics during the past half century.

Schultz

In a sense, Henry Schultz' work, as exemplified by his book *The Theory and Measurement of Demand,* (1938) was the counterpart to Douglas' studies of real wages and production functions. But Schultz' interest in methodology was far stronger than Douglas', and he worked hard to introduce recent developments in mathematical economics to Chicago students, as well as to train them in the use of multiple regression techniques.

His attempts at measurement met with a mixed reception from his colleagues. Both Douglas and Viner were sympathetic, but Knight was hostile and derisive.

---

[4] I shall not speak further of these men, because they had little impact upon or interest in the theoretical and ideological skirmishes of their colleagues.

[5] Douglas' non-academic career is described in his memoirs (1972).

Knight's opposition was based partly on a deep philosophical aversion to the quantification of economics, but may also have reflected annoyance with Schultz' intellectual style.

Like many of the early protagonists of mathematical methods in the social sciences, Schultz had an uncertain command of a limited mathematical technique at which, I was told by Lange, he worked very hard; his approach to economic theory was very formal. Knight's bent was precisely the opposite: indifferent to formal demonstration, he would confront theoretical arguments with counter examples, show inconsistencies—when possible, absurdities—in their assumptions, and stress the inadequacy of theoretical abstractions to cope with complex real-world phenomena. Knight was a man of insight and reflection, above all a critic. Schultz was a patient, meticulous and orderly research worker who "reported findings."

Whatever the cause, Schultz' attempts to disseminate mathematical economics and econometrics at Chicago had to overcome Knight's formidable opposition. Whether this opposition was responsible for the adverse opinion of Schultz held by some Chicago students (of the middle and late 1930s) is hard to say: Knight was not one to hide his views, and his opinions carried weight. Two of the students not favorably impressed by Schultz were Friedman and Stigler; they might have influenced others. However, there were other good students (for example, Martin Bronfenbrenner and Jacob Mosak) who always spoke highly of Schultz as did Lange himself.[6]

Lange

The appointment of Oscar Lange as assistant professor in 1938, met several departmental needs. Lange was an up-to-

the-minute young theorist, in the vanguard of the Keynesian Revolution who had acquired a considerable reputation as a mathematical economist as a result of studies in the theory of capital and in utility theory. His work on the use of the price system to allocate resources in a socialist economy was widely considered to be a definitive answer to the Mises-Hayek attack on the economic efficiency of socialism, and gave the Chicago department a leading participant in this debate. For the time, he had considerable expertise in mathematical statistics and econometrics and was expected to supplement Schultz in this area.

When Lange was appointed, he was considered a young man of promise. But within six months of his arrival, the death of Schultz in an automobile accident made Lange the senior mathematical economist-econometrician in the department. Lange had a fully developed perspective of economics which constituted a distinct alternative to the "Chicago View." The precise details are no longer important, but the essential points can be readily inferred from *Price Flexibility and Employment* (1944) the major work of his Chicago years, and from his 1945 article on methodology. His 1944 volume was intended as a challenge to the Chicago view of general equilibrium theory; and Friedman's highly critical review (1946) was a response.

Lange's very substantial impact on Chicago resulted from a coincidence of person and situation. At the outbreak of World War II, Chicago was in danger of losing its position as a leading center of economic research. Two of its major figures, Douglas and Schultz, had departed. Knight had lost interest in economics[7] and, in any event, had ceased research in economic theory. Even more, apart from Lange, there was no one at Chicago

[6] The statements in this paragraph are based on personal conversations.

[7] Personal conversation with Aaron Director.

who was a recognized leader of "recent developments in economic theory."

Lange's influence was due not only to his professional attainments, but also to his great personal charm and broad intellectual interests. In a department where conflicts of very strong personalities exacerbated intellectual differences, Lange's tact and disarming manner enabled him to remain *persona grata* to all. These same qualities made his presence a great asset in attracting other young economists to Chicago and made him an extremely attractive job candidate at any institution desiring to improve its economics department—and able to tolerate his outspoken socialist views.

This popularity extended beyond his colleagues to the graduate student body.[8] Like Viner's, his lectures were highly organized, but students were spared the ever-present threat of humiliation for errors of utterance or of inappropriate silence that was part of the Vinerian pedagogy (Bronfenbrenner, 1938). As Don Patinkin recalls, Lange's verbal reflexes were slow so that he would at times defer answering questions until the next class meeting in order to reflect on the matter; students found this very reassuring.

Almost invariably Lange was patient with student questions or arguments, regardless of their quality, a trait that was, and still is, very scarce on the Chicago scene. And he was polite, almost deferential, to his colleagues in discussion. In part this was simply good manners, but it also reflected the genuine respect he had for

them, especially for Knight and Viner.[9] However, this respect did not prevent him from insisting on the appointment of up-to-date theorists who were very different from those currently in the department. He was especially eager to get Abba P. Lerner but, failing to persuade his colleagues, he welcomed the appointment of Jacob Marschak and looked to him for help in making further appointments.[10]

Whether Lange's presence would have materially altered the course of departmental appointments during the rebuilding process after 1945 is moot. But it is not absurd to suppose that it might have done so, in which case the Chicago School might have died or, more likely, taken root elsewhere.

Knight, Viner, Simons, and Students

That what is now called Chicago economics could have been transplanted in the mid-1940s, is not implausible.[11] Though the ideas proved hardy, their roots in Chicago were quite shallow. Before the arrival of Knight and his student Simons, it would have been hard to identify a particular intellectual style among Chicago Ph.D.'s. Even in the 1930s, Chicago students were not readily identifiable by their view of economic analysis or of economic policy. Among graduate students or young instructors of my student

[9] This respect was tempered by his chagrin at their unwillingness to keep abreast of modern economic theory. His hero, among older economists still active, was Schumpeter.

[10] As of 1940–42, Lange often spoke to his intimates about the kind of Economics Department he would like to have, either at Chicago or elsewhere.

[11] An obvious candidate institution would have been Columbia. The Columbia–National Bureau nexus had a strong attraction for quantitatively oriented Chicago economists. Stigler was a Columbia Professor for ten years (1947–57); Becker for twelve (1958–70); Jacob Mincer remains at Columbia, etc. The National Bureau connection is reflected in the long affiliation of Becker, Friedman, Stigler and many other Chicagoans, as well as in the close personal relations of Friedman, Stigler, and Wallis with Arthur Burns who was Friedman's undergraduate teacher and long-time admirer.

[8] As reflected in an anonymous article (Bronfenbrenner, 1938) and in the recollections of Don Patinkin (1981, pp. 8–9, 25–26). The article was unsigned, but many of us students suspected the author to be Martin Bronfenbrenner. Bronfenbrenner has kindly agreed to acknowledge authorship, but desires that it be noted that he no longer holds all of the views there expressed. Patinkin's description of Lange as teacher, so far as it goes, agrees with my recollections. What is missing is Lange's impish sense of humor, and rare ability to project euphoria.

years at Chicago (1939–41), some (e.g., Yale Brozen, D. Gale Johnson, H. Gregg Lewis) were Chicago-style economists; others (such as G. L. Bach, Arthur Bloomfield, A. G. Hart, C. E. Lindblom, Jacob Mosak, David Rockefeller) would not usually be thought of as examples of the Chicago genre.

As of 1940, the Chicago "tradition" was of recent origin, and its spokesmen quite discordant. Knight's ideas were highly idiosyncratic and his expository style made few concessions to listeners or readers. Among the Chicago graduate student body he had many admirers, but only a few students. Fortunately, some of these were extremely able; notably, Friedman, Stigler and Allen Wallis.

The contributions to economic thought with which Knight is most readily identified (theory of the firm, uncertainty and profit, capital theory, social cost, etc.) are only tangentially related to the Chicago tradition. His contribution to the Chicago tradition was that of sage and oracle, rather than initiator of research programs. It was mainly through his personal impact on a few influential students that Knight affected the subsequent course of Chicago economics.

This is not to minimize either Knight's originality or his wide influence. It is to say that the impact of his ideas was widely diffused and not concentrated at Chicago. Like the profession at large, Knight's students absorbed his ideas, but did not use them as points of departure for their own work. Knight contributed to the formation of their minds, but did not influence the direction of their research, or participate in it.[12]

This limitation of Knight's influence was due largely to his sceptical view of empirical social science—including economics—and of its possible application to the improvement of public policy. He could—and did—vigorously support Henry Simons' retention in the Economics Department against strong opposition,[13] but it is doubtful that he could have approved *A Positive Program for Laissez Faire* (1934), or any other of Simons' policy-oriented tracts.

After 1945, if not earlier, Knight's outspoken disdain for empirical, especially quantitative, research set him completely apart from the main body of Chicago economists—including his own former students.[14] But the intellectual breach did not destroy the strong personal attachments. Knight had an affection for his protegés that he did not have for colleagues nearer his own age. Hostile to Douglas and Henry Schultz, his relations with Viner were probably "correct," but there is little evidence of cordiality. What relations they had must at times have been strained by Knight's refusal to cover the fact of disagreement with a fig leaf of politeness.[15] Cause and effect aside, Knight and Viner were not able to co-ordinate their views on research or departmental appointments; so far as I am aware they never tried to do so.

In contrast, the personal affection and mutual esteem in which Knight and his protegés held one another facilitated the collaborative efforts of the latter. The informal, but very effective, promotional aspect of the Chicago School sprang from the affinity group of Knight's students and

---

[12] Stigler's dissertation in the history of economic thought (1941), written under Knight's supervision might constitute an exception to this statement. However, Stigler's research in areas other than *Dogmengeschicte* is not particularly Knightian.

[13] Particularly from Douglas. My knowledge of this episode is derived from George Stigler.

[14] Of course, not all Chicago economists have become quantitatively oriented. Although more temperate in statement, Ronald Coase's views on quantification in economics are far closer to Knight's than to those of (say) Stigler.

[15] I can recall that Knight sold our theory class reprints of both Viner's "Cost Curves and Supply Curves" (1931) and of Roy F. Harrod (1934). He urged us to read the latter carefully because "it corrected all the errors" in Viner's article.

protegés that formed in the middle 1930s. The principal members of this group were Milton and Rose Director Friedman, George Stigler, Allen Wallis, Aaron Director and Henry Simons.[16]

The "baton passer" of the initial Chicago group, therefore, was Knight rather than Viner. There is irony in this fact: Viner's intellectual style was far closer than Knight's to that of the present-day Chicago economist. In addition to his historical scholarship, Viner was a careful, empirically oriented—though essentially non-quantitative—student of international trade and related questions of money and finance. He could, and did, establish research programs and enlist graduate students to participate in their development; he supervised far more doctoral dissertations than Knight[17] and was a much better classroom teacher.

But Viner's students never constituted a club. Dispersed in time and intellectual interest (e.g., T. O. Yntema, Jacob Mosak, V. F. Coe, Arthur Bloomfield and, at Princeton, Gary Becker) they had little in common other than their contact with Viner. Apparently Viner did not actively seek to keep his students near him, as Knight did, and his extensive involvement in governmental affairs (both in Washington and abroad) competed with whatever desire he might have had to become a focal point of intellectual activity. Whatever the explanation, the critical mass— in quality and numbers—necessary for the intergenerational transmission of an intellectual style formed around Knight rather

than Viner.[18] However much they respected Viner, the "Knight affinity group" was not personally close to him, and he was apparently not in sympathy with its activities or its ideology.[19]

As mentioned, the methodological views of the Knight affinity group were more nearly Viner's than Knight's, but far more quantitatively oriented than would have suited either.[20] In addition to this dif-

---

[16] In preparing this essay, I have been struck by the many strong expressions of intellectual indebtedness both of Chicago economists and legal scholars (such as Edward Levi and Robert Bork) to Aaron Director. Despite Stigler's repeated admonitions about the difficulty of imputing "influence," Director appears to have exercised a great deal of influence upon the principal figures in Chicago economics from the 1930s to the present.

[17] Stigler tells me that his own dissertation is one of the only two that Knight ever supervised to completion.

[18] By the middle forties, when Douglas returned from the war, he found "The university I had loved so much seemed to be a different place. Schultz was dead, Viner was gone, Knight was now openly hostile, and his disciples seemed to be everywhere." Douglas (1972, p. 128). Hyperbole aside, it is clear that Douglas perceived a change of intellectual climate in the community of Chicago economists from 1939–40 to 1945–46.

[19] I quote a letter from Viner to Patinkin, reprinted in Patinkin:

It was not until after I left Chicago in 1946 that I began to hear rumors about a 'Chicago School' which was engaged in organized battle for laissez faire and the 'quantity theory of money' and against 'imperfect competition' theorizing and 'Keynesianism.' I remained sceptical about this until I attended a conference sponsored by University of Chicago professors in 1951. The invited participants were a varied lot of academics, bureaucrats, businessmen, etc., but the program for discussion, the selection of chairmen, and everything about the conference except the unscheduled statements and protests from individual participants were so patently rigidly structured, so loaded, that I got more amusement from the conference than from any other I ever attended. Even the source of the financing of the Conference, as I found out later, was ideologically loaded. There is a published account of the preceedings of the Conference, but it does not include the program, etc. as presented to the participants to direct their discussion. From then on, I was willing to consider the existence of a 'Chicago School' (but one not confined to the economics department and not embracing all of the department) and that this 'School' had been in operation, and had won many able disciples, for years before I left Chicago. But at no time was I consciously a member of it, and it is my vague impression that if there was such a school it did not regard me as a member, or at least as a loyal and qualified member. In any case, I am not well-informed about the past or the present of such a 'school,' and therefore I have had nothing to contribute to the recent inquirers about the intellectual history of this putative 'school.' (1981, p. 266).

[20] Viner's attitude toward quantitative methods was tolerant, but reserved; see Viner (1958, pp. 41–49). Knight's view is epitomized by his remark, "The saying . . . 'where you cannot measure, your knowledge is meagre and unsatisfactory,' . . . very largely means in practice, If you cannot measure, measure anyhow!" Knight (1960, p. 166, fn. 18).

ference in research bent, the younger members of the group (Friedman, Stigler, and Wallis), were extremely good expositors and very effective advocates, qualities which Knight did not share. Their skill and energy, coupled with Knight's prestigious support, made them an effective and cohesive group—at the University of Chicago and elsewhere—in promoting their common ideas.

The older members of the group (Lloyd Mints, Aaron Director and Henry Simons), were also effective promoters of the group's ideas. Director was (and is) an extremely persuasive advocate of ideas and an extraordinarily effective intellectual catalyst. Henry Simons (who died in 1946 at the age of 47) is best known for a series of essays of which "A Positive Program for Laissez-Faire" (Simons, 1948) is the most famous. His work on personal income taxation (1938) is also important, but not central to the development of Chicago ideas. However, his teaching of Economics 201 (and 209) and his Syllabus for these courses, may have made an even greater contribution to the development of Chicago economics than his published writings.

The Training Program

To understand this contribution, I must briefly describe certain features of the Chicago Ph.D. program in Economics. At least since the early 1930s, all Ph.D. students have been required *(inter alia)* to pass two examinations in economic theory; one in price theory, one in monetary economics. These examinations have always been difficult, and the failure rate substantial. As the admissions policy of the Department has traditionally been lenient (i.e., give students of uncertain promise a chance), these examinations have functioned as a screening device for admission to candidacy for the Ph.D. The exam-takers, therefore, have always included a substantial number of uncertain and appre-

hensive students as well as embryonic winners of the Clark medal.

While any registered student may attempt the examinations, the normal procedure is to take the course sequences in price and monetary theory and then to prepare intensively for the examinations, usually as part of a small group of fellow students. The beginning course in the graduate price theory sequence, Economics 301, has traditionally been considered an essential part of the preparation.

Course 301, however, is itself difficult and not easily passed without substantial previous training. Because of gradual improvement in undergraduate training in economics and even more in mathematics during the past decade or two, beginning graduate students are now much better prepared than in Simons' time, and can usually start with 301. But, in the 1930s and early 1940s, upper-division undergraduates, Masters' candidates and inadequately prepared doctoral students, flocked to Simons' 201 (or 209, a more technical version of 201 for undergraduate majors in economics) to learn the rudiments of price theory together with Simons' view of how the economy functioned. As Patinkin puts it, "we all emerged from his classroom 'simonized' to some extent or other" (1981, p. 5).

For those who were successful, determined, or both, 201 or 209 was the prelude to 301, which Simons rarely if ever taught. The teaching of 301 has always been the prerogative of the department's "big guns" and over the years has been identified successively with Viner, Friedman, and Becker. Different though these economists have been in the foci of their research interests, they have had a certain commonality of pedagogical style that has given a continuing character to 301 and to the training program as a whole.

The common element is a combination of well organized presentation, seriousness of purpose, and strictness of standards. Course 301 has always been tough, and its teachers have been stern taskmasters. In class, inappropriate questions or erroneous answers are exposed without concern for the feelings of the inept offender. As already suggested, Viner was well-known for his lack of mercy.[21] While Friedman and Becker have not cultivated quite the same classroom manner as Viner, it is nevertheless understood that in their classes one hazards his utility level on his classroom performance.[22]

Together with preparation for the qualifying examinations, the Ph.D. theory courses constitute an acculturation process, normally lasting one to two years, whose end result is an economist with the Chicago style of thought. Part of a student cohort, in the training process the trainee makes friends and establishes a professional reputation that exerts a powerful influence on his subsequent career.

This, of course, often happens in professional training programs. What distinguishes the Chicago economics program from others is its power to imbue its matriculants with a distinctive approach to their discipline. I conjecture that this power is rooted in its rigid standards for a doctorate, applied both to the qualifying examinations and to the dissertation, and in the correlatively high failure rate. To obtain a Chicago Ph.D. one must learn to do certain specific and fairly difficult

things quite well, and the learning process inculcates distinctive habits of thought.

As a result of this training process, for over forty years the Chicago-trained applied economist working in such fields as Labor Economics, Public Finance, International Trade, Industrial Organization, Economic History or Economic Development has been well grounded in economic theory and disposed to apply it vigorously. For a long time this set him sharply apart from most other degree holders working in the same fields, the difference in training being much more noticeable among economists of average ability, or less, than among the more able. However, in the last decade or so, improvement in the general level of theoretical training among applied economists, due in part to the influence of Chicago-trained faculty teaching in other institutions, may have eroded the comparative advantage of a Chicago Ph.D.

The Transition: 1940–1946

Before describing the stylized habits of thought of Chicago economists—the Chicago View—let me give a brief summary of events to 1946: (1) In the 1930s the Chicago Economics Department contained a diverse group of individuals with differing ideas as to the proper course for the discipline in general and the Department in particular. (2) In the early to middle thirties,[23] a small group of Knight's students (including Simons, Director, and Mints) began to function in a loosely coordinated fashion to advance their common

[21] In fairness to Viner's memory, I should note that it was also known in my student days that he was very generous, both financially and in other ways, to needy students. I also recall Lange telling me, on several occasions, of Viner's successful efforts to help him rescue friends and political associates from Europe in 1939 and 1940.

[22] It is interesting to note that Viner's teacher, F. W. Taussig, apparently had much the same teaching style as Viner. This is recounted in some detail by Douglas (1972), pp. 33–35. Douglas survived his exposure to this pedagogy, and he and Taussig "became fast friends for the rest of his (Taussig's) life." Friedman was Viner's student and Becker was a student both of Viner (as a Princeton undergraduate) and of Friedman. So the sub-culture of 301 may have very long roots.

[23] The preface to Knight's *The Ethics of Competition* is suggestive of the timing. Dated March 1, 1935, it states that "the idea of publishing a collection of Knight's articles suggested itself to a small group who had attended a dinner on the occasion of Professor Knight's forty-ninth birthday, November 7, 1934, but not until all arrangements had been made and the selection of the contents completed was Professor Knight informed of the project." The signers were Milton Friedman, Homer Jones, George Stigler and Allen Wallis.

ideas. Many of these ideas were inspired by Knight, though he did not consistently espouse them. (3) In 1938–39, the "old" Chicago department experienced three shocks that effectively transformed it: the arrival of the Cowles Commission in October 1939; the death of Henry Schultz in November 1938; and the election of Paul Douglas to public office—Alderman—in November 1939 (implying substantial withdrawal from departmental affairs). These events, together with a pre-existing concern with failure to keep up with new developments in theory, generated pressure for rebuilding the department. (4) It was expected that Oscar Lange would play a leading role in the rebuilding process, and he did so during 1940–45. However, in 1945, he left academic life for a political career in Poland. His views on departmental appointments were generally similar to those of Marschak, Tjalling Koopmans and other members of the Cowles Commission who more or less succeeded to his role in departmental affairs. (5) The rebuilding process was delayed by World War II, at the end of which Viner left to go to Princeton. The institutionalist wing of the department was greatly reduced by the retirement of Millis (in 1940) and the departure of Leland for Northwestern in 1946. (6) During the war years, T. W. Schultz joined the department, and soon became its Chairman. In this role he provided departmental leadership that had long been missing. As leader, he mediated among contending factions while pursuing his own research programs.

By 1944, a fairly intense struggle was underway between Knight and his former students on one side, and the Cowles Commission and its adherents on the other. The struggle had several facets: research methodology; political ideology, and faculty appointments. It continued for almost 10 years, being terminated only with the departure of the Cowles Commission for Yale in 1953. The battle engendered a great deal of bitterness which still persists, though undoubtedly it is diminishing in intensity.

In retrospect, and quite likely in prospect (as of 1945), the key to the development and eventual dominance of the "Chicago View" was to unite Friedman, Stigler and Wallis on the Chicago faculty. This took 13 years to accomplish: Stigler was appointed to the Walgreen Professorship in the Graduate School of Business with a joint appointment in the Economics Department, in 1958; the other two were appointed in 1946—Wallis to the Business School, where he became Dean in 1955, and Friedman to the Economics Department.[24]

Friedman swiftly took over the intellectual leadership of one faction of the Department and energetically attacked the views and proposals of the others. His vigor in debate and the content of his arguments set the tone and public image of Chicago economics for at least a quarter century. The details of the ensuing intramural struggle would make interesting reading, but I have neither space nor first-hand knowledge of this episode of intellectual-institutional history. Accordingly, I interrupt the narrative at this point to attempt a description of the Chicago View. The thread of the narrative is resumed, briefly, in Section IV.

III. *The Chicago View*

Chicago economics has two facets: positive and normative. In my opinion it is the former that dominates, but recognition of the interrelation is essential. For expository convenience, I shall discuss each facet separately.

[24] The Economics Department had approved an offer to Stigler in 1946, but due to an unsatisfactory interview (with Stigler), the President of the University, Ernest Colwell, refused to approve it. The position was then offered to Friedman who (evidently) had better luck with the University Administration. My source for this anecdote is George Stigler.

Reder: Chicago Economics   11

Positive Economics

(a) Tight Prior Equilibrium (TP)

In essence the Chicago View, or what I term "Tight Prior Equilibrium" theory (TP), is rooted in the hypothesis that decision makers so allocate the resources under their control that there is no alternative allocation such that any one decision maker could have his expected utility increased without a reduction occurring in the expected utility of at least one other decision maker.

For Chicago and non-Chicago economists alike, this is a definition of Pareto optimality, which may or may not be associated with a model that yields particular testable hypotheses, depending upon whether certain further assumptions are made. Chicago economists typically make these assumptions while others often refuse to do so. For problems whose analysis does not require these assumptions—"pure theory"—I do not consider that there are any generic differences between Chicago (TP) and non-Chicago (DP—diffuse prior equilibrium) theorists.

The further assumptions may be summarized as follows: (1) *most* individual transactors treat the prices of all goods and services that they buy or sell, as independent of the quantities that they transact; (2) the prices at which individuals *currently agree* to transact are market clearing prices that are consistent with optimization by all decision makers; (3) information bearing on prices and qualities of all things bought and sold, present and future, is acquired in the quantity that makes its marginal cost equal to its price; i.e., information is treated like any other commodity;[25] (4) neither monopoly nor

governmental action (through taxation or otherwise) affects relative prices or quantities sufficiently to prevent either marginal products or compensation of identical resources from being approximately equal in all uses.[26]

None of the above assumptions is—or ever was—believed to hold exactly, but only as a "first approximation." That is, it is recognized that (a) apart from those traded on organized exchanges, commodities may be heterogeneous in various respects; (b) tastes, techniques and resources are all affected by random disturbances, as is information concerning prices and characteristics of goods and services, leading to transitory violations of assumptions (2) and (3); (c) relative to the total quantity traded, the quantity offered by any one transactor is subject to random variations, with consequent transitory violations of assumptions (1) and (4).

In the Chicago view, however, these random disturbances are such that it is possible to devise a stochastic analogue of the exact (non-stochastic) competitive general equilibrium model that has the following property: if for all commodities, expected price and expected quantity are treated as proxies for the corresponding

---

[25] This is the only one of the four assumptions about which I anticipate (some) disagreement. The assumption is not usually made explicit, though it is very often required for the validity of an argument. Without this assumption, there is no relation be-tween individual optimization and overall economic efficiency. However, the assumption is neither unambiguous, nor universally acceptable when clarified (see p. 23).

[26] It is to be emphasized that the goods and services mentioned in this paragraph are "ordinary" market commodities. They do not include elements of the legal system, political institutions, property rights, etc. as elements of choice; these are considered as data. In the past decade, one group of Chicago economists (see below, p. 26) has come to consider the political economy, rather than the economy, as the proper object of analysis and to apply economic theory (TP) to the task. But this is a relatively new development, even at Chicago, and there is considerable diversity of opinion among Chicago economists as to its propriety.

In this section of the paper (i.e., the part devoted to Positive Economics) Pareto optimality refers only to social choices defined over "ordinary" commodities, the definition usually adopted in discussion of the welfare gains from exchange.

price and quantity in the exact model, all propositions concerning partial derivatives of prices with respect to quantities (and of quantities with respect to prices) in the exact model will hold for the stochastic model as well, provided that we substitute "expected price" and "expected quantity" for "price" and "quantity," respectively.

Subject to exceptions noted below, TP further maintains that these propositions concerning partial derivatives are the *only* valid propositions of economic theory. This need not imply a belief that economic theory is a powerful tool for explaining price-quantity behavior; its power will vary with the character of the disturbances. But it does imply belief that there are no stable empirical relationships among prices, quantities and disturbances other than those with the aforementioned analogues in the exact general equilibrium model.

Mutual independence of all disturbances, and of each disturbance with respect to every expected price and expected quantity, would be sufficient to satisfy the requirements of TP. But such an assumption is not necessary; any of a wide variety of patterns of offsetting covariations would also suffice. So far as I am aware, no investigation has ever been made of the restrictions on the joint distribution of disturbances necessary for the validity of TP, and this is not the place to begin.[27]

Moreover, mutual independence of disturbances can be assumed to hold only under stationary (i.e., long run) conditions. At any given moment, the effect of long-term contracts or of durable assets acquired in the past exercises an influence on present behavior implying *(inter alia)* that current demand and supply sched-

ules are affected by past errors, including imperfect forecasts.

This is, I believe, generally accepted and is no more than recognition of the lagging effect of short-run disturbances, in the general spirit of Book V of Marshall's *Principles*. However, in applied work, adherents of TP have a strong tendency to assume that, in the absence of sufficient evidence to the contrary, one may treat observed prices and quantities as good approximations to their long-run competitive equilibrium values. Call this the "good approximation assumption."

This assumption enables an investigator to abstract from the effects of transitory market imperfections resulting in misallocation or underutilization of resources, etc. and to treat observed prices of inputs as measures of the opportunity cost of the imputed output associated with their use. Thus observed returns to similar resources in alternative uses may be compared; marginal productivities in different uses can be estimated from observed prices and so on, making it possible to use studies referring to different times and places as providing mutual confirmation, or for their inconsistency to signal researchable anomalies; and to treat findings in seemingly unrelated fields as means of estimating parameters not otherwise measurable.

Hard use of the good approximation assumption is a hallmark of Chicago applied research; but the assumption is not tested directly. Instead of investigating the descriptive accuracy of this assumption, or the precise extent of the resource misallocations caused by its failure to hold exactly[28] the Chicago style is to treat it

---

[27] Some years ago, I discussed this subject (1962, pp. 257–310). I consider this discussion inadequate and outdated, but I am not aware of any attempts to improve upon it.

[28] An important exception to this statement is Harberger's measurements of output loss from resource misallocation caused by monopolistic behavior (1954). Harberger found these losses to be small and the work was therefore accepted (at Chicago). But suppose the losses had been "large" (say, 25 per of potential GNP), would this have led to an abandonment of TP? My conjecture is negative; the measurement would have been attacked, both substantively

as a maintained hypothesis and apply it, using the resulting research findings as a test of TP.[29]

As the term TP, and even its concept, may appear unfamiliar in this context, let me explicate: as I perceive them, Chicago economists tend strongly to appraise their own research and that of others by a standard which requires *(inter alia)* that the findings of empirical research be consistent with the implications of standard price theory (as described above). Any apparent inconsistency of empirical findings with implications of the theory, or report of behavior not implied by the theory, is interpreted as anomalous and requiring one of the following actions: (i) re-examination of the data to reverse the anomalous finding; (ii) redefinition and/or augmentation of the variables in the model, particularly the permissible objects of choice and the resource constraints; (iii) alteration of the theory to accommodate behavior inconsistent with the postulates of rationality (constrained optimization) by one or more decision makers (resource

owners); (iv) placing the finding on the research agenda as a researchable anomaly.

TP implies shunning (iii): i.e., the subject matter of the tight prior is the adequacy of this approach to theory as an explanation of whatever behavior is considered as economic. It is not appropriate to characterize this prior as "dogmatic," and to suggest that it implies placing no credence in the possibility that (iii) is appropriate. It suffices to say that TP adherents—with variation among individuals—focus attention upon (i) and (ii) and, failing a quick resolution of the anomaly, move to (iv) but pay little attention to (iii). By contrast, DP adherents consider all possibilities, varying research strategy with circumstances, but showing no strong pre-disposition to neglect (iii).

(b) Problems of the Short-Run

An important class of situations in which it is difficult to maintain the good approximation assumption is where existing stocks of assets and/or preexisting contracts are non-optimal. If prices were completely flexible (i.e., differing from long-run equilibrium values only to the extent implied by transitory disturbances) then, subject to the *quantity* constraints created by past outlays and contractual commitments, all transactors would optimize at current prices and all markets would clear. However, as Chicago economists have always recognized, prices (especially wage rates) are sticky in the short-run. Thus there is a long-standing problem of reconciling the fact of price stickiness with the maintained hypothesis of continuous optimization.

While the problem is by no means solved, some progress on it has been made since the early 1960s. Stigler's work on search (1961, 1962b), and Becker's on the allocation of time (1965) have shown that expected utility maximization does not always lead to transacting at the lowest

---

and methodologically, and research would have proceeded on the assumption that the measurements were incorrect.

In my view, the attempt to measure "Harbergerian" triangles is alien to the spirit of TP because TP does not address the question of whether the deadweight losses attributable to departures from competition are "large" or "small." It is concerned only with whether such departures (i) invalidate propositions of comparative statics that assume competition or (ii) generate stable price-quantity relationships that are not deducible from TP.

While I believe TP to be the "true Chicago line," I fear that a good deal of Chicago discussion on the "unimportance of monopoly" has been fuzzy and interpretable either as a statement about the magnitude of welfare loss caused by monopoly or as a statement about the fraction of GNP produced in noncompetitive industries. Score this as a mark against my characterization of Chicago economics as a development of the implications of TP.

[29] For example: in applications of human capital theory, one does not usually measure the marginal productivity of labor directly, but assumes it to be equal to the relevant wage rate at each moment and estimates investment in training from the earnings profile.

quoted price for given quantity and quality. More important, recognition of the fact of *jointly owned* specific capital (Becker, 1964) has created awareness of the importance of long-term explicit and implicit contracts (especially the latter) that govern the distribution of the joint return over time. Although such contracts may relate wages and product prices to various indicia of currently observable economic conditions, the implied prices are independent of whether, temporarily, there may be better current alternative but unexploited opportunities for transacting.

While implicit contracts can be broken, it is clear that often it is efficient to sacrifice transitory gains (from transacting on better terms than the contract provides) in order to maintain a contractual relationship.[30] Thus, in the short run, transaction prices that are governed by contracts will follow the implicit and explicit terms of these contracts, possibly deviating substantially from what a continuously clearing spot market would imply.

If there is a spot market, concurrent with the contract market, the time path of the spot price may be quite different from that of the contract price. Moreover, the existence of contractual commitments will usually shift both the (short-run) supply and demand functions for the spot market, possibly making the (spot) market thin or even eliminating it altogether.[31]

The time path of prices under a long term contract is "quasi-determined" by the agreed (or understood) formula embedded in the contract.[32] TP implies that,

as of the moment of negotiation, the expected costs and returns to a long-term contract will satisfy the usual conditions of dynamic optimization by all transactors. But economic theory says very little about the day-to-day movements of prices and quantities during the life of the contract, beyond insisting that, *at every moment,* parties either observe or violate contracts as present expected value maximization (including the value of reputation) dictates. In this context, TP can accommodate a wide variety of behavior provided it can be rationalized as expected value maximazation; when the value of reputation is included in the maximand this requirement is not hard to satisfy. However, TP resists explanations of intertemporal price movements that are based solely on institutional or ethical imperatives such as John R. Hicks' concept of "fix-price."

In brief, the short-run time series behavior of prices and quantities has long been on the research agenda of TP adherents and others as well. Despite some theoretical progress cited above and some empirical investigations (notably Stigler and James Kindahl, 1970), attention to the problem(s) has been desultory and there is no consensus among Chicago economists as to how to apply economic theory when explaining intertemporal price-quantity behavior in markets where long-term contracts are important.[33] But, as al-

---

[30] This is discussed at length in Arthur Okun (1981), who felicitously designates behavior under long-term implicit contracts as resulting from an "invisible handshake."

[31] Dennis Carlton (1979) provides an excellent discussion of the relation of spot and contract prices where trading takes place simultaneously at both prices.

[32] It is essential to note that pricing formulae that (may be) inconsistent with continuous market clear-

ing must be—and are—accompanied by implicit rationing procedures that establish quantity conditioned delivery priorities. Such rationing procedures are an essential part of long-term contracts; indeed, desire to insure delivery is a primary reason for the existence of such contracts.

[33] I would add that, circa 1980, active research in this problem area is largely concentrated among labor economists analyzing career earning profiles, retirement dates, layoff patterns, etc. of workers with term attachments to single employers. Prominent examples of this type of research are James J. Heckman (1976), Edward P. Lazear (1979) and Sherwin Rosen (1976). While I believe that the findings of this body of research will fertilize research in the behavior of product prices (and quantities), this has not yet happened.

ready noted, there is continuing resistance to institutional explanations that are incompatible with the assumption of optimization as of the moment of decision making.

(c) Monopoly, Market Failure and Government Intervention

A major difference arises between TP and its logical complement, diffuse prior equilibrium (DP), from the manner in which they interpret and use empirical evidence bearing on price-quantity relations. TP theorists are far less willing than others to accept reports of irrational or inefficient behavior at face value, including money illusion, and typically seek to discredit or reinterpret such reports so as to protect the basic theory.

As with irrational behavior, Chicago concedes that monopoly is possible but contends that its presence is much more often alleged than confirmed, and receives reports of its appearance with considerable scepticism. When alleged monopolies are genuine, they are usually transitory, with freedom of entry working to eliminate their influence on prices and quantities within a fairly short time period. Where reports of monopoly are substantiated (by finding that observed behavior has been incompatible with rationality, assuming competition) the standard monopoly model or an appropriate alternative model involving small numbers of transactors is applied, but only to the particular market where the monopoly has been found. The effect of monopoly in one market (or a small set of inter-related markets) on price-quantity relations in other markets is assumed to be captured by the disturbance terms in the behavioral equations of the other markets, and not to affect relations among their expected quantities and expected prices: i.e., assumption (4) is assumed to hold. Normatively, Chicago economics says monopoly is bad; positively, it says

it is of infrequent occurrence and limited impact.[34]

As I interpret it, the TP view is that most of what appears to be monopoly is ephemeral, being eliminated by free entry. In addition, I interpret the TP view of the economy as embracing a large number of distinct products each of which is associated with a market that could be either competitive or otherwise. It also assumes a number of productive agents (factors), each with its own market, but far fewer than the number of product markets.

My interpretation of the TP view is that it supposes that prices in some subset of the product markets may be set monopolistically, but that this does not appreciably affect equilibrium prices in the factor markets which are (approximately) competitive.[35] Implicitly, the secondary importance ascribed to long-run monopoly reflects an (alleged) absence of interaction between deviations of equilibrium prices and quantities from competitive levels in any single product market, or combination of product markets, and equilibrium prices in the factor markets. Put differently, long-run monopoly is not important enough to invalidate the contention that prices of factors are good approximations to the opportunity cost of using them.[36]

---

[34] Nevertheless, there is a substantial literature of Chicago contributions to the analysis of non-perfect competition stemming from Stigler's work, summarized in 1968. Chicago has not failed to work on imperfectly competitive markets; but it has refused to treat the economy-wide allocation of resources as the outcome of interaction among imperfect competitors.

[35] An important qualification to this statement might be caused by the effect of unions on wages. However, there is no general agreement at Chicago, or elsewhere, as to how large this effect might be. In principle, strong unionism could require alteration of the assumptions of TP, but it has not done so thus far.

[36] While I believe the above description of the TP view of monopoly to be accurate in substance, I must acknowledge that it is a construction I have placed upon a variety of remarks, oral and written, made by Chicago economists.

Market failure or more generally failure of individual decision makers to achieve a Pareto-optimum, is treated like monopoly: an unusual situation, to be analyzed ad hoc but not requiring a shift of emphasis away from the basic competitive model. An example of this approach is Stigler's treatment of the "free rider" problem (1974).

Government intervention is—or in the 1930s was—also treated like monopoly: bad, but fortunately atypical and of limited impact on the economy. The practise still is to require that anyone claiming to explain inefficient behavior by a household or profit-seeking firm as the result of government intervention must specify the intervention, and demonstrate that it has had the alleged effect of making inefficient behavior privately optimal. But while the Chicago tradition has been to argue that monopoly is not very important (Stigler, 1941; Arnold C. Harberger, 1954), and is not growing in importance (G. Warren Nutter, 1951), obviously this cannot be said of government intervention. And it is possible that the authority of TP in *positive* economics could be successfully challenged on the grounds that "government is too important"; but this has not yet happened at Chicago.[37]

(d) TP in Historical Perspective

The distinctive character of TP would not have seemed nearly so pronounced before 1930. In 1922, Keynes wrote:

> The Theory of Economics does not furnish a body of settled conclusions immediately applicable to policy. It is a method rather than a doctrine, an apparatus of the mind, a technique of thinking, which helps its possessor to draw correct conclusions . . . Before Adam Smith this apparatus of thought scarcely existed. Be-

tween his time and this it has been steadily enlarged and improved . . . It is not complete yet, but important improvements in its elements are becoming rare. The main task of the professional economist now consists, either in obtaining a wide knowledge of relevant facts and exercising skill in the application of economic principles to them, or in expounding the elements of his method in a lucid, accurate and illuminating way . . . Generally speaking, the writers of these volumes believe themselves to be orthodox members of the Cambridge School of Economics. At any rate, most of their ideas about the subject, and even their prejudices, are traceable to the contact they have enjoyed with the writings and lectures of the two economists who have chiefly influenced Cambridge thought for the past fifty years, Dr. Marshall and Professor Pigou [1922, pp. v–vi].

Substitute Chicago for Cambridge and these remarks could have been written by Viner, as easily as by Keynes. But whoever the author, they would have occasioned little dissent among neo-classical economists prior to 1930.

This consensus was shattered in the 1930s, when theorists substituted imperfect and/or monopolistic competition for atomistic competition as the paradigm for the theory of price, and Keynes' *General Theory* in place of market-clearing general equilibrium, as the explanation of aggregate output and employment. By embracing non-perfect competition and the *General Theory*, a large part of the economics profession moved away from TP which had been the essence of economic theory since Adam Smith. This happened at almost the same time as Chicago moved both to sharpen the statement of TP and to propagate its spirit through what was, for the time, an unusually rigorous training program required of all Ph.D. students, including those who intended to do applied work. Thus in the early and middle 1930s, the neo-classical consensus was ruptured with Chicago holding fast to TP and, partly as reaction, sharpening some of its implications that had previously gone unstressed, though hardly ignored.

[37] Conceivably, the pre-occupation of an important group of Chicago economists with the positive explanation of governmental behavior as it affects the economy represents the beginning of such a challenge.

(i) *Non-Perfect Competition*

Especially repugnant to TP is the suggestion that price and marginal cost (or marginal product and input price) may vary independently of one another, or of quantity bought and sold, in response to shifts in the parameters of (monopoloid) demand or cost functions as these are imagined by transactors. For example, consider the suggestion that wage rates or product prices systematically respond (a) to variations in a decision maker's maximand (e.g., Baumol's Sales Maximization Hypothesis, 1959) or as a result of "satisficing" behavior (Herbert Simon, 1955; Oliver Williamson, 1967); or, (b) to the dictates of a societal or ethical norm (e.g., "just price" or "fair wage") or (c) to some unexplained shift in their anticipated price movements. Whatever their merits, such suggestions undermine the authority of neo-classical price theory in general, and TP in particular. As Hicks put it:

> . . . it has to be recognized that a general abandonment of the assumption of perfect competition, a universal adoption of the assumption of monopoly, must have very destructive consequences for economic theory . . . It is, I believe, only possible to save anything from this wreck—and it must be remembered that the threatened wreckage is that of the greater part of economic theory—if we can assume that the markets confronting most of the firms with which we shall be dealing do not differ very greatly from perfectly competitive markets [1939, pp. 83–84].

Diffuse prior equilibrium (DP) considers the above mentioned "other" explanatory factors as valid supplements or alternatives to the neo-classical hypothesis. Its adherents do not consider that showing an argument to imply (say) a failure of sellers or buyers to optimize provides a serious reason for rejecting it. So far as they are concerned, decision makers may or may not optimize; markets may or may not clear; resource units of equal productive capacity may or may not have equal mar-

ginal products in different uses, and their owners may or may not receive equal returns.

In their view a competitive general equilibrium model with all markets continuously clearing is but one of many possible models that a theorist may investigate or utilize in applied research, and has no valid claim to special consideration. This mounts a serious challenge to the procedure of cumulating the findings of separate pieces of research using the implications of competitive equilibrium (i.e., the good approximation assumption) to estimate parameters and/or magnitudes not directly observable. Without the presumption that the equalities implied by competitive equilibrium hold, the "burden of proof" shifts and an investigator must establish, case by case, the existence of any alleged equalities. This seriously inhibits the development of research programs of the Chicago style and gives a quite different direction to economic research (see below).

Free of the requirements of a neo-classical prior, since the early 1930s DP theorists have developed models embodying a wide variety of postulates to satisfy standards of logical rigor, findings of "stylized" facts of all sorts, consistency with various political programs, and so on. But with the possible exception of a requirement that compensated demand curves must be negatively inclined, DP theory imposes no restrictions on the permissible empirical implications of such models.

Many of the models that have been offered have pre-1930 counterparts, e.g.: institutional explanations of price-cost relationships. But before 1930, such explanations were not considered compatible with economic theory (i.e., neo-classical theory) and usually did not purport to be. Institutional or historical economics was then considered as providing an explanation of economic phenomena, and a philosophy of economic policy, alternative to neoclassical theory and laissez-faire. Theories of non-perfect competition represented a more or less conscious attempt to relax the assumptions of neo-classical theory to permit accommodation of these alternative viewpoints; Chicago regarded this attempt as misguided, and still does.[38]

(ii) *The General Theory of Employment*

Keynes' *General Theory* represented an even more fundamental challenge to neo-classical theory than the abandonment of atomistic competition. The crucial departure was a concept of equilibrium that permitted less than full employment of resources, especially labor. Both Knight's (1937) and Viner's (1936) reviews of the *General Theory* stressed the importance of this unacceptable innovation.

The paradigmatic tension between Chicago and adherents of Keynes' *General Theory* is an old and continuing story that needs no retelling.[39] Its fundamental cause is the implication of the *General Theory* that, for admissible values of exogenously determined variables, an equilibrium may be reached with less than full employment of the labor force and with the unemployed workers being unable to obtain employment even though they are willing to accept the same pay as those employed, or even less, and are no less productive.

In such "equilibria," exogenous increases in consumption expenditure (or in government transfers that have the effect of increasing consumption expenditure) may increase investment and thus the stock of capital while exogenous increases

in the rate of saving may have the reverse effect. Still further, *opportunities to use* resources, as distinct from the resources themselves, may become valuable and destruction of wealth may become a stimulus to investment and output.

The Chicago aversion to considering such situations as equilibria reflects more than desire to have research directed by a correct theory; it also reflects a concern with achieving and maintaining intellectual influence beyond the small community of researchers. A major expression of this concern, which is fully shared by Chicago's rivals, is effort to influence the teaching of economics to non-economists. The objective is to have other social scientists, lawyers, judges, legislators, bureaucrats, voters think about economics in terms of "correct" models; make the "right" assumptions; ask the right questions; etc.

While this is obviously related to a desire to influence public policy, it is not quite the same. Although models and factual presumptions may direct questions and fix prejudices, they do not guarantee conclusions; like Keynes' Cambridge School (of 1922), Chicago considers the teaching of correct economic principles to be an important part of its *professional* activity (e.g., through text book writing). The challenge presented by the *General Theory* to this activity was direct and, for at least three decades, very effective.

The particular features of the *General Theory* that challenge TP are the following:

(1) The existence of a stable aggregate consumption function (or any stable aggregate relation) that is not derivable by aggregation of consumption decisions of individual decision makers who treat long-run equilibrium values of all endogenous variables as parameters. The existence of such a stable aggregate relation implies either (i) that the model is inconsistent or (ii) that some individuals will not be able

---

[38] The Chicago view of imperfect competition and related methodological issues is discussed and debated in Friedman (1963), Stigler (1963), George C. Archibald (1961).

[39] For a recent skirmish, see James Tobin (1980) and Lucas (1981). It is almost half a century from Viner vs. Keynes to Lucas vs. Tobin, and both sides have become far more sophisticated in discussing matters related to unemployment, but the underlying issues remain the same.

to execute their decisions (i.e., will be quantity rationed).

(2) Belief that the wage rate (or any price) is rigid—or follows any specific long-run time path other than that which tracks equilibrium values—is inconsistent with the good approximation assumption. Either such belief is systematically in error, in which case it violates rational expectations[40] or, if not in error, the system will not tend to a Pareto-optimal equilibrium.[41]

In essence, TP implies the absence of stable "macro" relations (other than those obtainable from aggregation of optimal individual decisions) in a properly specified model. Thus acceptance of TP implies rejection of an autonomous macroeconomics and, at Chicago, what is elsewhere termed "macro" is, in orientation and substance, the analysis of the behavior of the money supply and its impact upon a competitive economy, both in long run stationary equilibrium and in response to shocks with various adjustment lags.

Macrodynamics, per se, is not incompatible with TP. TP can accommodate real shocks, monetary shocks, time lags of all kinds, etc. so long as stable relationships are compatible with continuous individual optimization. What TP cannot accommodate is macrostatics with one of the variables indicating the level of resource utilization; ultimately because such models imply (at equilibrium with less than full employment) the availability of free real

resources—free lunch—to the controller of the money supply.

(e) Methodology

The Chicago View I am attempting to describe is not a set of tenets or propositions to which all Chicagoans subscribe, but an approach to economic research. Were it not for fear of becoming involved in side issues, I would have suggested that Chicago economics is a scientific sub-culture in the Kuhnian sense, and spoken of the "Chicago Paradigm" (or family of paradigms), or of the "Chicago Scientific Research Program" (*pace* Imre Lakatos), rather than the Chicago View.[42]

Let me elaborate: initiation to the Chicago sub-culture is through a rigorous training program in which failure is for many a distinct possibility, and placement in a well defined pecking order a concern of all. Success is achieved by mastery and application of certain tools and concepts to obtain correct answers to analytical problems (Kuhnian puzzles). Correct answers must conform to definite criteria which are the fundamental characteristics of TP, e.g.: competitive markets must clear, decision makers must optimize, money illusion must be absent.[43] However imaginative, answers that violate any maintained hypothesis of the paradigm, are penalized as evincing failure to absorb training.

Correct answers to questions on Ph.D. prelims imply correct use of tools and concepts. An acceptable dissertation exhibits correct application of appropriate tools to an explanation of some empirical phenomenon that is relevant to one or another of the paradigms or research pro-

---

[40] TP long antedates the model of rational expectations originally presented by John F. Muth (1961). However rational expectations is very much in the spirit of TP, and no other well known model of expectations has this property. Accordingly, it is not surprising that "rational expectations" has had a very favorable reception at Chicago.

[41] As Tobin (1980, pp. 24–25) points out (in effect), a non-TP economy may embody rational expectations and its history may confirm the expectations of its participants. That is, TP readily accommodates rational expectations, but non-TP can also accommodate them—though with different consequences.

[42] For a lively discussion of the views of Thomas C. Kuhn and those of Lakatos as they apply to economics see the papers in Spiro J. Latsis (1976).

[43] The presence of money illusion implies an unexploited opportunity for the producers of money to increase real wealth by expanding the money supply.

grams currently being developed by the thesis supervisor. "Explanation" means either a demonstration that the phenomenon is compatible with the underlying theory, or the provision of such extensions of the theory as may be required.

The quality of a dissertation, or of any piece of research, depends upon the salience of the phenomenon studied for the associated research program; upon the difficulty of reconciling the phenomenon with the program; upon the breadth of implication of any innovations made in the program and, of course, upon the technical virtuosity exhibited in developing the innovations.

As in any "normal science," there is resistance to innovation, and ambivalence toward would-be innovators. The lowest level of an acceptable research project is one that applies a theory correctly in explaining some phenomenon, but without extending the theory in any way, e.g.: fitting a conventional earnings function to a new data set. Proceeding up the scale of scientific merit, we move to minor clarification of concepts through introduction of new distinctions which, although valid, do not greatly alter the established views of researchers. From there we proceed to analytical innovations of increasing salience to wider and wider groups of researchers, or to discoveries of important new phenomena, or measurements thereof, that require alteration of previously held views; and, at the pinnacle, to major theoretical innovations.

The greater the merit to which a given contribution aspires, the greater the resistance it encounters. This is partly because greater merit is associated with need for more fundamental adjustments in the research program to which the contribution is made. But it is also because merit increases with the breadth of the contribution's influence—the number and importance of the research programs that it disturbs. Thus a highly meritorious contribution is one that disturbs the activity of a wide circle of other researchers, and the more fundamental the disturbance the greater its merit.

On this view, scientific progress is a process of creative destruction. What is destroyed is the intellectual capital of other scientists whose resistance to accepting new contributions is not only understandable, but desirable; it is only by overcoming this resistance that the few genuine contributions can be separated from the more numerous invalid proposals.

While this process is not unique to Chicago economics, Chicago economics strongly exemplifies it. Chicago dissertations, typically, are associated with a particular workshop. Each of the more successful workshops is associated with one (or more) research programs sponsored by its director or other leading figures. Each program has unresolved theoretical problems and is confronted with empirical anomalies; dissertations are generated by the effort to surmount these difficulties. A common feature of all (or almost all) of these research programs is that they embody the Chicago View—TP.

But though the central tendency is clear, the adherence to TP is not uniform across workshops. In International Trade, for example, the facts of trade restriction and factor immobility make (even Chicago) researchers abandon the hypothesis that resources are allocated in an approximately Pareto-optimal manner. Also, the ubiquity of trade restrictions and/or state trading makes Chicago specialists in Trade far more ready to work with theories of "second best" and to consider optimal tariffs than their colleagues in (say) Industrial Organization would be to consider schemes of "optimal government regulation to offset oligopolistic output distortions."[44]

----

[44] I am indebted to Jacob Frenkel for an enlightening discussion of this matter.

The paradigmatic nature of TP gives its adherents a particular perspective upon empirical evidence. A new finding is, and should be, screened to see how it bears upon the findings of research programs in a number of related fields. Because in "normal science" it is presumed that the currently accepted theory is valid, new findings are accepted far more readily if they are consistent with the theory's implications, than if they are not. In the Bayesian sense, the prior on the findings of any piece of empirical research is that they are consistent with the established theory; the strength of the evidence required for acceptance of a finding is greater than otherwise if any of its implications are inconsistent with TP.

This posture of TP causes its adherents to distrust reports (from historians, journalists, practitioners of other social sciences, and from some economists) of behavior incompatible with the implications of economic theory. The resulting scepticism sharply distinguishes TP adherents from other economists who are willing, sometimes even anxious, to credit accounts of irrational and/or non-competitive behavior.[45] Where reports of irrational behavior reflect careful research, interesting intellectual confrontations may arise; however, this is not the place to explore this issue.

Adherents of any paradigm can be ac-

cused of dogmatism—holding excessively tight priors; Chicago economists have not been exempt from such charges. How tight a prior should be is a nice question, more easily judged ex post than at the moment of research decision—but never a simple matter. Circa 1980, some Chicago economists were inclined to disparage the standards of evidence applied in certain workshops other than their own, especially what they considered to be the manner in which excessively tight priors lead to inappropriately low standards for findings interpreted as consistent with the accepted theory, and excessively high standards for those that do not permit such interpretation.

The pros and cons of this matter cannot be usefully discussed in the abstract. Foolish or unlucky scientists can easily slide from "properly tight" to dogmatic priors and appear, ex post, to have been insensitive to evidence. But a mixture of misfortune and bad judgment can just as easily make an open-minded investigator appear a credulous bubble head willing to believe anything. There is no formula for "optimal tightness"; what is required is judgment and luck.

Resistance to paradigm-disturbing evidence is paralleled by reluctance to accept disruptive theoretical innovations. A theoretical innovator must squeeze between the rock: "if an innovation is consistent with what is known, it serves no useful purpose" and the hard place: "if inconsistent with what was previously believed, it must be wrong." If a theoretical innovation threatens an implication of TP, neither ingenuity and logical elegance in its development will count for much in gaining it acceptance. Only solid evidence that behavior is in accord with the proposed innovation, and cannot be reconciled with its rejection, will suffice; and the standards for accepting evidence offered in support of the innovation will be high. Consequently, at Chicago, a would-be theoreti-

---

[45] For example, TP adherents tend to give little weight to self-reports of participants in the economic process describing their motives, decision making processes, objectives, sources of information, etc. TP runs entirely in terms of prices, quantities and wealth: if observed behavior is consistent with the implications of TP, the self-reports are redundant; if the behavior is inconsistent with TP, but consistent with self-reports, the latter will be discounted, and the anomaly investigated; if the behavior supports TP, and is inconsistent with the self-reports, the self-reports will be ignored. DP theorists urge the contrary procedure: i.e., use whatever information we can get about decision maker's behavior regardless of its lack of consistency with TP; e.g., Tobin (1980, pp. 34–35), Simon (1976) and James L. Medoff and Katherine G. Abraham (1980).

cal innovator must be unusually self-confident and determined.

The TP emphasis gives a distinctive character to Chicago contributions to economic theory: either they involve redefinition of a key variable or restructuring of a model so as to reconcile empirical anomalies with theory, or extend the theory so that it applies to behavior previously considered intractable to economic analysis. In other words, Chicago-type innovations are "paradigm preserving" or "paradigm extending" rather than "paradigm shattering."

A few examples of Chicago-type innovations will clarify this statement:

(i) *The Coase Theorem (1960)*[46]

Before Ronald Coase's paper, technical externalities were thought to cause losses to injured parties that exceeded the gains to those causing them. "All" that Coase did was point out that on the maintained hypothesis that everyone is optimizing, and in the absence of transactions cost, failure of an injured party to induce (i.e., bribe) his injurers to desist implied that the marginal cost to the injurer, of desisting, was greater than the marginal benefit (of non-injury) to the injured. Absent transaction costs, this proposition can fail to hold only if varying the quantity of the externality drastically alters the distribution of wealth by changing relative prices (including shadow prices).[47]

In a sense, the Coase theorem is simply a convoluted definition of transaction cost;

nevertheless it has altered the way in which economists view externalities. It is now recognized that externalities are negative outputs, produced jointly with positive outputs, whose "consumers" must be compensated as the property rights of injurers and injured and the laws of liability determine.

What Coase did was to expand the concept of transaction and commodity to include purchase and sale of the right to inflict losses. This has enabled economists to apply standard economic theory to the analysis of the economic consequences of alternative assignments of property rights (and of tort liability) and even to explaining how such rights are assigned.

(ii) *Human Capital and Allocation of Time (Becker, 1964, 1965)*

While the idea that education and training may be treated as capital is at least as old as the *Wealth of Nations,* Becker (1964) gave it a greatly sharpened formulation which made it possible to consider time used for study and in acquiring work experience as proxies for investment in human capital, and thereby to organize a large body of previously unrelated data about a coherent theory. As part of the theory, he introduced the important distinction between general and specific capital without which it is impossible to reconcile on-the-job training with individual optimization by both the worker and the employer.

Whether the theory of the allocation of time is part of the theory of human capital, or a separate contribution, can be debated elsewhere. However, by explicitly introducing the time constraint (common to all decision makers) as a resource limitation additional to those normally included in the consumer budget, Becker opened a new and wide range of phenomena to analysis by conventional tools of economic theory.

---

[46] At Chicago as elsewhere, the initial reaction to the Coase theorem was incredulity. A piece of Chicago folklore, told me by others (and confirmed by Coase), is how one evening in the late 1950s, but prior to his appointment at Chicago, Coase converted a large group of Chicago economists—including most of the resident leaders—from sceptics to believers in "The Theorem."

[47] The significance of this qualification is not always appreciated at Chicago. Not a few Chicago economists like to argue as though the efficiency locus of an economy were invariant to the distribution of wealth within it.

(iii) *The Theory of Search (Stigler, 1961, 1962b)*

The one-price competitive market has been the paradigm for the theory of price determination since Adam Smith, and even earlier. Yet, neo-classical economists had long been aware that a large part of economic activity occurs in situations where transactors, although strongly competitive, confront different equilibrium prices associated with varying modalities of service, delivery, etc. (Viner, 1921).

Stigler showed that the one-price market was not inherent in the structure of TP, but arises only in the special case where the cost of information about offer prices is negligible and transaction costs are identical for all possible trading pairs (e.g., on an organized exchange). Without these conditions, equilibrium implies not a single price, but a distribution of prices whose variance (and other moments) is related to the cost of acquiring information—search. Thus in the presence of search cost the existence of multiple prices was shown to be compatible, even required, by efficiency. Not only was TP vindicated, but its range of applicability (to such phenomena as search, turnover, and frictional unemployment) was greatly increased.

(f) Search and Cost of Information

Where search activity and, more generally, acquisition of information become important inputs of economic activity the concept of efficiency becomes more complex. As stated at the outset of this section (assumption 3, p. 11), I understand TP to imply that information is acquired by each decision maker in the quantity that makes its marginal cost of acquisition equal to its marginal return. But what does it mean to "acquire information?" If one is searching for prices quoted by alternative suppliers or for the technology to produce a particular product or for expert appraisals of

a city's restaurants, etc., one hires a shopper or a technical expert, or buys a restaurant guide as circumstances require, *provided* he knows the "location" of the market for the relevant service. But the meaning of this condition is not obvious.

For many real life decisions, much of the relevant information is too technical, and expert opinions too diverse, for even the educated layman to feel capable of becoming informed. Often one's actual, and possibly one's optimal, procedure is to hire or somehow obtain the advice of an "expert." But which "expert?" How is the expert to be selected? Typically, by recommendation of a more or less expert selector of experts and so on, leading either to an infinite regress or to acting on the advice—informed or otherwise—of an individual one trusts for reasons exogenous to the model.

The process of acquiring information is akin to proceeding down a logical tree, where at the initial branch point (and possibly others as well), the cost of acquiring additional information—even if finite—varies greatly with the information with which the individual is initially endowed. Viewed in this way, differences in equilibrium stocks of information across individuals reflect differences in the cost of acquiring information which, in turn, reflect differences in endowed stocks of information (e.g., information transmitted through family environment, etc.).

Thus assimilating differences in cost of acquiring information to differences in endowed (i.e., inherited) human capital facilitates treating information as an input into productive processes on the same footing as any other input. In general, this is the procedure normally adopted by TP adherents.

But non-TP adherents often object to this approach, sometimes contending that the marginal cost of acquiring information is a parameter of an individual's utility function; sometimes arguing as if differ-

24   *Journal of Economic Literature, Vol. XX (March 1982)*

ences in cost of information across decision makers were akin to differences in wealth, and sometimes seeming to advance both claims.

At a formal level, the disagreement between TP adherents and others is not, in my opinion, very important. What TP would attribute to exogenous differences in endowed human capital, non-TP would ascribe to exogenous differences in cost of acquiring information: TP-adherents tend to minimize the importance and/or stress the transitory nature of such differences while non-TP economists tend to build models that assume their quasi-permanence.

For example, "dual economy" models that postulate differences in technology are rarely, if ever, constructed by TP adherents. These models require that there be unexplained differences in the cost of acquiring information or differences in tastes for using the technologies.[48] I might add at this point that non-TP economists often assume, without much supporting argument, that if one individual or group seems to have less information than another there is a prima facie case for the state "giving" the information to the less well informed. TP adherents are likely to insist (in effect) on a calculation of costs and benefits of the information transfer.

(g) Survivor Principle

Extensive use of the "survivor principle" is characteristic of TP. Long implicit in accounts of division of labor and specialization,[49] its classic statement is Armen A. Alchian (1950), and its most famous application is Stigler's explanation of the distribution of firm sizes (1968). In its weak form, the survivor principle says that competition will lead to the selection of lower cost methods of performing any task so that in the long run the surviving method(s) will be those associated with lowest cost.

But TP says more than this: it holds that at any moment the expected cost of the method actually in use will be "close" to that of the least cost method available. In individual cases, deviations of actual from least cost methods are interpreted as reflections of changes in technology or factor prices that had been unanticipated when the productive technique was adopted. Thus the strong form of the survivor principle says that, at any moment of time, the decision rules being followed come close to minimizing the expected cost of doing whatever each decision maker is attempting.

The survivor principle, strong form, therefore, is one aspect of the good approximation assumption; its applicability varies with the problem. The principle works quite well in explaining behavior of traders on organized exchanges, particularly markets for financial assets; traders following inefficient behavioral rules lose wealth and are eliminated. It is not surprising, therefore, that the Finance workshop which focuses on the explanation of returns to financial assets should be identified with a very active and successful TP research program based on the notion of efficient markets and the underlying Modigliani–Miller (M & M) Theorem.[50] Where returns to comparable resources

---

[48] Becker and Stigler (1974) argue that differences in tastes are an inappropriate element in any explanation of cross-sectional differences in individual or group behavior.

[49] For example, Keynes

. . . they (economists) have begun by assuming a state of affairs where the ideal distribution of productive resources can be brought about through individuals acting independently by the method of trial and error in such a way that those individuals who move in the right direction will destroy by competition those who move in the wrong direction . . . [1926, p. 28].

[50] The M & M theorem (1958) is a very Chicagoish proposition which I did not include in the list of Chicago contributions to economic theory because it was the invention of two Carnegie Tech professors. However, soon after its publication (1958) Merton Miller came to the Chicago Business School where he has long been the recognized doyen of the Finance group.

in alternative uses converge to a unique equilibrium value more slowly, the explanatory power of the survivor principle is reduced correspondingly.

Normative Economics

In discussing the Positive aspect of Chicago economics, I have emphasized its persisting characteristics; these are associated with TP. The Normative or policy oriented side can be better understood by emphasizing the changes that have occurred over the past half-century.

(a) Political Economy

Whether the Populist strain in Henry Simons' *A Positive Program for Laissez Faire,* ever truly reflected a consensus of the views of the younger members of the Knight affinity group must be left an open question. Surely it could not have reflected Knight's own views, though for the present purpose that is unimportant. But if, during the thirties and forties, Friedman, Stigler, et al. had any reservations about the Positive Program, they did not avow them publicly. Moreover, the main themes of *A Positive Program* were very close to the public policy positions that members of the Knight affinity group were taking (in the late thirties and early forties), so that it is reasonable to consider it more or less representative of a common view.

Superficially, *A Positive Program* seems entirely compatible with the pursuit of scientific economics; and for many years it was so considered. However, in recent years, increasing disagreement on this question has seriously divided the Chicago School. Before discussing the intellectual evolution that caused the disagreement, let me briefly describe what happened.

Soon after coming to Chicago, Friedman began to combine economic research with advocacy of specific proposals for socio-economic reform (negative income

tax, substitution of publicly subsidized private schools for public schools, making participation in social security voluntary, abolishing licensure for doctors, volunteer army in lieu of the draft). All of these reform proposals involved either increased use of the price system, substitution of private for public production, replacement of legal compulsion by voluntary—financially induced—private co-operation, or a mixture of all three. In an important sense, they reflected the spirit of *A Positive Program;* most Chicago economists did and still do agree with most of them, and they have become identified—both to the profession and to the general public—as the Chicago View on economic policy. The problem that has arisen is not with the particular policies espoused, but with the compatibility of policy advocacy per se with the practice of scientific economics.

After the middle 1940s, Stigler's intellectual development diverged from Friedman's. Although continuing his interest in the history of thought, the focus of his research was upon various aspects of industrial organization (oligopoly, entry restriction, search, anti-trust and, above all, behavior of regulated industries). In these studies, the interaction between political and economic variables increasingly intruded upon the *positive* explanation of observed behavior, with the result that Stigler became unwilling to analyze problems on the assumption that the economist-reformer could move the economy in a desired direction simply by persuading a beneficent ruler, constrained by prices but otherwise omnipotent, to behave appropriately. In particular, he objected to the assumption that a ruler, and *a fortiori* a reformer, could ignore the need to obtain political support and the effect of economic policies in attracting that support.[51]

[51] As Stigler puts it:
This new focus of economic studies of regulation changes the economists' role from that of reformer to

But this assumption is precisely what economists generally, and Friedman especially, have relied upon in giving policy advice. For almost four decades Friedman has counselled his fellow economists to recommend what they considered sound economic policy, regardless of perceived political practicability. He has told us that our political judgments are seriously defective and that, in any case, it is our professional obligation to give our best advice and let the recipients make decisions as best they can. Without gainsaying the considerable merit in this counsel it is obviously incompatible with a view of society that holds economics and politics to be a seamless web.

In effect, Stigler has come to think of political decision makers as endogenous participants in a political-economic process. As such, their behavior is to be interpreted as a response to pressures exerted by their constituents who are, in turn, responding to the perceived effect of possible government action upon their utility levels. So viewed, politicians are incapable of acting on advice as to the promotion of the general welfare, and unlikedly to be much interested in receiving such advice.[52] Their concerns, indeed their

only possible concerns, are getting re-elected or otherwise retaining office, and advancing in political influence.

By so accentuating the positive, Stigler has virtually eliminated the normative and left reformers (and anti-reformers) with nothing to latch onto. From Smith to Keynes to Friedman, reformers have all been deluded or, since TP precludes such an interpretation, agitating for their own amusement or private advantage. The implication is that economic science and concern with influencing public policy have little synergism and there is no reason for individuals interested in the former to be engaged in the latter.[53]

In view of this, it is not surprising that many of the younger Chicago economists are quite apolitical.[54] In current lunch time discussions, the political question is at least as likely to be: "Why take the time and trouble to vote?" as it is: "For whom should one vote?" Nevertheless, the aversion to government activity built into the Chicago sub-culture remains strong (see below, pp. 28–29).

Fortunately, affection and good sense have prevented serious intellectual disagreement from causing any breach of personal relations between Friedman and Stigler. The high value they place on these relations, however, may have inhibited public debate of the serious issues involved in the disagreement. But despite the lack of public debate the fact of the disagreement has been well-known at Chicago for the last decade.

In essence, the Stigler research program in Political Economy (see below) involves an attempt to extend TP to political

---

that of student of political economy. The change seems to me eminently desirable. Until we understand why our society adopts its policies, we will be poorly equipped to give useful advice on how to change those policies. Indeed, some changes (such as free trade) presumably are unattainable without a fundamental restructuring of the political system which we are unable to describe. A measure of restraint in our advice on policy would seem to be dictated by a sense of responsibility on the economists' part, and not only by the sense of caution of the body politic to whom we address the advice. [1975, p. xi].

[52] Sam Peltzman has pointed out to me that this goes too far. Economists still have an (important) advisory function as providers of technical information (e.g., calculation of costs and benefits of legislative measures). However, this is very different from giving advice on the overall desirability of particular policies. Peltzman also remarks that the effect of Chicago work on Regulation has been to alter the opinions of some regulators on the desirability of regulation, per se.

[53] In commenting on this paper, Stigler has remarked that he firmly believes that increasing scientific knowledge of the political-economic process will (ultimately) improve public policy making.

[54] The growing technical demands of the subject probably contribute to this phenomenon. I have no idea of whether political indifference among young economists is more prevalent at Chicago than elsewhere.

processes.[55] There is no formal statement of how the group or any of its members[56] proposes to model the determination of political events as the outcome of resource allocations of individual participants in the political-economic process. Formal statements of this kind, abstracted from concrete application, would be alien to the spirit of the program.

Nevertheless, the general drift of many discussions I have had with members of this research group about the application of economic theory to political behavior convinces me of the following statement: the Stigler program will consider suspect any implication of a model purporting to explain political behavior that does not have a precise analogue in TP (*a fortiori*, if the implication is inconsistent with TP) while identification of a TP analogue will count in the model's favor. Therefore, I conjecture that the implicit objective of the research program is to apply TP to the explanation of political behavior with the presumption that every proposition of TP will hold, and with the intention of making amendments only when observed behavior is clearly inconsistent with an appropriate analogue of TP.

The broad characteristics of a TP model of political economic behavior are generally agreed upon although many conceptual details require formulation. In essence, individuals are assumed to be rational and to have means of obtaining goods and services through the political system—political wealth—as well as by exchange through the market. Political

wealth includes votes, but may also include other sources of influence. Individuals striving to be political decision makers function analogously to entrepreneurs in seeking to form coalitions of political wealth owners by promising various benefits, etc.

The spirit of such models requires that they leave no place for concern with the general welfare to affect the political decision making process, except insofar as manifestation of such concern may be instrumental in accumulating political wealth. The impact of this characterization of economic policy making on the day-to-day work of economic researchers varies with their field of specialization. Among Chicago economists, students of Applied Microeconomics (e.g., Labor, Industrial Organization) are generally positive in orientation and (save for recommendations of deregulation) rarely offer proposals for improving public policy. Ergo, the Stigler research program creates no problems for them. On the other hand, students of Money or International Trade are still greatly interested in formulating optimal rules for governmental conduct. Despite great progress in analytical sophistication, under Lucas' direction as under Friedman's, the Money Workshop continues its concern with Simons' problem of specifying an optimal rule for governing the growth of the nominal money stock (Lucas, 1981, especially pp. 563–64).

But from the viewpoint of Industrial Organization, searching for rules of optimal behavior begs important questions: granted the "optimality" of some rule of behavior for (say) the monetary authority, what are the incentives for the authority to conform to the rule? What is the mechanism for selecting the individuals who are to make the decisions? What are the rewards for conforming to the rule selected and the penalties for departures in various directions and magnitudes? Until these and related questions are asked, and an-

---

[55] The Stigler research program of applying economic theory to political behavior is closely allied to a program, identified with Gary Becker, to apply economic analysis to the explanation of "sociological" phenomena, and yet a third program, identified with Richard Posner, to use economics to study the workings of the legal system. The Becker and Posner programs are discussed, briefly, below (pp. 34–35).

[56] The general outlook (which is in fairly rapid evolution), may be inferred from Stigler (1975) and Peltzman (1976).

swered, proposing optimal rules for the management of the nominal monetary stock is as inappropriate as proposing optimal rules for regulating industry X. However, despite trenchant criticism of the effectiveness of attempts to improve the behavior of industry X through regulation Stigler (1975) and his associates have never attempted to apply their analysis of regulation to the question of whether, and under what conditions, a monetary authority with the legal capacity to depart from a proposed behavioral rule could be expected to adhere to it.[57] Reconciling the Stigler theory of "regulatory capture" with the behavior of the Federal Reserve System, and with the Simons–Friedman–Lucas view of optimal rules, would be an interesting exercise.

(b) Voting Power

In the positive study of political economy there is no room for normative judgments on the distribution of voting power, but this did not always inhibit Chicago economists. The normative attitude of economic liberals toward the suffrage has often been wobbly, and Chicago has been no exception. In general, the conventional

attitude among 20th century Americans is "one man-one vote," and in most matters Chicago economists are conventional. But the implications of political rationality combined with the presence of a large stock of client-voters in a Welfare State gives pause to anyone concerned with economic efficiency.

"The offer of alms increases the supply of beggars"[58] is a thought that is readily appreciated by an adherent of TP. And the idea of an interaction of voting beggars with alms-offering politicians is suggestive of a maleficent cobweb cycle, the outsweeping of which might require the disenfranchisement of the poor. But this is one bullet that Friedman seems reluctant to bite. With uncharacteristic tentativeness, he quotes Dicey:

> Surely a sensible and a benevolent man may well ask himself whether England as a whole will gain by enacting that the receipt of poor relief, in the shape of a pension, shall be consistent with the pensioner's retaining the right to join in the election of a Member of Parliament. [And goes on to comment]: the verdict of experience in Britain on Dicey's question must as yet be regarded as mixed [1962, p. 194].

Simons' view was, if anything, even more ambiguous:

> Democracy . . . implies an inclusive electorate, if not universal adult suffrage, and moral, intelligent electors—although qualitative selection for suffrage, with universal eligibility to qualify, should not be hastily ruled out [1948, p. 8].

Obviously the meaning of "qualitative selection" can vary with the reader. However "universal eligibility to qualify" does not suggest a tropism for a franchise restricted to the non-dependent.

(c) Monopoly and the State

Whatever their ambivalence, or pudicity, on the voting franchise, Chicago econ-

---

[57] While this is hardly the place for a full dress discussion, it should be remarked that the positive theory of nominal money supply has been surprisingly neglected at Chicago. Simons' and Mints' discussions of money supply are entirely normative, i.e.: how should banks be regulated to achieve desired results?

Friedman (1959, pp. 4–7) addresses the problem explicitly, but concludes that production of money is too susceptible of fraud and contract breach to leave the competition of individual private producers to determine its quantity. But as Benjamin Klein (1974) has pointed out, Friedman simply assumes without argument that the private interest of issuers and potential holders of fiduciary money would not suffice to develop methods of privately certifying the redemption value of the issue of any given bank and thereby give an incentive to each to limit its issue. Why are fraudulent bankers more able to escape effective detection than quack doctors, dishonest repairmen, and the like from whose depredations legislators are always seeking to protect us by licensure? It may be that "money is different," but more argument is needed to establish the point.

[58] I do not know the author of this phrase; as George Neumann has pointed out, it is probably Simon Newcomb (1885), but I cannot find the exact quote.

Reder: Chicago Economics 29

omists have always been openly and strongly anti-statist. In the 1930s, and ever since, they have been opposed, resolutely, to government engaging in the regulation of private business, fixing of prices, or direct production of goods and services with the usual grudging exceptions for traditional public goods, e.g., defense, maintenance of public order, etc.[59] The reasons for this posture are well-known and need not be elaborated.

Among Chicago economists, the importance of resisting government growth relative to other social objectives has clearly increased since *A Positive Program*. Simons was willing to tolerate some increase in the role of government (ownership of natural monopolies and regulation—via the Federal Trade Commission—of corporate size and financial structure) in order to limit inequality, both of income and of power (1948, pp. 58–59). But this gene of Populism was not affixed to TP and it has proved recessive in the Chicago strain.

It was easier for Simons' successors than for him to perceive the potential for government expansion inherent in a program to regulate the size and financial structures of corporations. Early in his career, Gary Becker pointed out that "It may be preferable not to regulate economic monopolies and to suffer their bad effects, rather than to regulate them and suffer the effects of political imperfections" (1958, p. 109). A few years later, Friedman wrote:

> . . . monopoly arises to some extent because technical considerations make it more efficient or economical to have a single enterprise rather than many . . . There is unfortunately no good solution for technical monopoly. There is only a choice among three evils: private unregulated monopoly, private monopoly regulated by the state, and government operation. . . . It seems impossible to state as a general proposition that one of these evils is uniformly preferable to another. As stated in chapter ii, the great disadvantage of either governmental regulation or governmental operation of monopoly is that it is exceedingly difficult to reverse. In consequence, I am inclined to urge that the least of the evils is private unregulated monopoly wherever this is tolerable [1962, p. 128].

No doubt tolerance for the costs of private monopoly was promoted by belief that those costs were low: "I accept . . . as a fundamental empirical truth; the history of the American economy in the twentieth century testifies that a modest program of combatting monopoly is enough to prevent any considerable decline in competition" (Stigler, 1968, p. 297). Thus the perceived marginal cost of government action came to balance (or outweigh) the marginal benefit of reduced inequality of "income and power" that Simons had desired to combat.

A similar evolution occurred in the attitude toward Trade Unionism: Simons' antagonism toward union monopoly (1948, Chapter VI) has never been completely abandoned, but the emphasis has shifted from normative condemnation to positive analysis of their effects on wages and employment (as in Lewis, 1963). In addition, Simons' fear of unions as generators of inflation (1948) has been simply abandoned as reflecting an incorrect view of the determination of money supply (Friedman, 1951; for a contrary view, closer to Simons', see Reder, 1948).

In short, Simons feared and sought to limit concentrations of private economic power—both in unions and large corporations—as well as in government. Among later Chicagoans, fear of government became greater, or fear of concentrated wealth less, with the result that the spirit

---

[59] Even these traditional preserves for government action are under recurrent hostile scrutiny by Chicago economists eager to find yet another opportunity to replace public with private activity and to use prices to allocate resources. For example Becker and Stigler (1974) argue for the use of private law enforcers as substitutes or at least major supplements to the public police. (This piece was written well after the launching of the Stigler research program in political economy.) Numerous other examples could be offered.

of Populist reform became swamped by a general aversion to government activity beyond the "essential minimum."

While this aversion persists—and not least in the minds of Stigler and his research collaborators—it does not easily co-exist with the research program of applying economic theory to politics. If the actions of governments are inimical to the welfare of their citizens then, by the survivor principle, governments should be diminishing as resource users. Manifestly, this has not been the case—at least since 1929 (Peltzman, 1980). Rationalizations of government growth running in terms of duped voters are unacceptable for the same reason as explanations of consumer behavior that rest on allegations of delusion or irrationality.

The logic of TP implies that if governments are growing, they must be satisfying the demands of their customer-voters. Therefore the continuing aversion of Chicago economists to government activity must reflect some combination of (i) subcultural distaste, (ii) disapproval of the distribution of voting strength, or (iii) rejection of the implications of economic theory as applied to explaining political behavior. It is my impression that Chicago economists are very diverse in their views of these alternatives.

(d) Income Distribution

Simons' hostility to corporate bigness was closely allied to his desire to make the distribution of income more equal through progressive income taxation. This desire was not related in any way to TP and it has not survived in the Chicago tradition. Since Simons' death in 1946, Chicago interest in the income distribution has been almost if not exclusively positive, e.g.: Friedman (1953), Becker (1967), Richard A. Posner (1973), Sam Peltzman (1980). The contrast between Simons' tropism for equality and Posner's flat rejection of any such social objective is striking:

> Economics is a positive science. The economist has an important contribution to make to the debate over the appropriate distribution of income and wealth, but it is descriptive rather than normative [1973, p. 118].

(e) Immigration and Inequality

Like most protagonists of laissez-faire, Chicago economists have not paid much attention to the issue of freedom of immigration. By a straightforward extension of TP, equality of opportunity is a requirement of worldwide productive efficiency. It is also an ethical precept that, in most contexts has great appeal for classical liberals. But not where "Freedom to Choose" implies freedom to choose a national location. Simons' vehemence on this point is astonishing (though fully compatible with his strain of Populism):

> As regards immigration policies, the less said the better. It may be hoped that world prosperity, increased political security, and ultimate leveling of birth rates may diminish migration pressures. Wholly free migration, however, is neither attainable politically nor desirable. To insist that a free-trade program is logically or practically incomplete without free migration is either disingenuous or stupid. Free trade may and should raise living standards everywhere (and more if transportation were costless). Free migration would level standards, perhaps without raising them anywhere (especially if transportation were costless)—not to mention the sociological and political problems of assimilation. Equal treatment in immigration policy, or abandonment of discrimination, should likewise not be held out as purpose or hope. As regards both export of capital and import of populations, our plans and promises must be disciplined by tough-minded realism and practical sense [1948, p. 251].

Clearly, Simons' egalitarianism was less than species-wide.

Friedman is more sensitive to the ethical claims of potential immigrants than Simons. However, he tempers his advocacy of free entry with the qualification that the existence of welfare programs that provide guarantees of minimum income

Reder: Chicago Economics 31

regardless of productivity makes free immigration to the U.S. undesirable.[60]

I think this qualification raises an important point: with few, if any, exceptions developed countries provide minimum income guarantees for their inhabitants. These minimum guarantees are well above the earning power of most workers in less developed areas, and vary with per capita income across developed countries. Thus, freedom of immigration is likely to cause substantial income transfers within high per capita income countries as well as gains for immigrants.

Apart from compensating differentials to offset locational preferences, free immigration would cause rapid equalization of per capita incomes across countries accomplished mainly by leveling downward the incomes of the more affluent. Like Simons and Friedman, I resist this prospect.

However, I am firmly of two minds on the issue of free immigration. Both freedom of opportunity and world wide efficiency of economic organization require freedom of choice in location. Intellectual defense of resistance to the implied redistribution of income and (possibly) of political power requires a quite sharp reformulation of the normative principles of traditional liberalism and the associated goal of an open society.

Normative and Positive: The Interrelation

The anti-statist view of Chicago economists has two closely related, but distinct rationales: one of these is positive, the other normative. The positive rationale stems from TP and is accepted by virtually all Chicago economists. Disposition of resources is by primary units, individuals or families, whose well being is the object of social organization. In disposing of their resources primary units sometimes find it advantageous to employ agents to save their own time or to avail themselves of

greater skill. But use of agents, per se, always dissipates part of the gain from division of labor because agents have their own utility functions to optimize. Though restrained by the monitoring activity of the principal, the self-seeking of the agent always causes some diversion of resource yield.

The state is considered an agent, and one that is exceedingly difficult to monitor or to control. Therefore the state is to be shunned as an inefficient instrument for achieving any given objective—it is better sought privately—and objectives that cannot be achieved except through the state are to be scrutinized carefully and sceptically. Either the political process will frustrate the achievement of the goals altogether, or will drastically alter them in the process of achievement and, in any case, waste resources.

The argument of the preceding paragraph is sufficient basis for a generally adverse view of government intervention. Any reformer must either refute it, or minimize its importance. And it is a line of argument freely used by those who also accept the normative rationale.[61] But it is different from the normative rationale for anti-statism: this rationale holds that it is wrong to entrust the control of resources to government officials no matter what social objectives they may be pursuing (faithfully and efficiently). Control of resources, and the power that goes with it, *ought* to be retained by their owners. Even if property owners should wish (as such wishes are revealed through the political process) to alienate resource control to the state and its functionaries, such alienation should be resisted as wrong. I believe that it is this normative view that distinguishes laissez-faire conservatives from mere sceptics of the political process.

These two strains of anti-statist thought

---

[60] Oral discussion following initial lecture in the *Free to Choose* series.

[61] So far as I am aware, all who accept the normative rationale also accept the positive, but the reverse does not hold.

are not easily disentangled. The normative strain is held by a set of Chicago economists much smaller than the total, but a group which I believe would include most of the original Knight affinity group. An intellectual portrait of this group, many of whom would be members of the Mt. Pelerin Society, would be quite different from a description of Chicago economics although the relation of the two can be (and has been) the subject of many a lunch table conversation.

Graphically, I would describe the relation by two overlapping circles: one would be labelled "Chicago-style economists" and the other "Friends and members of the Mt. Pelerin Society." The small overlap of the two contains some of the most prominent and influential members of either group whose particular ideas are quite distinct from those in the non-overlapping portions of either circle.

IV. *Chicago Economics Since the Cowles Commission*

The history of Chicago economics since 1953 can be summarized very briefly. The departure of the Cowles Commission came soon after a tragic illness greatly curtailed the activity of Lloyd Metzler. Specializing in International Trade, Metzler was an outstanding member of his generation of Keynesian general equilibrium (DP) theorists. Together with the departure of the Cowles group, his incapacitation greatly reduced the intellectual diversity of Chicago economists.

A Friedman Era

These events occurred at the peak of Friedman's professional activity. For many years, during the fifties and sixties, a steady stream of papers on money, methodology, price theory, the consumption function, public policy proposals, etc. kept economists at Chicago and elsewhere, busy reacting to various Friedman initiatives. Outside Chicago—and in this period I was an outsider—the force of Friedman's ideas was very strong; at Chicago, it must have been even stronger.

On a wide variety of issues, one was led—drawn into—defining one's own position by reference to Friedman's views. Agree or disagree, one had to come to terms with his ideas: given the power of these ideas, his debating skill, and the force of his personality, it was not surprising that students and colleagues tended to agree with him more often than not. And even when managing to disagree, or continue in disagreement, they came away with a very firm impression of the case for the opposing view.

This exposure to the force of Friedmanian argument became a distinguishing and shared characteristic of Chicago economists, faculty members and students. However they might disagree with him on one or a number of issues, awareness of the strength of Friedman's case led Chicago economists to become interpreters of Friedman's views to uncomprehending outsiders. ("Milton may be wrong, but surely not for the reasons the outsiders are alleging.") Being conscripted as his interpreters had the effect, in the 1950s and early 1960s, of making all Chicago economists appear to be dominated by Friedman and, I suspect, had the further effect of bringing them much closer to his views than they would otherwise have come.

Personality aside, the "explanation" for this state of affairs is that during the decade and a half following World War II, the bulk of the economics profession believed that the doctrinal "revolutions" of the 1930s were successful and that they provided an intellectual rationale for the New Deal–Fair Deal reforms of the 1930s and 1940s and various proposed extensions (e.g., guarantees of full employment). In coming to these beliefs, the strong elements of validity in the neo-classical position were overlooked and the infirmities of the state as a vehicle for social change were brushed aside. Friedman saw the opportunity for scientific and ideological achievement inherent in this disequilibrium and exploited it brilliantly. But by the later 1960s, this disequilibrium had been largely corrected; outsiders had heard Friedman's messages and Chicago economists visiting at other campuses no longer had to serve as sometimes eager, sometimes semi-reluctant, interpreters.

Faculty Appointments

As Chicago economists are hardly a random sample of the profession, even after adjustment for quality, the characteristics of their ideas are influenced by the selection process. As it always has been, a major criterion for appointment is professionally recognized excellence: Chicago still wants to be the leading center of research and graduate instruction. The key term is "professional recognition": Friedman noted in 1974 that of the 13 Clark medal winners to that date, nine were teaching (or had previously taught) at Chicago at the time they received the award, and two of the other four had received offers of a position. Among these nine were several who could not possibly be described as TP adherents and some who had been leading professional opponents of Friedman's views both on policy and positive economics.

Professional recognition is not to be confused with popularity in the media: the latter is tolerated only if accompanied or preceeded by substantial scientific achievement. Ideally, professional recognition is the reflection of demonstrated ability to initiate research programs and attract other esteemed researchers to collaborate. In practise, offers from appropriately competitive institutions are treated as good proxies for demonstrated research leadership, provided there is promise of the latter. In this respect Chicago is no different from other leading schools.

There are, however, differences between Chicago and some of its leading competitors in appraising the quality of those below the very pinnacle of professional recognition. For example, there is a divergence of view as to the value of a certain type of abstract theorist with naysayers more influential at Chicago than at most other leading centers.

A second difference between Chicago and other institutions concerns the appraisal of applied economists, the quality of whose performance is measured by the interest and reliability of their empirical findings rather than by theoretical ingenuity or display of technical virtuosity. In these (numerous) cases, adherence to TP becomes very important. Inconsistency of empirical findings with the implications of TP, especially if the investigator is not greatly concerned about the inconsistency, is considered to be poor performance. This standard is markedly different from that applied in some other places where the criteria for *theoretical* performance—and hiring—are very similar to Chicago's.

In this paper, I have paid little attention to the development of Chicago ideas in the various applied fields. This neglect in no way implies that there has been lack of results important to these sub-fields, or to economics generally. My narrow focus is due primarily to my concentration upon explaining the evolution of a few central ideas that characterize Chicago economics. It also reflects the fact that the Chicago tradition has not been carried on, without major hiatus, in any of the applied fields with the exception of Labor Economics.

In Labor, Gregg Lewis integrated the TP theoretical approach with Douglas' empirical style. From Lewis the baton passed to his students: first to Albert Rees and, after Rees left for Princeton in the mid-sixties, to Gary Becker and later to James Heckman (a non-Chicago Ph.D.) and to Sherwin Rosen (Rees, 1976).

34   *Journal of Economic Literature, Vol. XX (March 1982)*

Stable Preferences and Endogenization

The inner dynamic of TP has not yet been fully worked out. As described above, ongoing research is attempting to explain not only the production of commodities but also of legislation as the result of attempts by self-seeking suppliers and office seekers to satisfy equally self-seeking customers and voters. But what determines the distribution of buying power (wealth) and voting power? And what generates the tastes or preferences that determine what individuals will do with what economic and political resources they possess?

The determinants of the distribution of "political power" are being studied at the Center for the Study of the Economy and the State, where research on Political Economy is conducted. The "explanation" of preferences is being attempted by Gary Becker who proposes to treat them as endogenous, but unchanging—stable. Such an assumption implies that changes or differences in behavior are to be attributed to changes in technology or in resource endowments that cause shifts in relative factor prices, but not to exogenous shifts of tastes. As Becker puts it: "The combined assumptions of maximizing behavior, market equilibrium and stable preferences, used relentlessly and unflinchingly, form the heart of the economic approach as I see it" (1976, p. 5). He (Becker) goes on to make it clear that he regards the economic approach as comprehensive, applicable to all human behavior (1976, Chapter 1).

Adding the assumption of stable preferences to TP, implies a fundamental modification of the theory, adding to its predictive power and correspondingly increasing its vulnerability to refutation. Becker's augmentation of the range of application of the theory—to cover all human behavior—may not involve a funda-

mental change, as the theory's field of application has never been explicitly delimited. However, it invites application of economic theory to subject matter that economists, and others, have hitherto regarded as non-economic, e.g.: marriage, fertility, divorce, the legal system, accidents, discrimination, etc. And the invitation has been widely accepted by economists at Chicago and elsewhere.

The extension of economic theory to politics by Stigler and associates; to the analysis of the legal system by Richard A. Posner and William P. Landes, and to a wide variety of "sociological" phenomena by Becker, is intellectually exciting and has had an important impact on economics at Chicago in the last decade. (It is important to note that these extensions of subject matter are independent of the assumption of stable preferences, although the two have been associated.) Finally, I should add that there is substantial disagreement among Chicago economists both as to the fruitfulness of assuming stable preferences and the validity of economic analysis when applied to seemingly non-economic subjects.[62]

Associated with the assumption of stable preferences, but logically distinct, is the "thrust for endogenization." A leading manifestation of this tendency is Stigler's attempt to explain—and constrain—the behavior of political decision makers, but it is not the only one. Becker suggests, albeit tentatively that preferences may be endogenous (1976, p. 145, no. 2); Posner has argued that the Common Law (prior to the 20th century) tended to locate liability with the party to whom cost of loss prevention was lowest, etc.

Endogenization usually involves application of the survivor principle to explain-

---

[62] This sentence is not an attempt to cloak my own views: I am sceptical about "stable preferences," but enthusiastic about (some of) the new applications of economics.

ing the characteristics of some entity. The entity may be firm size, but it might also be (say) the Gini coefficient of a country's income distribution if that coefficient could be related to (say) the cost of riot prevention. Successfully to endogenize a new variable is to enhance the explanatory power of economics, and there is much interest in such achievements. However, it must be noted that where variables are made "endogenous," they can no longer serve as objects of social choice.

To the extent that variables are endogenized—choice is explained—"society's" freedom of choice is seen as illusory. Freedom appears to consist not in power of choice, but (*pace* Hegel) in recognition of necessity. This is not a likely conclusion for followers of Adam Smith, and surely not one they desire, but one from which they can be saved only by failure of this direction of research.

To avoid the possibility of misinterpretation, let me state explicitly that I know of no Chicago economist who is prepared to say that it would be scientifically fruitful, or even possible, to "explain" all variables of interest to social choice makers by a political-economic model. I am certain that there is considerable diversity of opinion among Chicago economists of the present time as to how far it will prove fruitful to push endogenization. However, I am also quite sure that a substantial body of Chicago economists (including the present writer) feels that using economic theory to explain observed political attitudes and values is both appropriate and potentially fruitful.

Many Chicago economists, therefore, especially those in Applied Microeconomics (e.g., Labor, Industrial Organization, Law and Economics, Economics of the Family) have moved toward becoming disengaged analysts of the political-economic-social process rather than defend-

ers of laissez-faire; but though the mode may be moving toward pure analysis, both styles are still discernible. However, we are all now a long way from the Henry Simons who held that it was "'immoral' to accept as inevitable what is itself immoral" (1948 p. vii).

V. *Conclusion*

The remarkable success of the Chicago School during the third quarter of this century was due in large part to the fact that it was able to take a leading role both in scientific research and in providing a rationale for political conservatism. That it could fill this dual role was due to the fortunate combination of scientific talent and expository skill possessed by both Friedman and Stigler, but perhaps even more to the bankruptcy of intellectual conservatism at the end of World War II.

The combined effect of the Great Depression in discrediting laissez-faire capitalism, and of Hitler in rendering suspect every type of nationalist-conservative doctrine, was to leave the political right with very little intellectual support. While there were other spokesmen for laissez-faire (e.g., the Mises group), the professional esteem and academic positions of Friedman, Stigler, and Wallis, as well as their skill in non-technical communication, gave them a tremendous advantage in competing for attention and support from the conservative public during the decades following 1945.

This temporary competitive advantage made it possible for them and their protegés to adhere rigidly to their principles, both in science and ideology, without making concessions to the prejudices of gold bugs, protectionists, supporters of the military draft, etc., and without losing their support. The Friedman–Stigler policy position was too attractive ideologically, and too successful as propaganda, for hesitant conservatives to refuse support.[63]

By the late 1960s, however, the near monopoly was over. A "New Right" had emerged containing a broad spectrum of conservative positions as well as a variety of articulate spokesmen; laissez-faire is only one of the ideological vehicles for the expression of conservative attitudes. As a result, the influence of the successors of Friedman and Stigler outside the profession, and among the ideologically oriented within the profession, is likely to be much less than their mentors have enjoyed. However, few if any of the successors have equal taste or aptitude for the role of ideologue.

Temporary advantage existed in methodology as well as ideology. During the fifties and sixties, the identification of Chicago with TP economics was a source of great strength. While TP may have repelled some pure theorists whom Chicago would have wished to attract, it also made Chicago stand out as the place at which to do TP-oriented empirical research. But here again, success has given rise to a small swarm of imitators, so that at present Chicago has lost much of its one-time advantage. In various established fields of economics, including Finance, Chicago remains outstanding; but there now is keen competition from several other institutions where TP-oriented research programs are currently flourishing.

To retain its position of leadership, Chicago must continue to innovate. The research programs in Political Economy, Law and Economics and Social Interactions constitute important efforts in this direction and, clearly, these programs have roots deep in TP. However, they represent a marked change in subject matter from what was Chicago economics a quar-

ter century ago, or from the main stream of neoclassical economics at any time in the past. Such an extension entails greater risk than "mere" seeking to advance the frontier of well established fields of research. But acceptance of such risks may be the price of pre-eminence at this stage in the development of TP.

REFERENCES

ALCHIAN, ARMEN A. "Uncertainty, Evolution and Economic Theory," *J. Polit. Econ.*, June 1950, 58(3), pp. 211–21.

ARCHIBALD, GEORGE C. "Chamberlin versus Chicago," *Rev. Econ. Stud.*, Oct. 1961, 29(1), pp. 1–28.

———. "Reply to Chicago," *Rev. Econ. Stud.*, Feb. 1963, 30(2), pp. 68–71.

BAUMOL, WILLIAM J. *Business behavior, value and growth.* New York: Macmillan, 1959.

BECKER, GARY S. "Competition and Democracy," *J. Law Econ.* Oct. 1958, 1, pp. 105–09.

———. *Human capital: A theoretical and empirical analysis.* New York: National Bureau of Economic Research; distributed by Columbia University Press, 1964 (1st ed.), 1975 (2nd ed.).

———. "A Theory of the Allocation of Time," *Econ. J.*, Sept. 1965, 75(3), pp. 493–517.

———. *Human capital and the personal distribution of income: An analytical approach.* Ann Arbor: Institute of Public Administration, University of Michigan, 1967.

———. *The economic approach to human behavior.* Chicago: University of Chicago Press, 1976.

BRONFENBRENNER, MARTIN. "By Degrees," *Daily Maroon* (student newspaper, University of Chicago), Nov. 16, 1938.

———. "Observation on the 'Chicago School(s)'," *J. Polit. Econ.*, Feb. 1962, 70(1), pp. 72–75.

CARLTON, DENNIS W. "Contracts, Price Rigidity and Market Equilibrium," *J. Polit. Econ.*, Oct. 1979, 87(5), Part 1, pp. 1034–62.

COASE, RONALD H. "The Problem of Social Cost," *J. Law Econ.*, Oct. 1960, 3, pp. 1–44.

COATS, A. W. "The Origins of the 'Chicago School(s)'?" *J. Polit. Econ.*, Oct. 1963, 71, pp. 487–93.

DOUGLAS, PAUL H. *In the fullness of time.* New York: Harcourt Brace Jovanovich, 1972.

FRIEDMAN, MILTON. "Lange on Price Flexibility and Employment: a Methodological Criticism," *Amer. Econ. Rev.*, Sept. 1946, 36, pp. 613–31.

———. "Some Comments on the Significance of Labor Unions for Economic Policy," in *The impact of the union.* Edited by DAVID MCCORD WRIGHT. New York: Harcourt Brace, 1951, pp. 204–34.

———. "Choice, Chance and the Personal Distribution of Income," *J. Polit. Econ.*, Aug. 1953, 61(4), pp. 277–90.

———. *Essays in positive economics.* Chicago: University of Chicago Press, 1953 (2).

---

[63] In "support" I include grants for research, conferences, and so forth. But also, and more important, I include access to conservative politicians and business leaders, and to the media.

————. *A program for monetary stability.* New York: Fordham University Press, 1959 [1960].

————. *Capitalism and Freedom.* Chicago and London: The University of Chicago Press, 1962.

————. "More on Archibald versus Chicago," *Rev. Econ. Stud.*, Feb. 1963, *30*, pp. 65–67.

————. "Schools at Chicago," *University of Chicago Magazine*, Autumn 1974, pp. 11–16.

———— AND KUZNETS, SIMON. *Income from independent professional practice.* New York: National Bureau of Economic Research, 1945.

HARBERGER, ARNOLD C. "Monopoly and Resource Allocation," *Amer. Econ. Rev.*, Papers and Proceedings, May 1954, *44*(2), pp. 77–87.

HARROD, ROY F. "Doctrines of Imperfect Competition," *Quart. J. Econ.*, May 1934, *48*(2), pp. 442–70.

HECKMAN, JAMES J. "A Life-Cycle Model of Earnings, Learning and Consumption," *J. Polit. Econ.*, Aug. 1976, *84*(4), Part 2, pp. S11–44.

HICKS, SIR JOHN R. *Value and capital.* Oxford: The Clarendon Press, 1939.

KEYNES, LORD JOHN M. Introduction to HUBERT D. HENDERSON. *Supply and demand.* London: Nisbet, 1922.

————. *The end of laissez-faire.* London: Hogarth Press, 1926.

KLEIN, BENJAMIN. "The Competitive Supply of Money," *J. Money, Credit, Banking.* Nov. 1974, *6*(4), pp. 423–53.

KNIGHT, FRANK H. *Ethics of competition.* New York and London: Harper, 1935.

————. "Unemployment and Mr. Keynes's Revolution in Economic Theory," *Can. J. Econ. Polit. Sci.*, Feb. 1937, *3*(1), pp. 100–23.

————. *Intelligence and democratic action.* Cambridge: Harvard University Press, 1960.

KUHN, THOMAS C. *The structure of scientific revolutions.* 2nd ed., Chicago: University of Chicago Press, 1970.

LANGE, OSCAR. *Price flexibility and employment.* Cowles Commission Monograph. No. 8; Bloomington, Indiana: Principia Press, 1944.

————. "The Scope and Method of Economics," *Rev. Econ. Stud.*, *13*(1), 1945, pp. 19–32.

LATSIS, SPIRO J., ed. *Method and appraisal in economics.* Cambridge: Cambridge University Press, 1976.

LAZEAR, EDWARD P. "Why Is There Mandatory Retirement," *J. Polit. Econ.*, Dec. 1979, *87*(6), pp. 1261–84.

LEWIS, H. GREGG. *Unionism and relative wages in the United States.* Chicago: University of Chicago Press, 1963.

LUCAS, ROBERT E., JR. "Tobin and Monetarism: A Review Article," *J. Econ. Lit.*, June 1981, *19*(2), pp. 558–67.

MEDOFF, JAMES L. AND ABRAHAM, KATHERINE G. "Experience, Performance and Earnings," *Quart. J. Econ.*, Dec. 1980, *95*(4), pp. 703–36.

MILLER, HENRY L., JR. "On the 'Chicago School of Economics'," *J. Polit. Econ.*, Feb. 1962, *70*, pp. 64–69.

MODIGLIANI, FRANCO AND MILLER, MERTON H.

"The Cost of Capital, Corporation Finance and the Theory of Investment," *Amer. Econ. Rev.*, June 1958, *48*(3), pp. 261–97.

MUTH, JOHN F. "Rational Expectations and the Theory of Price Movements," *Econometrica*, July 1961, *29*(3), pp. 315–35.

NEWCOMB, SIMON. *Principles of political economy.* New York: Harper, 1885.

NUTTER, G. WARREN. *The extent of enterprise monopoly in the United States.* Chicago: University of Chicago Press, 1951.

OKUN, ARTHUR. *Prices and quantities: A macroeconomic analysis.* Washington, D.C.: Brookings Institution, 1981.

PATINKIN, DON. *Essays on and in the Chicago tradition.* Durham, N.C.: Duke University Press, 1981.

PELTZMAN, SAM. "Toward a More General Theory of Regulation," *J. Law Econ.*, Aug. 1976, *19*(2), pp. 211–40.

————. Growth of Government," *J. Law Econ.*, Oct. 1980, *23*(2), pp. 209–87.

POSNER, RICHARD A. "Economic Justice and the Economist," *The Public Interest, 33,* Fall 1973, pp. 109–19.

REDER, MELVIN W. "The Theoretical Problems of a National Wage-Price Policy," *Can. J. Econ. Polit. Sci.*, Feb. 1948, *14*(1), pp. 46–61.

————. "Wage Differentials in Theory and Measurement," in *Aspects of Labor Economics,* New York: National Bureau of Economic Research, Special Conference series 14. Princeton: Princeton University Press, 1962, pp. 257–310.

———— AND NEUMANN, GEORGE R. "Conflict and Contract: The Case of Strikes," *J. Polit. Econ.*, Oct. 1980, *88*(5), pp. 867–86.

REES, ALBERT. "H. Gregg Lewis and the Development of Analytical Labor Economics," *J. Polit. Econ.* Aug. 1976, *84*(4), Part 2, pp. 3–8.

————. "Douglas on Wages on the Supply of Labor," *J. Polit. Econ.*, Oct. 1979, *87*(5), Part 1, pp. 915–22.

ROSEN, SHERWIN. "A Theory of Life Earnings," *J. Polit. Econ.*, Part 2, Aug. 1976, *84*(4), pp. S45–67.

SAMUELS, WARREN J., ed. *The Chicago School of political economy.* East Lansing: Michigan State University, Graduate School of Business Administration, 1976.

SAMUELSON, PAUL A. "Paul Douglas's Measurement of Production Functions and Marginal Productivities," *J. Polit. Econ.*, Oct. 1979, *85*(5), Part 1, pp. 422–39.

SCHULTZ, HENRY. *The theory and measurement of demand.* Chicago, Ill.: The University of Chicago Press, 1938.

SIMON, HERBERT A. "A Behavioral Model of Rational Choice," *Quart. J. Econ.*, Feb. 1955, *67*(1), pp. 99–118.

————. "From Substantive to Procedural Rationality," in *Method and appraisal in economics.* Edited by SPIRO J. LATSIS. Cambridge: Cambridge University Press, 1976, pp. 129–48.

SIMONS, HENRY C. *Personal income taxation.* Chicago: University of Chicago Press, 1938.

———. *Economic policy for a free society.* Chicago: University of Chicago Press, 1948.

SIMONS, HENRY. *A positive program for laissez faire; some proposals for a liberal economic policy.* Chicago, Ill.: The University of Chicago Press, 1936.

STIGLER, GEORGE J. *Production and distribution theories, the formative period.* New York: MacMillan, 1941.

———. "The Economics of Information," *J. Polit. Econ.,* June 1961, *69*(3), pp. 213–25.

———. "On the 'Chicago School of Economics': Comment," *J. Polit. Econ.,* Feb. 1962a, *70,* pp. 70–71.

———. "Information in the Labor Market," *J. Polit. Econ.,* Oct. 1962b, *70*(5), Part 2, pp. 94–105.

———. "Archibald versus Chicago," *Rev. Econ. Stud.,* Feb. 1963, *30,* pp. 63–64.

———. *The organization of industry.* Homewood, Ill.: Richard D. Irwin, 1968.

———. "Director's Law of Public Income Redistribution," *J. Law Econ.,* April 1970, *13*(1), pp. 1–10.

———. "Free Riders and Collective Action: An Appendix to Theories of Economic Regulation," *Bell J. Econ. Manage. Sci.,* Autumn 1974, *5*(2), pp. 359–65.

———. *The citizen and the state; essays on regulation.* Chicago: University of Chicago Press, 1975.

——— AND KINDAHL, JAMES K. *The behavior of industrial prices.* National Bureau of Economic Research, distributed by Columbia University Press, (1970).

TOBIN, JAMES. *Asset accumulation and economic activity; reflections on contemporary macroeconomic theory.* Chicago: University of Chicago Press, 1980.

VINER, JACOB. "Cost Curves and Supply Curves," *Zeitschrift fur Nationalokonomii,* Sept. 1931, *111*(1), pp. 23–46.

———. "Mr. Keynes on the Causes of Unemployment," *Quart. J. Econ.,* Nov. 1936, *51*(4), pp. 147–67.

———. *The long view and the short.* Glencoe, Ill.: The Free Press, 1958.

WALL, DAVID, ed. *Chicago essays in economic development.* Chicago: University of Chicago Press, 1972.

WILLIAMSON, OLIVER E. *The economics of discretionary behavior.* Chicago: Markham, 1967.

Journal of Economic Literature
Vol. XVII (June 1979), pp. 477–502

A Branch of Economics is Missing: Micro-Micro Theory

By HARVEY LEIBENSTEIN

Harvard University

and

Institute for Advanced Study
Princeton, New Jersey

I wish to thank James Dean, James Medoff, Richard Day, Victor Goldberg, Albert Hirschman, Gordon Winston, Persio Arida, and the editor for helpful comments.

I. *Introduction*

IN THE LIFE HISTORY of most sciences there are movements toward the study of larger aggregates or toward the detailed study of smaller and more fundamental units. My impression is that in most fields the movement toward the study of more micro units has predominated. Yet in economics in the 1930's the movement was in the macro direction. Both physics and biology (in the last three decades) have made great strides by studying smaller and smaller entities— physics by studying more minute fundamental particles and biology by studying the fundamental elements determining genetics. In a general sense economics has not been moving in this direction, although some work of this nature exists. The purpose of this paper is to review some samples of the work that exists and to argue that this area must become a major field of economic research and study.

The question of how individuals in mul-tiperson firms influence firm decisions seems like such a natural question to ask that it is amazing that it is not part of the formal agenda of economists as a profession. Of course it has been asked, but not by present-day economists in their professional capacity. In other words, micro-microeconomics has never become an established field. For the most part, theorists have not only not raised this question, but they have continued to develop micro the-, ory in such a way as to discourage economists from raising this question. Part of the reason for this lies in the maximizing and optimizing biases of conventional micro theory, and part can be ascribed to the consequences of the long period required to refine the theory so that elements that did not fit the basic model were discarded.[1]

[1] Both Alfred Marshall in *Industry and Trade* [33, 1923] and Frank Knight in *Risk, Uncertainty and Profit* [21, 1921] considered intra-firm elements. However these considerations have certainly dropped out of modern microeconomic analysis. They do not appear to be necessary elements of the main-line neoclassical model.

478   *Journal of Economic Literature, Vol. XVII (June 1979)*

A frequently-used metaphor is that the firm behaves *as if* it possessed a "black box," which drives the firm *as if* it were an individual, irrespective of size. One way of looking at micro-micro theory is to suggest that the micro-micro problem is the study of what goes on *inside* the black box. Does the multiperson firm face the same problems as the one-man firm? What are the components of the black box? From this point of view, micro-micro theory is concerned with *intrafirm* behavior and relations or with the interaction of persons within the firm and their influences on firm behavior. Outside the degenerate case of the one-man firm, for which the boundary between micro and micro-micro disappears, the distinction between the two types of theories, micro and micro-micro, is unambiguous.

An obvious question is the relation between firm owners and firm members. Does the owner completely control, through contracts or other means, what others in the firm do? Can costs be understood without first answering this question? It would be platitudinous to argue that only to the extent that intraorganization activities are understood can costs of production be understood. But this is not a view that one gets from traditional micro theory, which simply asserts that costs are minimized. Hence, we have at least one reason why we should be interested in micro-micro theory. Another is whether the picture of the firm we get by analyzing the internals of the black box independently from conventional theory leads to a view of the firm consistent with conventional micro theory.

For the most part these questions are not answered in the conventional texts; and from this standpoint micro-micro theory may be said to be missing. However, there are other writings that come close to investigating some aspects of this problem. While these writings are too voluminous to review in detail, it is useful to review them on a broad brush basis in order to see whether a valid argument can be made that micro-micro theory as a branch of economics is missing, for the most part. Further, I will argue that this branch represents at this point a natural and useful research frontier.

To carry out this task we will examine, (1) complex objective functions, (2) the work of the Carnegie school, (3) what I have referred to elsewhere as X-efficiency theory, and (4) some related writings that do not fit easily into any of these categories.

II. Complex Objective Functions versus Micro-Micro Theory

There are at least two ways of trying to create alternatives to the traditional micro theory: One is to change the objective function of conventional theory, while the other is to start by creating micro-micro theories. These two approaches are not the same, although they are sometimes confused for the same thing. In this connection it is of interest to look at several well known "complex objective function" theories: those associated with the names Tibor Scitovsky, William J. Baumol, Robin Marris, and Oliver E. Williamson.

Scitovsky's theory appeared in the 1940's [44, 1943]—and his work may be looked at as the paradigm for the others. According to Scitovsky, the neoclassical assumption that an entrepreneur maximizes profits as well as satisfaction implies that the entrepreneur's choice between more income and more leisure is independent of his income. This presupposes a special hypothesis about the psychology of the entrepreneur such that his profit-seeking activities will continue unabated as his income increases. In contrast to the neoclassical entrepreneur, Scitovsky's entrepreneur trades income for leisure as his income rises. Whether or not entrepreneurs in general maximize profits can only be determined empirically. In this model there is no distinction between entrepreneurs, owners, and managers.

Baumol suggested an objective function that emphasized sales maximization subject to a profit constraint [5, 1959]. Baumol came to this conclusion as a result of his work with a business consulting firm. The profit constraint has something to do with the belief that the stockholders have to be satisfied in some sense. However, there is nothing in Baumol's theory that determines what the profit constraint ought to be. Nevertheless, for any given positive profit constraint, Baumol was able to demonstrate that he could get qualitive results different from the conventional profit maximizing model.

The growth maximization model developed by Robin Marris [30, 1963] is in some respects different from Baumol's, but is similar to it in spirit. Clearly there are similarities between growth and sales maximization, but they need not be the same thing. Thus, reinvestment is important in the Marris model. Furthermore, the Marris model finds a solution for the profit constraint; *i.e.*, profits must not be so low as to reduce the value of the stock to a degree that a takeover bid is probable. Presumably the manager's position is vulnerable to the introduction of new owners. Thus Marris's managers work out trade-offs between the utility of growth versus the utility of profits so that the position of management is not threatened.

Williamson [50, 1963] developed a model that has greater similarity to Scitovsky's than to Baumol's and Marris's. Williamson assumes that managers control the firm and are in a position to divert profits for the benefit of management—but only indirectly. Profits belong to the stockholders. Managers cannot cut into profits after the fact—that is, after they have been earned. But managers can lower profits by increasing expenses. Thus Williamson implicitly assumes that there exists a class of expenses, a subdivision of

all expenses, which is for the benefit of managers. Some examples come easily to mind: lavish offices, carpets, extra secretarial services, entertainment budgets, and so on. Other "benefits" may be more subtle and be related to taking it easier than otherwise—which manifests itself in organization slack.

In any event, because of managerial discretion, expenses are higher and profits lower than would be the case under profit maximization. In this model we visualize the manager (or managers) deciding, as it were, on the distribution between profits and management perquisites so as to maximize the utility of a profits-perks mix.

If we combine all four of these models, we can come up with a composite objective function. Under such a function the managers would maximize the utility of a function whose arguments would include: profits, sales, the growth rate, and managerial perquisites. By changing the arguments, we can develop almost any number of different complex objective function models.

There are problems with such a vision of firm behavior. A basic one has to do with the distinction between a single decision-maker versus group decision-making. Do groups decide the same way as individuals do? Are the same ideas as meaningful for groups as they are for individuals? These are fundamental questions that permeate many aspects of our discussion. We shall treat them in this section only in connection with the problem of complex objective functions. Consider Williamson's function. Is the "Manager" who decides between profits and "enjoyable expenses" an individual or a group? If there is only *one* manager, than no problem arises. It makes sense for the manager to maximize a utility function. Such a person can decide between the utility of profit versus the utility of perquisites disguised as expenses. What meaning can we give to the notion of maximizing utility of a group

480   *Journal of Economic Literature, Vol. XVII (June 1979)*

of individuals? How is the decision made between different individuals' evaluation of the utility of more versus less profits?

The main point of all this is that the basic question of micro-micro theory is not answered by the complex objective function approach. It retains the black box of conventional micro theory, but changes the assertion about the behavior of the black box. These remarks are not intended as a criticism of Williamson or of any of the other authors involved. They did not set out to solve a micro-micro problem but to make micro theory more realistic. In this they succeeded. Nevertheless, these models do not handle the problems that arise when we shift from the single person dictator-manager case to the multi-person case. In general, it would seem reasonable to expect that (1) the larger the management group, the greater the number of arguments in the objective function and (2) the larger the potential perquisites to be distributed among managers, the greater the problem.

The essence of the problem is the size of the management group and the relation of various members to each other. For different individuals there are likely to be differences in power and similarity or conflicts of interests that arise. Many organizations allow for conflict resolution through a hierarchical system so that differences among lower status individuals can be resolved by higher status individuals. But despite a hierarchical power structure, informal degrees of influence may play a significant role. Hence, the multiperson situation as such creates difficulties in determining how "utilities" are distributed, and what meaning can be attached to utility maximization where actual or potential conflict exists. In other words, there is no reason to assume that any system of conflict resolution necessarily results in "joint maximization."

A single individual can be presumed to have a unique objective function, at least

at any one time. But do two individuals necessarily have the same objective function? Whatever the answer, this is clearly a legitimate question. By adding enough arguments it may always be possible to presume that a utility function exists for any number of individuals. Thus if $U_a (X_1, X_2)$ and $U_b (X_3, X_4)$ are two objective functions for individuals A and B, a combined function $U (X_1, X_2, X_3, X_4)$ may be formed where each X_i stands for a different subobjective. But is all this meaningful if there are hundreds of X's? Clearly, the "team sense" of the management group must become attenuated as sub-objectives multiply. Does the sum of all the individual objectives, or some subset of these, add up in a way to a group objective? At least in some cases one can argue that there is a sense of group objectives that differs from the sum of individual objectives.

For a multiperson group such as a committee or a group of committees, maximization of utility may be an inappropriate concept. There is the game-theoretic problem made famous in the John von Neumann and Oskar Morgenstern's *Theory of Games* [38, 1944]. If an individual (or decision-maker) does not control all the variables, then maximization by any decision-maker may be impossible. This is one essential of the games of strategy problem. If A controls options X_1 and X_2, while B controls X_3 and X_4, the outcome depends on how each chooses. There is no necessary way for A or B to choose a maximum *individually*. Whether or not they can do so jointly (*i.e.*, cooperatively) is another matter. In the same sense, if management is a multiperson group, there may be no way to guarantee maximizing the utility of the group. Also, "forced" cooperation may also not yield a maximum. Suppose part of the value for some of the managers is noncooperation in some instances. Cooperation may reduce the utility of some individuals who enjoy an individualistic (non-cooperative) stance. The most likely outcomes are situations in which some gain and others lose. Thus a maximum in the Pareto superior sense may be ruled out in such instances. In sum, groups involve potential conflict, which puts into question certain basic concepts that are applicable to individuals.

III. *"Semi Micro-Micro Theory"*— *The Carnegie School*

The set of ideas developed by Herbert Simon, his colleagues, and those (many of whom were at one time or another at Carnegie-Mellon University) who were influenced by his ideas, will be referred to as the Carnegie school ideas. (See Kalman Cohen and Richard Cyert [9, 1975].)

In general, the writings of the Carnegie school contain an extremely rich set of ideas about the internal operations of firms. This point cannot be overemphasized. A major concern of many of these writers is organization theory and the analysis of a variety of intraorganizational problems. Thus, anyone searching for ideas in this area would be well advised to pursue the work of this group. At the same time, from the standpoint of our problem area there are difficulties with this body of literature. It has not resulted in an alternative to the existing neoclassical paradigm, although it may contain the raw materials for constructing one or more such alternatives. These remarks are not intended as a criticism of what has been achieved, but indicate the boundaries of the effort to date.

This set of ideas is rather difficult to place in terms of the dichotomy established for purposes of this paper. Most of the central ideas do not of themselves imply a micro-micro model. To start with, consider Simon's famous concept, *satisficing*. Satisficing behavior is an alternative to maximizing behavior. However, it could be applied just as easily to an individual decision-maker, or a group, or a multiperson firm. It substitutes a different decision criterion for maximization or optimization, but it does not of itself imply that we go inside the firm for this purpose.

The same can be said for a number of other concepts. Richard Day [12, 1964; 13, 1975] has attempted to summarize the essentials of the Carnegie approach in a terse and useful way for our purposes. He lists ten basic characteristics, one of which is (1) satisficing. Let us look briefly at the others and see to what extent they involve a micro-micro approach. These are: (2) bounded rationality, (3) multiplicity of goals, (4) sequential attention to goals, (5) feedback, (6) standard operating procedures, (7) resistance to change except under "duress," (8) coalitions to resolve conflicts, (9) organizational slack to stabilize coalitions, and (10) maintenance of viability. In Day's list, eight of the ten characteristics are not *necessarily* related to an essentially micro-micro approach. Most of them are related to the departure from the perfect rationality assumption. The two that are related to the *insides* of the firm are (8) "coalitions to resolve conflict," and (9) "organizational slack to stabilize coalitions." But we are not presented with a theory of intra-firm coalitions. That is, we are not told how coalitions are formed, who gets into a coalition, who remains outside, who gets what in a coalition, and so on. Of course, ideas not necessarily related to micro-micro models may be extremely useful in developing such models. Thus, the notions of (3) multiplicity of goals, (6) standard operating procedures, and (9) organizational slack lend themselves readily to the creation of micro-micro type simulation models. However, both the spirit and essence of the ideas, as far as I understand them, are that the firm itself is a coalition, and organizational slack exists to maintain that coalition.

I find it extremely difficult to judge the depth of the micro-micro concern of the

Carnegie school approach. Interpreters and summarizers have not emphasized that aspect. To the extent that emphasis exists, it is on the substitutes for the maximization assumption. Where the Carnegie school is contrasted with the neoclassical position, it is almost invariably the case that the deviations from rationality are emphasized. The elements usually discussed are satisficing, aspirations, bounded rationality, multiplicity of goals, standard operating procedures, and feedback.

An essential difficulty in treating the Carnegie school is that one cannot ask what the Carnegie economic model is and expect to be shown a specific article or book and to be told, "This is it"—at least, not in the sense in which a good graduate (or high level intermediate) text represents neoclassical theory or in which Gerard Debreu's book [15, 1959] or Kenneth Arrow and Frank Hahn [4, 1971] represents modern general equilibrium theory. From this point of view the text by Cohen and Cyert is of considerable interest [9, 1975]. The authors present both the standard neoclassical theory of the firm and some Carnegie school writings, as well as other alternatives. One of the authors, Cyert, has been a major contributor to the work of the Carnegie school and with James G. March wrote *The Behavioral Theory of the Firm* [11, 1963].

In their text Cohen and Cyert face the contrast between the Carnegie school and the orthodox approach. It is of interest that they step away from the possible conflict between the two types of theories and search for a conciliation between the two views. Some quotations from the Cohen and Cyert book are of interest:

> At this level of generality, we think that the results deduced from a set of assumptions which include utility and profit maximization are perfectly acceptable. If we wish to predict how a *particular* household or firm will behave, then assumptions this general will not be satisfactory. [9, 1975, p. 51.]

> Subjectively rational decision models of the type proposed by Simon represent a promising alternative to the usual models of economists which implicitly assume that great knowledge and computational ability are possessed by decision makers. Evidence suggests that Simon's approach to economic decision making is likely to provide good explanations and predictions of the actual decision-making behavior of consumers and businessmen. [9, 1975, p. 308.]

But earlier we read that

> The analysis of microeconomics assumes rational behavior by individual economic agents. The usefulness of this analysis for answering questions involving the allocation of resources among broad economic sectors, such as markets or industries, does not necessarily depend upon the extent to which consumers actually do maximize their utilities and business firms actually do maximize their profits. [9, 1975, p. 289.]

The view taken seems to be that for industry-wide or larger problems the neoclassical approach is appropriate, while those involving predictions of specific firm behavior may be aided by applying some of the newer theories. Obviously there is an unresolved procedural difficulty here. If a theory will not predict the behavior of a firm, can it predict the behavior of a collection of firms? The foregoing is not to suggest that there is no satisfactory answer to this question, but somewhere this question should be investigated. Perhaps Cohen and Cyert felt that their text was not the place to do so.

At the same time one gets the impression from the Cyert and Charles Hedrick paper [10, 1972, p. 409] that the authors share the "growing uneasiness with the neoclassical approach," and they conclude that "the problem is clearly difficult, but we wonder whether economics can remain an empirical science and continue to ignore the actual decision-making process of real firms."

Yet the view represented by the quotations may be consistent with the present status of Carnegie school theories. The impression that one gets is that there is no general Carnegie school model. Rather, what we have is a set of ingredients; we are asked to work out specific recipes of our own from these ingredients. Sample recipes already exist. These are the simulation models presented in Cyert and March's *The Behavioral Theory of the Firm* [11, 1963] and elsewhere. While these simulation models are examples of the approach, they need not be consistent with any more general Carnegie school theory. Each simulation model represents a single case. Since the bounds of the simulation model are not constrained by a more general theory, it would seem reasonable to assume that we cannot determine in advance whether the simulation model is consistent with the neoclassical model. (See also William Baumol and Maco Stewart [6, 1971] on this point.)

In general, the Carnegie school view of the firm may be said to be made up of two components, both of which are related to the problem of deviation from rational decision-making. These two elements are: (a) the ingredients that enter into the decision process and (b) the likelihood that various sub-objectives of the firm will be inconsistent. Frequently, the organizational sub-goals considered are (a) a production goal, (b) an inventory goal, (c) a sales goal, (d) a market share goal, and (e) a profit goal. Different members of the coalition, which is made up of those who run the firm, may espouse different goals, and bargaining takes place between them in order to solve this problem. However, except for the statement that organizational slack is likely to enter as a means of conflict resolution, the Carnegie school does not present a theory of how these various conflicting elements are resolved. Essentially two elements would be necessary in order to make the theory exist and "move," so to speak. One would be a theory of goal determination by the firm from components (sub-goals) taken from within the firm and the other a theory of conflict

resolution of such sub-goals. Hence, it seems fair to say that while there are elements in the Carnegie approach that suggest the ingredients of specific micro-micro models, these elements are still incomplete, or the elements have not been selected and put together in such a way as to form a competing theory. As far as I could judge, the specific authors do not appear to claim much more for the Carnegie school approach.[2] Nevertheless, the Carnegie school approach has been extremely useful in providing the raw materials for simulation models based on assumptions that differ from the maximizing paradigm. Furthermore, as micro-micro theories are developed in greater depth, they are bound to use some of the existing Carnegie school ideas or ideas that overlap with them.

There is a large and growing literature that looks at various problems internal to organizations from an optimizing standpoint, and which are quite likely of interest to those concerned with micro-micro theory. We cannot review this literature (although such a review would be useful), but it may be helpful if we point to some examples. For the most part the authors do not ask what the behavior relations are but seek to provide optimal solutions to predetermined organizational problems. Thus James A. Mirrlees considers the optimal relations between reward administration and the monitoring of performance [35, 1976]. Joseph Stiglitz considers some related questions concerning internal incentives, lack of information about performance, piece rates, monitoring problems, *etc.* [48, 1975]. Roy Radner's and Jacob Marschak's work on the theory of teams is concerned with the information aspects of team work [41, 1972]. Radner and Michael Rothchild look at the allocation of effort from a similar standpoint [42,

[2] Baumol and Stewart [6, 1971, pp. 122–23] appear to agree with this assessment.

1975]. An essential aspect of these papers is to recognize an organizational problem and to find an optimum solution. It is of interest that the various papers do not deal with the question as to whether or not organizations seek, find, or use optimum solutions. A paper by Day and E. Herbert Tinney takes a somewhat different approach [14, 1968]. Their model has two departments, an engineering department whose objective is to minimize cost and a sales department with a profit maximizing objective. They show that a response to success and failure mechanism leads to dynamic behavioral trajectories consistent with the neoclassical model. It would be of interest to rework the exercise based on other behavioral assumptions for the two departments. On the whole this growing body of literature is of considerable importance, since it helps to fill out some of the theoretical possibilities about the nature of the "black box."

Another body of literature tangential but not unrelated to our problem seems to be inspired by Ronald Coase's famous article, which attempts to explain why firms should emerge [8, 1937]. Coase tried to answer the question in terms of the idea that firms save on transaction costs. Two especially noteworthy contributions are those of Armen Alchian and Harold Demsetz [2, 1972] and Oliver Williamson [51, 1975]. Alchian and Demsetz argue that as individual (cottage industry) production efforts become more complicated, monitoring the work or work results is required, and the firm provides internal monitoring activities more cheaply than do individuals working in isolation.

Williamson examined the problem much more extensively in *Markets and Hierarchies* [51, 1975]. There he analyzes the advantages of shifting transactions from the market to hierarchical structures. Williamson begins by analyzing the advantages of the most basic grouping of people within the firm, the peer group— advantages both to members of the group and to the overall efficiency of the firm. He then considers the advantages of vertical integration, which culminates in the multidivisional structure. While Williamson does acknowledge the possibility of conflict between workers and managers and is concerned with how the firm can elicit consummate rather than perfunctory cooperation from the workers, he does not discuss in any detail the inefficiencies of the peer group and/or hierarchical structures. While Williamson does not provide a micro-micro model, since that is not his problem, the book does contain innumerable useful ideas and insights for those interested in constructing micro-micro models.

IV. General X-Efficiency Theory as a Micro-Micro Theory

I have referred to my work that attempts to explain the phenomenon of X-efficiency as General X-Efficiency theory. In this section I want to consider how this work fits the concept of a micro-micro theory. Unlike conventional micro theory, it is unrealistic to assume that readers have read any of the expositions of X-efficiency theory. Hence this treatment will be disproportionately long. Of course there is no necessary connection between length and importance. At the same time I do not wish to use very much of this space to present another fairly full exposition. This part of the paper cannot be self-contained. What I wish to do instead is to indicate in a few pages (once again) a few basic elements of the theory to the extent necessary for purposes of this article. Readers interested in a fuller treatment can check the references.

We shall focus on five elements of X-efficiency theory: (1) selective rationality (degree of maximization deviation); (2) in-

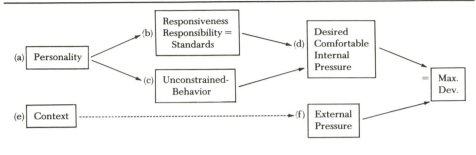

DIAGRAM 1

dividuals as basic decision units; (3) effort discretion; (4) inert areas; and (5) organizational entropy. In the neoclassical theory, maximization is the counterpart to selective rationality. The other elements are of a micro-micro nature and have no neoclassical counterparts.

Under selective rationality individuals select the extent to which they deviate from maximizing behavior. If two individuals *A* and *B* are faced with the same flow of opportunities and constraints (note that the constraints are attached to the opportunities) and *A attends* to all the opportunities and constraints, while *B* attends to only half of them, we can say that *B* deviated from maximizing behavior by 50 percent. The degree of maximization deviations depends on the elements indicated in the scheme shown on DIAGRAM 1. Personality is defined in terms of (b) a taste for responsiveness to opportunities and constraints within certain standards of behavior and (c) a simultaneous taste for "irresponsible" or unconstrained behavior. The standards of behavior include moral constraints reflected in attitudes toward trust, honesty, lying, altruism, group solidarity, sacrificing for group objectives, and so on, which play a role in behavior. The compromise between (b) and (c) that the personality makes leads to a most "comfortable" degree of internal pressure

which, if everything were in the person's control, would determine the degree of maximization deviation. Maximization deviation is a measure of selective rationality. However, the economic context (e) in which the individual finds himself may impose a higher degree of external pressures than desired internal pressure, and hence the interaction between (d) and (f) determines the actual degree of maximization deviation. That is, pressures from peers (horizontal relations) and authorities (vertical relations) within the firm determine a degree of selective rationality different from what the person would choose in the absence of such pressures.

Now, we assume that firm membership contracts are incomplete.[3] The simplest case to consider is the one in which the individual is told what payment he is to receive but not how much effort he has to put forth. Hence effort discretion exists. Effort has four dimensions: activities *A*, pace of activities *P*, quality of acts *Q*, and time duration and sequence *T*. One value for each dimension yields an *APQT* bundle or effort point. Individuals will usually

---

[3] The fact that such contracts usually involve an indefinite future in which both reliability and flexibility are simultaneous requirements implies the necessity of effort discretion. See Ian R. MacNeil [28, 1974] and Victor Goldberg [18, 1978] on the significance of such contracts.

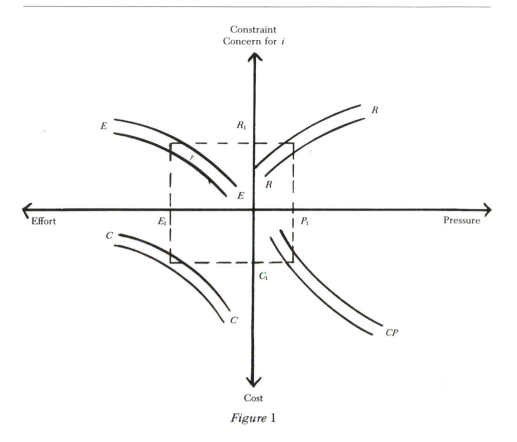

Figure 1

interpret their jobs (firm membership role) in terms of a subset of related effort points (to allow for variable demands on effort), which we will refer to as an effort position.

The idea of inert areas indicates the existence of effort points or of "positions" (whether effort positions or other types of option choices), so that if one is at one position associated with a certain utility one does not move to another position associated with a higher utility. The reason is that there is an "inertial cost" in moving from one position to another, and for the positions in the inert area, the inertial cost of moving is greater than or equal to the utility gain.

In diagramatical expositions inert areas will usually be reflected by "fat" curves. Now, it should be clear that the most important distinction between the X-efficiency theory and the neoclassical model of the firm is the fact that in X-efficiency theory the individual is the basic atomic unit. This by itself assures that the theory will be a micro-micro theory. If we add to this the assumption that effort discretion exists for every firm member, in part because employment contracts are incomplete, then clearly everyone in the firm helps to determine output, and hence each and every individual's choice helps to determine the cost of production.[4]

When an individual joins the firm, he is likely to be given bits of information that give him various clues that help him to guess the range of the area of effort discretion. In addition his perception of (1) the horizontal (or peer group), (2) the vertical (or hierarchical), and (3) the historical influences helps to guide him in his choice.[5] These constraining influences help to determine his choice. They are based on the likely reactions of others. That is, on the likelihood of approval or disapproval (1) on the basis of what is or is not done traditionally, (2) from peers, and (3) from those who are "authorities" or more specifically, those who are hierarchically above and below him.[6] These ideas are illustrated with the aid of *Figure* 1 above.

In quadrant I the abscissa *P* indicates the pressure that the firm imposes on the individual. The curve *RR* indicates how external pressure is translated into constraint concern by the individual. In quadrant II constraint concern becomes the

independent variable, which in turn determines, through the function *EE*, the effort put forth. In quadrant III the curve *CC* translates effort into the cost of the production per unit contributed by the individual. In quadrant IV cost is the independent variable, and the curve *CP* shows how the firm reacts to the cost attributed to individual *i* by putting pressure on the individual. The greater the cost, the greater the pressure by the firm to reduce cost.

The essence of the relations in *Figure* 1 is shown in *Figure* 2. Constraint, concern, and effort are intermediate variables between pressure and cost. Hence, in *Figure* 2, in which the two variables are cost and pressure, the curve $C_i(P)$ indicates cost for the *representative* individual *i* as a function of pressure (suppressing *R* and *E* in *Figure* 1) and $P_i(C)$ as pressure imposed by the firm as a function of cost. The intersection between these two curves reflects an equilibrium between the representative individual *i* and the firm. If we start at a nonequilibrium point, we can see that there exists a cobweb pattern of reactions that leads back to the equilibrium position *E* in *Figure* 2. Other dynamic sequences are also possible. Space considerations do not permit a discussion of the relations between representative individuals, nonrepresentative individuals, and the firm.

Another idea related to effort discretion is organizational entropy. Entropy is used in the sense of a tendency towards disorganization. An individual chooses his effort position on the basis of what he expects the horizontal and vertical relations to be. However, if he discovers in the course of his activities that the horizontal and vertical constraints are much weaker than he anticipated, then he is likely to shift to those effort points within his effort position that he prefers, and which are less likely to be connected with the objectives of the firm. Hence we visualize this

---

[4] Mainline theory must assume implicitly that employment contracts are complete, or that supervision is precise and makes up for contractural incompleteness, if we are to have a conventional production function.

[5] We do not specify exact choice criteria nor do we assume a uniform choice procedure used by all individuals. Behind these ideas is the implicit assumption that different individuals will use different information search and different decision procedures. For each individual the search and decision procedures reflect the degree to which a person's behavior deviates from maximizing behavior. We do assume that once the activities reflecting these procedures fall into the inert area that this ends the search for options that can yield superior results. It would take us too far afield to go into details on these matters here.

[6] The authority-sanction-approval mechanism is an important part of the internal structure of the organization; *i.e.*, it is part of the insides of the "black box." The "voice" versus "exit" modes of behavior, analyzed by Hirschman [19, 1974] are part of this structural mechanism, both for imposing and for resisting pressure within the firm.

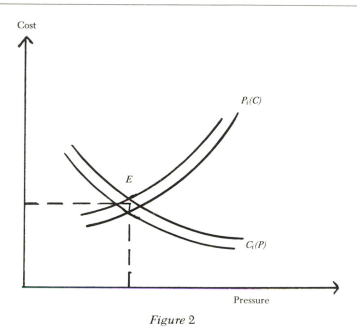

Figure 2

movement, when it manifests itself, as a process of organizational entropy. In *Figure* 2 it may be shown as a limited upward shift of the $P_i(C)$ curve. Thus we see in the figure that cost rises as entropy increases take place. However, an entropy increase may not manifest itself. We visualize the firm as an arena in which management struggles against the latent entropy force inherent in the organization and in effort discretion. If the management struggle is equal to the latent entropy then, of course, actual entropy increases will not be observed; *i.e.*, the curve $P_i(C)$ will not rise. But in any event we see the entropy force as a *latent* cost increasing process within the firm.

Figure 3 is similar to *Figure* 2 except that it aggregates the situation for all individuals. Aggregation is not simple. There is a distribution problem involved, which we will ignore in this brief exposition. For

every level of aggregate pressure that the firm imposes, there is a distribution of pressures over individuals. Let us assume that pressure is the same for all individuals. We write p_{ij} to mean that for every individual i, the pressure is j. We can then obtain aggregate $P_j = \Sigma_i p_{ij} = n p_{ij}$ for n individuals. For each pressure level P_j we can now add up the costs and obtain the aggregate cost-pressure function C, and in a similar manner the aggregate pressure-cost function P.

The level of aggregate pressure P_j depends not only on cost but on influences outside the firm. Referring to the firm under analysis as firm A, if prices of competing firms are low compared to the cost level in a given firm A, then the members of the management team in A will feel more pressure to try to do something about costs than if prices in other firms were relatively high. We may visualize a

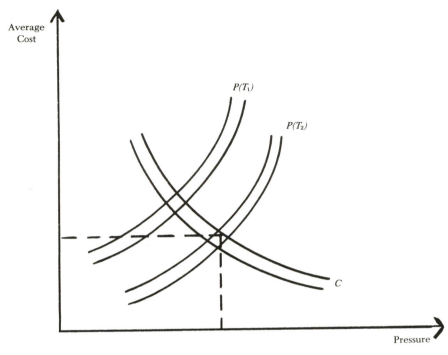

Figure 3

situation in which competing prices are low as a "tight" environment. Alternatively, if competing prices are high, it is a "loose" environment. Clearly the pressure that the management[7] imposes *inside* the firm will depend not only on cost but also on the level of environmental tightness. Thus for a tighter environment T_2 we show the P curve below what it would be for the looser environment T_1. As shown in *Figure* 3, equilibrium costs turn out to be lower under T_2 than under T_1. Of course, price is only one manifestation

[7] Every so often we use "management" as a linguistic shorthand to avoid getting into the problem of the distribution of activities among members of management teams. Of course, we have in mind that individuals impose these pressures on others.

of environmental tightness—since we visualize environmental tightness as a more general concept than degree of competition. However, this is not the place to go into this matter.

Firms do not necessarily accept the degree of tightness—they can also attempt to determine it or contribute to its determination. We refer to activities whose aim is to reduce tightness as sheltering activities. In other words, the firm tries to find a shelter from competition for its high cost activities. First note that a substitute for reducing costs (fighting entropy) is to reduce tightness; *i.e.*, to change the environment. Thus pressure activities on firm members and sheltering activities are substitutes for each other. Examples of sheltering activities are the following: entering into price agreements, activities that help maintain price agreements, product differentiation, activities such as advertising, developing trademarks, engaging in market share agreements, entering into mergers, political activities to obtain price supports, tariffs or other restrictions on trade, and so on. The function of such sheltering activities is to reduce the impact of competition in the industry, or by possible entrants, in order to maintain or raise the existing price or prices charged by the firm in question. Thus, in general, the aim of sheltering activities is to increase the capacity to raise prices without excessive loss of sales. Of course, the firm in question need not initiate such activities. In part it may engage in such activities by acquiescing to or supporting the sheltering activities of others. Thus, in the price leadership situation following the price leader is a type of sheltering activity. Similarly, supporting political activities to increase a particular tariff is a sheltering activity that is likely to be approved by both management and trade unions that represent some or all of the workers within the firm. Thus sheltering activities are facilitated by various organizational networks, which permits the flow of support from inside the firm to industry-wide organizations, to political parties, and to governments.

From the point of view that we are taking, the opposite of sheltering activities are entrepreneurial acts—*i.e.*, those activities that set up new units, or expand existing units, in competition with existing firms. Thus anybody who sets up such units increases the response to an existing high price or to price increases. Hence, entrepreneurial activities have the effect of putting pressure on firms to reduce their prices. These activities are of course determined not by specific existing firms but by the entire economy. This is not the place to present a theory of entrepreneurship; however, consistent with X-efficiency theory we have to start with imper-

fect markets. (See Leibenstein [26, 1978, ch. 3].) Hence, our markets are characterized by *gaps* in input availabilities as well as obstacles that manifest themselves in less than equal access to inputs. Hence, in order to start a new firm, an entrepreneur must have the capacity to overcome the gaps and the obstacles in imperfect markets. He also has to be an *input completer* in the sense that less than the complete marshaling of inputs would not fulfill the entrepreneurial function. Obviously there are limits to the supply of gap fillers and input completers. Without going into detail as to all the elements that determine the supply of entrepreneurship, it seems likely that the higher the price, the greater the entrepreneurial supply. Also the lower the price, the greater the inducement to engage in sheltering activities.

For ease in exposition it is useful to consider simultaneously both sheltering and entrepreneurial activities. At any given price, sheltering activities would be aimed at raising or maintaining that price, while entrepreneurial activities would generally result in a lower price. However, an inadequate supply of entrepreneurial activities, *e.g.*, a level that would not replace all the firms going out of business during any period, would have the opposite effect. Now, both sheltering and entrepreneurial acts cost money, time, or both. Thinking of time in terms of the pecuniary value of its opportunity cost, we can use the monetary cost of entrepreneurial and sheltering acts as a measure of both. When we speak of both sheltering and entrepreneurial acts simultaneously, we shall refer to them as *environmental acts*, since they are essentially environment altering activities.

There are some intermediate steps in this analysis that will be left out. In a many-firm industry each firm contributes to sheltering or entrepreneurship or both, but no single firm can determine the environment. Hence what we illustrate in *Figure* 4 are the activities for all firms in

Leibenstein: On Micro-Micro Theory   491

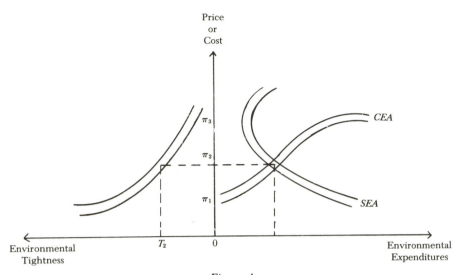

Figure 4

the industry, including that of latent entrepreneurs not currently in the industry.

It is also worth noting that with respect to sheltering activities a possible free-rider problem can arise. Each firm gains from the sheltering acts contributed by others. It is possible that there are cases for which the sheltering cost for each contributor is less than the gain to them if all firms do not contribute. A nonmaximizing model can help us out of the dilemma, since only non-profit-maximizers can be expected to act in such a way that they help to create a sheltered environment even if the gain of doing so is less than the cost when there is no assurance that others will contribute simultaneously. The reader will recall that the components of selective rationality include "moral" notions. Executives of firms may feel that their industry "ought" to be organized so as to weaken "unfair" competition.

In the right quadrant of *Figure* 4 we show the supply of environmental activities *SEA*, the consequences of environ-

mental activities *CEA*, and the interaction between these two functions, which determines the equilibrium degree of tightness in the market. The abscissa measures environmental acts in terms of expenditures on such activities, while the ordinate measures the expected long run average price. The shape of the *SEA* curve reflects the expectation that at high prices entrepreneurial acts dominate, while at low prices sheltering acts dominate; while at some level of intermediate prices there is neither great enthusiasm for entrepreneurship nor much-felt need for sheltering. Now the curves *CEA* reflect the consequences of environmental acts.[8] We

[8] Entrepreneurial *(E)* and sheltering *(S)* acts are each assumed to be separate functions of price. Each point on the *SEA* curve reflects the sum of the entrepreneurial and sheltering acts at that price. Thus each point on the ordinate reflects a determinate mix of *E* and *S* acts. Points on *CEA* reflect the consequences of that mix as reflected in the *SEA* curve. A more detailed theory would start with a model of the determination of the specific contribution of each firm to the *SEA* curve. Space limitations prohibit a consideration of this problem here.

consider the *CEA* function only between prices π_1 and π_3. We assume that this is the segment of sustainable prices. Above π_3 the consequences of the mixture of entrepreneurial and sheltering acts are such that the price cannot be sustained. Hence no values on the *CEA* curve are shown above π_3. The shape of *CEA* presumes that the consequences of sheltering activities dominate as prices rise from π_1 to π_3. *CEA* would be downward sloping if the opposite were the case. The point of intersection at π_2 determines the equilibrium level of environmental activities, and its related degree of tightness is shown in the left quadrant. This analysis could be developed in much greater detail, but for present purposes it is sufficient to simply indicate that there are incentive elements, which generate activities that determine environmental tightness, which is then transmitted to the firm in question. This determines the pressure-cost relationship, which in turn gives the cost-price relationship, which in its turn determines the cost area of the commodity.

For present purposes we focus attention on *Figures* 1, 2, and 3, which are concerned with the micro-micro aspect of the theory. We note that the choice of effort positions by individuals essentially determines the cost attributed to each individual. Of course, the degree of organizational entropy and the extent to which managers and their effort activities are induced to fight entropy are also part of the firm picture. In addition the reader should recall that all curves are drawn in the four figures as "fat curves" in order to reflect the existence of inert areas. The significance of this is considered later.

Our theory also allows for the special case in which entrepreneurship is so vigorous that it induces a very high degree of tightness, which in turn forces a degree of pressure so that firms either minimize costs or do not survive. However, we must note that this is a very special case, one

not likely to exist in most industries. Thus the micro-micro theory enables us to distinguish the environmental micro-micro conditions for perfect competition as against what is probably the normal situation of some form of imperfect competition, and hence the case in which costs are not minimized.

We have argued in an earlier section that one of the problems a micro-micro theory is likely to face is the resolution of possibly conflicting choices by firm members. We now consider very briefly to what extent X-efficiency theory handles this problem. A primary resolution mechanism lies in the existence of inert areas. Without inert areas the choices of *A* and *B* could easily conflict if they impinge on each other; but with inert areas many choices made by *A* that affect *B* lead to no response by *B*, and the same is true of *B*'s choices that affect *A*.[9] The larger the inert areas, the larger the nonconflict area, or mutual non-response area. If the inert areas do not resolve potential conflicts, at least two other mechanisms exist that help. These are horizontal or peer group pressures and vertical pressures, especially that of superiors on subordinates. Finally the system of authority and the persuasive sanctions available to authorities come into play. These mechanisms are usually sufficient for the day-to-day operations of the firm. Of course, some areas of conflict remain, and some extraordinary mechanisms may have to be used, *e.g.*, external mediation or arbitration in the settlement of strikes.

This general set of ideas does lead to some different conclusions than the neoclassical model. Among these are: (1) the cost of a commodity is not independent of the price of the commodity; (2) except in the extreme circumstances firms do not

[9] Mutually consistent inert areas would also allow for the persistence of repressed conflict in the organization.

minimize costs; (3) cost of production has a tendency to rise toward the price level; and (4) there is no production function independent of the environment of the firm and the history of the firm.

V. *To Maximize or Not to Maximize*

In considering alternatives to conventional micro theory, one of the questions that arises is how to handle the usual maximization assumption. At present the maximization postulate has an unusually strong hold on the mind set of economists. To examine why this is the case would take us too far afield into the sociology of the profession. Suffice it to say that in my view the belief in favor of maximization does not depend on strong evidence that people are in fact maximizers. In this section we will (a) consider some arguments usually put forward in favor of the maximization postulate and (b) suggest some reasons why it is reasonable to relax the maximization assumption in developing micro-micro theories.

It should be clear on the basis of what has been argued heretofore that micro-micro theory does not depend on dropping the maximization assumption—but it helps. In part, this point will be argued in this section. However, the essence of micro-micro theory is the behavioral unit; *e.g.*, shifting to the individual rather than to the firm or to the household. Clearly a theory of the firm can start with the assumption that each individual member maximizes something or other, the simplest assumption being the maximization of utility. There are problems with this idea, but let's ignore these while we examine some possibilities and implications.

We may ask (1) whether individual utility maximization will or will not be consistent with firm maximization, and (2) what it is that firms maximize. Consider the case of a two-person firm. One possibility is for the two to attempt to achieve a joint maximum. The nature and limitations of this approach are already exemplified in the Edgeworth box diagram, in the large literature on bargaining, and in von Neumann and Morgenstern's *Theory of Games* [38, 1944]. Such situations are usually characterized by simultaneous possibilities for *both* cooperation and conflict. The so-called contract curve in the box diagram indicates that for every choice off the curve there is a superior position on it. But once on the curve the cooperative aspects are exhausted, and movement along the curve implies that a gain for one will be counterbalanced by an equal loss to the other. Thus, even if it were in the interest of firm members to maximize the size of the pie, they would still face a pie-dividing problem. Furthermore, the situation need not be a zero-sum game. Tactics that determine pie division can affect the size of the pie. It is this latter possibility that is especially significant. That is, one of the questions we have to raise is whether, if we want an individual maximization theory, that theory should be allowed to reflect the possibility that the struggle over pie division can affect size.[10]

An argument could be developed to the effect that individual utility maximization would destabilize intrafirm behavior. Suppose that every member of a firm is a utility maximizer. How would such people behave? By definition they would respond

[10] A somewhat related way of looking at this problem is to note that intrafirm behavior involves free-rider elements and that it can be characterized as a prisoner's dilemma type of problem. But there is frequently a resolution of such problems if we take "ethical" or superego considerations into account. Note that these elements are contained in the non-maximizing selective rationality approach. Each may prefer the other person to do the work, but if each has a strong sense of a "fair" day's work, despite the fact that it is against his best interest to do so, then the free-rider prisoner dilemma aspects of the problem can be overcome. The reader will also note that in our discussion of sheltering similar free-rider prisoner's dilemma situations arise, and similar possible resolutions may exist.

to every "data" change that would affect them. Since such data changes are numerous and frequent in most firms and markets, such individuals would be constantly interested in changing their jobs inside or outside the firm. At the same time they would be interested constantly in renegotiating their contracts. The transaction costs created by the constant search for even a slight advantage may be low for each individual, but quite high in the aggregate for the firm as a whole. One could easily develop a model the result of which would be that firms would prefer to hire people who would act *as if* they had inert areas of a reasonable size. Better still, the firm would prefer sincere non-maximizers.

The main argument against the maximization postulate is an empirical one—namely, people frequently do not maximize. Of course, this standpoint argues that while postulates simplify reality, we are not free to choose counterfactual postulates. Hence, from this point of view a superior postulate would be one under which maximizing behavior is a special case, but non-maximization is accommodated for as a frequent mode of behavior.[11]

We now turn to some of the arguments usually brought forth in favor of the maximization hypothesis. One point must be made clear before we start. We shall not argue against maximization as a description of behavior under the circumstances under which such a description is accurate. In other words, the view to be taken is that maximization as a description of behavior is an empirical question. It is either universally true or not. I believe there is evidence that it is not universally true. On the whole it is rare to find anyone

[11] One may argue in favor of a maximization postulate as a convenient research strategy. This may be best for some problems and not for others. It seems to me one cannot say anything on this question *a priori*.

arguing that maximization is a universal description of behavior despite the ubiquity of the assumption. It is an assumption that is most frequently stated rather than supported.

A position frequently taken is that maximization is invariably true if only we take into account (a) the right considerations and/or (b) enough considerations. Thus if on the basis of some consideration it appears that maximization has not taken place, then it is only because an additional consideration has not been taken into account. Thus if an economic agent has not appeared to have maximized profits, it is only because leisure has not been considered. If it had been, it would be reasonable to presume that the agent had maximized the utility of a function made up of both profits and leisure. Similarly, if a two-argument function does not appear to have been maximized, then a three-argument function would solve the problem. And so the argument goes. This type of thinking has an extremely strong hold on the economics profession. In one form or another I have heard it put forth in a number of seminars. Yet this argument has serious flaws. We now turn to examine the form of this argument, and the appropriate response to it, although we cannot examine all variants of the argument.

(1) The first point to be considered may appear to be linguistic, although in this case it is also logical. Words have to be used in such a way that they do not contradict their essential meaning. Thus, in using the word "maximization," we must of necessity assume that non-maximization is meaningful in the same context. Otherwise the word maximization is robbed of its meaning. And obviously we are not using the word maximization appropriately if we rob it of its meaning. If we say that there are three options, *A, B,* and *C,* valued at 3, 7, and 10, then the person who maximizes chooses *C* valued at 10. But by the same token we must imply the *possi-*

bility of non-maximization; that is, someone could choose options *A* or *B*.

Now suppose someone chooses option *B*. How shall we judge such a choice? One possibility is to say that this represents non-maximizing behavior. But what of the argument that this really reflects maximizing, but that other considerations are involved so that the valuation of *B* is really greater than *C*, and furthermore, that similar arguments apply in *all* cases. Now this approach goes counter to the appropriate use of words. This approach *essentially* denies the possibility of non-maximization, since every choice that is made is interpreted as maximization; it robs the assertion of "maximizing" of meaning. It says no more than people behave as they do. Giving the name "maximization" to what people do does not add information. In fact it is most likely to hide information and to deter questions about what is actually happening.

An approach sometimes used explicitly is the tautological interpretation of utility maximization. This is similar to the approach considered in the previous paragraph except that it has the virtue of being explicit rather than implicit. From this standpoint not only is everyone assumed to maximize all the time, but non-maximizing behavior is *assumed* to be out of the question. Essentially, this says that whatever people do, they are somehow maximizing utility, without specifying the components they add or subtract from the individual's utility. Since all behavior is subsumed under this view, it essentially says nothing more than people do what they do. There is an extraneous assertion that is added on to the notion that people do what they do, which suggests that when they do what they do they are also maximizing utility. Clearly the concept that people do what they do is non-falsifiable and unrelated to the proper use of the word maximization.

(2) A nontautological approach must

lead to the conclusion that whether or not maximization takes place is an empirical question. This is not to suggest that with present methods we can always determine whether or not maximization is in fact taking place.[12] Rather, it simply says that the appropriate use of the term of maximization or non-maximization involves the idea that in principle one could check it on the basis of empirical data. Obviously not all empirical questions can be handled with current techniques.[13] This is true at some time or other in all sciences.

Herbert A. Simon in his 1978 Ely lecture argues that where scarce decision resources (*e.g.*, computational, search, or attention means) are involved, optimizing decision procedures may not be rational. Thus, he argues that an ". . . important direction of research in computational complexity lies in showing how the complexity of problems might be decreased by weakening the requirements for solution—by requiring solutions only to approximate the optimum, or by replacing an optimality criterion by a satisficing criterion" [47, 1978, p. 12]. This yields an additional reason for not using the maximizing postulate.

(3) If maximization is to include all types of behavior and all types of tastes, we have to raise the question of how we should handle a taste for nonmaximizing behavior. In that case we would come up against assertions of the following types: That a person is maximizing when he behaves in accordance with his taste for non-maxi-

---

[12] Of course in some cases we can tell. In his Ely lecture [47, 1978], Herbert A. Simon cites the work of Howard Kunreuther *et al.* to the affect that decisions to buy flood insurance depended more on personal experience with floods than with a knowledge of the rates, objective risks, or even subjective beliefs about these facts.

[13] A desirable convention that would avoid some confusion would be for writers to indicate explicitly whether they are using maximization in a tautological or nontautological sense.

mizing. Obviously there is a contradiction in the notion that a person is maximizing when he is not maximizing.

(4) In the discussion in the previous section, we have suggested a nonmaximization model in which statements were made about the psychological attributes of an individual and about inertial costs. It has sometimes been argued that when such costs are taken into account that what appears to be a nonmaximization approach turns out to be maximization. Such an approach involves a very significant distinction: The distinction between statements about the personality of an individual and statements about his behavior. To say that someone's inertial cost is clearly zero is a statement about his personality. It indicates how he feels about making a certain type of choice. It does not discuss how an individual behaves when faced with alternatives. The inertial cost idea explains *why* a person behaves in a certain way. It does not indicate *how* he behaves. The statement that a person is a non-maximizer is an assertion about *how* he behaves. If these two elements are confused, the "why" and the "how," then we end up with a tautological interpretation of maximization, an interpretation that robs the concept of maximization of its meaning.

(5) A very important element in any conceptual scheme is whether the scheme allows us to ask interesting questions. The difficulty with assuming maximization is that within this assumption we cannot raise the question of what happens when behavior is of a non-maximizing sort and, even more important, we cannot raise the question of what happens during the interaction between those individuals who maximize and those who don't. Does a maximizer have an advantage over a nonmaximizer? Can the careful calculator victimize the incomplete calculator? Clearly there are a host of interesting questions involving such interactions that should be

investigated. It may turn out that part of the important element of micro-micro theory depends on interacting behavior between individuals who are calculating to very different degrees.

(6) We have argued in previous sections that conflict resolution is likely to be an important aspect of micro-micro behavior. In a sense, maximizing behavior by interdependent individuals is the opposite of conflict resolution; whereas some forms of non-maximizing behavior allow for considerable latitude of accommodation between competing objectives.

Dropping the maximizing postulate is likely to raise a host of interesting questions; one of the most important of which is the determination of the set of decision processes actually used within a group. This question is brushed under the rug, so to speak, by assuming maximization. It may turn out that the mix of decision processes used within a firm, or a group of firms, has important economic implications. We do not know the answer, but it would seem exciting to open up the question.

VI. *Summary and Conclusions*

In a number of the natural sciences, at various times, there has been a special sense about some areas of study—the sense of a *research frontier.* I am told that in physics, microbiology, and in some branches of chemistry, there is a clear sense of such a frontier. Investigators in these fields frequently know and agree where fruitful work can take place, and they usually have a lively sense of where in fact it is taking place. James Watson's book, *The Double Helix* [49, 1968], dramatizes those aspects in which there is clearcut convergence of a number of investigators in a number of disciplines, almost inexorably toward the discovery of the structure of DNA and the relationship of the structure to its capacity to replicate itself.

Economics as a science has never had a clear sense of a research frontier. Investigators work in a variety of subdisciplines without much convergence. Economics as a discipline has changed gradually, but there is still considerable controversy as to whether the new stuff is any truer than the old. As a profession we have become more mathematical, but that does not mean we know any more about the world of economic phenomena. The closest thing to the opening up of a research frontier occurred in the 1930's in the wake of the so-called Keynesian revolution. Probably a better name would have been the macroeconomic revolution. While there is still much to know, the work of an army of investigators resulted in changing the face of economics—basically, the formalization of *macro*economics. The current spate of multiequation forecasting models, which depend on computers to derive results quickly, may be looked upon as the end product of this type of work. But outside of the macroeconomic breakthrough of the thirties, there is very little that has occurred in the twentieth century that we can point to as a research frontier.

The point of the above discussion on the idea of a research frontier is to suggest that micro-micro theory has the potential for becoming such a frontier. To start with, a great deal of accumulated information already exists on the major entity to be studied—the individual. Biologists, psychologists, and sociologists already know a great deal about individual behavior in a variety of contexts, including economic contexts. The findings in the field of industrial psychology may be useful to our understanding of how individuals function in firms. But much more important than the actual facts about individual behavior are the various *techniques* developed in these disciplines to study individual behavior in organizational contexts. Every discipline develops its own special questions, and the questions most pertinent to industrial psychologists or sociologists may not be the most pertinent ones for economists. While we frequently cannot use the answers developed in these fields, we can use their methods of inquiry, albeit refined to our own needs and standards.

Microeconomics has avoided the study of individuals, but that is no reason why we should continue to do so. After all, once we change the central questions to the ones pertinent to micro-micro theory, we can investigate the empirical elements. At the very least we can observe individual behavior in economic contexts. Also, we can submit individuals to questionnaire surveys, as well as to try to observe them in experimental settings. The main point is that individuals are the most fundamental and the easiest units to observe. Once economists really get into micro-micro-economics, they can gather their own data, the data exactly relevant to their concerns and questions; test their hypotheses; and obtain results.

The basic point is that individuals within organizational contexts are likely to be easier to study than individuals generally. Furthermore, individuals are easier to study than multiperson firms as units. This argument is difficult to develop rigorously. No such attempt will be made. Rather, we hope to indicate some of the components of the argument in the hope of suggesting that the general argument is a reasonable one. It would seem almost self-evident that it would be easier to study individuals in limited sets of contexts rather than in all contexts. In some sense this implies that by choosing our contexts very carefully we may be able to get close to laboratory experiments. The ideal would be to find organizational contexts that are as close to being identical as possible and to see in what way individuals behave differently, given different values of the independent variables in such contexts. Obviously there are likely to be different degrees to which it may be possible to find contexts that are similar, but in which only one of the few independent variable values differs. In general it would seem that by reducing the variety of behavioral contexts, it should be very much easier to study individual behavior.

The argument is somewhat more difficult when we compare the study of individuals versus the study of firms. One would think it would be easier to find units of firms that have greater similarity to each other than would firms as entities. For example, it might be easier to find similarity in plants than in firms, or in some sub-units of plants, than in firms. Hence, through the careful selection of some sub-units, it would be easier to study individuals than through the study of gross aggregate entities as units. Furthermore, once we accept the idea that we should look at what goes on inside the firm, it is almost self-evident that there are some researchable areas inside the firm. Of course, these two approaches, the study of the individual and the firm as units, are not by any means mutually exclusive. We would normally expect that information gained from each approach separately would turn out to be complementary.

Near the boundary of micro-micro theory there exists a number of models, most of which fall into the category of multivariable objective functions. The firm, or some persons or group within the firm, is presumed to maximize a utility function with many arguments. Typical arguments are growth, profits, managerial perquisites, leisure, and so on. We argued that while these models are of considerable interest in that they relax some of the conventional assumptions of micro theory, they may be viewed only as embryonic micro-micro theories. Although these models do separate owners from managers and are concerned, to some degree, with the relations between these two groups, they do not handle the problems

of potential conflict within multiperson managerial groups. Other studies, such as the theory of teams, are also just within the micro-micro boundary. The team may be a portion of a firm rather than the entire firm, but such studies are usually normative or prescriptive, rather than behavioral.

The work of the Carnegie school can be interpreted as being within the micro-micro framework, but the Carnegie framework is at present too incomplete a system to permit determinate conclusions. The simulation models inspired by or based on Carnegie school ideas are usually single case models. Other works that fall into this general category, although not directly based on the Carnegie school or considered here (*e.g.*, Eliasson, Nelson, and Winter, *etc.*) represent deviations from neoclassical theory, which yield results by using different decision criteria. However, these works are not primarily concerned with disassembling the black box of standard theory. They are, nevertheless, within the boundaries of micro-micro theory.

I have argued that my own work, which I have referred to as General X-efficiency theory, is a micro-micro theory. Since the individual is the irreducible analytical unit, models developed on this basis fit under the micro-micro rubric. At the present stage of development its focus is primarily on the factors responsible for cost determination. The basic decision-makers are *individuals* who, through their effort-discretion choices, determine cost of production.

In our discussion of various alternatives to neoclassical theory, the problem of giving meaning to "group utility functions" turned out to be troublesome. Intra-firm discretion of various sorts is a related or similar characteristic of many models. In both cases there are problems of resolving conflicts. We cannot give a general answer, but one form of resolution is through the notion of inert areas. If one's position falls into an inert area, conflict is no longer pursued.

Micro-micro theories, as they now stand, are far from being as well developed as neoclassical theory—especially the perfect competition case. In part this is one reason why it may be a candidate to become a fruitful research area. Different scholars will approach this area from different standpoints. In my view progress is most likely to be made if we drop at least some of the assumptions of conventional theory. Obviously the most important assumption that has to be dropped is the one under which firm behavior is visualized as if it is the behavior of a single individual.

An area where, in my experience, a good deal of controversy is likely to arise is the relaxation of the maximization hypothesis. In *Section* V an argument was presented in favor of relaxing this particular postulate. Nevertheless, it seems to me that at the present stage this is not an either/or question. It may be useful to work out models either on the basis of utility maximization or on the basis of nonmaximizing behavior. My own preference is toward models in which maximization represents a special case within a larger range of possibilities. In part, this reflects the notion that it would be useful to experiment with interrelations within firms in which some individuals are more calculating than others.

One of the difficulties in working in this area is that at the present time many economists appear to have strong feelings about the maximization hypothesis. Although strong feelings are understandable, given a century-long tradition within the profession of using maximizing-optimizing models and given the handiness of the mathematical tools available for maximizing models, nevertheless, they are not sufficient reasons to ignore the possibility of nonmaximizing models. Such

models should be judged by their results and not by the criterion as to whether or not the model uses a specific hypothesis such as the maximization postulate.

Given that most sciences have moved from the study of less to more micro aspects, it would seem reasonable to cultivate this area in economics—especially to study intra-firm units and intra-firm individual behavior. But in addition to following a general scientific trend, there are intrinsic reasons to intensify our work in the micro-micro area. A body of work already exists, which suggests ways of studying these problems in greater depth. We should take advantage of the fact that we can observe intrafirm behavior and study such behavior intensively. A great deal of literature already exists in allied fields, such as industrial psychology, some of whose results can be incorporated into intra-firm models. And last but not least, it would seem natural at this stage to pursue work on micro-micro elements in order to check the consistency of the implications of what we know and what can be learned about intra-firm behavior with the postulates *and* implications of mainstream micro theory.

References

1. ALLISON, GRAHAM T. "Conceptual Models and the Cuban Missile Crisis," *Amer. Polit. Sci. Rev.*, Sept. 1969, *63*(3), pp. 689–718
2. ALCHIAN, ARMEN A. AND DEMSETZ, HAROLD. "Production, Information Costs and Economic Organization," *Amer. Econ. Rev.*, Dec. 1972, *62*(5), pp. 777–95.
3. ARGYRIS, CHRIS. "Management Information Systems: The Challenge to Rationality and Emotionality," *Manage. Sci.*, Feb. 1971, *17*(6), pp. B275–92.
4. ARROW, KENNETH J. AND HAHN, FRANK H. *General competitive analysis.* San Francisco: Holden-Day, 1971.

5. BAUMOL, WILLIAM J. "The Revenue Maximization Hypothesis," in *Business behavior, value and growth*. New York: Macmillan, 1959, pp. 45–53.

6. _____ AND STEWART, MACO. "On the Behavioral Theory of the Firm," in ROBIN MARRIS AND ADRIAN WOOD, eds. [32, 1971], pp. 118–43.

7. CAIRNCROSS, ALEC. "The Optimum Firm Reconsidered," *Econ. J.*, Supplement, March 1972, *82*(325), pp. 312–20.

8. COASE, RONALD H. "The Nature of the Firm," *Economica*, Nov. 1937, (4), pp. 386–405.

9. COHEN, KALMAN J. AND CYERT, RICHARD M. *Theory of the firm: Resource allocation in a market economy*. Second edition. Englewood Cliffs, N.J.: Prentice-Hall, [1965] 1975.

10. CYERT, RICHARD M. AND HEDRICK, CHARLES L. "Theory of the Firm: Past, Present, and Future; An Interpretation," *J. Econ. Lit.*, June 1972, *10*(2), pp. 398–412.

11. _____ AND MARCH, JAMES G. *A behaviorial theory of the firm*. Englewood Cliffs, N.J., Prentice-Hall, 1963.

12. DAY, RICHARD. "Review of Cyert and March, *A Behavioral Theory of the Firm*," *Econometrica*, July 1964, *32*(3), pp. 461–65.

13. _____. *Behavioral economics*. Madison: University of Wisconsin, Social Systems Research Institute, 1975.

14. _____ AND TINNEY, E. HERBERT. "How to Cooperate in Business without Really Trying: A Learning Model of Decentralized Decision Making," *J. Polit. Econ.*, July–August 1968, Pt. I, *76*, pp. 583–600.

15. DEBREU, GERARD. *Theory of value*. New York: Wiley, 1959.

16. EDWARDS, RICHARD C. "Individual Traits and Organizational Incentives: What Makes a 'Good' Worker?" *J. Hu-*

man Res., Winter 1976, *11*(1), pp. 51–68.

17. ELIASSON, GUNNAR. *Business economic planning*. New York: Wiley; Stockholm: Swedish Industrial, 1976.

18. GOLDBERG, VICTOR P. "Protecting the Right to Be Served By Public Utilities," in *Research in Law and Economics*. Vol. 1. Forthcoming, 1978.

19. HIRSCHMAN, ALBERT O. "Exit, voice, and loyalty: Further reflections and a Survey of Recent Contributions," *Social Science Information*, Feb. 1974, *13*(1), pp. 7–15.

20. JENNER, R. A. "An Information Version of Pure Competition," *Econ. J.*, Dec. 1966, *76*, pp. 786–805.

21. KNIGHT, FRANK H. *Risk, uncertainty and profit*. Boston: Houghton Mifflin, 1921.

22. LEIBENSTEIN, HARVEY. "Organizational or Frictional Equilibria, X-Efficiency and the Rate of Innovation," *Quart. J. Econ.*, Nov. 1969, *83*(4), pp. 600–23.

23. _____. "Notes on X-Efficiency and Technical Progress," in *Micro aspects of development*. Edited by ELIEZER B. AYAL. New York: Praeger, 1973, pp. 18–38.

24. _____. "Aspects of the X-Efficiency Theory of the Firm," *Bell J. Econ.*, Autumn 1975, *6*(2), pp. 580–606.

25. _____. *Beyond economic man*. Cambridge, Mass.: Harvard University Press, 1976.

26. _____. *General X-efficiency theory and economic development*. New York and London: Oxford University Press, 1978.

27. LINDBECK, ASSAR. "The Efficiency of Competition and Planning," in *Planning and market relations*. Edited by MICHAEL KASER AND RICHARD PORTES. London: Macmillan, 1971, pp. 83–107.

28. MACNEIL, IAN R. "The Many Futures of Contracts," *Southern California Law Rev.*, May 1974, *47*(3), pp. 691–816.

29. MARGOLIS, JULIUS. "Analysis of the Firm: Rationalism, Conventionalism and Behaviorism," *J. Bus.*, July 1958, pp. 187–99.

30. MARRIS, ROBIN. "A Model of the Managerial Enterprise," *Quart. J. Econ.*, May 1963, *77*, pp. 185–209.

31. _____. "An Introduction to Theories of Corporate Growth," in MARRIS AND WOOD, eds. [30, 1971], pp. 1–36.

32. _____ AND WOOD, ADRIAN, eds. *The corporate economy: Growth competition and innovative potential.* Cambridge, Mass.: Harvard University Press, 1971.

33. MARSHALL, ALFRED. *Industry and trade.* London: Macmillan, 1923.

34. MEYER, JOHN R. "An Experiment in the Measurement of Business Motivation," *Rev. Econ. Statist.*, August 1967, *49*, pp. 304–18.

35. MIRRLEES, JAMES A. "Optimal Structure of Incentives and Authority within an Organization," *Bell J. Econ.*, Spring 1976, *7*(1), pp. 105–31.

36. NELSON, RICHARD R. AND WINTER, SIDNEY G. "Toward an Evolutionary Theory of Economic Capabilities," *Amer. Econ. Rev.*, May 1973, *63*(2), pp. 440–49.

37. _____ AND WINTER, SIDNEY G. "Neoclassical *vs.* Evolutionary Theories of Economic Growth—Critique and Prospectus," *Econ. J.*, Dec. 1974, *84*(336), pp. 886–905.

38. VON NEUMANN, JOHN AND MORGENSTERN, OSKAR. *Theory of games and economic behavior.* Princeton, N.J.: Princeton University Press, 1944.

39. OLSEN, E. ODGERS, JR. "The Effort Level, Work Time, and Profit Maximization," *Southern Econ. J.*, April 1976, *42*(4), pp. 644–52.

40. PENROSE, EDITH T. *The theory of the growth of the firm.* Oxford: Oxford University Press; New York: Wiley, 1959.

41. RADNER, ROY AND MARSCHAK, JACOB. *The economic theory of teams.* New Haven: Yale University Press, 1972.

42. _____ AND ROTHSCHILD, MICHAEL. "On the Allocation of Effort," *J. Econ. Theory*, June 1975, *10*(3), pp. 358–76.

43. RASMUSEN, HANS J. "Multilevel Planning with Conflicting Objectives," *Swedish J. Econ.*, June 1974, *76*(2), pp. 155–70.

44. SCITOVSKY, TIBOR. "A Note of Profit Maximisation and Its Implications," *Rev. Econ. Stud.*, 1943, *11*(1), pp. 57–60.

45. SIMON, HERBERT A. "A Comparison of Organisation Theories," *Rev. Econ. Stud.*, 1952, *20*(1), pp. 40–48.

46. _____. "Theories of Decision-Making in Economics and Behavioral Science," *Amer. Econ. Rev.*, June 1959, *49*, pp. 253–83.

47. SIMON, HERBERT A. "Rationality as Process and as Product of Thought," *Amer. Econ. Rev.*, May 1978, *68*(2), pp. 1–16.

48. STIGLITZ, JOSEPH. "Incentives, Risk and Information Notes Towards a Theory of Hierarchy," *Bell J. Econ.*, Autumn 1975, *6*(2), pp. 552–79.

49. WATSON, JAMES D. *The double helix: A personal account of the discovery of the structure of DNA.* New York: Atheneum, 1968.

50. WILLIAMSON, OLIVER E. "A Model of Rational Managerial Behavior," in CYERT AND MARCH [11, 1963], pp. 237–52.

51. _____. *Markets and hierarchies: Analysis and antitrust implications: A study in the economics of internal organization.* New York: Free Press, 1975.

52. _____. "The Economics of Internal Organization: Exit and Voice in Relation to Markets and Hierarchies," *Amer. Econ. Rev.*, May 1976, *66*(2), pp. 369–77.

53. WINTER, SIDNEY G. "Economic 'Natural Selection' and the Theory of the Firm," *Yale Econ. Essays*, 1964, *4*(1), pp. 225–72.

54. _____. "Satisficing, Selection, and the Innovating Remnant," *Quart. J. Econ.*, May 1971, *85*(2), pp. 237–61.

COMMENT

Substantive mountains and methodological molehills

E. ROY WEINTRAUB

A current fashion in economic argument requires economist X, who doesn't agree with Y, to accuse Y of having "a flawed methodology." The issue then becomes one of method, not substance. But since X and Y are merely economists, neither X nor Y is comfortable developing a useful methodological argument.

Sheila Dow's recent *JPKE* piece, on "Weintraub and Wiles: The Methodological Basis of Policy Conflict" (Spring 1981, pp. 325-39), develops a methodological critique of my survey of general equilibrium theory. Peter Wiles has spoken for himself. I would like here to suggest that since there are many real issues which divide Dow and me, it is not fruitful to argue methodology. I shall not, in what follows, attempt to restate the main argument of my *Microfoundations* (Cambridge: Cambridge Press, 1979). Instead, I shall try to organize some of its subsidary elements to focus the substantive issues.

Microfoundations surveyed recent work in general equilibrium theory which was developed to pose, and get partial answers to, questions that had been traditionally asked in macroeconomics. The material in Part II of the book effected that survey.

My approach was simple. The coherence, and sequence, of the models suggested the presence of what Lakatos defined as a "scientific research program."[1] I adopted the terminology "neo-

The author is Professor of Economics, Duke University.

[1] For a full and complete description of this topic, see Imre Lakatos, *The Methodology of Scientific Research Programs: Philosophical Papers*, Vol. 1, edited by John Worrall and Gregory Currie (New York: Cambridge Press, 1980, paperback edition). See also Volume II, which includes some additional papers.

Journal of Post Keynesian Economics/Winter 1982-83, Vol. V, No. 2   *295*

Walrasian program" for this sequence, believing then, and now, that "neoclassical" is not well-defined.[2] Since Keynesian economics had previously been viewed as a scientific research program in Lakatos' sense,[3] I suggested that the microfoundations of macroeconomics literature could be rationally reconstructed as an attempt to extend the range of the neo-Walrasian program to a variety of issues which were (Lakatosian) anomalies[4] for that program. I was, and am, aware that some of those issues (e.g., unemployment and inflation) were *not* anomalies within the Keynesian program.[5]

Any work in the history of science must select the materials to be studied in some coherent fashion. I was not interested in creating a Popperian "demarcation criterion"[6] which would define gen-

[2] "Neoclassical" appropriately refers to the marginalists of the late nineteenth century. Current use of the term is so loose that is is sensibly abandoned. Vivian Walsh and Harvey Gram's superb *Classical and Neoclassical Theories of General Equilibrium* fails to present a convincing case only in the last chapters where *modern* neo-Walrasian theory is linked to nineteenth-century economics. (See my review, in the *Journal of Economic Literature*, December 1980, pp. 1566-68.)

[3] The best single reference for this is certainly Axel Leijonhufvud's "Schools, Revolutions, and research programmes in economic theory," in Spiro Latsis, ed., *Method and Appraisal in Economics* (Cambridge: Cambridge University Press, 1976).

[4] "Thus an anomaly in a research programme is a phenomenon which we regard as something to be explained in terms of the programme. More generally, we may speak, following Kuhn, about 'puzzles': a 'puzzle' in a programme is a problem which we can regard as a challenge to that particular programme. A 'puzzle' can be resolved three ways: by solving it within the original programme (the anomaly turns into an example): by neutralizing it, i.e., solving it within an independent, different programme (the anomaly disappears); or, finally, by solving it within a rival programme (the anomaly turns into a counterexample)" (entire passage italicized in original). Imre Lakatos, "Falsification and the Methodology of Scientific Research Programmes," in Lakatos, p. 72.

[5] The existence of unemployment was a "puzzle" solved within the Keynesian program by Keynes, as in the first "resolution" suggested in Note 4. Inflation is a puzzle that post Keynesians believe they have solved following Keynes' lead.

[6] It is instructive to read of Lakatos' *rejection* of rigid demarcations between science and nonscience. "I advocate a primarily quasi-empirical approach instead of Popper's aprioristic approach for law-giving to science. I do not lay down general rules of the game *a priori*, so that, if history of science turns out to violate the rules, I would have to call the business of science to start anew. ... Up to the present day it has been the scientific norms, as applied instinctively by the scientific *elite* in *particular* cases, which have constituted the main yardstick of the philosopher's *universal* laws." Imre Lakatos,

eral equilibrium theory as "science" and Keynesian economics as nonscience. I *was* interested in providing a "logic of appraisal"[7] for the work I surveyed, and I believe that such a task was facilitated by the "research program" language.

This objective led me (unlike Dow) to reject Kuhn's terminology. "Paradigms" and "revolutions" and "normal science," while they can liven up a history of science, do not facilitate a logic of appraisal.[8] Kuhnian science, a developed science at any rate, cannot have coherent paradigms coexisting for any length of time.[9] Dow, believing Kuhn's framework to be the way to tell my story, ignores the simultaneous burgeoning of neo-Walrasian analysis *and* Keynesian analysis in the 1930s. She must, and does, tell a story of a Walrasian (Classical) view, a Keynesian revolution, a neo-Walrasian counterrevolution, and post Keynesian (counter-counter (?) revolution) restoration.

Such a view does some violence to the modern history of our discipline. Many facts don't fit this story. The *Ergebnisse* papers, for instance, appeared *before* the *General Theory*.[10] Kurt Gödel (!), in 1934, had already suggested the kinds of questions that would be asked in the 1970s.[11] Hicks, Lange, Klein, and Patinkin formed

---

"Popper on Demarcation and Induction," in Lakatos, op. cit., p. 153 (italics in original).

[7] For Lakatos, "Sophisticated Falsificationism thus shifts the problem of how to appraise *theories* to the problem of how to appraise *series of theories*," in "Falsification," p. 34. This paper is itself Lakatos' response to Kuhn's *Structure of Scientific Revolutions*. See especially pp. 90-93. In very brief outline, Lakatos demonstrated that Kuhn's rejection of naive falsificationism does *not* entail rejection of *all* falsificationism. The Kuhnian "paradigms" follow only if one throws away the "baby" of sophisticated falsificationism with the "bath" of oversimplified views of scientific progress.

[8] Ibid., pp. 52-86.

[9] For Kuhn, normal science can proceed only from an accepted paradigm.

[10] E.g., Abraham Wald, "Über die Productionsgleichungen der ökonomischen Wertlehre" (Part 1), *Ergebnisse eines mathematichen Kolloquiums*, Heft 7, (1934-35), untermitwirkung von K. Göden und A. Wald, herausgeben von Karl Menger, Franz Deuticke, Leipzig and Vienna, 1936, pp. 1-6. Karl Schlesinger's paper appeared in Heft 6 (1933-34), as did one of Wald's other papers.

[11] "In reality the demand of each individual depends also on his income, and this in turn depends on the prices of the factors of production. One might formulate an equation system which takes this into account and investigate the existence of a solution." In "Comment by Kurt Gödel," on Wald's paper (Note 10), translated in William Baumol and Stephen Goldfeld, eds. *Precursors in Mathematical Economics: An Anthology*, Series of Reprints of Scarce Works in Political Economy, No. 19 (London: LSE, 1968), p. 293.

a neo-Walrasian line which was perceived, correctly at the time, to support Keynesian ideas.[12] In Dow's Kuhnian terminology Hicks must have been a fifth-columnist or a (counter) revolutionary vanguard.[13]

I reconstructed the history differently. Having identified the neo-Walrasian and Keynesian programs, I could describe the development of the neo-Walrasian program without having to deny the simultaneous existence of a Keynesian alternative. The continuous existence, from the 1930s to the present, of the Keynesian program was *not* my subject matter. That existence however provided, and provides, a background context for the development of neo-Walrasian economics and, specifically, for the emerging microfoundations literature. The striving to supplant a rival program is one of the rich features of the Lakatosian framework.[14] It served its purpose adequately.

From this account, it is hard for me to understand Dow's claim that *Microfoundations* is part of a *Methodenstreit*.

Let me be more specific.

> Weintraub shares Wiles' preference for the Popperian scientific method in economics.... Any alternative (nonorthodox) methodology is dismissed with the familiar (implicit) accusation of being unscientific. (pp. 328-29)

Dow's evidence for this is a quote from my book which identifies a Marxist question as a nonquestion *within* the neo-Walrasian program. So what? "Stability of a competitive equilibrium" is a nonquestion in the Marxian program, too.[15]

[12] Compare, for example, the introductions to *Value and Capital, Price Flexibility and Employment, The Keynesian Revolution,* and *Money, Interest and Prices.* In what sense can it be asserted that these economists were engaged in subverting Keynes' ideas?

[13] I am saddened that even Hicks has been caught in this labeling miasma. For if "Mr. Keynes and the Classics" is so often cited by counterrevolutionaries, why then Hicks must be partly to "blame" for the success of the "counterrevolution" of the 1960s and 1970s. I find such reasoning to be both *post hoc ergo propter hoc* and ahistorical.

[14] "When two research programmes compete, their first 'ideal' models usually deal with different aspects of the domain (for example, the first model of Newton's semi-corpuscular optics described light-refraction. The first model of Huygaaens's wave optics [described] light-interference). As the rival research programmes expand, they gradually encroach on each other's territory and the *n*th version of the first will be blatantly, dramatically inconsistent with the *m*th version of the second." Lakatos, "Falsification," p. 71.

[15] Dow's view that I have a Popperian methodology is true to the extent that she means Lakatosian. But this, of course, means simply that I believe that the growth of knowledge may be appraised. See Note 6.

Dow goes on, quoting me correctly as saying:

> There should be little argument about the proposition that some sort of revivified, reconstituted general equilibrium theory is the only logically possible general link between microeconomics and macroeconomics. (p. 161)

Dow then states:

> This strongly supports the view that, in fact, given the impossibility of mixing general equilibrium theory and Keynesian theory, Weintraub is concerned with the search for a neoclassical macroeconomics founded on neoclassical microeconomics. (p. 329)

I rather think it supports nothing of the sort. It does suggest, however, that any family of models which purports to explain the propositions found *both* in a microtext *and* a macrotext is likely to have a general systems flavor. (E.g., a Leontief system goes partway to this end, and certainly focuses on systemic interaction. But it's hardly "neoclassical."[16])

These remarks illuminate but one part of a more fundamental misunderstanding. Simply put, some economists appear to believe that *any* attempt to extend neo-Walrasian theories to Keynesian problems is necessarily wrong-headed:

> Weintraub appears to believe that a process of reconciliation is already emerging, in spite of persistent ideological differences. . . . [The] developments in neo-Walrasian economics described by Weintraub represent an accommodation of macroeconomic concerns only *within* the neoclassical paradigm; as an accommodation of Keynes' contribution, they are, at the very least, misleading. (p. 326)

She goes on, a bit later, to complete this line of reasoning:

> Actually, the only possible reason why anyone would want to try to relate Keynesian "macro" concerns to neoclassical microeconomics is to shore up the neoclassical model at its publicly weakest point. . . . If Keynesian macroeconomics were to be taken at all seriously, it would be clear that it contains the denial of neoclassical economics at the micro, as well as the macro, level. (p. 331)

I find the anti-intellectualism of this position abhorrent. If Dow means what she says, then only post Keynesians are allowed to develop Keynesian ideas. To say, for example, that a neo-Walrasian does violence to Keynes' framework when he treats "uncertainty"

---

[16] I have even attempted to provide some sort of recipe for the kind of mixing that Dow says is impossible in "Catastrophe Theory and Intertemporal Equilibria," *Economie Appliquée*, Tome XXXIII, No. 2 (1980). pp. 303-15.

as "risk" is equivalent to a fundamentalist's charge that interpreting the Gospel According to Matthew using the Gnostic Gospels is sacrilege. *It may be thus,* but the investigation is relevant to the growth of knowledge, *which may be appraised independently*.

I therefore reject the claim that to take Keynesian concerns seriously, I must approach the Keynesian canon as a post Keynesian.

About halfway through the article, Dow shifts the discussion to substantive matters. She presents some propositions associated with post Keynesian economics and uses *this* framework, *not* methodology, to carry her critique forward.

> The methodology employed by post Keynesians, at different levels of aggregation, has two primary features by which it differs from neo-Walrasian methodology: equilibrium plays no central role, and economic systems cannot be fully determinate.... Such a notion tends to make orthodox economists nervous.... (pp. 331-32)

She goes on to state:

> This neo-Walrasian attachment to the concept of equilibrium has been protected by the notion that it is "scientific." But knowledge has in the meantime been evolving in the physical sciences. Developments of the quantum theory suggest ... an absence of equilibrium in the random movements of subatomic particles.... Post Keynesians are on the side of at least some of the scientific angels! (p. 334)

The first passage is clear. It suggests points of disagreement between the neo-Walrasian program and the Keynesian program. Since this was one of the motifs in *Microfoundations,* I have no quarrel with Dow here. Why she believes, then, that I would be "nervous" with this notion rather escapes me. I am, in fact, delighted that there are economists who work in different programs. I wish them success.[17]

[17] This statement goes to the heart of a major difference between Dow's views and my own, based on Lakatos: "The history of science has been and should be a history of competing research programmes.... The idea of competing scientific research programmes leads us to the problem: how are research programmes eliminated? ... Can there be any objective (as opposed to sociopsychological) reason to reject a programme, that is, to eliminate its hard core and its programme for constructing protective belts? Our answer, in outline, is that such an objective reason is provided by a rival research programme which explains the previous success of its rival and supercedes it by a further display of heuristic power.... But the novelty of a factual proposition can frequently be seen only after a long period has elapsed.... All this suggests that we must not discard a budding research programme simply because it has so far failed to overtake a powerful rival. We should not abandon it if, supposing its rival were not there, it would constitute a progressive problem shift ... it should be sheltered for a while from a powerful established rival." Lakatos, "Falsifications," pp. 69-71 (italics deleted).

The second passage, however, goes on to argue that my allegiance to the neo-Walrasian program is partially based on its scientific character. Presumably she would also believe that I identify post Keynesianism as a-scientific. Both propositions are mistaken. The issue is not one of science versus nonscience, or equilibrium as a "scientific" term,[18] but rather the *role* of equilibrium in the *neo-Walrasian* program. There are two competing Lakatosian research programs. The choice that an economist makes about which program to defend is not based on a demarcation criterion for "scientificness." Adherence is based on beliefs about the relative progressivity of those competing programs.[19]

Once it is recognized that Dow's paper defines one post Keyesian critique of new directions in the neo-Walrasian program, the issue becomes primarily one of substance, not method, since the two programs are different. The differences between them are only incidentally differences in method which arise from the internal heuristics which guide research within the program.

I attempted to show that the neo-Walrasian program could be (imperfectly) characterized by its Lakatosian hard core, which would consist of irrefutable (*within the program*) propositions[20] certainly including:

HC 1) Economic agents optimize;

HC 2) Economic agents pursue their self-interest;

HC 3) Economic agents act in markets.

The positive heuristic of this program would include such propositions as:

---

[18] Dow's appeal to quantum theory supports my argument, not hers. What happened, in fact, is that the deterministic mechanical equilibrium concept gave way to a broader, statistical equilibrium in the sense of distribution theory. As one of its severest detractors wrote, "The modern quantum theory in the form associated with the names of de Broglie, Schrödinger, and Dirac, operates with discontinuous functions . . . [and] the spatial functions which appear in the equations make no claim to be a mathematical model of the atomic structure. Those functions are only supposed to determine the mathematical probabilities to find such structures. . . ." Albert Einstein, "On the Method of Theoretical Physics," in *Einstein, A Contemporary Volume,* edited by A. P. French (Cambridge, Mass.: Harvard University Press, 1979) p. 314.

[19] "Incidentally, in the method of research programmes, the pragmatic meaning of 'rejection' [of a programme] becomes crystal clear: it means *the decision to stop working on it.*" Lakatos, "Falsification," p. 70, n. 4 (italics in original).

[20] It should be obvious that these propositions are not meant to be definitive. They represent my own attempt to articulate the defining characteristics of the neo-Walrasian program. I present them here only to sharpen points of disagreement.

PH 1) Create models, based on the hard core, which have coherent (equilibrium) outcomes; and

PH 2) Create models, based on the hard core, which have market implications.

The negative heuristic would include propositions like:

NH 1) Do not construct models which have no equilibria;

NH 2) Do not construct models which rely on institutional
change to produce coherent outcomes; etc.

Even at this level of programmatic description it is clear that the
Keynesian program is different, and fundamentally so. From
Shackle who doesn't believe that it is useful to model agents as
being *capable* of such optimizing, to Dow who is comfortable with
models that cannot possess equilibria, (post) Keynesians are certainly not neo-Walrasians.

Keynes once remarked that the task of an argument was not to
convict an opponent of error, but to *convince* him of error.

Frankly, I am not convinced by Dow. I am, however, open to
persuasion.[21]

I could be convinced by two distinct but related lines of argument.

The first would involve a demonstration that the neo-Walrasian
program was degenerating, and the second would involve a demonstration that the (post) Keynesian program was progressing.

Demonstrating the former would require, at best, arguments
showing repeated ad hoc adjustments of the neo-Walrasian hard
core in order to assimilate anomalies. It would further require a
relative absence of new empirical facts which were explicable
with theories derived from the hard core.

Neither am I aware of reduced scope for the program. Rather
than drawing in its extension over time, it has helped to explain,
in recent years, new facts from female labor force participation
rates to migration flows, from the relationship between race and
earnings to the decline in U.S. fertility.

Demonstrating the progressivity of the (post) Keynesian program would require, at a minimum, an articulation of the hard
core, and heuristics, of the (post) Keynesian program. Repeated

[21] "So no degree of commitment to beliefs makes them knowledge. Indeed
the hallmark of scientific behavior is a certain scepticism even towards one's
most cherished theories. Blind commitment to a theory is not an intellectual
virtue: it is an intellectual crime." Lakatos, "Science and Pseudoscience,"
in Lakatos, p. 1.

announcements of what post Keynesians do not believe does not constitute an investigative logic. Further, what are the successes of the program? What extension has there been in its domain? What previously inexplicable, or unrecognized, features of economic life has it illuminated? If Dow wishes to convince neo-Walrasians to abandon what seems to them to be a progressive research program, she must, at least, be willing to defend the relative progressivity of the (post) Keynesian program. Simultaneously, she must be willing to specify the circumstances under which she would be willing to move the other way. If there are *no* such circumstances, then we have no hope of communicating.

COMMENT

Substantive mountains and methodological molehills: a rejoinder

SHEILA DOW

Great mountains out of little molehills grow. I emphasized the importance of methodology in my discussion of Weintraub and Wiles (Dow, 1981) because I am convinced that most "real" issues which divide economists arise from methodological differences. As such, I was not accusing Roy Weintraub of having a "flawed methodology" but rather arguing that he did not carry over the methodological analysis in Chapter 1 of his book (1979) to the analysis of microfoundations.

Weintraub dismisses any discussion of methodology by "mere" economists on the grounds that we are not adequately equipped; we should leave such discussion to philosophers of science. But since we must use *some* method, should we not form opinions on the rationale for and implications of that choice? We do not, after all, leave the specification of production functions entirely to physicists, or of labor markets entirely to sociologists.[1]

Not wishing to prolong the debate about the relative merits of Kuhnian analysis, I accept that a Lakatosian approach may be preferable for theory *appraisal* within a body of theory; Kuhn's approach is however particularly illuminating when discussing relationships *between* bodies of theory. (As with economic theories, metatheories can only be chosen on grounds of usefulness with respect to some stated purpose, not on grounds of "correctness.") The paradigm concept allows bodies of theory to be categorized in terms of their world-view-plus-methodology. Weintraub himself implicitly employs this concept when he rejects potentially am-

The author is lecturer in Economics, University of Stirling, Scotland.
[1] I am indebted to Sidney Weintraub for this point.

biguous terms such as "neoclassical" in favor of "neo-Walrasian." The General Equilibrium method thus defines the boundaries of the paradigm with which he is concerned.

Much of the differences he perceives between us would be eliminated if he were to take the same approach to the equally potentially ambiguous term "Keynesian." (I admit that I may not have been sufficiently precise in my use of "labels.") Of course there can be no objection to neo-Walrasians trying to deal with the phenomenon of involuntary unemployment; far from it. But it is very misleading to talk of this phenomenon as a "Keynesian concern." The term "Keynesian," to a post Keynesian, implies the whole world-view-plus-methodology of the *General Theory*, and this cannot be expressed in terms of another methodology without becoming radically different. Hicks himself has recently, in this journal, elaborated on his conclusion that *IS-LM* analysis precludes most of the concerns expressed by Keynes (1980-81).

Now, in his reply to my article, Weintraub presents his book as a survey of work which provides microfoundations for a macroeconomic analysis of involuntary unemployment, *within the neo-Walrasian paradigm*. But throughout the book (even in its title) there are indications that this paradigm is being treated as being synonymous with economics. Indeed, Weintraub explicitly rejects alternatives to general equilibrium approaches to microfoundations in the passage from p. 161 reproduced again in his reply; but general equilibrium theory is *not* synonymous with general systems theory.

Weintraub highlights another source of misunderstanding when he asks for an articulation of the post Keynesian program. Apart from the fact that I provided a nutshell account of post Keynesian theory of inflation and unemployment in my article, there is a wide range of literature setting out a post Keynesian account of the economy,[2] as well as Harcourt's forthcoming survey paper. (The vastness of economics literature is only one reason why economists must be selective in their reading and thus in their theoretical framework.)

[2] The list of "successes" of the post Keynesian paradigm which Weintraub asks for must include at least the following: Robinson (1953-54), and subsequent work, on capital; Galbraith (1974) on the duality of industrial structure between oligopoly and small, competitive firms; Sidney Weintraub (1958) on profits and contracts and on inflation (in 1959 and subsequent publications); Davidson (1972) on money; and Minsky (1975) on financial instability. There is in addition a large post Keynesian literature on the theory and practice of economic policy.

More significantly, it seems from *Microfoundations* that Weintraub equates microeconomics with neo-Walrasian microeconomics: "To a microeconomic theorist, then, a study of the microfoundations of macroeconomics is coextensive with general equilibrium analysis" (1979, p. 10). Unfortunately, Weintraub is not alone in not acknowledging the existence of a microeconomic theory which sits much more happily with "Keynesian" macroeconomics; indeed, some of this literature explicitly deals with the two levels of aggregation together (see Dow and Earl, 1982, for a treatment of monetary economics with post Keynesian microfoundations).

In appraising the neo-Walrasian research program, Weintraub inevitably appraises it relative to other programs and appears to find them wanting. It is on this question that our fundamental disagreement rests: not on grounds of content so much as on grounds of methodology. Weintraub argues that economists can be persuaded to change research programs, having been convinced by argument and evidence. He states that he would be persuaded to doubt the value of the neo-Walrasian program if "repeated ad hoc adjustments" were made to the "hard core in order to assimilate anomalies," and if new facts were not explained by the theory. Now, I would be prepared to argue that the microfoundations literature Weintraub surveys represents "ad hoc adjustments" to the hard core and that these adjustments fail to explain adequately the persistence of involuntary unemployment. I have no doubt that Weintraub would *not* be convinced, since my supporting arguments would be expressed from outside the paradigm.

Similarly, a post Keynesian would argue that Weintraub's negative heuristic, NH2 ("do not construct models which rely on institutional change to produce coherent outcomes"), protects the neo-Walrasian paradigm from anomalies but at the same time prevents it from explaining or predicting economic events outside a very short period. At the same time, the extension of the paradigm to apply market analysis to such phenomena as changing fertility rates, with no reliance on an understanding of institutional change, does not appear to represent progress.[3] Again, our difference of opinion stems from our difference of method, and thus our difference of paradigm. The reasons for adopting a particular paradigm in economics are very complex (see Dow and Earl, 1981) and cannot be explained simply in terms of "convincing of error."

[3] I am indebted to Sidney Weintraub for these points.

Weintraub has made a valiant attempt at meeting Boland's criterion: "The only question of substance is whether a theorist is willing to say what it would take to convince him or her that the metaphysics used failed the test" (1981, p. 1035). But it is impossible to specify what constitutes an "ad hoc adjustment" to the hard core of a theory or a fact which is unexplained to the satisfaction of representatives of more than one paradigm without invoking what Boland calls the "metaphysics" (or world-views) underlying the paradigms. Unless there is scope for changing one's metaphysics, then Weintraub is right up to a point that communication is impossible between paradigms. An enormous amount of effort among economists over the years could have been put to more productive use if only it had been recognized that to talk across paradigms is to talk at cross-purposes; perhaps more important, a lot of acrimony could also have been avoided.

An explanation of methodological issues can thus be very constructive, pinpointing those areas where argument is fruitless and those areas where discussion is enlightening. As an analogy, it is fruitless to argue with someone from another culture about the relative merits of their customs. In order to understand the metaphysics of the customs, one must commit oneself to becoming part of that culture for some time. But without that commitment discussions between members of different cultures can still be most enlightening and mutually enriching. This mutual respecting of different territories is the appropriate basis for the tolerance which Weintraub advocates.

REFERENCES

Boland, C. L. "On the Futility of Criticizing the Neoclassical Maximization Hypothesis." *American Economic Review*, 1981, 71, 1031-36.

Davidson, P. *Money and the Real World*. London: Macmillan, 1972.

Dow, S. C. "Weintraub and Wiles: The Methodological Basis of Policy Conflict." *Journal of Post Keynesian Economics*, 1981, 3, 325-39.

_____, and Earl, P. E. "Methodology and Orthodox Monetary Policy." Paper presented at the Cambridge Journal of Economics Conference on the New Orthodoxy in Economics. Cambridge, June 1981.

_____. *Money Matters: A Keynesian Approach to Monetary Economics*. Oxford: Martin Robertson, 1982.

Galbraith, J. K. *Economics and the Public Purpose*. London: Andre Deutsch, 1974.

Harcourt, G. C. "Post Keynesianism. Quite Wrong and/or Nothing New?" *Thames Papers in Political Economy* (forthcoming).

Hicks, J. "*IS-LM*: an explanation." *Journal of Post Keynesian Economics*, 1980-81, 3, 139-54.

Minsky, H. *John Maynard Keynes*. New York: Columbia University Press, 1975.

Robinson, J. "The Production Function and the Theory of Capital." *Review of Economic Studies*, 1953-54, 81-106.

Weintraub, E. R. *Microfoundations: The Compatibility of Microeconomics and Macroeconomics*. Cambridge: Cambridge University Press, 1979.

Weintraub, S. *An Approach to the Theory of Income Distribution*. Westport, Conn.: Greenwood Press, 1958.

_____. *A General Theory of the Price Level, Output, Income Distribution and Economic Growth*. Westport, Conn.: Greenwood Press, 1959.

REVIEW OF SOCIAL ECONOMY

VOLUME XXXIX   OCTOBER, 1981   NUMBER 2

THE NEOCLASSICAL AND POST-KEYNESIAN RESEARCH PROGRAMS: THE METHODOLOGICAL ISSUES*

By Elba K. Brown**
University of Texas at El Paso

The debate about the Keynesian revolution rages on and on, seemingly never to end. It continues in various forms, sometimes referred to as the Cambridge controversy, sometimes as the post-Keynesian/neoclassical debate. By whatever name it is called, the essence of the debate is whether or not the post-Keynesian approach is a viable alternative to the well-established neoclassical view as an explanation of an aggregated economic process. Are these in fact alternative and contradictory research programs? If so, how should economists rationally choose one as the better explanation? The argument presented here is that two contradictory research programs do exist, resulting in quite different theoretical frameworks or approaches used to "explain" a dynamic macroeconomic process. The resolution concerning which of these alternative approaches is the better "explanation" involves the resolution of important methodological issues within the discipline of economics. Until there is consensus regarding what constitutes a "better" theory of a "better" research program, there can be no consensus in the science of economics concerning the appropriate approach.

A few words of caution are in order with respect to the interpretation of what follows. First, the concept of a research program is a framework for analyzing the basic contradictions between the two approaches. That concept and the difficulties in using it are discussed below. Second, in focusing in on two different approaches for ex-

*0034-6764/81/1001-111/$1.50/0.
** Assistant Professor of Economics.

111

plaining a macroeconomic system, it is impossible to easily categorize each and every economist as being in either one camp or another. Specifically, there are many areas where such classification cannot be made. For example, individuals working in general equilibrium theory are often more concerned with showing why a free market economy is *not* likely to be coordinated at a unique optimum rather than an analysis of how a coordinated outcome is achieved.

> There is by now a long and fairly imposing line of economists from Adam Smith to the present who have sought to show that a decentralized economy motivated by self-interest and guided by price signals would be compatible with a coherent disposition of economic resources that could be regarded, in a well-defined sense, as superior to a large class of possible alternative dispositions. . . . The proposition having been put forward and very seriously entertained, it is important to know not only whether it *is* true, but also whether it *could* be true. A good deal of what follows is concerned with this last question . . . [Arrow and Hahn, p. vii]

One is tempted to classify Kenneth Arrow and F. H. Hahn as neoclassical because of their use of the neoclassical general equilibrium framework. Yet their purpose is more closely associated with what will be described below as the "hard core" of the post-Keynesian approach. Third, one should not confuse the post-Keynesian/neoclassical debate with the monetarist/Keynesian (American) debate. And, finally, the purpose of this paper is not to debate all of the theoretical issues involved in this controversy, but rather to show that such debates are meaningless in the absence of any consensus with respect to the methodological and epistemological issues involved.

THE RESEARCH PROGRAM

The concept of a research program was developed by Imre Lakatos in an attempt to explain the evolution of a scientific discipline. [See Lakatos.] A research program is defined as a series of theories which share a common "hard core" belief. All of the theories in the program must be consistent with the "hard core" belief and the "hard core" of the program is "irrefutable" by the methodological decision of its protagonists. [Lakatos, p. 135] The postulates of the "hard core" are accepted, and the "negative heuristic" forbids testing or questioning of the "hard core" principles. It is important to understand that these "hard core" principles need not be well articulated. Indeed, the act of articulating the "hard core" principles may expose them to criticism and question.[1] In particular, one should not confuse the axioms of a theoretical framework with the "hard core" beliefs with which those axioms must be consistent. If the "hard core" beliefs are stated as the axioms of a theory or group of theories, the "hard core" is exposed to criticism and testing. As a research program progresses, the axioms of the theories in that program may have to change in order to protect the "hard core" belief. Rules of procedure in a scientific discipline are provided by the "positive heuristic"—a set of suggestions on how to change or develop the refutable part of the research program, the "protective belt."

The role of the research program in explaining the evolution of a science is that it defines the systematic framework within which each scientist works. The evolution of a discipline is described with respect to changes in the systematic framework. The rules for accepting such changes as scientific progress are discussed by Lakatos as rational decision-making within the discipline. The rules of demarcation set out by Karl Popper which provide grounds for selecting one theory over another are extended by Lakatos to apply to the selection of one research program over another. Lakatos' rules for appraising research programs are as follows:

> A research program is either progressive or degenerating. It is *theoretically progressive* if each modification leads to new unexpected predictions and it is *empirically progressive* if at least some of these novel predictions are corroborated. It is always easy for a scientist to deal with a given anomaly by making suitable adjustments to his program. . . Such manoeuvres are *ad hoc*, and the program is degenerating unless they not only explain the given facts they were intended to explain but also predict some new fact as well. . . One research program supersedes another if it has excess truth content over its rival, in the sense that it predicts progressively all that its rival truly predicts and some more besides. [Lakatos and Zahar, p. 369]

Just how helpful these rules can be in choosing between two research programs, however, is a significant question. As Toulmin points out, what precisely is meant by "prediction" and "novel fact" is am-

---

[1] Because "hard core" principles are seldom made specific, application of the Lakatosian concept is particularly difficult. Often the "hard core" of a particular research program is specified quite differently from one writer to the next.

biguous. [Toulmin, pp. 384-91] Recognizing that objectively determined knowledge is an unattainable goal, Lakatos admits that a methodological decision is required to determine the "empirical base" with which a theory is tested. Before an agreement about whether a program is "progressive" or "degenerating" can be reached, there must also be an agreement about what constitutes a "prediction" of a "novel fact." While it seems reasonable to assume agreement among individuals within a given research program, there is at least a likelihood that no consensus will exist between rival research programs. Different views as to what constitutes "progressive content," both theoretically and empirically would involve these methodological decisions. Thus, it is possible to get two conflicting research programs within a scientific discipline, each describing and working within a different systematic framework with no objectively determined scientific ground upon which one might be selected as better than the other.

If a different systematic framework is associated with each research program, then what constitutes "explanation" in terms of one framework will not necessarily be accepted as "explanation" in the other. Toulmin claims that Lakatos' modification of his use of prediction in the reconstruction of the Copernican research program's victory over that of Ptolemy calls for replacing the word "prediction" with "explanation" if it is consistent with an accepted systematic view of the world. For example, the observed throwing motion made by a child is said to predict and explain the subsequent breaking of window-glass *because* such an explanation is consistent with the accepted view that such movement is associated with throwing an object, and that hard objects thrown against window-glass with certain properties will cause the glass to break. The prediction that the motion of the child would result in the breaking of the window is also explanation because it fits into a systematic framework of thought consistent with our view of the world. In Toulmin's interpretation of Lakatos, it is prediction in the sense of explanation within an accepted systematic framework which identifies the "progressivity" of a research program. If there is no agreement about the appropriate systematic framework, agreement on what constitutes better predictions or explanations cannot easily be reached.

The "hard core" beliefs of the research program must be consistent with the view of the world which defines the systematic framework accepted by the protagonists of that program. Two contradictory research programs would have different frameworks, each consistent with its own "hard core." Thus, competing research programs would involve different notions about what constitutes predictive and explanatory power of a given theory. If we can identify the different "hard core" beliefs and the resulting differences in the systematic framework, we can better understand the nature of the debate between neoclassicists and the post-Keynesians.

THE RESEARCH PROGRAM EVIDENT IN THE WORKS OF KEYNES

There are different possible specifications of the neoclassical "hard core." The specification made by Spiro Latsis is most acceptable from my point of view. It is this specification I shall use as a comparison to the "hard core" evident in the works of Keynes and in the works of the post-Keynesians. Latsis describes the "hard core" of the neoclassical research program as follows:

(i) Decision-makers have correct knowledge of the relevant features of their economic situation.

(ii) Decision-makers *prefer* the best available alternative given their knowledge of the situation and of the means at their disposal.

(iii) Given (i) and (ii), situations generate their internal "logic" and decision-makers *act appropriately to the logic of their situation.*

(iv) Economic units and structures display stable, coordinated behavior. [Latsis, p. 22]

This notion of "stable and coordinated behavior" becomes in neoclassical macrotheory an ideal toward which the economic process is said to move, with policy prescriptions derived as those policies which would facilitate that movement. The coordinated outcome is implicitly accepted in neoclassical macrotheory and explicitly accepted in neoclassical welfare theory as a position toward which the economic process *should* move. The "efficient" allocation of resources is defined in neoclassical economics as a Pareto optimal allocation—one from which there is no *potential* Pareto improvement. [Mishan, p. 274] Assuming the desirable distribution criteria or social welfare function is determined outside the "positive" neoclassical theory [Blaug, pp. 143-46], the neoclassical economists considers such an allocation an "ideal" even though ". . . it is not possible to say, in general, that more efficient production confers an unambiguous welfare gain in the form of a potential Pareto improvement on the community or that a production optimum is better in the sense for the community than a nonoptimum." [Mishan, p. 348]

The Keynesian "hard core" contradicts the neoclassical "hard core" in two respects. First, decision-makers cannot have correct knowledge of the relevant features of their economic situation and, second, as a result, the system is not inherently stable and coordinated. The actual economic process does not automatically move toward an "efficient" allocation or production optimum. These differences are reflected in the framework of analysis used by each group.

The research program evident in the works of Keynes had the following characteristics. First, he did not hold that decision-makers have correct knowledge of the relevant features of their economic situation. In the *Treatise on Probability* Keynes clearly presents his epistemological views. "Knowledge" of the future can only be gained via induction from past experiences. What we can know is "direct" knowledge. Knowledge by induction is "indirect knowledge." We may have a "rational degree of belief" in the "indirect knowledge" of a proposition by perceiving a logical relation between the proposition and "direct knowledge." This logical relation Keynes termed probability.

Decisions between alternative courses of action must involve knowledge of the future. We must have, or believe ourselves to have, knowledge of the future consequences of each alternative in order to choose one alternative course of action over another. It appears that Keynes would argue that such "knowledge" of the future must be held with only a probable degree of certainty. But, Keynes was careful to stipulate the conditions under which a probability could be calculated. These conditions are seldom met in the course of everyday activity. Thus, in general, such probability calculations cannot be made.

> By uncertain knowledge, let me explain, I do not mean merely to distinguish what is known for certain from what is only probable. . . . About these matters there is no scientific basis to form any calculable probability whatever. We simply do not know. [Keynes, "The General Theory of Employment," in 1973b, p. 114]

Not only can probability calculations not be made in most situations, but comparisons of probability calculations cannot be made. Thus, for decisions made with reference to the future consequences of current actions, correct knowledge cannot be held.

Second, as a result of this lack of correct knowledge, Keynes would not accept the proposition that economic units and structures display stable, coordinated behavior. Coordination, in the sense that pre-reconciled plans yield a unique single-exit decision, does not exist. Single-exit decision situations are defined as "situations where one best course of action is uniquely prescribed by the structure of the situation according to some liberal conception of rational behavior." [Latsis, p. 19] Conversely, a multiple-exit decision situation "is physically and situationally open." It is physically open because the subsequent action does not appear to be narrowly circumscribed by available physical or physiological laws and conditions, and it is situationally open in the sense that the socioeconomic environment "does not (given the decision-maker's aims, interest, and objective) uniquely determine any particular course of action." [Latsis, p. 22]

The Keynesian "hard core," then, can be presented as follows:

(i) Decision-makers prefer the best available alternatives given their knowledge of the situation and the means at their disposal.

(ii) Decision-makers behave in a "rational" way, i.e., they use logic in their reasoning.

(iii) Decision-makers do not have correct knowledge of situation with respect to alternative courses of action. Although decision-makers are "rational," there is no information or "knowledge" about some alternatives with which a "rational" decision can be made.

(iv) Given (iii), economic units and structures do not display coordinated behavior. Expectations are not realized, and markets do not necessarily clear. A unique or ideal equilibrium does not result from individual decision-making. Multiple-exit decision situations are characteristic of the economic process.

"The positive heuristic" of a research program sets out the rules and procedures which the scientists follow. To determine what "positive heuristic" is associated with the Keynesian research program, we must investigate the methods used by Keynes and establish their consistency with the "hard core."

The most obvious feature, and perhaps the most controversial for our purposes, of Keynes' method was his use of comparative statics. Although, as Axel Leijonhufvud out, at the time "formal economic theory consisted almost altogether of static and comparative static models with mathematical solutions only for 'coordinated states' of the system" [Leijonhufvud, p. 91], the relevant question is whether or not the method of comparative statics is consistent with the Keynesian "hard core." I would argue that claims of inconsistency can only be made if we impose on Keynes a neoclassical notion of equilibrium. For Keynes, as for Marshall, equilibrium was simply a balance or resting place from which the economy would not move unless a change or movement occurred in one of the change producing factors. These factors were assumed constant (long-term expectations) and fulfilled (short-term expectations) in order to describe in formal terms the "equilibrium." These types of "equilibria" are compared in *The General Theory*. But, if use of comparative statics is taken to require that the "equilibria" being compared are such that all markets must clear as a result of maximizing behavior or the part of perfectly informed individuals, then that method would be inconsistent with the Keynesian "hard core." Specifically, it would conflict with the notions that individuals cannot have complete knowledge of their economic situation, and that, as a result, coordination of the economic process in the form of such market-clearing is not generally the case.[2]

In order to describe an "equilibrium," it was necessary for Keynes to assume the psychological factors constant and to assume short-term expectations fulfilled. However, the resulting model with a determinate solution should not be interpreted as a single-exit decision situation in the sense that given the expectations, one and only one course of action would be prescribed by the "rational" behavior of individual decision-makers. But, in order for an "equilibrium" to obtain, it must be necessary that the actions taken by individuals do not change, at least in the aggregate. Notice the subtle but distinct difference. It is here that Keynes must move from the analysis of individual decision-making to the resulting actions taken as a result of some type of decision-making which may or may not be capable of analysis.

[2] One will note that I have described the market-clearing notion of equilibrium associated with what Leijohnufvud calls the Neo-Walrasian research program. Leijohnufvud's thesis is that the neoclassical and Neo-Walrasian research programs are not the same. I would argue, however, that the "hard core" set out by Latsis for the neoclassical program does apply to both groups. It could be argued that the equilibrium concept is a notion in the "protective belt" which had to be changed in order to be consistent with mathematical proofs that a unique single-exit decision situation could exist for the economy as a whole, thus protecting the neoclassical "hard core" from the Keynesian attack. This thesis, however, will not be pursued here.

Choices between alternative courses of action with respect to future consequences cannot be "rational," yet such decisions are made and actions result.[3]

The aggregation of such actions determines aggregate employment and income. If these are to remain the same, as they must in order for an "equilibrium" to obtain, there must be nothing happening to induce change in those actions. A change in long-term expectations would more than likely induce change in actions with respect to long-term alternatives. But, exactly what that change will be, given a change in long-term expectations, or even in what direction cannot be uniquely determined. The economic process is characterized by multiple-exit decision situations. Indeed, it is the analysis of such changes and of the different repercussions possible as a result that is important.

Time is embodied in Keynes' notion of uncertainty. Choices between alternative courses of action necessarily involve the future, as the decision can only be made with reference to the future outcome associated with each alternative. It is precisely these future outcomes about which we are uncertain, and for which no probability calculations or comparisons can be made. Factors which are partially determined by long-term expectations can never be completely determined by the existing conditions.

> For example, the schedule of the marginal efficiency of capital depends partly on the existing quantity of equipment which is one of the given factors, but partly on the state of long-term expectation which cannot be inferred from the given factors. [Keynes, 1965, p. 246]

It is for this reason long-term expectations must be assumed constant in formulating an essentially "timeless" static model with a determinant solution. More importantly, however, it creates the multiple exit decision situation as a characteristic of the economic process. Thus, the Keynesian "equilibrium" model cannot be interpreted as a single-exit decision situation.

It must be made clear that Keynes was interested in analyzing changes in the economy, or the economic process over time. In the preface to *The General Theory*, Keynes criticizes his *Treatise on*

---

[3] It could be argued that such an approach is capable of greater empirical content than the orthodox approach, as the empirical observations are measurements or records of actions taken, not of an optimum desire, given certain assumptions.

Money because in it, "I failed to deal thoroughly with the effects of changes in the level of output." [Keynes, 1965, p. vii] But, he says of *The General Theory*, "This book, on the other hand, has evolved into what is primarily a study of the forces which determine changes in the scale of output and employment as a whole." [Keynes, 1965, p. vii]

The emphasis on change is closely tied to Keynes' notion of stability in the economic system. His view of the economic process was "that we oscillate, avoiding the gravest extremes of fluctuation in employment and in prices in both directions, round an intermediate position appreciably below full employment and appreciably above the minimum employment a decline below which would endanger life." [Keynes, 1965, p. 254] This apparent stability is due to certain special characteristics of the propensity to consume, the marginal efficiency of capital and the money rate of interest "about which we can safely generalize from experience, but which are not logically necessary." [Keynes, 1965, p. 249] Thus, for Keynes, the economy is constantly fluctuating between two extremes. However, the important differences between Keynes' and the neoclassical view is that these fluctuations are inherent in the system. It is not the case that the economic system is stable, and given a long enough period of time and no exogenous shock, full employment equilibrium will result. Change inducing characteristics are not exogenous; they are only exogenous to the static "equilibrium" model. Stability is discussed in terms of limits to those fluctuations, one limit of which is the case of full-employment. It is in this sense that Keynes contends that his theory is "a more general theory, which includes the classical theory with which we are familiar, as a special case." [Keynes, 1965, p. vii]

THE POST-KEYNESIAN RESEARCH PROGRAM

Our objective here is to analyze the differences in the neoclassical and post-Keynesian research programs.[4] In what sense is current post-Keynesian theory an extension of the program evident in the works of Keynes?

---

[4] By "post-Keynesian" we do not mean the American Keynesians. With the acceptance of the general equilibrium framework of IS-LM and the later extension of this with the addition of the labor market and the so-called Keynesian-neoclassical synthesis, American Keynesians have accepted the approach of the neoclassical framework. To show the insights of Keynes, the so-called "Keynesian constraints" must be added to the model. These simply have the effect of preventing adjustment to the full employment "market-clearing" equilibrium.

Consistent with the "hard core" belief that the economy is not automatically coordinated, the important questions for the post-Keynesians involve explanations of the actual observed behavior of the economic system. As Minsky points out, ". . . the explanation of systematic instability, rather than a tendency towards a stable equilibrium, became a key problem for economic analysis." [Minsky, p. 297] If one assumes that the economic process is not automatically coordinated at an optimal equilibrium, then explanations of movements of that process cannot be made in terms of movement toward a coordinated equilibrium, so the emphasis in post-Keynesian theory is placed on the discovery of what causes change.

> . . . the impact of both past history and expectations about the future on current decisions that are bringing about the change must be taken into account. [Eichner and Kregel, p. 1294]

> Post-Keynesians are thus ultimately concerned with the analysis of the economy in disequilibrium. [Eichner and Kregel, p. 1299]

An emphasis on change over time leads directly to an emphasis on growth and dynamics. However, growth cannot be explained by movement along an equilibrium path. Rather, the purpose is "to explain why, as the historical records bear strong witness, the expansion path of a free enterprise economy is likely to be so erratic." [Eichner and Kregel, p. 1296] What becomes important is to discover the main driving force of the economy and what endogenous features of the process lead to "systematic instability" or fluctuations.

The emphasis on growth and dynamics can be considered a logical extension of the Keynesian research program. Keynes was interested in what causes changes in investment and how those changes affect the level of output and employment. Recognizing that net investment means a change in the capital stock, it is logical that theories of growth should follow. Keynes used the method of comparative statics in order to isolate and discuss the major change-producing variables so that the fluctuations of the economic process could be explained. To achieve the same purpose, the post-Keynesians used the method of comparative dynamics. The difference in these methods is not substantial.

> . . . but the main topic of *The General Theory* was the consequences of a *change* in the level of effective demand within a

> short-period situation with given plant and available labor.
> The consequences of changing the stock of plant as invest-
> ment matures hardly came into the story . . .

> Once he (Keynes) had thrown off the incubus of Say's Law,
> the whole field of the long-period theory of accumulation
> remained to be explored. [Robinson, 1977, p. 1235]

The post-Keynesian emphasis on distribution can also be explained
as consistent with the Keynesian "hard core." Acceptance of the
marginal productivity theory of distribution would be inconsistent
with the "hard core" if its acceptance requires the belief that an automatically coordinated equilibrium state exists. The post-Keynesian
rejection of the marginal productivity theory of distribution rests on
the criticism that the return to capital cannot be determined unless
the capital-value aggregate could be specified. The prices of capital
assets cannot be explained until it is assumed "that equilibrium not
only now exists, but it has existed since the creation and will continue
to exist until the final holocaust." [Minsky, 1977, p. 301] Thus, the
marginal productivity theory of distribution involves the assumption
that equilibrium in the sense of coordinated states must be at least
possible. An alternative theory of distribution had to be developed
within the Keynesian research program, i.e., consistent with the Keynesian "hard core."

> This dissatisfaction with the traditional theory's explanation
> of the determination of factor prices, of the wage and profit
> rate, and thus of factor shares led to the search for a theory of
> distribution that was both logically sound and compatible
> with *The General Theory*. [Kregel, p. 423]

It should be noted that in addition to the impossibility of specifying
a capital-value aggregate, the acceptance of Keynes' view that the
level of employment could not be explained by marginal productivity
of labor alone led to the abandonment of the marginal productivity
theory of distribution. This, of course, is consistent with Keynes'
notion of non-market clearing equilibrium.

One other characteristic which can be interpreted as consistent with
the "hard core" of the Keynesian research program should be presented. The microeconomic base described by Eichner and Kregel as
a distinguishing characteristic of post-Keynesian theory does *not* require the assumption of perfect information or foresight on the part
of the individual decision-making units. The assumption of perfect
competition is not required.

As noted above, Keynes' notion of equilibrium cannot be construed as necessitating market-clearing as in Walrasian models. In dynamic analysis, the notion of equilibrium is translated into a steady rate of expansion. Post-Keynesian growth theory begins by describing the conditions required for such a steady rate of expansion. However, it must be clear that such conditions do not include full-employment or clearing of all markets in the Walrasian sense. Post-Keynesian analysis is considered complete when "discretionary income must be equal to discretionary expenditures." [Eichner and Kregel, p. 1309]

> This gives greater freedom to the analysis because, with only one set of flows that must be brought into balance before the chain of causal explanation can be considered complete, many other things—like the flow of those who would like to obtain employment or the desired portfolios of wealth holders —can remain out of balance. [Eichner and Kregel, p. 1301]

The significant difference between this view of equilibrium or steady expansion and the view requiring market-clearing is that the latter view associates simultaneity of determination in the model with causality.

One of the uses of static equilibrium has been to describe the system with a set of simultaneous equations, yielding a determinate system. The Keynesian system is not completely determined by the "givens" because the "independent" variables are those which can never be inferred from the given variables. For the post-Keynesians, as for Keynes, the notion of causality "is not the same as simultaneity of determination." [Eichner and Kregel, p. 1295]

> . . . a most reliable sign of distortion shows up any time the original Keynes' "clear-cut results" are obfuscated by the imposition of interdependences which transform Keynes' causally ordered relations into a system of simultaneous equations. [Pasinetti, p. 46]

Post-Keynesians do not call for abandonment of the equilibrium concept. However, caution in interpreting it as a point toward which the economy should or does move is expressed.

> The concept of equilibrium, of course, is an indispensable tool of analysis. . . . But to use the equilibrium concept one has to keep it in its place, and its place is strictly in the preliminary stages of an analytical argument, not in the framing of hypothesis to be tested against the facts, for we know perfectly well that we shall not find facts in a state of equilib-

rium. Yet many writers seem to conceive the long-period as
a date somewhere in the future that in equilibrium something
is true . . . then it somehow does not matter that every day
now and to come, it will not be true. [Robinson, 1962, p. 81]

Pasinetti uses a full-employment equilibrium model "as a logical
framework to answer interesting questions about what ought to happen if full employment is to be kept over time, more than as a behavioral theory expressing what actually happens." [Pasinetti, p. 119]

Thus, even though an equilibrium or steady rate of expansion may
be described within the post-Keynesian framework, neither is intended
to be used as a description of actual activity in the economy. Rather,
each of these concepts is intended to be a description of a situation
which is meant to be disturbed or changed. Equilibrium or a steady
expansion path represents a point of reference with which actual
economic activity can be compared.

The importance of the distinction between the uses of equilibrium
analysis and the notion of causality for the post-Keynesians, as distinct from the neoclassical view, can only be understood within the
context of the Keynesian research program. With the belief that the
economy does not automatically reach toward a market-clearing equilibrium, the purpose of economic analysis is to explain change or
movement of the system. Furthermore, the forces causing change may
be endogenous to the system. If a model of that system is completely
determined and causality is embodied in the simultaneity of determination, any explanation of change must be due to variables *not* included in the system, i.e., exogenous shocks. Yet, the Keynesian and
the post-Keynesian view are that instability and fluctuations result
from the normal operation of a developed economy. Thus, an interesting question to Keynes and to the post-Keynesians is the explanation of this endogenously created change.

THE APPROACHES COMPARED

The purpose of this paper is to compare the systematic framework
of the post-Keynesians and neoclassical research programs. I have
stated that the two programs are rivals in the sense that the "hard
core" associated with each program contradicts the other. It is my
contention that the Keynesian research program was originally
"grafted on" to the neoclassical program. Both originated from essentially the same works. Both accepted the principle that man is

"rational"—that he is teleologically oriented. The primary difference in the "hard cores" is the assumption that man can have complete knowledge with which to behave "rationally." The effect of this assumption is on the degree of coordination possible in a system where action is a result of "rational" individual choices. This placed the emphasis of the analysis directly on the macroeconomic level. The problem to be analyzed involved the degree of coordination of the whole economic process, not the individual actions. This made the Keynesian program appear to be applicable only to the aggregate level of economic activity. Since neoclassical theory up to that time had been primarily concerned with the analysis of individual actions or choices, the inconsistency between the two programs was not immediately obvious.

The reactions to the new Keynesian research program were mixed. The "conservative" reaction, as it is termed by Lakatos, was to begin a reinterpretation of the Keynesian program along neoclassical lines. [Lakatos, p. 144] This began the process that produced the "neoclassical-Keynesian" synthesis.

> While Keynes was still attempting to refine this new way to viewing economic phenomena . . . a number of other economists were trying to comprehend Keynes' ideas in terms of traditional theory. Hicks published a "potted version" of what he believed to be Keynes' central argument, using the famous IS-LM diagram of a general equilibrium system. This began a retrograde movement of modification, alteration, and distortion of the new paradigm to force it into the older neoclassical mold. [Davidson, pp. 276-77]

The development of these so-called "Keynesian" macroeconomic models indicates that better explanation involves the inclusion of more and more variables in a simultaneously determined model. Criticisms of the Samuelson-Hanson "cross" include the nondetermination of the price level and the insufficient treatment of the money-market. [Weintraub, pp. 45-46] The IS-LM framework was considered an improvement over the "cross" as it made equilibrium in the money market and equilibrium in the commodity market simultaneously determined. Thus, we see the development of "Keynesian" economics as a movement toward more comprehensive models exhibiting simultaneity of determination. The IS-LM framework, however, was still unable to show determination of the price level. To present a "plausible theory of inflation" the "Keynesians" had to

refer to the Phillips curve. The Patinkin model, which is said to illustrate the Keynesian-neoclassical synthesis, explains the price level
by making it also determined in the general equilibrium model.
Minsky summarizes the development of these "Keynesian" models
as follows:

> The journey through various standard models that embody
> elements derived from *The General Theory* has led us to the
> position that such Keynesian models are either trivial (the
> consumption-function models), incomplete (the IS-LM models
> without a labor market), inconsistent (the IS-LM models with
> a labor market but no real-balance effect), or indistinguish-
> able in their results from those of the older quantity-theory
> models (the neoclassical synthesis). [Minsky, 1975, p. 53]

The Patinkin model is said to illustrate the neoclassical-Keynesian
synthesis because non-clearing in the labor market is assumed possible only if money wages are rigid; or, in the Patinkin analysis, if
we assume such behavior in the labor market, the labor market is
said to be in disequilibrium, and adjustment to full-employment will
be delayed. [Patinkin, Ch. 13] The notion is that wage-rigidity is
"responsible for unemployment, involuntary unemployment disappears in the neoclassical world." [Minsky, 1975, p. 53] This conflicts
with Keynes' view that money wage stability gives price stability and
that wage flexibility might make things worse.

My purpose here is not to give a complete summary of current
neoclassical macrotheory, but to show that the method involves assuming a full-employment equilibrium and analysis of the economy
in terms of movement toward that ideal position. What are given as
"Keynesian" contributions to involuntary unemployment are those
things which either prevent the automatic adjustment back to equilibrium or prolong the adjustment period. Patinkin, rather than dis-
torting the labor supply curve of his model with the assumption that
labor has "money illusion" (rigid wages), simply refers to such behavior as sub-optimal. Thus, involuntary unemployment is a disequilibrium situation. The implication is that if labor would behave
"optimally" or "rationally," full employment would automatically be
achieved.

> This is the real impact of the innocuous tautology of the
> preceding section, not that involuntary unemployment can
> be defined away, but that it can have no meaning within the
> confines of static equilibrium analysis. Conversely, the es-

sence of dynamic analysis is involuntariness: its domain consists only of positions *off* the demand or supply curves. Indeed, it is this very departure from these curves, and the resulting striving of individuals to return to the optimum behavior which they represent, which provides the motive power of the dynamic process itself. [Patinkin, p. 323]

This is the primary distinction between the approach of the neoclassical research program and the post-Keynesian research program. The belief that "rational" behavior can and does lead to a coordinated or efficient outcome which is the "ideal" position for society is associated with the belief that the movement of the whole economic process can be analyzed as the return to that optimum. If the dynamic process can be explained as a movement toward equilibrium or the optimum, then forces that create instability or disequilibrium must be exogenous to the system. Instability must come from outside the normal operation of the economic process, and instability is explained as a result of interference in the otherwise smooth-functioning free market system.

As set out above, the primary characteristics of the post-Keynesian approach are, first, to look for the explanation of instability as endogenous to the operation of an economic process, and second, to explain the movement of an economic process in terms of variables, endogenous and exogenous, which produce change. They do not associate mathematical determinism of a model with causality or situational determinism in the economic process. Most importantly, they do not assume the system automatically moves toward the "efficient" or "ideal" level of output in the neoclassical sense. Their purpose is to "explain" the actual level of economic activity, not to ask what is preventing that activity from reaching some Pareto optimal position.

THE METHODOLOGICAL ISSUES

Acepting that two contradictory research programs do exist, what is the nature of the debate between these two groups? The debate goes on in terms of demarcation rules for accepting specific theories. As such rules are methodologically determined within the context of a given research program, one would not expect to find agreement between the two groups. We must look for what is accepted by each group as predictive power and explanation. Each group should be able to argue that their particular program is more "progressive" or better "explanation" than the other based on the methodological decision within each program as to what constitutes such "progressivity."

One of the major criticisms of neoclassical theory by the post-Keynesians is that the theory lacks contact with the "real world." Because the "hard core" of the post-Keynesian research program involves the belief that prereconciled coordination is not possible, a theory presented in these terms is unacceptable to them as an "explanation" of the real economic process. Under the influence of rules of demarcation described as naive methodological falsificationism, they reject equilibrium theory as a "metaphysical" theory: i.e., an equilibrium automatically obtained is a statement which is in direct conflict with an "observation" they treat as "unproblematical background knowledge"—man is *not* capable of perfect knowledge. Thus, equilibrium models and conclusions drawn from equilibrium models cannot and do not apply to the "observable" world.

One neoclassical defense against this criticism is that "explanation" is "prediction." The argument is that the assumptions of the model or theory need not be "realistic." The test of a good theory is how well it predicts.

> Complete "realism" is clearly unattainable, and the question whether a theory is realistic "enough" can be settled only by seeing whether it yields predictions that are good enough for the purpose at hand or that are better than predictions from alternative theories. Yet the belief that a theory can be tested by the realism of its assumptions independently of the accuracy of its predictions is widespread and the source of much of the perennial criticism of economic theory as unrealistic. Such criticism is largely irrelevant . . . [Friedman, p. 41]

Prediction is not defined, but it is apparently taken as probabilistic predictions of particular observed relationships with rules agreed upon within the neoclassical research program concerning what is acceptable as "good enough." It should be noted, however, that the model from which observable conclusions are deduced is an equilibrium model with the simultaneity of determination related to the notion of causality. So, it could be argued that "explanation" includes the need to develop what is in the neoclassical view as a single consistent treatment of the phenomena to be "explained."

It is also argued by some that a particular set of assumptions should be chosen over alternatives "on the grounds of the resulting economy,

clarity, and precision in presenting the hypothesis." [Friedman, p. 40]
Lakatos refers to this as the methodology of simplicism.

> I use this rather ugly term for methodologies according to
> which one cannot decide between theories on empirical
> grounds: a theory is better than another if it is simpler, more
> "coherent," more "economical" than its rival. [Lakatos and
> Zahar, p. 361]

It is important, of course, that the hypothesis suggest some implication that can be "readily checked with observation" or that they bring
out some "connection with other hypotheses dealing with related
phenomena." [Friedman, p. 41]

The important point is this: Consistent with the view that an
equilibrium or optimal state automatically results from the "rational"
actions of individuals, the driving force of the economic process is
assumed to be the movement toward that optimum. Thus, in the
neoclassical research program, an adequate or acceptable "explanation" of the actual movement of the economic process involves the
explanation of this movement toward equilibrium. The "predictions"
by which the theory is appraised consist of conclusions derived from
the equilibrium model. Assuming a change in one of the variables,
how must the other variables change in order to restore equilibrium?
Instability is not due to individuals behaving "rationally" and can
only be "explained" as the influence of exogenous shocks to the system. It is accepted that the economy is not at equilibrium and may
never reach equilibrium due to repeating exogenous shocks. How
good "predictions" must be in order to be "good enough" is a methodological decision within the research program. And, there is by no
means agreement even within the neoclassical camp with regard to
these methodological issues.

The post-Keynesian research program involves the "hard core"
belief that an economic process organized by "rational" individual
decision-making does not in principle automatically move toward coordinated optimum as described by full-employment equilibrium.
While accepting the notion that individuals attempt to maximize their
position, they reject the notion that such actions automatically result
in a well-coordinated or optimal economic state. Indeed, "rational"
individual decision-making may create instability. Therefore, the
driving force or actual movement of the economic process cannot be
"explained" as movement toward that equilibrium, and conclusions

regarding relationships between variables and causality as they exist in the economic world cannot be derived from the solution of the equilibrium model. Their "empirical" observations and "predictions" are derived from models which do not require completeness in the form of market-clearing equibibrium. How good their "predictions" are should also be appraised within the context of their own research program. And, the "explanation" of actual movement of the economic process involves the analysis of "rational" changes in behavior when expectations are not realized (endogenous source) and technological and physical constraints on long-run development (exogenous source). A primary endogenous source of instability is discussed as the fluctuation on the expected return from capital which results from changes in the level of the capital stock.

CONCLUSION

In conclusion, we must agree that at this time no *objective* way to choose between these two alternative programs may exist. Such a choice at the very least, requires some consensus as to what constitutes a better theory in terms of predictive and explanatory factors. The debate between the neoclassical and the post-Keynesian economists has been primarily in terms of rules of demarcation between theories. However, no agreement regarding what those rules should be has been reached even among members of the same program. It is not clear what the members of each of these programs would accept as a valid test of their theories. Debates on theoretical issues between members of the competing programs are meaningless as the terms are defined within the context of the two different research programs.

While there is substantial agreement about what constitutes the empirical base, the data being gathered from national income accounting, there are irreconcilable differences in the accepted framework or view of the world associated with each research program.[5] With no consensus concerning what constitutes explanation or pre-

---

[5] It should be emphasized that these irreconcilable differences apply primarily to macroeconomic theory. Neoclassical models developed in areas such as industrial organization in which the assumption of maximizing behavior is used without the assumptions of perfect competition, can be said to be more consistent with the post-Keynesian program than with the neoclassical program. The post-Keynesians accept the notion that man is "rational" in the sense that he attempts to maximize his net benefits. They reject the notion that such behavior on the part of all decision makers results in an automatically coordinated optimal state which is "best" for society.

diction, there is no consensus concerning which view is the appropriate approach for understanding the economic process. Those who believe the economy to be inherently stable and well coordinated, with instability a result of exogenous shocks preventing the system from reaching the implied "ideal," tend to fall in the neoclassical camp. Those who believe that a free-market economic process is not inherently stable, but generates within itself forces which create instability and fluctuations in the level of economic activity, will tend to side with the post-Keynesians.

Perhaps the only resolution to the debate is to adopt *subjective* criteria or criteria outside the theoretical framework based on the ability of the different approaches to meet the needs and goals of society. "The respect accorded to a discipline depends in the last resort on its power to serve society." [Mishan, p. xvii] The normative influences in neoclassical welfare theory have been made explicit. Even though both neoclassical and post-Keynesian macrotheory may attempt to be "value free," when policy prescriptions are made, the implicit beliefs as to what is "best" for society are involved. Exposing the "hard core" elements of the competing research programs may make the underlying beliefs explicit and, therefore, pave the way for discussion from which new criteria may emerge.

REFERENCES

Arrow, Kenneth J. and F. H. Hahn. *General Competitive Analysis,* San Francisco, 1979.

Asmakopulos, A. "Post-Keynesian Growth Theory," in *Modern Economic Thought,* edited by Sidney Weintraub, College Park PA, 1977.

Blaug, Mark. *The Methodology of Economics,* Cambridge, 1980.

Davidson, Paul. "Post-Keynesian Monetary Theory and Inflation," in *Modern Economic Thought,* edited by Sidney Weintraub, College Park PA, 1977.

Eichner, Alfred S. and J. A. Kregel. "An Essay on Post-Keynesian Theory: A New Paradigm in Economics," *Journal of Economic Literature, 13,* December 1975, pp. 1293-1314.

Keynes, John M. *Economic Articles and Correspondence (Towards the General Theory),* Vol. XIII of *The Collected Writings of John Maynard Keynes,* edited by Donald Moggridge, London, 1973a.

————. *The General Theory of Employment, Interest, and Money,* New York, 1965.

————. *Social, Political, and Literary Writings,* Vol. XIV of *The Collected Writings of John Maynard Keynes,* edited by Donald Moggridge, London, 1973b.

————. *Treatise on Probability,* Vol. VIII of *The Collected Writings of John Maynard Keynes,* edited by Donald Moggridge, London, 1973c.

Kregel, J. A. "Some Post-Keynesian Distribution Theory," in *Modern Economic*

Thought, edited by Sidney Weintraub, College Park PA, 1977.

Lakatos, Imre. "Falsification and the Methodology of Scientific Research Programmes," in *Criticism and the Growth of Knowledge*, edited by Imre Lakatos and Alan Musgrave, Cambridge, 1970.

———— and Elie Zahar. "Why Did Copernicus' Research Program Supersede Ptolmey's?" in *The Copernican Achievement*, edited by Robert S. Westman, Berkeley, 1975.

Latsis, Spiro J. "A Research Programme in Economics," in *Method and Appraisal in Economics*, edited by Spiro Latsis, Cambridge, 1976.

Leijonhufvud, Axel. "Schools, 'Revolutions' and Research Programmes in Economic Theory, in *Method and Appraisal in Economics*, edited by Spiro Latsis, Cambridge, 1976.

Minsky, Hyman. "An Economics of Keynes' Perspective on Money," in *Modern Economic Thought*, edited by Sidney Weintraub, College Park PA, 1977.

————. *John Maynard Keynes*, New York, 1975.

Mishan, E. J. *Introduction to Normative Economics*, New York, 1981.

Pasinetti, Luigi L. *Growth and Income Distribution*, Cambridge, 1974.

Patinkin, Don. *Money, Interest and Prices*, 2nd ed., New York, 1965.

Robinson, Joan. *Economic Philosophy*, Chicago, 1962.

————. "What Are the Questions?" *Journal of Economic Literature*, December 1977.

Toulmin, Stephen E. "Commentary," in *The Copernican Achievement*, edited by Robert S. Westman, Berkeley, 1975.

Weintraub, Sidney. "Hicksian Keynesianism: Dominance and Decline," in *Modern Economic Thought*, edited by Sidney Weintraub, College Park PA, 1977.

Let's Take the Con out of Econometrics

By Edward E. Leamer*

Econometricians would like to project the image of agricultural experimenters who divide a farm into a set of smaller plots of land and who select randomly the level of fertilizer to be used on each plot. If some plots are assigned a certain amount of fertilizer while others are assigned none, then the difference between the mean yield of the fertilized plots and the mean yield of the unfertilized plots is a measure of the effect of fertilizer on agricultural yields. The econometrician's humble job is only to determine if that difference is large enough to suggest a real effect of fertilizer, or is so small that it is more likely due to random variation.

This image of the applied econometrician's art is grossly misleading. I would like to suggest a more accurate one. The applied econometrician is like a farmer who notices that the yield is somewhat higher under trees where birds roost, and he uses this as evidence that bird droppings increase yields. However, when he presents this finding at the annual meeting of the American Ecological Association, another farmer in the audience objects that he used the same data but came up with the conclusion that moderate amounts of shade increase yields. A bright chap in the back of the room then observes that these two hypotheses are indistinguishable, given the available data. He mentions the phrase "identification problem," which, though no one knows quite what he means, is said with such authority that it is totally convincing. The meeting reconvenes in the halls and in the bars, with heated discussion whether this is the kind of work that merits promotion from Associate to Full Farmer; the Luminists strongly opposed to promotion and the Aviophiles equally strong in favor.

*Professor of economics, University of California-Los Angeles. This paper was a public lecture presented at the University of Toronto, January 1982. I acknowledge partial support by NSF grant SOC78-09479.

One should not jump to the conclusion that there is necessarily a substantive difference between drawing inferences from experimental as opposed to nonexperimental data. The images I have drawn are deliberately prejudicial. First, we had the experimental scientist with hair neatly combed, wide eyes peering out of horn-rimmed glasses, a white coat, and an electronic calculator for generating the random assignment of fertilizer treatment to plots of land. This seems to contrast sharply with the nonexperimental farmer with overalls, unkempt hair, and bird droppings on his boots. Another image, drawn by Orcutt, is even more damaging: "Doing econometrics is like trying to learn the laws of electricity by playing the radio." However, we need not now submit to the tyranny of images, as many of us have in the past.

I. Is Randomization Essential?

What is the real difference between these two settings? Randomization seems to be the answer. In the experimental setting, the fertilizer treatment is "randomly" assigned to plots of land, whereas in the other case nature did the assignment. Now it is the tyranny of words that we must resist. "Random" does not mean adequately mixed in *every* sample. It only means that on the average, the fertilizer treatments are adequately mixed. Randomization implies that the least squares estimator is "unbiased," but that definitely does not mean that for each sample the estimate is correct. Sometimes the estimate is too high, sometimes too low. I am reminded of the lawyer who remarked that "when I was a young man I lost many cases that I should have won, but when I grew older I won many that I should have lost, so on the average justice was done." In particular, it is possible for the randomized assignment to lead to exactly the same allocation as the nonrandom assignment, namely, with treated plots of land all being under trees and with nontreated plots of land all being away from trees. I submit that, if this is the outcome of the randomization, then the randomized experiment and the nonrandomized experiment are exactly the same. Many econometricians would insist that there is a difference, because the randomized experiment generates "unbiased" estimates. But all this means is that, if this particular experiment yields a gross overestimate, some other experiment yields a gross underestimate.

Randomization thus does not assure that each and every experiment is "adequately mixed," but randomization does make "adequate mixing" probable. In order to make clear what I believe to be the true value of randomization, let me refer to the model

$$(1) \qquad Y_i = \alpha + \beta F_i + \gamma L_i + U_i,$$

where Y_i is the yield of plot i; F_i is the fertilizer assigned to plot i; L_i is the light falling on plot i; U_i is the unspecified influence on the yield of plot i, and where β, the fertilizer effect, is the object of the inferential exercise. We may suppose to begin the argument that the light level is expensive to measure and that it is decided to base an estimate of β initially only on measurement of Y_i and F_i. We may assume also that the natural experiment produces values for F_i, L_i, and U_i with expected values $E(U_i|F_i) = 0$ and $E(L_i|F_i) = r_0 + r_1 F_i$. In the more familiar parlance, it is assumed that the fertilizer level and the residual effects are uncorrelated, but the fertilizer level and the light level are possibly correlated. As every beginning econometrics student knows, if you omit from a model a variable which is correlated with included variables, bad things happen. These bad things are revealed to the econometrician by computing the conditional mean of Y given F but not L:

$$(2) \quad E(Y|F) = \alpha + \beta F + \gamma E(L|F)$$

$$= \alpha + \beta F + \gamma(r_0 + r_1 F)$$

$$\equiv (\alpha + \alpha^*) + (\beta + \beta^*)F,$$

where $\alpha^* = \gamma r_0$ and $\beta^* = \gamma r_1$. The linear regression of Y on F provides estimates of the parameters of the conditional distribution of Y given F, and in this case the regression coefficients are estimates not of α and β, but rather of $\alpha + \alpha^*$ and $\beta + \beta^*$. The parameters α^* and β^* measure the bias in the least squares estimates. This bias could be due to left-out variables, or to measurement errors in F, or to simultaneity.

When observing a nonexperiment, the bias parameters α^* and β^* can be thought to be small, but they cannot sensibly be treated as exact zeroes. The notion that the bias parameters are small can be captured by the assumption that α^* and β^* are drawn from a normal distribution with zero means and covariance matrix M. The model can then be written as $Y = \alpha + \beta F + \varepsilon$, where ε is the sum of three random variables: $U + \alpha^* + \beta^* F$. Because the error term ε is not spherical, the proper way to estimate α and β is generalized least squares. My 1974 article demonstrates that if (a, b) represent the least squares estimates of (α, β), then the generalized least squares estimates $(\hat{\alpha}, \hat{\beta})$ are also equal to (a, b):

$$(3) \qquad \begin{pmatrix} \hat{\alpha} \\ \hat{\beta} \end{pmatrix} = \begin{pmatrix} a \\ b \end{pmatrix},$$

and if S represents the sample covariance matrix for the least squares estimates, then the sample covariance matrix for $(\hat{\alpha}, \hat{\beta})$ is

$$(4) \qquad Var(\hat{\alpha}, \hat{\beta}) = S + M,$$

where M is the covariance matrix of (α^*, β^*).

The meaning of equation (3) is that unless one knows the direction of the bias, the possibility of bias does not call for any adjustment to the estimates. The possibility of bias does require an adjustment to the covariance matrix (4). The uncertainty is composed of two parts: the usual sampling uncertainty S plus the misspecification uncertainty M. As sample size grows, the sampling uncertainty S ever decreases, but the misspecification uncertainty M remains ever constant. The misspecification matrix M that we must add to the least squares variance matrix is just the (prior) variance of the bias coefficients (α^*, β^*). If this variance matrix is small, the least squares bias is likely to be small. If M is large, it is correspondingly probable that (α^*, β^*) is large.

It would be a remarkable bootstrap if we could determine the extent of the misspecification from the data. The data in fact contain no information about the size of the bias, a point which is revealed by studying the likelihood function. The misspecification matrix M is therefore a pure prior concept. One must decide independent of the data how good the nonexperiment is.

The formal difference between a randomized experiment and a natural experiment is measured by the matrix M. If the treatment is randomized, the bias parameters (α^*, β^*) are exactly zero, or, equivalently, the matrix M is a zero matrix. If M is zero, the least squares estimates are consistent. If M is not zero, as in the natural experiment, there remains a fixed amount of specification uncertainty, independent of sample size.

There is therefore a sharp difference between inference from randomized experiments and inference from natural experiments. This seems to draw a sharp distinction between economics where randomized experiments are rare and "science" where experiments are routinely done. But the fact of the matter is that no one has ever designed an experiment that is free of bias, and no one can. As it turns out, the technician who was assigning fertilizer levels to plots of land, took his calculator into the fields, and when he was out in the sun, the calculator got heated up and generated large "random" numbers, which the technician took to mean no fertilizer; and when he stood under the shade of the trees, his cool calculator produced small numbers, and these plots received fertilizer.

You may object that this story is rather fanciful, but I need only make you think it is possible, to force you to set $M \neq 0$. Or if you think a computer can really produce random numbers (calculated by a mathematical formula and therefore perfectly predictable!), I will bring up mismeasurement of the fertilizer level, or human error in carrying out the computer instructions. Thus, the attempt to randomize and the attempt to measure accurately ensures that M is small, but not zero, and the difference between scientific experiments and natural experiments is difference in degree, but not in kind. Admittedly however, the misspecification uncertainty in many experimental settings may be so small that it is well approximated by zero. This can very rarely be said in nonexperimental settings.

Examples may be ultimately convincing. There is a great deal of empirical knowledge in the science of astronomy, yet there are no experiments. Medical knowledge is another good example. I was struck by a headline in the January 5, 1982 *New York Times*: "Life Saving Benefits of Low-Cholesterol Diet Affirmed in *Rigorous* Study." The article describes a randomized experiment with a control group and a treated group. "Rigorous" is therefore interpreted as "randomized." As a matter of fact, there was a great deal of evidence suggesting a link between heart disease and diet before any experiments were performed on humans. There were cross-cultural comparisons and there were animal studies. Actually, the only reason for performing the randomized experiment was that someone believed there was pretty clear nonexperimental evidence to begin with. The nonexperimental evidence was, of course, inconclusive, which in my language means that the misspecification uncertainty M remained uncomfortably large. The fact that the Japanese have both less incidence of heart disease and also diets lower in cholesterol compared to Americans is not convincing evidence, because there are so many other factors that remain unaccounted for. The fact that pigs on a high cholesterol diet develop occluded arteries is also not convincing, because the similarity in physiology in pigs and humans can be questioned.

When the sampling uncertainty S gets small compared to the misspecification uncertainty M, it is time to look for other forms of evidence, experiments or nonexperiments. Suppose I am interested in measuring the width of a coin, and I provide rulers to a room of volunteers. After each volunteer has reported a measurement, I compute the mean and standard deviation, and I conclude that the coin has width 1.325 millimeters with a standard error of .013. Since this amount of uncertainty is not to my liking, I propose to find three other rooms full of volunteers, thereby multiplying the sample size by four, and dividing the standard error in half. That is a silly way to get a more accurate measurement, because I have already reached the point where the sampling uncertainty S is very small compared with the misspecification uncertainty M. If I want to increase the true accuracy of my estimate, it is time for me to consider using a micrometer. So too in the case of diet and heart disease. Medical researchers had more or less exhausted the vein of nonexperimental evidence, and it became time to switch to the more expensive but richer vein of experimental evidence.

In economics, too, we are switching to experimental evidence. There are the laboratory experiments of Charles Plott and Vernon Smith (1978) and Smith (1980), and there are the field experiments such as the Seattle/Denver income maintenance experiment. Another way to limit the misspecification error M is to gather different kinds of nonexperiments. Formally speaking, we will say that experiment 1 is qualitatively different from experiment 2 if the bias parameters (α_1^*, β_1^*) are distributed independently of the bias parameters (α_2^*, β_2^*). In that event, simple averaging of the data from the two experiments yields average bias parameters $(\alpha_1^* + \alpha_2^*, \beta_1^* + \beta_2^*)/2$ with misspecification variance matrix $M/2$, half as large as the (common) individual variances. Milton Friedman's study of the permanent income hypothesis is the best example of this that I know. Other examples are hard to come by. I believe we need to put much more effort into identifying qualitatively different and convincing kinds of evidence.

Parenthetically, I note that traditional econometric theory, which does not admit experimental bias, as a consequence also admits no "hard core" propositions. Demand curves can be shown to be positively sloped. Utility can be shown not to be maximized. Econometric evidence of a positively sloped demand curve would, as a matter of fact, be routinely explained in terms of simultaneity bias. If utility seems not to have been maximized, it is only that the econometrician has misspecified the utility function. The misspecification matrix M thus forms Imre Lakatos' "protective belt" which protects certain hard core propositions from falsification.

II. Is Control Essential?

The experimental scientist who notices that the fertilizer treatment is correlated with the light level can correct his experimental design. He can control the light level, or he can allocate the fertilizer treatment in such a way that the fertilizer level and the light level are not perfectly correlated.

The nonexperimental scientist by definition cannot control the levels of extraneous influences such as light. But he can control for the variable light level by including light in the estimating equation. Provided nature does not select values for light and values for fertilizer levels that are perfectly correlated, the effect of fertilizer on yields can be estimated with a multiple regression. The collinearity in naturally selected treatment variables may mean that the data evidence is weak, but it does not invalidate in any way the usual least squares estimates. Here, again, there is no essential difference between experimental and nonexperimental inference.

III. Are the Degrees of Freedom Inadequate with Nonexperimental Data?

As a substitute for experimental control, the nonexperimental researcher is obligated to include in the regression equation all variables that might have an important effect. The NBER data banks contain time-series data on 2,000 macroeconomic variables. A model explaining gross national product in terms of all these variables would face a severe degrees-of-freedom deficit since the number of annual observations is less than thirty. Though the number of observations of any phenomenon is clearly limited, the number of explanatory variables is logically unlimited. If a polynomial could have a degree as high as k, it would usually be admitted that the degree could be $k + 1$ as well. A theory that allows k lagged explanatory vari-

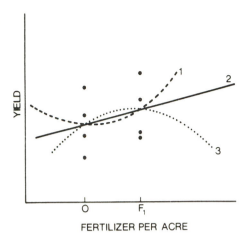

FIGURE 1. HYPOTHETICAL DATA AND
THREE ESTIMATED QUADRATIC FUNCTIONS

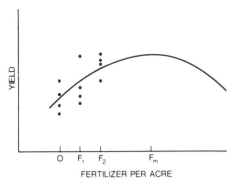

FIGURE 2. HYPOTHETICAL DATA AND
ESTIMATED QUADRATIC FUNCTION

ables would ordinarily allow $k + 1$. If the level of money might affect *GNP*, then why not the number of presidential sneezes, or the size of the polar ice cap?

The number of explanatory variables is unlimited in a nonexperimental setting, but it is also unlimited in an experimental setting. Consider again the fertilizer example in which the farmer randomly decides either to apply F_1 pounds of fertilizer per acre or zero pounds, and obtains the data illustrated in Figure 1. These data admit the inference that fertilizer level F_1 produces higher yields than no fertilizer. But the farmer is interested in selecting the fertilizer level that maximizes profits. If it is hypothesized that yield is a linear function of the fertilizer intensity $Y = \alpha + \beta F + U$, then profits are

$$Profits = pA(\alpha + \beta F + U) - p_F AF,$$

where A is total acreage, p is the product price, and p_F is the price per pound of fertilizer. This profit function is linear in F with slope $A(\beta p - p_F)$. The farmer maximizes profits therefore by using no fertilizer if the price of fertilizer is high, $\beta p < p_F$, and using an unlimited amount of fertilizer if the price is low, $\beta p > p_F$. It is to be expected that you will find this answer unacceptable for one of

several reasons:

1) When the farmer tries to buy an unlimited amount of fertilizer, he will drive up its price, and the problem should be reformulated to make p_F a function of F.

2) Uncertainty in the fertilizer effect β causes uncertainty in profits, *Variance* (*profits*) $= p^2 A^2 F^2 Var(\beta)$, and risk aversion will limit the level of fertilizer applied.

3) The yield function is nonlinear.

Economic theorists doubtless find reasons 1) and 2) compelling, but I suspect that the real reason farmers don't use huge amounts of fertilizer is that the marginal increase in the yield eventually decreases. Plants don't grow in fertilizer alone.

So let us suppose that yield is a quadratic function of fertilizer intensity, $Y = \alpha + \beta_1 F + \beta_2 F^2 + U$, and suppose we have only the data illustrated in Figure 1. Unfortunately, there are an infinite number of quadratic functions all of which fit the data equally well, three of which are drawn. If there were no other information available, we could conclude only that the yield is higher at F_1 than at zero. Formally speaking, there is an identification problem, which can be solved by altering the experimental design. The yield must be observed at a third point, as in Figure 2, where I have drawn the least squares estimated quadratic function and have indicated the fertilizer intensity F_m that maximizes the yield. I expect that most people would question whether these data admit the

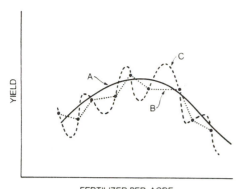

FIGURE 3. HYPOTHETICAL DATA AND
THREE ESTIMATED FUNCTIONS

inference that the yield is maximized at F_m. Actually, after inspection of this figure, I don't think anything can be inferred except that the yield at F_2 is higher than at F_1, which in turn is higher than at zero. Thus I don't believe the function is quadratic. If it is allowed to be a cubic then again there is an identification problem.

This kind of logic can be extended indefinitely. One can always find a set of observations that will make the inferences implied by a polynomial of degree p seem silly. This is true regardless of the degree p. Thus no model with a finite number of parameters is actually believed, whether the data are experimental or nonexperimental.

IV. Do We Need Prior Information?

A model with an infinite number of parameters will allow inference from a finite data set only if there is some prior information that effectively constrains the ranges of the parameters. Figure 3 depicts another hypothetical sequence of observations and three estimated relationships between yield and fertilizer. I believe the solid line A is a better representation of the relationship than either of the other two. The piecewise linear form B fits the data better, but I think this peculiar meandering function is highly unlikely on an a priori basis. Though B and C fit the data equally well, I believe that B is much more

likely than C. What I am revealing is the a priori opinion that the function is likely to be smooth and single peaked.

What should now be clear is that data alone cannot reveal the relationship between yield and fertilizer intensity. Data can reveal the yield at sampled values of fertilizer intensities, but in order to interpolate between these sampled values, we must resort to subjective prior information.

Economists have inherited from the physical sciences the myth that scientific inference is objective, and free of personal prejudice. This is utter nonsense. All knowledge is human belief; more accurately, human opinion. What often happens in the physical sciences is that there is a high degree of conformity of opinion. When this occurs, the opinion held by most is asserted to be an objective fact, and those who doubt it are labelled "nuts." But history is replete with examples of opinions losing majority status, with once-objective "truths" shrinking into the dark corners of social intercourse. To give a trivial example, coming now from California I am unsure whether fat ties or thin ties are aesthetically more pleasing.

The false idol of objectivity has done great damage to economic science. Theoretical econometricians have interpreted scientific objectivity to mean that an economist must identify exactly the variables in the model, the functional form, and the distribution of the errors. Given these assumptions, and given a data set, the econometric method produces an objective inference from a data set, unencumbered by the subjective opinions of the researcher.

This advice could be treated as ludicrous, except that it fills all the econometric textbooks. Fortunately, it is ignored by applied econometricians. The econometric art as it is practiced at the computer terminal involves fitting many, perhaps thousands, of statistical models. One or several that the researcher finds pleasing are selected for reporting purposes. This searching for a model is often well intentioned, but there can be no doubt that such a specification search invalidates the traditional theories of inference. The concepts of unbiasedness, consistency, efficiency, maximum-likelihood estimation, in fact, all the concepts of traditional theory, utterly lose their meaning by the time an applied researcher pulls from the bramble of computer output the one thorn of a model he likes best, the one he chooses to portray as a rose. The consuming public is hardly fooled by this chicanery. The econometrician's shabby art is humorously and disparagingly labelled "data mining," "fishing," "grubbing," "number crunching." A joke evokes the Inquisition: "If you torture the data long enough, Nature will confess" (Coase). Another suggests methodological fickleness: "Econometricians, like artists, tend to fall in love with their models" (wag unknown). Or how about: "There are two things you are better off not watching in the making: sausages and econometric estimates."

This is a sad and decidedly unscientific state of affairs we find ourselves in. Hardly anyone takes data analyses seriously. Or perhaps more accurately, hardly anyone takes anyone else's data analyses seriously. Like elaborately plumed birds who have long since lost the ability to procreate but not the desire, we preen and strut and display our t-values.

If we want to make progress, the first step we must take is to discard the counterproductive goal of objective inference. The dictionary defines an inference as a logical conclusion based on a set of facts. The "facts" used for statistical inference about θ are first the data, symbolized by x, second a conditional probability density, known as a sampling distribution, $f(x|\theta)$, and, third, explicitly for a Bayesian and implicitly for "all others," a marginal or prior probability density function $f(\theta)$. Because both the sampling distribution and the prior distribution are actually *opinions* and not *facts*, a statistical inference is and must forever remain an *opinion*.

What is a fact? A fact is merely an opinion held by all, or at least held by a set of people you regard to be a close approximation to all.[1] For some that set includes only one

person. I myself have the opinion that Andrew Jackson was the sixteenth president of the United States. If many of my friends agree, I may take it to be a fact. Actually, I am most likely to regard it to be a fact if the authors of one or more books say it is so.

The difference between a fact and an opinion for purposes of decision making and inference is that when I use opinions, I get uncomfortable. I am not too uncomfortable with the opinion that error terms are normally distributed because most econometricians make use of that assumption. This observation has deluded me into thinking that the opinion that error terms are normal may be a fact, when I know deep inside that normal distributions are actually used only for convenience. In contrast, I am *quite* uncomfortable using a prior distribution, mostly I suspect because hardly anyone uses them. If convenient prior distributions were used as often as convenient sampling distributions, I suspect that I could be as easily deluded into thinking that prior distributions are facts as I have been into thinking that sampling distributions are facts.

To emphasize this hierarchy of statements, I display them in order: truths; facts; opinions; conventions. Note that I have added to the top of the order, the category truths. This will appeal to those of you who feel compelled to believe in such things. At the bottom are conventions. In practice, it may be difficult to distinguish a fact from a convention, but when facts are clearly unavailable, we must strongly resist the deceit or delusion that conventions can represent.

What troubles me about using opinions is their whimsical nature. Some mornings when I arise, I have the opinion that Raisin Bran is better than eggs. By the time I get to the kitchen, I may well decide on eggs, or oatmeal. I usually do recall that the sixteenth president distinguished himself. Sometimes I think he was Jackson; often I think he was Lincoln.

A data analysis is similar. Sometimes I take the error terms to be correlated, sometimes uncorrelated; sometimes normal and sometimes nonnormal; sometimes I include observations from the decade of the fifties, sometimes I exclude them; sometimes the

---

[1] This notion of "truth by consensus" is espoused by Thomas Kuhn (1962) and Michael Polanyi (1964). Oscar Wilde agrees by dissent: "A truth ceases to be true when more than one person believes it."

equation is linear and sometimes nonlinear; sometimes I control for variable z, sometimes I don't. Does it depend on what I had for breakfast?

As I see it, the fundamental problem facing econometrics is how adequately to control the whimsical character of inference, how sensibly to base inferences on opinions when facts are unavailable. At least a partial solution to this problem has already been formed by practicing econometricians. A common reporting style is to record the inferences implied by alternative sets of opinions. It is not unusual to find tables that show how an inference changes as variables are added to or deleted from the equation. This kind of sensitivity analysis reports special features of the mapping from the space of assumptions to the space of inferences. The defect of this style is that the coverage of assumptions is infinitesimal, in fact a zero volume set in the space of assumptions. What is needed instead is a more complete, but still economical way to report the mapping of assumptions into inferences. What I propose to do is to develop a correspondence between regions in the assumption space and regions in the inference space. I will report that all assumptions in a certain set lead to essentially the same inference. Or I will report that there are assumptions within the set under consideration that lead to radically different inferences. In the latter case, I will suspend inference and decision, or I will work harder to narrow the set of assumptions.

Thus what I am asserting is that the choice of a particular sampling distribution, or a particular prior distribution, is inherently whimsical. But statements such as "The sampling distribution is symmetric and unimodal" and "My prior is located at the origin" are not necessarily whimsical, and in certain circumstances do not make me uncomfortable.

To put this somewhat differently, an inference is not believable if it is fragile, if it can be reversed by minor changes in assumptions. As consumers of research, we correctly reserve judgment on an inference until it stands up to a study of fragility, usually by other researchers advocating opposite opinions. It is, however, much more efficient for

individual researchers to perform their own sensitivity analyses, and we ought to be demanding much more complete and more honest reporting of the fragility of claimed inferences.

The job of a researcher is then to report economically and informatively the mapping from assumptions into inferences. In a slogan, "The mapping is the message." The mapping does not depend on opinions (assumptions), but reporting the mapping economically and informatively does. A researcher has to decide which assumptions or which sets of alternative assumptions are worth reporting. A researcher is therefore forced either to anticipate the opinions of his consuming public, or to recommend his own opinions. It is actually a good idea to do both, and a serious defect of current practice is that it concentrates excessively on convincing one's self and, as a consequence, fails to convince the general professional audience.

The whimsical character of econometric inference has been partially controlled in the past by an incomplete sensitivity analysis. It has also been controlled by the use of conventions. The normal distribution is now so common that there is nothing at all whimsical in its use. In some areas of study, the list of variables is partially conventional, often based on whatever list the first researcher happened to select. Even conventional prior distributions have been proposed and are used with nonnegligible frequency. I am referring to Robert Shiller's (1973) smoothness prior for distributed lag analysis and to Arthur Hoerl and Robert Kennard's (1970) ridge regression prior. It used to aggravate me that these methods seem to find public favor whereas overt and complete Bayesian methods such as my own proposals (1972) for distributed lag priors are generally ignored. However, there is a very good reason for this: the attempt to form a prior distribution from scratch involves an untold number of partly arbitrary decisions. The public is rightfully resistant to the whimsical inferences which result, but at the same time is receptive to the use of priors in ways that control the whimsy. Though the use of conventions does control the whimsy, it can do so at the cost of relevance. Inferences based on Hoerl and Kennard's conventional "ridge regression" prior are usually irrelevant, because it is rarely sensible to take the prior to be spherical and located at the origin, and because a closer approximation to prior belief can be suspected to lead to substantially different inferences. In contrast, the conventional assumption of normality at least uses a distribution which usually cannot be ruled out altogether. Still, we may properly demand a demonstration that the inferences are insensitive to this distributional assumption.

A. *The Horizon Problem: Sherlock Holmes Inference*

Conventions are not to be ruled out altogether, however. One can go mad trying to report completely the mapping from assumptions into inferences since the space of assumptions is infinite dimensional. A formal statistical analysis therefore has to be done within the limits of a reasonable horizon. An informed convention can usefully limit this horizon. If it turned out that sensible neighborhoods of distributions around the normal distribution 99 times out of 100 produced the same inference, then we could all agree that there are other more important things to worry about, and we may properly adopt the convention of normality. The consistency of least squares estimates under wide sets of assumptions is used improperly as support for this convention, since the inferences from a given finite sample may nonetheless be quite sensitive to the normality assumption.[2]

The truly sharp distinction between inference from experimental and inference from nonexperimental data is that experimental inference sensibly admits a conventional horizon in a critical dimension, namely the choice of explanatory variables. If fertilizer is randomly assigned to plots of land, it is conventional to restrict attention to the relationship between yield and fertilizer, and

to proceed as if the model were perfectly specified, which in my notation means that the misspecification matrix M is the zero matrix. There is only a small risk that when you present your findings, someone will object that fertilizer and light level are correlated, and there is an even smaller risk that the conventional zero value for M will lead to inappropriate inferences. In contrast, it would be foolhardy to adopt such a limited horizon with nonexperimental data. But if you decide to include light level in your horizon, then why not rainfall; and if rainfall, then why not temperature; and if temperature, then why not soil depth, and if soil depth, then why not the soil grade; ad infinitum. Though this list is never ending, it can be made so long that a nonexperimental researcher can feel as comfortable as an experimental researcher that the risk of having his findings upset by an extension of the horizon is very low. The exact point where the list is terminated must be whimsical, but the inferences can be expected not to be sensitive to the termination point if the horizon is wide enough.

Still, the horizon within which we all do our statistical analyses has to be ultimately troublesome, since there is no formal way to know what inferential monsters lurk beyond our immediate field of vision. "Diagnostic" tests with explicit alternative hypotheses such as the Durbin-Watson test for first-order autocorrelation do not truly ask if the horizon should be extended, since first-order autocorrelation is explicitly identified and clearly in our field of vision. Diagnostic tests such as goodness-of-fit tests, without explicit alternative hypotheses, are useless since, if the sample size is large enough, any maintained hypothesis will be rejected (for example, no observed distribution is exactly normal). Such tests therefore degenerate into elaborate rituals for measuring the effective sample size.

The only way I know to ask the question whether the horizon is wide enough is to study the anomalies of the data. In the words of the physiologist, C. Bernard:

A great surgeon performs operations for stones by a single method; later he

---

[2] In particular, least squares estimates are completely sensitive to the independence assumption, since by choice of sample covariance matrix a generalized least squares estimate can be made to assume any value whatsoever (see my 1981 paper).

makes a statistical summary of deaths and recoveries, and he concludes from these statistics that the mortality law for this operation is two out of five. Well, I say that this ratio means literally nothing scientifically, and gives no certainty in performing the next operation. What really should be done, instead of gathering facts empirically, is to study them more accurately, each in its special determinism...by statistics, we get a conjecture of greater or less probability about a given case, but never any certainty, never any absolute determinism...only basing itself on experimental determinism can medicine become a true science.

[1927, pp. 137–38]

A study of the anomalies of the data is what I have called "Sherlock Holmes" inference, since Holmes turns statistical inference on its head: "It is a capital mistake to theorize before you have all the evidence. It biases the judgements." Statistical theory counsels us to begin with an elicitation of opinions about the sampling process and its parameters; the theory, in other words. After that, data may be studied in a purely mechanical way. Holmes warns that this biases the judgements, meaning that a theory constructed before seeing the facts can be disastrously inappropriate and psychologically difficult to discard. But if theories are constructed after having studied the data, it is difficult to establish by how much, if at all, the data favor the data-instigated hypothesis. For example, suppose I think that a certain coefficient ought to be positive, and my reaction to the anomalous result of a negative estimate is to find another variable to include in the equation so that the estimate is positive. Have I found evidence that the coefficient is positive? It would seem that we should require evidence that is more convincing than the traditional standard. I have proposed a method for discounting such evidence (1974). Initially, when you regress yield on fertilizer as in equation (2), you are required to assess a prior distribution for the experimental bias parameter β^*; that is, you must select the misspecification matrix M. Then, when the least squares estimate of β

turns out to be negative, and you decide to include in the equation the light level as well as the fertilizer level, you are obligated to form a prior for the light coefficient γ consistent with the prior for β^*, given that $\beta^* = \gamma r_1$, where r_1 is the regression coefficient of light on fertilizer.[3]

This method for discounting the output of exploratory data analysis requires a discipline that is lacking even in its author. It is consequently important that we reduce the risk of Holmesian discoveries by extending the horizon reasonably far. The degree of a polynomial or the order of a distributed lag need not be data instigated, since the horizon is easily extended to include high degrees and high orders. It is similarly wise to ask yourself before examining the data what you would do if the estimate of your favorite coefficient had the wrong sign. If that makes you think of a specific left-out variable, it is better to include it from the beginning.

Though it is wise to select a wide horizon to reduce the risk of Holmesian discoveries, it is mistaken then to analyze a data set as if the horizon were wide enough. Within the limits of a horizon, no revolutionary inference can be made, since all possible inferences are predicted in advance (admittedly, some with low probabilities). Within the horizon, inference and decision can be turned over completely to a computer. But the great human revolutionary discoveries are made when the horizon is extended for reasons that cannot be predicted in advance and cannot be computerized. If you wish to make such discoveries, you will have to poke at the horizon, and poke again.

V. An Example

This rhetoric is understandably tiring. Methodology, like sex, is better demonstrated than discussed, though often better anticipated than experienced. Accordingly, let me give you an example of what all this

---

[3] In a randomized experiment with $r_1 = 0$, the constraint $\beta^* = \gamma r_1$ is irrelevant, and you are free to play these exploratory games without penalty. This is a very critical difference between randomized experiments and nonrandomized nonexperiments.

ranting and raving is about. I trust you will find it even better in the experience than in the anticipation. A problem of considerable policy importance is whether or not to have capital punishment. If capital punishment had no deterrent value, most of us would prefer not to impose such an irreversible punishment, though, for a significant minority, the pure joy of vengeance is reason enough. The deterrent value of capital punishment is, of course, an empirical issue. The unresolved debate over its effectiveness began when evolution was judging the survival value of the vengeance gene. Nature was unable to make a decisive judgment. Possibly econometricians can.

In Table 1, you will find a list of variables that are hypothesized to influence the murder rate.[4] The data to be examined are state-by-state murder rates in 1950. The variables are divided into three sets. There are four deterrent variables that characterize the criminal justice system, or in economic parlance, the expected out-of-pocket cost of crime. There are four economic variables that measure the opportunity cost of crime. And there are four social/environmental variables that possibly condition the taste for crime. This leaves unmeasured only the expected rewards for criminal behavior, though these are possibly related to the economic and social variables and are otherwise assumed not to vary from state to state.

A simple regression of the murder rate on all these variables leads to the conclusion that each additional execution deters thirteen murders, with a standard error of seven. That seems like such a healthy rate of return, we might want just to randomly draft executees from the population at large. This proposal would be unlikely to withstand the scrutiny of any macroeconomists who are skilled at finding rational expectations equilibria.

The issue I would like to address instead is whether this conclusion is fragile or not. Does it hold up if the list of variables in the model is changed? Individuals with different experiences and different training will find

[4] This material is taken from a study by a student of mine, Walter McManus (1982).

TABLE 1 — VARIABLES USED IN THE ANALYSIS

a. Dependent Variable
  M = Murder rate per 100,000, FBI estimate.
b. Independent Deterrent Variables
  PC = (Conditional) Probability of conviction for murder given commission. Defined by $PC = C/Q$, where C = convictions for murder, $Q = M \cdot NS$, NS = state population. This is to correct for the fact that M is an estimate based on a sample from each state.
  PX = (Conditional) Probability of execution given conviction (average number of executions 1946–50 divided by C).
   T = Median time served in months for murder by prisoners released in 1951.
  $XPOS$ = A dummy equal to 1 if $PX > 0$.
c. Independent Economic Variables
  W = Median income of families in 1949.
  X = Percent of families in 1949 with less than one-half W.
  U = Unemployment rate.
  LF = Labor force participation rate.
d. Independent Social and Environmental Variables
  NW = Percent nonwhite.
  AGE = Percent 15–24 years old.
  URB = Percent urban.
  $MALE$ = Percent male.
  $FAMHO$ = Percent of families that are husband and wife both present families.
  $SOUTH$ = A dummy equal to 1 for southern states (Alabama, Arkansas, Delaware, Florida, Kentucky, Louisiana, Maryland, Mississippi, North Carolina, Oklahoma, South Carolina, Tennessee, Texas, Virginia, West Virginia).
e. Weighting Variable
  $SQRTNF$ = Square root of the population of the FBI-reporting region. Note that weighting is done by multiplying variables by $SQRTNF$.
f. Level of Observation
  Observations are for 44 states, 35 executing and 9 nonexecuting. The executing states are: Alabama, Arizona, Arkansas, California, Colorado, Connecticut, Delaware, Florida, Illinois, Indiana, Kansas, Kentucky, Louisiana, Maryland, Massachusetts, Mississippi, Missouri, Nebraska, Nevada, New Jersey, New Mexico, New York, North Carolina, Ohio, Oklahoma, Oregon, Pennsylvania, South Carolina, South Dakota, Tennessee, Texas, Virginia, Washington, West Virginia.
  The nonexecuting states are: Idaho, Maine, Minnesota, Montana, New Hampshire, Rhode Island, Utah, Wisconsin, Wyoming.

different subsets of the variables to be candidates for omission from the equation. Five different lists of doubtful variables are reported in Table 2. A right winger expects

TABLE 2—ALTERNATIVE PRIOR SPECIFICATIONS

Prior	PC	PX	T	XPOS	W	X	U	LF	NW	AGE	URB	MALE	FAMHO	SOUTH
Right Winger	I	I	I	*	D	D	D	D	D	D	D	D	D	D
Rational Maximizer	I	I	I	*	I	I	I	I	D	D	D	D	D	D
Eye-for-an-Eye	I	I	D	*	D	D	D	D	D	D	D	D	D	D
Bleeding Heart	D	D	D	*	I	I	I	I	D	D	D	D	D	D
Crime of Passion	D	D	D	*	I	I	I	I	I	I	I	I	I	I

Notes: 1) *I* indicates variables considered important by a researcher with the respective prior. Thus, every model considered by the researcher will include these variables. *D* indicates variables considered doubtful by the researcher. * indicates *XPOS*, the dummy equal to 1 for executing states. Each prior was pooled with the data two ways: one with *XPOS* treated as important, and one with it as doubtful.

2) With five basic priors and *XPOS* treated as doubtful or important by each, we get ten alternative prior specifications.

the punishment variables to have an effect, but treats all other variables as doubtful. He wants to know whether the data still favor the large deterrent effect, if he omits some of these doubtful variables. The rational maximizer takes the variables that measure the expected economic return of crime as important, but treats the taste variables as doubtful. The eye-for-an-eye prior treats all variables as doubtful except the probability of execution. An individual with the bleeding heart prior sees murder as the result of economic impoverishment. Finally, if murder is thought to be a crime of passion then the punishment variables are doubtful.

In Table 3, I have listed the extreme estimates that could be found by each of these groups of researchers. The right-winger minimum of -22.56 means that a regression of the murder rate data on the three punishment variables and a suitably selected linear combination of the other variables yields an estimate of the deterrent effect equal to 22.56 lives per execution. It is possible also to find an estimate of $-.86$. Anything between these two extremes can be similarly obtained; but no estimate outside this interval can be generated no matter how the doubtful variables are manipulated (linearly). Thus the right winger can report that the inference from this data set that executions deter murders is not fragile. The rational maximizer similarly finds that conclusion insensitive to choice of model, but the other three priors allow execution actually to encourage murder, possibly by a brutalizing effect on society.

TABLE 3—EXTREME ESTIMATES OF THE EFFECT OF EXECUTIONS ON MURDERS

Prior	Minimum Estimate	Maximum Estimate
Right Winger	-22.56	$-.86$
Rational Maximizer	-15.91	-10.24
Eye-for-an-Eye	-28.66	1.91
Bleeding Heart	-25.59	12.37
Crime of Passion	-17.32	4.10

Note: Least squares is -13.22 with a standard error of 7.2.

I come away from a study of Table 3 with the feeling that any inference from these data about the deterrent effect of capital punishment is too fragile to be believed. It is possible credibly to narrow the set of assumptions, but I do not think that a credibly large set of alternative assumptions will lead to a sharp set of estimates. In another paper (1982), I found a narrower set of priors still leads to inconclusive inferences. And I have ignored the important simultaneity issue (the death penalty may have been imposed in crime ridden states to deter murder) which is often a source of great inferential fragility.

VI. Conclusions

After three decades of churning out estimates, the econometrics club finds itself under critical scrutiny and faces incredulity as never before. Fischer Black writes of "The Trouble with Econometric Models." David

Hendry queries "Econometrics: Alchemy or Science?" John W. Pratt and Robert Schlaifer question our understanding of "The Nature and Discovery of Structure." And Christopher Sims suggests blending "Macroeconomics and Reality."

It is apparent that I too am troubled by the fumes which leak from our computing centers. I believe serious attention to two words would sweeten the atmosphere of econometric discourse. These are whimsy and fragility. In order to draw inferences from data as described by econometric texts, it is necessary to make whimsical assumptions. The professional audience consequently and properly withholds belief until an inference is shown to be adequately insensitive to the choice of assumptions. The haphazard way we individually and collectively study the fragility of inferences leaves most of us unconvinced that any inference is believable. If we are to make effective use of our scarce data resource, it is therefore important that we study fragility in a much more systematic way. If it turns out that almost all inferences from economic data are fragile, I suppose we shall have to revert to our old methods lest we lose our customers in government, business, and on the boardwalk at Atlantic City.

REFERENCES

Bernard, C., *An Introduction to the Study of Experimental Method*, New York: MacMillan, 1927.

Black, Fischer, "The Trouble with Econometric Models," *Financial Analysts Journal*, March/April 1982, *35*, 3–11.

Friedman, Milton, *A Theory of the Consumption Function*, Princeton: Princeton University Press, 1957.

Hendry, David, "Econometrics—Alchemy or Science?," *Economica*, November 1980, *47*, 387–406.

Hoerl, Arthur E. and Kennard, Robert W., "Ridge Regression: Biased Estimation for Nonorthogonal Problems," *Technometrics*, February 1970, *12*, 55–67.

Kuhn, Thomas S., *The Structure of Scientific Revolutions*, Chicago: University of Chicago Press, 1962.

Lakatos, Imre, "Falsification and the Methodology of Scientific Research Programmes," in his and A. Musgrave, eds., *Criticism and the Growth of Knowledge*, Cambridge: Cambridge University Press, 1969.

Leamer, Edward E., "A Class of Prior Distributions and Distributed Lag Analysis," *Econometrica*, November 1972, *40*, 1059–81.

_____, "False Models and Post-data Model Construction," *Journal American Statistical Association*, March 1974, *69*, 122–31.

_____, *Specification Searches: Ad Hoc Inference with Non-experimental Data*, New York: Wiley, 1978.

_____, "Techniques for Estimation with Incomplete Assumptions," *IEEE Conference on Decision and Control*, San Diego, December 1981.

_____, "Sets of Posterior Means with Bounded Variance Priors," *Econometrica*, May 1982, *50*, 725–36.

McManus, Walter, "Bayesian Estimation of the Deterrent Effect of Capital Punishment," mimeo., University of California-Los Angeles, 1981.

Plott, Charles R. and Smith, Vernon L., "An Experimental Examination of Two Exchange Institutions," *Review of Economic Studies*, February 1978, *45*, 133–53.

Polanyi, Michael, *Personal Knowledge*, New York: Harper and Row, 1964.

Pratt, John W. and Schlaifer, Robert, "On the Nature and Discovery of Structure," mimeo., 1979.

Shiller, Robert, "A Distributed Lag Estimator Derived From Smoothness Priors," *Econometrica*, July 1973, *41*, 775–88.

Sims, C. A., "Macroeconomics and Reality," *Econometrica*, January 1980, *48*, 1–48.

_____, "Scientific Standards in Econometric Modeling," mimeo., 1982.

Smith, Vernon L., "Relevance of Laboratory Experiments to Testing Resource Allocation Theory," in J. Kmenta and J. Ramsey, eds., *Evaluation of Econometric Models*, New York: Academic Press, 1980, 345–77.

Bibliography

Abele, H., 'From One-Dimensional to Multidimensional Economics: "Paradigm" Lost', *Zeitschrift für Nationalökonomie*, vol. 31 (1971), pp. 45–62.

Agassi, J., 'Tautology and Testability in Economics', *Philosophy of Social Sciences*, vol. 1 (1971), pp. 49–63.

Alchian, A., 'Uncertainty, Evolution and Economic Theory', in Alchian, *Economic Forces at Work* (Indianapolis, Ind.: Liberty Press, 1977), pp. 15–35.

Alhadeff, D., *Microeconomics and Human Behavior: Towards a New Synthesis of Economics and Psychology* (Berkeley, Calif.: University of California Press, 1982).

Alter, M., 'Carl Menger and Homo Oeconomicus: Some Thoughts on Austrian Theory and Methodology', *Journal of Economic Issues*, vol. 16 (March 1982), pp. 149–60.

Applebaum, E., 'Radical Economics', in S. Weintraub, ed. (1977), pp. 559–74.

Archibald, G., 'The State of Economic Science', *British Journal for the Philosophy of Science*, vol. 10 (May 1959), pp. 58–69.

Archibald, G., 'The Qualitative Content of Maximizing Models', *Journal of Political Economy*, vol. 73 (February 1965), pp. 27–36.

Archibald, G., 'Refutation or Comparison?' *British Journal for the Philosophy of Science*, vol. 17 (February 1967), pp. 279–96.

Armstrong, J. S., *Long Range Economic Forecasting* (New York: Wiley, 1978).

Asimakopulos, A., 'Post-Keynesian Growth Theory', in S. Weintraub, ed. (1977), pp. 369–88.

Axelsson, R., 'The Economic Postulate of Rationality – Some Methodological Views', *Swedish Journal of Economics*, vol. 75 (September 1973), pp. 289–95.

Balogh, T., *The Irrelevance of Conventional Economics* (New York: Norton, Liveright, 1982).

Barry, N., *Hayek's Social and Economic Philosophy* (Atlantic Highlands, NJ: Humanities Press, 1979).

Barucci, P., 'The Scope and Method of Political Economy in the First Histories of Economics', in Coats, ed. (1983), pp. 125–36.

Basmann, R., 'Modern Logic and the Suppositious Weakness of the Empirical Foundations of Economic Science', *Schweizerische Zeitschrift Volkswirtschaft und Statistik*, vol. 111 (April 1975), pp. 153–76.

Battalio, R., *et al.*, 'Commodity-Choice Behavior with Pigeons as Subjects', *Journal of Political Economy*, vol. 89 (February 1981), pp. 67–91.

Battalio, R., Green, L. and Kagel, J., 'Income–Leisure Tradeoffs of Animal Workers', *American Economic Review*, vol. 71 (September 1981), pp. 621–32.

Baumberger, J., 'No Kuhnian Revolutions in Economics', *Journal of Economic Issues*, vol. 11 (March 1977), pp. 1–20.

Bausor, R., 'Time and the Structure of Economic Analysis', *Journal of Post-Keynesian Economics*, vol. 5 (Winter 1982–83), pp. 163–79.

Bear, D. V. T. and Orr, D., 'Logic and Expediency in Economic Theorizing', *Journal of Political Economy*, vol. 75 (April 1967), pp. 188–96.

Becker, G., 'Irrational Behavior and Economic Theory', *Journal of Political Economy*, vol. 70 (February 1962), pp. 1–13.

Bensusan-Butt, D., *On Economic Knowledge: A Sceptical Miscellany* (Canberra: Australian National University, 1980).

Black, R. D. C. 'The Present Position and Prospects of Political Economy', in Coats, ed. (1983), pp. 55–70.

Blaug, M., 'Kuhn versus Lakatos, or Paradigms versus Research Programmes in the History of Economics', in Latsis, ed. (1976), pp. 149–80.

Blaug, M., *The Cambridge Revolution: Success or Failure?*, revised edn. (London: Institute of Economic Affairs, 1975).

Blaug, M., *A Methodological Appraisal of Marxian Economics* (Amsterdam: North Holland, 1980a).

Blaug, M., 'A Methodological Appraisal of Radical Economics', in Coats, ed. (1983), pp. 211–45.

Blaug, M., *The Methodology of Economics: Or How Economists Explain* (Cambridge University Press, 1980b).

Boehm, S., 'The Ambiguous Notion of Subjectivism: Comment on Lachmann', in Kirzner, ed. (1982), pp. 41–52.

Boland, L., 'The Identification Problem and the Validity of Economic Models', *South African Journal of Economics*,vol. 36 (September 1968), pp. 236–40.

Boland, L., 'Economic Understanding and Understanding Economics', *South African Journal of Economics*, vol. 37 (June 1969), pp. 144–60.

Boland, L., 'Conventionalism and Economic Theory', *Philosophy of Science*, vol. 37 (June 1970),pp. 239–48.

Boland, L., 'Discussion: Methodology as an Exercise in Economic Analysis', *Philosophy of Science*, vol. 38 (March 1971), pp. 105–17.

Boland, L., 'Testability in Economic Science', *South African Journal of Economics*, vol. 45 (March 1977), pp. 93–105.

Boland, L., 'Model Specification and Stochasticism in Economic Methodology', *South African Journal of Economics*, vol. 45 (June 1977), pp. 182–9.

Boland, L., 'Time in Economics vs. Economics in Time: The "Hayek Problem"', *Canadian Journal of Economics*, vol. 11 (May 1978), pp. 240–62.

Boland, L., 'A Critique of Friedman's Critics', *Journal of Economic Literature*, vol. 17 (June 1979), pp. 503–22.

Boland, L., 'Friedman's Methodology vs. Conventional Empiricism: A Reply to Rotwein', *Journal of Economic Literature*, vol. 18 (December 1980), pp. 1555–7.

Boland, L., 'Satisficing in Methodology: A Reply to Fels', *Journal of Economic Literature*, vol. 19 (March 1981), pp. 84–6.

Boland, L., 'On the Futility of Criticizing the Neoclassical Maximization Hypothesis', *American Economic Review*, vol. 71 (December 1981), pp. 1031–6.

Boland, L., *The Foundations of Economic Method* (London: Allen & Unwin, 1982).

Boland, L., 'The Neoclassical Maximization Hypothesis: Reply', *American Economic Review*, vol. 73 (September 1983), pp. 828–30.

Boland, L., 'On the Best Strategy for doing Philosophy of Economics', *The British Journal for the Philosophy of Science* (December 1983), pp. 387–92.

Boland, L., 'On the State of Economic Methodology', in Samuels, ed. (1984).

Bordo, M., 'John E. Cairnes on the Effects of the Australian Gold Discoveries 1851–73: An Early Application of the Methodology of Positive Economics', *History of Political Economy*, vol. 7 (Fall 1975), pp. 337–59.

Bordo, M., 'Reply to Hirsch', *History of Political Economy*, vol. 10 (Summer 1978), pp. 328–31.

Bostaph, S., 'The Methodological Debate Between Carl Menger and the German Historicists', *Atlantic Economic Journal*, vol. 6 (September 1978), pp. 3–16.

Boulding, K., 'Do the Values of Science Lead to a Science of Value?' *Social Science Quarterly*, vol. 11 (March 1978), pp. 548–50.

Brandis, R., 'On the Current State of Methodology in Economics', in Samuels, ed. (1984).

Bray, J., 'The Logic of Scientific Method in Economics', *Journal of Economic Studies*, vol. 4 (May 1977), pp. 1–28.

Brennan, T., 'Explanation and Value in Economics', *Journal of Economic Issues*, vol. 13 (December 1979), pp. 911–32.

Brennan, T., 'Is Economics Methodologically Special?', in Samuels, ed. (1984).

Bronfenbrenner, M., 'Observation on the "Chicago School(s)"', *Journal of Political Economy*, vol. 70 (February 1962), pp. 72–5.

Bronfenbrenner, M., 'Radical Economics in America: A 1970 Survey', *Journal of Economic Literature*, vol. 8 (September 1970), pp. 747–66.

Bronfenbrenner, M., 'The "Structure of Revolutions" in Economic Thought', *History of Political Economy*, vol. 3 (Spring 1971), pp. 136–51.

Brown, E., 'The Neoclassical and Post-Keynesian Research Programs: The Methodological Issues', *Review of Social Economy*, vol. 39 (October 1981), pp. 111–32.

Buchanan, J., *What Should Economists Do?* (Indianapolis, Ind.: Liberty Press, 1979).

Buchanan, J., 'What Should Economists Do?', in Buchanan (1979), pp. 17–38.

Buchanan, J., 'Is Economics the Science of Choice?', in Buchanan (1979), pp. 39–63.

Buchanan, J., 'The Domain of Subjective Economics: Between Predictive Science and Moral Philosophy', in Kirzner, ed. (1982), pp. 7–20.

Caldwell, B., 'Two Suggestions for the Improvement of Methodological Work in Economics', *American Economist*, vol. 23 (Fall 1979), pp. 56–61.

Caldwell, B., 'Positivist Philosophy of Science and the Methodology of Economics', *Journal of Economic Issues*, vol. 14 (March 1980), pp. 53–76.

Caldwell, B., 'A Critique of Friedman's Methodological Instrumentalism', *Southern Economic Journal*, vol. 47 (October 1980), pp. 366–74.

Caldwell, B., 'Book Review: Mark Blaug, *The Methodology of Economics: Or How Economists Explain*', *Southern Economic Journal*, vol. 48 (July 1981), pp. 242–5.

Caldwell, B., *Beyond Positivism: Economic Methodology in the Twentieth Century* (London: Allen & Unwin, 1982).

Caldwell, B., 'The Neoclassical Maximization Hypothesis: Comment', *American Economic Review*, vol. 73 (September 1983), pp. 824–7.

Caldwell, B., 'Some Problems with Falsificationism in Economics', *Philosophy of the Social Sciences*, vol. 14 (1984).

Caldwell, B., 'Praxeology and Its Critics: an Appraisal', *History of Political Economy*, vol. 16 (Fall 1984).

Caldwell, B., 'Economic Methodology in the Post-Positivist Era', in Samuels, ed. (1984).

Caldwell, B. and Coats, A. W., 'The Rhetoric of Economists: Reply to McCloskey', *Journal of Economic Literature*, vol. 22 (June 1984), pp. 575–8.

Chalk, A., 'Concepts of Change and the Role of Predictability in Economics', *History of Political Economy*, vol. 2 (Spring 1970), pp. 97–117.

Chase, R., 'Adolph Lowe's Paradigm Shift for a Scientific Economics: An Interpretive Perspective', *American Journal of Economics and Sociology*, vol. 42 (April 1983), pp. 167–77.

Clark, A., 'Testability in Economic Science: A Comment on Boland', *South African Journal of Economics*, vol. 45 (March 1977), pp. 106–7.

Coats, A. W., 'Half a Century of Methodological Controversy in Economics: As Reflected in the Writings of T. W. Hutchison', in Coats (1983), pp. 1–42.

Coats, A. W., 'The Origins of the "Chicago School(s)"? *Journal of Political Economy*, vol. 71 (October 1963), pp. 487–93.

Coats, A. W., 'Is There a "Structure of Scientific Revolutions" in Economics?' *Kyklos*, vol. 22 (1969), pp. 289–96.

Coats, A. W., 'Economics and Psychology: The Death and Resurrection of a Research Programme', in Latsis, ed. (1976), pp. 43–64.

Coats, A. W., 'The Current "Crisis" in Economics in Historical Perspective', *Nebraska Journal of Economics and Business*, vol. 16 (Summer 1977), pp. 3–16.

Coats, A. W., 'The Culture and the Economists: Some Reflections on Anglo-American Differences', *History of Political Economy*, vol. 12 (Winter 1980), pp. 588–609.

Coats, A. W., 'The Methodology of Economics: Some Recent Contributions', *Kyklos*, vol. 35 (1982), pp. 310–21.

Coats, A. W., (ed.), *Methodological Controversy in Economics: Essays in Honor of T. W. Hutchison* (Greenwich, Conn.: JAI Press, 1983).

Coats, A. W., 'The Sociology of Knowledge and the History of Economics', in Samuels, ed. (1984).

Coddington, A., 'Positive Economics', *Canadian Journal of Economics*, vol. 5 (February 1972), pp. 1–15.

Coddington, A., 'Creaking Semaphore and Beyond: A Consideration of Shackle's *Epistemics and Economics*', *British Journal for the Philosophy of Science*, vol. 26 (May 1975), pp. 151–63.

Coddington, A., 'Keynesian Economics: The Search for First Principles', *Journal of Economic Literature*, vol. 14 (December 1976), pp. 1258–73.

Cohen, R. and Wartofsky, M. (eds), *Epistemology, Methodology, and the Social Sciences*, vol. 71, *Boston Studies in the Philosophy of Science* (Dordrecht, Holland: D. Reidel, 1983).

Collard, D., 'Swans, Falling Bodies, and Five-Legged Dogs', *Quarterly Journal of Economics*, vol. 78 (November 1964), pp. 645–6.

Cross, R., 'The Duhem–Quine Thesis, Lakatos and the Appraisal of Theories in Macroeconomics', *Economic Journal*, vol. 92 (June 1982), pp. 320–40.

Cyert, R. and Hendrick, C., 'The Theory of the Firm: Past, Present, and Future', *Journal of Economic Literature*, vol. 10 (June 1972), pp. 398–412.

Cyert, R. and March, J., *A Behavioral Theory of the Firm* (Englewood Cliffs, NJ: Prentice-Hall, 1963).

Dacey, R., 'Theory Absorption and the Testability of Economic Theory', *Zeitschrift für Nationalökonomie*, vol. 36 (1976), pp. 247–67.

Dacey, R., 'Some Implications of "Theory Absorption" for Economic Theory and the Economics of Information', in Pitt, ed. (1981), pp. 111–36.

De Alessi, L., 'Economic Theory as a Language', *Quarterly Journal of Economics*, vol. 79 (August 1965), pp. 472–7.

De Alessi, L., 'Reversals of Assumptions and Implications', *Journal of Political Economy*, vol. 79 (July 1971), pp. 867–77.

Deane, P., 'The Scope and Method of Economic Science', *Economic Journal*, vol. 93 (March 1983), pp. 1–12.

Devroey, M., 'The Transition from Classical to Neoclassical Economics: A Scientific Revolution', *Journal of Economic Issues*, vol. 9 (September 1975), pp. 415–39.

Dillard, D., 'Revolutions in Economic Theory', *Southern Economic Journal*, vol. 44 (April 1978), pp. 705–24.

Dolan, E. (ed.), *The Foundations of Modern Austrian Economics* (Kansas City, Mo.: Sheed and Ward, 1976).

Dow, S., 'Methodological Morality in the Cambridge Controversies', *Journal of Post-Keynesian Economics*, vol. 2 (Spring 1980), pp. 368–80.

Dow, S., 'Weintraub and Wiles: The Methodological Basis of Policy Conflict', *Journal of Post-Keynesian Economics*, vol. 3 (Spring 1981), pp. 325–39.

Dow, S., 'Neoclassical Tautologies and the Cambridge Controversies: Reply to Salanti', *Journal of Post-Keynesian Economics*, vol. 5 (Fall 1982), pp. 132–4.

Dow, S., 'Substantive Mountains and Methodological Molehills: A Rejoinder', *Journal of Post-Keynesian Economics*, vol. 5 (Winter 1982–83), pp. 304–8.

Dugger, W., 'Ideological and Scientific Functions of the Neoclassical Theory of the Firm', *Journal of Economic Issues*, vol. 10 (June 1976), pp. 314–23.

Dugger, W., 'Institutional and Neoclassical Economics Compared', *Social Science Quarterly*, vol. 53 (December 1977), pp. 449–61.

Dugger, W., 'Methodological Differences between Institutional and Neoclassical Economics', *Journal of Economic Issues*, vol. 13 (December 1979), pp. 899–909.

Dugger, W., 'Two Twists in Economic Methodology: Positivism and Subjectivism', *American Journal of Economics and Sociology*, vol. 42 (January 1983), pp. 75–91.

Dwyer, L., 'The Alleged Value Neutrality of Economics: An Alternative View', *Journal of Economic Issues*, vol. 16 (March 1982), pp. 75–106.

Dwyer, L., '"Value Freedom" and the Scope of Economic Inquiry: 1. Positivism's Standard View and the Political Economists', *American Journal of Economics and Sociology*, vol. 41 (April 1982), pp. 159–68.

Egger, J. 'The Austrian Method', in Spadaro, ed. (1978), pp. 19–39.

Eichner, A., 'Why Economics Is Not Yet a Science', *Journal of Economic Issues*, vol. 17 (June 1983), pp. 507–20.

Eichner, A. and Kregel, J., 'An Essay on Post-Keynesian Theory: A New Paradigm in Economics', *Journal of Economic Literature*, vol. 13 (December 1975), pp. 1293–314.

Fels, R., 'Boland Ignores Simon: A Comment', *Journal of Economic Literature*, vol. 19 (March 1981), pp. 83–4.

Finger, J., 'Is Equilibrium an Operational Concept?' *Economic Journal*, vol. 81 (September 1971), pp. 609–12.

Finn, D., 'Objectivity in Economics: On the Choice of a Scientific Method', *Review of Social Economy*, vol. 37 (April 1979), pp. 37–61.

Franklin, R. J. and Resnick, S., *The Political Economy of Racism* (New York: Holt, Rinehart & Winston, 1973).

Fraser, L. *Economic Thought and Language: A Critique of Some Fundamental Concepts* (London: A. and C. Black, 1937).

Frazer, W. and Boland, L., 'An Essay on the Foundations of Friedman's Methodology', *American Economic Review*, vol. 73 (March 1983), pp. 129–44.

Friedman, M., 'The Methodology of Positive Economics', in Friedman, *Essays in Positive Economics* (Chicago, Ill.: University of Chicago Press, 1953), pp. 3–43.

Friedman, M., 'Nobel Lecture: Inflation and Unemployment', *Journal of Political Economy*, vol. 85 (June 1977), pp. 451–72.

Fulton, G., 'Research Programmes in Economics', *History of Political Economy*, vol. 16 (Summer 1984), pp. 187–205.

Fusfeld, D., 'The Conceptual Framework of Modern Economics', *Journal of Economic Issues*, vol. 14 (March 1980), pp. 1–52.

Gafgen, G., 'On the Methodology and Political Economy of Galbraithian Economics', *Kyklos*, vol. 27 (1974), pp. 705–31.

Galbraith, J. K., 'On Post Keynesian Economics', *Journal of Post-Keynesian Economics*, vol. 1 (Fall 1978), pp. 8–11.

Garb, G., 'The Problem of Causality in Economics', *Kyklos*, vol. 17 (1964), pp. 594–609.

Georgescu-Roegen, N., 'Methods in Economic Science', *Journal of Economic Issues*, vol. 13 (June 1979), pp. 317–28.

Gill, F., 'Some Methodological Implications of the Marginal Revolution', *Australian Economic Papers*, vol. 20 (June 1981), pp. 72–82.

Good, I. J., 'Some Logic and History of Hypothesis Testing', in Pitt, ed. (1981), pp. 149–74.

Goodwin, C., 'Towards a Theory of the History of Economics', *History of Political Economy*, vol. 12 (Winter 1980), pp. 610–19.

Gordon, D., 'Operational Propositions in Economic Theory', *Journal of Political Economy*, vol. 63 (April 1955), pp. 150–62.

Gordon, S., 'Should Economists Pay Attention to Philosophers?', *Journal of Political Economy*, vol. 86 (1978), pp. 717–28.

Gordon, S., 'Social Science and Value Judgements', *Canadian Journal of Economics*, vol. 10 (November 1977), pp. 529–46.

Gordon, W., *Institutional Economics: The Changing System* (Austin, Tex.: University of Texas Press, 1980).

Grampp, W., 'An Episode in the History of Thought and Policy', in Coats, ed. (1983), pp. 137–53.

Green, F., *Empiricist Methodology and the Development of Economic Thought* (London: Thames Polytechnic, 1977).

Green, F., 'On the Role of Fundamental Theory in Positive Economics', in Pitt, ed. (1981), pp. 5–15.

Grether, D. and Plott, C., 'Economic Theory of Choice and the Preference Reversal Phenomenon', *American Economic Review*, vol. 69 (September 1979), pp. 623–38.

Grether, D. and Plott, C., 'Reply to Pommerehne, et al.', *American Economics Review*, vol. 72 (June 1982), p. 575.

Grossack, I. and Loescher, S., 'Institutional and Mainstream Economics: Choice and Power as a Basis for a Synthesis', *Journal of Economic Issues*, vol. 14 (December 1980), pp. 925–36.

Grunberg, E., '"Complexity" and "Open Systems" in Economic Discourse', *Journal of Economic Issues*, vol. 12 (September 1978), pp. 541–60.

Guthrie, W., 'The Methodological and the Ethical Context of Positive Economics: A Comment on McKenzie', *Journal of Economic Issues*, vol. 16 (December 1982), pp. 1109–16.

Guthrie, W., 'Methodological Diversity: Recognition, Responses and Implications', in Samuels, ed. (1984).

Hahn, F. and Hollis, M. (eds), *Philosophy and Economic Theory* (Oxford: Oxford University Press, 1979).

Hands, D. W., 'The Methodology of Economic Research Programmes', *Philosophy of the Social Sciences*, vol. 9 (1979), pp. 293–303.

Hands, D. W., 'Blaug's Economic Methodology', *Philosophy of the Social Sciences*, vol. 14 (1984), pp. 115–25.

Hands, D. W., 'The Role of Crucial Counterexamples in the Growth of Economic Knowledge: Two Case Studies in the Recent History of Economic Thought', *History of Political Economy*, vol. 16 (Spring 1984), pp. 59–67.

Hands, D. W., 'Second Thoughts on Lakatos', *History of Political Economy*, vol. 17 (1985).

Handy, R. and Harwood, E., *A Current Appraisal of the Behavioral Sciences*, 2nd revised edn. (Great Barrington, Mass.: Behavioral Research Council, 1973).

Harvey-Phillips, M. B., 'T. R. Malthus on the "Metaphysics of Political Economy": Ricardo's Critical Ally', in Coats, ed. (1983), pp. 185–210.

Hausman, D., 'Are General Equilibrium Theories Explanatory?', in Pitt, ed. (1981), pp. 17–32.

Hausman, D., *Capital, Profits, and Prices: An Essay in the Philosophy of Economics* (New York: Columbia University Press, 1981).

Hausman, D., (ed.), *The Methodology of Economics* (Cambridge: Cambridge University Press, 1984).

Hayek, F., *Individualism and Economic Order* (Chicago, Ill.: University of Chicago Press, 1947).

Hayek, F., 'Economics and Knowledge', in Hayek (1947), pp. 33–56.

Hayek, F., 'The Use of Knowledge in Society', in Hayek (1947), pp. 77–91.

Hayek, F.,*Studies in Philosophy, Politics and Economics* (Chicago, Ill.: University of Chicago Press, 1967).

Hayek, F., 'Degrees of Explanation', in Hayek (1967), pp. 3–21.

Hayek, F., 'The Theory of Complex Phenomena', in Hayek (1967), pp. 22–42.

Hayek, F., 'The Pretense of Knowledge', in Hayek, *New Studies in Philosophy, Politics, Economics and the History of Ideas* (Chicago, Ill.: University of Chicago Press, 1978), pp. 23–34.

Hayek, F., *The Counter-Revolution of Science: Studies on the Abuse of Reason*, 2nd edn. (Indianapolis, Ind.: Liberty Press, 1979).

Heilbroner, R., 'Economics as a "Value-free" Science', *Social Research*, vol. 40 (Spring 1973), pp. 129–43.

Heiner, R., 'The Origin of Predictable Behavior', *American Economic Review*, vol. 72 (September 1982), pp. 560–95.

Heller, W., 'What's Right with Economics?' *American Economic Review*, vol. 65 (March 1975), pp. 1–26.

Hendry, D., 'Econometrics Alchemy or Science?', *Economica*, vol. 47 (November 1980), pp. 387–406.

Hicks, J., *Capital and Growth* (Oxford: Clarendon Press, 1965).

Hicks, J., '"Revolutions" in Economics', in Latsis, ed. (1976), pp. 1–42.

Hicks, J., *Causality in Economics* (New York: Basic Books, 1979).

Hill, L., 'Social and Institutional Economics: Toward a Creative Synthesis', *Review of Social Economy*, vol. 36 (December 1978), pp. 311–23.

Hill, L., 'The Metaphysical Preconceptions of the Economic Science', *Review of Social Economy*, vol. 37 (October 1979), pp. 189–97.

Hirsch, A., 'Ideological and Scientific Functions of the Neoclassical Theory of the Firm: Comment on Dugger', *Journal of Economic Issues*, vol. 10 (June 1976), pp. 324–7.

Hirsch, A., 'The A Posteriori Method and the Creation of New Theory: W. C. Mitchell As a Case Study', *History of Political Economy*, vol. 8 (Summer 1976), pp. 195–206.

Hirsch, A., 'J. E. Cairnes' Methodology in Theory and Practice: A Note', *History of Political Economy*, vol. 10 (Summer 1978), pp. 322–8.

Hirsch, A., 'The "Assumptions" Controversy in Historical Perspective', *Journal of Economic Issues*, vol. 14 (March 1980), pp. 99–118.

Hirsch, A. and Hirsch, E., 'The Heterodox Methodology of Two Chicago Economists', *Journal of Economic Issues*, vol. 9 (December 1975), pp. 645–64.

Hollis, M. and Nell, E. J., *Rational Economic Man: A Philosophical Critique of Neo-Classical Economics* (Cambridge: Cambridge University Press, 1975).

Homans, G., 'What Kind of Myth Is the Myth of a Value-Free Social Science?', *Social Science Quarterly*, vol. 58 (March 1978), pp. 530–41.

Homans, G., 'Values in Social Science: Rejoinder', *Social Science Quarterly*, vol. 58 (March 1978), pp. 551–2.

Hutchison, T. W., *The Significance and Basic Postulates of Economic Theory*, reprint edn. (New York: Augustus M. Kelley, 1960).

Hutchison, T. W., 'Reply to Knight', *Journal of Political Economy*, vol. 49 (October 1941), pp. 732−50.

Hutchison, T. W., 'Professor Machlup on Verification in Economics', *Southern Economic Journal*, vol. 22 (April 1956), pp. 476-83.

Hutchison, T. W., *Positive Economics and Policy Judgements* (London: Allen & Unwin, 1964).

Hutchison, T. W., 'Testing Economic Assumptions: A Comment on Melitz', *Journal of Political Economy*, vol. 74 (February 1966), pp. 81−3.

Hutchison, T. W., 'On the History and Philosophy of Science and Economics', in Latsis, ed. (1976), pp. 181−206.

Hutchison, T. W., *Knowledge and Ignorance in Economics* (Chicago, Ill.: University of Chicago Press, 1977).

Hutchison, T. W., *On Revolutions and Progress in Economic Knowledge* (Cambridge: Cambridge University Press, 1978).

Hutchison, T. W., *The Politics and Philosophy of Economics: Marxists, Keynesians and Austrians* (Oxford: Basil Blackwell, 1981).

Jalladeau, J., 'The Methodological Conversion of John Bates Clark', *History of Political Economy*, vol. 7 (Summer 1975), pp. 209−26.

Jalladeau, J., 'Research Program versus Paradigm in the Development of Economics', *Journal of Economic Issues*, vol. 12 (September 1978), pp. 583−608.

Johnson, L., 'A Neo-Paradigmatic Model for Studying the Development of Economic Reasoning', *Atlantic Economic Journal*, vol. 8 (December 1980), pp. 52−61.

Jones, E., 'Positive Economics or What?' *Economic Record*, vol. 53 (September 1977), pp. 350−63.

Kagel, J., *et al.*, 'Demand Curves for Animal Consumers', *Quarterly Journal of Economics*, vol. 96 (February 1981), pp. 1−16.

Kahaneman, D. and Tversky, A., 'Prospect Theory: An Analysis of Decision Under Risk', *Econometrica*, vol. 47 (March 1979), pp. 263−91.

Kantor, B., 'Rational Expectations and Economic Thought', *Journal of Economic Literature*, vol. 17 (December 1979), pp. 1422−41.

Kapp, K., 'The Nature and Significance of Institutional Economics', *Kyklos*, vol. 29 (1976), pp. 209−32.

Karsten, S., 'Dialectics and the Evolution of Economic Thought', *History of Political Economy*, vol. 5 (Fall 1973), pp. 399−419.

Karsten, S., 'Dialectics, Functionalism, and Structuralism in Economic Thought', *American Journal of Economics and Sociology*, vol. 42 (April 1983), pp. 179−92.

Katouzian, H.,'Scientific Method and Positive Economics', *Scottish Journal of Economics*, vol. 21 (November 1974), pp. 279−86.

Katouzian, H., *Ideology and Method in Economics* (New York: New York University Press, 1980).

Katzner, D., 'On Not Quantifying the Non-quantifiable', *Journal of Post-Keynesian Economics*, vol. 1 (Winter 1978−79), pp. 113−28.

Kaufmann, F., *Methodology of the Social Sciences* (London: Oxford University Press, 1944).

Kenen, P. B., (ed.), *International Trade and Finance. Frontiers for Research* (Cambridge: Cambridge University Press, 1975).

Kirzner, I., 'Rational Action and Economic Theory', *Journal of Political Economy*, vol. 70 (August 1962), pp. 380−5.

Kirzner, I., 'On the Method of Austrian Economics', in Dolan, ed. (1976), pp. 40−51.

Kirzner, I., 'Philosophical and Ethical Implications of Austrian Economics', in Dolan, ed. (1976), pp. 75–88.

Kirzner, I., *The Economic Point of View*, 2nd edn. (Kansas City, Mo.: Sheed and Ward, 1976).

Kirzner, I. (ed.), *Method, Process, and Austrian Economics: Essays in Honor of Ludwig von Mises* (Lexington, Mass.: Lexington Books, 1982).

Klamer, A., *Conversations with Economists* (Totowa, NJ: Rowman and Allanheld, 1984).

Klamer, A., 'Levels of Discourse in New Classical Economics', *History of Political Economy*, vol. 16 (Summer 1984), pp. 263–90.

Klappholz, K. and Agassi, J., 'Methodological Prescriptions in Economics', *Economica* (February 1959), pp. 60–74.

Kmenta, J. and Ramsey, J. (eds), *Evaluation of Econometric Models* (New York: New York University Press, 1980).

Knight, F., '"What Is Truth" in Economics?' *Journal of Political Economy*, vol. 48 (February–December 1940), pp. 1–32.

Knight, F., 'A Rejoinder to Hutchison', *Journal of Political Economy*, vol. 49 (October 1941), pp. 750–3.

Knight, F., *On The History and Method of Economics* (Chicago, Ill.: University of Chicago Press, 1956).

Koopmans, T., 'Measurement without Theory', *Review of Economic Statistics*, vol. 29 (August 1947), pp. 161–72.

Koopmans, T., *Three Essays on the State of Economic Science* (New York: McGraw-Hill, 1957).

Koopmans, T., 'Economics Among the Sciences', *American Economic Review*, vol.69 (March 1979), pp. 1–13.

Kregel, J., *The Reconstruction of Political Economy: An Introduction to Post-Keynesian Economics* (London: Macmillan, 1973).

Kregel, J., 'Some Post-Keynesian Distribution Theory', in S. Weintraub, ed. (1977), pp. 421–38.

Krupp, S. (ed.), *The Structure of Economic Science: Essays on Methodology* (Englewood Cliffs, NJ: Prentice-Hall, 1966).

Krupp, S., 'Types of Controversy in Economics', in Krupp, ed. (1966), pp. 39–52.

Kunin, L. and Weaver, F., 'On the Structure of Scientific Revolutions in Economics', *History of Political Economy*, vol. 3 (Fall 1971), pp. 391–7.

Kunreuther, H. and Slovic, P., 'Economics, Psychology, and Protective Behavior', *American Economic Review*, vol. 68 (May 1978), pp. 64–9.

Lachmann, L., 'From Mises to Shackle: An Essay on Austrian Economics and The Kaleidic Society', *Journal of Economic Literature*, vol. 14 (March 1976), pp. 54–62.

Lachmann, L., 'Ludwig von Mises and the Extension of Subjectivism', in Kirzner, ed. (1982), pp. 31–40.

Lachmann, L., 'The Salvage of Ideas: Problems of the Revival of Austrian Economic Thought', *Zeitschrift für die gesamte Staatswissenchaft*, vol. 138 (December 1982), pp. 629–45.

Lancaster, K., 'The Scope of Qualitative Economics', *Review of Economic Studies*, vol. 29 (1962), pp. 99–123.

Lancaster, K., 'Economic Aggregation and Additivity', in Krupp, ed. (1966), pp. 201–15.

Latsis, S., 'Situational Determinism in Economics', *British Journal for the Philosophy of Science*, vol. 23 (August 1972), pp. 207–45.

Latsis, S., 'A Research Programme in Economics', in Latsis, ed. (1976), pp. 1–42.

Latsis, S. (ed.), *Method and Appraisal in Economics* (Cambridge: Cambridge University Press, 1976).

Latsis, S., 'The Role and Status of the Rationality Principle in the Social Sciences', in Cohen and Wartofsky, eds (1983), pp. 123–51.

Lavoie, D., 'From Hollis and Nell to Hollis and Mises', *Journal of Libertarian Studies* (Fall 1977), pp. 325–36.

Leamer, E. E., 'Let's Take the Con Out of Econometrics', *American Economic Review*, vol. 73 (March 1983), pp. 31–43.

Lee, F., 'The Oxford Challenge to Marshallian Supply and Demand: The History of the Oxford Economists' Research Group', *Oxford Economic Papers*, vol. 33 (November 1981), pp. 339–51.

Leibenstein, H., 'Allocative Efficiency vs. X-Efficiency', *American Economic Review*, vol. 56 (June 1966), pp. 392–415.

Leibenstein. H., 'X-Efficiency Xists – Reply to an Xorcist', *American Economic Review*, vol. 68 (March 1978), pp. 203–11.

Leibenstein, H., 'A Branch of Economics Is Missing: Micro-Micro Theory', *Journal of Economic Literature*, vol. 17 (June 1979), pp. 477–502.

Leibenstein, H., *Beyond Economic Man: A New Foundation for Microeconomics*, 2nd edn. (Cambridge, Mass.: Harvard University Press, 1980).

Leijonhufvud, A., 'Schools, "Revolutions," and Research Programmes in Economic Theory', in Latsis, ed. (1976), pp. 65–108.

Leijonhufvud, A., 'Life Among the Econ', *Western Economic Journal*, vol. 11 (September 1973), pp. 327–37.

Leinfellner, W., 'Marxian Paradigms vs. Microeconomic Structures', in Cohen and Wartofsky, eds (1983), pp. 153–201.

Leontief, W., 'Theoretical Assumptions and Nonobserved Facts', *American Economic Review*, vol. 61 (March 1971), pp. 1–7.

Lester, R., 'Shortcomings of Marginal Analysis for Wage-Employment Problems', *American Economic Review*, vol. 36 (March 1946), pp. 63–82.

Lester, R., 'Marginalism, Minimum Wages, and Labor Markets', *American Economic Review*, vol. 37 (March 1947), pp. 135–48.

Lindbeck, A. *The Political Economy of the New Left: An Outsider's View* (New York: Harper & Row, 1971).

Loasby, B., *Choice, Complexity and Ignorance: An Enquiry into Economic Theory and the Practice of Decision Making* (Cambridge: Cambridge University Press, 1976).

Lofthouse, S. and Vint, J., 'Some Conceptions and Misconceptions Concerning Economic Man', *Rivista Internazionale di Scienze Economiche e Commerciale*, vol. 25 (July 1978), pp. 586–615.

Lowe, A., *On Economic Knowledge: Toward a Science of Political Economics* (New York: Harper & Row, 1965).

Lowe, A., 'What Is Evolutionary Economics? Remarks Upon Receipt of the Veblen-Commons Award', *Journal of Economic Issues*, vol. 14 (June 1980), pp. 247–54.

Lucas, R. E. 'Methods and Problems in Business Cycle Theory', *Journal of Money, Credit, and Banking*, Supplement, vol. 12 (November 1980), pp. 696–715.

McCloskey, D., 'The Rhetoric of Economics', *Journal of Economic Literature*, vol. 21 (June 1983), pp. 481–517.

McCloskey, D., 'The Rhetoric of Economics: Reply to Caldwell and Coats', *Journal of Economic Literature*, vol. 22 (June 1984), pp. 579–80.

MacDougall, D., 'In Praise of Economics', *Economic Journal*, vol. 84 (December 1974), pp. 773–86.

Machan, T. R., 'The Non-Rational Domain and the Limits of Economic Analysis: Comment on McKenzie', *Southern Economic Journal*, vol. 47 (April 1981), pp. 1123–7.

Machlup, F., 'Marginal Analysis and Empirical Research', *American Economic Review*, vol. 36 (September 1946), pp. 519–54.

Machlup, F., 'Rejoinder to an Antimarginalist', *American Economic Review*, vol. 37 (March 1947), pp. 148–54.

Machlup, F., *Essays on Economic Semantics* (Englewood Cliffs, NJ: Prentice-Hall, 1963).

Machlup, F., *Methodology of Economics and Other Social Sciences* (New York: Academic Press, 1978).

Machlup, F., 'The Problem of Verification in Economics', in Machlup (1978), pp. 137–57.

Machlup, F., 'Operational Concepts and Mental Constructs in Model and Theory Formation', in Machlup (1978), pp. 159–88.

Machlup, F., 'Operationalism and Pure Theory in Economics', in Machlup (1978), pp. 189–203.

Machlup, F., 'The Ideal Type: A Bad Name for a Good Construct', in Machlup (1978), pp. 211–21.

Machlup, F., 'Ideal Types, Reality, and Construction', in Machlup (1978), pp. 223–65.

Machlup, F., 'Homo Oeconomicus and his Class Mates', in Machlup (1978), pp. 267–81.

Machlup, F., 'The Universal Bogey: Economic Man', in Machlup (1978), pp. 283–301.

Machlup, F., 'Are the Social Sciences Really Inferior?', in Machlup (1978), pp. 345–67.

Machlup, F., 'Theories of the Firm: Marginalist, Behavioral, Managerial', in Machlup (1978), pp. 391–423.

Machlup, F., 'Rejoinder to a Reluctant Ultra-Empiricist', in Machlup (1978), pp. 493–503.

MacKay, A., *Arrow's Theorem: The Paradox of Social Choice: A Case Study in the Philosophy of Economics* (New Haven, Conn.: Yale University Press, 1980).

Maddock, R., 'Rational Expectations Macrotheory: A Lakatosian Case Study in Program Adjustment', *History of Political Economy*, vol. 16 (Summer 1984), pp. 291–309.

McKenzie, R., 'On the Methodological Boundaries of Economic Analysis', *Journal of Economic Issues*, vol. 12 (September 1978), pp. 627–45.

McKenzie, R., 'The Non-Rational Domain and the Limits of Economic Analysis', *Southern Economic Journal*, vol. 46 (July 1979), pp. 145–57.

McKenzie, R., 'The Non-Rational Domain and the Limits of Economic Analysis: Reply to Machan', *Southern Economic Journal* vol. 47 (April 1981), pp. 1128–31.

McKenzie, R., 'The Necessary Normative Context of Positive Economics', *Journal of Economic Issues,* vol. 15 (September 1981), pp. 703–19.

de Marchi, N., 'The Case for James Mill', in Coats, ed. (1983), pp. 155–84.

de Marchi, N., 'The Empirical Content and Longevity of Ricardian Economics', *Economica*, vol. 37 (August 1970), pp. 257–76.

de Marchi, N., 'Anomaly and the Development of Economics: The Case of the Leontief Paradox', in Latsis, ed. (1976), pp. 109–28.

Margenau, H., 'What is a Theory?', in Krupp, ed. (1966), pp. 25–38.

Marr, W. and Raj, B. (eds), *How Economists Explain: A Reader in Methodology* (Lanham, Md: University Press of America, 1983).

Mason, E., 'The Harvard Department of Economics from the Beginning to

World War II', *Quarterly Journal of Economics*, vol. 97 (August 1982), pp. 383–434.

Mattessich, R., *Instrumental Reasoning and Systems Methodology: An Epistemology of the Applied and Social Sciences* (Dordrecht, Holland: D. Reidel, 1978).

Mayer, T., 'Selecting Economic Hypotheses by Goodness of Fit', *Economic Journal*, vol. 85 (December 1975), pp. 877–83.

Mayer, T., 'Economics as a Hard Science: Realistic Goal or Wishful Thinking', *Economic Inquiry*, vol. 18 (April 1980), pp. 165–78.

Mayo, D., 'Testing Statistical Testing', in Pitt, ed. (1981), pp. 175–203.

Melitz, J., 'Friedman and Machlup on the Significance of Testing Economic Assumptions', *Journal of Political Economy*, vol. 73 (February 1965), pp. 37–60.

Meyer, W., 'Values, Facts, and Science: On the Problem of Objectivity in Economics', *Zeitschrift für die gesamte Staatswissenchaft*, vol. 131 (July 1975), pp. 514–39.

Miller, H., 'On the "Chicago School of Economics"', *Journal of Political Economy*, vol. 70 (February 1962), pp. 64–9.

Miller, W., 'Richard Jones: A Case Study in Methodology', *History of Political Economy*, vol. 3 (Spring 1971), pp. 198–207.

Mini, P., *Philosophy and Economics: The Origins and Development of Economic Theory* (Gainesville, Fla.: University of Florida Press, 1974).

von Mises, L., *Epistemological Problems of Economics*, translated by G. Reisman (Princeton, NJ: van Nostrand, 1960).

von Mises, L., *Human Action: A Treatise on Economics*, 3rd revised edn. (Chicago, Ill.: Henry Regnery, 1963).

von Mises, L., *The Ultimate Foundation of Economic Science*, 2nd edn. (Kansas City, Mo.: Sheed, Andrews and McMeel, 1978).

Morgenstern, O., 'Descriptive, Predictive and Normative Theory', *Kyklos*, vol. 25 (1972), pp. 699–714.

Morgenstern, O., 'Thirteen Critical Points in Contemporary Economic Theory: an Interpretation', *Journal of Economic Literature*, vol. 10 (December 1972), pp. 1163–89.

Morgenstern, O., 'The Collaboration Between Oskar Morgenstern and John von Neumann on the Theory of Games', *Journal of Economic Literature*, vol. 14 (September 1976), pp. 805–16.

Musgrave, A., '"Unreal Assumptions" in Economic Theory: The F-Twist Untwisted', *Kyklos*, vol. 34 (1981), pp. 377–87.

Myrdal, G., *Objectivity in Social Research* (London: Duckworth, 1970).

Myrdal, G., *Against the Stream: Critical Essays on Economics* (New York: Vintage Books, 1975).

Nagel, E., 'Assumptions in Economic Theory', *American Economic Review Papers and Proceedings*, vol. 53 (May 1963), pp. 211–19.

Naughton, J., 'The Logic of Scientific Economics in Economics: A Response to Bray', *Journal of Economic Studies*, vol. 5 (1978), pp. 152–65.

Nelson, R. and Winter, S., *An Evolutionary Theory of Economic Change* (Cambridge, Mass.: Harvard University Press, 1982).

Ng, Y.-K., 'Value Judgements and Economists' Role in Policy Recommendation', *Economic Journal*, vol. 82 (September 1972), pp. 1014–18.

Nozick, R., 'On Austrian Methodology', *Synthese*, vol. 36 (1977), pp. 353–92.

O'Brien, D. P., 'Theories of the History of Science: A Test Case', in Coats, ed. (1983), pp. 89–124.

O'Brien, D. P., *Whither Economics? An Inaugural Lecture* (Durham: University of Durham, 1974).

O'Driscoll, G. and Rizzo, M., *The Economics of Time and Ignorance* (London: Basil Blackwell, 1984).

Papandreou, A., *Economics as a Science* (Chicago, Ill.: Lippencott, 1958).

Pfouts, R. W., 'Some Proposals for a New Methodology in Economics', *Atlantic Economic Journal*, vol. 1 (November 1973), pp. 13–22.

Phelps Brown, E., 'The Underdevelopment of Economics', *Economic Journal*, vol. 82 (1972), pp. 1–10.

Pitt, J. (ed.), *Philosophy in Economics*, vol. 16, *University of Western Ontario Series in Philosophy of Science* (Dordrecht, Holland: D. Reidel, 1981).

Pomerehne, W., Schneider, F. and Zweifel, P., 'Economic Theory of Choice and the Preference Reversal Phenomenon: A Reexamination', *American Economic Review*, vol. 72 (June 1982), pp. 569–74.

Pope, D. and Pope, R., 'Predictionists, Assumptionists and Relatives of the Assumptionists', *Australian Economic Papers*, vol. 11 (December 1972), pp. 224–8.

Pope, D. and Pope, R., 'In Defense of Predictionism', *Australian Economic Papers*, vol. 11 (December 1972), pp. 232–8.

Rashid, S., 'Richard Jones and Baconian Historicism at Cambridge', *Journal of Economic Issues*, vol. 13 (March 1979), pp. 159–73.

Reder, M., 'Chicago Economics: Permanence and Change', *Journal of Economic Literature*, vol. 20 (March 1982), pp. 1–38.

Redman, B., 'On Economic Theory and Explanation', *Journal of Behavioral Economics*, vol. 5 (Summer 1976), pp. 161–76.

Reed, M., 'Rationality and Neoclassical Economics', *Economic Forum*, vol. 10 (Summer 1979), pp. 91–3.

Reilly, R., 'Preference Reversal: Further Evidence and Some Suggested Modifications in Experimental Design', *American Economic Review*, vol. 72 (June 1982), pp. 576–84.

Remenyi, J., 'Core Demi-core Interaction: Toward a General Theory of Disciplinary and Subdisciplinary Growth', *History of Political Economy*, vol. 11 (Spring 1979), pp. 30–63.

Rivett, K., '"Suggest" or "Entail"? The Derivation and Confirmation of Economic Hypotheses', *Australian Economic Papers*, vol. 9 (December 1970), pp. 127–48.

Rivett, K., 'Comment on Pope and Pope', *Australian Economic Papers*, vol. 11 (December 1972), pp. 228–32.

Rizzo, M., 'Praxeology and Econometrics: A Critique of Positivist Economics', in Spadaro, ed. (1978), pp. 40–56.

Rizzo, M. (ed.), *Time, Uncertainty and Disequilibrium: Exploration of Austrian Themes* (Lexington, Mass.: Lexington Books, 1979).

Rizzo, M., 'Mises and Lakatos: A Reformulation of Austrian Methodology', in Kirzner, ed. (1982), pp. 53–74.

Robbins, L., *An Essay on the Nature and Significance of Economic Science*, 2nd edn. (London: Macmillan, 1935).

Robbins, L., 'On Latsis's *Method and Appraisal in Economics:* A Review Essay', *Journal of Economic Literature*, vol. 17 (September 1979), pp. 996–1004.

Robbins, L., 'Economics and Political Economy', *American Economic Review*, vol. 71 (May 1981), pp. 1–10.

Robinson, J., *Economic Philosophy* (Chicago, Ill.: Aldine, 1962).

Robinson, J., 'Foreword' to Kregel (1973), pp. ix–xiii.

Robinson, J., 'What Are the Questions?' *Journal of Economic Literature*, vol. 15 (December 1977), pp. 1318−39.

Rogers, C., 'Rational Expectations and Neoclassical Economics: The Methodology of the New Classical Macroeconomics', *South African Journal of Economics*, vol. 50 (December 1982), pp. 318−39.

Rosefielde, S., 'Economic Theory in the Excluded Middle between Positivism and Rationalism', *Atlantic Economic Journal*, vol. 4 (Spring 1976), pp. 1−9.

Rosefielde, S., 'Post-Positivist Scientific Method and the Appraisal of Non-Market Economic Behavior', *Quarterly Journal of Ideology*, vol. 3 (Spring 1980), pp. 23−33.

Rosenberg, A., *Microeconomic Laws: A Philosophical Analysis* (Pittsburgh, Pa.: University of Pittsburgh Press, 1976).

Rosenberg, A., 'Can Economic Theory Explain Everything?' *Philosophy of Social Science*, vol. 9 (1979), pp. 509−29.

Rosenberg, A., 'A Skeptical History of Microeconomic Theory', in Pitt, ed. (1981), pp. 47−61.

Rothbard, M., 'In Defense of "Extreme Apriorism"', *Southern Economic Journal*, vol. 23 (January 1957), pp. 314−20.

Rothbard, M., 'Praxeology: The Methodology of Austrian Economics', in Dolan, ed. (1976), pp. 19−39.

Rotwein, E., 'On "The Methodology of Positive Economics"', *Quarterly Journal of Economics*, vol. 73 (November 1959), pp. 554−75.

Rotwein, E., 'Empiricism and Economic Method: Several Views Considered', *Journal of Economic Issues*, vol. 7 (September 1973), pp. 361−82.

Rotwein, E., 'The Methodological Basis of Institutional Economics: Comment on Dugger', *Journal of Economic Issues*, vol. 13 (December 1979), pp. 1029−33.

Rotwein, E., 'Friedman's Critics: A Critic's Reply to Boland', *Journal of Economic Literature*, vol. 18 (December 1980), pp. 1553−5.

Rousseas, S., 'Paradigm Polishing versus Critical Thought in Economics', *American Economist*, vol. 17 (Fall 1973), pp. 72−8.

Rousseas, S., 'Wiles' Wily Weltanschauung', *Journal of Post-Keynesian Economics*, vol. 3 (Spring 1981), pp. 340−51.

Salanti, A., 'Neoclassical Tautologies and the Cambridge Controversies: Comment on Dow', *Journal of Post-Keynesian Economics*, vol. 5 (Fall 1982), pp. 128−31.

Samuels, W. (ed.), *The Chicago School of Political Economy* (East Lansing, Mich.: Association for Evolutionary Economics and Michigan State University, 1976).

Samuels, W., 'Roy Weintraub's *Microfoundations:* The State of High Theory, A Review Article', *Journal of Economic Issues*, vol. 13 (December 1979), pp. 1019−28.

Samuels, W., 'Economics as a Science and its Relation to Policy: The Example of Free Trade', *Journal of Economic Issues*, vol. 14 (March 1980), pp. 163−85.

Samuels, W., 'A Necessary Normative Context of Positive Economics?' *Journal of Economic Issues*, vol. 15 (September 1981), pp. 721−7.

Samuels, W., (ed.), *Research in the History of Economic Thought and Methodology* (Greenwich, Conn.: JAI Press, 1984).

Samuels, W., 'Comments on McCloskey on Methodology and Rhetoric', in Samuels, ed. (1984).

Samuelson, P., 'Problems of Methodology − Discussion', *American Economic Review Papers and Proceedings*, vol. 53 (May 1963), pp. 231−6.

Samuelson, P., 'Theory and Realism: A Reply', *American Economic Review*, vol. 54 (September 1964), pp. 736−9.

Samuelson, P., 'Economic Forecasting and Science', *Michigan Quarterly Review*, vol. 4 (October 1965), pp. 274–80.

Samuelson, P., 'Professor Samuelson on Theory and Realism: Reply', *American Economic Review*, vol. 55 (December 1965), pp. 1164–72.

Sawyer, M., *Theories of the Firm* (New York: St. Martin's Press, 1979).

Schoeffler, S., *The Failure of Economics: A Diagnostic Study* (Cambridge, Mass.: Harvard University Press, 1955).

Schoemaker, P., 'The Expected Utility Model: Its Variants, Purposes, Evidence and Limitations', *Journal of Economic Literature*, vol. 20 (June 1982), pp. 529–63.

Schumpeter, J. A., *History of Economic Analysis* (New York: Oxford University Press, 1954).

Shackle, G. L. S., *The Years of High Theory: Invention and Tradition in Economic Thought 1926–1939* (Cambridge: Cambridge University Press, 1967).

Shackle, G. L. S. *Epistemics and Economics: A Critique of Economic Doctrines* (Cambridge: Cambridge University Press, 1973).

Shackle, G. L. S., 'Means and Meaning in Economic Theory', *Scottish Journal of Political Economy*, vol. 29 (November 1982), pp. 223–34.

Shubik, M., 'A Curmudgeon's Guide to Microeconomics', *Journal of Economic Literature*, vol. 8 (June 1970), pp. 405–34.

Shupak, M., 'The Predictive Accuracy of Empirical Demand Analyses', *Economic Journal*, vol. 72 (September 1962), pp. 550–75.

Simon, H., 'From Substantive to Procedural Rationality', in Latsis, ed. (1976), pp. 129–48.

Simon, H., *Models of Discovery and Other Topics in the Methods of Science*, vol. 54, *Boston Studies in the Philosophy of Science* (Dordrecht, Holland: D. Reidel, 1977).

Simon, H., 'Rationality as Process and as Product of Thought', *American Economic Review Papers and Proceedings*, vol. 68 (May 1978), pp. 1–16.

Simon, H., 'Rational Decision Making in Business Organizations', *American Economic Review*, vol. 69 (September 1979), pp. 493–513.

Simon, H., *Reason in Human Affairs* (Stanford, Calif.: Stanford University Press, 1983).

Skinner, A., 'Adam Smith: Rhetoric and the Communication of Ideas', in Coats, ed. (1983), pp. 247–63.

Slovic, P. and Lichtenstein, S., 'Preference Reversals: A Broader Perspective', *American Economic Review*, vol. 73 (September 1983), pp. 596–605.

Smith, V. (ed.), *Research in Experimental Economics* (Greenwich, Conn.: JAI Press, annual).

Smith, V., 'Experimental Economics: Induced Value Theory', *American Economic Review*, vol. 66 (May 1976), pp. 274–9.

Smith, V., 'Microeconomic Systems as an Experimental Science', *American Economic Review*, vol. 72 (December 1982), pp. 923–55.

Smyth, R. (ed.), *Essays in Economic Method* (London: Duckworth, 1962).

Spadaro, L. (ed.), *New Directions in Austrian Economics* (Kansas City, Mo.: Sheed, Andrews and McMeel, 1978).

Stanfield, R., 'Kuhnian Scientific Revolutions and the Keynesian Revolution', *Journal of Economic Issues*, vol. 8 (March 1974), pp. 97–109.

Stanfield, R., 'Phenomena and Epiphenomena in Economics', *Journal of Economic Issues*, vol. 13 (December 1979), pp. 885–98.

Stewart, I., *Reasoning and Method in Economics: An Introduction to Economic Methodology* (London: McGraw-Hill, 1979).

Stewart, I., 'Views of Economic Ignorance', in Samuels, ed. (1984).

Stigler, G., 'On the "Chicago School of Economics": Comment', *Journal of Political Economy*, vol. 70 (February 1962), pp. 70–1.

Stigler, G., 'The Influence of Events and Policies on Economic Theory', in Stigler, *Essays in the History of Economics* (Chicago, Ill.: University of Chicago Press, 1965).

Stigler, G., 'Has Economics a Useful Past?' *History of Political Economy*, vol. 1 (Fall 1969), pp. 217–30.

Stigler, G., 'The Xistence of X-Efficiency', *American Economic Review*, vol. 66 (March 1976), pp. 213–16.

Stigler, G. and Becker, G., 'De Gustibus Non Est Disputandum', *American Economic Review*, vol. 67 (March 1977), pp. 76–90.

Stigler, G., 'The Process and Progress of Economics', *Journal of Political Economy*, vol. 91 (August 1983), pp. 529–45.

Streissler, E., *Pitfalls in Econometric Forecasting* (London: Institute of Economic Affairs, 1970).

Suppe, F. (ed.), *The Structure of Scientific Theories*, 2nd edn. (Urbana, Ill.: University of Illinois Press, 1977).

Sweezy, A., 'The Interpretation of Subjective Value Theory in the Writings of Austrian Economists', *Review of Economic Studies*, vol. 1 (June 1934), pp. 176–85.

Sweezy, P., 'Toward a Critique of Economics', *Review of Radical Political Economics*, vol. 3 (July 1971), pp. 59–66.

Tarascio, V., *Pareto's Methodological Approach to Economics: A Study in the History of Some Scientific Aspects of Economic Thought* (Chapel Hill, NC: University of North Carolina Press, 1966).

Tarascio, V., 'Intellectual History and the Social Sciences: The Problem of Methodological Pluralism', *Social Science Quarterly*, vol. 56 (June 1975), pp. 37–54.

Tarascio, V. and Caldwell, B., 'Theory Choice in Economics: Philosophy and Practice', *Journal of Economic Issues*, vol. 13 (December 1979), pp. 983–1006.

Theil, H., *Applied Economic Forecasting* (Amsterdam: North Holland, 1966).

Thoben, H., 'Mechanistic and Organistic Analogies in Economics Reconsidered', *Kyklos*, vol. 35 (1982), pp. 292–306.

Thompson, H., 'Adam Smith's Philosophy of Science', *Quarterly Journal of Economics*, vol. 79 (May 1965), pp. 212–33.

Tisdale, C., 'Concepts of Rationality in Economics', *Philosophy of Social Science*, vol. 5 (1975), pp. 259–72.

Vaughn, K., 'Subjectivity, Predictability, and Creativity: Comment on Buchanan', in Kirzner, ed. (1982), pp. 31–40.

Veblen, T., 'Why Is Economics Not an Evolutionary Science?' in M. Lerner, ed., *The Portable Veblen* (New York: The Viking Press, 1948), pp. 215–40.

Vickers, D., 'Formalism, Finance, and Decisions in Real Economic Time', in Coats, ed. (1983), pp. 247–63.

Viner, J., *The Long View and the Short* (Glencoe, Ill.: The Free Press, 1958).

Ward, B., *What's Wrong With Economics?* (London: Macmillan, 1972).

Watts, M., 'The Non-Rational Domain and the Limits of Economic Analysis: Comment on McKenzie', *Southern Economic Journal*, vol. 47 (April 1981), pp. 1120–2.

Weber, M., *The Methodology of the Social Sciences*, ed. E. A. Shils and H. A. Finch (Glencoe, Ill.: The Free Press, 1949).

Weintraub, E. R., 'The Microfoundations of Macroeconomics: A Critical Survey', *Journal of Economic Literature*, vol. 15 (March 1977), pp. 1–23.

Weintraub, E. R., *Microfoundations: The Compatibility of Microeconomics and Macroeconomics* (Cambridge: Cambridge University Press, 1979).

Weintraub, E. R., 'Substantive Mountains and Methodological Molehills', *Journal of Post-Keynesian Economics*, vol. 5 (Winter 1982–83), pp. 295–303.

Weintraub, E. R., 'On the Existence of a Competitive Equilibrium', *Journal of Economic Literature*, vol. 21 (March 1983), pp. 1–39.

Weintraub, S. (ed.), *Modern Economic Thought* (Oxford: Basil Blackwell, 1977).

Weisskopf, W., *The Psychology of Economics* (Chicago, Ill.: University of Chicago Press, 1955).

Weisskopf, W., *Alienation in Economics* (New York: Dutton, 1971).

Weisskopf, W., 'The Method Is the Ideology: From a Newtonian to a Heisenbergian Paradigm in Economics', *Journal of Economic Issues*, vol. 13 (December 1979), pp. 869–84.

Whitaker, J., 'John Stuart Mill's Methodology', *Journal of Political Economy*, vol. 83 (October 1975), pp. 1033–50.

White, L., 'Methodology of the Austrian School', *Center For Libertarian Studies, Occasional Paper Series*, No. 1 (New York, 1977).

Wible, J., 'Friedman's Positive Economics and Philosophy of Science', *Southern Economic Journal*, vol. 49 (October 1982), pp. 350–60.

Wible, J., 'The Rational Expectations Tautologies', *Journal of Post-Keynesian Economics*, vol. 5 (Winter 1982–83), pp. 199–208.

Wilber, C., 'Empirical Verification and Theory Selection: The Monetarist-Keynesian Debate', *Journal of Economic Issues*, vol. 13 (December 1979), pp. 973–82.

Wilber, C. and Harrison, R., 'The Methodological Basis of Institutional Economics: Pattern Model, Storytelling, and Holism', *Journal of Economic Issues*, vol. 12 (March 1978), pp. 61–89.

Wilber, C. and Hoksbergen, R., 'Current Thinking on the Role of Value Judgments in Economic Science: A Survey', in Samuels, ed. (1984).

Wilber, C. and Wisman, J., 'The Chicago School: Positivism or Ideal Type', *Journal of Economic Issues*, vol. 9 (December 1975), pp. 665–79.

Wilde, L., 'On the Use of Laboratory Experiments in Economics', in Pitt, ed. (1981), pp. 137–48.

Wiles, P., 'Ideology, Methodology, and Neoclassical Economics', *Journal of Post-Keynesian Economics*, vol. 2 (Winter 1979–80), pp. 155–80.

Wiles, P., 'Methodology and Ideology: Reply', *Journal of Post-Keynesian Economics*, vol. 3 (Spring 1981), pp. 352–8.

Williams, P., *The Emergence of the Theory of the Firm* (London: Macmillan, 1978).

Winter, S., 'Economic "Natural Selection" and the Theory of the Firm', *Yale Economic Essays*, vol. 4 (Spring 1964), pp. 225–72.

Wiseman, J. (ed.), *Beyond Positive Economics? Proceedings of Section F of the British Association for the Advancement of Science* (New York: St Martin's Press, 1983).

Wisman, J., 'The Naturalistic Turn of Orthodox Economics: A Study of Methodological Misunderstanding', *Review of Social Economy*, vol. 36 (December 1978), pp. 263–84.

Wisman, J., 'Toward a Humanist Reconstruction of Economic Science', *Journal of Economic Issues*, vol. 13 (March 1979), pp. 19–48.

Wisman, J., 'The Sociology of Knowledge as a Tool for Research into the History of Economic Thought', *American Journal of Economics and Sociology*, vol. 39 (January 1980), pp. 83–94.

Wong, S., 'The F-Twist and the Methodology of Paul Samuelson', *American Economic Review*, vol. 63 (June 1973), pp. 312–25.

Wong, S., *The Foundations of Paul Samuelson's Revealed Preference Theory: A Study by the Method of Rational Reconstruction* (London: Routledge & Kegan Paul, 1978).

Woodbury, S. A., 'Methodological Controversy in Labor Economics', *Journal of Economic Issues*, vol. 13 (December 1979), pp. 933–55.

Worland, S., 'Radical Political Economy as a "Scientific Revolution"', *Southern Economic Journal*, vol. 39 (October 1972), pp. 274–84.

Worswick, G. D. N., 'Is Progress of Economic Science Possible?' *Economic Journal*, vol. 82 (March 1972), pp. 73–86.

Zarnowitz, V., 'Prediction and Forecasting, Economic', in D. L. Sills (ed.), *International Encyclopedia of the Social Sciences* (New York: Macmillan, 1968), vol. 12, pp. 425–39.

Zellner, A., 'Causality and Econometrics', in K. Brunner and A. Meltzer (eds), *Three Aspects of Policy and Policy-Making: Knowledge, Data and Institutions*, Supplement to the *Journal of Monetary Economics*, vol. 10 (1979), pp. 9–54.

Zinam, O., 'Search for a Logic of Change in Economic Theories: Evolution, Revolutions, Paradigmatic Shifts and Dialectics', *Rivista Internazionale di Scienze Economiche e Commerciale*, vol. 25 (February 1978), pp. 156–88.